Streaming Media Delivery in Higher Education:

Methods and Outcomes

Charles Wankel
St. John's University, USA

J. Sibley Law
Saxon Mills, USA

A volume in the Advances in Higher
Education and Professional Development
(AHEPD) Book Series

Senior Editorial Director:	Kristin Klinger
Director of Book Publications:	Julia Mosemann
Editorial Director:	Lindsay Johnston
Acquisitions Editor:	Erika Carter
Development Editor:	Mike Killian
Production Editor:	Sean Woznicki
Typesetters:	Keith Glazewski, Milan Vracarich, Jr. & Deanna Zombro
Print Coordinator:	Jamie Snavely
Cover Design:	Nick Newcomer

Published in the United States of America by
Information Science Publishing (an imprint of IGI Global)
701 E. Chocolate Avenue
Hershey PA 17033
Tel: 717-533-8845
Fax: 717-533-8661
E-mail: cust@igi-global.com
Web site: http://www.igi-global.com

Library of Congress Cataloging-in-Publication Data

Streaming media delivery in higher education : methods and outcomes / Charles Wankel and J. Sibley Law, editors.
    p. cm.
 Includes bibliographical references and index.
 Summary: "This book is both a snapshot of streaming media in higher education as it is today and a window into the many developments already underway, forecasting of areas yet to be developed"-- Provided by publisher.
  ISBN 978-1-60960-800-2 (hardcover) -- ISBN 978-1-60960-801-9 (ebook) -- ISBN 978-1-60960-802-6 (print & perpetual access) 1. Internet in higher education. 2. Streaming technology (Telecommunications) I. Wankel, Charles. II. Law, J. Sibley, 1969-
 LB2395.7.S77 2012
 378.1'7344678--dc23
                              2011016796

This book is published in the IGI Global book series Advances in Higher Education and Professional Development (AHEPD) (ISSN: 2327-6983; eISSN: 2327-6991)

British Cataloguing in Publication Data
A Cataloguing in Publication record for this book is available from the British Library.

All work contributed to this book is new, previously-unpublished material. The views expressed in this book are those of the authors, but not necessarily of the publisher.

Advances in Higher Education and Professional Development (AHEPD) Book Series

Jared Keengwe
University of North Dakota

ISSN: 2327-6983
EISSN: 2327-6991

MISSION

As world economies continue to shift and change in response to global financial situations, job markets have begun to demand a more highly-skilled workforce. In many industries a college degree is the minimum requirement and further educational development is expected to advance. With these current trends in mind, the **Advances in Higher Education & Professional Development (AHEPD) Book Series** provides an outlet for researchers and academics to publish their research in these areas and to distribute these works to practitioners and other researchers.

AHEPD encompasses all research dealing with higher education pedagogy, development, and curriculum design, as well as all areas of professional development, regardless of focus.

COVERAGE

- Adult Education
- Assessment in Higher Education
- Career Training
- Coaching & Mentoring
- Continuing Professional Development
- Governance in Higher Education
- Higher Education Policy
- Pedagogy of Teaching Higher Education
- Vocational Education

IGI Global is currently accepting manuscripts for publication within this series. To submit a proposal for a volume in this series, please contact our Acquisition Editors at Acquisitions@igi-global.com or visit: http://www.igi-global.com/publish/.

Titles in this Series

For a list of additional titles in this series, please visit: www.igi-global.com

Teacher Education Programs and Online Learning Tools Innovations in Teacher Preparation
Richard Hartshorne (University of Central Florida, USA) Tina L. Heafner (University of North Carolina at Charlotte, USA) and Teresa Petty (University of North Carolina at Charlotte, USA)
Information Science Reference • copyright 2013 • 569pp • H/C (ISBN: 9781466619067) • US $175.00 (our price)

Collaborative Learning 2.0 Open Educational Resources
Alexandra Okada (The Open University, UK) Teresa Connolly (The Open University, UK) and Peter J. Scott (The Open University, UK)
Information Science Reference • copyright 2012 • 378pp • H/C (ISBN: 9781466603004) • US $175.00 (our price)

Informed Design of Educational Technologies in Higher Education Enhanced Learning and Teaching
Anders D. Olofsson (Umeå University, Sweden) and J. Ola Lindberg (Mid Sweden University, Sweden)
Information Science Reference • copyright 2012 • 548pp • H/C (ISBN: 9781613500804) • US $175.00 (our price)

Streaming Media Delivery in Higher Education Methods and Outcomes
Charles Wankel (St. John's University, USA) and J. Sibley Law (Saxon Mills, USA)
Information Science Publishing • copyright 2011 • 492pp • H/C (ISBN: 9781609608002) • US $195.00 (our price)

Technology Integration in Higher Education Social and Organizational Aspects
Daniel W. Surry (University of South Alabama, USA) Robert M. Gray Jr. (University of South Alabama, USA) and James R. Stefurak (University of South Alabama, USA)
Information Science Reference • copyright 2011 • 428pp • H/C (ISBN: 9781609601478) • US $180.00 (our price)

Critical Design and Effective Tools for E-Learning in Higher Education Theory into Practice
Roisin Donnelly (Dublin Institute of Technology, Ireland) Jen Harvey (Dublin Institute of Technology, Ireland) and Kevin O'Rourke (Dublin Institute of Technology, Ireland)
Information Science Reference • copyright 2010 • 448pp • H/C (ISBN: 9781615208791) • US $180.00 (our price)

Virtual Environments for Corporate Education Employee Learning and Solutions
William Ritke-Jones (Cybermations Consulting Group, USA)
Business Science Reference • copyright 2010 • 426pp • H/C (ISBN: 9781615206193) • US $180.00 (our price)

www.igi-global.com

701 E. Chocolate Ave., Hershey, PA 17033
Order online at www.igi-global.com or call 717-533-8845 x100
To place a standing order for titles released in this series, contact: cust@igi-global.com
Mon-Fri 8:00 am - 5:00 pm (est) or fax 24 hours a day 717-533-8661

Editorial Advisory Board

Table of Contents

Detailed Table of Contents

The aim of this chapter is to highlight essential criteria required to set up streaming media server within higher education institutions. It explores different types of video content, highlights the importance of streaming media technology by differentiating between the traditional Web server software and streaming media server software. This is then followed by the explanation of different streaming media protocols and how the video content gets transported from the streaming media server to students' computer. The chapter also explores different types of methods used to deliver streaming videos over the Internet, different streaming media software, encoding software and encoding parameters used for converting high definition/quality videos into streamable quality. Section 3 of this chapter highlights the importance of folder and file naming conventions, exploring essential video metadata which is required to create and manage video files, Digital Rights Management technology to securely deliver video over the Internet and how to publish a video on the Internet.

Video is generally seen as a passive, primarily didactic teaching method, an approach at odds with contemporary cross-cultural training, which tends to emphasize highly interactive "experiential" methods. In this chapter we draw on contemporary theories of learning to argue that video-based cross-cultural training is, in fact, more flexible than it is given credit for, and can play an important role in developing learners' cultural intelligence. In doing this, we outline several practical and creative ways in which video can be used to develop cultural intelligence.

Using streaming video for recording and playing back lectures has become a widespread extra feature for lectures in higher education. There is a wide variety in ways of recording these lectures and making them available. The main form is live lectures that are recorded with slides synchronized with the audio and video of the lecturer. These lectures are recorded, placed online via a University portal, students typically study these materials just before an examination of assignments. But many more ways of using Weblectures are possible. This chapter describes 5 didactic models of using Weblectures. These are: checking back attended lectures, checking back missed lectures, flexible learning, presentation skills, and re-use. The models can help to make decisions for the form in which lectures can be used, and steer technical developments.

In the last ten years, the world has witnessed immense advances in media and Internet technologies. Through examination of the use of social media, virtual collaboration platforms, and live streamed access to images, graphics, and video, this chapter offers a new approach to education which calls for leaders to use technology to inform and connect teachers, students, and the community. Similar to the changes in the entertainment industry, educational institutions can adopt an interactive, collaborative, and socially aware model of knowledge creation to engage more students and encourage innovation in issues of global scope. The value of making this change is examined through curricula that stress multidisciplinary projects and provide hands on experiential learning. Lacking the market forces of the entertainment industry, being primarily supported by public funds, education institutions face more legal, political and business model barriers. However, the benefits of digital media so far outweigh the risks that the next decade will see the emergence of learning environments that provide as much of a quantum leap in pedagogy as did the advent of the printing press more than five hundred years ago. Examples of the emotional appeal of digital media combined with the relatively low cost of scaling with the Internet are provided as impetus to overcome resistance to change in creating new institutions of learning.

This chapter shows how the authors have used video streaming as a central component of a rich-media, online learning environment incorporating podcasting and advanced Internet technologies to promote deep learning while educating for social change. In the first part of the chapter we discuss the design and pedagogy of our award-winning course. Various aspects of our technological and teaching innovations are highlighted. We discuss the factors that impelled us to rethink ways of creating online, rich-media learning environments, and move toward innovation. We explain the principles, ideas, and concepts that have grounded our approach and inspired us to embrace video streaming, podcasting, and advanced Internet technologies. We unpack a fundamental assumption: deep learning and educating for social change are made possible by an acceptance and understanding of the radical intertwining of learner, educator, technologist, and technology. In sum, we draw on our course to illustrate enactive, online teaching-and-learning.

Chapter 6

In this chapter, we present the case study into the effectiveness of using streaming media reusable learning objects to teach practical/technical skills in pattern cutting for undergraduate fashion students. We discuss our research methodology and our experimental design. We also share our findings, and outline how we propose to take the streaming media based teaching method further.

Chapter 7

This chapter focuses upon a case study of an online higher education intervention – an interactive resource the author has devised as an aid to the teaching and learning of undergraduate digital video editing (DVE). This resource specifically addresses drama and fiction postproduction principles, practice and techniques. The repository, which includes streamed materials available to download, guides the student through the film production process in a step-by-step way (for students), with suggested class based activities and tasks using the materials (for tutors). The resources include the script, all planning documentation, all production paperwork, and all rushes shot for different productions. The student/tutor navigates through these materials guided by a combination of voice-overs, video tutorials by those personnel involved in the production, and clips taken from the "making of" documentaries. This chapter explores the intervention within the wider context of higher education online teaching and through the lens of virtual learning environment pedagogic theory.

Chapter 8

In the not too distant future, university students will have trouble recalling a pre-YouTube or pre-podcast world. While streaming media in those formats has become ubiquitous in many areas of their lives through ease of use and dissemination, how does it factor into their learning? Should teachers in higher education utilize students' engagement with streaming media as teachable opportunities? Or, in lieu of teachers intentionally choosing to use streaming media, what about the potential for it to be imposed on them for logistical or operational reasons and the effects of that on student learning and teaching? Building upon prior work that has been done on the use of streaming media in higher education, this chapter will examine it from several teachers' perspectives with a focus on their decision-making processes, implementations, challenges, and opportunities. From their experiences, a set of grounded guidelines for using streaming media in higher education will be developed and offered as starting points for others interested in trying this in their teaching.

Chapter 9

Dierdre Burke, University of Wolverhampton, UK
Brian Barber, University of Wolverhampton, UK
Yvonne Johnson, University of Wolverhampton, UK
A. Nore, University of Wolverhampton, UK
C. Walker, University of Wolverhampton, UK

This chapter reports on a project to explore the potential of a mobile learning device (Apple iTouch iPod) to enhance student field visits to local places of worship, which are part of the Religious Studies degree programme. Places of worship are a valuable resource for student learning, but often the value of the visit is linked to the quality of information and the style of presentation by the faith informant. In addition, there is a particular problem for university students who need to go beyond basic information about history and artifacts to explore key concepts in situ. The project is a collaboration between staff and second year students to develop podcasts on local places of worship, which have been trialed by first year students. These podcasts include a range of media: video, audio, images, text, and hyperlinks to offer a rich learning experience. The podcasts link to theoretical issues in the study of religion to enhance the development of appropriate literacies for the discipline of Religious Studies. The chapter reports on the range of technical and other issues encounters, the way we responded to them, and our overall assessment of the potential applications for mobile learning during field visits.

Chapter 10

Deborah H. Streeter, Cornell University, USA

In this chapter, the author draws from her experience of building a library of digital video since the mid-90s with her eClips team and using it in the classroom. The chapter will focus on: 1) strategies and practical tips for using video inside and outside the classroom to engage learners and respond to short attention spans and 2) guidelines for educators who wish to create their own rich media collections because they need content that has a very specific focus and/or mirrors their learner population more appropriately in terms of demographics.

Chapter 11

Amanda E.K. Budde-Sung, The University of Sydney, Australia
Anthony Fee, The University of Sydney, Austral

Today's business classes are increasingly diverse, with students from all around the world. Teaching international business and cross-cultural management classes to student audiences that are themselves already nationally diverse can pose challenges, but can also provide unique opportunities to bring real experience and varying perspectives into the classroom. Video can be an effective tool in teaching diverse student groups and capitalizing on the diversity present in the classroom. This chapter presents some of the challenges that these diverse student audiences present, as well as practical suggestions for using video to help overcome those challenges and make use of the diversity in the classroom to the benefit of all students' learning.

The Information Resources and Technology Department of Drexel University has developed an ambitious, flexible streaming media system to help Drexel faculty use various types of media in their teaching. This system, Drexel DragonDrop, allows faculty to upload a wide variety of file types and then encodes and converts them to media files that students (and others) can easily access and view. This chapter focuses on how the system simplifies the use of video applications specifically for those who teach writing or writing-centered courses; a number of specific teaching applications will be described. As has been discussed throughout this book, video enables a number of innovative teaching practices, but instructors often have to solve core distribution and access issues that Drexel's system largely eliminates, allowing faculty to focus on creative teaching uses of technology.

Technologies used to enhance, augment, or replace traditional course content have been widely examined. With few exceptions, study of these technologies focuses on the effects of the technologies in isolation. Only a few discussions have attempted to evaluate multi-technologies and their contribution to effective learning for online students. This chapter looks at the traditional learning styles and creates a model for robust, multi-technology, student learning-centered approach to optimize student learning in online classes in a business school. It finds that a well-designed, multi-technology approach results in better student performance, more satisfied students, and greater cost-benefit for the business school. The results have been adapted into course design to create a new kind of resource for online course deployment.

Chapter 14

In this study, we are interested in the question "what motivates students to use webcast?" Most technology acceptance studies have focused on extrinsic (utilitarian) motives (increase in efficiency, ease of use and effectiveness, etc.) to explain the use of e-learning systems. However, recent research suggests that intrinsic (hedonic) motivations, like attractiveness and enjoyment play an important role as well.

Chapter 15

In an increasingly interconnected world, it is highly important that professors and researchers alike not only find cost-effective solutions to further their work but also methods to inspire their students to go beyond the traditional methods. This chapter aims to show a couple of examples of successfully integrating new media features in the teaching and research of new media emphasizing their effectiveness as well as their innovation, involvement, and surprise factors. Furthermore, the methods suggested are easy-to-use, and mostly accessible on a non-fee basis. Additionally, the chapter reviews a series of platforms that allow live video broadcasting such as Yahoo! Messenger, Windows Live Messenger, Skype, Oovoo, Google Talk, PalBee, TokBox, PalTalk, TinyChat, TimZon, VoiceThread, Ustream.tv, and Livestream giving some examples where they could be used in the daily teaching process. Finally, a call for more cross-cultural teaching and collaborative projects is launched.

Chapter 16

This chapter explores the rise of public online video in higher education as both a compliment to and a potential replacement for traditional means of teaching students. Firstly there is a brief history of the recording and delivery of the moving image, followed by a review of the public video platforms currently available and being used by academics. The use of public online video in higher education is then examined from the perspective of the students who may watch such videos, the academics who may make them, and the institutions for whom these academics may work. A key conclusion is that whilst public online video has the potential to turn a few academics into powerful online brands, increasingly, most other academics are likely to spend less time lecturing and more time supporting students and mashing online video content.

Chapter 17

As of early 2010, 117 nations mandate or allow the use of International Financial Reporting Standards (IFRS). On November 14, 2008, the SEC issued its proposed roadmap for U.S. companies to adopt the new international accounting standards. As a result firms nationwide are beginning to prepare for adoption of IFRS. However, many U.S. business schools are still lagging in the teaching of the new standards and attribute their slow movement to the lack of educational materials. While several IFRS textbooks are beginning to appear on the worldwide market, and several innovative curriculum developments are occurring, the teaching materials are still considered sparse. This chapter examines an emerging and impressive source of IFRS teaching materials that includes professional and institutional Webcasts and online videos. The available IFRS Webcasts are first surveyed, and then pedagogical strategies are suggested for a variety of accounting courses. This technology-based media offers both professors and students alike numerous educational benefits and opportunities. Our experience with these "cyber-guest" lecturers has inspired an innovative Inter-University IFRS Online Video Competition amongst our two universities.

Alastair Tombs, University of Queensland, Australia
Doan Nguyen, University of Queensland, Australia

This chapter presents a case study of the development of dramatized video cases as a resource for use in teaching marketing. It explains the benefits of developing and the pitfalls with making this sort of interactive media. The benefits of using dramatized video scenarios as a teaching resource are: a) they facilitate problem based learning, b) they provide the student with a realistic view of the ethical decisions that are faced by marketing managers, and c) they keep the class learning at the same pace. The development of a multi-platform format means that the videos can be streamed into lectures and tutorial groups, published as streaming content on Web based platforms such as Blackboard and/or downloaded onto students' mobile phones and iPods. However, the problems associated with developing this sort of resource are the cost and time required to make a high quality and credible dramatized case study.

Patricia Genoe McLaren, Wilfrid Laurier University, Canada
Lori Francis, Saint Mary's University, Canada
E. Kevin Kelloway, Saint Mary's University, Canada

With the advent and growth of the virtual generation, educators need to understand the worlds that their students inhabit, and how to make use of those worlds within an academic setting. Within this chapter, we present the characteristics of the virtual generation and the unique challenges involved in engaging the members of the generation in the classroom. We address online learning, its benefits and negatives, and how it differs from the more specific topic of learning in a virtual world. We discuss the capabilities that virtual worlds offer as learning environments, and how these capabilities relate to current learning theories. We end the chapter with a discussion of considerations that are involved in creating a virtual learning environment. Examples of learning within virtual worlds are included throughout the chapter.

Catharine Jenkins, Birmingham City University, UK
Andrew Walsh, Birmingham City University, UK

This chapter discusses the challenges for higher education raised by socio-cultural, technological, and pedagogical developments. The authors' response as experienced healthcare educators was to develop videos and e-learning objects as part of a blended approach to training mental health nursing students. The authors describe the initiative, discuss progress, analyse outcomes, and highlight implications for practice. The chapter ends by drawing wider conclusions about use of streaming media within professional education.

Rajiv Kumar, Indian Institute of Management Calcutta, India
Abhishek Goel, Indian Institute of Management Calcutta, India
Vidyanand Jha, Indian Institute of Management Calcutta, India

This chapter is an auto-ethnographic account of three instructors of Organizational Behavior (OB). It begins with an introduction to our approach of deriving learning using auto-ethnography. It then highlights the challenges faced by us when we tried to use our interactive style of content delivery in the online format. Such challenges became pronounced while using case-study discussions as a tool for teaching OB. The nuances of experiences with the technology and environment of a virtual classroom per se are also discussed. The dilemmas, modifications, and outcomes are highlighted with key learning for instructors and participants.

Rajiv Kumar, Indian Institute of Management Calcutta, India
Abhishek Goel, Indian Institute of Management Calcutta, India
Vidyanand Jha, Indian Institute of Management Calcutta, India

Several scholars have described the advantages of online education. The Indian market for business management education is also increasingly accepting this mode of delivery. This case presents the history and policy environment leading to origin, design, and delivery of a one-year online management education program by a leading business school in India. The technological and marketing support received from a partner organization is presented. The structure of this program, along with the unique challenges faced in operationalizing such a program with limited resources is also highlighted. The interplay between program administrators, business school, faculty members, program participants, and service provider is discussed. The authors illustrate various enablers and impediments faced, and derive key points of learning.

Foreword

If you are reading this book, odds are you're an intellectual, an instructor, or just interested. And *interested* you should be.

While I may teach at some of the world's best known film schools, I too am stunned, dizzied, even frightened by the massive wave of technology that is bearing down on us all like a tornado in a trailer park.

It's too much for a human to keep up with. Even low-grade robots have trouble. We all think of Star Trek as a peek into our technical future, but think about it—their "communicators" served only one function. An iPhone's 100,000 apps can serve 100,000 functions. Even the "tricorder" only did three things. So there, Gene Roddenberry!

While no one person can grasp everything in New Media—it is evolving too quickly—one *group* can. A group of highly dedicated minds like the authors of this book. My hat is off to them. (However, I will keep my socks on.)

This compilation is a line in the sand. It defines where we are today, and summarizes it in a way that can be absorbed and put to use.

Society is evolving at an ever-quicker rate every day, and change is the only constant. This book will challenge you to change, but remember, change is a good thing. We either adapt or die.

Okay, well, "die" might be a bit harsh, but adaption in this case will result in more engagement from the students, more challenges to you, and a much more interesting course of study for everyone. That may result in more pay, but if not, I beseech you not to sue the authors. (The publishers have so much more money.)

Streaming media in the classroom allows you several minor miracles:

- You can be in two places—or thousands of places—at once.
- You can gather information from thousands of places, and demonstrate it in a smooth, flowing matter in minutes.
- You will look cool to your students. (Never undervalue that, my friends.)

Remember, if a picture is worth a thousand words, a video is worth a million. My guess is that you can only spit out about a half a million words per class. So enjoy the book, relish in the unknown, and good luck.

Frank Chindamo
President and Chief Creative Officer, Fun Little Movies
Adjunct Professor, University of Southern California, School of Cinematic Arts,
Associate Professor, Chapman University's Dodge College of Film and Media Arts
UCLA, Instructor
Mobisode/Webisode Writing/Production

Frank Chindamo *is the President and Chief Creative Officer of Fun Little Movies. FLM specializes in the development, production and distribution of original content for global distribution on mobile phones, the Internet, and portable devices. Its mission is to contribute to love and to laughter by providing fun, funny, advertiser-friendly comedy to every person on Earth. Fun Little Movies was the first U.S. company to produce comedic films for mobile phones worldwide, and launched as a channel on Sprint TV in 2004. FLM's "Fun Funny Phone Films" have won 23 awards. In Feb. 2009, they took the Grand Prize at Mobile Content World in Barcelona in the MoFilm awards, given by Kevin Spacey. See http://www.mofilm.com/blog/2009/02/19/english-as-a-second-language-wins-the-grand-prize-at-the-mofilm-mobile-festival-2009/. They've also won CTIA's "World Smallest Film Festival" and two Golden Eagles at the American Cine' Awards, as well as The Content Award at Cannes in 2008, over MTV and Orange. FLM was also a finalist at: The Cannes Film Festival for Best Short Film, the 2008 Mobile Content Award in London, the 2008 and 2009 Mobile Excellence Awards, and the 2006, 2007 and 2009 Mobile Entertainment Magazine Awards for Best Video. Fun Little Movies have aired on numerous TV networks worldwide including HBO, Showtime, CBS, Playboy, MTV, and Comedy Central. FLM's mobile comedy can be watched on iPhones, Sprint, Verizon, Nokia, MSN Mobile, and ATT mobile phones, on Babelgum.com, MSN.com, Revver.com, Vuze.com, and many other top video sites, and on other mobile and Internet platforms. FLM has been a cover story or featured in CNN, the BBC, Forbes Magazine, the L.A. Times, the NY Times, the Washington Post, Variety, Hollywood Reporter, CBS, and Wired Magazine.*

Preface

There is no question to the fact that online video is as ubiquitous today as any phenomenon of the past. Countless hours of digital video are uploaded to various online video platforms such as YouTube.com and Facebook.com every minute. Online video has become so prevalent in the online life of Internet denizens that at a recent YouTube Partner Meeting, employees of the company touted YouTube.com as the second largest search engine in the world, second only to its parent company's search engine: Google (http://www.RocketsTail.com). An interpretation of this fact might suggest that some large portion of people looking for information online are looking for videos instead of text, audio, or other forms of information dissemination. Extrapolate the notion of a video platform being the second largest search engine in the world to its impact on knowledge acquisition and learning, and one can easily watch a paradigm shift as it happens. (Note that YouTube only began in 2005).

Faced with the incredible changes underway, it only makes sense for educators of all kinds to not only note the ubiquity that streaming media has gained in the lives of their students, but to embrace and appropriate the technology in their efforts to impart knowledge. Some of the largest companies in the world have utilized various services provided by companies like WebEx.com, which offer the capability to stream "virtual live training" experiences with an instructor on a Web camera in one location while students participate from their own locations via their own Web cameras. However, these kinds of learning experiences only scratch the surface in terms of uses of streaming media to enhance the educational experiences of all kinds of students. This book is focused on higher education, but certainly the applications extend far beyond the halls of higher learning to business, secondary education, and even to the primary levels of learning.

Streaming Media Delivery in Higher Education: Methods and Outcomes aims to provide insight and practical knowledge to those interested in leveraging these specific new media to enhance learning. It is both for the educator and the practitioner. It is for any reader seeking a snapshot of many ways streaming media are being used in education today, from iPod enhancement to didactic models for Web lectures, to virtual guest instructors, virtual worlds, and more. As the first book of its kind to cover the depth and breadth of this topic, the authors of these chapters have provided incredible insight into streaming media today.

ABOUT THE CHAPTERS

Chapter 1: *Streaming Media Management and Delivery Systems* by Nipan J. Maniar

Taking a technical look at the essentials of a streaming media server, Nipan Maniar also explores how streaming media requires a different set of specifications than traditional Web servers. Additionally, this chapter explores issues of metadata and digital rights management. Though a more technical approach to the topic, Maniar captures some of the key elements to successfully delivering streaming media.

Chapter 2: *The Link in the Lesson: Using Video to Bridge Theory and Experience in Cross-Cultural Training* by Anthony Fee and Amanda E.K. Budde-Sung

Anthony Fee and Amanda E.K. Budde-Sung make the case that video-based cross-cultural training plays an important role in developing learner's cultural intelligence. They outline a number of ways in which online video can be used toward this end. Their case is pitted against traditional perspectives of video as passive and didactic and suggests that it is, in fact, the opposite.

Chapter 3: *The Next Step for Use of Streaming Video in Higher Education: Didactic Models for Weblectures* by J. C. Winnips, G. J. Verheij, and E. M. Gommer

Winnips, Verheij, and Gommer assess historic uses of streaming video in higher education and suggest alternate uses, as well. Focused especially on Web-lectures, they suggest that streaming media permits a more creative and flexible learning environment. Additionally, they provide five didactic models for using Web-lectures.

Chapter 4: *Digital Provide: Education Beyond Borders* by Neerja Raman

Neerja Raman examines recent advances in media and Internet technologies, specifically social media, virtual collaboration platforms, and live streaming and their implications on learning environments and pedagogy. As an assessment of the benefits of adopting resulting changes in the entertainment industry in education, this chapter suggests that certain kinds of curricula and projects are especially suited to the new technology. It further suggests that low cost and heightened emotional appeal serve as an impetus to overcome resistance to the adoption of these new media.

Chapter 5: *Using Video Streaming in an Online, Rich-Media Class to Promote Deep Learning While Educating for Social Change* by Diane Zorn and Kelly Parke

Diane Zorn and Kelly Parke examine their award-winning course. The chapter examines the learning environment and design as well as teaching practices. Additionally, it covers how their design and pedagogy works against fundamental and prevalent values underlying the culture of higher education that desperately need changing. Finally, they outline the theory behind the practice explaining the principles, ideas, and concepts that grounded their approach.

Chapter 6: *The Effectiveness of Streaming Media Clips in Skills Teaching: A Comparative Study* by Andrew Saxon and Sheila Griffiths

Andrew Saxon and Sheila Griffiths examine the use of streaming media as part of Virtual Learning Environment (VLE) at Birmingham City University Institute of Art and Design, UK. As a case study, they consider the extent to which the streaming media method can replace traditional face-to-face teaching, and pedagogical aspects of how the media worked through the VLE in a blended learning setting. In addition to discussing their research methodology, they explore how to take streaming media based teaching further.

Chapter 7: *Teaching Off-Line Digital Video Editing On-Line: An Exploration into Editing and Postproduction Digital Pedagogic Practice* by Sarah Atkinson

Sarah Atkinson presents a case study where streaming media was used as an aid to teaching and learning undergraduate digital video editing. This chapter explores resources and methodologies involved. Additionally, it contributes to the dialog regarding the wider context of higher education online teaching and through the lens of virtual learning environment pedagogic theory.

Chapter 8: *In the Current or Swimming Upstream? Instructors' Perceptions of Teaching with Streaming Media in Higher Education* by Billy O'Steen, Arin Basu, and Mary Allan

O'Steen, Basu, and Allan address the following questions: How does streaming media factor into learning? Should teachers in higher education utilize students' engagement with streaming media as teachable opportunities? Or, in lieu of teachers intentionally choosing to use streaming media, what about the potential for it to be imposed on them for logistical or operational reasons and the effects of that on student learning and teaching? This chapter examines the issues from several teachers' perspectives with a focus on their decision-making processes, implementations, challenges, and opportunities.

Chapter 9: *iPod Enhancement for Field Visits in Religious Studies* by Deirdre Burke, with Brian Barber, Yvonne Johnson, A. Nore, and C. Walker

Burke, Barber, Johnson, Nore, and Walker report on uses of a specific mobile learning device to enhance student field visits in religious studies. This chapter reports on technical and other issues the authors encountered and how they responded to them. Additionally, they provide an assessment of the potential applications for mobile learning during field visits.

Chapter 10: *Using Digital Stories Effectively to Engage Students* by Deborah H. Streeter

Deborah Streeter reports on the rich media collection at Cornell University (Cornell's eClips of more than 14,000 units) and their utilization in learning. Specifically, she discusses strategies and practical tips for using video inside and outside the classroom. Additionally, she provides guidelines for educators wishing to create their own rich media collections.

Chapter 11: *Unleashing Dormant Diversity: Insights on Video, Culture, and Teaching Diverse Student Groups* **by Amanda E. K. Budde-Sung and Anthony Fee**

Amanda Budde-Sung and Anthony Fee discuss some of the key issues of teaching international business and cross-cultural management to audiences, which are, themselves, diverse. This chapter presents some of the challenges that these diverse student audiences present, as well as practical suggestions for using video to help overcome those challenges.

Chapter 12: *Streaming Media for Writing Instruction: Drexel's Streaming Media Server and Novel Approaches to Course Lessons and Assessment* **by Scott Warnock**

Scott Warnock analyzes Drexel University's DragonDrop system, which allows faculty to upload a wide variety of file types and then encodes and converts them to media files that students (and others) can easily access and view. This chapter focuses on how the system simplifies video use as well as describing a number of teaching applications, particularly for those who teach writing or writing-centered courses. Additionally, this assesses how Drexel's system eliminates distribution and access issues, which are common to many instruction environments.

Chapter 13: *Effective Online Courses in Business Administration: Expanding Course Design to Activate Diverse Learning Styles* **by David L. Sturges**

David Sturges explores the blending of a multiplicity of technologies with traditional learning methods and their contribution to online learning. This chapter looks at the traditional learning styles and creates a model for robust, multi-technology, student learning-centered approach to optimize student learning in online classes in a business school. Additionally, it looks at the results and how they have been utilized in course design focused on online course deployment.

Chapter 14: *Utilitarian and Hedonic Motivations in the Acceptance of Web Casts in Higher Education* **by Peter van Baalen, Jan van Dalen, Ruud Smit, and Wouter Veenhof**

Baalen, Dalen, Smit, and Veenhof present and discuss the results of a study on the adoption of webcasts by students in higher education. This chapter explores what motivates students to use webcasts. Whereas most technology acceptance studies have focused on extrinsic (utilitarian) motives (increase in efficiency, ease of use and effectiveness, etc.) to explain the use of e-learning systems, this chapter extends the research model by including intrinsic (hedonic) motivations they may contribute to use webcasts. Additionally, the chapter includes some directions for future research.

Chapter 15: *Streaming Live: Teaching New Media with New Media* **by Ana Adi**

Ana Adi provides examples of successful integration of new media features in the teaching and research of new media emphasizing their effectiveness as well as their innovation, involvement, and surprise factors. Additionally, the chapter reviews a series of platforms that allow live video broadcasting. Finally, this chapter calls for more cross-cultural teaching and collaborative projects.

Chapter 16: *The New Chalk and Slate? Public Online Video in Higher Education* by Christopher Barnatt

Christopher Barnatt explores the rise of public online video in higher education as both a compliment to and a potential replacement for traditional means of teaching students. The use of public online video in higher education is then examined from the perspective of the students who may watch such videos, the academics who may make them, and the institutions for whom these academics may work. Finally, this chapter draws some conclusions about the impact of the integration of online video into the learning environment.

Chapter 17: *IFRS Cyber-Guest Lecturers: A Pedagogical Resource for Professors and an Inspiration for Student Online Video Projects* by Mark Holtzblatt and Norbert Tschakert

Mark Holtzblatt and Norbert Tschakert examine the lagging education around International Financial Report Standards (IFRS) at many U.S. business schools and suggest that professional and institutional webcasts and online videos provide a viable method to overcome the lack of other educational material readily available. This chapter examines an emerging and impressive source of IFRS teaching materials particularly in these media. Additionally, it assesses the educational benefits and opportunities these technology-based media offer.

Chapter 18: *Developing Interactive Dramatised Videos as a Teaching Resource* by Alastair Tombs and Doan Nguyen

Alastair Tombs and Doan Nguyen present a case study of the development of dramatized video cases as a resource for use in teaching marketing. This chapter assesses both the benefits of these kinds of dramatized videos as well as some of the downsides. Additionally, they explore platforms and delivery as expanding the possibilities of the medium.

Chapter 19: *Higher Education in a Virtual World* by Patricia Genoe McLaren, Lori Francis, and E. Kevin Kelloway

McLaren, Francis, and Kelloway present the characteristics of the virtual generation and the unique challenges involved in engaging the members of the generation in the classroom. This chapter addresses online learning, its benefits and negatives, and how it differs from the more specific topic of learning in a virtual world. Additionally, this chapter provides examples of learning within virtual worlds throughout the text.

Chapter 20: *Use of Blended E-Learning Resources in Higher Education: An Innovation from Healthcare Training* by Catharine Jenkins and Andrew Walsh

Catharine Jenkins and Andrew Walsh explore the challenges for higher education raised by socio-cultural, technological, and pedagogical developments. The chapter discusses the authors' use of videos and e-learning objects as part of a blended approach to training mental health nursing students. The authors describe the initiative, discuss progress, analyse outcomes, and highlight implications for practice.

Chapter 21: *Medium Matters: Experiences of Teaching Online in India* by Rajiv Kumar, Abhishek Goel, and Vidyanand Jha

Kumar, Goel, and Jha provide an auto-ethnographic account of three instructors of Organizational Behavior (OB). The chapter explores their approach and highlights the challenges they faced when attempting to use an interactive style of content delivery in the online format. Additionally, the chapter discusses the dilemmas, modifications, and outcomes, and highlights key learning for instructors and participants.

Chapter 22: *Online Business Education in India: A Case Study* by Rajiv Kumar, Abhishek Goel and Vidyanand Jha

Kumar, Goel, and Jha present the history and policy environment leading to origin, design, and delivery of a one-year long online management education program by a leading business school in India. This chapter discusses the technological and marketing support received from a partner organization, as well as the structure of the program, along with the unique challenges faced in operationalizing it. The authors illustrate various enablers and impediments faced, and derive key points of learning.

CONCLUSION

One of the first collections of its kind, these chapters together paint a picture of a growing and changing world; one that is both virtual and physical and that is as diversely multi-faceted as the many people who either teach or learn (or both). This book is both a snap shot of streaming media in higher education as it is today and a window into the many developments already underway, and in some cases, a forecast of areas yet to be developed. As a resource, this book serves both as an explication of many practices, including their possibilities and pitfalls, as well as recommendation of the many areas where opportunities for development lie.

Charles Wankel
St. John's University, USA

J. Sibley Law
Saxon Mills, USA

Acknowledgment

We have unbounded gratitude to Patti Law, our talented collaborator and managing editor, whose contributions to this endeavor exceed ours in many ways.

Charles Wankel
St. John's University, USA

J. Sibley Law
Saxon Mills, USA

Chapter 1
Streaming Media Management and Delivery Systems

Nipan J. Maniar
University of Portsmouth, UK

ABSTRACT

The aim of this chapter is to highlight essential criteria required to set up a streaming media server within Higher Education Institutions. It explores different types of video content and highlights the importance of streaming media technology by differentiating between the traditional Web server software and streaming media server software. This is then followed by the explanation of different streaming media protocols and how the video content gets transported from the streaming media server to students' computer. The chapter also explores different types of methods used to deliver streaming videos over the Internet, different streaming media software, encoding software, and encoding parameters used for converting high definition/quality videos into streamable quality. Section 3 of this chapter highlights the importance of folder and file naming conventions, exploring essential video metadata which is required to create and manage video files, Digital Rights Management technology to securely deliver video over the internet, and how to publish a video on the Internet.

CONTENT (VIDEO)

The aim of this section is to investigate and review the types of streaming media content Higher Education offers. To review current streaming media services within UK Higher Education, the internet was searched using Google's advanced search methods looking for higher education institutions that deliver streaming media videos. Interviews were carried out with Higher Education librarians and academics. The search criteria and interviews were restricted to UK Higher Education domain, keeping in mind that the Higher Education sector globally has similar objective and encourage sharing best practice to enhance the student learning experience.

DOI: 10.4018/978-1-60960-800-2.ch001

Review suggested that within Higher Education, videos are generally divided into two categories:

- Own Produced video
- Licensed video

Own Produced Video

Own produced video are produced by Higher Education institutions using their own services and under its editorial responsibility, in general with its own production facilities. Terms of use and code of practice is decided in house to meet their requirements An institution may decide to make their video globally accessible or restrict their video to geographical location or validate access via login technology.

Licensed Video

A Higher Education institution can purchase a license (Educational Recording Agency, 2009) which allows its staff members to record television broadcasts for educational purposes, which can be distributed using streaming media technologies to students. However majority of such licenses contain terms of use and guidance to follow. For example: A video can only be delivered within restricted geographical boundary, video must be tagged with appropriate metadata and institutions must follow accepted code of practice for monitoring authorized access to licensed video.

Steaming media technology (Yan-Jun & Li, 2003) has made it possible to publish such videos online for instant access as oppose to traditional methods of delivery such has video tapes or DVDs.

STREAMING MEDIA

The word 'streaming media' refers to the technology that allows the continuous flow of multimedia over the internet. Video is a type of multimedia that combines both visual and audible components. Streaming Media in Higher Education refers to the real time delivery of audio/video over the networks. In computer science, network is a group of two or more computers linked together. Connected group of networks is called Internet. Internet connects groups of computer networks together regardless its geographical location, forming a single network in which any computer from any group can share information with any other computer globally. One way of accessing shared information located on the Internet is using a technology called World Wide Web (WWW). WWW contains a set of protocols to transmit different types of information. The protocol defines a common set of rules and signals that computers on the network use to communicate. Hyper Text Transfer Protocol (HTTP) is the set of rules for transporting information (text, graphic images, sound, video, and other multimedia files) on the World Wide Web. Information transported using HTTP can be viewed using a Web Browser. A Web Browser is a software application for retrieving, presenting, and transporting information on the World Wide Web. However the speed in which information can be transported is dependent upon the Internet Bandwidth. In the context of Internet, Bandwidth is defined as the maximum amount of information that can be transmitted over the internet per second. It is measured in bits per second. Streaming videos can be delivered using HTTP protocol using traditional web server which hosts WebPages. However, use of a streaming media server is highly recommended for streaming video instead of traditional web server.

Streaming Media Server vs. Traditional Web Server

Following are the differences between streaming media server and traditional web server for streaming videos over the internet (Nelson, 2009):

- A Traditional web server is designed to send maximum amount of data at any given time based on the available internet bandwidth, but it is not the best way to send a streaming video file. Ideally, the data for streaming video should be delivered in real time based on the video file size and not based on the available internet bandwidth (Buford et al, 2010).
- A Streaming media server creates a communication channel with the viewer's computer (student), which enables the server to receive feedback information and send data accordingly maintaining a smooth flow. This enables media server to allow multiple users to watch a streaming video at the same time without any interruptions.
- Web servers do not support multiple-bit-rate (MBR) video. When a video file streams from a Web server, the quality of the delivery is not monitored and the bit rate cannot be adjusted, which can cause the playback quality to vary during the duration of the stream and can result in a poor user experience.
- Web servers cannot use the preferred delivery protocol User Datagram Protocol (UDP) for streaming media, so delivery of a stream is more likely to be interrupted by periods of silence while the player buffers data.
- Web servers do not support live streaming or multicast streams.
- Web servers do not support indexed files. (Indexing provides users with a means of fast-forwarding and rewinding through a file that is streaming.)
- A streaming media server includes built-in monitoring and logging capabilities with which you can gather valuable information about your streaming media session and its audience.

Streaming media can utilize different transport protocols and application protocols as oppose to HTTP, which are discussed in the next section.

Transport Protocols

After the student s' computer has connected to the server, the content can be delivered through either User Datagram Protocol (UDP)(Kurose, 2010)or Transmission Control Protocol (TCP)(Krasic et al, 2001). The difference between these two protocols is how the students' computer acknowledges the receipt of data packets.

Transmission Control Protocol (TCP)

The Transmission Control Protocol (TCP) is a protocol developed for the internet to send data from one network device to another. It uses Internet Protocol (IP) to transmit information across the internet and is commonly referred to as TCP/IP. TCP is a connection oriented protocol and is optimized for accurate delivery rather than timely delivery, and therefore, TCP sometimes incurs relatively long delays (in the order of seconds) while waiting for out-of-order messages or retransmissions of lost messages.

User Datagram Protocol (UDP)

Like TCP, UDP is a protocol developed for the internet to send data from one network device to another and uses Internet Protocol (IP) to transmit information across the internet. UDP is a connection less protocol, optimized for timely delivery of data rather than a accurate delivery, and therefore, UDP is faster and more efficient compared to TCP. UDP traffic also enjoys a high-priority status on the Internet, making it a fairly smooth, uninterrupted ride for media running over the public network. Overall, it's suited to media, which is more sensitive to variances in bandwidth availability than short-session TCP traffic. There has been a fair amount of discussion regarding whether or not trafficking data over UDP is as secure as on TCP, but from a pure streaming standpoint, UDP is the preferred option.

TCP and UDP delivery method is used in conjunction with streaming media application protocols to deliver streaming videos.

STREAMING MEDIA APPLICATION PROTOCOLS

HTTP Streaming

HTTP streaming is a mechanism for sending data from a Web server to a Web browser in response to an event. It is achieved through several common mechanisms. In one such mechanism the web server does not terminate the response to the students' computer after data has been served. This differs from the typical HTTP cycle in which the response is closed immediately following data transmission. The web server leaves the response open such that if an event is received, it can immediately be sent to the students' computer. The data otherwise would have to be queued until the student's computer's next request is made to the web server. The act of repeatedly queuing and re-requesting information is known as the Polling mechanism. Typical uses for HTTP streaming include market data distribution (stock tickers), live chat/messaging systems, online betting and gaming, sport results, monitoring consoles and Sensor network monitoring. HTTP uses TCP rather than UDP, since reliability is critical for web pages with text. HTTP protocol usually uses port 80 or 8080.

Real Time Streaming Protocol (RTSP)

RTSP was developed by the Multiparty Multimedia Session Control Working Group to establish and control media sessions between end points. Clients of media servers issue VCR-like commands, such as play and pause, to facilitate real-time control of playback of media files from the server. Most streaming servers use the Real-time Transport Protocol (RTP) for media stream delivery; however some vendors implement proprietary transport protocols. The RTSP default port is User Datagram Protocol (UDP)/Transmission Control Protocol (TCP) 554.

Microsoft Media Services (MMS)

MMS is a proprietary transport protocol developed by Microsoft that is primarily used with Microsoft Windows Media Server to transport media stream over the internet to the Windows Media Player. The MMS default port is User Datagram Protocol (UDP)/Transmission Control Protocol (TCP) 1755.

Real Time Messaging Protocol (RTMP)

RTMP is a proprietary transport protocol developed by Adobe Systems (formerly developed by Macromedia) that is primarily used with Adobe Flash Media Server to transport media stream over the internet on students' computer. Students' can play flash video using Adobe Flash Player software. The RTMP default port is User Datagram Protocol (UDP)/Transmission Control Protocol (TCP) 1935.

TCP and UDP delivery method is used in conjunction with streaming media application protocols to deliver streaming videos. RTSP, MMS, RTMP can be used in conjunction with either UDP or TCP, while HTTP streaming only supports TCP at this time.

STREAMING MEDIA TRANSIMISSION TYPES

There are three transmission types in use to transmit streaming media from the streaming media server in conjunction with appropriate application protocol and transport protocol:

Unicast Streaming

A Unicast stream is a one-to-one connection between the server and a students' computer, which means that each student receives a distinct stream and only those students that request the stream receive it. You can deliver content as a unicast stream from either an on-demand or a broadcast publishing point (Figure 1).

Unicast streaming offers the benefits of interactivity between the player and server, easier setup, and multiple-bit-rate streaming capability. However, the number of users that are able to receive unicast streams is limited by the bit rate of the content and the speed of the server network. A large unicast audience can quickly overwhelm a network or server. Consider using unicast streaming if (Microsoft, 2009):

- You want to take advantage of multiple-bit-rate encoding and intelligent streaming.
- Your projected audience size and content bit rate is compatible with the capabilities of your network and server.
- You require a detailed student log.
- Your network is not multicast-enabled.

Multicast Streaming

Multicast streaming is a one-to-many relationship between a server and the students' computer receiving the stream. With a multicast stream, the server streams to a multicast IP address on the network, and students receive the stream by subscribing to the IP address. All students receive the same stream and do not have control of content playback (Figure 2). As there is only one stream from the server regardless of the number of students receiving the stream, a multicast stream requires the same amount of bandwidth as a single unicast stream containing the same content. Using

Figure 1. Unicast streaming

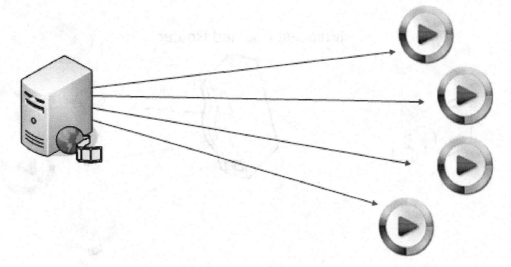

Required Components
Windows Media Services
URL:
(mms://ondemand.xyz.edu/filename.wmv)

Student access to Live Broadcast video files
(mms:/ondemand.xyz.edu/filename.wmv)
OR
Video can be embedded within a webpage
(http://ondemand.xyz.edu)

a multicast stream preserves network bandwidth and can be useful for low bandwidth local area networks. However you will need a multi cast enabled router to enable this feature.

Multicast streams are less demanding on the server and network but may require network modification for multicasts and regular network traffic to coexist effectively. Consider using multicast streaming if [2]:

- You are broadcasting content to a large audience, and network bandwidth and server capacity are limited.
- Your network is multicast-enabled.
- You are delivering high quality high bandwidth content.

Reflected Multicast Streams

Reflected multicast streams take live media from another source, such as a radio or TV broadcast, and stream it out to viewers as a series of unicasts.

Figure 2. Multicast streaming

Streaming Media Method

Following are the three methods which can be used with the above mentioned transmission types:

On-Demand

On-demand streaming provides "anytime" access to a pre-recorded video. In this scenario, each user independently requests access to watch the video via internet, so everyone experiences the video from the beginning with the facility of rewinding and fast forwarding the video streams anytime during the play. On-demand describes a method of delivering content that uses unicast transmission to stream the content only when the client requests it from the server. Each client that requests a stream usually has full control of the stream and can fast-forward, rewind, pause, and restart the content. This is because unicast on-demand publishing points provide a unique data path for every client that requests content.

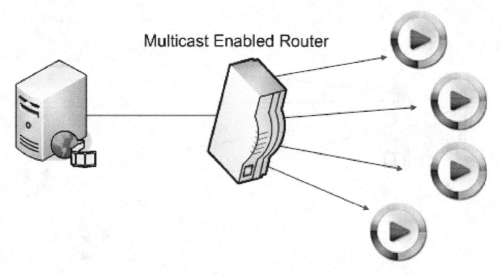

Required Components
Windows Media Services
URL:
(mms://ondemand.xyz.edu/filename.wmv)

Student access to Live Broadcast video files
(mms:/ondemand.xyz.edu/filename.wmv)
OR
Video can be embedded within a webpage
(http://ondemand.xyz.edu)

Multicast Enabled Router

Live

Live events such as lectures, seminars, conferences, tutorials can be streamed over the internet with the help of streaming media server live broadcasting software. For example Windows media encoder compresses the live video from a microphone, video camera, or other recording device in real time and broadcasts it live so the students experience the event as it happens. Quick-Time Broadcaster and flash media live encoder do similar jobs.

Simulated Live

Streaming media server can simulate live broadcasts by creating playlists of pre-recorded video files. As with live broadcasts, all users connecting to the stream see the same point in the simulated live broadcast at the same time, which creates a simulation of watching a live event. Since the event actually is not live, broadcasting software is not required.

Video streams delivered using on-demand, live and simulated live broadcasts are not stored on student's computer, which makes streaming media an attractive option.

To conclude:

- You can stream prerecorded videos using unicast over HTTP, MMS, RTSP, RTMP or other proprietary protocol for streaming video over UDP/IP or TCP/IP. UDP is preferred protocol for streaming prerecorded videos.
- You can stream a live video broadcast using unicast or multicast over MMS, RTSP, RTMP or other proprietary protocol for streaming over UDP/IP or TCP/IP. Multicast over UDP is a preferred protocol for live video broadcast.
- You can stream simulated live videos using unicast or multicast over HTTP, MMS, RTSP, RTMP or other proprietary protocol for streaming over UDP/IP or TCP/IP. Multicast over UDP is preferred protocol for streaming simulated live videos.

Streaming Media Server Software

Table 1 are few examples of industry standard streaming media servers.

Preparing Content for Streaming

Videos are by default captured using video camera in an uncompressed file format, which are not streamable. Uncompressed video files require massive bandwidth, making it impossible to send them over the internet for streaming. That's why it is necessary to compress, or encode your video before streaming. The process of compressing uncompressed video files into a streamable compressed format is called Video Encoding. This process is carried out by a software application referred to as Video Encoder.

Video Encoder

Video encoders are assembled with video compression codec which reduces the quality and size of the original video in order to make it streamable. Table 2 shows a few examples of industry standard

Table 1. Streaming media server software

Streaming Media Server Software	Supported Streaming File Format
Windows Media Server	Advanced System Format (ASF) Audio Video Interleave (AVI) Windows Media Video (WMV) Motion Picture Expert Group (MPG)
Flash Media Server	Flash Video (FLV)(F4V)
QuickTime Streaming Server	QuickTime (MOV) QuickTime (M4V) MPG-4 Part14 (MP4) H.264

video encoders, video codec and streaming media file formats.

First choose the streaming media server platform and then choose the video encoder which can produce appropriate streaming video file format. There is no point in using Flash Media Encoder if you want to use windows media server because flash media encoder will produce flash video (.flv) file format, which is not supported by windows media server. Most video encoders are loaded with pre-defined encoding parameters, which may suit or may not suit your encoding requirements. However video encoders allow you to edit pre-existing parameters or you can create your own custom encoding parameters from scratch.

Video Encoding Parameters

The quality and file size of an encoded video will rely heavily on the following settings [Adobe, 2009; Microsoft, 2009; QuickTime, 2009]:

Bits per Second

For a streaming video, Bits per second refers to the amount of data transmitted by video file per second over the internet. Bit rate measurements are in bits per second (bps) or kilobits per second (Kbps). The higher the bit rate the better an image quality. For streaming videos over the internet, the video bit rate (bits per second) is of vital importance. If the available internet bandwidth is less than the bit rate of the video file, the playback of the file will be interrupted. Usually, insufficient bandwidth will result in either the video being skipped or a pause in playback while more data is buffered. For Example: A video file encoded at 700 kbps will not play smoothly on 500 kbps internet bandwidth, but a video file encoded at 400 kbps will play smoothly on 500 kbps internet bandwidth. It is vital to know your students' internet bandwidth in-order to encode video file at appropriate kbps. To address this issue, a video encoder provides choice of few methods of encoding: Constant Bit Rate (CBR), Peak Variable Bit Rate (VBR) also referred as ABR (Average Bit Rate), and Multiple Bit Rate (MBR) encoding modes, each optimal for particular playback or streaming scenarios.

CBR encoding is designed to work optimally in a variety of streaming scenarios. The bit rate remains fairly constant and close to the target bit rate over the course of the stream, which guarantees consistent playback. The disadvantage of CBR encoding is that the quality of the encoded

Table 2. Video encoders

Video Encoders	Supported Video Codec	Supported Streaming File Format
Windows Media Encoder	Windows Media 9	Advanced System Format (ASF) Audio Video Interleave (AVI) Windows Media Video (WMV) Motion Picture Expert Group (MPG)
Flash Media Encoder	VP6 Sorenson Spark H.264	Flash Video (FLV)(F4V)
Sorenson Squeeze	Windows Media 9 VP6 Sorenson Spark H.264	Advanced System Format (ASF) Audio Video Interleave (AVI) Windows Media Video (WMV) Motion Picture Expert Group (MPG) Flash Video (FLV)(F4V) QuickTime (MOV) QuickTime (M4V) MPG-4 Part14 (MP4)

content is not constant. As some pieces of content are more difficult to compress than others, some parts of a CBR stream are of lower quality than others. In addition, CBR encoding gives you inconsistent quality from one stream to the next. In general, quality variations are more pronounced at lower bit rates.

Peak VBR encoding which is also referred as ABR encoding is designed to work optimally in high bandwidth scenarios and is especially suited for encoding content that is a mixture of simple and complex data. The encoder allocates fewer bits to the simple parts of the content, leaving enough bits available to produce good quality for the more complex portions. Content with consistent data (for example, a "talking head" news story) would not benefit from VBR encoding. However, when it is used on content with varying complexity, VBR encoding produces a much better output than CBR encoding, even if both methods produce files of identical size. In some cases, a VBR-encoded file might have the same quality as a CBR-encoded file that is twice as large because the VBR encode compresses the less complex portions much more than the CBR method does. However, VBR would give more bandwidth to complex portions, unlike CBR encoding.

MBR encoding is designed to adjust to fluctuations in bandwidth. It combines several bit rates into a single encoded file. When the file is accessed, the server determines the appropriate bit rate based on the available bandwidth, and then serves the encoded file at the optimal bit rate. If the available bandwidth decreases for any reason, a stream at a lower bit rate can be served. With a lower bit rate, there is a decrease in quality as well. This suits a scenario if you are targeting students with varying bandwidth for example (200 kbps to 700 kbps).

Multi-pass encoding, also known as 2-pass or 3-pass encoding, is a technique for encoding using multiple passes to keep the best quality. The video encoder analyzes the video many times from the beginning to the end before the actual encoding

process. While scanning the file, the encoder writes information about the original video to its own log file and uses that log to determine the best possible way to fit the video within the assigned bit rate limits. Multi-pass encoding is an option used along with CBR, VBR or MBR encoding.

Video Image Size

Video is made up of images (frames). An image is made up of distinct colors. A color is represented by Pixel. Number of Pixels are calculated using image dimensions (width x height). Higher the image dimension better is the image quality. For video encoding, best practice is to either use the same image dimension as the source video image size or reduce the image size to compliment the encoding parameters (Table 3). If your source video image size contains a High Definition image size 1280x720 (16:9), then the recommended streaming image size will be lower than 1280x720. An ideal streaming video image size can be calculated based on number of simultaneous connections supported by streaming server, server storage space, institution internet bandwidth for delivering video to simultaneous users and the internet bandwidth connection speed of your students' computer.

Table 3. Video image size

4:3 Aspect Ratio	Maximum Pixels per image	16:9 Aspect Ratio	Maximum Pixels per image
160 x 120	19200	160x90	14400
240x180	43200	240 x 135	32400
320 x 240	76800	320x180	57600
480 x 360	172800	480 x 270	129600
512x384	196608	512x288	147456
40640 x 480	307200	640 x 360	230400

Frames per Second

A frame per second is the number of still images that make up one second of a moving video image. Higher frame rates generally produce smooth motion of the video. High Action videos such as sports videos may require 30 frames per second while low action video such as talking head may require fewer frames per second. Higher the frames per second larger will be the video file size. Frames per second also affect video image quality.

Key Frame

A key frame is a point in encoded video where the data for the entire frame is transmitted, rather than just the changes. Key frames are generally inserted when there is a scene change; they are also inserted at regular intervals to improve seeking. The key frame setting is the minimum time between points where the encoder will insert key frames (they may be inserted more often automatically, if necessary). Decreasing the distance between key frames can improve the quality of the video, but also significantly impact the overall file size. If you plan to edit the encoded video, reduce the distance between key frames to improve edited quality. If you want to minimize the file size, increase the key frame value, for example, to 20 seconds. If you use a longer key frame distance, additional key frames are inserted when necessary; for example, when a scene changes. Keep in mind, though, that a long key frame distance will affect both the ability to seek within the video and the amount of time a user may need to wait for video in a multicast scenario.

Buffer Size

The bit rate and quality of content fluctuate within the confines of the buffer size. A larger buffer size enables more bits within the buffer range to be allocated to complex scenes. For example, if you set the buffer size to 10 seconds, the codec may

choose to allocate x number of bytes to the first 8 seconds, and the rest during the last 2 seconds. This allows for the more complex parts of the video to have more bits allocated within the buffer. Typically, increasing the buffer will improve overall quality. However, it also increases the delay between the time when the user requests the content, and the playing starts. For download-and-play scenarios, increasing the buffer size has little impact on this delay. For lower bit rates, it is recommended to increase the buffer size. For higher bit rates, increasing the buffer size has a smaller impact on quality.

Video Image Quality (Smoothness)

Video image quality determines the tradeoff between sharp images and smooth motion. A video appears smooth when objects move easily from one position to another on the screen, and the edges of objects are not jagged. It appears clear when images and motion are well-defined and clearly delineated. The bit rate setting determines the number of bits that can be allocated over a period of video. Based on this setting, the codec can choose to include more frames, which results in the images appearing smoother. However, each frame uses fewer bits. With a higher video smoothness value, the codec may include fewer frames. This increases the number of bits allocated per frame, resulting in sharper images; however, because there were fewer frames, the image may not appear as smooth. The video smoothness setting only comes into effect when there are not enough bits to encode at the specified frame rate, and a tradeoff must be made. At higher bit rates, this value can be increased. If you are dropping frames during encoding, consider decreasing video smoothness. You can adjust the image quality to be smoother or clearer. Increasing the clarity can affect the frame rate, depending on the video. For example, if your video contains a lot of motion, increasing the clarity may decrease the frames rate. In addition, increasing the clarity results in a higher bit rate requirement and may also necessitate increasing the buffer size.

Deinterlace

Deinterlacing is the process of converting interlaced scanned video image into a progressive scanned (non-interlaced) image. Progressive scanning scans each line (or row of pixels) in a sequential order, while Interlace scanning scans each line in an alternate order. Interlaced scanning is used with the analog display (i.e TV). Progressive scanning is used with the digital display (i.e Computer). Streaming video is used with the digital display (i.e Computer), so it is essential to compress interlaced video into a progressive video.

Uploading Videos on the Server

It is easy to manage and upload videos on the server, if it is handled by a single user. However for Higher Education institutions there will be more than one user who would like access to streaming media server in-order to upload their videos. Individual academics may ask for direct access to the server in-order to upload their videos, although it becomes very hard to manage the content if there are more users. Best practice needs to be followed for naming folders, video files name conventions and video encoding parameters to maintain the quality of videos being uploaded. Folder and file naming conventions should have consistent titling which will help colleagues to share information and to locate accurate information quickly. For example: If I am a lecture based in the School of Creative Technologies, teaching Streaming Media Technologies, who requests a direct access to centralized streaming media server. I have uploaded some videos for one of my units. One of the ways to to go about naming the folder and video file is to apply a unique code (UCSMT01) for my unit Streaming Media Technologies. Majority of the institutions will have a unique code assigned to individual units. The folder will be created

based on the unique unit code (UCSMT01) and administrative access will be granted to me for the folder. There are several benefits of this approach. If I leave the institution or stop teaching this unit, my administrative rights can be replaced to whom so ever takes over this unit. This makes management of the content much easier and less time consuming. For uploading video files it is advisable to use a web based uploading platform so that individuals can perform all the steps from uploading to publishing videos online. Below are the steps which are involved in the process:

Step 1: Login

It would be advisable to setup a sub domain i.e. http://ondemand.xyz.edu to host a streaming media website, which can be an institutional gateway to the streaming media service. Applications such as Shibboleth or Novell Access Manger can be used to enable single sign-on access to the service so that academics don't have to memorize different login accounts or go through the registration process. The Shibboleth System is standards based, open source software package for web single sign-on across or within organizational boundaries. It allows sites to make informed authorization decisions for individual access of protected online resources in a privacy-preserving manner. The Novell Access Manager is access management product from Novell, successor to the iChain product. It supports single sign-on for web applications. Before academics can start uploading the content it is important to raise awareness regarding the regulations and standards associated with the usage of video/audio based learning by prompting them to read and accept the terms and condition before they can start using the streaming media service.

Step 2. Sample Declaration Form [5]

The University of XXX has adopted the declaration form shown in Table 4 to protect the University and

University staff from breaching any regulations and standards associated with the usage of video/audio based learning content via World Wide Web.

Step 3. Customized Webpage

After academics accept the terms and conditions they can be forwarded to their streaming media homepage, which may contain a library search facility and upload facility for adding video content. After uploading video content, it is recommended to add mandatory metadata to the video before it could be published online. Managing video content can be a time consuming task if not labeled properly. It is crucial to manage video content in a systematic manner so that it is easy to locate offline and easily searchable online. Metadata is information about an informational resource, be it an article, image or video. It is valuable in the storage and retrieval of information. A library catalogue is an example of Metadata. There are metadata formats defined by Dublin Core Metadata Element Set, SMIL (Synchronized Multimedia Integration Language), Media RSS, the Internet Archive's metadata format and many other organizations. However to make streaming video files searchable on the internet

(Library catalogue) and extranet (video search engines), it is essential to get the metadata right. Table 5 shows the core video metadata elements constructed keeping higher education in mind.

SECURE STREAMING

It is important to make videos accessible via the internet to reach a larger audience, grant easy and instant access regardless of time and geographical location; however embedding such programs within the curriculum raises several issues about copyright infringement.

For Example: Institutions within United Kingdom can join the Educational Recording Agency (ERA) licensing scheme to legally use radio and television programs as a teaching tool. The licensing scheme has two types of licenses – ERA License and ERA Plus License.

1. ERA License

ERA grants licenses in accordance with the licensing scheme, which has been certified by the Secretary of State under Section 35 of the Copyright, Designs and Patents Act 1988 ('the

Table 4. Declaration form

	Title	First Name	Last Name/Surname
Name:			
Department:			
Email:			

I (as named above) request the University of XXX to copy the files/ CD(s)/ DVD(s)/tape(s) (as specified in the section below) onto the Streaming Media Server and make them available to students.
I declare that: (Please tick all that apply)
☐ I created the files and am the rightful owner of them.
☐ The files are to my certain knowledge in the public domain or are otherwise
not subject to copyright and may be copied without express permission from the
author.
☐ The files are copied lawfully under the provisions of a licence agreement or
with the express permission of the copyright holder.
☐ The files were obtained from XXX free-to-air television or radio.
I agree to indemnify University of XXX for any liability or cost incurred as a result of actions taken by any copyright holder arising from making media accessible via World Wide Web.
I have read and agreed to the terms specified in the Streaming Media User Agreement.
Signed: _____ Date:_____

Table 5. Video metadata

User Details	
First Name Last Name	
Email	Contact address of the academic
Unit Code	Unit code is a unique course/subject identifier. Single user may be assigned to more than one unit.
Video Details	
Title	Title defines the name of the video. For Example: Birth of Education
Description	Video Description is a statement that represents video in words.
Keywords	Video Keywords are the words that may be used by viewers to search the videos. Keyword is made up of terms or phrases that are related to the video.
Comment	Comment is a written explanation or criticism or illustration that is added to a video.
Running Time	Running time is the length of time that a video runs.
Category	Category is defined as a group, often named or numbered, to which items are assigned based on similarity or defined criteria
Thumbnail	Video Thumbnail is a screen shot of the video image which is reduced to low-resolution. It is typically used to display search results along with the title.
Language	The language in which the video is broadcasted.
Subtitles	Subtitle is a translation of foreign dialogue of a video, usually displayed at the bottom of the screen.
Channel of Broadcast	In broadcasting, a channel is a range of frequencies assigned by a government for the operation of a particular television station or radio station. In common usage, the term also may be used to refer to the station operating on a particular frequency.
Date of Broadcast/Recording	Date of broadcast is the date on which the program was first transmitted.
Technical Details	
Identifier	Identifier defines the URL of the streaming video file. For Example: mms://xyz.ac.uk/birthofeducation.wmv
Resolution	Resolution is the video image size, which is measured in pixels (width x height).
File Format	A file format is a particular way to encode information for storage in a computer file.
File Size	File size measures the size of a computer file. Typically it is measured in bytes with a prefix. The actual amount of disk space consumed by the file depends on the file system.
Bit Rate	A bit rate is the amount of information (or bits) that is transferred per second (bit per second or bps).
Licensing Details	
Institutional Contact	Name of the person who is responsible for licensing the content. This field is for administrative purposes. Iin case of a copyright breach, this field might prove helpful.
Copyright Holder	Name of the copyright holder. This field is for administrative purpose.
License Start Date	Which date the video license starts from.
License Expiry Date	Which date the video license expires. This field may enable your system to bring a video offline on the expiry date.
Broadcasting Restrictions	It defines the access level of the video i.e can a student watch video only within the campus, or within a geographical boundary or using login protocol regardless of the geographical boundary.

Act'). The Licenses issued by ERA under Section 35 authorize the following activities:

- Recording from broadcasts made in the UK of the works and performance owned or represented by ERA members. Recordings may be made by or on behalf of an educational establishment;
- Electronic communication of licensed recordings within an educational establishment.

The ERA Licensing Scheme sets out a published tariff per full-time student (or equivalent) by the type of educational establishment, i.e. Primary, Secondary, Further and/or Higher education. The tariff is calculated per student per annum. i.e. For licenses issued between 1 April 2007 and 31 March 2008 the tariff is 30 pence per student for Primary education, 52 pence for Secondary education, 98 pence for Further education and £1.55 per student for Higher education.

Traditionally, staff at educational establishments are recording such programs on a cassette, CD/DVD and playing it in a classroom or making it available to borrow on request. ERA recommends that institutions ask students to sign a declaration to confirm the material will be used only for legitimate non-commercial educational purposes.

Educational institutions are coming under increasing demand to make courses available online. However under this ERA license, institutions are not permitted to make recordings accessible to students and teachers online.

2. ERA Plus License

In order to make recordings accessible online, ERA has introduced an additional license called ERA Plus license. Institutions can buy ERA Plus license as an addition to make recordings available online to registered students within United Kingdom. However, institutions that have bought ERA plus license or are planning to buy an ERA

plus license may not have the technology to deliver recorded programs online in accordance with the ERA Plus license agreement. Potential technology to deliver audio and video files over the internet to achieve television like experience is called "Streaming Media" and the technology to deliver protected recorded programs is called "Digital Rights/Restriction Management".

Streaming Secure Files Over the Internet (Maniar, 2007)

DRM is a proven platform that makes it possible to protect and securely stream content for playback on a computer, portable devices, and network devices. Using DRM, videos can be protected to ensure its delivery to authenticate users (i.e. students) in an authorized environment.

Microsoft Windows Media Rights Manager is the technology that allows you to package Windows Media DRM files and issued licenses. Macromedia Flash and Apple Quick time also offers similar facilities. If you decide to use Microsoft streaming server, you can use Windows Media Rights Manager to encrypt a given video file, lock it with a key, and bundle additional information from the content provider. This results in a packaged file that can only be played by the student who has obtained a license. Figure 3 shows a 4 Step process to implement Microsoft DRM technology.

1. **Establishing a Windows Media Server**
   Install Windows Media Services on a computer running Windows server platform. The role of this server will be to deliver streaming video files via internet.
2. **Establishing a DRM server**
   Install Windows Media Rights Manager and Internet Information Services Manager on a computer running Windows 2003 server. The role of this server will be to package video files with DRM encryption and to

Figure 3. Microsoft DRM

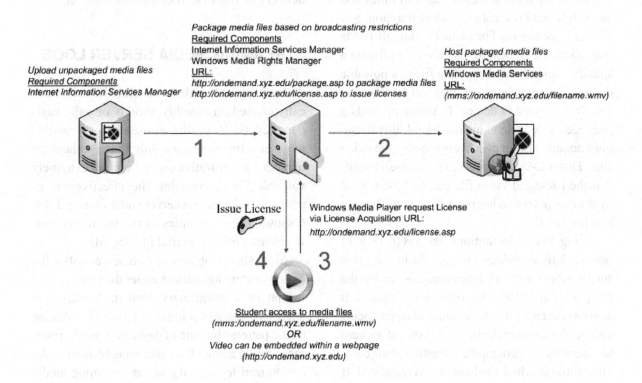

WINDOWS MEDIA DIGITAL RIGHTS MANAGEMENT

authenticate and authorize students request for a license.

3. **Packaging**

Windows Media Rights Manager provides packaging scripts to encrypt the video files. These packaged files get encrypted and locked with a key. Then other information is added to the video file, such as the URL from where the license can be acquired.

4. **Distribution**

The packaged file can be placed on a DRM server for download, on a Windows Media server for streaming, distributed on a CD, or e-mailed to students.

License Acquisition

To play a packaged video file, the students will have to acquire a license key to unlock the file. The process of acquiring a license begins automatically when the student attempts to play the packaged video file. Windows Media Rights Manager sends the student to a registration/login page where authentication and authorization takes place.

Playing the Video File

To play the encrypted video file using windows media encoder, the students' will need a direct URL to a video (mms:// ondemand.xyz.com/filename. wmv) or a webpage URL where the video is embedded.(http://ondemand.xyz.com/foldername/ filename),This should support the file format and DRM as well as allowing students' to input it into the web browser or video player.. If you are using Microsoft, students will need windows media player installed on their computer, if you are using Macromedia Flash, students will need flash player, and if you are using Apple QuickTime, students will need QuickTime player. Students' can then play the file according to the rules or rights that are included in the license. Licenses can have different rights, such as start times and dates, Internet Protocol protection, duration, and counted operations. For instance, default rights may allow the student to play the video file on a specific computer and copy the file to a portable device. Licenses, however, may not be transferable from device to device. If a student sends a packaged video file to his/her friend, this friend must acquire his/her own license to play the video file. This PC-by-PC licensing scheme ensures that the packaged video file can only be played by the computer that has been granted the license key for that file.

Using DRM, institutions can keep track of license delivery, which can provide information such as who downloaded the license, when was the file played and how many times it was played. It also has the capability to accommodate protocols such as detection of the Internet Protocol address to determine the geographical location of the computer through which the license was requested. If students save streamed files to their computer or redistributed it to friends, their friends still need a license key to play the saved file thus protecting the files. In order to implement Microsoft DRM technology, institutions have to sign an evaluation agreement with Microsoft to download and evaluate Windows Media Rights Manager software development kit, which contains Microsoft DRM technology. Macromedia Flash streaming server

also provides similar technology called Adobe Media Rights Management server to secure the delivery of flash video content on internet.

STREAMING MEDIA SERVER LOGS

A server log is a log file (or several files) automatically created on monthly, weekly or daily basis (Boer, 2010). These files are usually not accessible to general Internet users, only to the webmaster or other administrative users. Logs are extremely valuable for determining the effectiveness of your streaming media server and its usage. Table 6 shows a few examples of the log file entries, which are typically stored in a log file.

Most streaming media web servers offer the option to store log files in either the common log format or a proprietary format. A statistical analysis of the server log may be used to examine traffic patterns by time of day, day of week, referrer, or user agent. It is recommended to make customized logs available via streaming media website for academics, so that they can view the usage of their video files. Last but not least, it is essential to have a streaming media user agreement in place to protect your institution's regulations and standards associated with the usage of learning content. Below is a sample streaming media user agreement.

Table 6. Log file entry examples

Log Entry	Description
Student's Computer IP Address	Streaming media server will log the IP address of student's computer, used for watching streaming video.
Date of watching	On which date was streaming video accessed
Time	Time when student watched the video.
Duration	Length of time, student watched the video
Video Bit Rate	The quality of video streamed to the student.
Average Bandwidth	Average bandwidth (in bits per second) at which the student was connected to the streaming media server.

SAMPLE STREAMING MEDIA USER AGREEMENT [MANIAR, 2008]

Introduction

The University of XXX has adopted the following "Streaming Media Service User Agreement" to protect the University and University staff from breaching any regulations and standards associated with the usage of video based learning content via World Wide Web. It will be applicable to staff, who are using technology and equipment owned, operated, and administered by the University. The standards set forth in this document have been established to ensure the integrity and consistency of video streams using university technology and equipment for placement on the World Wide Web. This service will be made available to staff of University of XXX on request. The primary goal of the service is to support teaching and learning activities.

This agreement addresses stored (archived) streaming media files.

The University of XXX Streaming Server will be the single point of media streaming from the University network to the World Wide Web. Streaming will not be allowed through the Internet firewall from a departmental server.

All streaming media files are expected to abide by the Streaming Media User Agreement including copyright regulations and technical standards.

The University of XXX reserves that right to limit the number of streams per user if necessary during times of multiple streaming events.

Any inappropriate use of the streaming media service will be investigated. Video/s will be taken off-line immediately on notice and further action plan will be discussed by Streaming media user group.

Definition of Streaming Media

Streaming Media in higher education refers to the real time delivery of video over the networks. Following are the list of potential streaming media platforms:

- Windows Media
- Quicktime
- RealMedia
- Flash

Each platform uses different proprietary protocols to encode and play media files. The University of XXX initially will support only one platform (Windows Media). Based upon the usage and popularity, the University of XXX may look into supporting other platforms.

Terms and Conditions of Use

Staff using streaming media service, are required to be responsible for the following:

- Legal considerations, including copyright permissions and releases, and privacy issues.
- Technical considerations, including image and sound quality, file size, format, and production values.
- Public relations considerations.

Uploaded video files must be appropriate for their intended purpose, of high production value and quality, and consistent with University standards for public presentations and representations. Scheduling considerations with other promoted events or content will also be reviewed.

Encoding Pre-Existing Material

To request a pre-existing videotape, digital file, or DVD be made available as streaming video files please contact XXX. Staff making requests will be asked to:

- provide information about the source of the content, including producer and copyright holder,
- complete permission forms or provide releases obtained,
- indicate the purpose and the intended audience of the material,
- provide a proposed date for the file to be available on the server,
- indicate the length of time the material will be made available on the server, and
- provide a reason why streaming media seems appropriate for the intended audience.

Upon request, the content will be converted (if necessary) to appropriate digital video files and mounted on the server for the approved time period. All care will be taken to provide a robust, reliable and timely service. The streaming media service is available to University of XXX staff at no cost. There will be no restrictions on the total amount of video or audio, which can be uploaded but the University of XXX reserves the right to refuse requests either because they are excessive or because existing staff or resource commitments do not permit further work to be undertaken. Staff should fill out a request for accessing media server at least 4 weeks prior to its intended usage.

The University of XXX reserves the right to refuse to encode or upload any material deemed unsuitable for streaming. This may be for reasons of poor quality or possible copyright breach or any other reason. All staff are required to obtain copyright clearance, before uploading media files onto the server. If staff are unsure whether material can be copied and distributed to students via the streaming server, they should contact XXX.

Questions about this User Agreement should be directed to XXX.

CONCLUSION

Looking at the educational benefits, theoretical arguments, effectiveness of video as a teaching medium and having streaming media as a delivery platform combined with the tools to make video based learning interactive and more effective, we feel that it is essential to invest in Streaming Media Technology. The streaming media market has grown over the years spearheaded by the entertainment industry. With time, it's accessibility over the internet is becoming easier, faster and its existence is becoming ubiquitous on the World Wide Web. Content providers are supporting the delivery of their content over streaming media and next generation students will want to see such technology being used and closely embedded within their educational process. The educational potential has been realized by a small number of pioneers and is now becoming recognized by the mainstream. There will be a growth in the demand of delivering streaming videos on to mobile phones for teaching and learning activities with the advances in the mobile technology. However Digital Rights/Restriction Management plays an important role to protect the delivery of the learning content. The success of Streaming Media Technology within Higher Education will be imminent with the increase in the support of ubiquitous environment. In terms of implantation of the service, it might be cost effective to outsource the service to streaming hosting service provider as opposed to designing and implementing the service in-house. However it all depends on institutional preferences. Consider the cost of hardware, software license, storage space, performance enhancement, delivery, backup, and maintenance. It is highly recommended to compare the cost of in-house service with the outsourcing service, before making any decisions.

REFERENCES

Adobe. (2009, November). *Flash media server family*. Retrieved from http://www.adobe.com/products/flashmediaserver/

Boer, J. (2010)... *International Journal of Continuing Engineering Education and Lifelong Learning, 20*(1), 40–53.

Buford, J., Kerpez, K., Luo, Y., Marples, D., & Moyer, S. (2010). Network-aware peer-to-peer (P2P) and Internet video. *International Journal of Internet and Multimedia Broadcasting.* (Article ID 283068).

Educational Recording Agency. (2010, August). *What does ERA license?* Retrieved from http://www.era.org.uk/what_license.html

Jennings, C. A. (2010). *System and method for streaming media.* US Patent 7,689,706, 2010 - Google Patents.

Krasic, C., Li, K., & Walpole, J. (2001). *The case for streaming multimedia with TCP, Lecture Notes in Computer Science* (pp. 213–218). Springer.

Kurose, J. F., & Ross, K. W. (2010). *Computer networking* (5th ed.). Boston, MA: Pearson Education, Inc.

Li, Y.-J., & Zhang, L. (2003). The streaming - media technology. *Journal of Dali College.*

Maniar, N. (2007). Digital rights management for ERA plus license. British Universities Film and Video Council. *Viewfinder, 68.*

Maniar, N. (2008). *Digital media management and delivery system. Report to ELearning Steering Group Committee.* UK: University of Portsmouth.

Nelson, D. (2009). *Getting started with Windows Media Services 9 Series.* Retrieved from http://www.microsoft.com/windows/windowsmedia/howto/articles/IntroHosting.aspx

Quick Time. (2009, November). *Streaming.* Retrieved from http://www.apple.com/quicktime/technologies/streaming/

Windows Media Services. (2009, November). *Deployment guide.* Retrieved from http://technet.microsoft.com/en-us/library/cc730848(WS.10).aspx

Chapter 2
The Link in the Lesson:
Using Video to Bridge Theory and Experience in Cross-Cultural Training

Anthony Fee
The University of Sydney, Australia

Amanda E.K. Budde-Sung
The University of Sydney, Australia

ABSTRACT

Video is generally seen as a passive, primarily didactic teaching method; an approach at odds with contemporary cross-cultural training which tends to emphasize highly interactive "experiential" methods. In this chapter we draw on contemporary theories of learning to argue that video-based cross-cultural training is, in fact, more flexible than it is given credit for, and can play an important role in developing learners' cultural intelligence. In doing this, we outline several practical and creative ways in which video can be used to develop cultural intelligence.

INTRODUCTION

In the past fifty years cross-cultural training has evolved from 'chalk-and-talk' didactic approaches that tended to target culture-specific knowledge, to more experiential pedagogies that reflect current theories of learning (Brislin and Yoshida 1994; Fowler and Blohm 2004). We strongly believe in the benefits, indeed the necessity, of experience-based learning in order to develop cultural intelligence. However, in this chapter we suggest that video, when used in a way that aligns with contemporary learning theories, can be used to bridge the highly abstract knowledge required to be culturally intelligent, and the authentic cross-cultural interactions in which such knowledge is applied. As a pedagogical tool for developing cultural intelligence, video provides both flexibility and rigor that often go unrecognized. Our aim in this chapter is to highlight the breadth of pedagogically-sound uses of video in cross-cultural training. In doing so, we share some practical examples of the ways in which

DOI: 10.4018/978-1-60960-800-2.ch002

we have used video in our own cross-cultural training classes.

The chapter contains four sections. First, it provides an overview of cross-cultural training (CCT) approaches and learning outcomes, including the components of cultural intelligence. Next, it identifies problems with current 'experiential' approaches to CCT, before explaining why video may help overcome some of these problems. In doing so, it outlines three different pedagogical uses for video in CCT and provides examples from our own CCT programs. The chapter concludes by identifying some issues that arise in using video in CCT, as well as canvassing some sources of relevant content.

CROSS-CULTURAL TRAINING: FROM DIDACTIC TO EXPERIENTIAL

We use the term 'video' to refer to audio visual material in all its forms, from amateur clips available on the Internet, to television commercials, to extracts from stylized motion pictures. It includes documentary or 'reality' style footage depicting natural interaction between people, as well as highly scripted dialogue; video produced for training purposes or for other purposes. It can include DVD, videotape, or digital AV files, and can range from extracts of just a few seconds to several minutes in duration. We define 'cross-cultural training' as any formal training or education program designed to empower learners with the knowledge and skills to facilitate effective cross-cultural interaction (Black and Mendenhall 1990). This definition is intentionally broad. It encompasses learning that occurs within different settings, including schools, universities and corporate training rooms. It also includes training for various purposes, from generic undergraduate or postgraduate courses, to specific pre-departure preparation for expatriates, or targeted corporate diversity programs.

Forms of CCT are often classified based on the method used, with a distinction being made between cognitive or *didactic* approaches which emphasize the transfer of cultural knowledge and information, and interactive or *experiential* learning approaches, which aim to engage learners emotionally through participation in authentic or simulated cross-cultural interactions (e.g. Gudykunst, Guzley and Hammer 1996; Fowler, et al. 2004). For instance, written cultural briefings and standard 'chalk and talk' lectures are classified as didactic, while role plays and authentic cross-cultural group discussions are experiential (Gudykunst, et al. 1996).

Early forms of CCT were based on the dominant university model focusing on didactic/cognitive methods. While simple, inexpensive and flexible (Black, et al. 1990) this model has been criticized for its inability to accurately replicate 'real world' situations, for presenting learners with pre-defined problems rather having learners discover or identify problems themselves, and for placing learners in a passive, rather than active, position (e.g. Harrison and Hopkins 1967). These criticisms led to the development of experiential learning approaches to CCT, which first appeared in the late 1960s. Experiential learning models aim to engage the learners emotionally through participation in real or simulated cross-cultural interaction.

In reality, rather than being purely didactic or purely experiential, CCT approaches differ in terms of their orientation, and a range of approaches are available between these two extremes. Figure 1 presents a framework, slightly adapted from an earlier model (Black and Mendenhall 1989), representing some commonly used approaches in CCT. As per Black and Mendenhall, three categories of pedagogical activities are identified, those which require learners to: (1) comprehend cognitive information, (2) analyze cultural situations, or (3) engage in cross-cultural interactions.

Activities range from the strongly didactic-oriented on the left-hand side to the highly expe-

Figure 1. Forms of cross-cultural training

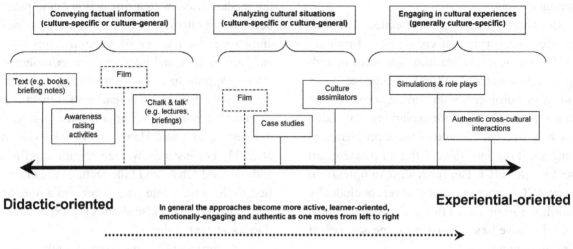

Adapted from Black and Mendenhall (1989)

riential approaches on the right. As one moves along the continuum from left to right, activities becomes more interactive, learner-centered, emotionally and cognitively engaging, and authentic. Video has generally been viewed as a passive, primarily didactic, teaching approach (Harris and Kumra 2000). As shown in Figure 1 in dashed boxes, Gudykunst *et al.* (1996) classify it as purely didactic, while Black and Mendenhall rank 'film' lower than case studies, non-interactive language training, and cultural assimilators in terms of degree of training rigor (1989). This didactic perspective is at odds with the current trend in education (Knowles, Holton and Swanson 1998), and in cross-cultural training in particular (e.g. Bhawuk and Brislin 2000; Yamazaki and Kayes 2004), towards experiential learning as a richer and more effective method. Thomas and Inkson (2003) argue that becoming culturally adept is fundamentally experiential, occurring during social interactions with people from other cultures. Some training programs tend to rely solely on experiential learning through either authentic or simulated cross-cultural interaction (e.g. Thiagarajan 2003), although combining this with didactic content is generally seen as most

effective (Tan and Chua 2003; Earley and Peterson 2004b). In their model, Black and Mendenhall (1989) claim that experiential training is the most rigorous form of training because it enables greater 'reproduction proficiency' (p 523) through the modeling and imitation of culturally appropriate behaviors.

However, successful cross-cultural interaction requires more than behavioral capabilities – indeed, poorly informed imitation of behaviors may be detrimental, rather than beneficial (Earley and Ang 2003). Researchers now recognize that the cultural intelligence (CQ) required to operate effectively in a range of cultural situations calls for a complex amalgam at least three distinct sets of capabilities and skills: cognitive capabilities, behavioral skills, and emotional engagement (Earley, et al. 2003). Key elements of each component of CQ are summarized graphically in Figure 2 and outlined briefly below.

The cognitive component of CQ incorporates the cognitive knowledge and abilities that help an individual cope in unfamiliar cultural situations. This includes knowledge about the specific culture(s) with which the individual is engaging, as well as understanding culture more broadly,

Figure 2. Building blocks of cultural intelligence (CQ)

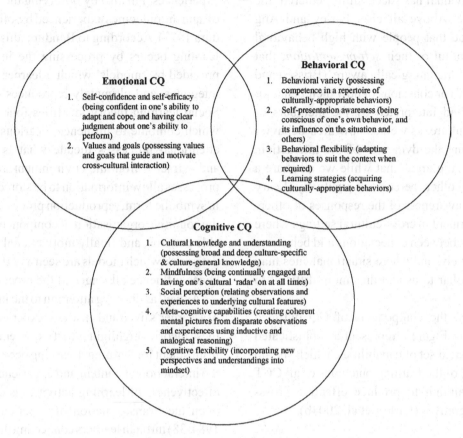

Emotional CQ

1. Self-confidence and self-efficacy (being confident in one's ability to adapt and cope, and having clear judgment about one's ability to perform)
2. Values and goals (possessing values and goals that guide and motivate cross-cultural interaction)

Behavioral CQ

1. Behavioral variety (possessing competence in a repertoire of culturally-appropriate behaviors)
2. Self-presentation awareness (being conscious of one's own behavior, and its influence on the situation and others)
3. Behavioral flexibility (adapting behaviors to suit the context when required)
4. Learning strategies (acquiring culturally-appropriate behaviors)

Cognitive CQ

1. Cultural knowledge and understanding (possessing broad and deep culture-specific & culture-general knowledge)
2. Mindfulness (being continually engaged and having one's cultural 'radar' on at all times)
3. Social perception (relating observations and experiences to underlying cultural features)
4. Meta-cognitive capabilities (creating coherent mental pictures from disparate observations and experiences using inductive and analogical reasoning)
5. Cognitive flexibility (incorporating new perspectives and understandings into mindset)

Adapted from Earley and Ang (2003)

including how cultures differ, and the ways in which culture can influence attitudes and behaviors (Thomas, et al. 2003; Thomas 2006). Because much cultural knowledge is tacit and hence cannot be learned by asking (Shiffrin and Schneider 1977), cultural patterns must be inferred through observation and interaction. Thus CQ also requires high levels of *social perception*, the capability to observe people and situations thoughtfully, and to relate these observations to underlying features or understandings of culture. This necessitates *mindfulness* during cross-cultural interactions (Thomas, et al. 2003; Thomas 2006), 'a flexible state of mind in which we are actively engaged in the present, noticing new things and sensitive to context' (Langer 2000: 220), as well as the metacognitive capabilities to piece together pat-

terns of behavior to create a coherent picture of a culture, situation or person.

The second of the three building blocks of CQ is emotional CQ, which refers to an individual's willingness and desire to interact with a new culture (Earley, et al. 2003). Emotional CQ requires high levels of *self-confidence* (Earley and Mosakowski 2004a) and *self-efficacy* (Earley, et al. 2003) to cope and persist with the uncertainties and misunderstandings that punctuate much cross-cultural interaction (Bandura 1982), rather than withdrawing and disengaging. A person's values and goals that encourage cross-cultural interactions and direct attention and actions during such encounters are also important motivational forces (Earley, et al. 2003). The final component of CQ comprises the behavioral skills that demonstrate that an individual has successfully 'entered' the new culture. Above all else, Earley and Ang (2003) argue that people with high behavioral CQ are mindful of their *self-presentation*; that is, they are 'dramaturgically aware' (Brissett and Edgley 1990) or conscious of how their behavior is viewed and interpreted by the members of the target culture, as well as how their behavior is influencing the dynamics of the interaction. Earley and Ang argue that while we all share a concern that others perceive us positively (Leary 1996), this awareness of the responses of others is more pertinent in cross-cultural settings where mismatches between expectations and behaviors are more likely, and where situational cues may be less familiar to us and thus more difficult to recognize.

Together, the components of CQ outlined above and in Figure 2 represent a sophisticated and interrelated set of capabilities, which should form a core of the learning outcomes of all CCT programs aiming to produce effective cross-cultural operatives (Earley, et al. 2004b).

DEVELOPING CQ: THE PROBLEM WITH EXPERIENTIAL APPROACHES

Interactive CCT approaches have their pedagogical underpinnings in both experiential and social learning theories. In brief, experiential learning theory posits that learning takes place through the day-to-day experiences and problems that people face as part of their lives (Dewey 1938; Kolb 1984). According to Kolb (1984), this occurs through a cyclic process that includes four stages: (1) having a *concrete experience*, (2) making sense of this experience through *reflective observation*, (3) *abstract conceptualization*, during which the learner develops hypotheses or theories, and finally, (4) *active experimentation*, whereby these theories are tested in practice. Building on similar foundations, social learning theory argues that individuals learn not only from their own personal

experiences, but also by observing the behaviors of, and the outcomes experienced by, others (Bandura 1977). According to Bandura, this vicarious learning occurs by processing the information provided by 'models' which a learner observes, integrates, and ultimately reproduces or adapts. Social learning theory identifies four processes which combine to influence vicarious learning: attentional processes dictate what is observed and extracted from the environment, retentional processes allow information to be stored mentally in symbolic form, reproduction processes involve the cognitive organisation of components into usable patterns, and finally motivational processes determine which models are seen as valuable, and hence influence all stages of the process.

As well as drawing attention to the importance of a learner's lived and vicarious experiences, what these theories highlight is that experience alone is insufficient for learning. Learning occurs through the interaction of content and experience, and the effectiveness of learning activities is contingent upon the 'transformation of experience' (Kolb 1984: 38) through learners connecting theories and knowledge about how the world operates, stored as cognitive knowledge, to their lived and vicarious experiences. Only by doing this can experiences be processed and categorized correctly, integrated with existing knowledge, successfully adapted, and employed at appropriate times.

For many of the building blocks of CQ, the gap between the cognitive knowledge (abstract conceptualization) and authentic cross-cultural interactions (concrete experience) is vast, and this presents challenges for learners to create 'a dialogue' between experiences and the theory that is required for learning to occur (Schön 1983). There are two main reasons for this. Firstly, the cognitive knowledge necessary for CQ is highly abstract. Culture-general knowledge comprises intricate psychological processes like categorization, stereotyping, attribution biases, and cognitive dissonance that are intangible and invisible, difficult for learners to code symbolically before being organized into new patterns and used. Similarly, the core of culture-specific knowledge – a society's values, beliefs, and assumptions - is usually tacit or sub-conscious (Hall 1976; Shiffrin, et al. 1977; Van Vianen, De Pater, Kristof-Brown and Johnson 2004). It cannot be learned by asking and must instead be inferred from the visible elements of a culture, like the behaviors, institutions, and artifacts that a learner observes or experiences. The highly tacit nature of this knowledge increases the risk that, without proper guidance, a particular learning cue will go unnoticed or be incorrectly coded, and thus a learning opportunity missed (Bandura 1977).

The second challenge of developing CQ through experiential activities stems from the complexity of intercultural experiences. Authentic cross-cultural interactions are not optimal learning environments. They create multiple simultaneous stimuli and distractions that can impede learners' ability to notice, accurately interpret, or categorize learning cues (Bandura 1977; Kolb 1984). They also create stress and uncertainty about one's own behavior that can be overwhelming and can inhibit one's attention to the environment (Black, et al. 1990). To successfully learn from cross-cultural experiences learners must engage in these interactions with the confidence and self-efficacy (motivational CQ), as well as the awareness, social perception, and metacognitive abilities (cognitive CQ) to be aware of, open to, and able to process 'the legitimacy and importance of different behavior' (Thomas, et al. 2003: 69-70). In short, learners may need to possess a base level of CQ already in order to learn experientially from their cross-cultural interactions; a situation that is rarely the case. In-class simulations and role plays may reduce the uncertainty associated with authentic intercultural interaction; however these are generally viewed as a poor alternative to authentic interaction because of their 'componential artificialities at each stage of the communication process' (Al-Arishi 1994: 345) and questionable

learning outcomes (e.g. Taylor 1982; Bruschke, Gartner and Seiter 1993; Bhawuk, et al. 2000).

Thus cross-cultural educators face a dilemma: how do we create opportunities for learners to develop a base level of CQ that will prepare them sufficiently to be able to learn from their cross-cultural experiences, often in the face of limited resources and time?

VIDEO: LINKING THEORY AND EXPERIENCES

One way to bridge the didactic/experiential divide in CCT is with carefully planned and pedagogically-sound video-based learning activities. Video can contribute to components of CQ which are not addressed in other forms of CCT. Of particular interest are some of the cognitive and behavioral skills of CQ which are frequently ignored in other forms of CCT, like social perception, self-presentation and advanced metacognition (Earley, et al. 2004b). When used in ways that draw on contemporary theories of learning, videos are a flexible and creative CCT approach with potential applications in each of the three pedagogical categories identified in Figure 1. Firstly, as a means of conveying factual cultural-specific and culture-general information, video can make abstract concepts more tangible, engaging, and realistic than most didactic approaches (Fischer and Boynton 2007) This provides a platform for more effectively developing some of the cognitive skills and self-efficacy required to be culturally intelligent. Secondly, video case studies provide a richer, more flexible and more authentic analytical resource than standard written cases, and can be powerful tools for developing metacognitive and social perception capabilities (cognitive CQ). Finally, video can make important contributions to experiential learning by modeling culturally-appropriate behaviors and enhancing self-presentation awareness (behavioral CQ). In brief, video provides a valuable bridge between the abstract concepts (cognitive knowledge) and complex interactions (experiences) that characterize cross-cultural learning. Table 1 summarizes some key uses, pedagogical advantages, and learning outcomes of video in CCT for each of the three categories identified in Figure 1.

The following sections examine the usage of video in CCT and provide several examples from our own experiences using video in the cross-cultural classroom.

1. Conveying Cultural Information

Video can make abstract cognitive knowledge more concrete through visual representation. Culture-general and culture-specific knowledge forms an important component of CQ (Earley, et al. 2003), and an equally critical platform for learning (Kolb 1984). However, its intangible nature can create difficulties for learners using this knowledge to make sense of experiences. For example, how can CCT instructors help learners recognize the visual signals that indicate when one is being categorized as an 'out-group' member rather than an 'in-group' member, or the behaviors and demeanor that demonstrate comfort (or discomfort) in unfamiliar cultural surroundings? Similarly, how can learners become skilled at inferring a culture's underlying values from the behavior of its people, or the structure of its institutions? In our experience instructor-facilitated video is a highly effective way to demonstrate, and hence reinforce, these vague cultural concepts. It allows students to observe the behavioral and other visible elements that represent or accompany these concepts, and so provides a scaffold that can help learners relate these to their own experiences (Wilkinson 2001). Table 2 provides examples of ways in which we have used video content to demonstrate some of these abstract concepts.

In using video in this way the selection of appropriate content is critical. Learners must see the relevance of the material and its importance to current (or future) cross-cultural encounters.

Hence, efforts must be made to choose content that is germane and interesting. Situations that the learners perceive as similar to their own are likely to result in greater attention and empathy, and thus greater emotional engagement (Black, et al. 1990). One way to increase the relevance of video content is to involve learners in selecting content by, for instance, asking them to search online video content sites in order to find and share pertinent content; the chapter by Budde-Sung and Fee in this volume provides an example of this. Taking this one step further is the *Cross-cultural Video Production Project* at the SUNY Center for Collaborative Online International Learning (COIL), Purchase College, New York. The project has involved students in New York writing and then creating short video clips with partner students from other cultures, via an iterative (and innovative) process of collaboration. At the completion of the project, each group of students views, discusses, and analyses the cultural similarities and differences in the completed videos.[1]

Video also provides a conduit through which the perspectives of people from different cultures can be introduced to the class (Fowler, et al. 2004). Learners are more likely to retain and recall the ideas, views, and behaviors of models with perceived status and interpersonal attractiveness (Bandura 1977), and for this reason we have found it a particularly useful way to bring 'outside experts' (Garcia 2008) to the classroom. This use of video is an efficient and convenient substitute for guest speakers. It enables a wider range of speakers than might be otherwise available, as well as greater flexibility in how the input is used. We have streamed extracts from publicly available interviews and presentations by a range of expert 'guests' including Steve Jobs (Apple Inc, USA), Sir Richard Branson (Virgin Group, UK), Ricardo Semler (Semco SA, Brazil), and Kofi Annan, the Ghanaian former Secretary General of the United Nations. Most recently, the speech by United States President Barack Obama at Cairo

Table 1. Overview of uses of video in cross-cultural training

Method	Pedagogical Benefit	Learning Outcomes (CQ)
1. Conveying Cultural Information		
a. Demonstrating a Cultural Concept - Use video to demonstrate visual aspects of abstract and tacit psychological concepts. e.g. in/out group categorization, disconfirmed expectancy, non-verbal communication, cultural values.	1. Provides an authentic visual model that reinforces a concept and facilitates retention (social learning theory - SLT). 2. Serves as a stepping stone between abstract concept and concrete experience (experiential learning theory - ELT).	Cognitive CQ: • Social perception (relating observations and experiences to underlying cultural features). • Meta-cognitive capabilities (creating coherent mental pictures from disparate observations and experiences using inductive and analogical reasoning).
b. Outside Voice – Use video of interviews, quotes or speeches from 'experts', practitioners or relevant informants (e.g. Bill Gates or Ban Ki-moon discussing the importance of culture in international business/diplomacy; repatriates discussing issues related to expatriation or repatriation).	1. Use of models with status and interpersonal attractiveness increases attention, retention and motivation to learn (SLT). 2. Cheaper, more convenient and more flexible than guest speakers (e.g. can be edited and shown at different points during a class, or re-used).	Cognitive CQ: • Culture-general or culture-specific knowledge. Emotional CQ: • Motivation (promoting values and goals that guide and motivate cross-cultural interaction). • Self-efficacy (creating more accurate understanding of practical applications of concepts).
c. Virtual Visits – Use video to show conditions, behaviors or institutions in a particular culture, country, city, or cultural event. In pre-departure training, use video to provide a realistic view of the office environment, living quarters, work colleagues etc.	1. Enables rich vicarious learning with greater emotional engagement than text or photographs (SLT). 2. As an authentic and realistic alternative (or precursor) to a site visit, increases anticipatory adjustment and enables cognitive rehearsal (SLT).	Emotional CQ: • Self-efficacy (developing a more accurate understanding of reality, thus promoting anticipatory adjustment and reducing culture shock). Cognitive CQ: • Culture-specific knowledge. • Social perception (relating observations and experiences to underlying cultural features). • Meta-cognitive capabilities (creating coherent mental pictures).
2. Analyzing Cultural Situations		
a. Critical Incident Analysis – Use video showing authentic cross-cultural interaction for analytical purposes (e.g. diagnose communication successes or failures, anticipate future problems, identify evidence of cultural intelligence).	1. More cognitively and emotionally engaging than written cases/incidents and cultural as-similators (SLT). 2. Less susceptible to 'framing' than written cases, and thus more realistic (i.e. problem-finding). 3. Control over the incident or model being observed (SLT).	Cognitive CQ: • Social perception (relating observations and experiences to underlying cultural features). • Meta-cognitive capabilities (creating coherent mental pictures from disparate observations and experiences using inductive and analogical reasoning). • Cognitive flexibility (incorporating new perspectives and understandings into mindset).
b. Assessment Activity – Use video as 'cases' for assessment or evaluation. These can be brief extracts or full movies with cross-cultural references. The focus of the activity can be adjusted to emphasize particular learning outcomes (e.g. culture-specific vs culture-general knowledge).	1. Relevant vicarious (concrete) experience for reflection and abstract conceptualization (ELT). 2. More cognitively and emotionally engaging than written cases/incidents (SLT). 3. Used as a group activity, encourages peer learning by providing students with a common shared experience to reflect on and discuss.	Cognitive CQ • Cultural knowledge & understanding (broad and deep culture-specific & culture-general knowledge). • Social perception (relating observations and experiences to underlying cultural features). • Meta-cognitive capabilities (creating coherent mental pictures).
3. Engaging in Cross-cultural Interactions		
a. Modeling Behaviors – Use video to model and rehearse culture-specific behaviors (e.g. the process of business greetings in particular cultures).	1. Enables cognitive and behavioral rehearsal in a controlled environment (SLT). 2. Cheaper, more convenient and more flexible than real models (e.g. can be edited or re-used). 3. Control over the incident or modeled behavior facilitates cognitive rehearsal (SLT). The instructor (or learner) can pause or replay to focus on different aspects (e.g. verbal & non-verbal communication aspects).	Cognitive CQ: • Social perception (relating observations and experiences to underlying cultural features). Behavioral CQ: • Behavioral variety (developing a repertoire of culturally-appropriate behaviors). • Self-presentation awareness (being conscious of own behavior, and its influence on the situation and others). Emotional CQ: • Self-confidence & self-efficacy (having clear judgment and confidence about one's ability to perform).
b. Recording Interactions – Record learners interacting in controlled environments and use the video for feedback and to enhance self-presentation awareness. Interaction may include authentic cross-cultural interaction (e.g. multicultural groups participating in problem solving or idea-generating activities), or simulated interactions (e.g. role play of a cross-cultural negotiation).	1. Enables behavioral rehearsal in a controlled environment (SLT). 2. Less stressful than authentic interaction outside the training room, thus enables greater self-awareness during interaction. 3. Enables reflection and observation comparing learners' perceptions (during interaction) and in hindsight (upon watching the interaction) (ELT). 4. Timely assimilation of feedback.	Behavioral CQ: • Self-presentation awareness (being conscious of own behavior, and its influence on the situation and others). • Behavioral variety (competence in a repertoire of culturally-appropriate behaviors). Cognitive CQ: • Mindfulness (being conscious of the situation; activating one's cultural radar). • Social perception (relating observations and experiences to underlying cultural features). Emotional CQ: • Self-confidence & self-efficacy (having clear judgment and confidence about one's ability to perform).

Table 2. Examples of using video to demonstrate abstract concepts

Contact theory specifies a number of conditions that should be present during cross-cultural interactions in order to promote positive, rather than prejudicial, interaction (Allport 1979). Among these conditions are interdependent cooperation, equal status, and authority support. Our experience has been that, while most learners can relate to this on a conceptual level, they struggle to visualize what these 'ideal' conditions might look like, and how they might influence a cross-cultural interaction. We have effectively used segments of the documentary 'Indecently Exposed', part of Jane Elliot's 'Blue Eyes, Brown Eyes' series, as powerful examples of how the conditions of contact theory might shape an interaction. In these video recordings of cultural awareness training seminars, the instructor Jane Elliott intentionally discriminates between participants with blue eyes and those with brown eyes, with the objective of having the blue-eyed majority experience the prejudice that, in her words, "brown-eyed folk confront daily." We usually precede the video by introducing the concept (abstract conceptualization) and asking students to consider how the presence, or otherwise, of these conditions might influence a cross-cultural interaction (active experimentation). Students then view a segment of the video which demonstrates the interaction between the two groups, and between the groups and the instructor. During the viewing we pause the video and label features of the interaction according to the components of contact theory (concrete experience). Following this, we ask students to reflect on and later share their own experiences in a cross-cultural interaction, and to consider to what extent the conditions were present, and how they might have been 'improved' (reflection and observation).

In a similar way we have used one segment of the recent Michael Moore documentary 'Sicko' to exemplify core cultural dimensions. The DVD version contains a pithy case study, not included in the original film, of Norway. We have used this to demonstrate the 'visible' aspects of common cultural dimensions like masculinity/femininity and short- /long-term orientation (Hofstede 1997) by asking students to identify 'evidence of cultural values' using a model that links values, attitudes and behaviors (Adler 2002). We have also used the same extract to demonstrate potential paradoxes and inconsistencies that might be evident in a culture (Osland, et al. 2000).

Likewise, CNN footage, widely available on YouTube, that shows the former United States President George W. Bush performing a traditional sword dance in Saudi Arabia is an excellent (positive) example of CQ. Specifically, we use this brief clip to exemplify two components of CQ: (1) the importance of one's willingness to engage in cultural rituals that are alien and which may create embarrassment or discomfort, but which have cultural significance to others (emotional CQ), and (2) the advantage of having appropriate cultural knowledge and behaviors to demonstrate competence and a degree of comfort when performing such behaviors (cognitive and behavioral CQ). This clip is especially effective because it can disconfirm a perception that some learners have, rightly or wrongly, that George Bush would lack CQ. Upon first viewing of the clip, his apparent discomfort and embarrassment lead some students to assume the video is a negative, rather than positive, example of CQ. However, once viewed in light of the target learning outcomes, it becomes a vivid exemplar of the nuances (and challenges) of being culturally intelligent.

University on 9 June 2009 contains several references to the importance of cultural awareness, and cross-cultural understanding and communication; we recently used video extracts of this speech at the start of a CCT program to motivate cultural learning and to provide a broader context for some of the program's learning outcomes. One benefit of this approach to using video is that it allows the instructor to introduce role models that disconfirm cultural stereotypes. This can provide a useful counterpoint during the learning of overarching cultural dimensions (e.g. Hofstede 1997) which, while contributing useful cognitive knowledge, simplify the complexities of a culture (Osland and Bird 2000). In addition to professional and amateur secondary sources of video, primary content can also be created and edited for specific purposes. For instance, rather than inviting a guest lecturer for a particular seminar, the lead author recorded a 35-minute interview with a global business proprietor (a surfboard manufacturer and exporter). The interview has been edited with different sections used across a number of seminars dealing with the specific issues raised.

In a similar way, video enables students to undertake 'virtual visits' to locales in a way that is more realistic than other forms (in lieu of, or as a precursor to, an actual visit). This use has particular value for expatriate pre-departure training programs. The portability, affordability, and quality of digital video recording equipment makes it easy for host-culture staff or incumbent expatriates to give pre-expatriates an authentic flavor of the working and living conditions that they will experience in the host-culture prior to arrival. This, in turn, can enhance anticipatory adjustment and reduce culture shock and placement failure (Black, Mendenhall and Oddou 1991; Caligiuri, Phillips, Lazarova, Tarique and Bürgi 2004).

2. Analyzing Cultural Situations

A second use of video is as an analytical tool. It enables learners to observe and analyze authentic situations, including cross-cultural interactions, as a cultural anthropologist might, but with two distinct advantages. Firstly, it reduces the stresses and complexity that can impede learning by removing the learner from the interaction (i.e. learners are observers without being participants). This is not intended to replace authentic cross-cultural interaction; however it does provide a buffer that allows learners to develop the cognitive and metacognitive capabilities necessary to be culturally intelligent in a staged way by acting as a 'stepping stone' that bridges theory and experience. Secondly, the analysis can be facilitated by an informed instructor, a process which can aid more accurate coding and retention (Bandura 1977), as well as being shared amongst a cohort of learners via discussions and group analysis. This group-based case analysis reduces the potential that learners will view interactions ethnocentrically, and increases the chance that learners will begin to recognize their own cultural frames of references (i.e. self-awareness). Wilkinson (2007: 10) suggests that open discussions, rather than tightly structured analysis questions, can create 'new meanings beyond those preconceived by instructors.' In our experience, video footage of authentic cross-cultural interactions is much more effective for analytical purposes than scripted dialogue, which tends to be less natural no matter how accomplished the actors. In addition,

we have found that video depicting ambiguous interactions – for instance, where the cause of a miscommunication is open to several interpretations – results in discussions that are the most stimulating and developmental.

As an analytical tool, video also provides a richer and more realistic medium for learning than written text. One criticism of didactic approaches to CCT is that they tend to encourage logical, unemotional participation when much cross-cultural interaction is emotionally charged (Harrison, et al. 1967; Wilkinson 2007). Video is more cognitively and emotionally engaging than standard didactic approaches (Fowler, et al. 2004; Wilkinson 2007). Perhaps more pertinently, written cases dealing with cultural interactions are susceptible to framing by the author. By necessity, they contain descriptions of relevant cues and 'trigger incidents.' Hence learners are led to pertinent stimuli or behaviors, even when the author avoids attribution and communicates these in a purely descriptive way. Thus the text highlights aspects that might not be as obvious in real life, and so learners are presented with pre-defined problems rather than having to discover and interpret these cues among dozens of others in a dynamic interaction (Hopkins 1999). Even the best written case studies suffer from this. For instance, the following extracts from two separate cross-cultural scenarios ask learners to consider what mistakes American business people (Bob and Paul respectively) make during cross-cultural business interactions:

Then Saade inquired about the health of Bob's elderly father. Without missing a beat, Bob responded that his father was doing fine, but that the last time he saw his father at the nursing home several months ago he had lost a little weight. From that point on, Saade's demeanor changed abruptly ... (Ferraro 2006: 45);

During some of the negotiations with the Venezuelan firm, Paul brought the presentation down to an informal level of speech. He noticed that the Venezuelans were listening attentively and seemed to follow the ideas and business plan he presented. He was joking around and talking like "one of the boys" since he was confident about the Latin business atmosphere. The Venezuelans listened politely until the end of the presentation. When Paul was finished, they thanked him and he left. A week later Paul's manager called him into his office ... The Venezuelan firm (had) called his company and refused to do business with them in the future. (Tolbert and McLean 1995: 123)

In each case, the cause of the breakdown of the relationship requires some cultural knowledge and interpretation; however, identifying the 'trigger incident' is clear from the context and the fact that only certain information is available for interpretation. What written text cannot do well is capture the breadth of competing and complex visual, verbal, and non-verbal cues that genuine interactions produce, and which culturally intelligent communicators must make sense of and respond to. Video captures this dynamism of cross-cultural interaction more effectively (Summerfield 1993) by presenting 'a broader array of communication signals' (Wilkinson 2007: 5), and thus retains the complexity, ambiguity and emotion inherent in cross-cultural interaction. It is therefore better able to develop learners' skills in observing and interpreting situational cues than text-based cases. For the same reasons, video-based case analysis can be used as an assessment and diagnostic tool that enables more discriminating evaluation of students' performance. It can also enable a more accurate identification of learning outcomes that might require further attention. Table 3 outlines just a few of the ways we have used video for analytical purpose.

Even culture assimilators (Triandis 1995; Bhawuk 2001), which require learners to actively interact with a written scenario, are limited in the extent to which they can meaningfully simulate intercultural interactions. Cultural assimilators are widely used in CCT, and comprise brief written scenarios describing cross-cultural encounters or misunderstandings, a question or problem relating to the scenario, and a list of alternative solutions from which to choose (Triandis 1995). Learners select the alternative that they feel best explains the scenario, and then read an explanation about why the selected alternative is appropriate or inappropriate. Learners work through the alternatives until the correct response is located, and therefore assimilate feedback immediately on the accuracy of their attributions. As well as presenting learners with brief (typically 80-100 word) pre-packaged scenarios, the descriptions provided in written cultural assimilators are stripped and 'irrelevant materials dropped' (Fiedler, Mitchell and Triandis 1971: 97) and thus distilled of some of the complexity so common in intercultural interactions.

Video can enable a similar process of analysis followed by immediate feedback whilst preserving many more implicit and explicit environmental 'signals' that allow deeper, and more realistic, analysis. Used in this way, video can effectively create an 'empathy experience' (Longo and Longo 2003; Weber and Haen 2005) by asking learners to imagine themselves within a particular cross-cultural situation. Learners can be encouraged to imagine appropriate (and inappropriate) behaviors and possible consequences of these. Following such an activity and related discussion, students can be shown the continuation of the video to see whether their predictions or preferred behaviors were, in fact, enacted, and what the outcomes were. This provides immediate assimilation of feedback in the same way that traditional cultural assimilators do. Because learners have been asked to put themselves in the 'mind and body' of characters, they are emotionally engaged and thus the feedback is highly salient.

Table 3. Examples of using video to analyze cultural situations

We use a brief (5 minute) extract of the film 'Lost in Translation' as a 'critical incident' analysis with two aims: to develop learners' metacognitive skills, and to highlight the importance of self-presentation to CQ. The film's central character is Bob Harris, a wealthy American entertainer. During a short visit to Tokyo, Harris (played by actor Bill Murray) has reason to take a female friend to a hospital. Immediately prior to and during the hospital visit Harris demonstrates a number of behaviors that could be viewed as 'culturally autistic', a term coined by Early and Ang to describe those low CQ individuals who, during cross-cultural interactions, lack awareness of salient environmental cues and are indifferent to the way they are being perceived (Earley, et al. 2003: 157). However, this interpretation of the video is not unambiguous. Harris looks comfortable, relaxed even, and appears to enjoy and succeed in the interactions despite the clear communication challenges (including no common language). He uses chopsticks fluently. At one point he communicates effectively, at least at some level, with an elderly Japanese woman in the hospital's waiting area by echoing her words and intonation. One approach that we find particularly effective is to show this extract to learners (concrete experience) prior introducing the target concept. In discussions following this initial viewing learners usually highlight the humor in some of the interactions, or the efforts made by Harris to communicate. Several criticize Harris' demeanor or attitude during the interactions. Importantly, most students view the extract through the eyes of Harris, the main character. Following this discussion we go on to introduce the concept of cultural autism (abstract conceptualization), and in particular how such behaviors might be perceived or evaluated by others. Later, learners watch the video extract again, this time through the prism of the concepts learned. Most learners view the interaction very differently, generally from the perspective of the people with whom Harris has interacted. For many learners this is a revelation, and has led to engaging class discussions about how such behaviors can create or reinforce negative stereotypes. Viewing the same extract in very different ways has also proven to be a powerful reinforcement to students about their own (CQ) development. It is worth noting that while the film 'Lost in Translation' received critical acclaim and some awards, it has also been criticized, at least in the popular press, for its portrayal of Japanese characters (Day 2004), a point we highlight when using it.

Another approach we use to develop metacognitive skills through video case studies is Personal, Cultural, Structural (PCS) analysis (Thompson 2006), which asks learners to delineate situational causes at the personal, cultural, and structural levels (e.g. What *personal* issues might be influencing the situation? What *cultural* aspects like stereotypes, assumptions, or cultural dimensions are evident? What about *structural* aspects, like class, race, gender?). This has been particularly useful in analyzing cross-cultural conflict situations, as it often facilitates subsequent discussions of relevant theories and/or strategies that might be useful for resolving such a conflict, like the Cultural Grid (Pedersen and Pedersen 1989) which emphasizes how cultural differences can lead to a mismatch between behaviors and perceived intentions. Slightly different again is an approach that draws inspiration from customized training videos developed by the Human Resource Research Organization (Kraemer 1973). This involves collating videos from a number of different situations and contexts, each presenting a slightly different manifestation of a common aspect of culture. For instance, we have collated a number of video clips, each less than two minutes in duration, that show people in different situations and from different cultures communicating in a way that demonstrates high-context communication (Hall 1976). These come from documentary movies, motion pictures, televised reality programs, and television advertisements from a number of countries. Prior to teaching the relevant concept, we ask learners to view the sequence of clips and develop hypotheses about cultural influences and patterns they observe. Unlike Kraemer's videos, which used actors in scripted scenarios, these represent authentic interaction or, in the case of the advertisements and movies, a script not specifically written to highlight a cultural learning outcome. However, like Kraemer, we use this method primarily to improve learners' metacognitive abilities that enable them to recognize patterns of cultural influence beyond the scenarios viewed.

3. Engaging in Cross-Cultural Interactions

One way to ease the stress of authentic cross-cultural interactions is to allow students to observe and 'rehearse' modeled behaviors in the safe environment of the classroom. Video is therefore a non-threatening way for learners to develop new cognitive maps, integrate knowledge and behaviors, and rehearse behaviors without risk of embarrassment and failure. As a means of learning modeled behavior it has the advantage of requiring 'symbolic associations based on observed relationships between behaviors and consequences' (Black, et al. 1990: 126). This is likely to be especially attractive to novices, shy learners, or learners from particular cultures – for instance, people with high levels of uncertainty avoidance, who may be less willing to experiment with new behaviors in ambiguous or unfamiliar situations

(Hofstede 1997). Combining such modeling with culture-general information encourages recall and facilitates improved reproduction (Bandura 1977), as well as promoting self-efficacy that contributes towards the learners' motivation and persistence, even when the behaviors they imitate might be imperfect (Black, et al. 1990; Earley, et al. 2003). Video allows rehearsal to be staged, beginning with cognitive rehearsal - for instance, asking learners to imagine themselves within observed situation - and followed by behavioral rehearsal, during which learners enact particular behaviors. Doing this assists more accurate coding and retention, and thus more likelihood that an individual will succeed in learning the modeled behavior (Bandura 1977). Pause and play-back options allow greater attention to modeled behaviors, and increase the likelihood that the modeled behavior will be encoded and stored accurately by learners, and hence retained in a form that can be correctly reproduced (Bandura 1977). While modeling culturally intelligent behaviors such as tolerating ambiguity or withholding judgment

is valuable, observing inappropriate behaviors like ethnocentrism or intolerance can be equally powerful vicarious learning experiences (Black, et al. 1990). Table 4 outlines one way we have used video in this way recently.

A second use of video when engaging in cross-cultural interaction is to record learners during controlled interactions. These might include authentic cross-cultural interactions (e.g. team problem solving among a multicultural group), or in-class simulations like the 'Synthetic Cultures Laboratory' (Pedersen and Ivey 1993). By doing this in a controlled setting, the instructor can create an environment conducive to learning, and choose specific experiences that are relevant, thereby reducing negative factors that may inhibit a learner's motivation or engagement with the new culture (Tan, et al. 2003). While recording learners during cross-cultural interaction can have evaluative uses (e.g. Falsgraf 1994), we believe its main benefits are diagnostic. It provides learners with direct feedback about their performance and enables reflection and observation on

Table 4. Example of using video to facilitate cross-cultural interaction

Social learning theory suggests that novel behavior is difficult for learners to retain and reproduce, and so gradually increasing the complexity of models can enhance learning (Bandura 1977). This is difficult to achieve without using customized training videos, but it can be approximated. For instance, we have been able to effectively increase complexity by repeated viewings of the same (brief) critical incident over a number of seminars, each time asking learners to focus on a particular aspect related to a specific learning outcome. This priming serves to filter out some complexity. In subsequent viewing, learners can be asked to incorporate additional cues or to broaden their objective in watching the video, and thus extend the models they perceive. One video that has been especially useful in doing this is the documentary film 'The Men Who Would Conquer China.' The film centers on the relationship between two business partners, an American and a Hong Kong Chinese, as they explore business opportunities in China. Among the many authentic interactions that the 'fly on the wall' documentary depicts is a meeting between the two men and a group of (potential) business partners representing a large Chinese bank. The footage of this meeting, and the events immediately preceding and following the meeting (approximately four minutes in total), is particularly 'thick with culture.' It demonstrates several theoretical concepts (cognitive CQ) and behaviors (behavioral CQ) that we include in our CCT programs. These include both positive and negative role models of several facets of cross-cultural communication like the use of interpreters, concept checking, non-verbal communication, and high- and low-context communication, as well as features specific to cross-cultural negotiations (e.g. the stages of negotiations, the role of cultural informants, and cultural variables in the negotiation process). With appropriate priming, we have been able to show this multiple times with students, each time focusing on a specific aspect. Without this priming, more subtle features of the interaction are often overlooked. After these features are highlighted and modeled, we use a custom-made role-play scenario that draws heavily on the details that emerge in the video as a basis for an interactive negotiation within the class. The video thus becomes the model for a class-based experiential activity (controlled cross-cultural negotiation) that enables behavioral rehearsal. Where time and resources allow, the option exists to record the negotiations, and thus introduce an additional 'loop' of feedback and learning.

this experience (Kolb 1984). Such usage is most effective with small groups as a means of promoting self-presentation awareness. Being able to view themselves as 'cultural' beings in a detached way provides learners with a strong 'cognitive confrontation' (Stewart 1966: 302) that can help them to understand and prepare for adjusting their cognitive frames of reference (Stewart 1966; Tan, et al. 2003). It also allows learners to critically view specific behavioral elements. Asking learners to review the video and diagnose their performance with the instructor or others during the activity debrief is also beneficial, as it enables the shared development of metacognitive skills. One simple approach to doing this is a variation of Pedersen's 'Multicultural Group Process Recall' (2004), designed to help group members understand the complex dynamics of multicultural teams. To do this, record a cross-cultural group interaction of around 20-30 minutes duration. Then, soon after, play the recording back to the group. Ask group members to stop the playback at particular times that they feel were pertinent – for instance, a time they recall feeling confused or frustrated, when they did not (or could not) share something during the discussion, or when a particular response or exchange was especially revelatory. During the playback, encourage them to ask questions to each other about the group processes (e.g. 'Why didn't you make that point earlier?' or 'How did you feel when I said that?'). Finally, group members can be asked to identify patterns of behavior they observe across the duration of the interaction. As this chapter has stressed, doing so is much easier once participants are removed from the heat of the cross-cultural interaction.

USING VIDEO IN CCT: CHALLENGES AND RESTRICTIONS

Using video in CCT is not without its problems. Dialogue may be difficult to understand because of poor sound, strong accents or the pace of speech, a particular problem when speakers (or learners) are using a second language (see Budde-Sung & Fee, in this volume, for suggestions for dealing with this). Perhaps a more significant issue for instructors relates to copyright laws, which can restrict what, how, and to whom video content is shown. For instance, although the technology exists, copyright restrictions prevent most commercially produced films from being edited for use in class, even for educational purposes. Copyright laws regarding the educational use of audio visual materials differ greatly around the world, and continually evolve in response to 'existing and emerging technologies, international agreements, and the need for reasonable balance between users and creators of copyrighted works' (Noel and Breau 2005: ii). Thus, instructors wishing to use video should check the legal obligations and restrictions within their own country. Most countries' laws will allow for limited showing of copyrighted material in the classroom in non-profit education institutions. By way of example, in the United States the *Copyright Act of 1976* contains a classroom 'exemption' that allows copyrighted video material to be shown in a classroom environment as long as four criteria are met: (1) the video is shown in a face-to-face classroom environment (i.e. not posted online); (2) the video is shown as part of the actual teaching activities of the course (not as a reward or other reasons external to the learning objectives of the course); (3) the video is used only by the instructor and/or the students enrolled in the class; and (4) the classroom is in a non-profit educational institution (U.S. Copyright Act of 1976, Section 110 (1)). For corporate training and other for-profit educational situations, the copyright issue is not an insurmountable obstacle. Permission can be requested from the copyright holder, with an explanation of the intended use. Alternatively, class syllabi can require learners to purchase their own copy of a DVD, just as many courses require participants to purchase textbooks and other class materials. YouTube videos can be streamed without violating copyright laws.

As well as the issue of copyright, purchase/rental agreement contracts mean that some DVD or video copies may be restricted to 'private' or 'domestic' use only. A public showing of that video, including within a class, might violate the terms of that contract. For this reason, most educational institutions have rules about how and where their instructors rent or buy video content. Instructors should check with their institution's legal department to see, for instance, if there are preferred providers, or if videos should be rented in the institution's name rather than the instructor's name.

CONCLUSION

This chapter has identified a number of ways in which video can be used in CCT to enhance CQ. In brief, we hope to demonstrate that video is a flexible, convenient and - when used in ways consistent with contemporary learning theories - pedagogically-sound approach to teaching CQ. It provides a range of teaching options and contributes to learning outcomes that are not well met by other techniques (Earley, et al. 2004b). This is not to say that video should take priority over other forms of pedagogy, particularly authentic cross-cultural experiences which are invaluable to developing CQ (e.g. Thomas, et al. 2003). Experiential learning (and assessment) activities remain the central plank of our CCT programs. However when used appropriately, video can be a valuable addition to an instructor's repertoire of approaches. Because our own experiences are in management education, many of the examples we present in this chapter have a business and management focus. However, the techniques can be applied equally well in any context where improved cultural awareness or knowledge is required, from health care to hospitality to law enforcement.

A plethora of secondary video content can be accessed relatively easily. Innovative sources are now available via the Internet, and the video search engine *blinkx* (http://www.blinkx.com/about) facilitates searching online video via specific keyword/s. Online content available includes professional and amateur video productions on YouTube (www.youtube.com/), Hulu (http://www.hulu.com/), OurMedia (http://www.ourmedia.org/), and other similar sites, depicting a range of relevant content like authentic cross-cultural interactions, news and current affairs reports, as well as information or training programs dealing specifically with cross-cultural issues. Multinational organizations like the *United Nations* (http://www.un.org/apps/news/html/multimedia.shtml) and the *World Trade Organization* (http://www.wto.org/english/res_e/webcas_e/webcas_e.htm#intro), to name two, provide relevant multimedia and webcasts via the Internet. The website of the United States Government Bureau of Educational and Cultural Exchange, *ExchangesConnect* (http://connect.state.gov/), hosts numerous culture-specific videos. Dedicated educational sites are also a source of valuable resources. For instance, Cornell University's eClips Internet site categorizes and makes available original video and transcripts of interviews and presentations by business leaders (http://eclips.cornell.edu/homepage.do). Similarly, London Business School's 'Survival of the Fastest' YouTube channel (http://www.youtube.com/survivalofthefastest) provides pithy video clips that, while dealing primarily with business leadership issues, can be analyzed for embedded (cultural) assumptions or communication patterns, as well as triggers for other cultural awareness activities.

Outside the Internet, a number of Hollywood motion pictures deal explicitly or implicitly with cross-cultural and diversity issues (for a comprehensive list see Tejeda 2008). However, we endeavor to balance our use of films from Anglo cultures with extracts of films made in a variety of cultural contexts, including Iran, South Korea, India ('Bollywood'), and Nigeria ('Nollywood'). Television – via its current affairs, reality, documentary and drama shows, as well as advertisements - is rich with content that can be used creatively in teaching CQ; indeed, we find it difficult to watch television now without seeing something that we could use in a CCT seminar. Hunt (2001: 633) persuasively argues for the use of television characters and shows in management education because 'the cultural values and priorities they reflect may be quite realistic.' The content of free-to-air television is increasingly being made available in formats that can be used by educators through licensing partnerships with bodies such as *Screenrights* in Australia and New Zealand (see http://www.screenrights.org/ and http://www.enhancetv.com.au/). Additionally, the accessibility, affordability and portability of digital video recording equipment mean that primary video content can be created relatively cheaply with limited technical knowledge.

REFERENCES

Adler, N. J. (2002). *International dimensions of organizational behavior* (4th ed.). Cincinnati, OH: SWCP.

Al-Arishi, A. Y. (1994). Role-play, real-play, and surreal-play in the ESOL classroom. *ELT Journal, 48*(4), 337–346. doi:10.1093/elt/48.4.337

Allport, G. W. (1979). *The nature of prejudice*. Reading, MA: Addison-Wesley.

Bandura, A. (1977). *Social learning theory*. Prentice-Hall.

Bandura, A. (1982). Self-efficacy mechanism in human agency. *The American Psychologist, 37*(2), 122–147. doi:10.1037/0003-066X.37.2.122

Bhawuk, D. P. S. (2001). Evolution of cultural assimilators: Toward theory-based assimilators. *International Journal of Intercultural Relations, 25*, 141–163. doi:10.1016/S0147-1767(00)00048-1

Bhawuk, D. P. S., & Brislin, R. W. (2000). Cross-cultural training: A review. *Applied Psychology: An International Review, 49*(1), 162–191. doi:10.1111/1464-0597.00009

Black, J. S., & Mendenhall, M. (1989). A practical but theory-based framework for selecting cross-cultural training methods. *Human Resource Management, 28*(4), 511–539. doi:10.1002/hrm.3930280406

Black, J. S., & Mendenhall, M. E. (1990). Cross-cultural training effectiveness: A review and a theoretical framework for future research. *Academy of Management Review, 15*(1), 113–136.

Black, J. S., Mendenhall, M. E., & Oddou, G. (1991). Toward a comprehensive model of international adjustment: An integration of multiple theoretical perspectives. *Academy of Management Review, 16*(2), 291–317.

Brislin, R., & Yoshida, T. (1994). *Intercultural communication training: An introduction*. Thousand Oaks, CA: Sage.

Brissett, D., & Edgley, C. (Eds.). (1990). *Life as theatre*. Hawthorne, NY: Walter de Gruyter.

Bruschke, J. C., Gartner, C., & Seiter, J. S. (1993). Student ethnocentrism, dogmatism, and motivation: A Study of Bafa Bafa. *Simulation & Gaming, 21*(1), 9–20. doi:10.1177/1046878193241003

Caligiuri, P., Phillips, J., Lazarova, M., Tarique, I., & Bürgi, P. (2004). The theory of met expectations applied to expatriate adjustment: The role of cross-cultural training. *International Journal of Human Resource Management, 12*(3), 357–372.

Day, K. (2004, 24 January). Totally lost in translation. *The Guardian Newspaper*. Retrieved on December 11, 2008, from http://www.guardian.co.uk/world/2004/jan/24/japan.film

Dewey, J. (1938). *Experience and education*. New York, NY: Collier Books.

Earley, P. C., & Ang, S. (2003). *Cultural intelligence: Individual interactions across cultures.* Stanford, CA: Stanford University Press.

Earley, P. C., & Mosakowski, E. (2004a). Cultural intelligence. *Harvard Business Review*, (October): 139–146.

Earley, P. C., & Peterson, R. S. (2004b). The elusive cultural chameleon: Cultural intelligence as a new approach to intercultural training for the global manager. *Academy of Management Learning & Education*, 3(1), 100–115. doi:10.5465/AMLE.2004.12436826

Falsgraf, C. D. (1994). *Language and culture at a Japanese immersion school.* University of Oregon, Unpublished doctoral dissertation.

Ferraro, G. P. (2006). *The cultural dimensions of international business* (5th ed.). Upper Saddle River, NJ: Pearson Prentice Hall.

Fiedler, F. E., Mitchell, T., & Triandis, H. C. (1971). The culture assimilator: An approach to cross-cultural training. *The Journal of Applied Psychology*, 55(2), 95–102. doi:10.1037/h0030704

Fischer, B., & Boynton, A. (2007). Out of this world high performing teams: A video tour. *Academy of Management Learning & Education*, 6(3), 412–428. doi:10.5465/AMLE.2007.26361630

Fowler, S. M., & Blohm, J. M. (2004). An analysis of methods for intercultural training . In Landis, D., Bennett, J. M., & Bennett, M. J. (Eds.), *Handbook of intercultural training* (3rd ed., pp. 37–84). Thousand Oaks, CA: Sage.

Garcia, R. (2008). *Integrating video clips in classroom teaching.* In Knowledge Development and Exchange in International Business Networks: 50th Annual Meeting of the Academy of International Business, Milan, Italy, 30 June to 3 July 2008: Academy of International Business.

Gudykunst, W. B., Guzley, R. M., & Hammer, M. R. (1996). Designing intercultural training. In Landis, D., & Bhagat, R. (Eds.), *Handbook of intercultural training* (2nd ed., pp. 61–80). Thousand Oaks, CA: Sage.

Hall, E. T. (1976). *Beyond culture.* New York, NY: Doubleday.

Harris, H., & Kumra, S. (2000). International manager development: Cross-cultural training in highly diverse environments. *Journal of Management Development*, 19(7), 602–614. doi:10.1108/02621710010373278

Harrison, R., & Hopkins, R. L. (1967). The design of cross-cultural training: An alternative to the university model. *The Journal of Applied Behavioral Science*, 3(4), 431–460. doi:10.1177/002188636700300401

Hofstede, G. (1997). *Cultures and organisations: Software of the mind, intercultural cooperation and its importance for survival.* New York, NY: McGraw-Hill.

Hopkins, R. S. (1999). Using Videos as Training Tools. In Fowler, S. M., & Mumford, M. G. (Eds.), *Intercultural Sourcebook: Cross-Cultural Training Methods* (*Vol. 2*, pp. 73–112). Yarmouth, ME: Intercultural Press.

Hunt, C. S. (2001). Must see TV: The timelessness of television as a teaching tool. *Journal of Management Education*, 25(6), 631–647. doi:10.1177/105256290102500603

Knowles, M. S., Holton, E. F., & Swanson, R. A. (1998). *The adult learner: The definitive classic in adult education and human resource development* (5th ed.). Houston, TX: Gulf Professional.

Kolb, D. (1984). *Experiential learning: Experience as the source of learning and development.* Englewood Cliffs, NJ: Prentice-Hall.

Kraemer, A. J. (1973). *Development of a cultural self-awareness approach to instruction in intercultural communication.* Alexandria, VA: Human Resources Research Organization. (Technical Report # 73-71).

Langer, E. J. (2000). Mindful learning. *Current Directions in Psychological Science, 9*(6), 220–223. doi:10.1111/1467-8721.00099

Leary, M. R. (1996). *Self-presentation: Impression management and interpersonal behavior.* Boulder, CO: Westview Press.

Longo, R. E., & Longo, D. P. (2003). *New hope for youth: Experiential exercises for children and adolescents.* Holyoke, MA: NEARI Press.

Noel, W., & Breau, G. (2005). *Copyright matters!* 2nd edition. Ottawa, Canada: Council of Ministers of Education Canada, Canadian School Boards Association, and Canadian Teachers' Federation.

Osland, J. S., & Bird, A. (2000). Beyond sophisticated stereotyping: Cultural sense-making in context. *The Academy of Management Executive, 14*(1), 65–77. doi:10.5465/AME.2000.2909840

Pedersen, A., & Pedersen, P. (1989). The cultural grid: A framework for multicultural counseling. *International Journal for the Advancement of Counseling, 14*(4), 299–307. doi:10.1007/BF00123258

Pedersen, P. B. (2004). *110 experiences for multicultural learning.* Washington, DC: American Psychological Association.

Pedersen, P. B., & Ivey, A. E. (1993). *Culture-centred counseling and interviewing skills.* Westport, CT: Greenwood/Praeger.

Schön, D. A. (1983). *The reflective practitioner. How professionals think in action.* London, UK: Temple Smith.

Shiffrin, R. M., & Schneider, W. (1977). Controlled and automatic human information processing: Perceptual learning, automatic attending and a general theory. *Psychological Review, 84*(2), 127–190. doi:10.1037/0033-295X.84.2.127

Stewart, E. C. (1966). The simulation of cultural differences. *The Journal of Communication, 16*(4), 291–304. doi:10.1111/j.1460-2466.1966.tb00043.x

Summerfield, E. (1993). *Cross cultures through film.* Yarmouth, ME: Intercultural Press.

Tan, J.-S., & Chua, R. Y.-J. (2003). Training and developing cultural intelligence. In Earley, P. C., & Ang, S. (Eds.), *Cultural intelligence: Individual interactions across cultures* (pp. 258–303). Stanford, CA: Stanford University Press.

Taylor, B. P. (1982). In search of real reality. *TESOL Quarterly, 16*, 29–42. doi:10.2307/3586561

Tejeda, M. J. (2008). A resource review for diversity film media. *Academy of Management Learning & Education, 7*(3), 434–439. doi:10.5465/AMLE.2008.37029279

Thiagarajan, S. (2003). *Design your own games and activities: Thiagi's templates for performance improvement.* San Francisco, CA: Pfeiffer.

Thomas, D. C. (2006). Domain and development of cultural intelligence: The importance of mindfulness. *Group & Organization Management, 31*(1), 78–99. doi:10.1177/1059601105275266

Thomas, D. C., & Inkson, K. (2003). *Cultural intelligence: People skills for global business.* San Francisco, CA: Berrett-Koehler.

Thompson, N. (2006). *Anti-discrimination practice* (4th ed.). New York, NY: Palgrave Macmillan.

Tolbert, A. S., & McLean, G. N. (1995). Venezuelan culture assimilator for training United States professionals conducting business in Venezuela. *International Journal of Intercultural Relations*, *19*(1), 111–125. doi:10.1016/0147-1767(94)00027-U

Triandis, H. C. (1995). Culture specific assimilators. In Fowler, S., & Mumford, M. (Eds.), *Intercultural sourcebook* (*Vol. 1*, pp. 179–186). Yarmouth, ME: Intercultural Press.

Van Vianen, A. E. M., De Pater, I. E., Kristof-Brown, A. L., & Johnson, E. C. (2004). Fitting in: Surface- and deep-level cultural differences and expatriates' adjustment. *Academy of Management Journal*, *47*(5), 697–709. doi:10.2307/20159612

Weber, A. M., & Haen, C. (2005). *Clinical applications of drama therapy in child and adolescent treatment*. New York, NY: Routledge.

Wilkinson, L. C. (2001). *Uses of moving pictures in intercultural education*. Seattle, WA: Seattle University, Unpublished dissertation (Ed. D).

Wilkinson, L. C. (2007). A developmental approach to uses of moving pictures in intercultural education. *International Journal of Intercultural Relations*, *31*(1), 1–27. doi:10.1016/j.ijintrel.2006.08.001

Yamazaki, Y., & Kayes, D. C. (2004). An experiential approach to cross-cultural learning: A review and integration of competencies for successful expatriate adaptation. *Academy of Management Learning & Education*, *3*(4), 362–379. doi:10.5465/AMLE.2004.15112543

ENDNOTE

[1] Details of the project can be found at: http://coilcenter.purchase.edu/index.php?option=com_content&task=view&id=22&Itemid=141 [Last accessed 1 June 2009].

Chapter 3
The Next Step for Use of Streaming Video in Higher Education:
Didactic Models for Weblectures

J.C. Winnips
University of Groningen, The Netherlands

G.J. Verheij
University of Groningen, The Netherlands

E.M. Gommer
University of Twente, The Netherlands

ABSTRACT

Using streaming video for recording and playing back lectures has become a widespread extra feature for lectures in higher education. There is a wide variety in ways of recording these lectures and making them available. The main form is live lectures that are recorded with slides synchronized with the audio and video of the lecturer. These lectures are recorded, placed online via a University portal, students typically study these materials just before an examination of assignments. But many more ways of using weblectures are possible. This chapter describes 5 didactic models of using weblectures. These are: checking back attended lectures, checking back missed lectures, flexible learning, presentation skills, and re-use. The models can help to make decisions for the form in which lectures can be used, and steer technical developments.

1 INTRODUCTION

In the past, many attempts have been made to capture the minds of our best university lecturers, and open up those bright minds to the world. Ideally this should happen in an interactive way, via tutoring systems, expert systems, or computer based training, so that the "boxed up" lecturer can respond to the students needs. But there are other ways. One of the moments when the lecturers mind opens up to the learner is during lecturing. With lectures captured, stored and made available for

DOI: 10.4018/978-1-60960-800-2.ch003

re-viewing we can now reproduce the experience, and store a bit of the lecturers' thoughts for use when studying.

Recording lectures, and presenting them on the Web is not new (see for example Winnips & McLoughlin, 2001). But increasingly faster networks, and better streaming technologies have caused a rise in the amount of Universities that capture lectures. A study by Leoni & Lichti (2009) with participants of 150 Universities showed that 118 of these Universities are working on implementation of weblectures. In Europe, Universities that are piloting with weblectures seem to be taking off too. For example, in the Netherlands, Universities such as University of Utrecht (Russel et. al. 2008), University of Groningen (Hofman & Wieling, 2009) and University of Twente (Gommer & Bosker, 2008) have evaluation studies available from pilots with weblectures, and projects have been done, such as Triple L (http://www.triple-l-project.nl/) with Universities collaborating on the use of weblectures.

Apart from Universities starting up the use of weblectures, students demand them. At the University of Groningen weblectures form a part of the election programme in student politics. Student fractions SOG (2009) and Calimero (2009) argue for weblectures to be made available via the University's learning environment, and have advertised this in their election programmes.

There are several publications pointing towards the effectiveness of weblectures, showing effects on motivation, or learning perception. Day (2008) found significant effects on learning via weblectures as compared to similar types of multimedia presentations. Further, comparing a more traditionally taught course to a course taught with weblectures significantly improved perception of learning, and satisfaction. Wieling and Hofman (2009) found that students who attended few lectures had relatively more benefit from viewing online lectures then students who attended many lectures. In a study by Jadin et. al. (2009) differences were found when compar-

ing weblectures with and without additional text presented. Analysis of learner actions revealed that students who were repeating fragments of video outperformed students who navigated away from fragments and studied external web links. In this case the learning strategy turned out to be the most important determinant for outcomes, and not the mode of presentation. So, how can we help students to use learning strategies in studying weblectures? A way to do this could be to start at the design phase, and integrating weblectures into teaching while keeping a didactic model in mind.

The momentum for use of weblectures is there, but what is happening with all these materials that are being produced? How are weblectures implemented in courses? Students demand weblectures, but do they learn from them? Can we support lecturers to integrate weblectures in their course design? How do we support students to use learning strategies? In this chapter we argue that key to the success of implementation of weblectures is not the technology, but how they are implemented and integrated in courses. To help implementation, five didactic models for best practices of using weblectures are identified. From these models and evaluation data, pointers for future development of this service at universities are gathered.

2 WEBLECTURES

Throughout recent years, many forms of recording lectures have emerged, many of them helped by software companies. Leoni and Lichti (2009) found some of the most prominent tools that are currently used: Camtasia Relay (http://www.techsmith.com/camtasiarelay.asp), Echo360 (http://www.echo360.com/), Mediasite, (http://www.sonicfoundry.com/) and ProfCast (http://www.profcast.com/). These tools allow production of a wide variety of weblecture forms.

Day (2008) defines weblectures as "multimedia presentations that integrate talking head and torso video, audio, lecture slides, table of contents, and navigation controls, which are made available via the web (streaming or download)." The lecturers video is synchronised with the lecture slides so that students can browse back and forth in the presentation, can repeat fragments, and search for fragments via the table of contents. Figure 1 gives a typical screen for the student side of lecture capture, made with Sonicfoundry's Mediasite at the Universite of Twente.

Weblectures are typically presented via presentation portals. Via these portal sites students can search for lectures, and browse collections based on course content. Some examples of widely used repositories of weblectures can be found at: Academic Earth (http://academicearth.org/), Weblectures.net (http://videolectures.net/), and Youtube Edu (http://www.youtube.com/education?b=400).

A variation on this theme is available from iTunes U (http://www.apple.com/education/mobile-learning/) which allows students to take lectures with them in their iPhones and iPods. iTunes U only provides the video and audio of the lecture. Access to iTunes U is open to anyone, and videos can be played on any computer. Figure 2 gives an example of one of the most downloaded lectures from iTunesU.

Via initiatives such as iTunes U considerable interest has been raised in the lectures of Walter Lewin. In an article in The New York Times (Rimer, 2007), the lectures of Walter Lewin are praised, describing reactions and questions of the fanmail received. But these lectures are not just top downloads from iTunes, they also rank high in Google's video search, and on YouTube. Some weblectures have even "gone viral". They are being spread over the Internet by users commenting, blogging, and sending on the link to the lecture. A lecture on law by Professor James Duane where he is quoted: "don't talk to the police" gives over 266.000 hits on Google. Weblectures are not just spreading over University students, they spread over the Internet as well.

Apart from viewing lectures, the other side is recording them. Figure 3 gives a typical recording setup, as used at Universit of Groningen in the Netherlands. An operator at the back of the

Figure 1. Typical Videolecture as recorded at the University of Twente, recorded with Sonicfoundry's Mediasite

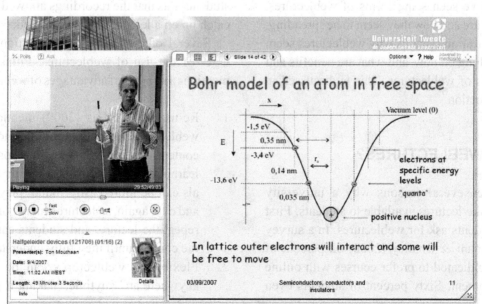

Figure 2. One of the most downloaded videos from iTunesU, Walter Lewin explaining kinematics of free fall via experiments with a monkey

lecture room views the recording, and can zoom, pan and tilt the camera.

So we've seen some forms of weblectures, what they are and how they seem to be spreading. But the question remains why weblectures seem to be catching on now, and what are benefits and drawbacks of weblectures. This is discussed in the next section.

3 WHY WEBLECTURES?

There are several reasons why a university would make lectures available to students. First of all: students ask for weblectures. In a survey by Veeramani & Bradley (2008) 82 percent of students indicated to prefer courses with online lecture content. Sixty percent of students even

indicated that they would pay for lecture capture services. The main advantage as mentioned by students was that the recordings allowed them to catch up on a lecture they had missed.

Several others publications mention advantages of the use of weblectures. Filius (2009) mentions a number of advantages of weblectures:

1. Re-usability: Filius (2009) mentions that weblectures offer opportunities to re-use content. Adding lectures to a repository of learning materials can make sure that materials can be more easily found, played over and over again, so lecturers may not have to repeat the lecture, and students can repeat the content until they fully understand it.

2. Flexibility: weblectures can be viewed anywhere and anytime, making it possible

Figure 3. Typical setup for an operator recording weblectures at the University of Groningen

for students to study where and when they want.

3. Variety: Using weblectures adds to the variety of presentation of learning materials, thus catering for more learning styles.

4. Cost: Production of weblectures is relatively cheap, as lectures are provided anyways. Cost of bandwith and cameras are no longer a big issue. What can become costly is time for post-processing of recordings.

So, the advantages are there, and for students it seems an easy choice, as weblectures are often provided as "something extra" with a course. When you buy a car, and you can get air-conditioning for free, would you not want it?

But not all lecturers are directly enthusiastic about weblectures. Most of the disadvantages of using weblectures are be experienced on the lecturers part:

1. Opening up the classroom: Some lecturers find it obtrusive that their classroom is opened up to a wider audience. It can be very confronting to view back a lecture that may not be an entire success, and some lecturers and faculties are reluctant to share their materials as they fear losing students when their lectures can be seen anyways ("Will they still visit my lecture?").

2. Copyrights: some lecturers have used materials in their presentations that may not be cleared for copyrights. Opening up their lectures on the web exposes this problem.

3. Without additional didactics viewing weblectures is rather passive. Weblectures seem to fit with a passive learning model, where a learner is receiving information, instead of actively constructing meaning. Demetriadis and Pombortsis (2007) critised weblectures for lack of interaction and lack of possibilities to ask and clarify questions.

In this chapter we hope to add to the didactics of using weblectures, so that through the actual use of weblectures students will become more engaged, and some of the arguments against weblectures are countered.

4 DIDACTICS FOR USING WEBLECTURES

Jadin, et. al. (2009) found that learning outcomes in a course were mainly influenced by the learning strategy that were employed by the students, and not on the presentation of the materials itself. In their experiment, participants (n=28) learned from a video based e-lecture with or without a written transcript. Qualitative analysis showed that the learning outcomes were significantly influenced by learner strategy, and not by the presentation modality. So not only the way of presentation of materials is important, but for a large part also how students deal with materials that are presented to them. When students view lecture materials, and constantly "wander off", learning will suffer. So, we need to ask the question how we can engage students to view online lectures.

Two possibly routes can be seen: either to make the materials more attractive, or to change the way of interaction with the materials. Going down the first route will mean that more attention has to be paid to edit materials after they have been recorded, or change the recording setting to make materials more attractive. Recordings could be made in a studio, where more possibilities are available for repeating and improving lecture fragments. Through editing afterwards examples and animations can be brought in.

The other possibility to engage students is to change the way that students interact with lectures. By building them in into courses, students can use weblectures as one of the ways to receive support for their learning. This changes the focus of viewing lectures. Instead of viewing weblectures as something extra, that could be a nice addition to a course, weblectures are seen as a necessary part of the learning materials. Weblectures can help to increase flexibility of education, for example when students will not be able to attend all lectures, or it may become necessary to offer courses for a second time in the lecture year. Different types of use of weblectures will require different ways of setting them up, and integrating them in courses. The didactic models as outlined in section 7 will guide setting up these models.

5 COPYING SUCCESSFUL COURSE DESIGNS

The goal of using didactic models is to describe the ordering and organisation of learning activities and materials, to be able to re-use them in a different situation. When it is possible to extract the design of a course by taking the didactic model, it will become possible to implement successful course designs into a new situation. In this way we will be able to spread innovation by copying of good examples.

A way to describe those good examples is via the use of design patterns. A design pattern "conveys the core of the solution to some relevant, recurring design problem" (Alexander, 1979). Originally, design patterns were used to offer citizens a set of resources to help them (re)shape their environment. The notion of design patterns was then picked up within the field of software engineering, using it to describe software design problems and to represent models for solving them. Design patterns can be used to solve educational design problems as well, as Goodyear (2005) describes:

- They provide the teacher-designer with a comprehensive set of design ideas
- The provide designs in a structured way, making the relationships between components easy to understand

- They combine a clear articulation of a design problem and a solution, offering a rational containing the pedagogical philosophy, research based evidence, and experiential knowledge of design
- They offer the encoding of this knowledge in such a way that it supports an iterative, fluid process of designing as used by teachers/designers in higher education

Patterns have been used to describe various educational design problems, such as "teaching seminars effectively" (Fricke & Voelter, 2000) or "keeping students active" (Bergin, et. al. 2009, retrieved from http://www.pedagogicalpatterns. org/). In Australia, the AUTC project created resources for lecturers in higher education to extract patterns from good examples, and create learning designs (see http://www.learningdesigns.uow. edu.au/). Although the authors do not specifically mention to have used patterns to describe their design, a similar approach was followed to create resources for lecturers around "digital didactics" (Baars, et. al., 2008).

There is a wide variety of describing design patterns (Dimitriadis, et. al., 2009), but in general (Fricke and Völter, 2000) they are described by:

1. a name
2. the problem description, including the goal
3. Solution outline (with consequences and drawbacks),
4. Examples: including attention points for preparation and use
5. Additional implementation information.

This framework is used to describe the examples as extracted from practice, in order to help application of the models, and steer technical developments.

6 WHICH DIDACTIC MODELS?

As we saw earlier, many universities are working on the implementation of weblectures, often responding to a demand from students, or copying the technology from their sister Universities. Relatively little attention is paid to the use of the lectures by students: What problem is solved by recording and re-distributing weblectures?

The situation at University of Twente seems to be typical for many Universities. A pilot was done to investigate offering weblectures as a standard service within the university (Gommer & Bosker, 2008). For this pilot, a total of 15 courses were recorded, using Mediasite (http://www.sonic-foundry.com/) as the recording software. During the pilot, the project members recorded the way of using the weblectures, which grew into the didactic models as presented here. These models were mainly formed by listening to the wishes of lecturers, and fitting in the weblectures in the actual course situation. Literature and projects that were being carried out concurrently were studied as well. Via presentations the models were further refined (Gommer, 2008; Winnips & Verheij, 2009). Five didactic models emerged:

1. Checking back attended lectures: students check back especially difficult parts of lectures they have attended. Typically, students check back materials directly before an examination or delivery of an assignment. Currently this seems to be the most dominant model.
2. Checking back missed lectures: Due to scheduling problems or illness, students were not able to attend a lecture. They can catch up on course content online.
3. Flexible learning: The flexible learning model can be used to help shape a second entry point for a course, use a course for different target groups, or remediate entry knowledge. This can be useful when universities want to increase learner flexibility for scheduling,

or provide a means for increasing student efficiency through their programmes.

4. Evaluating presentation skills: Video can be used to help students and staff improve presentation skills by viewing and reflecting on their own presentation.

5. Re-use: Recordings can be made for use in a portal or repository, for re-use in other courses, or for other groups of students.

Other projects, such as Triple L (2008) have investigated the use of weblectures, resulting in variations of didactic models, and different configurations. The experiences of the Triple L project have been taken into account in the models, as described. Many applications of weblectures can be thought of, and the models can be extended in many ways. To enable decision making amongst the models, we have tried to keep the number of models limited, list examples with the models, and included future use of the models with the descriptions.

7 DIDACTIC MODELS FOR USE OF WEBLECTURES

This section describes the five didactic models, along the presentation format as used by Fricke and Voelter (2000). The name and goal of the model is given, the problem is described, the solution outline is provided, examples are given, and additional implementation information is provided. To support future decision making about the use of the models, thoughts and directions for future developments of these models are added. Via this format the model can be applied within other settings in higher education.

7.1 Checking Back Attended Lectures

Problem Description

A drawback of lectures is that they don't offer much flexibility. Each course only provides one opportunity to attend lectures, and often studying for an examination takes place when the lecture series has finished. Students are dependent on their own notes and reading materials, which is not always enough to fully understand the course content. When studying for a resit of an examination this problem is even more prominent as the lectures were a long time ago.

Solution Outline

This model is quite common within Higher education. Lectures are recorded and presented via a portal site, so that students can access the lectures at their own time and pace. Slides and video of the lecturer are synchronised, and students can jump back and forth in the lecture by selecting a slide or moving the slider bar under the video. Formulas or writing on the blackboard can also be recorded, by zooming in, or by using an electronic writing pad.

Students view back parts of lectures that were not understood by browsing though the presentations as extra help when studying. This can be done in preparation for an examination, or to prepare a practical session. When formulas are explained in the lecture, the weblecture enables the learner to view back the steps that were taken to build up the formula. To enable doing this, either a high quality video recording or a digital drawing tablet is necessary. An operator can zoom in on the lecturers´ writing, thus capturing the formula that is being written. When a digital drawing tablet is used the source can directly be captured, achieving a higher quality.

An often heard drawback would be that students might start to miss out on lectures, as they know that the lectures are recorded. Evaluation data (see section 9) shows that only a very small part of students sees weblectures as a replacement for live lectures. This way of making lectures available could support negative student behaviour of delaying studying until the last moment, just before an examination. Using assignments and grading these could counter this, as described in Model 3, flexible learning.

Examples

A course on educational design is making extensive use of guest-lecturers, who present their expertise area in a very condensed way. Students often can't grasp the lecture content directly, and need to view back the recordings in order to be able to use them for writing a report. Students use the weblectures when writing their report, selecting the fragments they need. A similar use happens when studying for an examination.

As this is the most typical form of using weblectures, many examples and portals are available online, as also described in section 3.

Additional Implementation Information

There are many attention points when recording lectures. To name a few: questions from the audience need to be recorded, or the lecturer should repeat the question before answering. Recording formulas and writing on the blackboard should be organised (either by zooming in on the blackboard, or by using an electronic writing tablet). Pauses in the lectures can be cut out. Some weblectures should be password protected to avoid problems with copyrighted materials as used by the lecturer.

Lecturers need support to record weblectures. This needs to be organised on a University or University department level. Software needs to be bought to record lectures, and server space needs to be setup to make weblectures available via a portal. Further, to integrate weblectures with course content, they need to be imported into an electronic learning environment. This can be done by manually placing links from the weblecture portal into an electronic learning environment, but this process can also be automated Burdet et. al. (2009).

Apart from technical consequences, the process of recording weblectures need to be organised. Will there be operators to record? Who will place weblinks in the electronic learning environment? What will be done with technical problems? How can University lecturers request the recording of a weblecture?

Future

Viewing back attended lectures is the dominant model as used in universities. Still many advances can be made to this model, on recording of lectures but also on didactics. For recording, work is being done on automation of recordings, and removing the need for operators to install hardware and track lecture movement. As described by Burdet et. al. (2009) many aspects of recording lectures can be automated by building in the hardware into new lecture rooms, and integration of recording facilities into the lecture room. Many lecture rooms now have buttons to start projection facilities and dim the lights. Why not add a button to start lecture recordings, which are automatically integrated into the learning environment afterwards? Face tracking is now available on many consumer webcams. With a similar technique, the lecturer can be tracked which decreases the need for an operator.

The way of using the weblectures didactically can be extended to make students more active during lectures, to provide feedback to the lecturer during the lecture, and possibly to improve contact between lecturer and students after the lecture. Improving feedback and contact between students and lecturers may lead to more engagement of students with their study. This in turn may decrease dropout of students (Winnips, Verheij, & Beldhuis, 2009).

This model is similar to the model of a "live" lecture, as described in the Triple L project (Triple L, 2008), and more authors have experimented on the use of Web 2.0 technology to augment weblectures (Ketterl, 2009). Transmitting live lectures is possible with most software products for lecture capture. But enabling question asking is currently lacking. Therefore, a prototype was built to enable question asking during the lecture, using Twitter (http://www.twitter.com) and Twitterfountain (http://www.twitterfountain.nl). This prototype is then embedded into the Blackboard environment of the University of Groningen. Figure 4 shows the prototype, as seen from Blackboard.

When live lectures are transmitted, students can view the lectures from a distance, as well as comment and respond to lecturers questions. A tag for a course can be agreed on, in a similar way as tags are nowadays often used for professional conferences. Storing comments and questions will ensure that this technology is useful for the second model as well, as students can still respond and react to questions when they are viewing a lecture afterwards.

7.2 Checking Back Missed Lectures

Problem Description

When students have missed a lecture, the written course materials are often not enough to fully grasp course content. Still they need the lecture to be able to pass for a final examination. Further, sometimes lecturers fall ill during a lecture series, with no opportunity to catch up on the course content due to a full agenda of students, or due to scheduling difficulties.

Solution Outline

Making recorded lectures available helps students who missed a lecture catch up. When a lecturers has been ill, and there is no possibility to make up for the missed lecture, it is possible to record the lecture afterwards, without students. Students can then view the lecture at their own time and place.

Consequences of this way of recording is that students can miss lectures, without missing out on course content. This is especially helpful for part-time students living further away from university, or when other day-time obligations make it impossible to attend the lecture. When scheduling difficulties can make it impossible for students to attend a lecture, they can still complete the course without attending all lectures. Evaluation at the University of Twente (section 9) shows that 52% of the students used the recorded lecture to catch up on a lecture they had missed due to illness or schedule problems.

A possible drawback is that students may start to miss lectures on purpose. Evaluation (section 9) shows that 20% of students at the University of Twente have skipped one or more lectures, as they knew it was recorded.

Examples

In a course on Media design the lecturer has to miss a lecture because of illness. Scheduling problems prevented a repeat of the lecture with students present. So the missed lecture was recorded in an empty lecture hall, to make the lecture series complete. This enabled students to repeat the lecture in their own time. For the lecturer this required more "acting skills" then normally. Lectures with students present are more vibrant, and lecturers can see student reactions and respond to questions. With no audience present it was harder to keep going with the lecture. A further consequence was that the lecture content became more condensed, as the lecture was focused purely on the course content, and interactions with students (taking time) were left out.

Figure 4. Prototype of live comments during a (web)lecture as integrated in Blackboard. Comments during a lecture are shown here via a Flash object, but could also be integrated via an RSS feed.

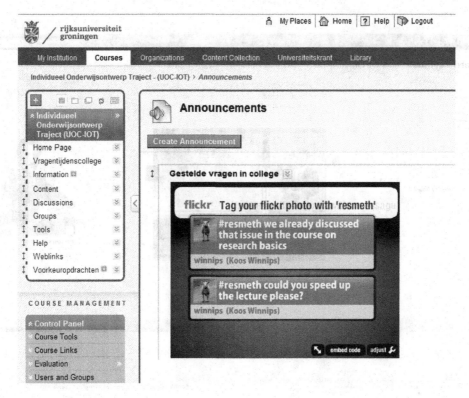

Additional Implementation Information

For this model of using a weblecture, no additional implementation considerations are necessary, as the current use is similar to the first didactic model.

Future

Following the advances on the first model of weblectures, enabling live comments on weblectures could have the added effect of increased interaction after a lecture. Students can read comments as provided, and react after the lecture has finished. Thus, a model for "augmented lectures" can be made with the goal of increasing student participation and thus increase time-on-task. An increase of time-on-task can decrease learner dropout. Tiernan and Grudin (2000) have found promising results on the use of a system for collaborative multimedia annotation. Systems for collaborative annotation are available (Schroeter, et. al., 2006), and are integrated with weblectures. Figure 5 provides an example of an extended video player, as used by Microsoft's Tuva project (http://research.microsoft.com/apps/tools/tuva/index.html).

More examples of video annotation systems are available such as the video notes project by Charleton University (http://videonotes.carleton.ca/author.html). Even Youtube now allows for commenting on videos. A next question is wether these systems can be used to increase student participation after a lecture, and how to apply them with a proper didactic model in universities learning environments.

Figure 5. Augmented lectures as demonstrated by the enhanced video player of the Tuva project. Shown are the weblecture comments, a timescale with locations of extra materials, notes, and extra materials.

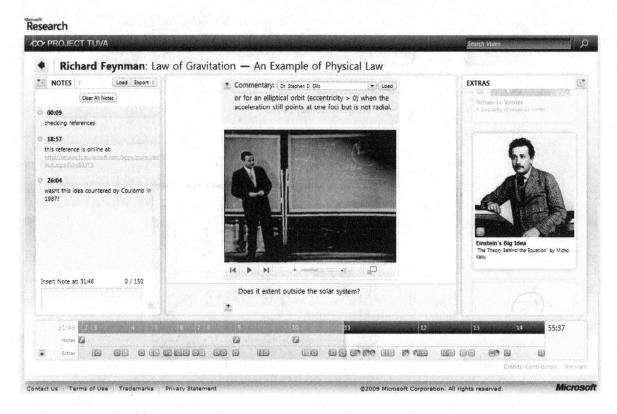

7.3 Flexible Learning

Problem Description

With students, and study programmes of students becoming more flexible, the entry knowledge of students who enter a course is getting more varied. Getting students on the right entry level (remediation) can cost a lot of time, taking away time for the actual course content. On the other hand, when entry knowledge is not remediated, large percentages of students will fail the course.

Solution Outline

Using a different course model can prevent dropout of students, with limited time of lecturers. A possible solution to this is the use of a "task-based" model to design courses (Dekker et.al., 2004).

Students are required to provide proof of their performance by submitting tasks. Before the start of a course, the ways of providing feedback on tasks, and the way of providing rewards for task performance is well thought out. Support for tasks is provided face-to-face and online. Weblectures are a part of the support provided, and are helpful as they are a very efficient way to produce multimedia materials. In contrast to the first two models, weblectures are not viewed as a means to understand course content, but are necessary as support to be able to perform a task. So, a learner may get stuck in a task they are trying to perform, and need to watch a certain fragment in a weblecture to be able to solve the problem. This fragment of the weblecture can be a bit of explanation about theory, a procedure for solving an equation, or an example of the task solved by someone else.

Examples

A masters' programme on Sustainable Energy Technology includes a course on Basic Chemistry. Students are allowed to enter this Master's programme with a wide variety of Bachelor's degrees: Electrical Engineering, Physics, Informatics and even Maritime Technology. The programme itself is cooperation between three Universities. In addition to the differences in entry knowledge, this means that students travel back and forth between the Universities. To cater for this variety, a course on Basic Chemistry is designed to level out differences in learner level on this topic. Tasks are designed, in the form of a series of online multiple choice tests, for which the software was provided with the book on Basic Chemistry. A one hour weblecture supports students to get the basics of chemistry, helps to vary media use in the course, and is efficient to produce for the lecturer. When the course has finished, the weblecture can be re-used for students entering late into the programme, and to brush up entry knowledge in other courses.

Additional Implementation Information

Design and implementation of courses within this model for flexible learning is not easy. For many lecturers, who have mainly been teaching courses face-to-face, based on a book and lectures this model is a variation from the ordinary. A lot of research has been carried out on models for flexible and blended learning (see for example Collis & Moonen, 2001) and in Universities blended learning is becoming a known factor. With the advent of electronic learning environment such as Blackboard (http://www.blackboard.com/) lecturers have access to powerful tools to make learning more flexible. But using these tools with an appropriate didactic model is a process that is slow to change in Universities. This model for flexible learning is an addition to the "toolbox" that is available for lecturers. It is applicable in situations where entry knowledge is varied, and

learner locations and schedules may demand flexible learning. For application of the model advice from an educational technologist may be required, or further study in resources in the area of online flexible learning.

Future

Software for recording weblectures is normally used in a lecture room, using professional hardware. But making these tools available to lecturers can increase their options for recording short lectures themselves. With a webcam, and screen-recording software (such as Camtasia: http://www.techsmith.com/camtasia.asp), webcasts can be made, making short clips that explain key points of a course. This can be used for software demonstrations, as shown in Figure 6, but also to record a lecturers "favourite stories". When lecturers record these stories as fragments, students can find them back by making them available in the electronic learning environment. In this way the lecturer can invest time in answering questions or discussing with students instead of repeating the story.

University of Groningen is currently setting up training for lecturers on "How to explain a topic in a five minutes video". Separate for this, the software for recording these (http://www.presentations2go.eu/) is being made available in the standard workplace setup of lecturers. Making these tools available to lecturers is a step to increase the use of short weblectures. Further experimentation could be done to study its effects.

7.4 Evaluation of Presentation Skills

Problem Description

Learning to give a good presentation is a skill that is required in many areas. Lecturers are judged by students on their abilities to present. Students are required to have conversation skills, and to carry out interviews. A problem is that it is hard to

Figure 6. Screencast with short explanation on the topic of "control engineering" (from: http://www. ce.utwente.nl/rtweb/files/camtasia/financieringsmodel/)

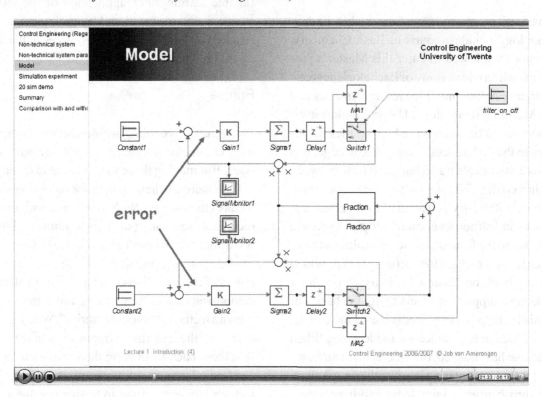

judge a presentation afterwards without a proper registration of the event.

Solution Outline

Recording presentations of students or lecturers enables good evaluation and reflection afterwards. Lecturers and students can view back their presentations, skip back and forth in fragments of lectures, and select good and bad parts of presentations.

The hardware and software setup that is used for recording standard lectures can be used for evaluation of lecturers' presentations. For recording students' fragments it may be necessary to build a separate setup that can be used by many students at the same time, and can be operated by students themselves. Added to this, it would be useful to be able to cut fragments out afterwards and use them to send to an evaluator.

A drawback is that universities may not like the idea that lecturers view back their lectures afterwards for improvement. Therefore a closed and password protected environment is necessary, providing a safe environment to practice. A worst-case model for a University would be a student edited collection of lecturing fragments with the worst bad examples of University lectures. However, a search on Youtube.com on "bad lectures" or "boring lectures" reveals none to very little fragments.

Examples

In a course on "Presentation skills" students prepare a presentation of 10 minutes each, and present this during the lecture. The whole lecture is recorded. Afterwards, students write a reflection on this lecture, discussing their points for improvement.

During teacher training lecturers record their lectures, and study them at home afterwards. During a coaching meeting, the lecturer shows the fragment to the coach and fellow lecturers, and asks for feedback on a part of the lecture that didn't go well.

Other examples of using weblectures reflection are: analysis of work in project groups, bedside manners for training medical students, and safety regulations for chemical students.

Additional Implementation Information

It is possible to use weblectures for evaluation of presentations using common lecture recording software, such as Mediasite or Camtasia. For selection of fragments, additional software can be used. Via the virtual cutter (http://video.surfnet.nl/virtualcutter/select_file.php?lang=en) fragments of videos can be cut out, and presented as a separate weblink, thus making it possible to present short fragments of video for evaluation.

Future

The Dividu project (http://info.dividu.nl/, Admiraal et. al., 2008) has focused on building a web environment for presenting and evaluating video materials. This was used for beginning teachers and dentists to study model behaviour and reflect on their behaviour. Via a process of reflection on action (Schön, 1983) students study their own work, and select fragments as examples of competences achieved, thus creating meaningful learning. Similar models can be used for other skills, and could be extended for synchronous use, for example by using videoconferencing.

7.5 Re-Use

Problem Description

Each university has their brilliant lecturers, and stories that need to be captured for history. Only students present at this university can see this lecturer in action, and after retirement their lectures can't be seen. Recording can be done with the aim of using them at a different moment.

Solution Outline

Recording lectures makes extra attention to recording quality worthwhile. A setup can be used with multiple cameras. Editing afterwards makes sure the best possible quality is reached.

Stored weblectures can be re-used. Tagging of materials will help to re-use specific fragments of the lecture, and finding them back. Tagging could be done by hand, or automatically.

Examples

A course with a series of guest lectures is recorded. The next year, different guest lecturers are invited, lecturing about the same topics. Students can view back last years lectures, and contrast the views of the lecturers. Further, a recording from a well known professor is used for promotion activities, and in a course for first year students, as it provides an especially good overview of recent developments in the area.

Students in two programmes participate in the course "Introduction to mechanics". Recordings of lectures are made in programme A. Programme B, scheduled in the next semester, uses the recorded lectures. The time that is saved by not repeating the lectures is invested on practicals.

A programme of Industrial design has a lecturer with special expertise on packaging of products. Their lectures are used at a sister institute, where this expertise is not available. In return, lectures on `Product design` from the sister institute are used.

Additional Implementation Information

Recording lectures with the aim of making them re-usable involves extra cost, for recording, but also for storing and making them retrievable. Multiple cameras can be used for recording, involving extra hardware, and extra operator time. When lectures are recorded without students, the decision can be made to repeat and improve fragments. Editing can take place after recording to add effects, or to remove or add fragments. Extra care in assignment of tags to the materials can be taken to improve retrieval of the materials. The designers of the lectures need to make decisions on the payoff of this extra effort. What quality is needed to fit the goal? How many times will this lecture be re-used? How big is the audience? How long will this content last? Is there additional pr-value?

Future

Recording high quality lectures is, as many of the other models, not new. However, improvements are under way to make these lectures, and lecture fragments more readily available. Some ways to open up these materials can be to tag materials, or by allowing groups of users to add their own tags to lecture materials. Alternatively true speech recognition can be used to transcribe the contents of the lecture. Further the lectures can be integrated into existing repositories in a better way. As described by Winnips & Portier (2008) by integrating materials into University systems, finding them back by users can be ensured, and repository systems can be created that fit the daily workflow of lecturers and students. Weblectures can be integrated into the University's electronic learning environment, tagged, and made available in the standard electronic search services of the University.

Didactically, re-use of recorded weblectures will fit best with the flexible learning model.

After recording high-quality lectures they can be integrated and re-used in other courses.

Overview of Didactic Models

Table 1 provides an overview of the five models for use of weblectures. This table can help decision making for lecturers and support staff to choose didactic models and think through implications for use of technology.

At the University of Twente, evalaution data regarding the use of weblectures is gathered. The next section discussed this evaluation.

8 EVALUATION

At the university of Twente the use of weblectures has been evaluated in the year 2008. This evaluation focused on the first two didactic models: checking back attended, and missed lectures as these models were the most used at the University of Twente. The main question for evaluation was whether the added value of weblectures for learning was sufficient in order to justify offering weblectures as a standard service at the University of Twente. Added value is operationalised in terms of the 4E-Model (Collis & Moonen, 2001). This model gives the added value of an ICT innovation as experienced by its users. Chances of success for the innovation are predicted by the 4 factors:

- Educational effectiveness: in what sense do weblectures help to improve the educational process, or to improve results of students?
- Ease of use: How user friendly is the application? What are practical advantages of using weblectures?
- Engagement: How engaged is the lecturer with application of weblectures? How much fun is it for students?
- Environmental variables: Which external factors influence the success of the use of

Table 1. Main characteristics of didactic models for weblectures

	1. Checking back attended lectures	2. Checking back missed lectures	3. Flexible learning	4. Presentation skills	5. Re-use
Goal of recording	Support for study of learning materials	Support for study of learning materials	Efficient way of producing multimedia materials, learner support	Reflection on (own) experience, help to evaluate own presentation skills	Creation of high quality content for re-use, pr value
Motivation of students to view lecture	Repeating a lecture fragment that was not understood or forgotten	Catching up on a missed lecture	Information in a weblecture is needed to complete a task	Reflection on own presentation or lecture	Learning something new (getting insights from top scholars)
Examples of software used	Mediasite, Echo360, Camtasia	Mediasite, Echo360, Camtasia	Screencast software (Camtasia, Wink)	Various, from standard weblecture set, to consumer videocamera)	Mediasite, Echo360, Camtasia, editing software
Operator needed?	Yes, could possibly be automated	Yes, could possibly be automated	Yes, lecturer could also record themselves (short clips)	Yes, for students presentations, students can operate	Yes
Typical time of use by students	Just before examination	After the lecture, during lecture series	Scheduled in via assignments in electronic learning environment	Directly after a presentation	Directly till years after the lecture
Expiry of lectures	1-2 years	1-2 years	3-4 years, or longer	Can be used once	More than 4 years
Editing necessary?	Very little editing	Very little editing	Very little	Editing is done to reflect on own performance	Yes
Length of fragments	Typically 1.5 hours	Typically 1.5 hours	5 minutes to 1 hour	Varied, from short presentations to full 1.5 hour lectures	Typically 1.5 hours
Future development	Automation of recordings, tagging, live lecture, more interactivity	Automation of recordings, tagging, live lecture, more interactivity	Evaluation of more widespread use	Fragment selection, annotation, commenting, synchronous use	Tagging, use in flexible learning model

weblectures? Such as availability of technical and educational support and availability of budgets.

These four factors together determine the vector sum. When the vector sum reaches a specific threshold value the ICT application will be accepted in an organisation, as staff and students experience enough added value. This can be seen in Figure 7.

Apart from added value, technical aspects were evaluated, to help setup the system for use as a standard service at University.

Method

To answer these questions, questionnaires were designed, and open interviews were held with lecturers. Five courses were evaluated, and a total of 169 students filled out the questionnaire (giving a response rate of 62%). Five of the participating lecturers were interviewed. A summary of the results is given below.

Results

In general, students are positive about this initiative. First, they indicate to find weblectures helpful

Figure 7. Representation of the 4E model. The vector sum of the 4 factors determines the success of an innovation (Collis & Moonen, 2001).

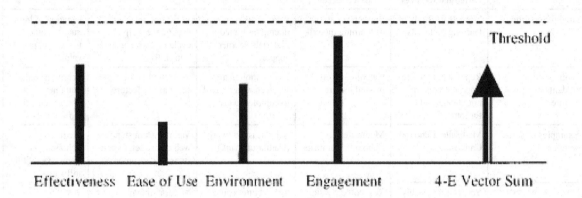

and useful, especially for repeating difficult parts of lectures when preparing for an examination, doing assignments, or when studying missed lectures. A number of students explicitly mentions using weblectures when they have missed a lecture.

Lecturers are positive about the results of the pilot. It went well, after some technical glitches at the start, when one or more lectures were not recorded and a recording got lost. They see the use of the using weblectures for their students, and get positive feedback from their students.

Use of weblectures was good: 28% of the students has viewed all weblectures that were available. 10% of students did not see any of the weblectures. Consequently, 62 percent did see some of the lectures. The time they invested in viewing lectures was over 4 hours for 30% of students, 38% spent 1 to 4 hours viewing lectures, and 22% viewed one hour or less.

Added Value

Added value is described in terms of the 4E model (Collis & Moonen, 2001).

Effectiveness

When asking students, 32% indicate that weblectures has helped them score higher for their courses. 63% indicate to have understood course content better, and 67% indicate that weblectures have helped to prepare for an examination or assignment. For one of the courses, that is perceived as difficult, and has many students resitting the examination, 81% students indicated that weblectures helped them understand course content better, and were useful for preparation for the examination (75%).

Lecturers see the main added value for students mainly in model 1 and 2: supporting study for examinations and assignments, and when studying for assignments.

A worry as often expressed by lecturers is: don't my students stay away from my lectures when they know all is recorded? This seems true for a small part: 20% of students indicated to have missed a lecture as they knew it was recorded. So, could weblectures replace live lectures? Students don't seem to think so, as 75% do not think weblectures are a replacement for regular lectures. But there are other uses for the recordings, as predicted in didactic model 2 (checking back attended lectures). Students (52%) have used the recordings when they could not attend due to illness, or scheduling problems.

All five lecturers stated they want to use the weblectures again next year. Two of these state they want to record the whole lecture series again. The other three either want to re-use existing recordings, or record one or two lectures that went missing, to complete the lecture series. All of the lecturers see possibilities for recording more of the own lectures, or lectures of colleagues.

Ease of use: 54% of students indicate they could learn more efficiently (faster) by the use of weblectures. Again, the course that was perceived by many students as difficult gave an even higher rate, where 69% of students found they learned more efficiently. Technically, students were satisfied with the quality of the recordings, although 25% of students indicated they had problems in viewing the recordings. Mainly this was caused by the use of operating systems (Macintosh, Linux) or software (Firefox, Opera, Safari) that were not fully compliant with the recording software (Mediasite).

Lecturers appreciated the very little time it has cost to them to record and make weblectures available.

Engagement: 77% of students indicated to have liked viewing weblectures. Some of the lecturers had worries about feeling inhibited when they knew they would be recorded. These worries did not become reality, as the lecturers either did not pay attention to the recording set and operator at all, or they got used to it after the first lecture. Also students indicated they were not disturbed by the recordings.

A few lecturers explicitly mentioned enjoying to see themselves back on video (model 4), as well as learning from viewing their performance.

Environment

Lecturers appreciated the technical support that was provided. Even when using a fixed setup in the future, lecturers indicate that operators could be helpful. Operators can help with the recording system at the start of the lecture, and operate the camera during the lecture, for example when the lecturer moves around, or starts writing on the blackboard.

The lighting of the recordings was not always sufficient, but audio was. Lecturers gave priority to the audio in the recordings.

Added Value?

Evaluation data gives a positive message. Students are satisfied, and indicate, not only to have liked, but also to have learned from weblectures. Staff had some worries, but all staff members are willing to continue the use of weblectures, and offer courses to record other courses, either their own, or courses from colleagues. Practically, the demand for weblectures was felt with the project team as well. The project started as a small scale project, recording weblectures for 10 courses. After a first information meeting, with lecturers crowding the small room wherein this was booked, the 10 pilot courses were booked full, and the project group couldn't (and didn't want to) restrict themselves to the initially planned 10 courses. University of Twente now offers weblectures as a standard service.

9 CONCLUSION

Although it is hard to formally calculate a vector sum by using the 4E-model, it seems that recording of weblectures was well worth it. Students and lecturers are enthusiastic and see value in effectiveness (learning) and ease of use. Availability of weblectures enables students to better prepare for examinations and assignments (model 1), and to repeat missed lectures (model 2). Especially in courses that are perceived as difficult, whereby many students need to resit the examination, the need for weblectures seems highest. So, the use of weblectures should focus on these.

Apart from using models 1 (checking back attended lectures) and 2 (checking back missed lectures) lecturers saw added value for the use of weblectures in model 4: presentation skills. This is further demonstrated by the use videorecordings in teacher training programmes and projects, such as Dividu.

The fifth model (re-use) was mentioned by lecturers, but possibly the value of this model is more on a university level. Making lectures available can be good for promotional value of a University as a whole, as demonstrated by lectures in iTunesU and on AcademicEarth.

Flexible use of lecture material (model 3) is relatively little mentioned, and little used. However, we do see growth in this model. With learning programmes becoming more flexible, courses need to become more flexible as well. Supporting students with fragments of recorded video can be a good an efficient way to provide additional learning support.

The models as described here were found in practice. Innovations can be made to all of these models by getting more experience in the same practices, by new technical developments, and research advances. Viewing back lectures can be extended by viewing live lectures, whereby web 2.0 techniques allow direct contact between the lecturer and learners, such as asking questions, and guiding the direction of the lecture. By storing comments and annotations, the second model (missed lectures) can be extended as well, by allowing students to be active when they are viewing back a missed lecture. Flexible use of the lectures is a model with much promise, as the possibilities we have inside our learning environments are not fully used, added flexibility can offer more choice for students and lecturers. At the University of Groningen we are working on the possibilities of recording small fragments of lecture material in a five minute video. This will allow lecturers to easily add multimedia support materials in their courses. The "presentation skills" model is resulting from, and has been used in teacher train-ing programmes, as well as projects. The re-use model offers many possibilities for improvement on finding back fragments, and using them in the model for flexible learning.

Weblectures offer many opportunities for learning, and students are positive about the extra possibilities offered. But to make students active students extra attention should be paid to the actual use of weblectures, and how they are built into education. This chapter offers five didactic models. For lecturers and educational support staff these models can help to make choices for use of weblectures in courses. This can then guide technical advances. To make students more active and to support learning activities extension to the first three models are proposed, by integrating more interaction possibilities into the first two models, and studying the effectiveness of the third model. With the popularity of weblectures rising a great rate advances in research may well be overtaken by practice.

REFERENCES

Admiraal, W., & Janssen, J. Pijls, M., & Gielis, A.M. (2008, May). *Transfer between learning and practice: The use of Web-based video in higher education.* Paper presented at the Annual conference on human resource development international. Lille, France. Retrieved October 30, 2009 from http://info.dividu.nl/docs/paper_HRDI.pdf

Alexander, C. (1979). *The timeless way of building.* New York, NY: Oxford University Press.

Baars, G., Wieland, A., Deinum, J. F., van de Ven, M., D'haese, I., & van de Linde, E. (2008). *Digitale didactiek: practische stappenplannen voor het gebruik van ICT in het hoger onderwijs* [Digital Didactics: practical procedures for using ICT in Higher Education]. Utrecht, The Netherlands: Lemma.

Bergin, J., Eckstein, J., Manns, M. L., & Sharp, H. (2009). *Patterns for active learning*. Retrieved October 23, 2009 from http://www.pedagogical-patterns.org/

Burdet, B., Bontron, C., & Burgi, R. (2009). Lecture capture, what can be automated? *Educause Quarterly Magazine, 30*(2). Retrieved November 7, 2009, from http://www.educause.edu/EDUCAUSE+Quarterly/EDUCAUSEQuarterlyMagazineVolum/LectureCaptureWhatCanBeAutomat/157454

Calimero. (2009). *Verkiezingsprogramma Calimero* [Election programme student fraction Calimero]. Retrieved October 21, 2009, from http://lijstcalimero.nl/verkiezingsprogramma-2009/

Collis, B. A., & Moonen, J. (2001). *Flexible learning in a digital world: Experiences and expectations*. London, UK: Kogan Page.

Dekker, P. J., Wagemans, L., Winnips, J. C., Clement, M., Loonen, J., & Rasenberg, J. (2004). *Zelfstandig leren in een digitale leeromgeving: Handboek voor het ontwerpen van taakgericht onderwijs [Self-reliant learning in an electronic learning environment: Handbook for the design of task-based learning]*. Utrecht, The Netherlands: Digitale Universiteit. Retrieved November 6, 2009, from http://www.surffoundation.nl/nl/publicaties/Pages/DU-publicatie-Handboeken-Zelfstandig-Leren.aspx

Demetriadis, S., & Pombortsis, A. (2007). E-lectures for flexible learning: A study on their learning efficiency. *Journal of Educational Technology & Society, 10*(2), 147–157.

Dimitriadis, Y., Goodyear, P., & Retalis, S. (2009). *Using e-learning design patterns to augment learners' experiences, 25*(5), 997-998.

Filius, R. (2009). *Handleiding Weblectures in de Universiteit Utrecht*. [Weblectures manual at the university of Utrecht]. Utrecht, The Netherlands: Universiteit Utrecht, IVLOS. Retrieved October 19, 2009 from: http://cms.let.uu.nl/lecturenet/uploads/documents/Handleiding%20weblectures%20mei%202009.pdf

Fricke, M., & Völter, M. (2000, July 10th). *Seminars: A pedagogical pattern language about teaching seminars effectively*. Workshop presented at the EuroPLoP2000 Conference, Irsee, Germany. Retrieved October 23, 2009 from: http://www.voelter.de/data/pub/tp/tp.pdf

Gommer, E. M. (2008, December). *Use and effectiveness of online video lectures*. Presentation at Online Educa 2008, Berlin.

Gommer, E. M., & Bosker, M. (2008). Videopilots UT: naar een standaarddienst voor registratie en aanbod van colleges via het Internet. [Videopilots UT: towards a standard service for registration and presentation of weblectures]. Unpublished project report. Enschede, The Netherlamds: University of Twente.

Goodyear, P. (2005). Educational design and networked learning: Patterns, pattern languages and design practice. *Australasian Journal of Educational Technology, 21*(1), 82–101.

Jadin, T., Gruber, A., & Batanic, B. (2009). Learning with e-lectures: The meaning of learning strategies. *Journal of Educational Technology & Society, 12*(3), 282–288.

Ketterl, M., Mertens, R., & Vornberger, O. (2009). Bringing Web 2.0 to Web lectures. *Interactive Technology and Smart Education, 6*(2), 82–96. doi:10.1108/17415650910968099

Leoni, K., & Lichti, S. (2009). *Lecture capture in higher education*. Evanston, IL: Northwestern University. Retrieved November 6th, 2009 from http://www.it.northwestern.edu/bin/docs/classrooms/LC_survey.pdf

Mayer, R. E. (2003). *Multimedia learning*. Santa Barbara, CA: Cambridge University Press.

Rimer, S. (2007, December 19). At 71, Physics professor is a Web star. *The New York Times*. Retrieved November 8th, 2009, from http://www.ny-times.com/2007/12/19/education/19physics.html

Schroeter, R., Hunter, J., Guerin, J., Khan, I., & Henderson, M. (2009). *A synchronous multimedia annotation system for secure collaboratories*. 2nd IEEE International Conference on E-Science and Grid Computing (eScience 2006). Amsterdam, Netherlands. Retrieved November 6, 2009, from http://www.dart.edu.au/publications/escience2006.pdf

SOG. (2009). SOG Verkort verkiezingsprogramma [short election programme student fraction SOG]. Retrieved November 6, 2009, from http://www.studentenorganisatie.nl/new/index.php?library/download/16

Tiernan, S. L., & Grudin, J. (2001). *Fostering engagement in asynchronous learning through collaborative multimedia annotation* (MSR-TR-2000-91). Redmond, VA: Microsoft Research. Retrieved November 7, 2009, from http://research.microsoft.com/apps/pubs/default.aspx?id=69315

Triple, L. (2008). *Triple L Project Wiki tool*. Retrieved October 21st, 2009, from http://www.iis-communities.nl/portal/site/triple-l

Veeramani, R., & Bradley, S. (2008). *Insights regarding undergraduate preference for lecture capture*. Retrieved October 19th, 2009, from http://www.uwebi.org/news/uw-online-learning.pdf

Wieling, M. B., & Hofman, W. H. A. (in press). *The impact of online video lecture recordings and automated feedback on student performance*. Article accepted for publication, Computers & Education (2009).

Winnips, J. C., & McLoughlin, C. (2001, June). Six WWW based learner supports you can build. In C. Montgomerie & J. Viteli (Eds.), *Proceedings of EDMEDIA 2001*, (pp. 2062-2067). Chesapeake, VA: AACE.

Winnips, J. C., & Portier, S. (2008). *Creating content and not sharing it: Why is it so quiet in so many repositories?* Paper presented at Online Educa 2008, Berlin.

Winnips, J. C., & Verheij, G. J. (2009, June). *Didactic models for the use of videolectures*. Paper presented at Diverse 2009, Aberystwyth, UK. Retrieved on November 6th, 2009, from http://echo360.aber.ac.uk:8080/ess/echo/presentation/3e9be7dc-097d-4a83-a7c7-778d905cc314

Winnips, J. C., Verheij, G. J., & Beldhuis, H. (2009, December). *Interactive large scale lectures: From clothespins to Twitter mashups*. Paper accepted for the Conference: Student Mobility and ICT: Dimensions of Transition. Amsterdam, December 2009.

Chapter 4
Digital Provide:
Education Beyond Borders

Neerja Raman
Stanford University, USA

ABSTRACT

In the last ten years, the world has witnessed immense advances in media and Internet technologies. Through examination of the use of social media, virtual collaboration platforms, and live streamed access to images, graphics, and video, this chapter offers a new approach to education which calls for leaders to use technology to inform and connect teachers, students, and the community. Similar to the changes in the entertainment industry, educational institutions can adopt an interactive, collaborative, and socially aware model of knowledge creation to engage more students and encourage innovation in issues of global scope. The value of making this change is examined through curricula that stress multidisciplinary projects and provide hands on experiential learning. Lacking the market forces of the entertainment industry, being primarily supported by public funds, education institutions face more legal, political and business model barriers. However, the benefits of digital media so far outweigh the risks that the next decade will see the emergence of learning environments that provide as much of a quantum leap in pedagogy as did the advent of the printing press more than five hundred years ago. Examples of the emotional appeal of digital media combined with the relatively low cost of scaling with the Internet are provided as impetus to overcome resistance to change in creating new institutions of learning.

BORN DIGITAL

More media will be created in the next 4 years than in the last 40,000 years combined concludes a UC Berkeley study (Lyman & Varian 2000) and most of it will be multimedia created by novices

to media production. Documents are born digital and media creation is no longer controlled by the privileged few. The advent of relatively inexpensive digital video cameras, cheap storage and free platforms like YouTube, GoogleDocs and iTunes has created new opportunity in how we create and share content, how we trade and how we commu-

DOI: 10.4018/978-1-60960-800-2.ch004

nicate. In terms of quantity, the amount of "user generated" content far outstrips "professional" content and is typically, available at no charge. Net-Geners (Tapscott, 1998) get information from the internet before they get it from a book. They comprise kids, teens, the eldest are graduating college and entering the workforce and to them information is born digital, shared digitally and need not become print or be shared face-to-face to be compelling. In fact, old fashioned text competes with slick multimedia productions for attention and amusement of the young who are often more comfortable with digital information than print.

The combination of *books that are born digital* and a generation that is vested in *digital experiences* is novel and will be a disruption for education and pedagogy.

Education 2.0: A Business Model in Transition

MIT, in 2001, was one of the first universities to make its courseware available online- free. Yet an MIT degree today is just as expensive as ever and by and large, universities have been slow to change their business model. K-12 education is even further behind. That does not mean change is not happening elsewhere.

"How Web-Savvy Edupunks Are Transforming American Higher Education" (Kamenetz, 2009) is a convincing argument of a change in the making through availability of free online courses, Wiki universities and Facebook-style tutoring networks. KnowledgeWorks Foundation (http://www.futureofed.org/) believes that over the next decade, the most vibrant innovations in education will take place outside traditional educational institutions because of an entrenched gap between bottom-up developments in education and the traditional top-down hierarchy that is currently in place. They write: *If you think our future will require better schools, you're wrong. The future of education calls for entirely new kinds of learning environments. If you think we will need better*

teachers, you're wrong. Tomorrow's learners will need guides who take on fundamentally different roles. As every dimension of our world evolves so rapidly, the education challenges of tomorrow will require solutions that go far beyond today's answers." 2020 Forecast, *Creating the Future of Learning,* is their tool to redefine how learning is organized, who comprises the broad school-community and what the actual experiences of learners will be like in the future. They predict that "the validity and role of formal institutions of education will be challenged by key forces of change and will be reconsidered by an expanding group of stakeholders."

Expanding stakeholders in education include students and society at large. On-line interaction and public acceptance of digital media have created patterns of social and institutional behaviors which open up new possibilities for education innovation. A student in college today is more likely to have applied online than mailed a paper application, researched colleges on the web rather than the local library (if there even is a local library – e.g. in India computer-internet access may be easier than physical library access), even downloaded lectures on iTunes. He may submit a video instead of an essay. Face-to-face conversations, books, paper and pencil have lost none of their power, but content that is born digital i.e. created with a computer, digital camera or video and then made accessible over the internet or broadband has an enhanced reach and hence is creating a new generation of learners with expectations and the ability to go beyond traditional barriers of geography, class and society.

The jury is still out on the phenomenon of media explosion. How does one judge quality, authenticity and veracity of digital content? How does one resolve conflicting web information? And what about copyrights? But one thing is certain: the lure of digital media for today's youth is real and tangible. Wikipedia, the free online encyclopedia, (http://en.wikipedia.org/wiki/Main_Page) may not be "authenticated" content but is still the first click of search queries. Social media has crept into business and learning. For example, in 2009, Facebook has 200 million visitors; corporations and senators are on Twitter; webisodes (web episodes) supplement regular TV programming. It follows that architects of Education 2.0- future education- *predict that traditional universities will find themselves on the wrong side of history*, alongside newspaper chains and record stores unless they incorporate technology to reduce cost and improve the education experience. "If universities can't find the will to innovate and adapt to changes in the world around them," writes David Wiley of Brigham Young University "universities will be irrelevant by 2020."

From news to nano-technology, for the latest developments, one reaches out to the web first not print, and reaches out to books for the basics only. Research and innovation is as likely driven by industry as universities. At such a time when we're all working smarter and faster, pedagogical methods and coursework must also adopt the internet with streaming, in conjunction with video-capture so content is updated in real time, else there is a risk of being perceived as obsolete or worse incorrect (e.g. scientific study changed status of planet Pluto- now downgraded from planet to dwarf-planet) as in the case of encyclopedias in print. Science and technology are updated at the speed of Internet and so must be the shift in institutions of higher education,

SHIFT HAPPENS

Change is messy. Social change is messier. Technology fuelled socio-political change is messiest of all. With globalization and climate change the world has shrunk and divisions between public and private funding, local and global issues, real and potential profits, geography and community are in disarray. Education, as the key to an open, inclusive, compassionate mindset, holds the key to world peace and a human centered, values

based ethos. Hence educational institutions, if they choose to, can enlist and advance technologies that help create a change for a better world. There are benefits to be harnessed for immediate change as well as transformational change that require further research and development.

A Burning Platform

Corporate change is often inspired with the image of a burning platform: better risk jumping off (into the unknown) than cling (where death is certain) to a platform on fire. There is no doubt that education at all levels, university as well as K-12 requires rethinking. At this time, *high cost and limited reach are burning platforms for educational institutions*. In "Liberating Learning: Technology, Politics and the Future of American Education" the authors (Moe and Chubb, 2009) convincingly cite data on how fewer teacher can deliver better education, even to geographically dispersed students, through on-line methods. Additionally, they argue, technology can also be instrumental in circumvention of political blocking from vested lobby group. Access anywhere - inner cities, remote rural areas, or even at home schools – to high quality content provides educational material at fractional cost. Indeed companies like Educomp (http://www.educomp.com/) have shown that they can provide quality tutoring with an on-line model and they are growing. Higher education institutions are taking note. Recently, Duke University Pratt School of Engineering launched its online learning program, saying "*Streaming online courses engages modern students, deepens relationships with key constituencies.*"

Looking ahead, with additional advances in technology, changes to education can be anticipated that make learning relate to life issues e.g. engage students through problem solving mode. These include aspects of education that have to do with social and emotional relevance. For far too long, educational methods have favored the analytical mindset with separation of science and math and have left the creatives behind with arts and literature providing limited job potential. It is common to find foundations and public funds being the only source of income for those who choose a career in soul-supporting activities such as music and live theatre. This has had a negative impact on the relevance of education as perceived by early stage learners leading to the current situation in the United States where we see declining interest in science and math. Complex information has to be delivered clearly at all levels of education. In doing so, much of the science and technology curricula have become so siloed and segmented that they have lost relevance to life.

BENEFITS OF DIGITAL

Incremental Benefits of Digital Engagement

Improved Access - Boston research firm Eduventures (http://www.eduventures.com/) estimates that in the last decade popularity of online classes increased more than tenfold. 11% of the approximately 18.5 million U.S. college students took most of their classes online in fall 2008, up from 1% a decade ago. Online higher education will generate revenue of $11.5 billion in 2009. Former General Electric CEO Jack Welch was persuaded to invest in the Chancellor University System which plans to offer most courses online by an entrepreneur, Michael Clifford, who also launched Grand Canyon Education and Bridgepoint Education (Glader, 2009). What is interesting to note is that Mr. Clifford has *a background in broadcasting, not education.*

Reduced Cost- California Governor Arnold Schwarzenegger's *"digital textbook initiative"* calls for California's 6.2 million public school students to move away from hardbound chemistry and calculus books and embrace texts in electronic form (Hull, 2009). Digital textbooks can be a way to save money from expensive physical books.

The state budget for textbooks and instructional material is $350 million in San Jose Unified where a single Algebra book for 9th graders costs the district $64.77. Once again publishers resist the idea as intriguing but without a business model while the push and support is from disruptive sources, like the CK-12 Foundation (http://www.ck12.org/flexr/) in Palo Alto, whose mission is to reduce the cost of textbooks. CK-12 Foundation's Flexbook Platform is an online system for collaborative, custom-collated, self publishable educational content that can be adapted for individualized needs in the form of digital textbooks (http://about.ck12.org/about-us/technology). Amazon.com has done much to popularize and develop the digital book Kindle, and it is matter of time, before prices of such devices come down and quality improves.

Potential Benefits of Digital Engagement

Greater Interaction - Furthermore, it's not just about cost – it's about getting students excited about learning. "If I want to understand a Calculus problem, I could click on a link in a digital textbook, watch someone else solve it – over and over again." CK-12 has created pilot digital books and found improved student performance. It is not difficult to imagine an e-book product that goes "live" to demonstrate an abstract concept with pictures and audio. Vook, (http://vook.com/), pronounced like the word book but with a "V" is a San Francisco startup aiming to bring the worlds of video and books together on the Internet, through multiple applications, devices and platforms.

Collaboration, not Competitive Style of Learning - The entire social dynamic of a classroom with its hierarchical structure and emphasis in grades produces a competitive rather than a collaborative mindset which in industry students must un-learn as they start working in teams. The social media phenomenon has proved that the natural mode of learning is collaborative and digital experiences are naturally easier to share and less hierarchical than static books and papers.

Transformational Benefits of Digital Engagement

Multimedia information has emotional as well as intellectual appeal especially when it is timely and in the moment, creating connectedness and compassion across a diverse people. That is understandable. Seeing is believing. What is less obvious, but even more important, digital media create a heart head bridge within an individual – or a soul-brain connection where something that makes sense analytically also appeals emotionally allowing for an ethos, a value system, to make tradeoffs that benefit society over the self. If the body is the hardware and behaviors the software, values are the operating system of a human being. Given that the better part of life when growing up is spent in school, educations models would do well to instill a personal ethic.

Heart-Head Bridge: Emotional Appeal and Collective Intelligence

The connected world is expanding–both broadcast and interactive media (cellular, web, cable). Then, is mass media the quantum jump for knowledge innovation like print and books were long ago? The emotional impact of image and video is evident and undisputed and the reason the web has overtaken print journalism. In education too, emotional understanding is important because while algorithms must be written to be understood, emotions must be experienced. Writing requires language. Experience requires imagery (plays, movies, face-to-face communication). Digital media delivers analytical as well as emotional understanding to create a heart-head connection. This bridge enables a move *from individual intelligence to collective intelligence*. Like diverse teams that create more value, collective intelligence integrates individuals' experiences to achieve greater breadth without losing depth. Between entertainment and education, digital media are in different stages of adoption and hence the benefits of collective intelligence beckon but are as yet unrealized. The evolutionary process of developing collective intelligence has been classified into the 4C's of social media (Mishra, 2009) as content, collaboration, community and collective intelligence, with content being pervasive (because it is easy and visible) now but collective intelligence (being invisible and hence difficult) still a distant dream (Table 1).

The 1:9:90 Rule where it takes 1 person to create (change leader), 9 people to curate (current experts) and 90 people to consume (market makers and future experts, leaders) is now in effect for digital content. For the remaining Cs, different institutions are at different stages of value utilization and creation – from global corporations which may be co-creating value with their customers

Table 1. Society and social media

	Easy	**Moderately Difficult**	**More Difficult**	**Most Difficult**
Evolutionary Steps	*Content*	*Collaboration*	*Community*	*Collective Intelligence*
Visible Benefit	Creators -> Curators -> Consumers	Collective Action -> Co-creation -> Conversations	Size + Strength + Social Objective	Implicit or explicit Reputation + recommendation
Visible Impact/ Value	Popularity -> The 1:9:90 rule	Dialog across distance -> Heart-Head bridges	Social Connectedness	Innovation to address global issues
Institution Stage	*Educational Institutions*	*Government Institutions*	*Multinationals, Global supply chains*	?

and suppliers to educational institutions which are just now bringing content online. Leaders may expect collaboration and social connectedness across different stakeholders while market makers are not yet ready for change. This has led to a global dilemma. The *economic distance* between the rich and the poor has increased since the poor are worse off in getting an education (computer literacy is now a required job skill – like reading, writing and math). On the other hand, global access in the field of entertainment as well as news, broadcast and mobile, (television has penetrated even the poorest economies) has reduced *social and cultural distance* because community lines are no longer defined by geography but by digital media access.

Technology purveyors firmly hold on to the belief (original attribution to Alan Kay, computer scientist, known for his early pioneering work on object-oriented programming and windowing graphical user interface design) that the best way to predict the future is to invent it. Innovation starts with education. The heart-head bridge of collective intelligence, as shown in Table 2, predicted by 1:9:90 rule and the evolutionary nature of value creation holds the promise of a future world we would want to invent.

Literacy, Education and Value Creation

Over time, education institutions have evolved into one way information transaction systems because increasingly complex information must be delivered clearly and persuasively at all levels of learning. This model has also worked its way into what we usually mean by distance learning. While useful, this model is limiting for teachers as well as students in their ability to co-create innovation value. Student-brains are not used enough while teachers are over-extended. Futurists use knowledge of the past (Cornish, 2005) to predict knowledge of the future and the fundamental tools are memory, intelligence and imagination which have not changed over time, and still constitute the greatest world asset. But science and technology has changed, creating shifts in sources of value creation as outlined in Table 3.

In the post 1980s world, for the first time in history, it is possible to define *aristocracy to be the middle classes*, for a better world for more of the world population. By enabling learning across disciplines and across diverse communities, education institutions can foster more creativity and innovation than they do mow. In much the same

Table 2. How digital education can change the world

Today	Tomorrow	Transformational
Lower cost	Economic inclusion	Heart-Head Connection
Greater reach	Social Inclusion	Collective Intelligence
Emotional engagement	Cross Cultural Understanding	Engage all 7 billion in innovation and value creation

Table 3. The evolution of the sources of value creation

Dates	Pre 1500s	1500 to 1750	1750 to 1980	Post 1980
Era	Agrarian	Guild	Industrial	Information
Value source	Land	Craft/ Trade	Manufacturing	Intellectual Property
Infrastructure	Irrigation	Transport	Power	Communication
Aristocracy	Barons	Merchants	Industrialists	Knowledge Workers

way a consumer is enlisted in value co-creation (Krishnan & Prahalad, 2008) by a business, teachers can enlist students and other stakeholders in knowledge creation. This is especially necessary in a global climate where actions (e.g. consumption habits affecting global climate) in a particular geography alter the economics in a different geography. The basic definition of literacy and value has now been expanded to include the global context of cross-cultural, cross community understanding and value for all - not at the expense of some in service of others. Hence an added function of education is the need to deliver good economics which then breeds good politics; instill an ethos of human values that lead not just to good citizenship but global citizenship.

Why Now? The issue with disruptive technologies is that traditional players take time to examine and change business models. In education, where market forces are less of a factor than in other areas, like entertainment, the change will come only after the value proves to be overwhelmingly compelling. Beyond cost and access, it is the heart-head link provided by digital content that is proving to be the compelling value. The 1:9:90 rule is having visible effects in content creation, and the promise of collective intelligence beckons. At its best, digital media have the ***power to entertain, educate and bring people closer*** together for a better world. In terms of reach, multimedia is to print what print was to orality.

Walter J.Ong in his book "Orality and Literacy" writes:

"Contrasts between electronic media and print have sensitized us to the earlier contrast between writing and orality."

With inexpensive print, the oral tradition of knowledge creation evolved to include many more people than was possible before. But in the process, close human-human interaction got de-emphasized. With multimedia, being closer to a face-to-face experience in terms of emotion and immediacy, there is an opportunity to bring back a more natural learning model and also expand inclusion.

BACK TO NATURE

Till now, media were produced, primarily by professionals, for consumption in entertainment and education industries which have different business models. Education is primarily a public sector activity and entertainment is market driven, private sector funded. This is now changed with user-generated media far outstripping professional media in sheer quantity and being available for free. Now, there is an opportunity to create crossover advantages across the two industries. The entertainment industry, including news, is in the process of reinventing itself. Educational institutions, are taking a more evolutionary approach to include on-line classes and video capture of lectures. Social Media services such as Facebook, although currently designed for entertainment, in the future may be tailored for educational purposes. What social media bring to education is a "back to nature" approach by engaging the heart and mind, a combination of orality and writing.

Born in 1623, Blaise Pascal classified the two extremes of reason and emotion as skepticism or dogmatism, where both extremes generate conflict. "We come to know truth not only by reason but even more by our heart" he said and education has been considered the backbone of society because school is where we learn to balance the two for best decision-making (Raman, 2003) in the service of the self as well as society. But with the rigorous separation of disciplines- science or arts- the integration of heart and head understanding, or how what we learn in school relates to life, is difficult to teach.

Studies examining the use of video and user generated content show that this gap in pedagogy can be bridged with digital content and provide new pathways to learning.

Video for Education

After School Program: Saori Fotenos (Digital Vision Fellow, 2007) decided she could turn the lure of media into literacy training for disaffected youth. Children and youth living on the streets have a self-destructive behavior and are at high risk for diseases and HIV, drug addiction and violence. In Brazil there are at least 23 million youngsters nationwide at such risk. They are, typically, functionally illiterate, have low self-esteem and are unmotivated. Traditional methods of reaching out to them to participate in a literacy or job curriculum program have failed.

"It works because the technology is taught from aninverseperspective by starting first with multimedia and then returning to text and word processing"

Video is a key part of the landscape today (e.g. music videos) and Fotenos and co-researchers observed that *youth are confident with video as a medium. This key insight combined with the observation that children are interested in themselves and their friends* became the fundamental principle behind *Vamos Blogar* (Lets Blog!) - a pilot program that would take advantage of the ubiquitous presence of media in contemporary pop-culture to improve literacy and enhance employability.

By leveraging existing open source, multimedia web log technology, *Vamos Blogar* created an authoring environment that serves as a communications curriculum for low-literacy urban youth. A field-study done to gauge effectiveness of the approach found that children were not threatened by the technology like they are with educational text materials. The pilot demonstrated that unmotivated, high risk youth can be drawn out to communicate and subsequently learn skills by participating in creating content which is personal and allows peer interaction (Fotenos, Wiedemann, Kautz 2007). In Brazil alone there

are 3200 tele-centers and teachers can be trained cost effectively through workshops of tele-center coordinators. Deployment costs are highly leveraged because the multimedia blogging platform is free, content is generated by users and the growing tele-center infrastructure is the vehicle for propagation and scaling.

Higher Education- As the general interest in creating and viewing personally made videos continues to increase, questions arise over how educators can incorporate these videos into standard coursework. Management schools, which already incorporate on-line learning, have been some of the first to embrace user generated videos. What are the pedagogical benefits of a video assignment? How should one structure the assignment and incorporate it into a course's overall learning objectives? Professor Paul Olk, The University of Denver, Daniels College of Business, created a workshop to study these questions. It incorporated video application to Organizational Behavior and Business Strategy courses to facilitate incorporation of a student-generated video assignment into their management courses.

K-12- Even more compelling is the use of student videos for grades K-12. Adobe Youth Voices (AYV) provides access to multimedia tools and training, to youth, teachers, and program leaders. Using video, audio, digital photography, animation, and web design, the program enables youth to explore and comment on their world and take an active role in their communities. The results in terms of motivation, engagement and social responsibility have been encouraging in cases where traditional education methodologies failed. In India, AYV (in partnership with American India Foundation) reached out to 260 young participants from 25 schools in two different cities, to create and share documentaries and photo essays they had created. Films had titles like Home Work, Do I Know My Fundamental Rights and Little Mind. In doing so they were addressing socio-economic, education, environment and other community issues in a personal heartfelt way and not as a distant, theoretical educational exercise. The educators' attributed success to a combined heart-mind approach: "when all the five senses of a human being are employed, which collectively enhance creativity in a person, they act in the right manner" (DElight, 2008).

Game Technology for Learning- Tetris turned 25 in 2009. Truly a landmark, the computer game Tetris was so easy to learn and engaging to play that it became the tool of choice for teaching computer skills to people who had never seen a computer- for *how do you teach about something that cannot even be imagined? You don't. You just allow the experience to happen and learning follows*. Tetris succeeded where workbooks and manuals failed by getting people over their inherent inhibitions about operating in an incomprehensible environment (computer). Today interactive game technology is being used to teach a range of subject: from financial skills to clean water and climate change (Digital Vision Program, rdvp.org).

EVOLUTION OF KNOWLEDGE

Around 40,000 BC, media production existed exclusively in the form of images on cave walls. To see one of those images you had to go to the cave. The cave would not come to you. One can imagine that the reason these images existed at all is that they were an outlet for human creativity. Like music, which also has existed since earliest recorded history (Sound Bytes from UCB study - http://www2.sims.berkeley.edu/research/projects/how-much-info/soundbytes.html

), such art forms were an addendum to more fundamental survival skills like orality or language. With or without tools, making these images was hard work but there they were. From this, we can infer that art and imagery was important to people, satisfying a need beyond survival. Today, if you have access to a computer and internet you have access to images, video, text, sound, graphics – in real time, at the click of a button, without leaving your physical space – from all over the world.

Influence of Language, Printing and Video- Around 100 AD paper technology became available and cave images evolved into image-like characters to take advantage of this new thing which had the benefit of being portable. One could draw or write that important missive, seal it, give it to a messenger and communicate reliably across distance in one's own words. *The notion of writing became associated with the notion of language* for communication. People who carried these important messages became recipients of trust and hence powerful as did the people who could create and decipher these missives. But writing on paper was still hard work and not something lightly undertaken. At this time, universities and other schools of learning created manuscripts to capture the thoughts of the wisest of the wise.

Year 1450 saw the invention of the printing press and writing in its modern form appeared. Language took on supreme importance as verbal and written communication could be linked. The written document could be mass produced and hence quickly became affordable and easy to transport. This was a big social change: for the average person, the source of knowledge shifted from a human being to a paper document.

Universities and institutions of learning evolved to take advantage of printing technology to educate and spread knowledge to many more people than was ever possible before. It was at this time that the notion of literacy evolved to become synonymous with knowledge and learning. *Language, in the oral form remained a communication vehicle but literacy, the ability to read and write a language, became the knowledge vehicle.* Images were still hand drawn hence a cottage industry and remained an art form.

One million books with textual content take up one million megabytes or one terabyte.

Five million books, approximately all printed material published in the world each year, if expressed in ASCII format could be stored in 5 terabytes. The storage cost of five terabytes is virtually insignificant compared to the cost of creating or printing the original content. This means that entire libraries can be digitized and the information becomes accessible to anyone with a computer and internet.

Year 2000 saw the appearance of digital capture devices. Digital image and video content proliferated when digital cameras and scanners became affordable and ubiquitous. A picture is worth a thousand words and now picture taking can be done easily by many more people than ever before. Thus from a technology perspective it seems almost too obvious to say that the current trend of data explosion offers great business opportunity. Toshiba has introduced a one terabyte home DVD recorder (Ricker, 2006). Using "nanopatterning" technology IBM hopes to improve storage capacity 250 times in just a few years (McMillan, 2004). Storage technology will certainly not be the roadblock to information access.

Evidence abounds that there is growth in the acceptance and use of digital media for lecture capture and extracurricular purposes. MIT and others make quality digital education content available. An increasing number of schools, colleges, and universities are taking advantage of free distribution platforms such as YouTube and iTunes while others are creating their own. Supporting this trend for educational institutions is an increasing focus on collaboration and sharing between corporations (Riismandel, 2009a) which is providing the impetus for technological advancement. Thus YouTube has launched YouTube EDU (www.youtube.com/edu) which aggregates content uploaded by colleges and universities. Creative Commons (http://creativecommons.org/) is a non-profit organization devoted to expanding the range of creative works available for others to build upon legally. Collaboration environments such as HP Halo and Cisco Telepresence system facilitate a face-to-face experience for globally dispersed teams. A number of startup companies are in the business of capturing meetings, seminars,

lectures and creating archives that are indexed for later retrieval and reference. Livestream (http://www.livestream.com/) advertises its platform as technology that delivers a "live experience". Conference organizers can attract a global audience with a combination of Livestream and Skype without learning difficult production values. The prestigious Tech Awards (http://www.techawards.org/) that recognize technology for human benefits encourage digital education. The 2009 education innovation awardees were recognized: "GeoGebra (International): Dynamic Mathematics for Everyone is a free, open-source software to display and practice geometry and mathematics that will help achieve rapid diffusion of information and quicker comprehension. *GeoGebra* created web-based, open-source software to visualize and practice geometric-based mathematics. http://www.geogebra.org/. The Khan Academy (International): High school students around the world need informal, clear explanations that can be reviewed at a leisurely pace to supplement their formal learning. *The Khan Academy* created hundreds of free educational videos in math, statistics, physics, and finance using drawing software. The "blackboard" style videos are accessible via the internet and hosted on YouTube. http://www.khanacademy.org/." With so much infusion of energy in the field, it is natural to expect changes in education delivery models.

Education Delivery Platforms- There is no ideal platform for hosting course content with limited overhead and education delivery. There is no standardization in this field either. As yet. Some universities are developing their own platforms while others are partnering. Also software companies are broadening their market base by seeking university business. Thus, Ektron Inc., a technology provider in web content management software, is expanding its market by working with customers in the higher education industry (http://www.ektron.com/customers/) to meet their unique online needs. Platform enhancements include "engagements with multiple audiences including current and prospective student". A platform that can assist education institutions in better representing their offerings online and that can help them to form a more direct line of communication with their audience is required. Across the world, the Indian university, Amrita (http://www.amrita.edu/) has developed a multi-media platform A-VIEW (http://www.amrita.edu/research/Amrita%20E-Learning%20Research%20Lab.html) for distance learning. The system is intended to broadcast classroom lectures live to students who would otherwise not be able to have access to campuses or teachers. The development effort brought together several US Universities as well as Indian universities as well as the government of India. Because of the partner-oriented development effort, the platform has already seen significant adoption in India. The entrepreneurial startup, market based approach is also live and well. Orlando, Florida based startup Neulio, (http://www.crunchbase.com/company/neulio) has a free platform for anyone looking to create an online course to educate via distance learning. Created as part of the University of Central Florida Incubator Program Neulio uses "software as a service" approach to enable users to easily create and share video or audio instructional course content. With Neulio users can create lessons within a course and maintain a course flow via quizzes or password gates, to keep viewers or listeners from jumping ahead. The idea of creating Neulio stemmed from assisting an educational institution with setting up distance learning programs and once the technology is proven, Neulio plans to get paying customers to achieve sustainability.

While confusion exists between platforms that use technology as a distance learning tool (where it is pure delivery model) versus the new model (sometimes called Learning 2.0 since it is based on Web 2.0 technology) that is interactive and collaborative and has a wider stakeholder base, it is only a matter of time till the concepts merge to create platforms that deliver the benefit of tra-

ditional institutions as well as the new benefits of internet media. The market forces for this merge are sizable since it is possible to reduce cost and improve reach through the use of digital media and educational institutions have access to students who are technically astute and hence less wary of new unproven technology.

FROM TEACHING TO LEARNING

A study on how digital media are changing education by MacArthur Foundation (MacArthur Briefing, 2009) supports the need for a change in education: "to stay relevant, learning institutions need to focus on participatory learning — learning by doing, which engages young people in their education and can be prompted and facilitated through using digital media".

The shift from a teaching (one way knowledge transfer) to learning (co-creation of knowledge) model is possible because of the following enablers of internet and digital:

- *Interactivity*
  - Interaction capability in spite of physical distance of diverse people
  - Interaction capability with the media itself in an engaging way- like games
- *Connectivity*
  - Emotional connection because of image and video
  - Real-time responses lead to dialogs- collaboration
- *Open systems*
  - User-generated media has freed content from burdensome copyrights
  - Creativity becomes king – internet readers decide who gets recognition

Evolution in hardware, software and networking including mobile networks has created these enablers and are listed in Table 4.

Technology Gaps- Because digital media use evolved much like print media, the underpinning technologies are resource intensive and currently an inhibitor to realizing its full potential. Capture, computation, transmission, storage, databases, information retrieval – all use technologies developed for text. For example, video search (Riismandel, 2009b) still requires text annotation. Furthermore educational materials also have evolved to replace a text-style delivery model which is optimized for printed books, rather than a more human centered model of learning which would be interactive and emotionally, socially and culturally aware. Moreover, the advances in mobile phone penetration have created possibilities for collaboration and knowledge transfer that were unimaginable ten years ago.

RESEARCH AREAS FOR TRANSFORMATIONAL IMPACT

Besides the high cost of hardware for emerging economies, software research also remains in its infancy. The platforms developed so far work well for lowering distribution costs but have barely touched on the human-technology-human perspective. The connection that interactive and digital media provide across distance, across diverse people falls in these categories:

- **Assumption: digital media > text + images + audio + video**

  ◦ Technology gap: search for video is text oriented; no automated indexing
  ◦ Multimedia metadata standardization
  ◦ Graphical display of complex data with relationships synthesis
- **Emulate Human Perceptual System:**
  ◦ Visualization techniques: systems (like the eye+brain system) that automatically separate foreground –background data, categorize and organize
  ◦ Lifelike collaboration systems: e.g. virtual, augmented or mixed reality systems
- **Emulate human interaction: digital communication > human-computer-text communication**
  ◦ New human-human interaction focused platforms e.g. game technology
  ◦ 100x improved access, cost reduction
  ◦ Take advantage of what computers do well with digital media – e.g. signal processing
  ◦ In parallel develop object, text and other human patterns

Social Learning in the Digital World

Stanford University, Media-X program (http://mediax.stanford.edu/about.html) specializes in supporting research that cuts across disciplines to promote change innovation which requires collaboration across diverse competencies. Media X collaborates with industry to bring together Stanford's interactive technology research with

Table 4. Key technology milestones

Timeline	1960	1970	1980	1990	2000	2010
HW Enabler	Mainframe	PC	CD-ROM	Internet	Broadband	Mobile

Timeline	2000	2002	2004	2006	2008	2010
SW Enabler Example	Open dictionary: Wikipedia	Experiential environments: Second life	Web 2.0, Facebook, Flickr	iPhone	Mashup Apps, Video for lecture capture	Mixed, Augmented and Virtual Reality

companies committed to technical advancement in basic issues about the design and use of interactive technologies. The *research focuses on people and technology* - how people use technology, how to better design technology to make it more usable (and more competitive in the marketplace), how technology affects people's lives, and the innovative use of advanced communication technologies in research, education, art, business, commerce, entertainment, communication, national security, and other walks of life. To involve all stakeholders, MediaX holds regular workshops for the community. For example, "mixed media and mixed realities in support of remote collaboration" http://mediax.stanford.edu/remote.html) is a workshop about remote-presence and ubiquitous computing applications that are increasingly valuable in creating a sense of "being there" and "co-action". This workshop explores of collaboration technologies as they are integrated and start to form an ecosystem that links collocated, remote, and mobile knowledge workers, including telepresence, telepresence robots and avatars, sensors and control, mobile devices, interactive rooms, physical and virtual team neighborhoods.

Heart-Head Research: Empirical studies as well as experience with digital environments, confirm that there is no replacement for human, direct face-to-face contact and as such there is no replacement for an expert, mentor or a teacher in the learning process. "The fusion of virtual and physical worlds for advanced communications represents a new field of interdisciplinary inquiry," says Byron Reeves, Professor of Communication (http://hstar.stanford.edu/cgi-bin/?hstar_leadership), Co-Founder of Media X and, the Human Sciences Technologies Advanced Research Institute, at Stanford University. While computer-aided 'physical worlds' with digitized documents, media and information exchange are the basis of most corporate work these days the question of synchronizing or harmonizing virtual worlds with physical worlds has not been studied in much depth. One MediaX and National Science Foundation sup-

ported project led by Professor Anthony Wagner (Chen, Shohamy, Ross, Reeves & Wagner, 2009) "*Impact of Social Belief on the Neurophysiology of Learning and Memory*" asks the research question: how does belief in the social status of an instructor providing performance-based feedback impact learning and subsequent memory representation? Early results are documented in the research paper. The project is based on previous research which provides background:

- Combining physical i.e. human and virtual: Learning is enhanced when subjects believe that a virtual character with whom they are interacting is controlled by a human as opposed to a computer.
- What happens in the human brain- "The medial temporal lobes support flexible episodic learning - the ability to generalize experiences to new stimuli or context. We observe that the basal ganglia support incremental, feedback-based learning of stimulus-response associations that are relatively inflexible and both memory systems are modulated by midbrain activity, and may be influenced by social belief, feedback value, and arousal."

The research methodology was Acquired Equivalence paradigm where subjects learn that two stimuli are equivalent (i.e., lead to the same outcome), and then are tested to see whether they generalize that equivalence to a novel situation. Some preliminary results indicated by observed brain activity show:

- Combined physical and virtual is effective - Subjects who believed they were participating in social learning were better able to generalize acquired knowledge to novel situations. Skin conductance increases during learning were predictive of generalization, suggesting that arousal is related to the acquisition of flexible conjunctive representations.

- More research - The difference in generalization between groups was evident, suggesting that arousal is not the only factor affecting generalization. fMRI results show distinct networks of regions that track performance (hippocampus, putamen, subgenual cingulate), outcome uncertainty (midbrain, caudate) and outcome valence (ventral striatum). Right hippocampus and right amygdala show different patterns of activity in the social (Avatar) and nonsocial (Agent) groups.

Thus the relationship between social conditioning and learning must also be taken into account in distance learning and collaboration.

Heart-Head Coursework: Borders are not binding when it comes to internet digital media. Geography, religion, color, race, economic or social status are irrelevant if the equalizer is the internet. The Peace Innovation course offered by Persuasive Technology Lab (http://captology. stanford.edu/) is an example interactive, collaborative learning presented in a transformational way through "use of new technology to invent peace". The course is based on the idea that new technologies such as mobile phones and web 2.0 are great tools of persuading people into believing (belief formation) and behaving in a certain way. Global engagement is encouraged (http:// fromgoodtogold.blogspot.com/search/label/ Video%20Peace) to give voice to the majority that believes in peace for social harmony versus war and students experience technology as well as social learning.

The Wild Card: Mobile Phones

While basic research in digital learning has stayed tethered to the computer, the transformational applications that require movement of business information have been happening in the mobile telephony space. Phones compensate for poor infrastructure and require much less energy (electricity) to operate, making markets efficient and unleashing entrepreneurship. Lower costs and business model innovations in India, China and Africa give rise to predictions that in next decade pretty much anyone who wants a mobile phone will have one. This is not true for the computer. Today the internet and computer are linked but broadband mobile is soon to be a reality making it possible for the internet (i.e. digital communication or content) to be de-linked from the computer (Mobile Marvels, 2009). Indeed, low cost computers like netbooks could potentially be given away with long term mobile broadband contracts just as mobile handsets already are in some cases (Finishing the job: Mobile Marvels – pg 18) leading to a new direction in software for education. Application innovation in the mobile-phone space is exploding – from rural banking – mobile money- to farming to politics to medicine to data-gathering. So far education remains a holdout. So it makes sense to predict that innovators will tap into mobile telephony for internet education delivery because these same developing economies are also largest markets for education. Technology innovations for the computer like the $100 laptop (http://laptop.org/ en/, one laptop per child- OLPC) have so far been unable to deliver. Meanwhile netbooks, smaller, cheaper computers have crossed the $200 barrier to become a growing segment of the computer market and now phones that you hold in your hand (to look at a screen- versus one you hold to the ear) are changing the perception of what applications are possible for cheaper devices with smaller visual real-estate. India's "Bonsai Netbook" (Sakshat Computer, http://keznews. com/5329_Sakshat___10_laptop_from_India) is targeted at a price point of $10. The jury is still out on what device will eventually become sustainable in the marketplace but there is no doubt that an iphone like device, a phone held in the hand rather than held to the ear, or a small computer, will become a platform for information disbursement which could include educational materials. The village-phone model pioneered by Grameenphone – where a village-woman leases a phone and goes around the village charging a small fee from people who want to make phone calls as a business – lends itself well to small inexpensive devices that link to a network through mobile broadband for education and learning. With greater access will come greater innovation in technology for education and it may well be driven by mobile phone penetration in the emerging economies.

The Learning Model- Education, experience and action with their different values can be integrated to create a new learning model (Table 5) that goes beyond traditional approach of (Multisilta, 2009) teaching and studying and involve the greater community to form a wider stakeholder base.

In this model it is not imperative that internet based education content be distributed free. Quality is most important and revenue models to offset implementation costs are viable. Pay per view (for periodic viewing) as well as the subscription model (e.g. distance learning) as well as a combination of the two apply. Increasingly, institutions offer courses online as part of the regular curriculum giving students flexibility in housing options to cut costs. Additionally, the learning model facilitates partnerships with industry, government and NGOs who are not on a school or university calendar and expands the stakeholder base for education.

CONCLUSION

Images on stone were in evidence 40,000 years ago. Paper was invented in China around 100 AD though the use of Papyrus was seen 3000 years ago (http://www.paperonline.org/history/history_frame.html). The first modern style university was in ancient India and teachers were revered as keepers of knowledge and enjoyed immense power. Fifteen hundred years later, the Gutenberg Press was invented in Europe and documents, manuscripts and books could be mass produced for the first time. Text, which aids analytical thinking allowed science and technology to flourish. Thus books have been revered since printing was invented as repositories of knowledge and people with access to books were in a better position to create new knowledge, new social wealth. Digital "books" are multimedia and easy to create, even for non-professionals, with relatively inexpensive equipment. After several hundred years of development in formal education methodologies based on printed media, shared digital media now present a potential to synthesize creativity with analytics and emotional

Table 5. Teaching, studying, learning

Reflective Teaching (Behaviorism)	Purposive Studying (Cognitive)	Action Learning (Collaborative)	Meaningful Learning (Open)
Exploratory	Cultural	Reflects	Reflected
Reciprocal	Dialogic	Collaborates	Cultural
Group investigation	Critical	Sets goals	Shared
Through simulation	Communal	Pro-active	Integrated
Master-Novice	Contextual	Feels responsible	Adopted
Socratic	Reflective	Explores	Internalized
	Individual	Discusses	Autonomous
	Cumulative	Integrates	Co-constructed
	Game based	Builds knowledge	Participatory
	Experiential		Engaged
	Multimodal		Critical
	Responsible		Well-structured

and intellectual knowledge. Emotional engagement favors collaboration over competition and group plus individual intelligence. The world-wide reach of telecom broadband as well as the advent of inexpensive computers offers the potential of including 4 billion minds, currently excluded from the education system, in solving issues of global scope like climate change.

Educational institutions that take advantage of the phenomenon of born digital can invent a future we would want.

ACKNOWLEDGMENT

Sincere thanks to Reuters Digital Vision Program (2003-2008) and Media-X at Stanford University for the opportunity and access to research media technologies applied to education and for their support and guidance.

REFERENCES

Chubb, J. E., & Moe, T. M. (2009). *Liberating learning: Technology, politics, and the future of American education*. San Francisco, CA: Jossey-Bass.

Cornish, E. (2005). *Futuring: The exploration of the future* (p. 134). Bethesda, MD: World Future Society.

DElight. (2008, July 8). *Adobe youth voices year end event – Delhi*. Retrieved from http://aifde.blogspot.com/2008/07/ayv-year-end-event-delhi.html

Fotenos, S., Wiedemann, L., & Kautz, J. (2007). *Vamos blogar (let's blog): Integrating two worlds through technology*. Paper presented at DigitalStream 2007. California State University, Monterey Bay, Seaside, CA, USA, March, 2007. Retrieved June 30, 2009, from http://php.csumb.edu/wlc/ocs/viewabstract.php?id=34&cf=1

Glader, P. (2009, June 22). The Jack Welch MBA coming to the Web. *The Wall Street Journal*. Retrieved from http://online.wsj.com/article/SB124562232014535347.html

Hull, D. (2009, June 17). Gov. Schwarzenegger wants California's schools to adopt digital textbooks. *San Jose Mercury News*. Retrieved from http://www.mercurynews.com/breakingnews/ci_12602248?source=rss

Kamenetz, A. (2009, September 1). How Web-savvy edupunks are transforming American higher education. *Fast Company*. Retrieved from http://www.fastcompany.com/magazine/138/who-needs-harvard.html

Krishnan, M. S., & Prahalad, C. K. (2008). *The new age of innovation: Driving cocreated value through global networks*. New York, NY: McGraw-Hill Professional.

Lyman, P., & Varian, H. R. (2000). *How much information?* Retrieved July 10, 2006, from http://www.sims.berkeley.edu/how-much-info

MacArthur Foundation. (2009, September 21). *Digital media are changing how young people learn*. Chicago, IL: The MacArthur Foundation. Retrieved from http://www.macfound.org/site/c.lkLXJ8MQKrH/b.4462309/apps/s/content.asp?ct=7510783

McMillan, R. (2004, December 17). IBM researchers eye 100T-byte tape drive. *IDG News Service*. Retrieved from http://www.itworld.com/041217ibmtape

Mishra, G. (2009, May 17). *The 4Cs social media framework*. Retrieved June 27, 2009, from http://www.gauravonomics.com/blog/the-4cs-social-media-framework/

Multisilta, J. (2009). Activity theory approach to designing learning activities in social media. Accepted to *International Journal of Web Engineering and Technology* (IJWET).

Raman, N. (2003). *The practice and philosophy of decision making: A seven step spiritual guide.* North Charleston, SC: BookSurge Publishing.

Report, E. S. (2009, September 26). *Mobile marvels: A special report on telecoms in emerging markets.* Retrieved September 26, 2009, from http://www.economist.com/surveys/download-SurveyPDF.cfm?id=14488868&surveyCode=%254e%2541&submit=View+PDF

Ricker, T. (2006, June 22). *Toshiba's RD-A1 HD DVD recorder with 1TB disk.* Retrieved from http://www.engadget.com/2006/06/22/toshibas-rd-a1-hd-dvd-recorder-with-1tb-disk/

Riismandel, P. (2009a). *Advanced learning: Education year in review: The use of video in higher education has moved beyond mere lecture capture.* Streaming Media, Feb/Mar 2009. Retrieved August 26, 2010, from http://www.streamingmedia.com/Articles/ReadArticle.aspx?ArticleID=65390&PageNum=3

Riismandel, P. (2009b). *Class act: Making educational video more accessible.* Streaming Media, June/July 2009. Retrieved August 26, 2010, from http://www.streamingmedia.com/Articles/ReadArticle.aspx?ArticleID=65494

Tapscott, D. (1998). *Growing up digital: The rise of the net generation.* New York, NY: McGraw-Hill.

Wagner, A., Chen, J., Shohamy, D., Ross, V., Reeves, B., & Wagner, A. D. (2009). *The impact of social belief on the neurophysiology of learning and memory.* Research work was supported by grants from the National Institute of Mental Health (5R01–MH080309), National Science Foundation, (NSF#0354453), and Stanford University's Media X program. Retrieved from http://hstar.stanford.edu/cgi-bin/?research_centers

Chapter 5
Using Video Streaming in an Online, Rich–Media Class to Promote Deep Learning While Educating for Social Change

Diane Zorn
York University, Canada

Kelly Parke
York University, Canada

ABSTRACT

This chapter shows how the authors have used video streaming as a central component of a rich-media, online learning environment incorporating podcasting and advanced Internet technologies to promote deep learning while educating for social change. In the first part of the chapter we discuss the design and pedagogy of our award-winning course. Various aspects of our technological and teaching innovations are highlighted: first, we have developed a highly flexible and customizable learning environment that addresses different learning styles, and which includes choice of mode of delivery, choice of amount of skills practice, and choice to effect changes to the course-in-progress. Second, we use design and teaching practices that facilitate deep learning through cognitive apprenticeship, such as modeling, coaching, and scaffolding (Weigel, 2002). Third, our design and pedagogy works against fundamental and prevalent values underlying the culture of higher education that desperately need changing, such as aggressive competitiveness, scholarly isolation, lack of mentoring, and valuing of product over process (Damrosch, 1995). These points are illustrated in the online course description that follows.

In the latter part of this chapter, we outline the theory behind our practice. We discuss the factors that impelled us to rethink ways of creating online, rich-media learning environments, and move toward innovation. We explain the principles, ideas, and concepts that have grounded our approach and inspired us to embrace video streaming, podcasting, and advanced Internet technologies. We unpack a fundamental assumption: deep learning and educating for social change are made possible by an acceptance and understanding of the radical intertwining of learner, educator, technologist, and technology. In sum, we draw on our course to illustrate enactive, online teaching-and-learning.

DOI: 10.4018/978-1-60960-800-2.ch005

BACKGROUND AND OVERVIEW

The authors co-designed a rich-media, online learning course for which Zorn developed the pedagogy and course material and which she leads as the course instructor, at York University in Toronto, Canada. She grades students' work with the assistance of a teaching assistant. Parke chose the technologies, designed the technology interface, and adapted the technologies to meet the needs of the course, the students and Zorn. Parke teaches innovation at the Schulich School of Business at York University, and along with a team of people at York's Faculty Support Centre oversees the use of the technology used in teaching-and-learning.

The course is called Reasoning About Morality and Values. It is a full-year, first-year undergraduate course, and was first offered in summer 2005. The most recent version of this course, offered in 2009/2010, comprises an in-class section with 60 enrolled students and a corresponding, fully online section with 150 enrolled students. The online section has one teaching assistant; the in-class section has none. It is one of many general-education, modes-of-reasoning courses offered at York University. However, it is York's only fully online, rich-media course and has the distinction of being the second course in Canada to provide lectures in video podcast format. It was awarded the United States Distance Learning Association 2008 Silver Award for Excellence in Distance Learning Teaching ("York Recognized as a Leader in Distance Education," 2008). It was also nominated for both the 2006 Council of Ontario Universities Award for Excellence in Teaching with Technology, and the 2007 Commonwealth of Learning Excellence in Distance Education Teaching Award for Distance Education Materials.

An interdisciplinary course, it aims to produce effective students and citizens by teaching skills most needed by first-year university students (namely, critical thinking, essay-writing, and reading comprehension) and skills required to participate fully as a citizen of a liberal democracy (namely, critically evaluating what is read or heard, clearly and cogently expressing and supporting one's views, and rational decision-making). The course design, pedagogy, and choice of course materials takes an antidomination approach. The issues, topics, cases, examples, and course content focus on morality and values.

The course is cumulative, skills-based, and multimodular. Module 1 begins by studying argument and argumentation. Module 2 emphasizes informal fallacies in everyday logic. Module 3 focuses on conceptual analysis, Module 4 on passages and issues analysis, and Module 5 on argument analysis. Weekly homework, two fully online tests, and an assignment consisting of analysis of a passage and an article assess the students' ability to analyze and criticize arguments. Since this is a skills-based, not a content-based course, the weekly homework plays the important role of providing the opportunity to practice the skills learned in class.

Classes are three hours in length. The first hour and 50 minutes consists of minilectures (Young, 2008, 2009), punctuated by collaborative learning exercises, with corresponding worksheets that students need to complete. In-class and online students complete the same worksheets. In-class students are divided into learning teams to complete the collaborative learning exercises. Examples of collaborative learning exercises are: viewing a video (DVD or YouTube), discussing, answering questions about it, and collaboratively filling out individual worksheets; listening to pieces of music and applying skills taught in class; completing tasks using skills taught in class and reporting findings as learning teams to the entire class. Zorn moves around the room and brings the microphone to each student, so that all dialogue and discussion is properly video streamed for the online students. The remaining 50 minutes is a workshop session.

The content, technology, and pedagogy have met objectives for essay-writing, critical thinking, and reading comprehension in a fully online, skills-based, student-centered, and reciprocally adaptive learning environment. The design uses student collaboration, video, audio, text, and exercises, which, together with the weekly homework, promote deep learning. The choice of video streaming, rich-media-capture technology has addressed the problem of how to teach skills and practices fully online while enabling modeling, coaching, and mentoring of behaviors and practices (e.g., argument and conceptual analysis). These enabling objectives are met by capturing and synchronizing images of Zorn lecturing with: (a) PowerPoint slides containing examples, steps, strategies, techniques, and concepts involved with the skills; (b) document camera projector images depicting the practice of work in progress; and (c) the Internet as a resource (e.g., databases, video clips).

The choice of video-streamed lectures, video and audio podcast format, and a WebCT platform (Blackboard) has addressed the challenges of York University as a commuter campus and the students' need for mobile learning. The WebCT (Blackboard) course management system has met the need for a fully online learning environment, delivering the course in an enactive and student-centered format, including real-time chat rooms, a virtual office, discussion rooms, nonlinear, user-friendly interface, video welcome messages, Ombuds Buddies, private learning teams, and coaching/mentoring videos. The course also has an accompanying Facebook User Group site (Facebook). Students' avatars (graphic representations of persons) also have the option to meet Zorn's avatar in Second Life (Second Life), a 3D virtual world, for virtual office hours.

A systematic design and multimedia product development process has been followed. The first step in the process is to digitally record the lecture material using Sonic Foundry's Mediasite technology (Mediasite). The in-class lecture is video recorded. The rich-media lecture material is also converted to Adobe Systems' Flash media by MediaLandscape software (MediaLandscape)

to ensure playback compatibility for the Mac platform. The rich-media capture technology has facilitated the creation of searchable, self-paced learning modules that are critical for this online environment. The user controls empower the students to stop, rewind, search, and print notes—all from the same interface. The course design has taken advantage of these player features to promote interactivity and allow the opportunity for discovery.

Rich media was an important choice for the technologist as well. Statistics are kept on how many times and when modules have been accessed. Information is also available on the country of origin from which the user accesses the system. This origination information has given us a global picture of our online community. The access information has also been critical for instructor feedback as the course is in progress. For example, if one learning module has been accessed more than other modules, it is clear what material has to be emphasized during the exam preparation.

Mobile learning capability is a reality for most of our students. Many students have access to MP3 players or portable video players such as the Apple video iPod. To add another dimension to the course, enhanced audio and video podcasts have thus been created. Creating this possibility has allowed even more integration with a student's lifestyle. We have chosen the unique approach of having referenced PDF files for each module. PDF referencing is done by time stamps on the individual pages that refer to the v-cast. RSS feeds contain both the v-cast and referenced PDF file.

Impacts on student learning have been variously assessed. Survey data have been collected anonymously at the end of the summer 2006 course offering, again at the end of the 2007/2008 version, and during the 2009/2010 running of the course. A summary of the survey data is available. Mediasite metrics have been collected and Ombuds Buddies have been used throughout all versions the course. (Ombuds Buddies are discussed in "Highly Flexible and Customizable E-Learning

Environment," below.) The survey data have shown the following:

- 10 percent of the class view the lectures on a video iPod about half of the time, frequently, or almost always;
- 54 percent of the class appreciate having the option to listen to the lectures on an MP3 player;
- 93 percent of the class say that the online format is a good way for them to learn; and
- 78 percent prefer online learning to an in-class format.

The Mediasite metrics have shown that students rewatch the lectures before the midterm test, and that more coaching has been needed for the conceptual analysis steps.

DESIGN AND PEDAGOGY

Highly Flexible and Customizable E-Learning Environment

In this section, we discuss the ways we have used video streaming, podcasting, and advanced Internet technologies to allow for a highly flexible and customizable enactive online learning environment. Students have several options from which to choose:

- when, where, and how the course is delivered;
- learning options that address their individual learning styles;
- how much practice they need at the skills they are learning; and
- to make changes to the course while it is in progress.

Choice of Mode of Delivery

Students in both the in-class and the fully online section have the choice of where, how, and when they would like to attend class. Students enrolled in the in-class section can attend in person one night of the week for a 3-hour class. Students in the fully online section have the option to tune in to the live webcast during the in-class session, including the workshop session, or watch the class on their PC or Mac, download the class from iTunes as an audio (MP3) file or a video (MP4) file to be viewed on a video iPod or any other hand-held device that will play MP4 files, including the Sony PlayStation Portable.

Students can also customize the mode of delivery individually; for example, Mediasite allows students to play the lectures at double speed and maintain the same audio pitch. This is used for review purposes as a way to speed-watch sections. This option meets the needs of ESL (English as a Second Language) students who may need to view and listen to the lecture at a slower pace. This option also meets the needs of digital learners who are multitaskers (Tapscott, 2009, pp. 106–110) and choose to speed the lecture up with the aim of watching it in less time.

Our learning environment has also allowed students to interact with and customize software components. For example, the WebCT (Blackboard) calendar function is not static. It can be altered for personal use, allowing it to act as a place to keep more than basic date information.

Addressing Different Learning Styles

Another aspect of a highly flexible, enactive learning environment is how different learning styles can be addressed. There is neither a common definition nor a unified theory of *learning style* (Cassidy, 2004; Desmedt & Valcke, 2004; Hall & Moseley, 2005; Merriam, Caffarella, & Baumgartner, 2007). Toye (1989) has defined learning styles as "attempts to explain learning variation between individuals in the way they approach learning tasks" (quoted in Merriam et al., 2007, p. 407), while Cranton's (2005) definition is "preferences for certain conditions or ways of learning, where learning means the development of meaning, values, skills, and strategies" (quoted in Merriam et al., 2007, p. 407). Merriam et al. (2007) note that although scholars are not in agreement about which elements constitute a learning style, learning-style inventories seem to be "useful in helping learners and instructors alike become aware of their personal learning styles and their strengths and weaknesses as learners and teachers" (p. 409).

Bonk and Zhang's (2008) R2D2 Model illustrates the ways that our online teaching-and-learning environment addresses different learning styles. Their model consists of four phases, corresponding to four types of learners: Read, Reflect, Display, and Do (Bonk and Zhang, p. 5). Sample technology resources and tools for each type of learner accompany each phase (Bonk & Zhang, p. 5). The R2D2 Model adapts and extends the work of several scholars of learning styles for online teaching-and-learning (Fleming & Mills, 1992; Kolb, 1984; McCarthy, 1987). For example, Fleming and Mill's (1992) VARK (visual, aural, read/write, and kinesthetic) approach to learning styles plays a central role in the R2D2 Model.

Read. The "Read" phase represents people with a dominant auditory and verbal learning style—those who prefer words, sounds, and spoken or written explanations. Examples of sample technology resources suited for the auditory and verbal learner are podcasts, online PDF documents, audio files, PowerPoint presentations, online portals, course announcements, help systems, FAQs, Webquests, online newsletters, e-books, and online journals (Bonk & Zhang, 2008, p. 5).

Our course addresses the learning style of auditory and verbal learners in the following ways. Students can download all class sessions (including workshop sessions) as audio podcasts, using Apple's iTunes digital music and video player. Audio presentations are also provided from the authors of the students' textbooks. Every class session has corresponding PowerPoint presentations that are downloadable from either the WebCT course platform (Blackboard) or through iTunes. Links to downloadable PDF documents are available throughout the course. Such documents may include: the weekly handouts and worksheets; samples of graded assignments that are accompanied by audio podcasts explaining grading criteria and assignment expectations; graded homework accompanied by audio podcasts taking up the homework; and workshop session worksheets accompanied by audio podcasts of the session. The WebCT course platform (Blackboard) is itself a kind of portal for the students. Its features include: an email system; synchronous and asynchronous, text-based discussion rooms (including announcements discussion room, coaching messages discussion room, and "Prof and TA never enter here"); interactive calendar, showing all homework and assignment due dates and other significant, university-wide academic dates; and a virtual office in which to meet with the professor and discuss with her, using real-time, text-based chatting. (For screen prints, see Appendix 1: Discussion Rooms, Appendix 2: Interactive Calendar, and Appendix 3: Real-Time Student Lounges and professor's Virtual Office.)

The course's web site home page consists of 15 graphic icons, each with a text heading beneath. Eight of the 15 icons have expanded textual explanation beneath the main text heading. The site addresses the navigation needs of verbal learners by including a text-based, at-a-glance, drop-down menu of all the lobbies, halls, and rooms on the site. For students who choose not to use the drop-down menu, every graphic icon on the site is accompanied by written text. Students can choose to click on the graphic image or on the written text to move about the site. When a student clicks on the written text that accompanies a home page graphic icon, the written text is repeated in the banners of the corresponding lobbies, rooms, or halls, often with more detailed textual explanation.

The choice of wording for the text is designed to be language-comfortable to the digital generation (Tapscott, 1996, 2009). Here are three examples, quoted directly from the home page:

- Main heading beneath graphic icon: "Technology Training Hall." Text beneath main heading: "How to use the course site. Well, do you want to ace the course or not? So, don't ignore this!"
- Main heading beneath graphic icon: "Lecture Halls." Text beneath main heading: "If you are allergic to work, do not enter these rooms. If you plan to fail this course, avoid this room like the plague."
- Main heading beneath graphic icon: "Coaching and Mentoring Hall." Text beneath main heading: "Come on in and take a long drink of water! Everyone needs some extra help once in a while. People with photographic memories or geniuses need not enter."

For a screen print of the drop-down menu and home page, see Appendix 4: Pull Down Menu, and Appendix 5: Home Page.)

Reflect. Our online teaching-and-learning environment also addresses Bonk and Zhang's (2008) "Reflect" phase. This phase refers to people with a dominant reflective and observational learning style—those who prefer to reflect, observe, view, and watch learning (p. 5). Reflective and observational learners make careful judgments and view things from different perspectives; they enjoy reflection, self-testing, review, and reflective summary writing. Examples of sample technologies suited for reflective and observational learners are blogs, synchronous chats, online exams, writing aids, electronic portfolios, asynchronous discussion, reflective writing tools, online review and self-testing aids, and expert videos or performances. The course includes synchronous chats, two online tests, and a portfolio assignment. Online review and self-testing aids are included as required, as well as optional online weekly homework and online practice tests and exercises.

Display. The course also addresses Bonk and Zhang's (2008) "Display" phase, which refers to people who are predominantly visual learners—those who prefer diagrams, concept maps, flowcharts, timelines, pictures, films, and demonstrations. Examples of sample technologies suited for visual learners are concept mapping and timeline tools, interactive news, video streamed content, online videos, virtual field trips and tours, animations, whiteboards, videoconferencing, online charts, graphs and visualization tools, video blogs (vblogs), and vodcasts.

All class and workshop sessions are provided as video streamed presentations synchronized with PowerPoint slides when viewed on a PC or Mac, without the slides when viewed on a hand-held device. Video streamed welcome messages from the professor and authors of the students' textbooks are provided on the home page. Also, video streamed coaching and mentoring presentations can be found throughout the site. For example, each Module of the course in the site's Lecture Halls has a welcome/coaching from the professor. (For screen prints, see Appendix 6: Video streamed Presentation, Appendix 7: Video streamed Author Presentation, and Appendix 8: Video streamed Welcome Message from Professor.) Links to online videos are provided with almost every class session. (For a screen print of a class session with links to videos, see Appendix 9: Class Videos.) All videos include text worksheets as PDF and Word docs for verbal learners and include a "doing" component. Concept and learning objective maps are also provided. As well, students are given the option in homework to learn to depict arguments in linear diagram form, arrow diagram form, or concept form.

Do. The "Do" phase refers to people who are dominantly tactile and kinesthetic learners—those who prefer role play, dramatization, cooperative games, simulations, scenarios, creative movement and dance, multisensory activities, manipulatives, and hands-on projects. Examples of technologies suited for tactile and kinesthetic learners are simulations, online games, wikis, digital story-telling and movie making, real-time cases, video scenarios, survey research, continuous stories, groupware and other collaborative tools, role play, and debate tools. Real-time cases, role playing, and debate format are used in the in-class and workshop session and then video streamed for those students in the fully online session.

A pilot-project, role-playing game will be introduced in the final module of the most recent version of the course (March–April, 2010). This will be the first online role-playing game we have attempted. The game is based on Professor David Wiley's open-source model used at Brigham Young University, Utah, in which students choose a character (an artisan, a bard, a merchant, or a monk), go on learning quests together, and gain experience points ("Introduction to Open Education 2009," 2009; Young, 2009). A 1-hour phone conversion with Professor Wiley convinced Zorn that the model he used for a sample group of less than 10 master's-level students could work even better with a class of 60 in-class and 150 online students.

Finally, consider the following example that illustrates a way in which our course addresses all four types of learners, in one room on the home page of the course web site. In the Coaching and Mentoring Hall, students can click on a Module of the course to get coaching. Information about assignment grading criteria and requirements are provided in this room, along with other helpful coaching and mentoring. When they enter an assignment information room for a specific assignment, the page provides them with written information and requirements for the assignment. Within the text are links to PDFs of actual, previously graded assignments with comments and grading bubbles, used with the permission of the student and all references to the student's

identity removed. Accompanying the PDFs are links to audio or video streamed presentations of the professor explaining the grading criteria and assignment information.

Choice of Amount of Skills to Practice

The course enables students to customize their learning experience by allowing them to choose how much practice they need to learn the skills taught in the course. Students can choose between two streams of homework, required and optional. Required homework is completed online in the Submit Homework Room. Answers to required homework are posted in the Coaching and Mentoring Hall after the due date. Also, video streamed presentations of the professor taking up the homework, including a student question-and-answer period, are provided as downloadable audio and video podcasts through iTunes, or webcasts that can be viewed on a PC or Mac. Extra, optional homework is provided in the Coaching and Mentoring Hall, with all the answers also available. (For print screens, see Appendix10: Submit Homework Room, Appendix 11: Sample Homework from Submit Homework Room, and Appendix 12: Required and Optional Homework from Coaching and Mentoring Hall.)

Choice to Effect Changes to the Course-in-Progress

The course uses Ombuds Buddies as a central way to allow students to effect changes to the course while it is in progress. Zorn's aim is to do whatever she can to ensure that students have a voice in the course, and, when possible, to make changes to the course before it is over. (Students are informed that there are some aspects of the course that simply cannot be changed 2 weeks after the course begins without violating Senate Policies.) It is Zorn's hope that students will feel comfortable enough to contact her directly with concerns, complaints or suggestions for change. If, however, students would like to remain anonymous, they can use one of the course's Ombuds Buddies. These are students who pass messages anonymously from other students to Zorn. To ensure that the student learning experience is enjoyable and the best that she can offer, Zorn asks for volunteers in the class to be Ombuds Buddies. Students are informed that Ombuds Buddies are not Teaching Assistants, and that they will not answer questions about course material, but rather only handle concerns, complaints, or suggestions. Within the Basic Information Centre is a Contact an Ombuds Buddy Room. Also, the web site includes a dedicated discussion room that both Zorn and the TA have promised not to enter, called Post Questions & Comments for Students—Prof NEVER Looks Here. There may be issues and concerns being discussed in this room that Zorn can respond to. An Ombuds Buddy will anonymously forward such concerns.

Here are three concrete examples of issues forwarded by Ombuds Buddies that resulted in changes to the course. In one case, students found that one question on a test was too hard, simply pitched at a higher skill level than had been addressed before the test. Many students emailed Ombuds Buddies who in turn informed Zorn of the concern. Zorn then consulted with the TA, course instructors of other sections of the same course, and the Area Coordinator. The general view was that this one question had been too difficult. Zorn dropped the question from the test. In a second example, students emailed the Ombuds Buddy because they felt that during one part of one Module the course material was being covered too quickly, moving too fast. Zorn was able to provide video streamed presentations reviewing material in the Coaching and Mentoring Hall, and she extended the due date of the corresponding assignment that tested these skills. A last example concerns the choice of how much practice, in the form of homework, students wanted in doing the skills they were learning. In the most recent ver-

sion of this course, students emailed the Ombuds Buddies, distressed that there was far too much homework. Zorn addressed this concern by adding two streams of homework, required and optional. Students were then able to customize their learning experience and make choices about how much practice they preferred.

PROMOTING DEEP LEARNING IN AN ONLINE TEACHING-AND-LEARNING COURSE

Our course addresses the problem of how to connect deep learning and e-learning. It shows how deep and durable learning can be achieved in a fully online, rich-media learning environment that uses WebCT (Blackboard), video streaming or webcasting, and video and audio podcasting. We do not advocate the use of technology for its own sake, a view in keeping with the conclusions of a study that answered the question "what do faculty want?" (Chizmar & Williams, 2001): "Faculty want instructional technology driven by pedagogical goals" (p. 19).

The biggest pedagogical challenge in creating this course has been to ensure the deep learning of skills. The course is almost entirely skills-based, rather than content-based. When the course was being designed, many faculty members expressed concerns about two common myths that needed to be debunked: first, that only content, not skills, could be taught online; and, second, that certain subjects could not be taught online, such as critical thinking, conceptual analysis, and argument analysis.

One faculty member had twice previously attempted online versions of this course. He had then thrown his hands up and the air and said, "These skills cannot be taught online." His attempts, however, were made before video streaming, podcasting, and advanced Internet technologies.

The courses he had developed were two versions of an online Modes of Reasoning course. The first was offered five times: 2000/2001, 2001/2002, 2002/2003, summer 2003, and 2003/2004. Each online section had an enrollment of between 60 and 80 students and each was offered in conjunction with a separate in-class section offering the same course material. Students enrolled in the in-class version had access to all online materials. Demographically—in terms of number of years in their program, grade point average, age, and how far along they were in university—there was no difference between the students in his online and in-class sections. The course was delivered in Lotus' Learning Space without the added advantage of recently developed rich-media approaches. The faculty member wrote all of the lectures and provided them to the students as PDFs. No audio or video elements were used. The course, designed without interactive elements, involved some asynchronous discussion and a lot of reading of documents that the faculty member had spent many months writing. The faculty member stated that this early online version fell short of meeting the learning objectives.

The same faculty member later developed a hybrid version of his original design to address problems with the course. The hybrid section was offered once in the summer 2004. In this version, students attended two classes a week for 12 weeks; each class was 3 hours in length, one in-class and one online. They met once a week rather than twice a week. Students also attended an in-person, 3-hour, inaugural workshop at the beginning of the course. Less than half of the students enrolled in the class attended this workshop. The faculty member stated that the hybrid section worked slightly better, but not well enough.

Video streaming, podcasting, and advanced Internet technologies solved the problems faced by this faculty member in the two earlier versions of his course. In the remainder of this section, we discuss the ways in which these technologies enabled deep learning of skills.

A Definition of Deep Learning

Weigel's (2002) model of depth education outlines the clear differences between deep and surface learning. His explanation, adapted from Noel Entwistle's (2001) research on assessment to promote deep learning, states that deep learners:

... relate ideas to previous knowledge and experience... look for patterns and underlying principles... check evidence and relate it to conclusions... examine logic and argument cautiously and critically... are aware of the understanding that develops while learning... become actively interested in the course content. (Weigel, p. 6)

On the other hand, surface learners:

... treat the course as unrelated bits of knowledge... memorize facts and carry out procedures routinely... find difficulty in making sense of new ideas presented... see little value or meaning in either courses or tasks... study without reflecting on either purpose or strategy... feel undue pressure and worry about work. (Weigel, p. 6)

Deep learning is rooted in conditionalized knowledge that specifies use contexts, metacognition that involves monitoring and reflecting on one's level of knowledge, and communities of inquiry or practice.

Cognitive Apprenticeship Learning

Cognitive apprenticeship (i.e., traditional apprenticeship learning applied to thinking or cognitive skills) is the learning methodology best suited to achieve the aims of deep learning (Weigel, 2002). Van Weigel (2002) has set out six teaching practices and course design strategies that facilitate cognitive apprenticeship (Collins, 1991; Collins, Brown, & Newman, 1989) in online learning environments: modeling, coaching, scaffolding, articulating, reflecting, and exploring (Weigel,

2002, pp. 10–11). Below we discuss the ways in which our course design and pedagogy illustrate the first three methods.

Modeling. When it comes to teaching cognitive skills, modeling—showing someone how something is done—is necessary for deep learning. Consider the skill of playing golf, for example. One cannot teach golf without showing learners how to position their hands on the golf club, how to take a proper swinging stance, how to plant their feet on the ground, and so on. Modeling cognitive skills such as concept and argument analysis involves "the externalization of internal cognitive processes" in which "the teacher puts her mind on display, walking her students through her approach to a problem making explicit the internal steps she took and strategies she used along the way" (Weigel, 2002, p. 10).

Video streaming technology makes this possible. It is thus a central way to achieve modeling in online learning environments. In our course, the rich-media capture technology, Mediasite, facilitates the creation of searchable, self-paced webcast presentations that are synchronized with PowerPoint slides, live Internet, or a doc-cam projector (a projector with a built-in document camera). Using this video streaming technology, Zorn has been able to demonstrate a step-by-step process of concept or argument analysis captured as a live and video podcast or presentation.

Coaching. In coaching, an instructor observes students in the classroom and gives feedback for improvement. Van Weigel (2002) notes that:

... whereas modeling emphasizes the student's role as observer, coaching requires teachers to observe students in the performance of some task or skill (usually in the context of problem solving) and to ask questions or to offer feedback on the student's performance. (p. 10)

Video streaming technology has enabled Zorn to coach students in several ways. For example, she sometimes provides students PDFs of graded homework with comment bubbles and an accompanying webcast of her taking up the homework on a doc-cam projector. Rich-media capture technology, Mediasite, has allowed Zorn's image and voice to be synchronized with a doc-cam projector of the homework. Mediasite's seek-and-search capability has made it easy for students to review only the sections that need attention, thus maximizing their study time.

Scaffolding. Scaffolding refers to the various ways that a teacher and a learning community help in the construction of knowledge; for example, hints and aids built into the curriculum designed to help students complete a task. The WebCT platform (Blackboard) has allowed Zorn to provide her students with a Coaching and Mentoring Hall on the course website's home page, containing video streamed presentations and podcasts of assignment information, grading criteria, and much more. Also, in order to avoid any "creepy treehouse effect" (flexknowlogy, 2008), Zorn set up a Facebook user group for students of the course to use as an alternative meeting place.[1]

The course also provides scaffolding with a Technology Training Hall. The following text on the home page describes this area:

Welcome! You have entered the lobby of the course Technology Training Hall. As the course instructor, I realize that I cannot erase social, political, and economic inequities among the students in this course. I also realize that despite my most democratic intentions, not everyone will feel comfortable in this course. Given these two provisos, there is something that I can do. I can make sure that everyone in the course knows how to use the technology. That is what this room is all about. Click on the icons below to learn how to view and use the lecture and site technology fully and to your advantage.

The Technology Training Hall includes video streamed presentations—including classes, workshop sessions, coaching and mentoring messages—on how to view and use the video streaming technology in the most beneficial ways. Students learn how to slow down or speed up the viewing speed. Slowing down video streamed presentations is advantageous for ESL students. Speeding up the video streamed presentations is helpful for digital learners who wish to multitask by viewing the presentations in less time. Students also learn how to use the Slide View function of the Mediasite video streaming technology for review purposes. To view the instructor talking about a specific slide or captured image, they can select a particular PowerPoint Slide, doc-cam projection, or live Internet capture.

The Technology Training Hall also includes an online code of conduct, information about how to subscribe to the course RSS feed through iTunes, how to join the Facebook user group, and how to use Second Life, 3D virtual technology (to meet with Zorn's avatar), a graphic representation of a person, or another student's avatar, in the Modes of Reasoning Building in Second Life. Once in this building, students can discuss course material and issues while sitting in comfortable chairs in a glass building with a view of water.

The Hall also includes a Troubleshooting Problems with Technology video streamed presentation that discusses possible problems that students may encounter using the technology and how to avoid these problems. The Hall also provides a video streamed presentation of Zorn explaining how to use basic WebCT (Blackboard) course features. Free plug-ins are also provided in the Hall, such as Adobe Acrobat, Media Player, and PowerPoint Viewer.

Teaching Against Prevalent Values and Educating for Social Change

The features of our enactive online learning environment discussed in the above sections point to the ways in which an enactive approach can educate for social change. These features in combination educate against the fundamental and prevalent values underlying the culture of higher education that desperately need changing: aggressive competitiveness, scholarly isolation, lack of mentoring, and valuing product over process (Damrosch, 1995).

Our customizable learning environment includes the following features:

- choice of mode of delivery;
- addressing of different learning styles;
- choice of amount of skills practice;
- choice to effect change to the course in progress;
- promotion of deep learning through cognitive apprenticeship learning, via coaching, modeling, scaffolding, articulating, reflecting and exploring; and
- foundational mentoring, including a Coaching and Mentoring Hall, video streamed welcome, coaching and mentoring messages throughout the site, coupled with dedicated asynchronous and synchronous discussion rooms and a Facebook user group.

Our use of video streaming, podcasting, WebCT (Blackboard), and advanced Internet technologies encourages behaviors and teaches values that promote social change by demonizing scholarly isolation, exiling aggressive competitiveness, valuing the learning process over the learning product, and embracing mentoring.

We are most proud of the mentoring and reciprocally adaptive course features that create comfort, collaboration, and community. Foundational mentoring features include video welcome messages on the home page, coaching messages throughout the site, modeling of expectations, skills, and practices in the form of sample assignments and homework, grading criteria videos, and a private discussion room dedicated to students only. The reciprocally adaptive features of the course include Ombuds Buddies and the ability to respond to information (metrics) gathered by

Mediasite technology. For example, Mediasite enables the instructor and technologist to see which lectures have been viewed more often, enabling us to change the course in response to students' needs. The organic fluidity and adaptability of this course structure has necessarily encouraged and strengthened the experience for student, technologist, and instructor alike, allowing the course to evolve in progress.

As well as contributing to the improvement of the culture of higher education, our innovative course improves the quality of education by going far beyond what is possible in a conventional classroom, through mobile learning and the students' ability to customize their learning environment and learning style.

THEORY BEHIND THE DESIGN AND PEDAGOGY

In the latter part of this chapter, we outline the theory behind our practice, drawing on our course to illustrate enactive online teaching-and-learning.

Teaching and Design Values and Behaviors That Need Changing

A starting point in our discussion was the following headline that appeared in the *Toronto Star's* online news source on April 6, 2009: "Profs blast lazy first-year students: Wikipedia generation is lazy and unprepared for university's rigors, survey of faculty says" (Rushowy, 2009). The headline suggests that facing current and future challenges may be like climbing a greased pole, to borrow Donna Haraway's phrase (1991, p. 188). Rushowy's key points are that college and university professors feel their students are less mature, rely too much on Wikipedia, and "expect success without the requisite effort." In their view, a decline in student preparedness began years ago but has more recently accelerated. Rushowy (2009) quotes several instructors who all agree that wider social issues, possibly the fault of the students, underlie

these themes. One instructor said: "We are basically trying to deliver a quality education on our campuses for a cohort of students who need extra attention to succeed." A fourth-year undergraduate student who worked at a library at the University of Toronto reports that "many students can't even ask for help. Partly, it's generational, the attitude and sense of entitlement they have." A faculty member said: "What the questionnaire reveals is a serious challenge that we are facing in the system. We are teaching students from what is basically an under-resourced secondary school system."

In presenting views about limited educational resources or a decline in student preparedness, Rushowy (2009) offers one defensible interpretation of the results of the questionnaire. We offer an alternative view. Rather than attributing the problem to lazy students and an under-resourced secondary school system, we would like to shine a light on the following fundamental and prevalent values underlying the culture of higher education that desperately need changing: aggressive competitiveness, scholarly isolation, lack of mentoring, and valuing product over process (Damrosch, 1995). Damrosch (1995) traces these shared learned values and behaviors to the birth of the university in the Middle Ages. He argues that

... much of this stability results from the university's ability to change constantly at a local level while varying little in many basic ways, so that contemporary concerns can coexist with very archaic procedures and values. Sedimented levels of history overlay one another, punctuated by igneous extrusions from the deep past. (p. 18)

Limited resources and budget cuts are seasonal: they come and go, depending on the health of the economy. But the shared values and collaboratively learned behaviors that are most relevant to the problems identified in the star.com article, and that have the most significant impact on teaching, learning, and creativity in North America, are the ones Damrosch (1995) mentions.

Confronting Habits of Inattention

These "holdover" (Damrosch, 1995, p. 18) values from the Middle Ages currently contribute to what Megan Boler (1999, 2004) calls " inscribed habits of inattention" (Boler, 1999, p. 180) in online teaching-and-learning. Course design and teaching practices in online learning environments reflect these taken-for-granted, shared, and collaboratively formed values and behaviors. Habits of inattention are learned ways of seeing and acting that can prevent one from seeing differently. They direct one's perceptions and actions, and limit one's ability to respond to students' needs in online learning environments. These are fundamentally emotional habits, driven by the avoidance of feelings of discomfort, feelings that most North Americans are simply not skilled at staying with, such as fear, disappointment, and uncertainty (Chödrön, 1997, 2001; Epstein, 1995, 1998; Hanh, 2005; Watts, 2000). Unfortunately, for the most part, North Americans are trained to run and hide from these unfamiliar feelings of discomfort when designing online learning environments. The authors had to use practices of mindfulness awareness to notice our habits of inattention in design and teaching and to stay with our discomfort in order to enable student-centered, highly participatory, engaging e-learning environments that would promote deep learning while educating for social change.[2]

Our enactive approach to online teaching-and-learning began by practicing unlearning emotional habits of inattention, through: befriending the fear of the unfamiliar, and living the assumption that rich media (i.e., online learning environments using advanced Internet technologies) can take us far beyond what is possible in a conventional classroom; staying with the uneasiness of not being the expert, to enable collective learning and to let a space for power to emerge from deep and durable learning methods that blur the lines between learner, instructor, technologist, and technology; and staying with and noticing the fear of losing control and of uncertainty, in favor of what is happening: emergent, collective teaching-and-learning.

For example, we have had to notice and practice unlearning certain ways of seeing and acting concerning online learning environments that had become obstacles. Three such habits of inattention are the association of high-quality learning with the in-class experience; the disassociation of teaching and research; and the tendency to see online learning environments as *created* or *constructed*. We discuss these emotional habits below.

Habit of associating high-quality learning with in-class courses. First we had to learn to let go of associating high-quality learning and the in-class experience. This habit can be expressed in the idea that "good" online learning environments are ones that replicate the in-class experience (Twigg, 2001), for example. We found that the emotional element of this habit was located in fear of the unfamiliar, and the profound need to feel that we are on safe ground as teachers. Twigg (2001) observes that "the problem with applying old solutions to new problems in the world of online learning is that these applications tend to produce results that are 'as good as' what we have done before" (p. 4). Only by letting go of this expectation were we able to practice new approaches that went beyond producing *no significant difference* between online teaching-and-learning and teaching-and-learning that takes place in a physical classroom. To paraphrase Twigg (2001), our focus shifted to what we could do with technology that we could not do without it (p. 9). We have needed to broaden our idea of a "high-quality" learning experience to mean greater individualization of learning experiences for students. The best e-learning environments would no longer begin with the thought "all students need..." We have learned that video streaming, podcasting, and advanced Internet technologies such as social networking sites, wikis, and blogs, can meet the needs of diverse students when, where, and how they want to learn. Living this habit of inattention could have prevented us from seeing that advanced Internet technologies could take online learning environments far beyond what is possible in a conventional classroom.

Habit of disassociating teaching and research. A second habit of inattention we have confronted is the disassociation of teaching and research. The emotional core of this habit, we have found, is an unhealthy attachment to power and the fear of being found out as an impostor—the fear that we don't know what we are talking about. The habit of bifurcating research and teaching leads to favoring a "banking" model of education, which views instructors as exclusive experts who deposit information in students' heads (Freire, 2003, pp. 71–86). The banking model, ineffective at promoting deep, durable learning, works even less effectively in e-learning environments. High-quality online learning environments call for instructors to employ cognitive apprenticeship models of education that require instructors to coach, mentor, facilitate, and model learning (Weigel, 2002, pp. 9–11). This tendency towards a false dilemma between research and teaching is an obstacle to creating e-learning environments that are highly participatory and that promote deep rather than surface learning (Weigel, 2002, pp. 5–6)

Habit of seeing online courses as constructed. A third habit of inattention is the tendency to see online learning and community as created or constructed. The emotions associated with this habit, we have discovered, are uncertainty and the fear of losing control. The habit is grounded in the idea of the "clockmaker hypothesis," the notion of a godlike instructor who must directly intervene to create the online learning environment because the complexity of e-learning and online communities requires it. Afterwards, according to this hypothesis, the creator steps aside, only acting to maintain the universe he created, perhaps repairing various mechanisms and replacing parts. This habit of inattention perpetuates the false idea that e-learning environments are mechanistic, rather than the complex, dynamic,

and self-organizing systems they are—a view that is founded in a misconception of the activities of teaching and learning.

REPLACING SELF-ACTION AND INTERACTION WITH ENACTION

In the remainder of this chapter we discuss the ways that our innovations in online teaching and course design have been enactive, rather than self-active or interactive.

The enactive approach is a form of collective, emergent teaching-and-learning and a technology innovation and design that redefines our concept of learner, educator, technologist, and technology. No longer are these roles we can occupy only one at a time. In fact, we are all these things simultaneously, and only by allowing all the relationships to exist simultaneously do we foster a truly enactive learning environment that can promote deep learning and social change.

Traditional lines that demarcate these roles are blurring, opening up the possibility to experience something new and genuine. Letting go of the model of interactive education and embracing an enactive approach can create an unsettling feeling as the ground constantly shifts; but the possibilities are boundless, as we position ourselves to engage simultaneously from all perspectives. This synergistic growth can be empowering. More importantly, staying with the discomfort and uncertainly of this shifting ground allows the roles of learner, educator, technologist, and technology to dynamically, reciprocally, evolve.

The broad enactive perspective (as discussed in Bateson, 1979, 1987; Johnson, 1987; Lakoff, 1987; Lakoff & Johnson, 1980, 1999; Maturana, 1975, 1980; Maturana & Varela, 1980, 1987; Varela, 1987; Varela et al., 1991) has helped to put self-organization, emergence, complexity, autopoiesis, non-linearity, dynamical systems theory, and a new conception of embodiment, experience, and ethics at the forefront of educational theory, research, and pedagogy.

Enactive online education fundamentally rethinks what it means to learn and think. Davis and Sumara (1997) present an enactivist model of cognition and contrast it with popular notions that pervade formal education. They cite the example of a year-long study in a small, inner-city elementary school to illustrate this model of cognition. They argue that cognition does not occur in individual minds or brains, but in the possibility for shared action. They suggest that an enactivist theory of cognition requires teachers and teacher educators to reconceive the practice of teaching, by blurring the lines between knower and known, teacher and student, school and community. They explain that "learning might be better understood as mutually specifying, co-emergent, pervasive, and evolving practices that are at the core of our culture's efforts at self-organization and self-renewal" (Davis & Sumara, p. 123).

Davis and Sumara understand learners as reciprocally intertwined with and emergent from relationships with others and their world or environment. With reference to a question about fractions posed to a group of 12-year-olds, Davis (1995) shows that mathematical knowledge is "simultaneously about the dynamic co-emergence of knowing agent-and-known world, of self-and-collective" (p. 8). He uses the enactive concept of "structural coupling" and complexity theory to argue that mathematical knowledge is neither subjective nor objective, but rather emerges out of shared action. It is neither a process nor a product; rather, the two are inseparable. Davis explains that "mathematical knowledge is like the subject matter of a conversation. It exists only in conversing, and its nature, its structure, and its results can never be anticipated, let alone fixed" (p. 4). Enactive education requires a theory of parthood relations in order to describe and explain "collectivities that arise in the co-specifying activities of diverse, relatively independent, dynamic, and interacting agents" (Davis & Sumara, 2002, p. 425). Davis

(1995) draws on an enactive account of selfhood as "tied closely to the co-evolving identities of those around us" (p. 7), and an enactive mereology (theory of the relations of part to whole and the relations of part to part within a whole) in which the whole unfolds from the part and is enfolded in it (p. 7).

The central hypothesis of the broad enactive approach to cognition is that natural cognitive systems are subject to the enaction of a world and mind on the basis of a history of embodied action (Thompson, 1996, p. 128). In this model, the online learning environment and online learning take form as a result of emergent, self-organized processes that span and interconnect students, teachers, technologists, software, hardware, and online resources. The act of knowing involves the complex interplay of brain, body, world, and technology. We do not believe that learning is constructed actively and interactively online, a commonly held constructivist view. We believe that learning, mentorship, discussion, and community emerge over time out of reciprocally evolving relationships between our students, technologies, software, hardware, online resources, the technologist, the course instructor, and the teaching assistants.

The authors see online learning environments as constantly evolving dynamic systems. We view the online course site we created as an open, nonlinear, dynamic system, following dynamic systems theory; it is an area of mathematics used to describe the behavior of complex systems. The course site is "open" in the sense that it is not confined to an interaction between student, teacher, and course materials. It dynamically interacts with its environment; for example, it travels with students on their iPods and MP3 players, and extends from the private learning team/tutorial rooms to students' MSN messaging. Our course constantly reaches beyond the confines of its design and reciprocally evolves via interactions characterized by nonequilibrium, since without such interaction the course cannot maintain its structure or function.

Our learning environment exhibits self-organization and emergent processes at multiple levels. Emergence involves both upward and downward causation. Instructors and technologists are changed by learners and learners are changed by instructors and technologists. Instructors, learners, and technologists change and are changed by environments. Learning environments are changed by instructors, technologists, and learners. Instructors, learners, learning environments and technologies become inseparably coupled Technologies, software, and hardware evolve through our interactions with them, and so on. The processes crucial for the success of the course cut across technology-student-instructor-technologist divisions.

A central condition for the possibility of online rich-media learning environments that promote deep learning and educate for social change is a new idea of *action*. If we—as technologists, designers, educators, learners, and administrators—are to begin the long, gradual, uncomfortable, and rewarding practice of befriending current challenges, we need to courageously replace the widespread ideas of *self-action* and *interaction* with the notion of *enaction*.

Self-Action, Interaction, and Enaction

Three main ways of understanding the activity of online rich-media teaching-and-learning and the technologies themselves have been *self-action*, *interaction*, and *enaction*. These three main approaches have not all been present from the inception of distance education and the balance of trends in the literature has changed from an exclusive dominance of the self-action approach to a coexistence of all three in contemporary research and practice.

The first concept, *self-action*, underlies the earliest forms of distance education, such as correspondence courses. These were pioneering online courses that employed written lectures and (more recently) audio lectures. The approach saw distance teaching-and-learning as a matter of self-action and correspondingly created distance learning courses that emphasized student self-direction. The assumption was that students learned better when they took control of their own learning. From this standpoint, good distance teaching involved creating an environment and support infrastructure that encouraged student self-action.

Dewey and Bentley (1973) note that the self-action model views "things... as acting under their own powers" (p. 121). The problem with the self-action approach, we now know, is that deep and engaged learning does not happen under one's own powers. As a matter of fact, the most viable cognitive scientific theories about how the human mind operates show that humans learn through sharing and collaboration (Bransford, Brown, & Cocking, 2000; Fischer & Immordino-Yang, 2008). This research supports the view that online teaching-and-learning cannot originate from self-action, but rather must emerge from a reciprocal, mutually codetermining relationship between a brain, a body, and a world; between educators, learners, technologists, and technology.

The second distance education model of action is *interaction*. This view is the most pervasive and well-documented approach in online teaching-and-learning theory and practice. Dewey and Bentley (1973) describe interaction as a system "where thing is balanced against thing in causal interconnection" (p. 121). The interactive model assumes that e-learning has separate constituent parts that "act" on each other to create or construct teaching-and-learning; constituent parts such as learners, educators, technologists, assistants, course materials, and the technologies themselves. Interactivity is seen as leading to learning; therefore, according to this model, the most viable and effective e-learning environments would be the ones that offer the most interactive learning experiences. The main problem with the interactive model is that teaching-and-learning is not caused or created; rather, it is enacted, and it emerges.

Influences on an Enactive Approach in Education

Dewey and Bentley. *Enaction* sees action as transactive, rather than self-active or interactive.[3] Dewey and Bentley's (1973) concept of transaction has characteristics very similar to the concept of enaction. For these authors, transaction emphasizes the temporal aspect of things in action, where interaction understands things in action as spatial. In transaction, "[a] 'thing' is in action,... [an] 'action' is observable as [a] thing,... [and] all the distinctions between things and actions are taken as marking provisional stages of subject matter to be established through further inquiry" (p. 137). In interaction, on the other hand, things in action are "primarily static" (Dewey & Bentley, p. 137). Thus, in the relationship of organism and environment, interaction presupposes that organism and environment are distinct, "substantially separate existences or forms of existence" (Dewey & Bentley, p. 137).

Concerning the object of knowledge and learning, transaction is a procedure that includes observing the ways that people use language and "other representational activities connected with their thing-perceivings and manipulations" (p. 137). Interaction, on the other hand, assumes that what can be known consists of "little 'reals' interacting with or upon portions of the flesh of an organism to produce all knowings up to and including both the most mechanistic and the most unmechanistic theories of knowledge" (Dewey & Bentley, 1973, p. 137). So, in contrast with self-action and interaction, we could say that transaction sees the activity of online teaching-and-learning as inseparable.

Finally, in terms of inquiry in general, "[t]ransactional observation is the fruit of an insistence upon the right to proceed in freedom to select and view all subject matters in whatever way seems desirable under reasonable hypothesis, and regardless of ancient claims on behalf of either minds or material mechanisms, or any of the surrogates of either" (Dewey & Bentley, 1973, p. 137). By contrast, interactional views are dogmatically asserted, insisting "on establishing its procedure as authoritative to the overthrow of all rivals" (Dewey & Bentley, 1973, p. 137).

Varela. The term *enaction* was first coined by Varela "in the summer of 1986 in Paris when he and Thompson began writing *The Embodied Mind*" (Thompson, 2007, p. 444). Thompson noted that enaction literally means the

... action of enacting a law, but it also connotes the performance of carrying out of an action more generally. Borrowing the words of the poet Antonio Machado, Varela described enaction as the laying down of a path in walking: "Wanderer, the road is your footsteps, nothing else; wanderer, there is no path, you lay down a path in walking." (Varela, 1987, p. 63, quoted in Thompson, 2007, p. 13)

The three interrelated postulates of the broad enactive approach are:

- *Embodiment*. The mind is not located in the head, but is embodied in the whole organism embedded in its environment.
- *Emergence*. Embodied cognition is constituted by emergent and self-organized processes that span and interconnect the brain, the body, and the environment.
- *Self-other co-determination*. In social creatures, embodied cognition emerges from the dynamic co-determination of self and other. (Thompson, 2001, p. 3; see also Thompson, 2007, p. 13)

The enactive approach is a theory of mind, a specific kind of emergence theory, and a method of examining experience (Zorn, 2010). A broad enactive approach (Torrance, 2006) was espoused by Varela, Thompson, and Rosch (1991) and

Thompson (2007). It has its roots in cognitive science; dynamical, non-linear systems; complexity theory; and two phenomenological traditions of direct experience, continental European philosophy and the Buddhist discipline of mindfulness awareness (Thompson, 2007; Torrance, 2006; Varela et al., 1991).

Enactive education has been flourishing in the decade and a half since the publication of *The Embodied Mind* (Varela et al., 1991).

Davis and Sumara. Zorn's (2010) research shows that the enactive approach in education, beginning in the mid 1990s till the present, consists of two successive major phases,[4] which co-exist in the literature today. The first phase, from the mid 1990s till the present, applies the "broad enactive approach," which examines teaching, learning, and education with a focus on what it is to be an agent with an embodied mind and a lived cognition, including a general account of dynamic co-emergence and self-other co-determination. The second phase, from the early 2000s till the present, uses the "narrow complexity view." This phase studies teaching, learning, and education as dynamic, co-emergent phenomena through the lens of complexity theory or science in general, and adaptive, self-organizing systems theory in particular.

The broad enactive perspective in education has the potential to fundamentally rethink the ideas of teaching, learning, curriculum, leadership, epistemologies, and the purposes of schooling (Zorn, 2010). The broad view, most pronounced in the literature from the late 1990s forward, draws on the work of Maturana (Maturana, 1975, 1980, 1987; Maturana & Varela, 1980), Varela (Varela, 1987; Varela et al., 1991), Bateson (1979, 1987), and Lakoff and Johnson (Johnson, 1987; Lakoff, 1987; Lakoff & Johnson, 1980, 1999).

The clearest formulations and strongest argumentation in a broad enactive approach to education are reflected in the work of Davis and Sumara (Davis, 1993, 1995, 2004, 2005, 2008; Davis & Sumara, 1997, 2002, 2007; Sumara &

Davis, 1997). Davis and Sumara, along with other enactive philosophers of education, often distinguish an enactive perspective from a social constructivist framework as a paradigmatic interactive orientation (Davis, 1996; Davis & Sumara, 1997, 2002, 2007; Merriam et al., 2007, pp. 291–294; Sumara & Davis, 1997).

Continental European phenomenology and Buddhist psychology. [2] We were also influenced in our enactive approach to online teaching-and-learning in our course by the theory and practice of two kinds of phenomenology: Continental European phenomenology and Buddhist psychology (Varela et al., 1991, pp. 217–260). Phenomenology is both a "style of thinking" and a "special type of reflection or attitude about our capacity for being conscious" (Varela, 1996, p. 335) that involves a disciplined examination of human experience and its direct, lived quality. All phenomenological approaches share a belief in the irreducible, fundamental nature and status of direct experience (Varela, 1996, p. 334). The enactive approach, like phenomenology, believes that the body is something that we live directly and that "all knowledge necessarily emerges from our lived experience" (Varela, 1996, p. 336).

Buddhist psychology uses a method of examining experience it calls mindful awareness (Varela et al., 1991, pp. 21–26, 217–260). In our course we embraced mindfulness awareness as a way of examining the online learning experience with the purpose of "becoming mindful, to experience what one's mind is doing as it does it, to be present with one's mind" (Varela et al., 1991, p. 23). This approach requires a constant and vigilant responding, listening and adapting to the online environment. The condition for the possibility of this sort of dynamic change is a letting-go of the need to have complete control over learning environments.

MOVING TOWARDS ENACTIVE TECHNOLOGIES IN EDUCATION

Current technology trends in education can be seen to be grounded in an enactive approach that draws on the three interrelated enactive postulates of embodiment, emergence, and self-other codetermination. With all of the challenges that the world faces from energy, pollution, social justice and sustaining life on the planet, we need to innovate to survive. Innovation simply defined is finding a way of doing something better. Human-technology relations are evolving away from self-action or interaction and towards enaction. Technologies can be seen to be no longer created or constructed, but rather dynamically coemerging with humans. For example, each of the six technologies indicated in *The 2009 Horizon Report* (Johnson, Levine, & Smith, 2009) that will significantly impact the choices of learning-focused organizations within the next five years are enactive technologies: mobiles, cloud computing, geo-everything, the personal web, semantic-aware applications, and smart objects. Tools such as Twitter, Camtasia, Adobe Captivate, and iPhone, among others, and social networking sites, such as Facebook, MySpace, LinkedIn, and others, are best understood as transactive (Dewey & Bentley, 1973, pp. 120–124) or enactive rather than self-active or interactive. These technologies suggest that e-learning is entering an era of enaction. Self-action and interaction are no longer viable ways of understanding or living with these technologies because they are "emergent processes" (Thompson, 2007, pp. 37–65).

The enactive approach to online teaching-and-learning, like the enactive approach as a cognitive-scientific theory, originates from cognitive science, phenomenology, and dynamic systems theory. In this view, the act of knowing emerges from a reciprocal, causal interaction of brain, body, and environment. Mental or cognitive processes are seen as the result of embodied sensorimotor activity embedded in an environment (Thomp-

son, 1999, p. 7). From this perspective students, instructors, technologists, technologies, software, and hardware are inseparable intertwinings that enact each other; they are not independent realms.

Online teaching-and-learning coemerges transactively across complex dynamic systems. User, technologist, and the technologies themselves are codetermined or structurally coupled (Stiegler, 1994, pp. 157–158): "Structural coupling refers to the history of recurrent interactions between two or more systems that leads to a structural congruence between them" (Thompson, 2007, p. 45; see also Maturana, 1975; Maturana & Varela, 1987, p. 75). These relationships are very much like how the human body functions and evolves to adapt to a new environment (as discussed in Thompson, 2007, pp. 37–65). We and the technologies can be seen to coevolve together, a process profoundly different from how we traditionally understand interacting with technology.

Technology is essentially an extension of the human body.

Here are some examples of enactive technologies.

Mobile computing. Hand-held devices such as phones will dominate the personal computing landscape, with enough computing power to complete most average computing tasks. The designs that are being used are adaptive to the user and are becoming ultimately configurable.

Cloud computing. Virtualized computing resources that adapt to the computing required, cloud computing is also self organizing and takes the computing load off the individual.

Geo-everything. Everything can be spatially identified by location on earth and, in turn, relational to everything else on earth. As you move though space you change the dynamic of that relationship.

The personal web. Customized, personal web-based environments that reflect the individual can be created.

Semantic-aware applications. Applications that can relate and adapt to make the ever-growing data on the web useful and contextual. The value increases with every action.

Smart objects. Smart objects have self awareness and know where and what they are. These devices are adaptive objects that can self-regulate. They bridge the gap between the real world and the digital world. In the future, many household appliances will be "smart," and adapt to our lives.

A reciprocally adaptive learning environment. The technologies and methodologies for the course were applied by developing an experiential design concept. Experiential design simply takes into consideration the factors that influence how the course is experienced on multiple levels. Some of the variables we took into consideration were language, culture, global location, and learning styles.

The original goal was to allow for access and participation—an interactive model. During the design stage we selected technologies and methodologies that were emergent in nature developing the model further, into an enactive model. We worked in partnership with software companies to make changes in the programs to allow for more feedback, so that the software itself could be reciprocally adaptive to the user. This logic spread through the rest of the course design and created fluidity in the design that not only made it adaptive to the user but also adaptive to the Internet environment. Rapid developments and changes in the technologies used with the Internet also forced this flexible design.

Designing a reciprocally adaptive environment was the key element to enable an enactive approach to online teaching-and-learning. During the development of this project at least one of the software companies involved applied a reciprocally adaptive model to developing new products—thereby transforming the company in the process. This enactive approach is now a key strategy that they use to compete in the marketplace.

Human/technology relations. Enactive technologies can be seen as a new type of experience of technology. Ihde (1974, 1979, 1983, 1993, 1990)

argues that there are three fundamental ways of experiencing technology that map onto an existential arc of body, interpretation, and otherness: experience *through*, *with*, and *among* technology. When experiencing the world *through* technology, technologies partially extend my bodily or perceptual experience; for example, when a hammer extends my arm by allowing my fleshy hand to drive a nail into a board. When experiencing *with* technology, humans interpret something about the world with technology (telescopes, microscopes, thermometers), and the technology may be experienced as other than oneself, (e.g., a dialogue box appears on our computer screen asking us to save something). When experiencing *among* technology, we are describing the background texturing of our daily lives (e.g., our air conditioning system).

These ways of experiencing technology correspond with three sets of human-technology relations along a continuum (Ihde, 1974, 1979, 1983, 1993, 1990): embodiment, hermeneutic, and alterity. Embodiment relations in which technologies is experienced as a *quasi-me* are at one end of the continuum. Alterity or *otherness* relations, in which technologies are experienced as a *quasi-other*, are at the other end of the continuum. Between the two sets of relations are hermeneutic relations "that both mediate and yet also fulfill my perceptual and bodily relation with technologies" through a reading process of my own (Ihde, 1990, p. 107). Through phenomenological analysis, Ihde showed that perception is embodied through technologies. The wearer of eyeglasses embodies eyeglass technology, or in Galileo's use of the telescope, he embodies his seeing through telescope technology, that is, "the technology is actually *between* the seer and the seen, in a *position of mediation*. But the referent of the seeing, that towards which sight is directed, is 'on the other side' of the optics" (Ihde, 1990, p. 73).

Enactive technologies join both ends of Ihde's continuum to form a circle in which embodiment and otherness intertwine, since enactive technologies emerge from the coupling of unitary structures of lived-body environments (Merleau-Ponty, 1962, 1963, 1973; Thompson, 2007; Varela et al., 1991).[5] Human-technology relations are entering an enactive evolutionary phase that can be seen to be "taking the *technē* out of technology" (Zorn, 1994, pp. 100–103).[6]

To understand and manipulate the technology/human interface, technology is developing a transparency layer in its complexity, reflecting the rise of the "prosumer." In his book *The Third Wave*, Alvin Toffler (1984) describes the prosumer as both producer and consumer. Technology companies have targeted this prosumer segment of the marketplace and have redesigned the technologies to satisfy that market segment allowing for the technology to change or be customized by the user. As an example, the consumer camcorder has developed to a level that rivals a professional broadcast camera in only a few short years. By giving prosumers access to high-quality technology, many spin-off applications have been developed. The slogan "broadcast yourself" should sound familiar, with over 100 million videos per month being watched at YouTube alone.

The enactive approach to the design and innovation of technology is indicative of the access and customization to the technology that has created a surge in a culture of participation. Henry Jenkins (n.d.) defined "participatory culture" as a culture:

1. with relatively low barriers to artistic expression and civic engagement;
2. with strong support for creating and sharing one's creations with others;
3. with some type of informal mentorship whereby what is known by the most experienced is passed along to novices;
4. where members believe that their contributions matter; and
5. where members feel some degree of social connection with one another (at the least they care what other people think about what they have created).

Not every member must contribute, but all must believe they are free to contribute when ready and that what they contribute will be appropriately valued.

CONCLUSION

This chapter makes four main points. First, habits of thinking and feeling inherited from the culture of higher education are getting in the way of creating viable, high-quality online learning environments. Second, video streaming, podcasting, and advanced Internet technologies have made obvious something that has been true all along: teaching-and-learning is not created or constructed but rather *enacted*. The focus in online teaching-and-learning therefore needs to be on enaction, rather than interaction. Third, an enactive approach can promote deep learning while educating for social change. Finally, current technology trends in education can be seen to be grounded in an enactive approach point, a new kind of human/technology relation.

REFERENCES

Bateson, G. (1979). *Mind and nature: A necessary unity*. New York, NY: Ballantine Books.

Bateson, G. (1987). Men are grass. In Thompson, W. I. (Ed.), *Gaia, a way of knowing* (pp. 37–47). Hudson, NY: Lindisfarne.

Blackboard. (n.d.). *Blackboard Inc* [Mobile technology software]. Retrieved from http://www.blackboard.com

Boler, M. (1999). *Feeling power: Emotions and education*. New York, NY: Routledge.

Boler, M. (2004). Teaching for hope: The ethics of shattering world views. In Liston, D., & Garrison, J. (Eds.), *Teaching, learning and loving: Reclaiming passion in educational practice* (pp. 117–131). New York, NY: RoutledgeFalmer. doi:10.4324/9780203465622_chapter_7

Bonk, C., & Zhang, K. (2008). *Empowering online learning: 100+ activities for reading, reflecting, displaying and doing.* San Francisco, CA: Jossey-Bass.

Bransford, J. D., Brown, A. L., & Cocking, R. R. (Eds.). (2000). *How people learn: Brain, mind, experience and school.* Washington, DC: National Academy Press.

Cassidy, S. (2004). Learning styles: An overview of theories, models, and measures. *Educational Psychology, 24*(4), 419–444. doi:10.1080/0144341042000228834

Chiel, H. J., & Beer, R. D. (1997). The brain has a body: Adaptive behavior emerges from interactions of nervous system, body and environment. *Trends in Neurosciences, 20*, 553–557. doi:10.1016/S0166-2236(97)01149-1

Chizmar, J. F., & Williams, D. B. (2001). What do faculty want? *EDUCAUSE Quarterly, 24*(1), 18–24.

Chödrön, P. (1997). *When things fall apart: Heart advice for difficult times.* Boston, MA: Shambhala.

Chödrön, P. (2001). *The places that scare you: A guide to fearlessness in difficult times.* Boston, MA: Shambhala.

Clotho Advanced Media Inc. (n.d.). *MediaLandscape* [Computer software]. Retrieved from http://www.media-landscape.com

Collins, A. (1991). Cognitive apprenticeship and instructional technology. In Idol, L., & Fly Jones, B. (Eds.), *Educational values and cognitive instruction: Implications for reform* (pp. 121–138). Hillsdale, NJ: Erlbaum.

Collins, A., Brown, J. S., & Newman, S. E. (1989). Cognitive apprenticeship: Teaching the crafts of reading, writing and mathematics. In Resnick, L. B. (Ed.), *Knowing, learning, and instruction: Essays in honor of Robert Glaser* (pp. 453–494). Hillsdale, NJ: Erlbaum.

Cranton, P. (2005). Learning styles. In English, L. M. (Ed.), *International encyclopedia of adult education* (pp. 111–117). New York, NY: Palgrave Macmillan.

Damrosch, D. (1995). *We scholars: Changing the culture of the university.* Cambridge, MA: Harvard University Press.

Davis, B. (1993). *Towards an ecological view of mathematics education.* Paper presented at a meeting of the Canadian Society for the Study of Education, Ottawa, Canada.

Davis, B. (1995). Why teach mathematics? Mathematics education and enactivist theory. *For the Learning of Mathematics, 15*(2), 2–9.

Davis, B. (1996). *Teaching mathematics: Towards a sound alternative.* New York, NY: Garland.

Davis, B. (2004). *Inventions of teaching: A genealogy.* Mahwah, NJ: Lawrence Erlbaum.

Davis, B. (2005). Teacher as consciousness of the collective. *Complicity, 2*(1), 85–88.

Davis, B. (2008). Complexity and education: Vital simultaneities. *Educational Philosophy and Theory, 40*(1), 50–65. doi:10.1111/j.1469-5812.2007.00402.x

Davis, B., & Sumara, D. (1997). Cognition, complexity, and teacher education. *Harvard Educational Review, 67*(1), 105–125.

Davis, B., & Sumara, D. (2002). Constructivist discourses and the field of education: Problems and possibilities. *Educational Theory, 52*(4), 409–428. doi:10.1111/j.1741-5446.2002.00409.x

Davis, B., & Sumara, D. (2007). Complexity science and education: Reconceptualizing the teacher's role in learning. *Interchange, 38*(1), 53–67. doi:10.1007/s10780-007-9012-5

Desmedt, E., & Valcke, M. (2004). Mapping the learning styles "jungle": An overview of the literature based on citation analysis. *Educational Psychology, 24*(4), 446–464. doi:10.1080/0144341042000228843

Dewey, J., & Bentley, A. (1973). Knowing and the known. In Handy, R., & Harwood, E. C. (Eds.), *Useful procedures of inquiry* (pp. 89–190). Barrington, MA: Behavioral Research Council.

Entwistle, N. (2001). Promoting deep learning through teaching and assessment . In Suskie, L. (Ed.), *Assessment to promote deep learning* (pp. 9–20). Washington, DC: American Association for Higher Education.

Epstein, M. (1995). *Thoughts without a thinker: Psychotherapy from a Buddhist perspective*. New York, NY: Basic Books.

Epstein, M. (1998). *Going to pieces without falling apart: A Buddhist perspective on wholeness—lessons from meditation and psychotherapy*. New York, NY: Broadway Books.

Facebook. (n.d.). *Social networking website technology*. Retrieved from www.facebook.com

Fischer, K., & Immordino-Yang, M. H. (2008). Introduction. In Fischer, K., & Immordino-Yang, M. H. (Eds.), *The Jossey-Bass reader on the brain and learning* (pp. xvii–xxii). San Francisco, CA: Jossey-Bass.

Fleming, N. D., & Mills, C. (1992). *VARK: A guide to learning styles*. Retrieved from http://www.vark-learn.com/english/index.asp

Freire, P. (2003). *Pedagogy of the oppressed*. New York, NY: Continuum.

Gadamer, H.-G. (1979). The problem of historical consciousness. In Rabinow, P., & Sullivan, W. M. (Eds.), *Interpretive social science: A second look* (pp. 82–140). Berkeley, CA: University of California Press.

Hall, E., & Moseley, D. (2005). Is there a role for learning styles in personalized education and training? *International Journal of Lifelong Education, 24*(3), 243–255. doi:10.1080/02601370500134933

Hanh, T. (2005). *Being peace*. Berkeley, CA: Parallax Press.

Haraway, D. (1991). *Simians, cyborgs, and women: The reinvention of nature*. New York, NY: Routledge.

Ihde, D. (1974). The experience of technology: Human-machine relations. *Cultural Hermeneutics, 2*, 267–279.

Ihde, D. (1979). *Technics and praxis: A philosophy of technology*. Dordrecht, The Netherlands: Reidel.

Ihde, D. (1983). *Existential technics*. Albany, NY: State University of New York Press.

Ihde, D. (1990). *Technology and the lifeworld: From garden to earth*. Bloomington, IN: Indiana University Press.

Ihde, D. (1993). *Philosophy of technology: An introduction*. New York, NY: Paragon House.

Introduction to open education 2009. (n.d.). In *Wikipedia*. Retrieved March 16, 2009, from http://opencontent.org/wiki/index.php?title=Introduction_to_Open_Education_2009

Jenkins, H., Clinton, K., Purushotma, R., Robison, A., & Weigel, M. (n.d.). *Confronting the challenges of participatory culture: Media education for the 21st century*. Retrieved from http://digitallearning.macfound.org/atf/cf/%7B7E45C7E0-A3E0-4B89-AC9C-E807E1B0AE4E%7D/JENKINS_WHITE_PAPER.PDF

Johnson, L., Levine, A., & Smith, R. (2009). *The 2009 horizon report*. Austin, TX: The New Media Consortium. Retrieved from http://www.nmc.org/pdf/2009-Horizon-Report.pdf

Johnson, M. (1987). *The body in the mind: The bodily basis of imagination, reason, and meaning*. Chicago, IL: University of Chicago Press.

Kolb, D. A. (1984). *Experiential learning: Experience as the source of learning and development*. Englewood Cliffs, NJ: Prentice-Hall.

Lakoff, G. (1987). *Women, fire and dangerous things: What categories reveal about the mind*. Chicago, IL: University of Chicago Press.

Lakoff, G., & Johnson, M. (1980). *Metaphors we live by*. Chicago, IL: Chicago University Press.

Lakoff, G., & Johnson, M. (1999). *Philosophy in the flesh: The embodied mind and its challenge to Western thought*. New York, NY: Basic Books.

Linden Research Inc. (n.d.). *Second Life* [Virtual world technology]. Retrieved from http://secondlife.com/

Maturana, H. (1975). The organization of the living: A theory of the living organization. *International Journal of Man-Machine Studies*, 7, 313–332. doi:10.1016/S0020-7373(75)80015-0

Maturana, H., & Varela, F. J. (1980). *Autopoiesis and cognition: The realization of the living*. Dordrecht, The Netherlands: Reidel.

Maturana, H., & Varela, F. J. (1987). *The tree of knowledge: The biological roots of human understanding*. Boston, MA: Shambhala Press/New Science Library.

McCarthy, B. (1987). *The 4MAT system: Teaching to learning styles with right/left mode techniques* (rev. ed.). Barrington, IL: Excel.

Merleau-Ponty, M. (1962). *Phenomenology of perception* (Smith, C., Trans.). London, UK: Routledge & Kegan Paul. (Original work published 1945)

Merleau-Ponty, M. (1963). *The structure of behavior* (Fisher, A., Trans.). Pittsburgh, PA: Beacon Press. (Original work published 1942)

Merleau-Ponty, M. (1973). *The visible and the invisible* (Lingis, A., Trans.). Evanston, IL: Northwestern University Press. (Original work published 1948)

Merriam, S. B., Caffarella, R. S., & Baumgartner, L. M. (2007). *Learning in adulthood: A comprehensive guide* (3rd ed.). San Francisco, CA: Jossey-Bass.

Rushowy, K. (2009, April 6). Profs blast lazy first-year students: Wikipedia generation is lazy and unprepared for university's rigours, survey of faculty says. *thestar.com*. Retrieved from http://www.thestar.com/News/Ontario/article/614219

Shieh, D. (2009, March 6). These lectures are gone in 60 seconds. *The Chronicle of Higher Education*. Retrieved from http://chronicle.com/article/These-Lectures-Are-Gone-in-60/19924

SonicFoundry. (n.d.) *Mediasite* [Webcasting and knowledge management software]. Retrieved from http://www.sonicfoundry.com/mediasite/

Stein, J. (2008, April 9). *Defining "creepy treehouse."* Retrieved from http://flexknowlogy.learningfield.org/2008/04/09/defining-creepy-tree-house/

Stiegler, B. (1994). Technics and time: *Vol. 1. The fault of Epimetheus* (Beardsworth, R., & Collins, G., Trans.). Stanford, CA: Stanford University Press.

Sumara, D., & Davis, B. (1997). Enactivist theory and community learning: Toward a complexified understanding of action research. *Educational Action Research*, 5(3), 403–442. doi:10.1080/09650799700200037

Tapscott, D. (1996). *Growing up digital: The rise of the net generation*. New York, NY: McGraw Hill.

Tapscott, D. (2009). *Grown up digital*. New York, NY: McGraw Hill.

Thompson, E. (1996). The mindful body: Embodiment and cognitive science. In O'Donovan-Anderson, M. (Ed.), *The incorporated self: Interdisciplinary perspectives on embodiment* (pp. 127–144). Lanham, MD: Rowman & Littlefield.

Thompson, E. (1999). *Human consciousness: From intersubjectivity to interbeing*. Retrieved from http://www.philosophy.ucf.edu/pcs/pcs-fetz1.html

Thompson, E. (2001). Empathy and consciousness. *Journal of Consciousness Studies*, 8(5/7), 1–32.

Thompson, E. (2007). *Mind in life: Biology, phenomenology, and the sciences of mind*. Cambridge, MA: Harvard University Press.

Toffler, A. (1980). *The third wave*. London, UK: Collins.

Torrance, S. (2006). In search of the enactive: Introduction to special issue on enactive experience. *Phenomenology and the Cognitive Sciences*, 4, 357–368. doi:10.1007/s11097-005-9004-9

Toye, M. (1989). Learning styles. In Titmus, C. J. (Ed.), *Lifelong education for adults: An international handbook* (pp. 236–232). Oxford, UK: Pergamon Press.

Twigg, C. (2001). *Innovations in online learning: Moving beyond no significant difference* [NCAT monograph]. Retrieved from http://www.thencat.org/Monographs/Innovations.html

University of Adelaide. (2008). *Research skill development and assessment in the curriculum* [Handbook for Research Skill Development Seminar]. Retrieved from http://www.adelaide.edu.au/clpd/rsd/otherfiles/RSD_hbk.pdf

Varela, F. J. (1987). Laying down a path in walking. In Thompson, W. I. (Ed.), *Gaia: A way of knowing—political implications of the new biology* (pp. 48–64). Hudson, NY: Lindisfarne Press.

Varela, F. J. (1996). Neurophenomenology: A methodological remedy for the hard problem. *Journal of Consciousness Studies*, 3(4), 330–349.

Varela, F. J., Thompson, E., & Rosch, E. (1991). *The embodied mind: Cognitive science and human experience*. Cambridge, MA: MIT Press.

Watts, A. (2000). *What is zen?* Novato, CA: New World Library.

Weigel, V. B. (2002). *Deep learning for a digital age: Technology's untapped potential to enrich higher education*. San Francisco, CA: Jossey-Bass.

YFile. (2008, May 6). York recognized as a leader in distance education. *YFile*. Retrieved from http://www.yorku.ca/yfile/archive/index.asp?Article=10445

Young, J. R. (2008, June 20). Short and sweet: Technology shrinks the lecture hall. *The Chronicle of Higher Education*. Retrieved from http://chronicle.com/article/ShortSweet-Technology/13866/

Young, J. R. (2009, October 29). Professor turns his online course into a role-playing game. *The Chronicle of Higher Education*. Retrieved from http://chronicle.com/blogPost/Professor-Turns-His-Online/4407

Zorn, D. (1994). *A hermeneutics of technology: Don Ihde's postmodern philosophy of technology* (Unpublished master's thesis). McMaster University, Hamilton, Canada.

Zorn, D. (2010). *Enactive approach to education* (Unpublished doctoral dissertation). Ontario Institute for Studies in Education/University of Toronto, Toronto, Canada.

ENDNOTES

[1] A creepy treehouse is: "... a place, physical or virtual (e.g., online), built by adults with the intention of luring in kids... [or] any institutionally created, operated, or controlled environment in which participants are lured in either by mimicking preexisting open or naturally formed environments, or by force, through a system of punishments or rewards" (flexknowlogy, 2008).

[2] Epstein (1995) has observed that mindfulness is a "distinctive attentional strategy" of Buddhism "in which moment-to-moment awareness of changing objects of perception is cultivated" (pp. 95–96). He distinguishes mindfulness from concentration (p. 132) and one-pointedness (p. 95). Concentration involves the "ability to rest the mind in a single object of awareness," whereas mindfulness involves the "ability to shift attention to a succession of objects of awareness" (p. 132). Mindfulness in Buddhist psychology is "the ability to know one's feelings without having to act on them, or be acted on by them, in an unconscious way" (p. xxi). Gendlin's (1978) concept of *focusing* was a Westernized version of Buddhist mindfulness awareness, in which one makes contact with a special kind of internal bodily awareness called a "felt sense" (Gendlin, p. 10), the "body's physical sense of a problem, or of some concern or situation. It is a physical sense of meaning" (Gendlin, p. 69). Focusing, when done properly, leads to "a distinct physical sensation of change" called a "body shift" (Gendlin, p. 7). Gendlin insisted that focusing is not an emotion (p. 10), not a mere body sensation (p. 69), and not just getting in touch with "gut feelings" (p. 69); it is the:... broader, at first *unclear*, *unrecognizable* discomfort, which *the whole* problem... makes in your body. To let it form, you have to stand back a little from the familiar emotion. The felt sense is wider, less intense [say, than emotions], easier to have, and much more broadly inclusive. It is how your body carries *the whole* problem. (p. 69)

[3] "Trans," derived from the Latin, means "across," "beyond," or "over." In such words as "transportation" and "transnational," "trans" suggests a covering or stretching over of an entire area.

[4] Zorn's characterization of the two major strands within the enactive approach in education was inspired by Steve Torrance's (2006) discussion of the two major strands within the enactive perspective.

[5] Essential to the enactive approach is the view of the lived-body environment as a unitary structure. The lived-body environment includes the world beyond the skin and the biological membrane of the organism (Thompson, 2001, p. 2). The lived body is intertwined with the environment and others in an interpersonal, human world, a unitary structure that emerges through the reciprocal interaction of brain, body and environment. Enactive cognitive science described this process as "structural coupling" (Varela et al., 1991). "The brain is structurally coupled to the body, and the body is structurally coupled to the environment" (Varela et al., p. 13). Merleau-Ponty (1968) used the term "intertwining the chiasm" to describe this kind of structural coupling. Recent neurobiological research has a complementary notion. Chiel and Beer (1997), for example, view adaptive behavior as the result of the continuous interaction between the nervous system, the body, and environment. The mind is seen as a

profoundly interwoven system incorporating complicated and highly dynamic aspects of brain, body, and world.

6 Gadamer (1979) explains the distinction between *technē*, technical know-how, and *phronēsis*, ethical know-how (p. 118). The former refers to the teachable, skill of the artisan and requires the making and executing of a plan. The latter term refers to concerns the unpredictable nature of actions.

Chapter 6
The Effectiveness of Streaming Media Clips in Skills Teaching:
A Comparative Study

Andrew Saxon
Birmingham City University, UK

Sheila Griffiths
Birmingham City University, UK

ABSTRACT

In this chapter, we present a small-scale comparative study into the use of streaming media Reusable Learning Objects (RLOs) in skills teaching. We consider the use of streaming digital video clips in the teaching of complex technical skills to Fashion Design students in large class sizes, drawing a comparison with the face-to-face demonstration model in widespread use in our curriculum.

INTRODUCTION

With the increase in UK undergraduate student numbers over the last five years, the three-year BA (Hons) Fashion Design course at Birmingham City University Institute of Art and Design, UK, has increased in size quite considerably, from 67 first-year students in the 2003-4 academic year to 135 in 2008-9. With much larger year groups, difficulties have emerged in the delivery of certain key technical aspects of the course, particularly in the area of pattern cutting.

DOI: 10.4018/978-1-60960-800-2.ch006

PATTERN CUTTING: THE MOVE FROM 2D TO 3D

Pattern cutting is the stage in fashion design where preparation of the finished garment begins. During this stage, the pattern cutter interprets the designer's sketch in order to draw and cut out paper patterns. These are in turn used to mark and then cut fabric pieces for subsequent sewing into garments. Once this skill is learned, students can transform their design ideas from sketches into fully fitted garments – it is the stage where the move from 2D to 3D takes place.

Students are taught the basics of pattern cutting during the first year of the course, enabling this process to begin. They learn 120 different pattern cutting adaptations, starting with simple bust dart manipulation working through to the more complex collar and rever drafting. When the individual adaptations are combined in different sequences the particular details determine the final form and look of a garment. Due to their number, their complexity, and the fact that they are used only at this particular stage in the process, many of the more esoteric adaptations tend to be easily forgotten, and students often seek out tutors for additional guidance in this area throughout the three years of the course.

Typically, pattern cutting is taught in a workshop setting, with a tutor demonstrating individual adaptations to the whole class. After a demonstration, each student is required to repeat the process at the cutting table facilitated by the tutor, thereby reinforcing the techniques taught to memory.

CLASS SIZE CONSIDERATIONS

We divide the year group into smaller teaching groups of between 25 and 30 students to create a more personalised learning experience. However difficulties are evident in the demonstration-based teaching of pattern cutting even to these smaller groups, as students can find themselves unable to adequately view the skill demonstrations, hindering their ability to perform the skills after the demonstration has ended.

Methods that would allow all students to view the skill demonstrations clearly were sought, and so the development of short video clips presenting the individual pattern cutting adaptations was begun. We filmed each adaptation from the pattern cutter's point of view, showing the demonstrator using pens, scissors and glue to mark, cut and stick the pattern. We shot close-up views of more intricate processes for clarity. After editing, all clips were dubbed with a voice-over narration explaining each step of the process. A simple controller offering play, pause, fast-forward and rewind was added prior to use. All 120 video clips were then presented to students online in a structured series of modules using Moodle – the Birmingham City University Virtual Learning Environment (VLE).

The video clips were originally intended to augment the face-to-face teaching sessions as an *aide memoire* used either during the module or afterwards. However, a stream of positive feedback from students who had used the clips provoked a further question: *Could we use the clips to replace the demonstrations?* And so our research question became: *Is student performance using video clips as good as or better than face-to-face classroom teaching?*

SKILLS TEACHING

There is little written regarding teaching practical skills to large class sizes in higher education, much of the literature on the teaching of large numbers of students seeks to address the problems associated with teaching theoretical topics within a lecture or seminar setting. Although splitting the larger lecture or seminar class into groups, for small group discussions or solving problems, as seen in Frederick (1987) is commonly advocated, this strategy would not support teaching of the practical or technical areas covered within the Fashion Design course. The main problem in the teaching of this material is the effect of group size on the students' ability to understand the subject matter being demonstrated.

Newberry (2003) recommends that Fashion Design courses should limit their annual intake to "25 students or less, if teaching is to be effective." This makes sense when taking into account the need to teach the practical and technical elements of such courses, as demonstrating skills to more than this number of students at a time becomes difficult. However, the advice sits in tension with the current drive to increase the participation rate of 18–21 year olds entering higher education, and may be somewhat unrealistic in the current climate. However, the use of smaller teaching groups in the Fashion Design programme has become the norm over the last four years as student numbers have grown.

BEFORE INDEPENDENCE COMES DEPENDENCE

During workshop sessions, the whole group of 30 students will distribute themselves around the cutting table to observe the demonstrations and make notes. At times, they may be standing three-deep, viewing the demonstration side-on or even upside-down; depending at which side of the table they stand in relation to the tutor. In this way, students can find themselves in a situation where they are unable to properly see and thus relate to the demonstration, resulting in an incomplete understanding of the skills being taught. This can result in high levels of dependence on the tutor by students and may lead to students losing confidence to perform some of the most basic tasks independently. This is a cycle that needs to be broken, but it is by no means a new problem, as highlighted by Gibbs (1992) who cautions against:

...spoon feeding in lectures, seminars and practical work, so that students become over-dependent on the information selected and provided by their teachers

Harvey & Knight (1996) remind us however, that before independence comes dependence, and in order for students to become independent they must first "know something about the issue in question – or know how to get the knowledge." That said, once these basic elements have been taught, students can and should be given the opportunity to develop and explore independently using trial and error which, according to Jarvis, Holford &

Griffin (2003) would allow them to take ownership of their learning whilst positively reinforcing correct behaviours. Naturally, students will make mistakes during the process of learning, some of which may be quite costly to themselves in terms of time and materials, but this is a process that needs to be endured. Pickford & Brown (2006) advise that "...students may need to be supported through making a lot of mistakes before they can become experts." It follows therefore that the practical and technical elements of the course need to be taught thoroughly and early enough within the course for students to be able to gain and practice the skills necessary to enable them to successfully compete within the fashion industry. 'Making' goes hand in hand with designing in Birmingham Institute of Art and Design courses, as we believe that the ability to implement their designs provides students with a competitive advantage borne of a deep understanding of making processes. Pickford and Brown (*ibid.*) explain that:

Students nowadays are expected to demonstrate skills and abilities that show they have mastered not only subject content but also the ability to put their learning into practice in real life contexts. Major initiatives in a number of countries, including the UK, focus on fostering students' employability, and research indicates that employers prefer to employ graduates who can demonstrate professionally related competencies as well as general key skills. In a range of professional and practical disciplines the 'ability to do' is equally as important as the 'ability to know'.

TEACHING CONSIDERATIONS

A key problem when teaching skills to large groups that have been subdivided is the time needed for preparation. Machemer & Crawford (2007) note that: "designing and testing active learning events can be time-intensive on already overloaded faculty schedules." Furthermore, when running multiple concurrent teaching sessions, careful scheduling of both academic staff and technician support is vital. Alongside the difficulties of preparation, are concerns regarding the time needed for delivery of learning sessions. Machemer & Crawford, (*ibid.*) caution against "…activities taking up too much time…and not being able to cover all the material" in the time available. This is a particular concern when teaching first year students, who need to learn the pattern cutting variations very early in the course, giving them time to gain experience in using the processes in order to gain mastery.

During the first year of the course students encounter a range of different modes of delivery in their learning, including: studio based instruction in design, drawing and illustration techniques, practical and technical workshop demonstrations, participation in design research and realisation exercises, CAD sessions, presentations and seminars. These learning sessions are normally tutor-led and face-to-face, in a studio or workshop setting. Learning resources, usually text or image based; are made available on the University VLE for students to access when needed.

The use of VLE's and associated e-Learning tools has become an important part of the student experience, and is a rapidly developing area in many institutions where we commonly see flexible and distance learning options with some courses now conducted entirely online. Our students are accustomed to using technology in their everyday lives; Prensky (2001) states:

…today's students think and process information fundamentally differently from their predecessors… They have spent their entire lives surrounded by and using computers, videogames, digital music players, video cams, cell phones, and all the other toys and tools of the digital age …they have little patience for lectures, step-by-step logic, and 'tell test' instruction.

Students are well versed in the use of online social networking tools, and communication for them is fairly instant. Accordingly, it is no surprise that they expect to use enabling technologies in all areas of their lives, including their learning, which Prensky (*ibid.*) points out ought to change in several ways:

This doesn't mean changing the meaning of what is important, or of good thinking skills. But it does mean going faster, less step-by step, more in parallel, with more random access, among other things.

Following Prensky's advice then, if pattern cutting were to be taught at a faster pace, relying less on step-by-step instruction and more in parallel, offering random access to the material, which would therefore need to be presented in bite-sized 'chunks', we might see improvements in student learning. Our chunks would be described by L'Allier (1997) as learning objects (LOs), which he defines as "the smallest independent structural experience that contains an objective, a learning activity and an assessment." With this in mind, the use of reusable learning objects (RLOs), which are defined by RLO-CETL (2009) as "web-based interactive chunks of e-learning designed to explain a stand-alone learning objective" for teaching pattern cutting and manufacture seems timely in our course context.

Learning, including learning of a practical and technical nature according to Duncan (2004) is:

…not achieved through 'delivering' content but through a series of learning activities…Learning design involves creating sequences of learning activities and these learning designs are themselves reusable learning objects.

The practical and technical elements of pattern cutting and manufacture are traditionally taught in bite-sized chunks. These discrete chunks of learning are made up from content and experience that has been assembled over several years. They can be delivered independently, but when sequenced together in different combinations can guide the student toward the creation of particular completed garments with each chunk still retaining its relevance at every stage. These chunks when developed into readily accessed, informative and easily navigated RLOs, form the first steps in the process that according to Ruiz, Mintzer & Issenberg, (2006):

... facilitate adaptive learning by offering the chunks of content that the learner needs in order to achieve an accepted level of competence.

However, whilst any learning object can be seen as potentially reusable, in order for it to be truly reusable it needs to be designed without context, for example, if the learning object contains references to prior learning with statements such as: "following on from last week" or "in the last session" it ceases to be reusable as a stand-alone learning objective.

The stand-alone element is important in the design of RLOs, as each should communicate a single learning objective which when used independently fulfils the given task without forming a step in a multi part process. That said, in the case of the pattern cutting RLOs the individual processes can be sequenced to create a finished garment in the same way that RLOs describing CAD processes can be used independently or sequenced to achieve different outcomes.

Optimally, when used in this way, RLOs can provide a highly student-centred learning experience, which according to Ruiz, Mintzer & Issenberg (*ibid.*) "…offers learners the ability to tailor their experience to their preferred learning needs."

Much literature concerning LOs, and RLOs in particular refers to generic learning, where the ability to use such objects across different subject areas with differing outcomes is seen as highly valuable. However, the nature of Pattern Cutting is such that RLO development within this

area would always be specific to Fashion Design, rather than being generic with other subject areas. Notwithstanding this, the pattern cutting RLOs can be used at all levels of the BA course, and by MA students.

THE COMPARATIVE STUDY

We set out to compare the effectiveness of two learning and teaching methods: traditional face-to-face demonstration and e-learning using streaming media. We used a mixed methods comparative study design to give us a rounded view of the participants' learning experiences. Both quantitative and qualitative data collection methods were used including an IT self efficacy questionnaire, pre- and post-study questionnaires designed to highlight 'distance travelled' by each student, a review of marks awarded for six assessable tasks and two post-study focus groups. The comparative study took place during November and December of 2008, in the Fashion Design workshop suite at Birmingham City University Institute of Art and Design, UK. Two areas of this suite were used: the cutting demonstration area, and the adjacent computer room. The study session involved the teaching of pattern cutting skills relating to six types of skirt: sheath, back vent, full circle, gathered front and yoke, gored and lower shaped full skirt. The skills required for the cutting of patterns for these skirts lie at the very simple end of the scale, as compared for example, with the cutting of a two-piece collar, which lies at the very difficult end of the scale. We felt that this selection was appropriate, as the effect of using the videos to teach pattern cutting was not yet known to us.

HOW THE SAMPLE WAS FORMED

The study group was formed by taking a systematic sample, followed by subsequent random sampling. Our initial sampling frame was taken from the university register of enrolled first year students, having first removed the names of any students who were known to have left the course, thus ensuring that our sampling frame was relevant, complete, precise and up-to-date (Denscombe 2007). An alphabetic listing of all 135 enrolled students attending the first year of the course was divided into five groups of 27 students; these groups were named 'A' to 'E' and were to be taught Pattern Cutting in rotation. We chose to draw study participants from group 'E', allowing the tutor for the Demonstration class to have had the chance to work with groups 'A' to 'D' beforehand, in order to familiarise with the material to be taught and the teaching approach to be used. Group 'E' was also scheduled to be taught at a time in the calendar when both of the authors had good availability and the necessary resources were available.

A random sample of 14 students was drawn from the 27 first-year students in Group 'E'. The first year course cohort is 96.6% female and 3.4% male, so perhaps unsurprisingly all 14 students in the random sample were female. Their mean age was 20.0 years (range 18-27). A strong gender bias, where female students greatly outnumber male students, is typical of our BA(Hons) Fashion Design course. These students all completed an informed consent form that was compliant with the University's Research Ethical Framework. The sample was then systematically subdivided into two groups, by sequentially assigning names with a '1' or a '2' in the list. One group of seven students was assigned to be taught using the traditional face-to-face classroom demonstration method, and the other group of seven students was assigned to be taught using the reusable learning objects, namely, the VLE-based streaming video clips. The former group was named the *Demonstration* group and the latter was named the *Video* group.

PRELIMINARY QUESTIONNAIRES

On arrival at the study session, prior to starting work, all 14 participants were asked to complete an eight item IT self-efficacy rating questionnaire using a five-point Likert scale, in order that a view could be achieved on the IT skills of the participants. Bandura (1995) defines self-efficacy as: "… beliefs in one's capabilities to organise and execute the courses of action required to manage prospective situations." We chose this approach, rather than for example, administering an IT skills test to participants because we felt that measuring this egocentric construct by means of self-reporting scales would produce a more rounded view of participant IT ability than would measurement of timings and error rates when performing selected IT skills in a computer skills test. Furthermore, Cassidy and Eachus (2002) note that: "Self-efficacy beliefs have repeatedly been reported as a major factor in understanding the frequency and success with which individuals use computers." For this reason, the self-efficacy approach was felt to be a better indicator of personal IT ability.

Before starting, participants were also asked to complete a Pre-Session questionnaire, which included three questions asking about prior use of: e-learning, video clips and animations for learning and a 16-item comprehension matrix of pattern cutting keywords intended to capture participants' existing knowledge level of pattern cutting terminology. The 16 items in the matrix included four keywords from each of four categories: 'newbie', 'basic', 'intermediate' and 'advanced'. The 'newbie' keywords – that a newcomer to pattern cutting might be expected to know – were: *Block, Clickers Awl, Set square* and *Metre rule*. The 'basic' keywords – that someone with only a basic understanding of pattern cutting might be expected to know – were: *Notches, Squared line, Stitch line* and *Grain line*. The 'intermediate' keywords – that someone with an intermediate understanding of pattern cutting might be expected to know were: *Body rise, Wrap, Collar fall* and

Bicep line. The advanced keywords – that someone with an advanced understanding of pattern cutting might be expected to know – were: *Collar diversion*, *Roll line*, *Scye* and *Break point*. These 16 keywords were placed in random order, and then presented in a 4x4 matrix on the questionnaire page. On the questionnaire we asked participants to: *"circle all of the pattern cutting terms that you are familiar with and can use."* In this way, a self-reported pattern cutting familiarity level for each participant prior to the study was made available. We chose a self-reporting format, as this takes into account each individual's own perceptions of self-efficacy at each of the tasks, giving a rounded view of what each participant felt that they could actually do. Cassidy and Eachus (*ibid.*) note: "Self-efficacy levels have been shown to be related to choice of task, motivational level and effort, and perseverance with the task." For this reason, the self-efficacy approach was felt to be a sound indicator of pattern cutting terms prior knowledge.

TWO TEACHING GROUPS

We then notified participants which group, Demonstration or Video, they had been allocated to. The Demonstration group worked in the cutting demonstration area of the workshop, and the Video group worked in the computer room. Both groups worked simultaneously, and members of one group were unable to observe or confer with members of the other group during the session. As our research question sought to compare student performance using the two methods: face-to-face demonstrations and streaming video clips, we had to firstly set up two distinct teaching protocols. One presenting a teaching session that would mirror as closely as possible the traditional face-to-face method of teaching already employed on the course, and the other, an efficient yet authentic learning and teaching environment for use by students who would be using the video clips as the basis for their learning. These are explained below.

DEMONSTRATION GROUP TEACHING PROTOCOL

The demonstration group were taught the skirt skills in the traditional way, as already used within the course for several years. Care was taken to employ an experienced pattern cutting tutor, who was provided with necessary curriculum materials by the module leader. The seven participants gathered around a large rectangular table to observe a demonstration of each stage of the skill, making personal sketches, notes and asking questions of the tutor as necessary. When the demonstration was complete, participants were then invited to perform the skill stage for themselves, using suitably large tables with all materials provided. The tutor facilitated the class by circulating around, answering questions and offering individual guidance as necessary. When all participants had completed the stage in question, they were asked to gather around the table again to receive a demonstration of the next stage. In this way, all of the skills were demonstrated and participants drew and cut their own patterns, which were handed in for assessment at the end of the session.

VIDEO GROUP TEACHING PROTOCOL

The video group were taught the skirt skills by using video clips that had been previously prepared by an experienced pattern cutting tutor. Adobe Flash video (flv) was used for the clips, as this meant that they would stream efficiently from the VLE to the computer, eliminating any waiting for files to download, and also providing good cross platform and browser compatibility. As noted earlier, the video clips were all shot from above using the same format, from the pattern cutter's eye view, showing the tutor performing the pattern cutting activity in close-up, with hands, measuring rules, squares and pencil being used as required to mark out the pattern, and scissors and glue being used for cutting and sticking. A narrative voice over was included, providing additional information.

Prior to the session, the video clips that were to be used had been uploaded onto the university VLE: Moodle, ready to be presented to students online in a structured module. Each participant was assigned a networked desktop computer, running Moodle in a web browser, to use during the session, and large tables were available with all necessary materials provided for pattern cutting. The tutor facilitated the class by circulating around, answering questions and offering individual guidance as necessary. Participants were free to view the clips as and when they saw fit, and to move freely between computer and table to measure, mark and cut their patterns. In this way, all of the skills were demonstrated and participants drew and cut their own patterns, which were handed in for assessment at the end of the session.

AFTER THE SESSIONS

On completion of the sessions, we asked participants to complete a post-session questionnaire, which included the same 16-item comprehension matrix of pattern cutting keywords used in the pre-session questionnaire, allowing a comparative view to be taken regarding knowledge before and after the session. The questionnaire also asked about the comprehensibility of the teaching method used, any difficulties encountered, the quality of teaching resources and participants' willingness to use the teaching method again.

All six practical work pieces undertaken by the participants during the session were collected at the end of the session for subsequent marking in the usual way. Participants were then thanked

for taking part in the study and the session was closed. Once the practical work had been marked, the grades were made available to the researchers for analysis.

One week later, after allowing time for post-session reflection, we held two Focus Groups, one for each participant group: Demonstration and Video. The focus groups sought to surface views and feelings about the experiences of the participants during the sessions. Both focus groups were recorded using a digital audio recorder placed on the table before the session, in full view of, and with the permission of all participants, and the audio was transcribed afterwards for content analysis. Selected comments from the focus group participants are shown in *italics* in both the Findings and the Focus Group Discussion sections below and are reproduced verbatim.

FINDINGS

IT Self-Efficacy Scores

The mean IT self-efficacy scores for each participant are shown in Figure 1. Participants 1 to 7 were in the Demonstration group and participants 8 to 14 were in the Video group. It can be seen that most of the participants rated their efficacy between 3 (Average) and 4 (High).

Prior Experience of Using Digital Media for Learning

Participants were asked whether they had ever used e-learning, video clips or animations previously for learning. As can be seen in Figure 2, most had not.

Pattern Cutting Comprehension Pre and Post Session

All participants completed the 16-item comprehension matrix of pattern cutting keywords before

Figure 1. Mean IT self-efficacy scores

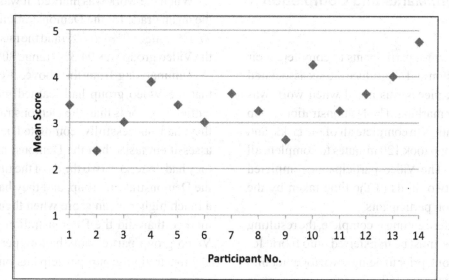

and after the teaching sessions. By comparing data from the two, we could arrive at a notion of 'distance travelled' by both groups.

As can be seen in Figure 3, the mean pre-teaching score for Demonstration participants was 4.9 keywords known (range 0-10), and the mean post-teaching score was 7.0 keywords known (range 3-11), which reflects a mean increase of 2.1 keywords known over the teaching session.

The mean pre-teaching score for Video participants was higher at 5.3 keywords known (range 1-10), but the mean post-teaching score was 12.1 keywords known (range 9-14), which reflects a mean increase of 6.8 keywords known. The Video participants were familiar with and felt that they could use more pattern cutting keywords than the Demonstration participants after the teaching sessions.

Figure 2. Prior use of e-learning, video clips or animation for learning

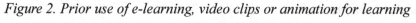

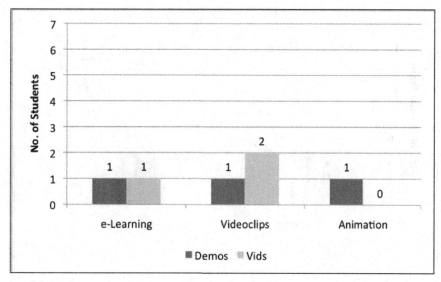

Time Taken, Marks and Completion Rates

The time taken for participants to complete their teaching session and to produce the six associated project work pieces was noted when work was handed in for marking. The Demonstration group took 180 minutes to complete all of the tasks, and the Video group took 120 minutes to complete all of the tasks. The Video participants completed the tasks in two thirds of the time taken by the Demonstration participants.

When pattern cutting is complete, the resulting paper patterns must be transferred onto fabric for final cutting out, prior to being sewn together into the finished garment. If the paper patterns contain any errors, then it will not be possible to make the garment from the fabric pieces, as they simply will not fit together. Only if the paper patterns are largely free from errors will it be possible to make a correctly finished garment. For this reason, the six project work pieces handed in by participants were each marked on a Pass/Fail basis. Three members of the Demonstration group completed all tasks correctly and five members of the Video group completed all tasks correctly.

When the work was marked, it was found that the mean grade for the Demonstration group was 77.1% (range 40% – 100%) and the mean grade for the Video group was 94.3% (range 80% - 100%).

Summarising from the above, it can be seen that the Video group had learned more pattern cutting keywords than the Demonstration group, they had successfully completed more of the assessment tasks than the Demonstration group, they had done so in two thirds of the time taken by the Demonstration group, and they had achieved a much higher mean score when their work was marked than did the Demonstration group. The Video group participants had outperformed the Demonstration group participants on every test measure.

Comprehensibility, Difficulty and Effectiveness Ratings

In the post-session questionnaire, participants were asked whether they could understand the Demonstrations that they had seen, or Video clips that they had used, and if they had experienced any difficulties during their learning session. Six of the Demonstration group participants stated that

Figure 3. Pattern cutting keywords known pre and post teaching

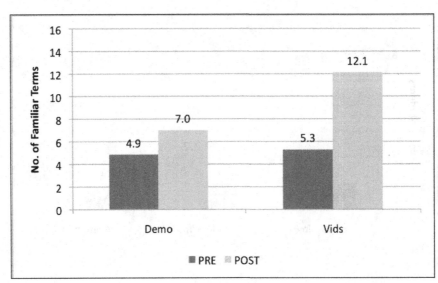

they could understand the demonstrations, and all seven of the Video group participants stated that they could understand the video clips.

Participants were also asked to rate how effective the demonstrations or video clips were for learning and to rate their quality, using a five-point Likert scale in both cases. The demonstration group gave a mean rating of 4.0 (range 3-5) for effectiveness, and a mean rating of 4.2 (range 4-5) for quality, and the Videos group gave a mean rating of 5.0 (range 3-5) for effectiveness and a mean rating of 4.1 (range 3-5) for quality.

Summarising from the above, it can be seen that participants from each of the groups rated the comprehensibility of the particular method that they had used highly, although a small number in each group had experienced problems along the way. Likewise, participants from each of the groups rated the effectiveness and quality of the particular method that they had used between high (mean score 4) and very high (mean score 5). In

two of the three measures, comprehensibility and effectiveness, the video clips were rated slightly higher than were the Demonstrations. In the quality measure however, the Demonstrations were rated very slightly higher than were the Video clips.

Most and Least Useful Aspects of the Methods and Willingness to Use Again

Participants were then asked to comment about what they found most and least useful about the demonstrations or video clips. Demonstrations group members' comments are shown in Table 1.

Video group members' comments are shown in Table 2.

Finally, in the post-teaching questionnaire, participants were asked if they would be happy to use the particular method of learning (demonstrations or video clips) that they had used again. Six participants in each group reported that they

Table 1. Demonstration group comments on most and least useful aspects of demonstrations

Participant	Demonstrations: Most Useful	Demonstrations: Least Useful
D1	*Shows a step-by-step way of making each pattern.*	*Sometimes can be made to seem more complex than they really are.*
D2	*Guess it was reassuring to know someone was there helping us.*	*Can't think of any.*
D3	*The teacher did all demonstrations slowly.*	*-*
D4	*-*	*-*
D5	*You find out exact measurements rather than having to guess and I could ask questions if I got stuck.*	*It takes a long time to watch demonstrations and then do patterns myself.*
D6	*You could ask again if something you didn't understand, you couldn't ask a computer.*	*Things were made to seem harder than they are, and tutor referring back to notes made me feel not confident.*
D7	*Measurements*	*Showing us how to draw in shapes for facings etc.*

Table 2. Video group comments on most and least useful aspects of video clips

Participant	Video clips: Most Useful	Video clips: Least Useful
V1	*To be able to see what we needed to make and compare with our own.*	*The lack of sound.*
V2	*You got to see and rewind and pause what happens.*	*It doesn't tell you the measurements you need.*
V3	*Being able to pause and work at my own speed as sometimes the group demos are too slow.*	*The camera angle distorts the shapes – e.g. right angles and distance through foreshortening.*
V4	*Everything.*	*-*
V5	*Pause and replay specific bits of each demonstration.*	*Might not work sometimes.*
V6	*Being able to pause and replay if something didn't make sense at first.*	*The videos can skip or freeze.*
V7	*Clearly explained, could make patterns in a tempo convenient for me.*	*Some movies couldn't be stopped, so I had to replay the whole a couple of times.*

would be happy to do this. Participants were also asked to give details about their reasons. Demonstration and Video group members' comments are shown in Table 3.

Summarising from the above, it is can be noted that many of the Demonstration group participants liked having a tutor present to ask questions of, either for reassurance or when stuck. Some were critical of the apparent complexity of the tasks at first glance, but stated that once tasks had been completed, their fears had proved unnecessary. The amount of time taken up by the demonstrations was also criticised.

Many of the Video group participants liked the ability to pause, rewind and play the clips to see things again, allowing them to work at their own speed. They were critical of some matters relating to content (lack of measurements) but mostly relating to technical matters (sound, camera angles, inability to stop clips playing) and fears that the technology might fail them in some way were also present (fear that the clips might not work and fear of clips skipping/freezing).

Members of each group were strongly supportive of the particular method that they had used, both citing matters relating to ease and convenience. Video group participants also liked the speed with which they were able to work, and the potential for off-site, out of hours use was noted.

FOCUS GROUP DISCUSSIONS

Audio from both focus groups was transcribed and reviewed. Where focus group participants expressed opinions on the teaching method that they had used, these were coded as being supportive (positive) or critical (negative). A frequency count of such utterances was then made, 62% of utterances made by Demonstration group members were positive and 38% were negative (n=26). 64% of utterances made by Videos group members were positive and 36% were negative (n=50). In each case then, around two-thirds of all utterances expressing opinion made by both Demonstration and Video group participants were positive. Most participants felt positively toward

Table 3. Demonstration and Video group comments on willingness to use learning method again

Demonstration Group		Video Group	
Participant	Comment	Participant	Comment
D1	*I've tried Moodle when doing my DS and find that much more simple and easy to follow than only be able to watch the demonstration only once.*	V1	*As I could see what mine was supposed to look like to see if I had gone wrong.*
D2	*To be honest it the best way for me to learn anything. It's easier/convenient/to the point.*	V2	*I would if it gave you measurements, however, it's not as good as a teacher as you can not ask questions if stuck etc.*
D3	*I prefer this method because it's been demonstrated clearly.*	V3	*Because it's quick and easy.*
D4	-	V4	*Easier. Learn quicker and more. See more. More clearly.*
D5	*This is probably my most preferred method as I can ask for help and ask questions. I also know exact measurements by asking.*	V5	*Can do it in your own time.*
D6	*I would use Moodle and ask a tutor if I had any problems. I couldn't sort on there, I would not just use purely tutorial help.*	V6	*The videos were clear and I could replay them as much as I liked.*
D7	*It was helpful to see someone else do it before I attempted it.*	V7	*It's very easy and accessible. I can use it at home if for some reason I can't come in.*

the particular teaching method that they had used. Selected participant statements will now be presented and discussed.

Demonstration Group Participant Statements in Focus Group

The Demonstration group particularly liked having the tutor present all of the time. *"I prefer like, with a teacher there 'cos you can like, ask them when you're stuck and stuff? I prefer it with a teacher there."*

They spoke of the reassurance provided, especially when carrying out complex, multi-stage procedures. *"It's just reassuring to know someone's there to help you…and to know you're doing it right."*

They also liked having the opportunity to ask questions and seek confirmation that they were getting the procedure right. *"It's like, the reassurance thing 'cos I panic a lot… Is this right? Is this right? And I'm too scared to continue further in case that part's wrong. 'Cos I've done that a few times… so I just like to have someone to tell me 'yeah, that's right'."*

Demonstration group members were particularly critical of the pace of the demonstration sessions, feeling that they went too slowly. *"…we have to wait around for her [the tutor] to draw lines and stuff…it ain't like Blue Peter either with 'Here's one I did earlier'."* They expressed frustration at having to wait until all members of the group had reached the end of the stage being demonstrated before continuing. *"…we had to like, wait for her, we had to see her demonstrations before we could do anything which was what slowed us down quite a lot."* One participant spoke passionately and at length about her frustration with a previous experience in the demonstration session. *"There's people are all at different stages and the demos go on for quite a long time it's just - you just wanna bang it out. Yeah, some people work really fast, some, like, don't, and then you're just sitting about for about, 20 minutes and you're doing nothing,* *just waiting. There was one like, she [the tutor] did an angle and just went and checked everyone had point seven, like, millimetres! Yeah, and that took ages, didn't it? And we were all sitting there like, 'oh m'God.' There's like half an hour just to check everyone's individual one and we were like, we could have finished the whole thing and got on to the next one by now."* Furthermore, Demonstration group participants were critical of an initial feeling of information overload, where a lot of detail needed to be assimilated quickly, which at first sight seemed to be intimidating. *"It gets quite stressful."* However, once participants had completed the task, they noted that this initial impression was erroneous. *"…she gives you loads of details and then you think 'oh my God, it's going to be really hard' and then it's not, when you actually do it it's alright."*

Video Group Participant Statements in Focus Group

The video group particularly liked the ability to pause, rewind and play the clips, so that they could review segments if they needed reassurance or had not understood something clearly first time around. *"…being able to pause it and being able to work faster 'cos the group's too slow."* It was also strongly felt that this had a positive impact on their rate of progress through the work tasks. *"There's like, being able to do it at your own speed, there's not being like, rushed by a teacher, or there's like, having to wait… or whatever to catch up stuff."* The short duration of the clips was also liked. *"…there's only like, seven minutes you've got the longest video and you can pause it when you get, you know, it's just too much… just go away and do up to that point."* Video group participants expressed a strong preference for using the clips as compared to observing a demonstration, as they felt that they learned more easily. *"It was just easier to watch a video than to - all try and cramp round a teacher and… see, well, think you've got it and then go away and you haven't... and I learned more easier, much easier."*

Video group members were particularly critical of the technical difficulties that they had encountered when using the clips. *"The only issue was that you couldn't hear it...we were all sitting there trying to hear it and then going away and hoping that we'd heard the right stuff. If there's headphones, that would be an idea."* Camera angles were also criticised, due to foreshortening. *"...some points the camera angle does distort some things so – an angle doesn't look... there's slight foreshortening of... the paper so you can't really tell what angles something is. If the camera zoomed in more on the paper like, if you showed something and then zoomed on...zoomed in on the, maybe like the lines she just drew, you could see."* A particular criticism centred on the lack of measurements given in the clips. *"I just think you could give like, more information on measurements 'cos sometimes we were just, like, ooh – shall we just guess how much that is or whatever?"*

CONCLUSION

Although we cannot generalise from our findings to the wider student population, we can draw conclusions locally, within the study participants, and in this way seek to "illuminate the general by looking at the particular." Denscombe (*op. cit.*).

1. Most participants rated their IT self-efficacy as between 'Average' and 'High' but most had not used e-Learning, video clips or animation previously for learning, so although fairly 'IT-savvy', most participants were new to e-Learning, suggesting that the use of e-Learning did not feature strongly in these participants' previous institutions (Further Education Institutions or Schools).

2. Comparing pre-and post-session 'comprehension of pattern cutting keywords' data shows that the Video group's 'distance travelled' exceeded that of the demonstration group quite considerably, with a mean pre-to-post-test increase in keywords known of 6.8 (Video) and 2.1 (Demonstration) respectively. This shows that the Video group participants had learned more of the keywords than the Demonstration group participants as a result of the teaching method used.

3. When comparing task completion rates, time taken and marks, the Video group outperformed the Demonstration group in each category. They successfully completed more of the assessment tasks than did the Demonstration group; in two thirds of the time, whilst achieving a much higher mean score when their work was marked. This quite convincingly shows large learning gains made by the Video group participants over the Demonstration group participants.

4. Participants from each group rated the comprehensibility, effectiveness and quality of the particular method that they had used highly, although a small number had experienced problems. This suggests that the learning and teaching philosophy and the delivery method underpinning both approaches was suitable to the material being taught.

5. Many of the Demonstration group participants liked having a tutor present while learning. The amount of time taken up by the demonstrations was criticised, as faster-working group members felt that they were having to work at the speed of slower-working group members, due to the need to ensure that all members of the group could perform the skills taught.

6. Many of the Video group participants liked the control offered by their ability to play, pause and rewind the clips, facilitating easy review. They also liked having the ability to work at their own pace. However, criti-

cisms were made regarding the content and regarding some key technical aspects.

7. Members of both groups were strongly supportive of the particular method that they had used, citing both ease and convenience. Video group participants also liked the speed with which they were able to work, and the potential for off-site, out of hours use was noted.

8. Analysis of the Focus Group transcripts supported the findings from the data.

IMPLICATIONS FOR THE FUTURE

Our students are changing, there is a need for us as educators to adapt our teaching to better fit the way in which they process information, giving them the opportunity to independently review new learning materials as and when necessary, leading to successful learning. By using online RLOs which can be accessed and revisited, paused and rewound as needed throughout the course, students can become more confident in their own abilities.

This small-scale one day comparative study of 14 students has shown that the students using RLOs to learn pattern-cutting skills outperformed the students who learned using traditional classroom demonstration methods, across all test measures. Technical difficulties need to be overcome however, namely issues with PC sound cards, the provision of headphones and networking issues. Content issues also need to be addressed, this may be because students, as discerning viewers of video media have high thresholds for quality.

Our findings from the current study are very encouraging; showing that student performance using streaming video-based RLOs in the teaching of skills for pattern cutting was far better than student performance using face-to-face classroom teaching.

We propose a further study, using a larger, representative sample of the incoming year-group, to permit a view on whether the convincing outcome noted in this study will be replicated with large numbers, helping us to determine whether we should move completely from face-to-face teaching of pattern cutting to the use of RLOs across the programme.

While the steadily increasing use of streaming media via the VLE in universities, and the accompanying increase in availability of online resources to support student learning during and outside of office hours must be welcomed, the time needed to develop high quality video and animation-rich RLOs, is considerable. Furthermore, most lecturers and supporting staff would probably need skilled technical support to assist their endeavours and would also need to be allowed the time and resources necessary to complete these projects successfully. It is hoped that this study may provide useful data to educators wishing to justify the use of streaming media in higher education to budget holders.

REFERENCES

Bandura, A. (1995). *Self-efficacy in changing societies*. Cambridge, UK: Cambridge University Press. doi:10.1017/CBO9780511527692

Cassidy, S., & Eachus, P. (2002). Developing the computer user self-efficacy (CUSE) scale: Investigating the relationship between computer self-efficacy, gender and experience with computers. *Journal of Educational Computing Research*, *26*(2), 169–189. doi:10.2190/JGJR-0KVL-HRF7-GCNV

Denscombe, M. (2007). *The good research guide for small scale social research projects* (3rd ed.). Berkshire, UK: Open University Press.

Duncan, C. (2004). *Leaning object economies: Barriers and drivers*. Retrieved August 10, 2009, from http://www.intrallect.com/index.php/intrallect/knowledge_base/white_papers/learning_object_economies_barriers_and_drivers

Frederick, P. J. (1987). Student involvement: Active learning in large classes . In Gleason Weimer, M. (Ed.), *Teaching large classes well*. San Francisco, CA: Jossey-Bass Inc.

Gibbs, G. (1992). *Improving the quality of student learning*. Bristol, UK: Technical and Educational Services Ltd.

Harvey, L., & Knight, P. (1996). *Transforming higher education*. Bristol, UK: Open University Press.

Jarvis, P., Holford, J., & Griffin, C. (2003). *The theory and practice of learning* (2nd ed.). Oxon, UK: Routledge.

L'Allier, J. J. (1997). *Frame of reference: NETg's map to the products, their structure and core beliefs*. NetG. Retrieved July 13, 2009, from http://netg.com/research/whitepapers/frameref.asp

Machemer, P., & Crawford, P. (2007). Student perceptions of active learning in a large cross-disciplinary classroom. *Active Learning in Higher Education*, *8*(1), 11. doi:10.1177/1469787407074008

Newberry, M. (2003). *A study of the UK designer fashion sector*. London, UK: DTI Publications.

Pickford, R., & Brown, S. (2006). *Assessing Skills and Practice*. Oxon: Routledge.

Prensky, M. (2001). Digital natives digital immigrants. *Horizon*, *9*(5), 1–4. doi:10.1108/10748120110424816

RLO-CETL. (2009). *Reusable learning objects Centre for Excellence in Teaching and Learning*. Retrieved August 7, 2009, from http://www.rlo-cetl.ac.uk

Ruiz, J. G., Mintzer, M. J., & Issenberg, S. B. (2006). Learning objects in medical education. *Medical Teacher*, *28*(7), 603–604. doi:10.1080/01421590601039893

Chapter 7
Teaching Off-Line Digital Video Editing On-Line:
An Exploration into Editing and Postproduction Digital Pedagogic Practice

Sarah Atkinson
University of Brighton, UK

ABSTRACT

This chapter focuses upon a case study of an online higher education intervention – an interactive resource the author has devised as an aid to the teaching and learning of undergraduate digital video editing (DVE). This resource specifically addresses drama and fiction postproduction principles, practice and techniques. The repository, which includes streamed materials available to download, guides the student through the film production process in a step-by-step way (for students), with suggested class based activities and tasks using the materials (for tutors). The resources include the script, all planning documentation, all production paperwork, and all rushes shot for different productions. The student/ tutor navigates through these materials guided by a combination of voice-overs, video tutorials by those personnel involved in the production, and clips taken from the "making of" documentaries. This chapter explores the intervention within the wider context of higher education online teaching and through the lens of virtual learning environment pedagogic theory.

DOI: 10.4018/978-1-60960-800-2.ch007

We are on the cusp of a global revolution in teaching and learning. Educators worldwide are developing a vast pool of educational resources on the Internet, open and free for all to use. These educators are creating a world where each and every person on earth can access and contribute to the sum of all human knowledge. They are also planting the seeds of a new pedagogy where educators and learners create, shape and evolve knowledge together, deepening their skills and understanding as they go.

(Cape Town Open Education Declaration, 2007)

1 INTRODUCTION

As a UK-based practitioner teaching university undergraduate video editing and post production for 7 years, I have faced constant challenges of sourcing and innovating visual materials with which to devise class-based teaching exercises, while managing growing student numbers and class sizes. To this end I have devised and developed an on-line teaching resource: *i-mpact* - Interactive Resource for Media Professionals and Academics Collaborating in Teaching (www.i-mpact.org.uk), within which to stream and allow access to relevant learning materials. The longer-term ideal of the project is that both students and colleagues across institutions will continually add and contribute to this resource.

My teaching of DVE has a dual focus. It incorporates an operational level – that is, teaching students how to drive the software and hardware in order to gain an in-depth working knowledge into the functionality of the different postproduction programmes. On the other-hand, tuition takes place on an aesthetic level – that is developing an awareness and understanding of the principles and practices of DVE – enhancing the student's appreciation and consideration of the audio and sound design, and the different visual styles, genres, approaches and aesthetics. The latter endeavour is centred on the history and craft of DVE itself, which I have approached in-class by using techniques such as visually demonstrating the act of cutting, primarily using visual examples from commercially available television and film footage. Students then practice these techniques and have the opportunity to develop their visual awareness, analytical skills and storytelling skills. These approaches sit within the wider remit of a higher education module of study within which transferable academic skills are also developed. For example, the student's critical and analytical skills are progressed within their experience of peer review and assessment when they are given the opportunity to critique one another's work.

In class sizes of 20 plus students, these teaching approaches have become ever more challenging in terms of ensuring equality of student experience. In terms of the classroom learning environment itself, many students are often positioned too far away from the screen on which the software interface is projected and demonstrated, and cannot fully see the intricacies of the interface and the smaller tools, icons and buttons therein. The diversity of student ability also leads to students working at varied paces. There is a definite need to support the class-based mode of delivery both within and beyond the classroom environment. The migration of some class-based content and the addition of supporting materials towards a blended learning approach within a virtual learning environment have therefore become inevitable. The concept of blended learning:

...is commonly associated with the introduction of online media into a course or programme, while at the same time recognising that there is merit in retaining face-to-face contact and other traditional approaches to supporting students, It is also used where asynchronous media such as

email or conferencing are deployed in conjunction with synchronous technologies, commonly text chat or audio (Macdonald, 2006, p.2).

Rather than viewing this content migration as an imposition, as an academic and professional compromise, I have been using the development of the *i-mpact* resource to look at ways to embrace and to use these opportunities to their best.

The overall aim of the *i-mpact* resource has been to align and adapt blended approaches with the cultural trajectory on which the mass inception that these technologies have taken us. That is, into the realms of web 2.0 phenomenon such as file-sharing, open source software, social networking, blogging, tweeting, modding and mashing-up.

2 VIRTUAL LEARNING WITHIN CONTEMPORARY HIGHER EDUCATION

In the last decade, we have witnessed the wide-spread use of online learning systems within module and course delivery within higher education institutions. The deployment of software such as *Blackboard,* a course management system (CMS) is now commonplace within UK based institutions. Other terms such as learning management system (LMS), learning content management system (LCMS), managed learning environment (MLE), virtual learning environment (VLE) (Weller, 2007, p. 2-3) account for similar manifestations of the CMS and have all become common language of teaching and learning in higher education.

The important emphasis that has been placed at instructional level on the use of such environments in terms of financial investment and course delivery has in part been attributed to the introduction of 'mass' higher education. Bach, Haynes and Smith define this at the point 'when a society moves from a position where an elite minority of

its population experience higher education to one where this becomes a large minority, or close to a majority' (2007, p.12). National and institutional initiatives to widen participation by actively re-cruiting first-generation or 'non-traditional' stu-dents to courses of higher education have also led to calls to re-think the more traditional modes of educational delivery. In addition, contemporary students increasingly have to contend with external financial pressures and have to balance ever more complicated home, work and life responsibilities. A recent article in the UK newspaper, the Daily Telegraph proclaimed;

Online learning is a phenomenal educational growth area that offers value for money, geo-graphical freedom and flexibility of delivery. Set-ting out his new framework for higher education recently, Lord Mandelson, the Business Secretary, said that the challenge for the next decade was "to offer a wider range of new study opportunities – part-time, work-based, foundation degrees and studying at home – to a greater range of people" and that universities should seek partnerships with the private sector to provide online education. (25th November, 2009)

Bach, Haynes and Smith also point to 'manage-rialism and a new bureaucracy in higher education' (2007, p.13) which has led to the mass inception of online learning support as well as technical developments have all fuelled developments into online learning environments. Basic institutional requirements tend to be that electronic versions of course materials, such as assignment briefs, lecture notes and glossaries of terms have to be uploaded prior to the delivery of classes. In addi-tion students may be required to engage with blogs, Wikis and other collaborative working spaces as part of their assessments. However, these environ-ments are sometimes criticised at an operational level, in part as a result of their inflexibility and un-usability. As Weller has observed;

It is becoming clear that common e-learning activities can't really be done by one application that has little or no knowledge of everything else on the network or the wider Internet. It's also becoming clearer that a single system that tries to combine all such functions is unlikely to do all of them equally well. Furthermore, one-size systems do not necessarily fit all institutions (in Weller, 2007, p.9).

The recent shift in the cultural use of technologies has also accelerated these changes. The Web 2.0 technological influence has meant that far more students are likely to have experience of these types of technologies when they arrive at university. They are likely to regularly engage in leisure pursuits, which involve social networking activities, and are adept at navigating and engaging with multiple streams of concurrent information. There is therefore a need for academic staff to adapt to these behaviours and expectations, and to accept the fact that students are likely to be monitoring the activity on their *Facebook* and *Twitter* pages in a minimized window during their access to computer laboratory class times.

It is interesting to note that there has been a shift towards the adoption of these technological principles within the filmmaking world. Director Matt Hanson has coined the term Cinema 2.0 as an obvious reference to Web 2.0 to describe this new approach to film making within his project *A swarm of Angels;*

I use Cinema 2.0 as a tongue-in-cheek label, but it conveys the idea that this is an amalgam of digital-age filmmaking techniques coupled with the social power of the Web. This is a way to create media and large-scale free cultural works. It's also about pushing the aesthetics and innovation of filmmaking"[1].

Hanson is currently developing two fictional scripts, the first *The Unfold*, which he will upload to a Wiki so that members of the so-called 'swarm' (the audience and participants of the Wiki) can amend and add to it. The second, *Glitch* has been developed by allowing the swarm the opportunity to vote on which story elements to retain and which to delete. The *Open Source Cinema Project* is currently creating a collaborative feature length documentary about copyright in the digital age. The director, Brett Gaylor, invites users to upload their own video content and then enables them to create online remixes of the footage using a mixer interface available through the web browser. Similarly, *Stray Cinema* operates under the same principles; users can download and remix content from the site to create their own edits of the fictional film. These can then be uploaded and entered into the competition, which is judged by visitors to the site.

It is through the study of such innovations that inspiration can be sought to apply these principles and approaches to the teaching of film making production and critical practices within higher education institutions.

After all, 'the underlying practice of web 2.0 tools is that of harnessing collective intelligence' (Mason and Rennie, 2008, p.2). Within the educational realm, the term VLE 2.0 has already been deployed by Weller within which he proposes open educational resources (OER) whereby 'universities and similar institutions make their academic material freely available online for anyone to use' (2007, p.149). The concept and development of OERs will be discussed a little later, but firstly it is important to further consider the effects that Web 2.0 technologies and their cultural take-up have had on filmmaking practice specifically in relation to the field of postproduction.

3 EXISTING INTERVENTIONS

There has been a proliferation of online browser-based DVE systems, which work within the framework of Web 2.0 technologies and architectures. These are not university based teaching systems, but are interesting examples of how off-line editing has been deployed within on-line environments. There have been several examples of companies using this technique for advertising purposes. The widespread introduction of domestic broadband services, through the technology of ADSL, which was launched in 2000, has led to the exploration of the potential of on-line video, and such systems allow for real time editing of video footage. McKinsey (1998) has suggested that TV advertising has been losing its impact for years and proposed that by 2010 it would be barely one-third as effective as it was in 1990, 'thanks to rising costs, falling viewership, ever-proliferating ad clutter, and viewers' TiVo[2]-fueled power to zip through commercials'. Several advertising campaigns have been created which utilise interactive technologies to engage the user in the postproduction process. In Spring 2005, the US car company Chevrolet, in their bid to increase sales of their new SUV model, the Tahoe, released a website inviting users to create their own thirty-second advertisement. Stock footage was uploaded to a website which viewers could access and edit together and add their own text captions. This resulted in numerous acts of virtual sabotage where users subverted the material and used their use of text to convey messages of environmental concern and protest. This highlights the potential problem of user control over content;

While interactivity often entails a built-in capacity to transform, shape or customise the text in accord with an author's wishes, it spurs on and sometimes encourages a desire to transform the text in ways that are out of the hands of the author and in accord with the individual wishes of an audience member or user (Cover, 2006, p.141).

In the case of the Chevrolet Tahoe, the intervention of an audience was detrimental to their brand. A similar campaign was available in the UK in 2007 by Volkswagen Golf (http://www.night-driving.com) in which all of the moving image footage of their original television advertisement was available to edit using the on-line editing software, *Jumpcut* (http://www.jumpcut.com). Finished versions could then be uploaded and entered into the competition to win the car. There are many social-network editing models on the web which require visitors to edit their own versions of short films, trailers and advertisements to then upload their creation for comment and ratings by other members of the community.

A counter movement to the commercial campaigns has been created within online communities such as *Trailer Mash* (http://www.thetrailermash.com), which enables users to remix, modify and upload commercial film content. *Brokeback to the Future* and *Goonies of the Caribbean* are examples of two hybrid trailers which are cut together from two commercial films by users of the site, other members of the community can then rate and comment upon them. More recently the UK TV channel E4 released a *Skins* editing competition, whereby viewers could download clips from the series, along with music in order to create their own trailers for the programme. This was very popular with the student demographic, and an activity, which many of my own students were keen to engage with.

These are all examples, which not only highlight the rapid development of internet technologies which have facilitated the manifestation of these types of projects, but that students are adept at engaging with this type of content.

4 POSTPRODUCTION VLEs

The purpose of my own pedagogic project was not to create an online editing system – but a supporting repository and teaching tool within which students could view materials and tutorials and then download high-resolution versions of the material used with which to practice the techniques with.

In terms of on-line content, which supports postproduction learning and development at the professional end of the scale, I have focussed on the *Avid* editing system. This is currently the software that is taught on the course, within which I incorporate *Avid's* own on-line VLE system – *The Avid Learning Excellerator* (*ALEX*) into my teaching.

The *ALEX* VLE system comprises of a number of modules, which the students can access online by logging into their own personal *ALEX* accounts. They have their own user profile, which tracks their progress through the modules, so that students can monitor the amount of the course they have successfully completed. The offering includes; Editing with Avid which 'covers all basic features of Avid, including capture, edit and trim, audio, titles, and output', a Color Correction course, in which students are able to; 'learn professional color correction skills, including shot-by-shot color correction using internal scopes', and a course entitled Creating Effects which 'covers basic effects, including segment and vertical effects, motion effects, nesting, and 3D Picture In Picture'. There are a total of 13 modules within the system, which in itself students found overwhelming. Students commented that;

'They HAD to be watched in order; otherwise you wouldn't understand what they were talking about'.

And that there were

'far too many videos to watch without enough time'.

There are quizzes, consisting of a list of multiple choice questions which the students can take at the end of each module to self-assess whether they have retained all of the information. The completion of the overall training package is assessed as an on-line multiple-choice exam, which the students have to achieve over 80% in order to pass. They would then receive an industry-recognised qualification as an *Avid Certified User* (ACU).

The training system uses video screen-capture software in order to demonstrate the different effects as they are performed within the interface and a voice over to verbally guide the student through the process. These are the available to view as Flash Movies within the browser or are available to download to watch through a portable device.

Students were questioned about their experiences of the training software. They were asked to provide comments on the positive and negative aspects of the systems in relation to their own learning, and their own professional and personal development.

When asked if they had improved their editing skills as a result of viewing the tutorials, the majority answered that they hadn't. Comments included;

'no, because to be a good editor you need to practice the things that were taught, but no one did. Just because someone has read or listened to the information doesn't mean they can execute it'.

'Not really, I learned a lot about computers, camera and wires more than editing, although learned what some of the editing terms meant'.

The pedagogic approach adopted by *ALEX* is didactic – information is fed to the students with little contextual detail, in terms of the production cycle, and no opportunities for interaction with any of the content (aside from the quizzes) is offered. *Alex*, as the *Avid* software is itself, is very much geared towards editors who already have a grasp and deeper understanding of the principles and processes of editing practice and, intuitively appreciate and inherently know why and where cuts should be positioned. Undergraduate students tend to approach the software without this knowledge, experience and ability. As such they face the dual challenge of learning (as I face the dual challenge of teaching) both the operational and creative aspects of DVE.

The practical and creative nature of this subject area, and the variety of students' preferred learning styles and approaches to the materials, are reflected in the varied responses to the use of the system. As Reynolds, Cayley, Mason (2002) have noted, the categorisations of approaches to learning have moved beyond the restrictive and somewhat stale nature of previous, outdated theorists, providing descriptions such as *Learning from novelty*, *Learning through experience*, *Learning through social interaction*, and *Learning and training* – in which an important distinction is made between training and teaching. This distinction is very apparent within the *ALEX* environment in which the focus is definitely on the training aspects of the system.

Within the *ALEX* system and indeed within any VLE that focuses upon the area of media production, there is therefore a definite need for the materials and tutorials to be placed back and to be referenced within their own production context, in order for them to gain meaning, and for the students to engage with them on a deeper pedagogic level. Grabinger and Dunlap have proposed *Rich Environments for Active Learning* (REALs) which;

Promote learning within authentic contexts, and encourage the growth of learner responsibility, initiative, decision-making, intentional learning and ownership over the acquired knowledge.

REALs should also provide an atmosphere that encourages the formation of knowledge-building learning communities. These communities encourage collaborative social negotiation of meanings and understandings among the members of the community. (in McPherson and Nunes, 2004, p.46)

5 ASSET GENERATION AND CONTEXTUALISATION FOR THE *I-MPACT* VLE

The concept of VLE 2.0 (Weller, 2007, p.149) was earlier cited and an excerpt from *The Cape Town Open Education Declaration*, which was written in September 2007 introduced this chapter. The Massachusetts Institute of Technology (MIT) was the first known institution to publish its own curricula, teaching and learning resources online. The MIT open courseware (OCW) system was established in 2001, and is available to access online today.

Many institutions and organisations have since developed their own open access learning sites such as *Jorum* (Jisc – Joint Information Systems Committee), *Edshare* (University of Southampton), *Humbox* (The Language, Linguistics and Area Studies Subject Centre, Higher Education Academy, UK) but as yet, there are no specific arts-based repositories. The Art Design and Media Higher education Academy Subject Centre are currently undertaking an-depth research project into Open Educational Resources (OER), this has yet to produce an operational repository. Such proposals are problematic within arts based communities and can often be met with resistance due to copyright issues, intellectual property rights and a reluctance to release materials over which the authors and artists perceive to have no creative or financial control.

Creative Commons licensing has been put in place to encourage the shared use of content within creative and artistic communities. With a Creative Commons license, the creator maintains the copyright but allows people to copy and distribute the work provided they give the creator the credit, and only on the conditions which the author or artist specifies. The widespread use of this licensing system has been an international success and many students are known to make use of this for their own assignment work when they want to incorporate elements such as incidental and theme music. However, it has not been so widely embraced within academic and educational communities in the realms of OER.

As such, a resource bank such as *i-mpact*, which includes all production elements from one programme/film in one repository, are difficult to obtain and also difficult to make use of due to copyright and licensing issues. Available resources also tend to be out dated and have little visual relevance to contemporary students expectations and sensibilities.

The *i-mpact* resource has initially overcome such issues by generating its own original materials at the outset. These were created within the university environment itself within a live teaching and learning project; a collaborative film project, which was delivered as part of the media production course provision.

The university at which I work offers a suite of media production courses, all of which have a vocational emphasis and aim to emulate professional industry practice in the approaches to teaching, learning and assessment.

The collaborative filmmaking project aimed to build professional awareness and practice and the overall emphasis throughout was on attaining high-end production values through real-world working conditions. This was achieved by deploying all Media staff (both academic and technical) and industry professionals (A Director of Photography, Grip and Camera operator) as key members of the production team. The emphasis was one of mutual collaboration between students, staff and professionals. Professional actors were cast in order to emphasise the actuality of the experience and to enable the professional film set feel.

The approach to the script was one of collaborative writing by a large group of students (namely the newly enrolled level 1 cohort). Similar collaborative film projects under development at the time of production included *A Swarm of Angels* (http://aswarmofangels.com) which involved multiple collaborators, exploiting Web 2.0 technologies in order to share and write a feature length script within an online environment.

The idea of the collaborative film project was to hand over this creative aspect entirely to the students. The script was created using a collaborative on line *Wiki* in which students could add, amend, and delete each other's work as the script developed. The students were provided with a story structure within which to work; the framework included three students from three different backgrounds following them from their decision points to apply to study at university, to their subsequent arrival and experience of the campus and university life.

The intensive shoot took place over the course of three days followed by a period of postproduction. On the shoot, the students were introduced to the concept of out of sequence shooting (that is that filming does not necessarily take place in the order in which the script is written) to maximise times spent on location.

All paperwork relating to the shoot, and the high-resolution rushes have been uploaded to the *i-mpact* resource.

As a result of the wealth of material that is included, the *i-mpact* resource is utilised across several other module/courses of study within the media field, not just within the area of postproduction. These include areas such as Scriptwriting, Screenwriting, Lighting, Camera work, Sound recording, Special Effects, Producing, Directing, and Acting for camera and Professional practice. By using this resource across several modules of study, students are enabled to make linkages between the different areas. They also gain an invaluable knowledge, appreciation and understanding of how teams and departments collaborate and work together. They gain insights into the intricate detail of the different disciplines and also an understanding of the overall production process, and the industry within which it operates.

For the purposes of providing professional quality footage, the collaborative film project deliberately used contemporary shooting styles and editing techniques (i.e. fluid camera work and fast paced cutting), which are familiar techniques that students are adept at consuming and also have the desire to create. Alongside the rapid development of media technologies, new styles of production will continue to manifest, and so the project addressed these changes. In the past, for the purposes of postproduction teaching, these materials have been sourced from the (US based) software companies *Apple* and *Avid*. Such visual materials that originate from exotic (and inaccessible; both culturally and physically) shooting locations, bear little relevance to a contemporary student's sensibilities.

As I have previously described, teaching DVE in a classroom computer laboratory environment usually entails tutorials – whereby students are provided with pre-recorded rushes[3] with which to practice the demonstrated techniques with. These are impossible to obtain from the commercial film and television examples that were previously described, since the films are already cut, fine-tuned, graded, and treated. In order for students to gain an authentic and valid experience of cutting the rushes of a production, elements such as the clapperboard need to be visible (so that the student can ascertain the shot and take number), and the off camera commands such as 'speed' 'action' and 'cut' need to be heard. Different 'takes' need to

be accessible too, so that students appreciate and gain an understanding of the importance of shot selection, being able to experiment with different 'takes' (variations of the same shot or sequence) so that they can make active and informed decisions about shot size, flow, pace, composition and continuity.

6 DESCRIPTION OF THE *I-MPACT* VLE

The *i-mpact* teaching resource has been devised to address the two challenges as articulated thus far; on the one hand to provide students with high quality rushes which they can access, use, manipulate, practice and experiment with (which in turn fosters and encourages a community which embraces OER), and on the other hand to develop an environment which encourages deeper learning which moves beyond a surface technical training model. It is proposed that this in part could be achieved through the encouragement of peer learning and peer collaboration. These aims collectively ensure that a key outcome of the module and the media production course itself is met; the improvement of the student's professional, creative and organisational approaches to their postproduction work.

It is not the intention that the *i-mpact* VLE replaces direct contact and face-to-face teaching within the classroom environment, but aims to enhance and reinforce the lessons learned by active engagement with the VLE. As with any practice-based, vocational subject area, much of the learning takes place independently when the students are given the opportunity to actively practice with the software and hardware tools. One student commented in response to the questionnaire that;

Examples shown on screen with very hands on approach was the best way of learning for my personal learning style.

The students of the university have direct access to the *i-mpact* site, through the internal computer network. This system could not be integrated into the university's own *Blackboard* site; as with most proprietary software; the university's own VLE is purpose built, and restrictive in terms of adaptability and modification. The issue of streaming media files outside of the university network due to bandwidth restrictions is also prohibitive. As Bonk, Kirkley, Hara and Dennen have noted when considering the potential teaching uses of generic university VLE systems;

While there are many asynchronous conferencing tools available, few have features that efficiently support the problem based learning (PBL) process for brainstorming, problem investigation, idea analysis and convergence, debating, collaborative writing and team production (Bonk, Kirkley, Hara and Dennen, 2001, p.85).

These latter learning experiences are an essential facet of the production-based student's pedagogic journey. In all other aspects of their class and assignment work, students are expected to work in production teams, to collectively conceptualise and synthesise the ideas upon which they collaborating. It is therefore important to emphasise the necessity of such approaches in their learning journeys, by ensuring that these approaches are consistent in all areas, which they study. As postproduction tends to be an exceptionally individual endeavour, it is important that the opportunities to engage in collaborative activities are available within the VLE itself.

The VLE utilises a screen capture software system *Camtasia Relay* with which to create a series of stream-able and downloadable mini tutorials and demonstrations, which are aimed at aiding the contextualisation of the editing and postproduction with the other aspects of the production process. The use of the software allows audio commentaries to be added to moving image footage, which can talk, guide and comment upon the process in real-time. The rushes used in the tutorials are then available for download so that the students can practice the techniques and use the footage for practical exercises and in their assignment work.

The tutorials and demonstrations are contextualised within the professional production cycle - therefore production elements such as the continuity sheets[4] and the scripts from the shoots are accessible which enables the student in to interpret the footage and then be aware of how the material should be captured and organised within *Avid*. This contextualisation of the material is crucial from a pedagogic point of view, since it enables cross-discipline linkages to be made with the other modules on the course – students themselves can begin to build up a broader understanding of the context and workflow of the entire film and television production cycle.

In addition to on-line tuition and practice - the *i-mpact* VLE encourages increased levels of critical reflection through informed peer feedback and commentary.

7 PEDAGOGIC APPROACHES WITHIN THE *I-MPACT* VLE

Weller has identified a number of modes of e-learning within VLEs such as community of practice/socio-cultural learning, resource-based learning, peer learning, content-led/instructivist learning, complex learning, problem-based learning, collaborative learning, instructor-led learning (2007, p.21-27).

The *i–mpact* resource has aimed to encapsulate all of these approaches. Within its modes of tuition it embodies instructor-led, resource-led and content-led learning. Within the context that I have framed these developments, of social and shared technologies; it is peer learning that is adopted as a predominant teaching and learning method of the *i-mpact* VLE. In order to tackle the teaching challenges that the online environment poses (since there is no face-to-face contact) it is necessary to investigate the potential of peer and collaborative learning. On the surface this is an expectation that the students may already have due to the high levels of participation with social-networking sites and technologies.

As Garrison et al have noted;

Peer learning is underpinned by a range of complex interactions, which include: peer learning (reading, reviewing, conceptualizing, critiquing), emotional, social, manipulating objects, questioning, responding etc. Thus, for peer learning to be effective in a technology-enhanced environment, it is important that the interactions consist of three core components: cognitive presence, teaching presence, and social presence (Garrison et al, 2000 cited in Rourke et al, 2001 in Juwah, 2006, p.175).

This level of interaction from both tutors and peers is of paramount importance to the success in terms of levels of engagement with the resource. A student response from the questionnaires revealed that;

I find feedback on my work useful from both peers and tutors although I feel I got more useful feedback from my peers, as they were more critical.

The form that this peer critique takes within the resource is that students upload their edited work onto the site to enable their peers to feedback and constructively comment on the work through the mode of a forum. Feedback is an important part of the higher education learning cycle, this tends to happen on a summative basis, when assessment work is marked and evaluated. With the increase in student numbers, and larger class sizes it is becoming increasingly difficult to provide in-depth feedback to students on a lesson-by-lesson basis, rendering the peer feedback facet of the resource all the more important to ensure. One student commented that;

'Feedback from our tutors is the best ever, because yes I find it helps me become a better editor its someone from the outside looking in. if you don't get other feedback from anyone you never see anything different or don't want to, as an editor you get used to looking at your own work but with someone else it helps change the little things'.

It is clear that receiving feedback fosters affirmation and confidence within the students, but is perceived by them as a really important facet of their learning and professional development.

A sense of ownership of the materials to the students is of great importance and worth to the students:

...students not only have a wider choice of resources and modalities of study materials from which to choose... but also come to share in the responsibility of identifying appropriate additional resources for the course and even contributing to the learning resources in a course (Collis, 1998, p.377).

Postproduction by its nature opens up possibilities for materials to be edited, manipulated, and their meanings changed by student intervention. The very process of editing is rooted in the techniques of the juxtaposition of images in order to make new meanings. This process was theorized by Lev Kuleshov in his concept of the Kuleshov effect. He describes the origins as follows;

During this time I created a montage experiment, which became known abroad as the 'Kuleshov Effect'. I alternated the same shot of Mozzhukhin [a Tsarist matinee idol] with various other shots (a plate of soup, a girl, a child's coffin), and these shots acquired a different meaning. The discovery stunned me - so convinced was I of the enormous power of montage. (1974, p.200)

Aligning this practice, and similar contemporary cultural technological practices to teaching and learning, can lead us to consider the potential of VLEs, and specifically their endorsement of the use of principles of OER.

For example, the practice of Modification, of Modding, has been an interactive trend prevalent in all forms of engagement with media, from the minor modifications of the personal appearance of avatars within gaming environments such as *Grand Theft Auto* and virtual environments such as *Second Life*, to full blown modification of computational source code to create whole new elements and levels of game play within gaming and virtual environments. This practice is characteristic of the inherently malleable form of new media and digital environments. There have been several examples in which commercial game engines have been used to modify and develop existing game architectures, environments and experiences. The original example was the game *Doom* (1993, iD Software) a first-person shooter played in a multiplayer networked environment which, from 1997 onwards, allowed users access to the source code to modify the software through scripting in order to create different levels of game play, which could then be uploaded and made available to other players. *Counter Strike (1999, Minh Le)* is the first example of a commercially successful entire game modification created in the original game environment of *Half Life (1998,*

Valve Software). 'With a published version of *CounterStrike* now available for purchase, things have gone full circle - audience members are now part of the next phase of production'. (http://zero. newassignment.net/filed/interview_michela_ledwidge_modfilms). A new genre of film modification has attempted to adapt these practices into the processes of film production. Examples of video based modification are evident within the You Tube community, where video is segmented, remixed and 'mashed-up'.

The artist Olivier Laric has released a modified version of Mariah Carey's promotional music video for her single *Touch My Body* (2008, http:// oliverlaric.com/touchmybody.htm). In this version Laric has replaced all visual content apart from the figure of Mariah, with green screen. This allows any user to replace the background content with alternative images using keying technologies available in most non-linear digital video editing packages. Users can then upload their own personal versions to *You Tube*.

A recent example of a 'remixable' or 'modifiable' film is *Sanctuary* (Dir: Michaela Lewidge, 2008). Currently in postproduction it is the first film of its kind, and will be released both as a theatrical feature, and in a remixable form. The remixable release will be available online through *Creative Commons* and will involve all the films assets being available to the viewing public to download, modify and remix.

Re-mixable films are films designed to permit explicit sampling of film assets. A film MOD (or modification) is like a game MOD, a modified version which you can experience as a bolt on (or replacement) to the original experience (http:// www.modfilms.com)

Within the example of *Sanctuary*, the CG character *Customisable Dude (CD)* can be manipulated and controlled, as can environments in which exchanges between characters take place (made possible by the fact that a majority of the scenes were shot against blue screen) These affects can take place on an individual user level, and can then take place collaboratively online to create a collective experience.

The principles of game and film modification can be applied to the OER trajectory in relation to the *i-mpact* resource. Looking towards future possibilities; in principle it is feasible that the postproduction of a short film can be undertaken in this collaborative way – with members of the student group editing, modifying and applying effects to the same piece of work. Currently, the limitations to bandwidth restrict the use of the network in this way, but this is the proposed next step, within the not so distant future within which bandwidth will be unlimited.

8 CONCLUSION

It would indeed be quicker to 'tell the students what they need to know' in a formal classroom lecture setting. Such a minimalist approach if applied to the online setting becomes about putting lecture notes on the web. (Bach, Haynes and Smith, 2007:58).

It is apparent from both wider discussions regarding current socio-technological behaviour within the student demographic and institutional use of VLEs in general to the more specific example of the *i-mpact* case study, that there is a need to move beyond the minimalist approach within contemporary learning spaces of undergraduate study. As revealed within my own observations and also noted by authors investigating these environments 'Effective learning needs to be collaborative and interactive' (Palloff and Pratt 1999; Bernard et al. 2000).

One would assume that adopting both collaborative and interactive modalities within the arts and media practice-based subject areas would be intuitively obvious since these approaches are clearly well suited to the arenas of problem and work-based learning. However, it is clear that such interventions, which involve instigating OER repositories across institutions has been and may well be met with resistance.

The next stage of the project is to encourage cross-institutional support of the repository in order to broaden its scope and possibilities – currently only internally generated materials from teaching and learning exercises to the one described herein and from student assignment work are available within the resource. It would be an achievement to be able to expand and diversify the resource through collaboration with media departments from other institutions.

The *i-mpact* resource and similar projects promote the need to embrace emergent technologies and their cultural use and encourage a move towards institutional digital repositories. Such endeavours ultimately aim for the utopian ideal of global learning materials and of educational internationalisation. Although an ideological concept, the educational benefits and opportunities offered by OER are invaluable and not just in the teaching of DVE but in other disciplines within the wider media field and within all arts-based subjects.

The Internet and related technologies have demolished traditional institutional boundaries to expertise and knowledge...the Internet gives everyone who seeks information access to resources once held within the ivory tower (Rudestam and Schoenholtz-Read, 2002, p.4).

A significant paradigmatic shift is now required within the HE sector; from one of prohibitive intellectual property rights and materials ownership resistance to one of open access, sharing, and modification, if we are respond to the individualistic learning styles, behaviours and expectations of a contemporary student demographic.

REFERENCES

E4. (2009). *Skins mash-up*. Retrieved from http://www.e4.com/skins/doitandwin/2641f7098510648 3801215a7f901a42d/entry-terms.e4

Avid Learning Excellerator. (n.d.). *Alex*. Retrieved from http://learn.avid.com/alex/lms/

Bach, S., Haynes, P., & Smith, L. J. (2007). *Online learning and teaching in higher education*. New York, NY: Open University Press.

Bonk, C. J., Kirkley, J., Hara, N., & Dennen, V. (2007). Finding the instructor in post-secondary online learning: Pedagogical, social, managerial and technological locations. In J> Stephenson (Ed.), *Teaching & learning online: Pedagogies for new technologies*. London, UK: Kogan Page.

Cape Town Open Education Declaration. (2010). *Unlocking the promise of open educational resources*. Retrieved from http://www.capetown-declaration.org/read-the-declaration

Collis, B. (1998). New didactics for university instruction: Why and how? *Computers & Education, 31*, 373–393. doi:10.1016/S0360-1315(98)00040-2

Cover, R. (2006). Audience inter/active: Interactive media, narrative control and reconceiving audience history. *New Media & Society, 8*(1), 139–158. doi:10.1177/1461444806059922

Jorum. (n.d.). Retrieved from http://www.jorum.ac.uk/

Juwah, C. (Ed.). (2006). *Interactions in online education: Implications for theory and practice*. London, UK: Routledge.

Kuleshov, L. (1974). *Kuleshov on film: Writings by Lev Kuleshov*. Berkeley, CA: University of California Press.

Macdonald, J. (2006). *Blended learning and online tutoring: A good practice guide*. Aldershot, UK: Gower.

Mason, R., & Rennie, F. (2008). *E-learning and social networking handbook: Resources for higher education*. London, UK: Routledge.

McPherson, M., & Baptista Nunes, M. (2004). *Developing innovation in online learning*. London, UK: Routledge. doi:10.4324/9780203426715

MIT. (n.d.). *Open courseware system*. Retrieved from http://ocw.mit.edu/index.html

Palloff, R. M., & Pratt, K. (1999). *Building learning communities in cyberspace: Effective strategies for the online classroom*. San Francisco, CA: Jossey-Bass Publishers.

Reynolds, J., Caley, L., & Mason, R. (Eds.). (2002). *How do people learn?* London, UK: CIPD.

Rose, F. (2006, December). Commercial Break. *Wired, 14*(12). Retrieved from http://www.wired.com/wired/archive/14.12/tahoe.html

Rudestam, K. E., & Schoenholtz-Read, J. (2002). *Handbook of online learning: Innovations in higher education and corporate training*. London, UK: Sage.

Telegraph. (2009, Nov 25). Online education grows apace. *Telegraph*. Retrieved November 28, 2009, from http://www.telegraph.co.uk/education/expateducation/6588855/Online-education-grows-apace.html

University of Southampton. (n.d.). *Edshare*. Retrieved from http://www.edshare.soton.ac.uk/

Weller, M. (2007). *Virtual learning environments: Using, choosing and developing your VLE*. London, UK: Routledge.

ENDNOTES

[1] http://zero.newassignment.net/filed/interview_matt_hanson_director_crowd_funded_open_s

[2] TiVo is one of a number of personal video recording systems (PVR), similar to Sky Plus in the UK

[3] so called because when films and programmes were shot on film – the runners would literally 'rush' with the cans of film to get them processed and screened to the director the end of each day

[4] These are notes taken by the script supervisor on the location of the shoot, detailing the shot and take numbers and notes relating to their position within the script and the contents and quality of each shot

Chapter 8
In the Current or Swimming Upstream?
Instructors' Perceptions of Teaching with Streaming Media in Higher Education

Billy Osteen
University of Canterbury, New Zealand

Arin Basu
University of Canterbury, New Zealand

Mary Allan
University of Canterbury, New Zealand

ABSTRACT

In the not too distant future, university students will have trouble recalling a pre-You Tube or pre-podcast world. While streaming media in those formats has become ubiquitous in many areas of their lives through ease of use and dissemination, how does it factor into their learning? Should instructors in higher education utilize students' engagement with streaming media as teachable opportunities? Or, in lieu of instructors intentionally choosing to use streaming media, what about the potential for it to be imposed on them for logistical or operational reasons and the effects of that on student learning and teaching? Building upon prior work that has been done on the use of streaming media in higher education (Chang, 2007; Phillips et al., 2007; Shepherd, 2003; Foertsch et al., 2002; Brahler et al., 1999), this chapter will examine it from several instructors' perspectives with a focus on their decision-making processes, implementations, challenges, and opportunities. From their experiences, a set of grounded guidelines for using streaming media in higher education will be developed and offered as starting points for others interested in trying this in their teaching.

DOI: 10.4018/978-1-60960-800-2.ch008

INTRODUCTION

In the not too distant future, many university students will have trouble recalling life before on-demand where most of one's needs were not individually delivered in the form and at the time desired. The spread of customer as delivery point has penetrated most aspects of the developed world such that many intellectual products are either portable or readily retrievable. Through searchable databases, pay-per-view films, podcasts, and You-Tube, physical attendance is no longer required in order to enjoy the content of a particular sporting event, religious service, or music concert. This type of delivery, streaming media, is defined by continuously present and transmitted text, image, data, voice, sound bytes, and video using a telecommunications network. While streaming media has become ubiquitous in many areas of life through ease of use and dissemination, how does it factor into the field of higher education? Should instructors in higher education utilize students' engagement with streaming media as teachable opportunities? Or, in lieu of instructors intentionally choosing to use streaming media, what about the potential for it to be imposed on them for logistical or operational reasons (e.g., an instructor who is required to teach two concurrent sessions with one face-to-face (FTF) and the other by video due to classroom size or scheduling constraints) and the effects of that on student learning and teaching?

The short answer to the first question above is that online learning, with streaming media being a possible method of its delivery, is increasingly becoming an economically powerful factor in higher education. The University of Phoenix's distinction of having the largest student enrollment of any higher education institution in the world suggests that online learning, and its related delivery methods, has been accepted by many as a legitimate and desirable way to engage in learning. The answers to the latter questions are a bit more difficult to definitively establish.

As the following review of literature about streaming media in higher education demonstrates, the research in this area appears to have been focused on how to teach with streaming media and less intent on exploring the ways in which instructors have come to use it and their beliefs about its effectiveness on supporting student learning. Within the research there are valuable tips and pointers as in the work by Brahler et al. (1999), but given the changing nature of technology, perhaps a less detailed view of using streaming media is more applicable over time. In order to evaluate the established suggestions about teaching with streaming media from the perspectives of instructors, three case studies will be presented and analyzed following the literature review.

REVIEW OF RELEVANT LITERATURE ABOUT STREAMING MEDIA IN HIGHER EDUCATION

In many instances, higher education instructors have quickly responded to new paradigms of training and information presentation for their teaching activities. As a result, large volumes of data are now streamed in educational contexts. In streaming, large amounts of textual, auditory, and visual data, often in conjunction and simultaneously, are distributed and sent in the form of packets that are then assembled in the client computer and can be either assembled and downloaded, or allowed to "stream" and reload on demand. The availability of high speed networks, new methods of data transfer that allow small quantities of data packaged in tandem, and the compression of data has opened up a new dimension of higher education. The purpose of this chapter is to first provide a brief description of the defining characteristics of streaming media, illustrate the rationale for its deployment and usage in higher education, outline the key limitations, and lay out a roadmap of its usage. Further, we shall present three case studies to show how these technologies have already been used in higher education.

Many higher education instructors have historically used media in their teaching. The use of computer graphics, animations, texts, and presentation software has been widely deployed throughout the world in higher education. In a limited sense, the streaming of information through television and radio signals to transmit educational content to distance education students has been in use since the early 1920's.

While these modalities of media transmission have been and continue to be widely used, they are also somewhat fragmented and contextually bound, and therefore what was possible through the print medium was not to be expected of a medium such as the moving images on television or primarily audio input based media applications in education such as CD's, radios, and other formats of audio files. Within the first decade of the 2000's, the availability of high speed networks, increased bandwidth, and the advancement of compression technologies (such as lossless compression and advancement in communication technology) has enabled a powerful convergence of textual, auditory, and visual data.

Learning Theories Related to Using Streaming Media

From a theoretical perspective, what role does streaming media play in higher education? We discuss this with regard to two related theoretical constructs on social communications – Social Presence Theory and Media Richness Theory - in the context of higher education. Social Presence Theory will be described first as it can be seen as a foundation for the implementation of Media Richness Theory. Essentially, Social Presence Theory (Short et al., 1976) is the belief that the social presence of others around a learner has an important influence on her or his learning. Therefore, media transmitted in a manner that allows both interactivity and a sense of others' presence

can influence learning, presumably in a positive manner. In a review of the role of social presence in fostering social learning in technology-enhanced environments, Tu (2000) found that the notion of social presence was essentially subjective and open to the learner's interpretation and was therefore inherently dynamic (Tu, 2000). This dynamic sense of social presence was dependent on three key components: social context, online communication, and interactivity. Tu concluded that, "whether one examines computer mediated communication as a learning environment … social presence must be examined."

Tu's findings and Social Presence Theory appear to be related to Biggs and Tang's (2007) suggestions about teaching and learning in higher education. In their constructivist model of education, teaching should be aligned with learning so that a learner constructs his or her own meaning through lived experience and in collaboration with others. For this to occur, the instructor and the learner form part of a social rubric where learning is defined by the social transactions that involve a sharing of skills and knowledge among the instructor, the individual learner, and fellow learners (Biggs & Tang, 2007). In addition, because situated context is important in the constructivist model, streaming media can add to that context because what is being experienced within it is not a physical, FTF context but is closer to it than other data transmission opportunities.

It may be argued that while the physical presence of the instructor and co-learners facilitates learning, it is not necessarily a requirement. However, any other social transaction process that facilitates the construction of meaning from lived experiences and allows for collaboration might foster constructivist learning, and therefore can be seen as meeting Biggs and Tang's idea of effective higher education teaching. Thus, the definition of social presence can be interpreted to mean that the consciousness of another person in an interaction and the "salience of an interpersonal relationship" is integral to teaching and learning

(Tu, 2000). It flows from social presence, then, that for media to create the social presence and foster communication, it needs to go beyond the mere presentation of data or, at the least, enable some interactivity between the learner and the media. Such media would have to be rich as opposed to the lean nature of text-based media applications (e.g., emails, documents, or static images).

Media Richness Theory (also known as Information Richness Theory) proposes that media differ in the ability to facilitate changes in understanding among communicators, and suggests that FTF is the gold standard of communication (Nardi & Whittaker, 2002; Wainfan L. & Davis P.K., 2004). Prevalent perceptions about FTF interactions suggest that they provide the richest and most effective medium for communication, providing verbal and non-verbal cues (Billinghurst & Kato, 1999; Daft & Lengel, 1986; Daft & Wiginton, 1979), while at the same time creating a sense of "being there" in each other's presence, or sharing a space (Goffman, 1963; Heeter, 1992; Schroeder, 2006).

The features described here highlight the social processes and the non-verbal exchange of information involved in communication between people in FTF communication:

1. Synchronous temporal turn taking interactions that enables the smooth alternation of speaker and listener who are co-present (Bosch, Oostdijk, & Ruiter, 2004),
2. Multidimensional information afforded by Mehrabian's "3 Vs" (Verbal, Vocal and Visual) (1971),
3. A sense of being with another or what Heeter (1992) refers to as presence and co-presence (Goffman, 1963; Schroeder, 2006).

These features are used by Media Richness Theory to rate different media according to the richness of information that they transmit (A.R. Dennis & J.S. Valacich, 1999). Daft & Lengel (1986), in classifying communication media ac-cording to the richness of information they can provide, rank FTF as the richest medium, seconded in decreasing richness by telephone; personal documents such as letters or memos; impersonal written documents, and numeric documents. The measurement of richness illustrates a medium's capacity for immediate feedback or synchronicity and the number of social cues and channels transmitted. High levels of richness equate to an improved sense of shared space, which is the crux of any communication activity.

Building on prior work by Baltes, Dickson, Sherman, Bauer, & LaGanke, (2002, p.159), and Wainfan and Davis (2004, p.5) describing relationships between degrees of synchronisation and levels of non-verbal cues across various media, Figure 1 shows the relations between levels of non-verbal cues and synchronisation and their creation of a sense of shared space.

The correlation between media richness and the levels of shared space can be explained using Social Presence Theory, which indicates the degree that communicants perceive the presence of each other (Biocca, Harms, & Burgoon, 2003; Goffman, 1963; Short, Williams, & B., 1976). We suggest that the more social cues that are transmitted and the more synchronicity that is present, then there will be more opportunity for people to perceive each other's presence and to experience a feeling of participating in a shared space of communication. Furthermore, the higher the levels of richness and creation of a sense of space, then the closer that mediated communication will resemble FTF (Allan & Thorns, 2009). Richer media, then, has the potential for the facilitation of: social perceptions, total socio-emotional communication, a positive socio-emotional climate, and the perceived ability to evaluate others' deception and expertise (A. R. Dennis & J. S. Valacich, 1999). Dennis and Valacich identified five media characteristics that can potentially affect communication in those ways. These include: immediacy of feedback, symbol variety, parallelism, rehearsability, and reprocessibility.

Figure 1. Media richness theory and sense of shared space

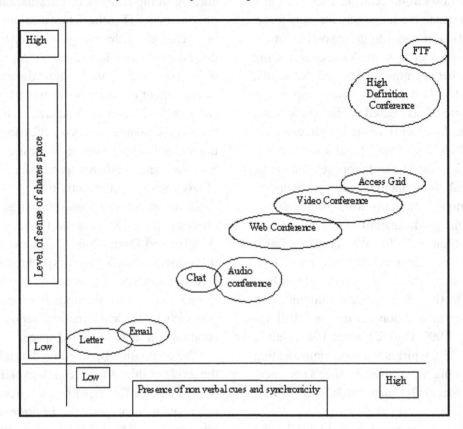

Immediacy of feedback indicates the extent to which the media allows users to provide feedback and is a measure of interactivity of the media with the viewer. In the context of streaming media in higher education, such immediacy may be achieved by the ability of the student to interact with fellow students and the instructor in real time, where a highly rich media tool such as videoconferencing or asynchronous interactivity is available.

Symbol variety of media refers to the number of communication channels it can provide. The two key assumptions that make the concept of symbol variety an essential characteristic of rich media are that, first, some types of information are easier to convey than other types depending on the format. Second, verbal and non-verbal symbols in media enable instructors to include

information beyond the words themselves when the message is transmitted. This plays itself out for some with the belief that human voice has an intrinsic power to explain complex topics. Carrying this notion further, when verbal and non-verbal symbols are removed, the corresponding loss of social presence that binds instructors and students makes their interactions more distanced and less immediate or personal.

Parallelism refers to the number of simultaneous conversations that are possible in the context of streaming media whereby the higher the parallelism, the richer the media. Rehearsability is essentially the extent to which the media allows the sender to modify or alter the messages before or during sending. And, reprocessibility is the extent to which the message in the media can be processed and reviewed by the receiver and sender such as in captured online chats or blogs.

In higher education, several features of Social Presence Theory and Media Richness Theory are applicable. From a social learning and social presence perspective, immediacy of feedback, symbol variety, and reprocessibility of the media are key to Biggs and Tang's constructivist teaching and learning model. Streaming media enables the clustering of a variety of information cues together, such that voice, data, video, and still pictures can all be located in one medium and transmitted. Also, since streaming allows the student to engage at the point of reception anytime, it facilitates reprocessing of information. Table 1 illustrates this through the applicability of Social Presence Theory and Media Richness Theory to using streaming media.

Perceived Benefits of Streaming Media

The degree to which specific media convey a heightened sense of immediate and personal reality would seem to enable them to lead to more effective or satisfying student experiences. This is especially true in higher education where instructors need to transmit complex concepts and skills to students. In a review of 409 distance education courses in the U.S., Adams et al. (2006) found that text-based and lean media such as emails were most frequently used, followed by video/broadcast media. They did not find that an e-mail driven community was an interactive mode of communication (Adams, 2006). Their conclusion suggests that the richness of media and use of simultaneous sensory cues in these courses was important in fostering a sense of community and active learning.

Similarly, in discussing the effectiveness of podcasts, Campbell (2005) has argued in favor of a set of key indicators of perceived benefits of streaming media in higher education. These include flexibility, context-insensitivity, ease of access, radio like ubiquity, power of the human voice, and the digital natives' effect (Campbell, 2005). The characteristics of flexibility and freedom from context are particularly applicable in the higher education setting where increasing numbers of students are enrolling as part-time, commuter, or distance students. Therefore, learning materials delivered to students on-demand (the "pull" factor) in a variety of rich formats (text, audio, video) provides an anytime and anywhere capability. The context freedom essentially indicates that a student can access all the audio and video components of the lectures, even at the workplace or at the convenience of home while attending to multiple tasks at the same time.

How streaming media has forced a rethink of the role of radio and the position of voice in teaching and learning warrants examination. Streaming media generally refers to continuously present and transmitted text, image, data, voice, sound bytes, and video using a telecommunications network. It may therefore be argued that radio and televi-

Table 1. Learning theories to support using streaming media in higher education

Learning Theory Applicable to Streaming Media	
Social Presence Theory (SPT)	SPT essentially posits that effectiveness of communication is dependent on the level of social presence. According to this theory, face-to-face interaction has the highest social presence and the further people get away from each other, the effectiveness of the interaction decreases.
Media Richness Theory (MRT)	MRT suggests that task performance will be improved when task needs are matched to a medium's richness. Media capable of sending rich information (such as media that streams simultaneous text, visual, and auditory feeds) are better suited to equivocal tasks or tasks that require multiple interpretations for available information compared to those that do not.

sion based educational content dissemination is, in essence, streaming media. Indeed, stream servers or podcasting servers are often referred to as internet radio stations. Podcasting is a form of digital media streaming (audio or video encoded files) where the receiver of the streamed media is a device that is connected to the internet receiving packets of audio or video data. The source media might be transmitted live or pre-recorded. The revision of the roles of internet radios may essentially be viewed as a resurgence of radios for the one-way transmission of educational materials – a practice that was highly popular among the distance educators in the early days of organizing distance education (Adams, 2006).

Streaming media enables an instructor to transmit a live or pre-recorded lecture to students. This allows students to perform multiple tasks at the same time as listening to a podcast. Moreover, the importance of streaming audio is rooted in audio signals being instrumental in fostering learning. Campbell (2005) has argued in favor of the power of voice as a medium that assures, provides meaning, and creates shared awareness. Through streaming media, instructors can tell stories, convey emotions, and provide real life examples that learners can use to create personal meaning – all of which are thought to foster learning (Campbell, 2005; Chan, Lee, & McLoughlin, 2006; Shephard, 2003).

One of the key advantages of streaming media that cannot be matched by any other form of media delivery of educational materials is the ability to track student activities and then tailor lesson components accordingly in order to personalize learning. Since streaming media uses a server to provide streaming videos for instruction or communication, logs of media server usage are generated when a learner plays, pauses, stops, forwards, or rewinds a clip of a teaching video. A record of media server logs can indicate for example, the file name of the streaming video that was accessed, the IP address of the computer that has accessed that streaming video, the time

and date that the streaming video was accessed and so on. From an instructor's perspective, this enables an instructor to review her or his teaching strategy and provision of materials and then make adjustments to better meet students' needs (S. Chang, 2007; Feeney, Reynolds, Eaton, & Harper, 2008).

Thus, while it appears that streaming media using rich media could be an effective method of teaching and learning, Adams et al.'s study suggests that actual adoption is considerably low, even within distance education courses. This raises the question of why streaming media using rich media is not used more in higher education, despite the perceived benefits summarized in Table 2.

Potential Limitations to Using Streaming Media

According to Adams et al., a possible driver of not using streaming media might be instructors' unfamiliarity and a reluctance in undertaking the perceived steep learning curve amidst demanding job duties. In addition to maintaining their content expertise, the instructor would be thrust into the new role of producing a rich media experience (Adams et al., 2006) to an increasingly discerning audience. In a review on the use of social networking software in higher education, Belderrain (2006) found that in addition to the considerations of cost and time involved in preparing and delivering the materials, there might be questions around potential conflicts of interests between what the university administration perceives as loss of control over students and the academic freedom that new media provides (Beldarrain, 2006). He also mentioned challenges around maturity of technology. Although this chapter was in the context of adopting social networking on university campuses, the ideas are applicable to making decisions about using streaming media as well, where similar situations around the accessibility of high-end technology, bandwidth, technical support

Table 2. Perceived benefits of using streaming media in higher education

Perceived Benefit	Description
Student engagement	Compelling student interaction and immediacy because of multiple media integration (Adams, 2006)
Flexibility	Enables anytime, anywhere education with internet connectivity, and flexibility of multitasking where a student can do a number of things while listening to or accessing podcasts or streaming media, ability to listen to other lectures of interest but not have to enroll for the full course, "frees eyes and hands" (Campbell, 2005; Chan, et al., 2006) (Chang, 2007)
Human voice	This is applicable not necessarily to streaming media in particular, but streaming media being associated with the power of human voice which in turn emphasizes a shared awareness where this shared space is between the learner and the Instructor, as well as there is a power in human voice that can explain phenomena and reinforces deep learning (Campbell, 2005; Chan, et al., 2006)
Builds community	This is in accordance with theories of constructivist learning (Biggs & Tang, 2007). Frequently, based around the streamed media
Ability to track	Media streaming can track access of students to the media at the packet level giving the instructor a fine grain control of which segments were viewed or repeated over and over again. This enables future control of tailoring lessons and so on (Chang, 2004)
Cost efficient	Lecture recordings and streaming them over the web is cost efficient way to produce great content (Morisse & Ramm, 2007); a consistent standardized learning at a lower cost (Feeney, et al., 2008)
Equity of access	Streaming media offers opportunities for equitable access to high quality media, including lectures. This allows students who are not able to attend lectures in person to experience the lectures offered in the class using technology and even download the lecture. The equity of access is an important consideration for university administrators.

and guidance, and learning context sensitivity for students are all key factors.

Others believe that adoption of streaming media might lead to a decrease in student attendance of classes. Morisse and Ramm (2007) reported their experiences of teaching computer science via podcasting where they created digital lectures and podcasted, which served as supplements for the FTF lectures. Initially, they used streaming media by using capture software of live lectures and then moved to using podcasting. They claimed that this led to a reorientation of the instructor's role to more like a guide or a coach in helping teach the core concepts. While the podcasts allowed students to navigate precisely to specific contents anytime and anywhere, there was a noticeable drop in student attendance at FTF lectures (Morisse & Ramm, 2007).

In another study on instructors' perceptions about the use and adoption of a lecture capture technology, Lectopia, in Australian universities, Chang (2007) also commented on the belief that media supplements or substitutes to lectures would

lead to decreased student attendance. Along with that concern by instructors, she found that there were others including: technological challenges (e.g., loss of bandwidth, immaturity of technology, and asymmetry of the technology at different locations where the streamed media was received) and the recognition that not all lecture styles are conducive to being captured and streamed.

While another study (Phillips et al., 2007) that collected the perceptions of both students and instructors about web-based lecture technologies (WBLT) also found that there was a shared concern about streaming media replacing physical attendance of lectures, there were some positive possibilities mentioned. These included the opportunity to review online delivery and align it with a variety of learning styles: "It allows students to review and add to their lecture notes points that they may have missed. It allows auditory learners to revise in a suitable way." This was expanded upon in the instructors' responses to a survey about the role of WBLT in assisting them to accomplish various goals of their physical lectures. The three highest ranking responses to the prompt, "WBLT has enhanced my ability to" were: impart a lot of information related to the subject (47.5%), make announcements to keep students up to date with events and course administration (46.8%), and provide a structured experience of the unit content (43.3%) (respondents could choose more than one answer). Thus, it appears that instructors in this study mainly saw WBLT as supporting the content aspect of the course in a "push" manner. Not surprisingly, the lowest ranking responses to the same statement above were: gauge students' understandings and then respond accordingly on the fly (12.8%), provide a routine for my students (15.6%), and provide group feedback to students (20.6%).

When considering using streaming media, it appears that instructors might acknowledge the perceived benefits but also may not see those as being worth the effort in advancing through the potential limitations as summarized in Table 3.

Characteristics of Using Streaming Media

The important question is, given all its pros and cons, are there certain defining characteristics of streaming media that we should focus on while considering its usage in higher education? The streaming process is essentially about sending small packets of information over a network. The client side software on the computer receives the media stream from the server side, stores it for the time being and then starts playing it while potentially receiving more information (Hartsell & Yuen, 2006).

This definition of streaming makes it clear that fixed media in any stored but not forwarded format are non-streaming media, irrespective of their digital status. Thus, books, journals, and CD's are not considered as streaming media. From the higher education instructors' perspectives, there are three forms of streaming media: text streaming, audio streaming, and video streaming. All these streams of information can be transmitted individually, or combined with each other. Some examples of text streaming include information transmitted through Twitter, really simple syndication (RSS) feeds, wikis (editable web pages), and blogs.

Audio streaming is probably the oldest technology in streaming applied to education so far. The use of radio started in 1923 and continues today through Internet radios, regular educational channels, and podcasts. Video streaming started with the use of television to promote educational materials in the 1950's and gradually picked up to promote interactive educational television shows where students had to be physically present in specific locations to view those shows, and now we are up to the stage of video podcasts. Podcasts fulfill the definition of streaming media because they are video/audio bytes that are transmitted over a network to the student's computer or a compatible device (e.g., mp3 player or iPod but neither is necessary for catching podcasting). The

Table 3. Potential limitations to using streaming media in higher education

Potential Limitation	Description
Steep learning curve	Non-familiarity of the instructor (Campbell, 2005; Adams, 2006)
Communication infrastructure	Dependent on robust networks, broadband packet loss, bandwidth issues (Beldarrain, 2006; Chang, 2007)
Low attendance	This has been cited by several authors (Chang, 2007; Morisse & Ramm, 2007) as restricting or limiting factors why faculty may not be willing to adopt media streaming since it gives the students a sense of deja vu. But then there have been proponents of media streaming for instance (Maag, 2006) who state that media streaming with active student participation in it is the very reason of increased student attendance in their programs.

student in this instance has the ability to review the content of the podcast over and over again, which is the characteristic of repeatability. Interestingly, Shephard (2003) in a review of streaming media in higher education, argued that one of the defining characteristics of streaming media is the ability of the students to "pull" information on demand. His other defining features were that media do not need to be downloaded and would start to play as soon as required. With broadband speed and increased memory space available, the image quality and viewing experiences have improved qualitatively (Shephard, 2003).

Bennet and Maniar (2008) argue that the ability to reprocess information at the student end, which is perceived as a benefit as an integral and desirable property of streaming, might send wrong messages when applied to classroom instructions. They claimed that using streamed media for lectures might even be detrimental to learning in falsely making the student believe that audio and lectures are the only means of knowledge acquisition. However, that would only be applicable if the instructor had led students to believe that that was the case through her or his course design.

The common thread among the characteristics of using streaming media in higher education described above and summarized in Table 4 is that they all focus on the student side of the teaching and learning experience.

Designing effective teaching and learning activities requires a considered choreography of a number of factors previously mentioned including: institutional context, disciplinary context, personal learning theories, benefits to students, potential limitations, and, ultimately, the implementation of a selection of characteristics or components. Once an activity has been designed and experienced by the students and instructor, some type of evidence is usually available in the form of student performance, feedback, evaluations and can be used to revise each part of the design process.

The above design and revision process is no different when using streaming media in teaching and learning and is represented in Figure 2 with the Analytical Framework for Considering the Use of Streaming Media in Higher Education. It is important to note several details in this figure with regard to the "fixed" or "flexible" boundaries in the design process. As illustrated with the solid,

Table 4. Defining characteristics of using streaming media in higher education

Defining Characteristic	Explanation
Integration	Include multiple entities in the same document (Adams, 2006)
Ubiquity	Can be accessed in multiple formats and minimum dependency (Beldarrain, 2006)
Flexibility	The student can be flexible in receiving the media anywhere anytime as long as connected to a network, and small packet based data transfer provide this element
Continuity	Streamed media unlike other forms of media has to flow into the device of the client or student in a continuous flow; it can be, but need not be stored for later access as long as the student can connect to the network
Repeatability	The ability of a student to repeat the streaming of the media.
Network	Presence of a network is a requirement as by definition video streaming indicates sending of packets of data in batches to a client computer over a network through cables and wireless systems. Because the data are being sent over a network, this supports the always on feature and the distinctive feature of streamed media to be available on demand by the student (Hartsell & Yuen, 2006)
Syndication	The media need to be pulled in by the learner. Occasionally, the media can be "pushed" by the instructor as well, thus confirming the concepts of both pushing and pulling of resources either on demand or by design over a specific period of time across a network.

or fixed, lines, many instructors have established views about their learning theories. These views have been honed and firmed up through their significant experiences as both students and instructors and it is often hard to move out of those perspectives. Save for the evidence of effectiveness that instructors rely on, everything else in the process is fairly fluid in that feedback one way or the other can influence and lead to changes in the instructional design as demonstrated in Figure 2.

This overall Analytical Framework will be used as a lens through which to view and compare the three instructors' case studies of using streaming media in higher education and provide readers with different contexts, instructional purposes, and perceived benefits. It is a unique combination of the literature about the major components of streaming media and can serve as guidance for other higher education instructors considering using it.

FINDINGS: THREE HIGHER EDUCATION INSTRUCTORS' PERCEPTIONS ON USING STREAMING MEDIA

In New Zealand, higher education consists of 19 polytechnic institutes, which are similar to U.S. community colleges in that they grant 2 year degrees and don't offer bachelor's, master's, or doctorate degrees, and 7 public, comprehensive universities. Admission and enrollment to the polytechs is open while for the universities it is

Figure 2. Analytical framework for considering the use of streaming media in higher education

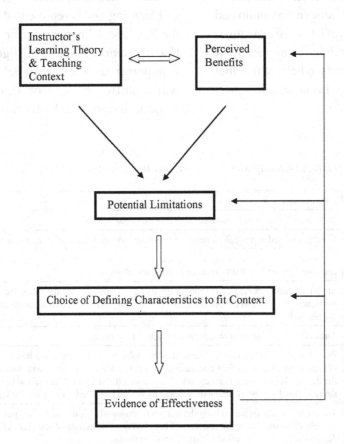

merit-based for students aged 20 and under and then open after that. Except for Massey University, most courses at the other polytechs and universities are primarily offered in FTF formats. Thus, outside of Massey, the concept of distance education is not a significant part of higher education for instructors and students in New Zealand.

That having been said, the potential for both full distance education or a blend of it with FTF is in place due to an increasing adoption of technology to enhance the delivery of courses in the form of Learning Management Systems (e.g., Blackboard, Moodle, and WebCT), a high speed network (the Kiwi Advanced Research and Education Network or KAREN) to allow for the use of interactive communication technologies like the Access Grid, and a governmental priority to improve internet access across the country. So, even though most higher education instructors in New Zealand do not solely rely on streaming media for their teaching, they are, at the least, aware of it as a growing option.

As this situation of a preponderance of FTF teaching amidst infrastructure changes that are enabling more usage of streaming media is similar to many other higher education institutions in Australia, Canada, U.K., and U.S, a closer examination of how three instructors at a particular university in New Zealand can be instructive, in general terms, as to what others in those countries might consider. To collect these instructors' perceptions about using streaming media, they participated in conversations and shared their stories. Their stories were then analyzed using the conceptual framework matrix described above to look for cross-case commonalities and discrepancies. From these comparisons, a collection of questions and considerations for using streaming media in higher education is offered with the caveat that further research, perhaps in the form of a widely administered quantitative instrument, would be helpful in confirming and revising the list.

Context of the Instructors

All three instructors who shared their stories of using streaming media hold tenured academic positions at a comprehensive university of 15,000 students that offers undergraduate, master's, and doctorate degrees in a range of fields. Most courses are delivered in a FTF format in lecture theaters, seminar rooms, laboratories, and field stations. The main user of distance technology is the College of Education, which utilizes several regional centers on both the South and North Islands as hubs through which courses are taught in a blend of online and hub-based interactions. Aside from that, the main use of technology on this campus is through Moodle with a large percentage of instructors maintaining at least a minimal course page. In addition to Moodle, many instructors across disciplines use PowerPoint as a teaching tool in their lectures.

This university would be categorized as a Research I institution in the U.S. Carnegie system with instructors required to maintain an active research agenda alongside their teaching and administrative responsibilities. To further highlight the role of research at higher education institutions in New Zealand, a nationally administered and competitive program, the Performance Based Research Fund (PBRF), was established in 2004. Through PBRF, individual instructors are evaluated and graded for their research productivity and their institutions are summarily rewarded with corresponding funding. In the previous funding round in 2006, this particular university was a close third in PBRF funding. Thus, as with U.S. institutions, research activity is more explicitly rewarded than teaching and thereby garners much attention by instructors and administrators.

Instructor A

"What's the best way of providing not just presentational material, but practice situations and opportunities for interaction that suit a whole raft of different kinds of students?"

Instructor A, who is not originally from New Zealand and received his degrees in Canada and New Zealand, is a well-established instructor and researcher in the field of linguistics with over 30 years of experience. He has created a successful balance of research and teaching as evidenced by his many publications and projects and receipt of the University's Teaching Medal, the highest honor provided for teaching. In addition to his reputation through his accomplishments, he is regularly sought out for his insightful thoughts and ideas about academia.

Despite being at the top of his field, he does not rest on his laurels and is always seeking ways to improve his teaching and research. It is no surprise that he would be an early adopter of new technologies in the classroom. So, his development of a specific usage for streaming media in the teaching of linguistics was both innovative and expected. He stated that his motivation for this innovation was based on the belief that every student learns differently: "For a student to learn flexibly is essentially saying that not every student learns the same way … you've got to try and see your way clear to thinking, what's the best way of providing not just presentational material, but practice situations and opportunities for interaction that suit a whole raft of different kinds of students."

To provide flexible learning for "a whole raft of different kinds of students," this instructor collaborated with colleagues in instructional technology to create a website that contained three main components: 1) recordings of what occurred in class, 2) podcasts and short videos of mini-lectures on specific topics, and 3) interactive quizzes to provide instant feedback. For him, the key to this course website was to allow students to access any of the above components anytime and anywhere. While recording the class lectures involves capturing what he'd be doing anyway, the mini-lectures and the interactive quizzes take considerably more time and effort to create. He

stated that his motivation for putting in the extra work on both centers around engaging and empowering the students with:

The mini-movies are 10-15 minutes long and the MP3s are around 3-4 minutes. They're all extension topics just to get people interested. [online] quizzes provide on-line tutorials for students. These give instant feedback on student understanding of terminology, concepts and capacity in the required analytic techniques.

He further noted that the online tutorials were particularly helpful in providing students in a large class with personalized opportunities to practice their analytical skills. "The first year course has got 180 people and obviously you can't go and talk to all of them, so you imaginatively have to put yourself in the position of asking how your material can be presented in a way that allows everyone the best access to learning. Part of that is presentational, but students also have to practice analytical skills."

As evidence that this approach is effective for students in his classes, he points to their performance: "Linguistics 101 has previously had a bimodal distribution with a strong peak at the top of the mark distribution and a somewhat smaller one in the fail range suggesting, rightly, that it is a mastery type course. Those who get it do well; those who don't, don't." However in 2004, the year he introduced the course website, "the distribution was trimodal with the same peaks as normal but with a further peak in the B range suggesting that the on-line resources may have pulled some of the students who would previously have failed into a respectable pass."

Additionally, he suggested that the presence of these materials online was the primary reason for the highest course evaluations he has ever received (4.8 out of 5 and 4.9 our of 5) with: "Educationally, the benefits are relatively easy to enumerate. Students appear more involved and motivated by having the extra resources available to them. The increase in these scores seems to have had more to do with the WebCT resources than any major changes in the lectures or course content." His use of streaming media is summarized in Figure 3.

Instructor B

"Because the course material was online, I was able to ensure better currency of content … plus the online material was available for campus and distance folk … and after a year, I chose to utilize some of the online modules for the on-campus students."

Like Instructor A, Instructor B has a well-regarded record of achievements in teaching and research. As a Senior Lecturer, she teaches in the areas of Visual Art Education, Professional Studies, and the use of Information Communication Technology (ICT) in education. In 2003, she developed GradNet, an online community site designed to provide support for teacher education graduates during their two-year provisional registration period.

Her emerging interest in the use of technology in education blended with her background as an artist and art educator to lead her to create a com-

Figure 3. Summary of instructor A's use of streaming media

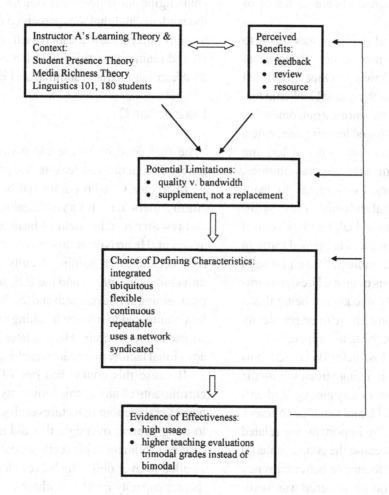

pletely streamed course experience in 2007. She attributes part of this decision to logistics with her desire to make the FTF course congruent with the distance course she was teaching. "Given that we had an existing paper-based version of the 'old' course and a quite different on-campus version, I designed the new course once, and developed both versions together in a parallel fashion. This ensured there was better congruency between them." She also indicated that her own experiences of being a student in a distance education course inspired her to give her students the same kind of flexibility around access, time, and location: "Flexible learning enables the student to make choices and to have some control over the time and place, and sometimes choices in the content of their learning. It also allows the instructor to make the best pedagogical choice in terms of delivery and approach."

Once the operational decision was made to teach with streaming media, her pedagogical choices included the following: "Once I'd defined the learning outcomes for the course I looked at two pathways to address those learning outcomes." In addition to the content-based learning outcomes, she saw streaming as supporting her underlying philosophies of creating learning communities, providing opportunities for students to learn transferable technological and collaborative skills, and leading students toward taking more control of the class. In her words, this happened through utilizing an online environment: "When I design courses, even on-campus courses, I design learning experiences that involve me not being there. I've gotten past believing I have to be physically present for effective learning to happen."

In addition to what Instructor B referred to as the "value of the C's" in using streaming media (Collaboration and Community among students, Congruency between FTF and distance courses), her fourth C is an equally important one related directly to Content: "Because the course material was online, I was able to ensure better currency of content ... plus the online material was avail-

able for campus and distance folk ... and after a year, I chose to utilize some of the online modules for the campus students." Thus, instead of being bound to materials that are selected before a class begins, she saw the flexibility of using current materials (newly published articles, websites, etc.) as being a key pedagogical benefit of using streaming media.

She is convinced of the value of using streaming media in her teaching through overwhelmingly positive student feedback such as, "I have grown in confidence in working online. The feeling of exposure has diminished substantially and I am enjoying contributing original thought to the forum, as well as learning from others." Alongside the benefits she has seen in shifting her FTF course online, she cautioned that it was initially challenging and time-consuming for both her and the students and that any perceived cost-savings are not realized due to the increased time of setting up and maintaining this kind of course. Her use of streaming media is summarized in Figure 4.

Instructor C

"The first decision to use video streaming was purely for operational reasons not pedagogical."

Instructor C, who completed his degrees in North America, is also a well established teacher and researcher in his field of business and management. He arrived at this university within the past decade after holding faculty positions at universities in Europe and the U.S. In addition to maintaining active research and teaching agendas, he volunteered to take on teaching an entry level course to the program. He was later joined by an additional faculty member in teaching this course.

Because this course has one of the highest enrollments of any at this university, it typically has several sections of lectures each semester. Due to a registration oversight that did not put a cap on the enrollment in his section, student numbers swelled to over 600, which exceeded the lecture theater capacity of 450. Without a viable option

Figure 4. Summary of instructor B's use of streaming media

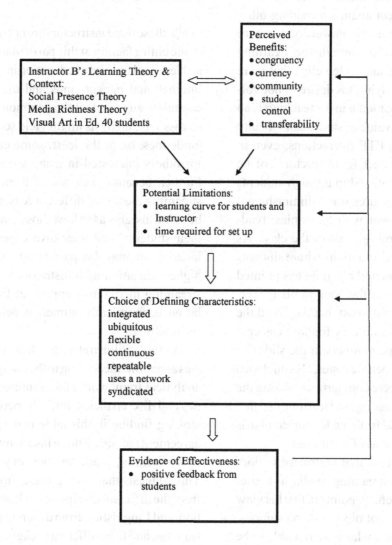

of opening another section for the 150-200 students who would have other schedule conflicts, he was forced to turn to streaming media in two ways as an essential component of his class. First, while conducting his lecture in person to 450 students in one lecture theater, he would be filmed and streamed into a nearby lecture theater with the remaining students. Second, his filmed lectures would now be recordings and could be made available for students to access anytime and anywhere. His reservations about doing so were

clear: "The first decision to use video streaming was purely for operational reasons not pedagogical." He elaborated on this point of not choosing to use streaming media for pedagogical reasons with: "If media streaming is used for teaching, students might substitute the video for class attendance. As a result, class attendance would fall and this leads to a disconnection between faculty and the students."

In addition to his belief that providing streaming media in the form of real-time and recorded lectures was not an effective contributor to student learning or student and faculty interaction, he saw a similar argument against providing other materials online such as his PowerPoint lecture slides, text-based media through the Learning Management System, and video clips that were shown in class. Underlying his desire to not voluntarily use streaming media in his teaching is an apparent belief in the value of student and faculty relationships through FTF interactions, even in large classes. A by-product, for Instructor C, of the dissolution of that relationship through students no longer attending lectures was a diminishment in students' engagement with the topics, readings, and overall learning goals of the class. As evidence, he described situations where students would come up to him and ask if he has pointed out the page numbers of the book in his PowerPoint slides. When he'd insist that they read the whole book, students said they found it easier if he mentioned the page numbers in the slides so that they could target specific pages. He concluded that this meant they were compartmentalizing the whole experience of reading and learning and that video streaming would further add to an emphasis on fragmentation instead of synthesis.

While it would seem that Instructor C does not see any role for streaming media in higher education, he was careful to point out that his view differs if students are not physically on campus. He felt that for students who were not able to be on-campus, then streaming videos might be useful, but not for students who can attend classes on campus. Instructor C also noted that it was not possible to wholly attribute decreased attendance to streaming media in that this was not an experiment under controlled conditions. His use of streaming media is summarized in Figure 5.

CONCLUSION AND IMPLICATIONS: CROSS-CASE ANALYSIS

While these three instructors are not representative of the entire faculty at this particular university or all New Zealand higher education instructors, their international backgrounds and disciplines vary enough to suggest that the common themes from a cross-case analysis might yield some lessons or guidelines, or, at the least, some considerations for others interested in using streaming media. Further, because each one of them came to use streaming media for different reasons, there may be some insights as to how those reasons affected their students' and their own experiences. This latter point may be particularly important for higher education administrators to reflect on as streaming media may appear, at first glance, to be an economically attractive delivery system for teaching.

As Table 5 illustrates, data from the three cases was assembled according to the components of the analytical framework and examined for similarities and discrepancies. Initially, perhaps the most striking finding in this table is the high level of agreement among all three instructors with regard to the defining characteristics they chose to use. This suggests that among these three instructors from the different disciplines of Business, Education, and Linguistics, from different philosophical leanings, and from different backgrounds, the characteristics for using streaming media as established in the literature are fairly fixed. In other words, streaming media in their instances looked pretty similar from an operational standpoint. So, that set of characteristics might be seen as a logistical starting point for any instructor considering using streaming media as seen in Table 5.

While the characteristics of each instructor's use of streaming media looked similar according to their accounts, the most variance appears to be in the two areas that are less operational and more philosophical: the instructors' learning theories and their perceptions of how using streaming

Figure 5. Summary of instructor C's use of streaming media

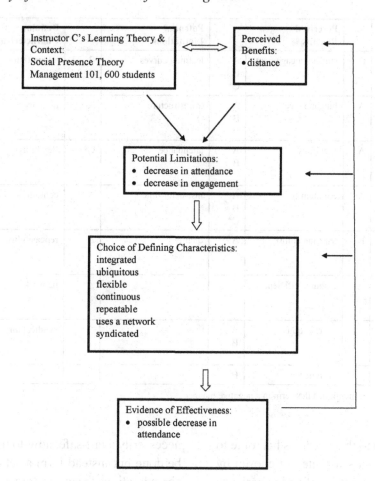

media would benefit students. Within these three cases, Instructor A and Instructor B appear more similar in both their learning theories and perceived benefits of using streaming media. They both see streaming media as being beneficial to students' academic performance and engagement with their particular subjects. Interestingly, they both also see streaming media as being beneficial to students' sense of community and belonging. For Instructor A, he viewed the technology as a bridge for personalizing students' experiences in a large class. For Instructor B, she viewed the technology as an opportunity to create a learning community that was not necessarily led by her. For both of them, these opportunities were seen to be

much more difficult or possible without streaming media.

As was clear through his statements about streaming media, Instructor C did not share those views of either Instructor A or Instructor B in believing that it could positively affect students' experiences on individual or communal levels. To the contrary, he came to the conclusion that it could have a negative impact on students' engagement with the academic material, their relationships with him, and their connection to the classroom community. Instructor C's belief that streaming media could be useful for students who are not physically on campus suggests that he is not anti-streaming media but just sees it as having a specific role for a specific group of

Table 5. Cross-case analysis

Learning Theory		Perceived Benefits		Potential Limitations		Defining Characteristics	
Social Presence	C	student engagement	A B C*	learning curves	B	integration	A B C
Student Engagement	A	human voice	A B	infrastructure	A	ubiquity	A B C
Multi-media, learning (Gardner)	A	flexibility	A B	attendance	C*	flexibility	A B C
Student-Centeredness (Biggs)	A	community	A B C*	instructor time	A B	continuity	A B C
Social Constructivism	B	tracking ability	A	quality	A	repeatability	A B C
Andragogy	A	resource efficient				network	A B C
		access equity	A B			syndication	A B C
		currency	B				

* indicates that the instructor mentioned that term in a negative manner

students. In addition to that, perhaps his route to using streaming media – a route not chosen by him – affected his perception of and experience with it. Table 6 is an attempt to overlay the ways in which all three instructors came to use streaming media with their perceived benefits of it in order to see what administrators and other instructors may want to consider before diving headfirst into streaming media.

Implications and Considerations for Using Streaming Media

From surveying the review of relevant research about using streaming media, the Conceptual Framework for Considering to Use Streaming Media, and the Case Studies findings, it is clear that a number of lessons have been learned by higher education instructors about using streaming media. These lessons presented below are not necessarily a fail-safe, how-to list of what should be done but instead form a set of questions and considerations for instructors to engage with and reflect upon prior to including a streaming media component to their instructional design.

- Rather than repeating in the class what is transmitted through media, it might be better to create a more enriched learning experience in the classroom based on student participation and discussion, and keep media streaming for transmission of difficult to understand and high impact materials. This might address the issue of reduced attendance to the class as some instructors have felt that to be the downside of media streaming.
- Involve students in the media streaming either in the process of media streaming or as part of content generation so that they can

Table 6. Spectrum of adoption of streaming media

Adoption of Streaming Media		
Minimal		**Maximum**
Instructor C	Instructor A	Instructor B
forced	chosen	chosen
supplemental resource	supplement resource	sole resource

feel some ownership in it. This can be in the form of instructor/student interactions that are then aired through media, or letting students create media and then the instructor could add to that for a co-created product (e.g., Maag's 2006 successful approach with nursing students).

- Instructors need to be able to match technology with the goals and aims of any given task for which they propose to use media.

- Content organization should be revisited when offered through media rather than traditional FTF classroom.

- Learners' accessibility and proficiency in using various media should be considered before incorporating it in teaching.

- Pros and cons (e.g., bandwidth, equipment accessibility, instructional technology assistance) for using media should be weighed.

- Using media when traditional teaching is occurring can enhance the learning if it is used to complement class activities. This, however, has implications for instructors' workloads and that should be taken into consideration.

SUMMARY

While one response to the emergence and infiltration of streaming media in many aspects of daily life might be to keep it out of the classroom, would this be blindly swimming upstream without recognizing the potential benefits of using it for teaching and learning? It is clear that the jury is still out with regard to definitively determining the effectiveness, or not, of using streaming media in higher education. Like most pedagogical decisions and practices, effectiveness is in the hands of the implementer – the instructor. To positively use streaming media in one's teaching, there must be a commitment to learn about it and a belief in its potential.

As the literature about streaming media in higher education and these case studies of some different uses demonstrate, there are particular learning theories, perceived benefits, potential limitations, and specific characteristics that appear to relate to one another such that they can be used as a formula or planning device. Along with the considerations that resulted from the prior research and these case studies, this chapter has offered some starting points to instructors considering streaming media. As motivation to use these starting points, one need to look no further than Marshall McLuhan's admonition that "the medium is the message" (2003). What is the message of higher education if the medium is not current?

REFERENCES

Adams, J. (2006). The part played by instructional media in distance education. *SIMILE: Studies In Media & Information Literacy Education*, 6(2), 1–12. doi:10.3138/sim.6.2.001

Allan, M., & Thorns, D. (2009). Being face to face - a state of mind or technological design. In Whitworth, B., & de Moor, A. (Eds.), *Handbook of research on socio-technical designing and social networking systems* (pp. 440–454). Hershey, PA: IGI Global Publications. doi:10.4018/978-1-60566-264-0.ch030

Baltes, B. B., Dickson, M. W., Sherman, M. P., Bauer, C. C., & LaGanke, J. S. (2002). Computer-mediated communication and group decision making: A meta-analysis. *Organizational Behavior and Human Decision Processes, 87*(1), 156–179. doi:10.1006/obhd.2001.2961

Beldarrain, Y. (2006). Distance education trends: Integrating new technologies to foster student interaction and collaboration. *Distance Education, 27*(2), 139–153. doi:10.1080/01587910600789498

Bennett, E., & Maniar, N. (2008). *Are videoed lectures an effective teaching tool? Biggs, J., & Tang, C. (2007). Teaching for quality learning at university: What the student does (Society for Research Into Higher Education)*. Mcgraw-Hill Publ.Comp.

Billinghurst, M., & Kato, H. (1999). *Collaborative mixed reality- merging real and virtual worlds*. Paper presented at the First International Symposium on Mixed Reality (ISMR 99), Berlin.

Biocca, F., Harms, C., & Burgoon, J. K. (2003). Towards a more robust theory and measure of social presence: Review and suggested criteria. *Presence (Cambridge, Mass.), 12*(5), 456–480. doi:10.1162/105474603322761270

Bosch, L. T., Oostdijk, N., & Ruiter, J. P. (2004). *Durational aspects of turn-taking in spontaneous face-to-face and telephone dialogues*. Paper presented at the Text, Speech and Dialogue Conference. Retrieved from http://www.hcrc.ed.ac.uk/comic/documents/

Brahler, C., Peterson, N., & Johnson, E. (1999). Developing online learning materials for higher education: An overview of current issues. *Educational Technology and Society, 2*(2). Retrieved on 5 October, 2009, from http://www.ifets.info/journals/2_2/jayne_brahler.html

Campbell, G. (2005). Podcasting in education. *EDUCAUSE,* Nov/Dec, 5.

Chan, A., Lee, M., & McLoughlin, C. (2006). Everyone's learning with podcasting: A Charles Sturt University experience. *Who's learning? Whose technology? Proceedings ascilite Sydney 2006.*

Chang, C. (2004). Constructing a streaming video-based learning forum for collaborative learning. *Journal of Educational Multimedia and Hypermedia, 13*(3), 245–264.

Chang, S. (2007). *Academic perceptions of the use of Lectopia: A University of Melbourne example.*

Daft, R. L., & Lengel, R. H. (1986). Organisational information requirements, media richness and structural design. *Management Science, 32*(5), 554–571. doi:10.1287/mnsc.32.5.554

Daft, R. L., & Wiginton, J. (1979). Language and organisation. *Academy of Management Review, 4*(2), 171–191.

Dennis, A. R., & Valacich, J. S. (1999). *Rethinking media richness: Towards a theory of media synchronicity*. Paper presented at the 32nd Hawaii International Conference on System Sciences, Hawaii.

Dennis, A. R., & Valacich, J. S. (1999). *Rethinking media richness: Towards a theory of media synchronicity.*

Feeney, L., Reynolds, P., Eaton, K., & Harper, J. (2008). *A description of the new technologies used in transforming dental education.*

Goffman, E. (1963). *Behaviour in public places: Notes on the social organisation of gatherings.* London, UK: The Free Press of Glenco.

Hartsell, T., & Yuen, S. (2006). Video streaming in online learning. *AACE Journal, 14*(1), 31–43.

Heeter, C. (1992). Being there: The subjective experience of presence. *Presence (Cambridge, Mass.), 1*(2), 262–271.

Maag, M. (2006). iPod, uPod? An emerging mobile learning tool in nursing education and students' satisfaction.

McLuhan, M. (2003). *Understanding media: The extension of man - critical edition.* Berkeley, CA: Gingko Press.

Mehrabian, A. (1971). *Silent messages.* Belmont, CA: Wadsworth.

Morisse, K., & Ramm, M. (2007). *Teaching via podcasting: One year of experience with workflows, tools and usage in higher education.*

Nardi, B. A., & Whittaker, S. (2002). The place of face-to-face communication in distributed work. In Hins, P. J., & Kiesler, S. (Eds.), *Distributed work* (pp. 83–113). Cambridge, MA: The MIT Press.

Phillips, R., Gosper, M., McNeill, M., Woo, K., Preston, G., & Green, D. (2007). Staff and student perspectives on web based lecture technologies: Insights into the great divide. *Proceedings ascilite Singapore 2007*, (pp. 854-864).

Schroeder, R. (2006). Being there together and the future of connected presence. *Presence (Cambridge, Mass.), 15*(4), 438–454. doi:10.1162/pres.15.4.438

Shephard, K. (2003). Questioning, promoting and evaluating the use of streaming video to support student learning. *British Journal of Educational Technology, 34*(3), 295–308. doi:10.1111/1467-8535.00328

Short, J., Williams, E., & B., C. (1976). *The social psychology of telecommunications.* New York, NY: John Wiley.

Tu, C.-H. (2000). On-line learning migration: From social learning theory to social presence theory in a CMC environment. *Journal of Network and Computer Applications, 23*(1), 27–37. doi:10.1006/jnca.1999.0099

Wainfan, L., & Davis, P. K. (2004). *Challenges in virtual collaboration: Videoconferencing, audio conferencing, and computer-mediated communications.* Santa Monica, CA: RAND National Defense Research Institute.

Chapter 9

iPod Enhancement for Field Visits in Religious Studies

Dierdre Burke
University of Wolverhampton, UK

Brian Barber
University of Wolverhampton, UK

Yvonne Johnson
University of Wolverhampton, UK

A. Nore
University of Wolverhampton, UK

C. Walker
University of Wolverhampton, UK

ABSTRACT

This chapter reports on a project to explore the potential of a mobile learning device (Apple iTouch iPod) to enhance student field visits to local places of worship, which are part of the Religious Studies degree programme. Places of worship are a valuable resource for student learning, but often the value of the visit is linked to the quality of information and the style of presentation by the faith informant. In addition, there is a particular problem for university students who need to go beyond basic information about history and artifacts to explore key concepts in situ. The project is a collaboration between staff and second year students to develop podcasts on local places of worship, which have been trialed by first year students. These podcasts include a range of media: video, audio, images, text, and hyperlinks to offer a rich learning experience. The podcasts link to theoretical issues in the study of religion to enhance the development of appropriate literacies for the discipline of Religious Studies. The chapter reports on the range of technical and other issues encounters, the way we responded to them, and our overall assessment of the potential applications for mobile learning during field visits.

DOI: 10.4018/978-1-60960-800-2.ch009

PLACE OF VISITS WITHIN RELIGIOUS STUDIES

Field visits are an important feature in our study of religions, enabling students to contextualise their theoretical study by exploring places of worship. This chapter shares our experiences in using the iPod Touch to enhance such visits. This project builds on a decade of developments linked to the use of technologies to enhance learning in this module *Religions in Wolverhampton.* This is an introductory level one module in which students explore the local religious landscape in a mix of class sessions and field visits. This approach provides a link between the theory and historical context provided in lectures and the findings on the ground in field visits. The module is innovative in terms of content, in setting religions within a local history framework, and innovative in approach in enabling students to develop their fieldwork skills alongside the ICT skills they use to present findings. The academic study of religion requires access to suitable materials for students to gain knowledge and develop their theoretical understanding. This has been a major challenge for this module due to the lack of published academic materials on religions in the locality, which has been addressed largely through the provision of electronic sources. Students are directly involved in this process as researchers, who are supported by the range of electronic sources, in their encounters with local religious communities.

Technology has been central to developments to make the study of local communities feasible in the absence of published sources for study. Thus, the institution's virtual learning environment and the development of a website on *Religion in Wolverhampton* made it possible to provide materials for local study. More recently the PebblePad webfolio opened up the possibility for interactive learning experiences which linked materials produced in past years with current research. These developments were reported by Burke, 2009, to explore aspects of e-Learning in dialogue. This

chapter takes the development a step further in assessing the contribution that the hand held iPod made to visits to places of worship,

These developments have resulted from a three way interaction between learners, the subject and technology. The learner category, for cutting edge technologies, has involved staff as well as students, and indeed staff from information technology (Dennet in Salmon et al. 2008) and the Institute for Learning Enhancement, as the application of technology in the new religious context required even IT experts to learn about situational issues. The subject aspect has been local religious communities, where our learning need has peeled away layers of information about particular communities. We have found this to be a kind of voyage of exploration as we discover more about the history, activities and practices of places, for example, previous visits to the Buddha Vihara did not uncover the historical collection held by the community, soon to be turned into a museum. Finally, the technology aspect has been crucial in offering new opportunities to access, process and record information about local religious communities.

This three way process has essentially been a dialogue between partners to explore potential applications of new technologies to learning situations. Thus, this chapter extends the dialogue to uncover the contribution of the iPod to learning during field visits to places of worship.

Religious Studies and e-Learning

Religious Education (RE), in schools, and Religious Studies (or Study of Religions or theology) in higher education settings, is a strange subject. Cognitive psychologists identified problems students may encounter understanding religion due to its abstract nature. Goldman (1965) recommended that materials be linked to the level of student cognitive 'readiness.' This recommendation was applied by Grimmitt (2000) and Jackson (1997) in strategies to support experiential encounters with religion. Explicit Religious Education built on such foundations to bring religious material into pupils' lives. Visits to places of worship have long been part of this process and are included in the experiences and opportunities recommended in *The National Framework for Religious Education* (QCA 2004) for secondary pupils. RE in schools has the two overarching aims of 'learning about' and 'learning from' religions.

The module *Religions in Wolverhampton* is set within the framework used by Grimmitt in his *Pedagogies of Religious Education* (2000), which defines pedagogic principles as 'general laws or substantive hypothesis about teaching and learning' (2000, p.18), which are then elaborated in terms of pedagogic strategies.

The pedagogic principle that underpins the approach in Religions in Wolverhampton, set out by Grimmitt (2000), is to offer students an experiential encounter with religion through a synchronic and diachronic study of religious communities. This approach recognises the gap between the way Western scholars categorise religions and the reality of lived experiences which can be accessed through 'ethnographic and personal accounts of religious life.' (Jackson, 1997, p.3). The pedagogic strategies employed to achieve this are based around field visits to local places of worship. Thus, local religious communities form the starting point for a study, which explores the historical origins of that religious community and the major phases of its development. Whole class field visits are an important part of this experiential encounter, and culminate in students researching communities in pairs and presenting their findings to the wider group, in person and through electronic means.

The theoretical foundation for this approach owes much to the work of Biggs. Firstly, Biggs, 1999, notion of 'constructive alignment,' is present in the construction of the curriculum, the interactive methods of teaching and learning, and finally the assessment tasks. Secondly, there is a focus on metacognitive skills, which goes beyond generic and study skills. Metacognitive skills are in essence involved with what a 'what learner does in new context.' (Biggs, 2003, p.94) Thus, the provision of electronic resources allowed students to interact with each religion, to learn facts, figures, and practical issues such as pronunciation of key terms through the sound glossary. This foundation was important in preparing students for their own visit and report on a particular religious community.

Visits in a Degree Programme

Visits outside educational venues are fraught with problems. They are difficult to set up, require authorization and risk assessments, and often involve complex transport arrangements. In addition it is necessary to check that the learning experience participants receive is appropriate for their programme of study. Chryssides and Geaves, 2007, set such 'pitfalls' against the 'extraordinary benefits' to be accrued from fieldwork, in their chapter on 'Fieldwork in the study of religion.' Whilst their primary focus is on ethnographic encounters with believers in traditions, much of their advice feeds into this consideration of field visits to places of worship. They set out a range of issues for consideration in this statement: "In the field, religions are messy, paradoxical and chaotic, and they feed on the irrational. Indeed, it could be argued that fieldwork is diametrically opposite to the scholar's rational process of ordering a faith tradition into neat packages of history, doctrine and practices." (2007, p.241)

The use of iPods offers a way to engage with three particular pitfalls in field visits. These concern a shared understanding of the purpose of visits; spokespeople being able to provide the information required, and finally the issue of a link between classroom study and the field visit. Each pitfall is to be considered before the section explores the potential of the iPod to address each challenge.

Firstly, a pitfall can arise if a common understanding on the aim and purpose of the visit is not shared by provider and participants. On one level local places of worship are geared up for school visits, for both primary and secondary pupils. Faith leaders or informants are guided by information from the local Agreed Syllabus on what they should cover in their input for the visit. However, for university students the situation is rather different. In Wolverhampton we are the only institute of higher education visiting local places of worship, and we are only likely to visit places once each year. This means that faith informants do not regularly talk to university students to gauge an understanding of the needs of university students on visits.

There is an additional issue in that each university visit is likely to have a specific and different purpose. For example, in the first year module *The Study of Religion* there is a group visit to a place of worship where we ask for a general introduction to the faith and students have to compare the presentation of the faith during the visit to the way the faith is presented in a textbook. This task helps students become aware of differences they are likely to encounter between insider and outsider sources, or between confessional and academic approaches. In the module *Religions in Wolverhampton* the purpose is again different in that visits to a range of places of worship aim to help students develop an understanding of how the communities developed and the challenges they face in the present. In other modules on specific religious traditions the visits have different purposes, on some occasions to see what happens during a festival or specific ritual observance.

Thus, there is great variety in the places we visit and the purpose of visits. This makes the process of negotiating a visit difficult as we are not asking for an 'off the peg' talk. In addition there are no set guidelines for a degree level visit to a place of worship that we can draw on to identify requirements, such as the approach to be taken and the detail required.

The second pitfall concerns the 'content' to be covered in the talk and the depth required. On the one hand places of worship have experts within the tradition, who possess the knowledge we seek to access on visits, in such cases it is just necessary to clarify the level required. However, in some cases the individuals who possess the depth of knowledge required may not have English as their first language, and thus struggle to find the words to convey their knowledge to students. If the majority of their contacts in this country have been with members of their own religious community, they may take aspects of knowledge about their religion for granted and thus not provide a full explanation for students. On the other hand it may be that people who act as faith informants in particular places do not have the in-depth knowledge required. Such individuals may be able to do a very good job in introducing school pupils to their faith, and will have developed an awareness of the types of questions that interest pupils. However, essentially one off university visits do not follow the same format and informants are unlikely to have developed a 'degree' level talk for students.

Thirdly, there is the pitfall identified by Carlson, that 'disconnected field visits can become moments of hiatus from the course, rather than an expression of it." (in Chryssides and Geaves, 2007, p. 249) This issue of 'hiatus' can occur when the approach or content of the talk during a field visit does not link to the classroom input. There is also the opportunity to remind students about key aspects of theory during the tour, so that a link is made to prior classroom exploration. Faith informants would not be able to make such links. Chryssides and Geaves recommend that students prepare for field visits by reading specific texts, that aspects of the visit are recorded to allow for a debriefing and a return to 'reread' such texts.

THE iPOD STUDY AND APPLICATION

The level of depth required for the talk can be accessed through discussion with the faith leader, who is more likely to give the time for a one off occasion that is recorded and put into a podcast for future use. There is also an issue about the depth of specific knowledge that can be provided during a tour. At St Peter's Church, for example, there are so many features that have such a rich history that one person is unlikely to be able to cover them all. Thus, prior research may be required to uncover details, and a form to record and access the information is needed.

Our aim in exploring the iPods is to gear the visits to our particular needs. This relates to the purpose of the visit- often faith informants have one talk and that is what you get whatever your aim is for the visit. Thus, we can develop tours to meet a variety of learning needs at different levels of study.

Thus, the iPod's functionality appears to meet our specific needs in allowing us to provide the depth and specificity of detail required for the particular learning need of the module.

Fieldwork in Religious Studies can take a variety of forms, in this study we are exploring the buildings that reflect the beliefs and provide the setting for practices. Thus, students are essentially encountering the building and interrogating the bricks and mortar for insights into the religious community that worship there. Other forms of fieldwork are likely to be ethnographical and be an encounter between students and the people who use the place of worship.

Students as Researchers

Dialogue as communication between participants and partners is central to Religious Studies. This builds on the 'conversational model' of teaching and learning, developed by Laurillard (1993) linking teacher and learner. Four second year students joined the project team to explore the ways that iPod could be used to explore local places. These students had completed the level one module *Religions in Wolverhampton* which was the focus for the project. The module is based around visits to local places of worship, starting with whole class visits and then moving to student led visits. Thus these students had already experienced the planning, guiding and evaluating a visit for other students to a place of worship. In the module they had worked in groups, for this research they worked individually on four different places of worship. The four places of worship selected for the project were chosen by individual students, based on their interests and the opportunities these places offered for the project. Three places had been involved in an earlier project with English Heritage, co-ordinated by a Religious Studies graduate, on 'Our Faith Buildings.' The resulting DVD provided a short video on each of these places which was incorporated into the tour for one of the places in the project.

The project team presented their findings to two Religious Studies conferences in 2009, firstly the *C4C 'Beyond the ordinary'* conference which explored creative approaches to teaching and learning in Religious Studies. The second presentation was at the *British Association for the Study of Religion* (BASR) conference which focused on the theme of places. This presentation allowed participants to experience aspects of the tour by way of standing in front of a poster of the place of worship. In addition a short report was provided by Burke at the *Higher Education Academy conference*, for the HEAT project (HEAT, 2009).

A short summary of each of the 'tours' is set out below by the student who put the tour together.

1. Text: The Collegiate Church of St Peter, Yvonne Johnson
2. Audio: Wolverhampton Buddha Vihara, Clare Walker
3. Audio and video: Latter Day Saints, Brian Barber
4. Collaboration: Wolverhampton Central Mosque, Aamir Nore

1. Text: The Collegiate Church of St. Peter, Yvonne Johnson

My experiences on the module *Religions in Wolverhampton* were very positive, so I was keen to be involved in the iPod project and decided to focus an independent study on the Collegiate Church of St. Peter which had been covered briefly in that module. The church is situated in the city centre next to the university and is passed by most students everyday, yet when questioned, representatives of the church commented that very few students visit the church. Moreover, considering the multicultural aspect of the City of Wolverhampton and its university, this project would offer a greater understanding of Christianity from the Church of England's perspective, informing students from other faiths about Christian beliefs and the history of Christianity in the city. Therefore my independent study would focus in depth on the historical aspect of this place of worship as well as exploring the practices of the Christian Church based on a field visit and tour of the Church, enhanced by the use of iPod. The use of iPod would focus and encourage mobile learning, especially those who are visual learners, and would be accessible to all students within the university. The iPod's impact on the tour would be evaluated by the current first year students on the module *Religions in Wolverhampton* to discover their perspectives on this style of learning.

The prospect of sharing the research in this way was an exciting opportunity as too often students in undergraduate study have little opportunity to share their research, other than in assessed presentation, but then you are too focused on your own presentation to take much note of what other students are doing. The iPod project was an ideal opportunity to offer a more modern approach to learning, and as the project podcast was to be added to the Wolf system at the university, more students would have access to this project at their leisure. It would also preserve the history of St. Peter's using new technology as well as encouraging and emphasising the important aspect of field visits which are so valuable to students.

It has been recognised that field visits provide a new dimension to study in addition to textual study. Chryssides and Geaves, 2007, outline the importance for study on living religions communities. Fieldwork offers the opportunity to enhance our understanding of a faith tradition by observing what it means to those who practise that faith, and by observing the place in which they worship. It also gives the student the opportunity to challenge their own perceptions of a faith, helping to form the identity of other faiths. When studying the faith in text books, the student should always question whether the religion discussed bears any resemblance to the religion practised, and fieldwork will confirm this.

Having decided on this project, the next stage was to approach St. Peter's Church for permission to carry out the research. Having a personal insight into the practices of the Church of England would be an advantage; however, one had to be aware that over familiarity can at times create its own problem, (Chryssides and Geaves, 2007) so making sure that phenomena would be explained fully and distancing oneself from the practices would be of paramount importance.

The first contact with the church was made during a visit when the church was open to the public. My initial contact was with the person who organised the opening times of the church, this person usually being available for any questions that the public may have, and she became my 'gatekeeper'. This term is explored fully in Chryssides and Geaves' text, and the importance of this person was considered at all times as she had the power to block access and finish the research before it had begun. As the gatekeeper was uncertain about the iPod aspect of the research, she introduced me to one of the team of Vicars and Curates at the church who gave his blessing to the project and who expressed great interest in the use of iPod. During future visits, many members of the church enquired about the progress of the project. They were particularly interested as the only source of information they had for visitors was the small but informative booklet by Hall-Matthews(1993). These members of the church became my unofficial 'gate openers' and their encouragement was greatly appreciated.

The gatekeeper was approached to arrange a visit in order for me to take photographs which would record the history of the church as it was in 2009, and would also greatly enhance the text, offering a visual dimension to the iPod therefore introducing an important aspect of learning.

Visual learning relates to the fundamental way which people take in information, using predominantly their eyes, and visual learners like to see how to do things, using illustrations to remember content, rather than talking or hearing about things. Maps, diagrams and photographs all enhance this style of learning, so the intention of adding photographs to the text and a tour diagram to the iPod presentation would encourage the visual learning experience. And, as most visual learners like to take notes and add lists, the use of the iPod encourages the visual learner to do so in their own time and at their own pace. A visual presentation also gives consideration to those students who have disabilities, no matter how small or large. Students who have physical disabilities may not be able to gain access to all parts of the church due to internal steps without additional help, so the photographs would enable them to see all aspects of the church. Similarly, those students in wheelchairs may not be able to view the misericords underneath the seats; the in depth detail of the photographs would ensure they do not miss out on the experience. Those students who have hearing disabilities and would not benefit from a talking tour as there is no loop system in the church at the present time, would benefit from the iPod. In addition those with learning difficulties can access the iPod at their own pace; taking the time they need, having the visual map to show the tour route. Consideration for those who cannot attend the church for this

field visit for whatever reason had been realised as the tour would be accessible from the Wolf system at the university.

Consideration had to be given as to whether mobile learning and the use of iPod would enhance the field visit. As already outlined in this text, mobile learning is considered a more modern approach to study, and as Clark reports, it is beginning to be recognised as an accepted form of learning in education. (in Mayer 2005.) It offers educational content around the clock at the student's convenience. It also makes web based research easy, providing students with suitable links, as the internet has taken on the role of an automated teacher as well as a being a source of knowledge. (Frechette, 2002 p.4) It can also be argued that it connects with students in a way that they already understand and enjoy. Lectures and presentations can be captured and published and downloaded from iTunes and transferred onto iPod or iPhones. Online tutorials are also possible. As technology moves forward, all types of learning have to be considered and this type of learning offers flexibility in a pleasurable way. Therefore, considering all the positive aspects of mobile learning this field visit could only be enhanced with its use.

The tour was initially made as a PowerPoint presentation and then uploaded on to the iPod. Immediately problems became apparent. When using the iPod, students had to be shown how to pause the slides manually as the automatic setting could not be altered and the automatic delay between slides was too long. Also the stretch touch facility would not function properly so that photographs, text and the tour map could not be stretched in the podcast. Therefore some aspects of the presentation were compromised.

I was encouraged with the feedback and the response to the tour using the iPod. The group of students confirmed that the iPod were useful for this type of tour and that the visual maps were extremely helpful. They confirmed that they had had no problems accessing the data as most had experience of iPod and iPhones. They also commented that the information was easy to understand. All stated that although they had not used this style of learning before they would like to use this style of learning and technology more often in their studies. They agreed that the visual representation of photography enhanced the learning experience, however not being able to stretch the pictures and text limited the iPod tour. They all decided that an audio commentary would also have enhanced the iPod experience. As there were no students with learning difficulties or special needs, including those with any hearing impairment, the evaluation as a visual learning experience could not be fully assessed, however, when the students present were asked for their opinion they agreed that it would help anyone with hearing problems, as there was currently no loop system in the church. A small percentage of students commented that they would have liked to have seen other aspects and objects within the church included in the tour but due to the limitations of the tour it was agreed that the most important aspects had been included.

The conclusion of the students was that the iPod was a useful way to help understand and explore the concepts of this Church and that the iPod enhanced the tour of the church, making it more exciting and interesting. One student did raise the point that it would be useful to always have an official guide of the Church present to whom questions could be raised, although in this instance, representatives of St. Peter's Church were in attendance to answer any queries. The iPod tour was also shown to the representatives of the church who were present. The representatives said that although they had never seen or used an iPod before they were keen to be shown how to use this technology. They were thrilled with the results and the depth of information provided on the iPod, and commented that all visitors to the church would certainly benefit if this technology was available.

In response to the issues raised concerning the limitations of the iPod and the feedback from the questionnaire, certain improvements were then made to the tour. Firstly, as the text, photographs and map could not be stretched, I included more slides within the presentation to allow for individual photographs on one slide and the text on another, therefore enlarging both aspects. I also made the text bold and included a slide with each individual position on the tour map to offer a clearer dimension of the point of reference within the tour. Secondly, as this presentation was focused on the visual aspect alone, I informed those fellow students who were also making iPod presentations concerning other places of worship within Wolverhampton of the importance of the audio application so that they could accommodate this facility within their iPod presentations. I am looking to develop my iPod tour by adding audio commentary in the near future, 'and have also made a copy of the presentation for the church.

In conclusion of the project, this iPod tour was a success. The tour was greatly enhanced by the technology and this imaginative learning experience was enjoyed by the students. As this tour of St. Peter's was the first one to be accessed by the first year students, the feedback allowed my fellow iPod researchers to learn from this experience and to use it to enable them to incorporate the feedback comments into their own presentations and tours. The tour is now accessible as a podcast on the university's Wolf system for students to use. As technology moves forward, the teaching methods within education must also move forward and this iPod learning experience has shown how the Religious Studies program at Wolverhampton University can incorporate new technology making the learning experience more enjoyable and stimulating for its students.

2. Audio: Wolverhampton Buddha Vihara, Clare Walker

My task was to develop a tour focusing primarily on the audio aspect of the iPod. This is to allow people to listen to a tour whilst looking at the features in the place of worship. The benefits of this type of information proviso are numerous. This type of tour would benefit students with any type of visual impairment as the information would be fed aurally without the need for reading. It would also benefit students who would like to gain more information about a particular faith or place of worship without the need of a lecturer to attend and provide the information; the tour can take place independently of any staff in attendance.

I chose the Buddha Vihara Buddhist Temple in Wolverhampton, I had visited the temple along with my classmates as part of the religions in Wolverhampton module, and remembered the temple quite vividly and it was this that prompted my choice of place of worship for this module.

This particular place of worship presented me with several problems and was a further reason for using this particular place of worship for the iPod tour. The Vihara was set up by immigrants from the Indian sub-continent, and is currently served by a resident monk and usually two visiting monks. The resident monk, who has been at the Vihara for many years, is fluent in English as well as several other languages although from Thailand. However, some of the visiting monks speak either very little or no English. By using the iPod to provide the essential information to the students, it overcomes the difficulties by both the user as well as providing the correct information from the Gatekeeper of the faith. In addition it is possible to address the problem of pronouncing key religious terms from a language other than English. These can be different to work out as the words are transliterations from another language which may bear little similarity to English.

To begin the planning of how this tour would best be put together I had to carry out some initial research into the uses primarily of the iPod and then to consider how the information would best be played through the iPod. I attended two lectures which included the use of the iPod and how to down/up load information, the use of Windows Movie Maker and how to put the two together. I also carried out some research on the internet, by looking at the Apple website and finally I checked out a couple of books from the Learning Centre to see how 'podcasting' may work and also adding albums/tracks/pictures. Another useful website was the Higher Education Academy that had some information on e-learning using PDAs.

I had in mind when I set out on this project, the idea of it being similar to the tours that people can take when visiting a museum, historical house or other large public venues, such as York Minster. The headset would be given to members of the public and then as they were walking around, the information would be passed through the headset.

The initial difficulty that I encountered was in that the places I had visited where these systems were in place, there is usually a number/signpost to say 'You are at point 13' and the headset could be programmed to play at that point automatically or the visitor could skip/enter the number to be at that point. As this is not an option, the easiest way I felt this could be done was by have a picture on the iPod corresponding to that particular point at the place of worship and then the visitor could 'play' that 'track'. The picture could be uploaded as album artwork. This has the advantage of being able to be paused/played at the visitors own pace, allowing them to move from point to point without have to pause at different points, as would needed to be done with Movie Maker/ podcast. Also if there is a large group walking around, the group can start at different points making it less invasive for members of the religious community.

In this first part of the Module, the aim was to provide a brief introduction of Buddhism but more importantly concentrate on the place of worship itself, how the community there developed and what happens in the place, as opposed to giving students a history of Buddhism. The primary focus will be to discuss briefly the life and works of Dr Ambedkhar, to whom the temple is dedicated, to look at the features of the temple and to cover how the place of worship is used. My part of the module for use of the iPod is to cover the audio aspect, and so my tour will include a few pictures but mainly as a reference point for the students to be aware of their situation in the temple and also to be used as a focal point for where the talk will take place. The audio aspect will consist of tracks with the picture being the album cover and the talk taking place with it. I shall also put together a tour on the iPod using moviemaker, but I do not feel this will work as well as the 'album/track version'.

To conduct the research I consulted several resources to give me a background of Buddhism in general to use this information as a basis to provide me with information prior to meeting with the 'gatekeeper' at the Vihara. According to Chryssides and Geaves, "the experiential dimension of the visit is brought into explicit relationship both with classroom experience and student reading" (2007, 248).

One of the immediate problems to come from the tour was that the 'playlist' that was loaded onto the iPod was reordered alphabetically. This caused a problem where the order that I had planned to show, was re ordered so that each track did not follow the list of the tour as it should have. To adjust this I will have to order them numerically first, followed by the title of the track to save any confusion.

The tour was conducted on May 5, the iPods had been synched prior to the visit with the information and a piece of paper was handed to each student with instructions on how the tour was to be done. Also given to each of the students was a questionnaire (included further down), for them to complete once the tour has been completed, which was structured as follows;

Audio Tour Evaluation of Buddha Vihara Temple
1. Was the tour long enough? Yes / No: Why?
2. Was there enough information contained for your needs? Yes/ No

If no, what further information would you require/ would you have liked to have seen?
3. What was the most positive aspect of the tour?
4. What could be done to improve the tour?
5. Would you have preferred a continuous play feature with pictures guiding you or did you feel the pictures in the album artwork provided you with enough information for a self guided tour?
6. Any other feedback?

The feedback was as follows:

All of the students felt that the tour was long enough and that there was enough information contained for their needs. All of the students felt that the audio tour was a good way to deliver the information. Several commented that it allowed them to look around the vihara and concentrate on the images there whilst being 'fed' the information rather than having to read it. Also several commented that they liked that there was a picture matching the place in the vihara that they were standing.

Improvements could be made so that the tracks are in order (as already mentioned above) as it caused confusion when to play the track. The majority of students said that they would have preferred a continuous play feature so that the tracks stayed in order to guide them around the temple, as they could pause it when necessary.

The majority of the feed back was positive about the concept of a individual iPod tour instead of being shown around by a member of the religion. The majority agreed that it would be useful to have a member of the community there in addition to the tour so than questions can be asked. Just two of the students, whilst acknowledging the benefits, would still prefer to be shown around by an 'insider' of the faith.

Following on from the tour, I feel that there are several changes that can be made to improve the tour. The numbering and correct order of the tracks is vital. Also to put the tour onto movie maker so that a continuous tour can be made. Once these are done it would be useful to conduct the tour again to see which the students prefer. Also the drawing more from the pictures in the meditation room would be useful so that the image on the iPod that are discussed can be directly related to objects within the room. An interactive 'quiz' or 'spot the item' type section on the iPod could be used to assess the learners intake of information. Also the English Heritage video from the 'Our Faith Buildings' on the vihara could be included. This would be particularly useful when it comes to demonstrating the kneeling to Buddha that is done when making an offering to Buddha after entering the meditation room. Finally it is my intention to go back to the vihara to gain access to the museum in the community centre and provide information to students about the artefacts that are contained there as well as further detail on the tour that has been raised from the evaluation.

3. Audio and Video Signing: Latter Day Saints, Brian Barber

The purpose of this project was to explore the possibilities of using the iPod touch to enhance the learning experience on field visits. Each member of the group had a certain quality of the iPod to focus on. This included the use of text, voice, interaction and being used by those who have hearing difficulties. As a group we went away with the iPod to experiment with them ourselves and gain firsthand experience while trying to research what they were capable of. The group varied in their own confidence towards technology. Some

were very confident and able while others it took a lot of patience and hard work.

From my own research it became apparent that iPod was not a replacement for lectures but certainly a useful addition and aid in the learning experience. I considered the following issues when organizing the tour. There was potential for more engagement leading to an increase with motivation towards learning from students. Students could work to their own level and understanding and playback any information they were unsure of. However the available information needed to be examined and students could also easily be passive. It becomes apparent that iPod provides a great opportunity for the willing student to have a much more interactive learning experience and at the same time the lazy student could go through the tour benefiting him very little.

My starting point for this project were my own experiences of technology used on tours. My main experience came from the Guggenheim museum in Bilbao. There you had a headset on with information in your own language given to you as you entered the building. At every piece of art you came across there was a number on the wall. You typed this number into your device where the information was then given to you by voice. It was this type of movement and freedom within the museum that I liked and tried to incorporate in the tour I made. One of the main differences with my own tour is that I will be using visuals as well as audio. The group got together and each person had their own specific area designated to them. Mine was to make the IPod tour accessible to those with hearing difficulties. Each member also had a different religious faith within Wolverhampton to research and organize the tour around that faith.

I decided to base my project around the The Church of Jesus of Jesus Christ of Latter-day Saint. This was because I had access to the building, members, and literature. The group met as often as possible to correlate thoughts and ideas together. Members of I.T also gave their time and advice to aid us in our efforts. From this I organized meetings with members of the church. This included full time missionaries who helped with explaining the beliefs of the church and how the church started. Interviews were also possible with some of the senior members of the congregation who described how the church had grown locally and how they purchased the land and built the chapel. The bishop was also helpful in explaining the organization of the church. This information was supported by relevant literature about the church. I then had to decide on certain key elements within the building to focus the tour around. Once this was achieved I started to write up a transcript of the information that I wanted to present. The next challenge was making this information available to those with hearing difficulties using the iPod. The tour was originally put onto a camera with an analogue file which needed to be converted to a digital file. I was able to record it straight onto a digital file and then transfer it into an MP4 file which could then be synced onto the iPod using iTunes.

There are about nine million people in the UK who are either deaf or hard of hearing. Many of these people were not born deaf but have had hearing difficulties during their life. There are about fifty thousand people who have BSL as their first sign language. Deaf people prefer to communicate in different ways depending on their own ability to hear, these include those that rely on BSL. Having friends and family who use BSL and doing BSL as an elective at university I was very excited about making my tour available to those who were deaf or hard of hearing.

I arranged an interview with one of the BSL interpreters at the university and spoke about the project with the idea of using iPods to increase learning and using BSL to particularly help those who are hard of hearing. This meeting was very beneficial as certain deaf issues were raised up about how to make the tour more accessible for deaf people and at the same time making it useful for those who could hear. It was concluded that a video of about two signers signing the informa-

tion would be best. Using two signers would give variety but not confuse the participants with too much diversity. The use of pictures I felt may have interrupted the information that was being presented. With a video of someone signing with a voice over allows those that can hear to listen to the information and those that can't hear could look at the BSL signer. As the tour is being taken at the place itself they would have a visual already in front of them. They would be a map of the building with a number code which will show which video track to play with the right place. She explained the difficulties in signing certain words such as names and places. These words needed to be finger spelt first which took time. So one difficulty was making the voice over match the time it took to film the signer. This took several attempts and the video itself might be a bit of a slow pace to compensate for the signing. The file itself was thirteen small videos which created one file, which was converted to an MP4 file.

Before the tour took place the iPods were synced with the tour and a map with references which identified the various places was provided. It was explained that they would need to identify which subject they wanted to listen to, then match the item on the map and go to the specific place before pressing the play button for the appropriate track. This offered great flexibility of movement but lacked structure as to which places to visit. After the tour the following questionnaire was handed to each student

1. Does using iPod support the learning experience? Please explain your answer
2. What could have been include or excluded to make the tour better?
3. What questions do you have about the Latter-Day Saints that was not answered in the tour?
4. Can you think of a better way to navigate around the building during the tour?
5. Any problems using the iPod during the tour? If yes please give details

6.   What would you change to make the tour better?

From the feedback which was given it became apparent that the use of iPod certainly helped the person to learn at their own pace by taking their own time around the tour. This flexibility helped to create a relaxed atmosphere. However there was only limited information available on each of the tracks which did not include any further references of information. The map was too small and could have been bigger with a possible planned suggested route. This would have helped with confidence with going from section to section. Each area of the building was covered with only the limited information which was provided. There were no suggestions for further reading or learning. This could have been solved with a select bibliography at the end of each section.

One way the tour could have been improved was to make it more interactive. The tour was quite static with no opportunities to interact with anyone or anything. The use of certain activities afterwards was suggested to help cement what was being taught. The tour was planned to help people with hearing difficulties. It would have been beneficial to have members of the deaf communities to have participated in the tour to see if it assisted them. The use of BSL meant that the voice was slower than normal speech. There was only one voice used throughout, one way this could have been improved was to use at least another voice or maybe two to add variety. However it was good to have a local accent explaining the church as it makes the tour more authentic.

In conclusion the tour itself was a success. It did support the learning experience of students. The use of iPod within tours are useful and enjoyable. The information which was given was clear and easy to understand and they were able to navigate around the building quite freely and with some confidence. To improve there will be more structure, interaction and diversity to the participant's attention.

4. Collaboration: Wolverhampton Central Mosque, Aamir Nore

My main aim was to select the main features of the Wolverhampton Central Mosque to reveal key aspects of faith and practice in Islam. This required research on Islamic beliefs and practices, as well as the history of the specific Muslim community. This is the largest mosque in Wolverhampton and receives more requests for school visits than they are able to accommodate. Thus, the Secretary from the mosque was interested to see iPods in action, and consider if they could help for future group visits to the mosque.

I have a strong interest in mobile technologies and eagerly explored research on eLearning so that I could develop an interactive tour on the iPod. Technology is critical to success in all aspects of modern life, especially education. Combining traditionally classroom based taught lectures with virtual technologies can transform learning and teaching by supporting a variety of learning styles, creating a more personalised experience for students and taking their learning beyond the classroom. E-learning is a new developing method based on an understanding of the attributes of technology as well as good planning and perfect supported electronic activities. This can cover a range of activities from the use of technology to support learning as part of a blended approach, to learning that is delivered entirely online. Whatever the technology, however, learning is the pivotal element. There are variety of ways in which e-Learning can be distributed to its audience, this can be done through visual learning, textual learning and through sign language. There are many advantages which e-Learning brings both to the students and the teachers and therefore it is seen as a successful teaching tool. Interaction stimulates understanding and the recall of information, it accommodates different learning styles, it allows students to access work any place any time, and it also allows students to take responsibility of their learning by building their self-knowledge and self-confidence. These are some of the advantages which are apparent to e-Learning.

This independent study focused on the Apple iPod Touch, this smart gadget is very useful for students as it allows students to store podcasts, word documents, sound clips, images, and videos. A pocket sized iPod, it can be carried anywhere allowing the students to access their work any place, any time. Apple report on educational developments: "Sparked by the enormous popularity of iPod and iTunes, mobile learning is changing education in a big way. Today Apple products are powerful enough to create a highly collaborative, interactive classroom" (Apple.com, 2009).

The tour around Wolverhampton Mosque took place on Tuesday 19th May 2009 at 9am. Before the start of the tour, I handed each student a questionnaire to get feedback from them on the tour, with any recommendations or changes. The students were familiar with using the iPod as they have been to various other places of worship with the same concept of using an iPod for the purpose of a tour.

The presentation consisted of audio, video, textual and photographic elements in order for the presentation and tour to be diverse as well as fun. The tour aimed to allow students to explore the main features of the mosque, to learn about the history of this particular mosque and to collaborate to complete the set questions. This tour introduced a collaborative learning experience for students, they had to share information to complete the tasks. Each person in the pair had a different podcast, one focusing on the particular mosque and one which provided general information about mosques. Questions required students to compare the features of the Central Mosque with features found in other mosques, this required students to share the information on their iPods with each other. Students reported favorably on this form of learning as they worked together to solve the puzzle. The material on iPods had been synchronized so that each student arrived at the same point at the same time. They felt that it

would have been useful to set one question out at a time rather than provide all questions at the start of the tour.. The students were satisfied with the layout of the presentation on the iPod as the text was clear, readable, well spaced and contained relevant information. As well as audio and video clips were concerned, they students were very happy that there was a diverse range of elements which put the information across.

Being present at the tour gave me the opportunity to experience first hand reactions and observations of students about how the presentation was setup and if they understood the context of the presentation. The President of the Mosque was available at the end of the tour to answer any questions from students.

The advantage of conducting this tour on an iPod is that it allows you to stop the tour, so you can go at your own pace and you are pressured to read the information. This feature may be particularly useful for students who like to take their own time in accessing information, or for students with learning difficulties.

Overall, the tour was very well conducted and was thoroughly enjoyed by the students. Mr Shah was fascinated by our interest in the Mosque was and very helpful indeed. As well as the information on the iPod, Mr Shah gave the opportunity to answer questions from the group. Students were very happy with the tour and would not recommend any changes.

In conclusion therefore, we can agree that using an iPod as a learning tool enhances a person's knowledge as well as making the tour fun and exciting. This method will become increasingly popular among many institutions who wish to adopt this approach towards enhancing learning.

Overall, I think the tour was successful in fulfilling the aim in trying to present the key features of the Mosque on an iPod. There are many aspects of the presentation which I would keep the same however, there maybe room for development. For example, as the Wolverhampton Central Mosque is a Sunni Mosque, it could have been a good idea to compare these features to those found in a Shia Mosque. The collaborative aspect could have involved students working together looking at the same features of two different strands of Islam.

OVERALL CONCLUSION

There were major technical problems in the development of the tours and getting them on to the iPods. Part of the problem was due to university systems and the set up of staff machines, as it was impossible to sync the iPods to the member of staff's desktop. This meant that other means had to be found to sync the iPods, either another member of staff's laptop or a student's own machine. This swapping from one machine to another led to the erasing of earlier programmes. These technical issues took a lot of time away from the consideration of learning engagement. These problems were largely due to our status as novices in using iPods for such learning encounters.

However, as complicated and frustrating as the technical challenges had been, the final product of the tours more than justified the effort. Student feedback noted that the iPods for tours enhanced their learning in four main ways.

Firstly, the individualized nature of learning made it possible for students to explore points at their own pace, and to return to particular aspects for review. The first tour was in a parish church which had over a thousand years of history and was packed with interlinked details. Thus, students were able to explore the links between aspects as they noted them and so make their own connections, returning to particular features as necessary. In addition at the Buddha Vihara students were able to sit and reflect in the meditation room as they assimilated a vast amount of information. Several students took this opportunity to go back to particular sections to check how they linked to later items.

Secondly, the variety of media used in the tours provided consolidation for learning by providing a textual, visual, aural or video commentary on each aspect of the tour. Thus the student encounter with each aspect was supported and extended, for example the visit to the Buddha Vihara was based around an aural commentary on each aspect. This commentary was supported by a picture which linked students to the particular aspects of the vihara so they could check they were in the right place. This form of support was the most successful, as it enabled students to engage fully with the feature of the Vihara, without the need to look down at the iPod. The audio commentary helped to examine Buddhist symbols in great detail, and thus supported and extended student engagement.

Thirdly, the collaborative tour undertaken at the mosque paired students up to encourage dialogue through the encounter with the place in relation to the content of the iPod tour. Two programmes were developed to enable students to explore the mosque from two perspectives. One student had a tour which focused on the actual features of the mosque they were in, while the other student had a tour which provided information about general features of a mosque. This enabled students to share information with each other, indeed collaboration was needed to complete the set tasks.

Fourthly, the iPods made it possible to tailor the tour to the content of learning at university. This was important as many places of worship have faith leaders who struggle to explain their beliefs and practices in English. In other places, where clear English details were provided, the informant struggled to provide the level of detail and analysis required for degree level engagement. In additional to the support for pronouncing terms for features in the place of worship, the tours also linked to key terminology for concepts and theories in Religious Studies. This ensured that the field visits were connected to the input in lectures, to allow for a discussion on aspects of theory and practice in the field. Additionally the approach linked to our aim of providing students with appropriate academic engagement, a factor that is very difficult to ensure when relying on a faith informant. We were able to ensure that details linked to lecture content and were suitable for the stage of learning students were at. At one level this meant that students were given sufficient depth and detail, but at the other ensured that their learning was not hampered by confusing detail.

Finally, this approach ensured that all students were provided with the support to enhance their learning. None of those involved in the project had visual or hearing challenges, but the project has identified ways that a range of media can be used to support learning: students with visual impairments can be supported by aural commentaries; students with hearing impairments can be supported with text and signing inputs. The success of this approach will feed into future field visits to provide the range of media to stimulate and support student learning.

Overall student feedback was that the iPods offered a way of supporting learning. Feedback from student participants, both the pilot group, and the project group, identified benefits and drawbacks to this use of technology. This data will be particularly useful in considering different student learning styles, and preferences for visual, auditory, verbal, kinaesthetic, social or solitary learning. The results will have a spin off for inclusion in developing materials to suit not only learning styles but also to provide extended access for students with disabilities who might otherwise have only restricted physical access to places of worship.

This exploration provides a snapshot of an attempt to harness technologies to enhance student learning. This process builds on Collis' notion of the 'contributing-student approach' to develop a 2.0 pedagogy, to fit technological developments, with students as 'co-creators' who are empowered to 'share, build, support, and manage their learning together, in their common context.' (Collis & Moonen, 2005, p.6)

REFERENCES

Apple Inc. (no date). *Learning with iPod touch and iPhone.* Apple in education. Retrieved December 9, 2010, http://www.apple.com/education/ipodtouch-iphone/

Biggs, J. (1999). *Teaching for quality learning at university.* Buckingham, UK: Society for Research in Higher Education & Open University Press.

Biggs, J. (2003). *Teaching for quality learning at university.* Maidenhead, UK: SHRE.

Burke, D. (2009). *Using mobile devices to enhance fieldwork.* Presentation at Higher Education Academy Conference July 2009. Retrieved from http://www.techdis.ac.uk/index.php?p=2_1_7_26_29

Burke, D. (2009). E-learning in dialogue: Using e-learning to explore the local religious environment. *Discourse: Learning and Teaching in Philosophical and Religious Studies, Special edition e-learning in dialogue, 8*(3).

Chryssides, G. D., & Geaves, R. (2007). *The study of religion: An introduction to key ideas and methods.* London, UK: Continuum.

Collis, B., & Moonen, J. (2005). *An on-going journey: Technology as a learning workbench.* Monograph (in Dutch, asfscheid rede) on occasion of their retirement from the University of Twente, Enschede, NL. (96pp). Retrieved 10th May 2008, from http://www.BettyCollisJefMoonen.nl/rb.htm

Fowler, C. J. H., & Mayes, J. T. (1999). Learning relationships from theory to design. *Association for Learning Technology Journal, 7*(3), 6–16. doi:10.1080/0968776990070302

Frechette, J. D. (2002). *Developing media literacy in cyberspace: Pedagogy and critical learning for the twenty-first-century classroom* (p. 4). Westport, CT: Praeger.

Goldman, R. (1965). *Readiness for religion.* London, UK: Routledge.

Grimmitt, M. (Ed.). (2000). *Pedagogies of religious education.* Great Wakering, UK: Mc-Crimmons.

Hall-Matthews, J. C. (1993). *The collegiate Church of St. Peter's Wolverhampton.* Much Wenlock, UK: Smith Publishers.

Jackson, R. (1997). *Religious education: An interpretive approach.* London, UK: Hodder & Stoughton.

Laurillard, D. (1993). *Rethinking university teaching.* London, UK: Routledge.

Mayer, R. E. (Ed.). (2005). *The Cambridge handbook of multimedia learning.* New York, NY: Cambridge University.

Projects, H. E. A. T. (2009). *Mobile technologies.* Techdis. Retrieved December 9, 2009, from http://www.techdis.ac.uk/index.php?p=2_1_7_27_2

Qualifications and Curriculum Authority. (2004). *Religious education: The non statutory national framework.* London, UK: QCA.

Salmon, G., Edirisingha, P., Mobbs, M., Mobbs, R., & Dennet, C. (2008). *How to create podcasts for education.* Maidenhead, UK: Open University.

Chapter 10
Using Digital Stories Effectively to Engage Students

Deborah H. Streeter
Cornell University, USA

ABSTRACT

Teachers in higher education interested in making use of streaming media can access more sources of video than ever before: news sites, popular media sites, YouTube, and Cornell eClips, the world's largest collection of short videos for educators (more than 14,000). Miller (2008) provides an impressive list of sources, along with a discussion of pedagogical rationale for using rich media. However, while supplies are numerous and demand from students is high, many educators lack the experience to integrate rich media effectively in their teaching. In this chapter, the author draws from her experience of building a library of digital video since the mid-90s with her eClips team and using it in the classroom. The chapter will focus on: 1) strategies and practical tips for using video inside and outside the classroom to engage learners and respond to short attention spans and 2) guidelines for educators who wish to create their own rich media collections because they need content that has a very specific focus and/or mirrors their learner population more appropriately in terms of demographics.

RICH MEDIA: THEN AND NOW

Picture an instructor in the mid-20th century using educational filmstrips to enhance classroom teaching. He inserts a spooled strip of 35 mm film into a projector and then advances it frame by frame while students listen to a recording (vinyl in the '60s, cassette tapes in the '70s) in which a distinctive "ding!" signals when to move forward. Fast forward to the present and envision an instructor simply clicking a mouse to play HD-quality video in the classroom. These two images demonstrate the tremendous change in what is available in the

DOI: 10.4018/978-1-60960-800-2.ch010

classrooms of then and now, but don't really tell us much about learners and teachers.

This chapter is a discussion of how new technological possibilities can be translated into effective learning tools and how instructors can effectively use new technologies such as video and audio clips—not only as the latest and greatest fad, but also as tools for active learning and effective engagement. In addition to exploring existing research on uses of technology in the classroom, digital storytelling, and effective learning environments, I draw from experiences with my eClips team building and using a library of digital video since the mid-90s as the basis for: 1) strategies and practical tips for using video inside and outside the classroom to engage learners and respond to short attention spans and 2) guidelines for educators who wish to create their own rich media collections because they need content with a very specific focus and/or content that mirrors the demographics of their specific learner population.

Technologies used in teaching can be delivered through many mechanisms: slide projectors, overhead machines, filmstrip projectors, TV, interactive whiteboards, VHS tape players, and computer projectors, to name a few. In my 23 years of teaching, I have used all of these and I believe that four seemingly small changes have created the most significant difference in the effectiveness of using technology with learners:

1. It is no longer necessary to turn out the lights to use technology.
2. In digital formats, the flow of information can now be easily started and stopped, enabling the instructor to deliver in bursts rather than in long segments.
3. Delivery devices are web-based and more mobile, making content equally available to teacher and learner.
4. Connectivity, facilitated by the Internet and the increasing availability of wide-area networks, allows for sharing of information in real time.

While this list may underwhelm the reader at first glance, consider the research on creating effective learning environments, which emphasizes that the physical environment in teaching is a critical element in creating optimal situations for student. For example, Vosko (1991), a space specialist who works on improving space for adult education, points out that when instructors pay attention to the physical space and technological possibilities, the learning environment can enhance interactivity. After teaching for 20 years with technology, I can vouch for the fact that today instructors are better able to take advantage of rich media due to changes in what is possible in displaying and manipulating the technology. These changes do not only avoid the physically disruptive aspects of earlier technological innovations (think of that dark room with a filmstrip projector and a tape recorder), but actually enhance the learning environment by creating new possibilities. In particular, these subtle changes in technology facilitate and amplify the ability the use digital storytelling in the classroom.

Consider how each element on the list impacts the learning environment. Although I have found little research on the impact of teaching in the dark, it has always seemed counterintuitive to me to turn off the lights in my classroom when presenting information. Pappas (1990) writes about the key physical aspects of conference settings, noting that lighting impacts participant interaction, with natural or bright lighting enhancing "general and intimate conversation and task performance." Put most of us in a dark, cool room and we expect sleep or entertainment to ensue, not dialogue, debate or active learning. Turning off the lights breaks the connection between the teacher and the learner. The instructor cannot get the needed feedback from the faces of the students and the students are cut off from the passion and energy of the teacher. High intensity projectors (LCD and DLP styles) have made a critical difference by eliminating the need to turn off the lights when using computer presentations. When telling a real world story through video, it is crucial to keep the connection between the listener and the speaker.

Information delivered by technology is now easier to stop and start, enabling instructors to blend it into their lectures and interactions with the class. This contrasts with audio and video products that have traditionally been available only in their longer forms. In the 1920s, radio programs, called the "textbooks of the air" (Cuban, 2001), were popular in education, and in later decades reel-to-reel films were installed in classrooms to show movies. But these innovations required a long attention span and the need to listen in a synchronous mode, in the case of radio. Fortunately, digitalized audio and video can be segmented with ease for more flexible use in the classroom. In addition, software programs, such as Keynote for the Mac and Powerpoint for the PC, allow easy insertion of media objects into presentations and make the movement between audio/video and other material seamless for the teacher. Instead of playing long uninterrupted pieces when using a digital story to engage students, an instructor can enrich the material with explanations, questions, and debate, creating a dialogue among the speaker, instructor and students.

Another important change has been the increasing mobility of the projection devices. Rather than relying on expensive installed equipment, teachers can now carry portable equipment in a small bag and move easily to various classroom settings. Technology companies like Mezmeriz (http://mezmeriz.com) are using robust carbon fibers to shrink efficient, wide-angle projectors so they can be embedded into mobile phones, laptops, video players, and smart phones. In addition, portability is helping extend the boundaries of the classroom. Because audio and video are available via the web, teachers and students both have easy access to content. For example, both students and teachers can listen to audio products on-the-go using MP3 devices and view video on cell phones as well as home computers. With these changes, the digital stories can be previewed outside of class, creating a ready environment for discussion inside the classroom.

Increased connectivity has also changed the nature of what is possible in the classroom. For example, I recently brought a team of entrepreneurs into my classroom each week for 15 minutes via Skype to talk about the evolution of their new startup business. Skiba (2008) discusses the various ways Twitter can be used to enable on-the-spot feedback and reporting and thus enhance active learning techniques, such as the One Minute Paper and Muddiest Point. Suddenly the classroom can operate in real time, offering an exciting array of possibilities. Connectivity has also enabled teachers to bring copyrighted material into the classroom, since playing the original material from the Internet (as opposed to illegal downloading) does not violate usage rules.

These four changes — teaching with the lights on, controlling the pace and duration of the information flow, having mobility, and the ability to be connected in real time — bring significant new possibilities into our classrooms. But the truth is, educators have seen many technological advances for use in the classroom heralded as game changing, only to be disappointed. It is fairly easy to find phrases such as "Technology holds great potential for revolutionizing education" (David, 1994), but scholars such as educational materials developer William D. Pflaum, who traveled across the country in 2001 talking with educators, reached the conclusion that technological change in the classroom was not living up to expectations.

The major factor in whether or not technology is effective in the classroom is the teacher, which will come as no surprise to most educators. More specifically, the attitude, training, and practices of teachers make all the difference. The remainder of this chapter is devoted to motivating educators to use audio and video effectively and to provide practical and specific advice on where to find and how to use rich media.

RESEARCH FINDINGS ON EFFECTIVENESS OF RICH MEDIA

Research in the late 21st century was focused primarily on whether using media would have a positive or negative impact on learning. In their excellent review of the debate, Marx and Frost refute the findings of Clark (1983), who claimed "media do not influence learning under any condition," and conclude that the true challenge is "harnessing the motivating impact of video without falling prey to its failings, shallow comprehension, trivialization, and lowered mental effort." By the turn of the century, it was clear that technology would have a lasting impact on the classroom. Hastings and Tracey (2004) argue that the Internet and the World Wide Web have become irreplaceable and have brought new possibilities to the educational landscape. Thus, they suggest that the debate be refocused away from *whether* and toward *how* use of media impacts education.

Looking at rich media (audio and video) in particular, Karpinnen (2005) notes that because of the relative novelty of the Internet, in-depth research on educational benefits of online videos "is still rather scarce." However, such studies are gradually coming to light. For example, Leet and Houser (2003) discuss using classic films to teach elementary concepts in economics, such as scarcity, market structures, public choice and rational ignorance. Sexton (2006) illustrates how he used video clips to teach 30 economic concepts. His experience has been that the clips help students retain important ideas and retrieve them from long-term memory. Likewise, Diamond (forthcoming, 2010) reports that his use of stories to teach the concept of "creative destruction" in economics has been successful. He points out that "stories are memorable and convincing." Rather than using full-length films or videos, Diamond keeps the focus on shorter, self-contained clips. He reports that clips "can be used to spark discussion, to help students remember certain concepts, or to just make the class more fun."

Video clips can be used for storytelling, a mechanism that humans have used to transfer knowledge for hundreds of years. Gallos (2007) identifies storytelling as "fundamental to the search for human meaning as well as a socially economic vehicle for conveying beliefs and values, for learning from experience, and for inspiring social action" and notes that use of stories through film and video speaks to various learning styles. Swap et al. (2001) describe the power of storytelling to transfer the explicit knowledge commonly transferred through systems and training in a corporate context, as well as transfer tacit knowledge, the personal and non-linear information. The paper draws on relevant research in learning and cognitive psychology to clarify how storytelling can be used most effectively. The authors note that cognitive research has shown that knowledge we retain in the unconscious is more likely to be used than that which is retrieved from memory. Accordingly, "because stories are more vivid, engaging, entertaining, …and because of the rich contextual details encoded in stories, they are ideal carriers of tacit dimensions of knowledge." Furthermore, they point out that "stories provide a simple way of combining verbal and visual information. If the story is sufficiently clear or dramatic, it will almost certainly stimulate visual images complementing the story line, providing a vicarious experience that results in a greater likelihood of being remembered." Although Swap and his co-authors were writing in 2001, they were prescient about information technologies, which they predicted should be designed keeping in mind the power of storytelling: "If stories are powerful in verbal form, their effect can be enhanced through the use of multimedia." Today, storytelling through digital media brings new possibilities into the classroom.

Digital video can also be effective because of its ability to engage students who live in a media rich world. Noting that students are surrounded with stimuli, Howard, et al. (2004) researched whether hypermedia can capitalize on "this contemporary sensory rich media environment and effectively employ multimedia effects to discipline-based learning." Their findings, which used Kolb's Learning Style Inventory (1981) to measure learning, showed that use of hypermedia created significant learning. Also referring to Kolb's measures, Tobolowsky (2007) found that video clips were effective in teaching a first year seminar series because students were able resonate with the movie clips she chose from films about college life (e.g., *National Lampoon's Animal House, Higher Learning, Buffy the Vampire, Undeclared*), creating a rich environment for discussion. Choi and Johnson (2005) compare learner perceptions in an online setting and find that instruction involving video is more memorable that traditional text-based instruction.

There have also been studies on how best to use audio products in education. Edirisingha and Salmon (2007) report on ongoing studies of effective podcasting, including among other uses, how they can be used as a strategy for teaching large cohorts in practical-based learning and to bring topical issues and informal content into the formal curriculum. Bongey (2006) shows the use of audio podcasting as an enhancement to student learning and found that it did not decrease student attendance. Griffin, et al. (2009), found that if online lectures had sychnronized audio and video files it was more effective than giving students the audio separately from the visuals.

Technology in and of itself is not a panacea for education. Marshall (2002) asserts that technology can help students make connections, and therefore learn, but he points out that if programs are not well designed or lack an instructional foundation, technology will not by itself create learning. Thus, it is critical to understand how and when to use video and audio in order to achieve desired learning outcomes. Snelson (2008) suggests that to gain practical insight into the potential value or pitfalls of rich media, more case studies are needed. What follows is a case study in how video and audio clips can be used in the teaching of entrepreneurship.

CASE STUDY: USING RICH MEDIA TO TEACH ENTREPRENEURSHIP

The Context of Entrepreneurship Education

Since the mid-90s, I have been teaching a course in startup business planning, as part of Entrepreneurship@Cornell, a university-wide program that stretches across the curriculum at Cornell University. When I began teaching the subject matter, I felt there was a strong need to breathe life into the relatively dry material. In addition, I felt many of the key concepts (value proposition, sustainable competitive advantage, cashflow) were deceptively simple and that students would not appreciate the importance of such ideas and the difficulty of implementing them in business unless I connected them to actual entrepreneurial stories. Although it was challenging at that time, as compared to 2009, I began to produce and use video content in my course.

Video Clips to Present Role Models

The concept I had when starting this project— and continue to cultivate—was the creation of a "virtual guest speaker panel." I wanted the ability to bring into my classroom an interesting and appropriate role model to tell a story, provide point of view, or give an explanation at any desired moment — without flying in a guest or wading through a case study. In the past I had been frustrated because the available options for introducing the real world commentary (guest speakers, full-length videos, case study reading) had to be presented asynchronously with the content to which I was trying to connect. By the time guests had arrived and started telling their entertaining tales, the lessons of the previous weeks seemed too distant for the students to connect the material with previous learning. Likewise, when I taught skills and techniques well after the guest appearance, I had trouble getting students to see how connected those stories were with their current work. I became obsessed with closing the gap between the real world and my classroom, desiring a fluid movement between concept and reality, between framework and example. I hit on a solution: I would do full-length interviews with entrepreneurs and other business experts and create shorter, edited clips from this material for use in class.

Using Microsoft PowerPoint, I inserted video clips directly into the flow of my lecture, enabling me to put context around the clip, which I did by providing an introduction and pointing to key things I wanted the students to listen for before I played the short clip. I aimed at a length of 1-3 minutes. (Interestingly, I find that 1 minute or less is ideal in my classroom today, some dozen years later.) Student feedback was extremely positive and has remained so through the years.

What I have observed is that my students become personally involved with the stories of these experts, linking the "virtual guest speaker" comments with the concepts presented in class and used in the course project (writing a business plan). The following is typical feedback I received from students: "I got so involved with hearing all the stories of these men and women. I was so interested by their plights, their success stories, their failed ventures, their startups, and their advice. I could hear their excitement and felt inspired to work harder to gain the success they had. Each person was completely different from the next and I was excited to hear more and more unique stories." My experience resonates with a point made by Diamond (forthcoming, 2010) who comments that the best clips: "… can reduce the cost to students of focusing on, and remembering, important issues. The clips can be even more valuable when they allow the students to see the issues from fresh perspectives, which can happen when the students have sympathy with the characters in the clips." Previous students are still able to recall with astonishing accuracy, certain phrases and points made by my virtual guest speakers, even years after they listened to eClips in my class.

Here are some examples of what I achieve using video clips in class:

- **Reinforce a point**. When a video clip of an entrepreneur is used to repeat an idea or concept just presented in class, it lends credibility and validity. For example, when teaching students the importance of cash flow, I use a clip of entrepreneur Earl Blanks (Party City Franchisee) saying, "Well you know, cash flow is very important. It is like the oil in a car. You know if you don't have oil in your car it smokes. It burns up. Cash is the same way with a business. You have to have cash. And I'll tell you, here's why. If you're running low on cash, you have employees to pay. You have a rent to pay as I mentioned earlier with the rent we were facing at Party City starting out. You have all these things to pay. So cash is very important. One of the things that's important about cash is to be able to project it. And to be able to know when you need it." The visual image of a car smoking and burning up is very effective in getting students to think more carefully about the cash flow statements in their business plans.

- **Present opposing points of view**. One subject of constant debate in entrepreneurship classes is whether entrepreneurs are born or made. I present two opposing points of view and allow the class to debate the subject. On the one hand, hotel entrepreneur Harris Rosen says: "One has to enjoy the pain almost. One has to believe in one's gut that everything, ultimately, will be fine and one has to be able to pick one's self up repeatedly and move on... I don't know if you can be taught that." On the other hand is Saaed Amidi, technology investor and founder of Plug & Play, saying "I really think my DNA is not any different. It's just what I've been exposed to."

- **Showing a diverse set of faces to the audience**. I can only designate so many classes to a guest speaker format, but with video clips, I am able to introduce dozens of role models to my class. Along the way, I ensure that there will be speakers of various genders, races, orientations, ethnicities, nationalities and other dimensions of diversity.

- **Provoke debate**. Students may feel constrained in criticizing or disagreeing with experts who are present in person. Not so with video clips. I have one particular speaker who has a very arrogant personality and makes broad-sweeping statements, which provoke strong disagreement from the student body. There are no barriers to encouraging energetic (and respectful) discussion of the speaker's viewpoints.

- **Provide relevant role models**. Entrepreneurs have many different personality types and interests, as do my students. In addition to the diversity dimensions mentioned above, I feel it is important to provide a wide variety of role models. Thus, at times I will use the relatively soft spoken person, at others someone who is exuberant and impulsive. It is equally important to share role models who are young (as young as 14!) and those with more experience (some are in their 80s) and at different stages, from startup, to growth to those who have harvested their businesses.

- **Share stories of those who have passed on**. Two of the people I have interviewed for my collection have since passed away. Their stories and journeys are captured and they continue to add their voices to entrepreneurship classrooms.

Finding and Selecting Appropriate Content

The abundance of free video available online represents rich opportunities, but the parallel challenge is trying to map such a broad array of materials to the precise needs of the classroom, a particular course and a specific topic. Video search engines, such as blinkx.com (http://blinkx.com) or clipblast! (http://clipblast.com) provide an imperfect solution to the problem, as it is still quite difficult to find precisely the right clip for the message you want to give to the class. Unlike visual media, it is not easy to scan large numbers of video to select just the right one, since to do so requires viewing the clip and reading the transcript (if available) to make sure the content is appropriate.

As an example, if one searches on the term "cash flow" in various video search engines, the first hits invariably have to do with the rap star Ace Hood singing about "knock, knock, bang, bang, where the cash at…" Educators are better off looking for videos within educational sites, where the content is more likely to be appropriate. Snelson (2008) recommends the list of sites found on the Web-Based Video in Education blog at: http://web-based-video.blogspot.com and also notes subscription-based sites such as Discovery Education Streaming (http://streaming.discoveryeducation.com/index.cfm) where educators can find pre-qualified content that will work in an educational context.

Although these solutions may work for some, there is no solution today for educators who want a short and focused path to video content, unless they are in a discipline in which specific collections exist. At least three existing video clip collections focus on relevant topics in entrepreneurship: Cornell's eClips collection (http://eclips.cornell.edu), Stanford's Education Corner (http://edcorner.stanford.edu), and Juniatia's JCEL Video Library (http://www.juniata.edu/services/jcel/video/index.html). Despite the careful organization of content evident in each of the collections, users still report that trying to find just the right clip is "like drinking out of a fire hose." Searching on "Cash flow" returns too many clips to easily review (94 in eClips, 8 in Edcorner and 14 in JCEL).

Once familiar with the organizational structure of each database it is easier to do a more effective search. For example, in Cornell's eClips collection, aside from keyword searching, one can search clips by theme or topic and then drill down using clip titles. Alternatively, a table is available (under the Entrepreneurs/Experts tab) in which the collection is displayed by name, company, industry, gender, age, and race, allowing the user to sort by any of the column headings.

Searching for targeted content remains a key challenge in the abundant world of free content. Time spent searching and viewing clips adds to the costs and can be discouraging, especially to new users. As the volume of content increases, especially considering the volume of user-generated video added to the Internet every day, the problem is likely to be exacerbated. Curating these collections and allowing for user-generated tags will take on even greater importance as the volume of clips grows.

Best Practices in Using Video Clips in the Classroom

Previous authors have touched on best practices in using video interactively with the class (Champoux, 1999; Bumpus, 2005; Richardson and Glosenger, 2006; Ventura and Onsman, 2009), and in this chapter I add my experiences to theirs. Based on my years of teaching with clips to enliven my classroom, I have identified three key areas of concern when using video in a classroom setting: download and playback issues, assembly instructions and presentation techniques.

Download and playback issues. A video clip can be accessed and played in one of two manners: 1) play in class from the Internet or 2) download the clip and play through presentation software

such as PowerPoint (PC or MAC) or Keynote (MAC). The advantage of the first option is that there is no need to store and retrieve the clip on your own computer. However, the delivery of the clip is dependent on having a robust connection to the Internet with enough bandwidth to play the clip in real time. Downloading the clip and using presentation software allows you to create a more seamless presentation, but does involve some knowledge of how to assemble a video-enhanced lecture (as discussed later in this chapter). Therefore, the simplest option, from a technology standpoint, remains playing the clip from the online source. Interestingly, a study entitled *Video Use and Higher Education: Options for the Future* (2009) surveyed librarians and teachers and reported that faculty and administrators "expect the sources of their video to shift from offline analog storage to online delivery."

One thing to keep in mind is that computers rely on specific media players to view video clips. Presentation software such as Keynote or PowerPoint require downloaded clips to be in a particular format (noted in the documentation). With media formats changing and evolving rapidly, it is important to have updated software and media players. "Unknown file type" and "codec not found" messages are usually indications of an out-of-date media player.

When using an older computer, video playback may stutter or be sluggish. Potential solutions include: 1) cleaning up a hard drive that is excessively full or 2) shutting down other processes if too many programs are running at once. Some inexpensive laptops and especially older laptops have very slow hard drives and CDRom drives, in which smooth video playback may be impossible. In addition, video will almost always play back better from the computer's hard drive versus a CDRom or USB removable drive (both may work fine depending on the speed of the CDRom or the quality of the removable drive). It is ideal to test playback on the computer that is to be used for presentation.

Most modern classrooms have some type of computer projection, ranging from devices rolled into the classroom for display to overhead computer projection to smartboards attached to player devices. In each case, for educators planning to play video clips through a computer, the key question is: How will sound be projected? Since projection is often used only for visual representations, which require no sound, it is not uncommon to find a classroom situation in which no provision has been made for playing the audio aspect of a video clip. When you are going to present in a room, be sure there is the ability to project sound. If you are in doubt, bring a small pair of computer speakers. I have found even a small set of speakers is big enough for a class of up to 100 people. Beyond that size, it is imperative to be able to plug into the room's own sound system. Finally, it is important to have control over sound, especially if you are playing more than one clip, since various clips may playback at different volumes.

Projected playback can be tricky, depending on the age of the computer. Lower end models (laptops, in particular) may not be able to play video on the laptop screen and the projector at the same time. In such a case, the user has to play the video through only the projector, and not the laptop screen by toggling one of the function keys (which one depends on the model of the computer.)

To summarize, consider the following checklist of logistical decisions:

- Choose whether to view clips directly from the Internet or from presentation software.
- If viewing clips directly from the Internet, make sure access and bandwidth are adequate at the projection site.
- Update computer media player.
- Optimize playback on computer through equipment choice or by making space and/or closing down other programs.
- If downloading, choose a video format compatible with the software.

- Test sound projection in classroom to be sure projected video plays sound at adequate level with option to control.

Assembly instructions. A presentation that involves video or audio clips can bring up both content issues and technical issues. From the content side, appropriate video placement is very important. I use the "80/20 rule" as an outside boundary; at the most, video should not make up more than 20% of the time in the classroom. For a 50-minute class, I do not use more than a total of 10 minutes of video, which may be broken down for shorter clips (for example, 3 2-minute clips, 2 1-minute clips and 4 30-second clips). The flow of the lecture/discussion dictates where the clips are inserted, but ideally they are distributed throughout the time period rather than being delivered back-to-back.

The steps for inserting video into a presentation vary by software package. Typically a blank slide is created and a series of steps allows the user to choose the clip to be inserted. When using PowerPoint 2007, go to the Insert tab, point to Movies and Sounds, and then click Movie from File and select the desired movie. In Keynote, select Insert/Choose and point to the relevant file. When inserting a video into a presentation, the software allows two options: playing the video automatically or when you click on the video. I prefer the latter option as it provides more control. In addition, I particularly like the ability in Keynote to start the video at any point and to start and stop the video any time during the playback. While this is possible in PowerPoint, it is not as user-friendly.

I find it useful to copy and paste the file name of the video and the transcript (if available) into the notes section of the presentation slide that includes the clip. I do this so that when I review the presentation for delivery at future dates, I need not replay the entire clip to remind myself of the salient points I wish to make. Cornell's eClips collection actually gives users the option to download an introductory slide for each speaker that contains a picture and some bullet points that present the speaker, including a bio in the notes section.

On the technical side, it is important to understand how presentation software (PowerPoint or Keynote) embeds video clips. Unlike clipart or photos, which become part of the presentation file and move with the file (for example, when moving from an external USB drive to another computer), video has a more complicated relationship with the video presentation. Files with either.ppt or.key extensions must have access to the original video clips file at the time of playback. Furthermore, during playback, the presentation software looks for the video clip file in the same place it resided at the time it was inserted. Thus, files have to be moved with care or all the associated video files will not be found by the presentation software and will be need to be re-inserted. For PC users, PowerPoint has a function called Package for CD that simplifies this process.

Here is checklist of issues to consider in the assembly process:

- Use no more than 20% of class time playing video content. Less is fine.
- Use flow of presentation to guide the clip placement, but aim to have video content distributed throughout class.
- Insert video and choose how it will play (immediately or on command).
- Cut and paste the transcript into the notes section.
- Download the introductory slide (if using eClips) for the speaker or create your own and insert in front of the slide containing the video.
- Move the presentation with care, making sure to either package up the videos through the software options or retain the file structure and storage of the clips.

Delivery techniques. Karpinnen (2005) notes that "videos are just one component in the complexity of a classroom activity system. The learning outcomes depend largely on the way videos are used as part of the overall learning environment, for example, how viewing or producing videos is integrated into other learning resources and tasks." In other words, the effective use of video depends on the way it is queued up by the educator, how attention is drawn to salient points and how it is integrated in the remainder of the learning experience.

It is critical for the educator to provide context for a video clip before playing it in class. By providing an introduction the teacher signals the listener that something new is about to happen in class and prepares the way for more careful listening. The approach resonates with the findings of Hooper and Hannafin (1991) who introduced the concept of "orienting" activities that prepare the learner by stimulating existing cognitive structures. Their findings would suggested that learning is enhanced and long term retrieval is more likely when orienting activities prepare the student ahead of media presentation.

To start the process, I use an introductory slide, with a picture and some bullet points describing the speaker while I am introducing the clip. As mentioned, introductory slides are pre-assembled and downloadable for all eClips speakers, but I also create my own if I am using content from a different source. When introducing a clip, I provide a description of the speaker and then say some variation of the following:

- "Listen carefully to see if you can catch her three main points about [topic]"
- "After listening, I'm going to ask if you agree with her."
- "Listen carefully to the beginning [or middle or end] of the clip, where he shows his central point."
- "I'm going to play the first part and then interrupt to ask you a question."

- "Here's what a real investor (or entrepreneur, or banker, or inventor) has to say about the ideas we have just been learning."

All of these cues are intended to help draw the learner's attention and to heighten his listening attitude.

I rarely turn off the lights to play a clip, unless absolutely necessary for visibility. I prefer to leave the lights on because I want to cultivate a sense of communication between the speaker, the classroom and me. I stop the clip at key points, repeating part of the comment or adding an idea, providing the illusion of give-and-take between us. Establishing this rhythm and connection between the content and the audience is an important part of effective storytelling. I narrate the clip in small pieces, while avoiding interrupting the virtual speaker so much as to be annoying. By involving the class at various points through asking for questions and opinions, I am building a relationship between the learners and the speakers, making the clip seem more similar to a live speaker.

In the following example, I will illustrate how I use clips in a typical presentation and when I "interrupt" the virtual speaker by pausing the clip to insert my comments (noted in italics). The actual clip can be accessed through Cornell's eClips Collection (select Entrepreneur and choose Pelletier.) The introduction provides evidence that the speaker, Dave Ahlers, is a credible expert (smart, trained at MIT, successful in a globally business and an active investor) and gives listeners an important reason — connected to their own self-interest — to listen to Dave's comments (he will be a business plan judge for their plans). The focus of this section of the presentation is on telling the "story" of how Dave approaches business ideas and plans. The clips allows you to follow the story of how Dave goes through a plan, page by page, ticking off (or not) his key checklist.

Instructor Comments: Listen carefully to this clip. We are going to hear from Dave Ahlers, an entrepreneur turned venture capitalist. He will be explaining the way an investor like him approaches a business plan. He's a fascinating guy, who has a PhD in Management and Computer Science from Carnegie Mellon – so he often approaches things with a technology/science mindset. His earliest business, in which he used a simulation in executive training, had clients in the financial services all over the world. He was also one of the founders of our local venture capital fund here in Tompkins County. And perhaps most importantly, he will be one of the business plan panelists at the end of the semester, so this is your chance to hear how he thinks about business plans, set-by-step

Clip. "First thing I look for — on my "good stuff list" — is it market driven?"

Pause the clip: What do you think he means by market driven ? – [some discussion will ensue with the class] – OK, let's listen because next he is going to talking about the need for the business to address a problem or "pain" on the part of the industry.

Clip resumes. "That is, does it start off with ABC industry has the following problem... and that I have sufficient data presented to me (because I am a busy guy) that says, "hey, the US Department of Commerce checks off on this, or each one of the Federal Reserve districts has a detailed report on business and it's usually once a quarter" -- that's been quoted. So I have lots of data supporting this, it's not just "I think that's the case okay."

Pause the clip: Why does he mention that he is a busy guy? It's because he does not want to have to dig up the facts. Your presentation of data in the plan helps free the investor from the need of certain types of "due diligence" – research – and sets the investor at ease about your conclusions. And the fact that the source is a government source makes a big difference in terms of credibility. Now he is going on to the next point, which includes the term "IP," meaning "intellectual property"

Clip resumes. "The second thing is that I have IP protection, and I know who owns the idea, that it's not you know ambiguous."

Pause the clip: What form does IP protection take and why does it matter? – [discussion ensues] –Now, pay attention to how he talks next about something we have heard time and time again – it's all about the team]

Clip resumes. "Third thing is that I have an experienced management team. I mean the entrepreneur doesn't have to be experienced but if he can get together a team that is, who is going to run the company, that's fine."

Pause the clip: This reinforces the idea we have heard before – that the entrepreneur needs to build a balanced and experienced team. Next, he is going to use the term PPM – it means a private placement memo, which is a legal document that outlines the risks

Clip resumes. "I am looking for an honest description of the risks involved, in the... the PPM it legally has to have this purchasing memorandum, and some of them are really good. All I want to know is, what are the risks and what do you think you can do -- not to eliminate them but to mitigate them. And what I don't want to see is that, here are all the risks but we have a bunch of bright guys... and the word I hate is "huge" - that we have huge markets, huge capabilities okay, this absolutely means nothing."

Pause the clip: What do you think he means here? - [discussion ensues] - Why is "huge" a dirty word here? Because when you describe with

an adjective, rather than showing the point with data, it is not convincing.

Clip resumes. "The revenue model will support growth. Lots of times you can have a revenue model but not one that will support you know reasonable growth. I want documentation on the scale up -- to know that both structurally the company is set to grow... I mean the way you could stop growing is that you have covenants put on the financials of the company by a bank that you should never have gotten the loan from in the first place, things like this could be actually be impediments as you go along. That's the revenue model."

Pause the clip: What is "reasonable" growth for a venture capitalist? [discussion ensues] What kind of multiple is he expecting? [discussion ensues] Next he'll address the competitive landscape.

Clip resumes. "The other aspect of it is the technological reality and then, then finally I want detailed intelligence on the competition and all your near term customers. All too often people will say well, they don't really appreciate what we have got and our competitors are all idiots, okay, sure that would be my list."

Pause the clip: Now listen carefully – he's going to talk about what type of thing will cause him to "ash can" the plan – put it in the garbage

Clip resumes. "The bad stuff and what would cause me to "ash can" it, would be any format errors whatsoever. If somebody misspells something, my god, if you can misspell it and not punch you know spellchecker, okay what did you do on all the other stuff, it's so much harder, I mean you get the easy stuff done. If there are missing charts and tables if there's more than a two-page executive summary, if there are large appendices with detailed excel spreadsheets that mean absolutely nothing given the early stage of the company, okay I don't bother."

Clip has ended. From what you just heard, who can tell me what are the "ash can" conditions that relate to presentation? [discussion ensues.]

It takes practice to pause in the right places, and sometimes it is tricky to start and stop (depending on the computer and the software). If difficulties are encountered, there is an alternative method for presenting the clip. For this example, the following list could be posted on the board along with instructions to students that they should listen for these key points, noting that a discussion will follow the playing of the entire clip:

- Market-driven
- Data (for credibility)
- IP – Intellectual Property
- Management Team
- PPM – Private Placement Memo
- Risk
- Revenue Model
- Intelligence on customers
- "Ash-can" factors

Note that even with this strategy, it might still be desirable to stop the clip part way through, just because 3 minutes is a long time to listen to video without any interruption.

Whether the clip is played in segments or without interruption, it is important to do a quick summary after the speaker is finished. Again, the idea is to create the feeling of connectedness to the course materials, so it may be useful to contrast the speaker to another source (book, lecture, another video clip) and also to note that the class will be "talking to him" again later in the semester or later in the presentation. The most important thing is to make the connection (through presentation and interaction) between the wisdom you are extracting from the story of the expert and the conceptual material or skills you are teaching in class.

OTHER CREATIVE USES OF RICH MEDIA

Audio in the Classroom

The chapter has focused on video until now, but audio content can also be extremely useful for educational purposes. If an audio clip is played while displaying a photo of the speaker (or other visual images), it is easier for the audience to make a connection with the speaker. A positive feature of audio is that when listening, students may not be influenced by personality factors, gestures, or visual tics that may be present in video formats. If the speaker is talking with relevant sounds in the background, such as a trading floor, or a manufacturing setting, it can make the clip sound more "real time" and relevant, whereas such noise in a video clip could be viewed as distracting. The mindset when listening to an audio source is more like that of radio listening, where the brain is trying to fill in details based on audible cues, while with video, the viewer is taking in much more data and extraneous noise is just one more thing to filter out.

It is more difficult to find short, focused audio than video. Most audio exists in podcast formats, which tend to be longer than 5 minutes. One exception is the eClips collection, which includes both full-length podcasts and associated shorter audio clips. These can be used in class while showing a visual of the speaker or a related picture.

Other Uses of Rich Media Outside of the Classroom

Both audio and video content can be useful outside the classroom and can move the timing and pacing of listening into the hands of the student. Here are some suggestions for how to use rich media outside class, along with examples drawn from my entrepreneurship classes.

1. **Create a listening list for class to review**. Most sites have a way to bookmark clips. In Cornell's eClips collection, the list can be annotated and published for students to hear outside class. Advantages include saving time in class and the opportunity for listeners to pause, rewind and review if needed. A disadvantage is that the act of listening is asynchronous with the conceptual learning in the classroom, which can lead to a disconnect between the clip and the related concepts.

2. **Ask students to find and share relevant video clips, with annotation, for use by the entire class**. Students, in general, are quite good at browsing and, in my experience, enjoy being involved in the selection of material.

3. **Have students create video or audio material**. The option of having students involved in user-generated content, such as interviewing experts or capturing an event or speaker that connects with class material, is appealing as an active learning strategy. In order for this method to be effective, students should be mentored on how to execute a strong interview. There is rich literature on the positive impact of involving students in digital storytelling (Meadows, 2003; Standley, 2003; Ohler, 2007; Fletcher and Cambre, 2009). Barrett (2005) presents a comprehensive literature review on the topic and concludes that digital storytelling, as executed by students brings together four student-centered learning strategies: student engagement, reflection for deep learning, project-based learning and the effective integration of technology into instruction. The website "Integrating Digital Story Telling in Your Classroom" (http://its.ksbe.edu/dst/) includes instructions for K-12 teachers, with excellent tips on video creation by students.

CREATING A COLLECTION OF DIGITAL VIDEO

Rich media is abundant, although much of it is not created or focused in a way that is appropriate for educational purposes. When YouTube launched in 2005, it opened up a channel that would become a rich playground for users to post and view user-generated video content, although finding the right clip for class among the millions of choices can be a challenge. A study from the Video and the Higher Education Project (2009) involving faculty and librarians from 20 institutions, reported that despite the abundance of existing video, 43% of the instructors answered yes to the statement "I can't find quality/appropriate material." The study also concludes that "technology, legal and other barriers continue to thwart faculty finding and accessing the segments of video they want for teaching and lectures." Educators may want to create custom content for a class or course, in order to target a particular topic or capture speakers with certain demographics that match the learner population. On most campuses, there are ready sources of storytelling (e.g., guest speakers, presentations, conferences) and it can be useful to create a collection that is targeted specifically to a particular set of learners and focused expressly on topics that relate to the curriculum. This section of the chapter provides guidelines and tips on how to approach creating educator-generated content.

Creating a Plan of Work

Even when creating a relatively small collection of video clips, it is ideal to map out a work plan for the project. Sketching out a timeline with specific milestones illuminates the many decisions to make along the way and provides a realistic idea if content will be ready to use on the desired launch date. Table 1 is a display of the various tasks to include on the timeline and estimated duration, based on my experience with eClips.

The initial work, which is "pre-production" in nature, includes clarifying the intended use of the collection and clarifying the strategic mission and goals. For example, it is important to determine whether the primary purpose of the collection is to address specific skills/topics or to present a particular range of role models and their storylines. In addition, it is important to consider whether the rich media is intended for use inside the classroom or to be used in an auto-tutorial manner, with users determining their own pathway through the material. Determining the core mission of the collection will help the educator make decisions about who to interview, how to frame the questions and how to choose an appropriate format and length of the final product. In addition, educators should think about the end users, their technology-readiness and whether they tend to approach information in a linear "deep dive" fashion or are more likely to simply browse and skim.

Early tasks also include choosing the size and scope of a project, including the number of videos and whether the end product will be primarily video or audio or some blend. For example, if the users are likely to listen on mobile devices, audio might be favored over video. However, if the primary use is in class or being viewed on a computer, the added visual impact of video is more effective. In addition, educators must decide how to capture, store and deliver the information, which will in turn dictate the budget. Other pre-production tasks include building a team (which could be a team of one or many, depending on the size and scope of the project) and creating materials to be used in preparing for the taping of the interviews or presentations. Depending on the nature of the project, the initial tasks outlined in the work plan might take a few weeks, but if the project is larger, it may take up to several months.

Running a pilot is a recommended next step in the work plan. Creating a small sample of the work that will make up the collection helps reveal problematic issues and provides a prototype, which may be used to obtain funding. A pilot might take up to a month, including setting up, executing the shoot, and evaluating the experiment.

If the project is continued after the pilot, a decision should be made about how the video will be stored. One option would be to use a storage and delivery mechanism such as a YouTube Channel or Vimeo. An alternative would be to use a content management system, such as the open-source Kaltura or a customized database such as the one created and used by the eClips team. Implementation of the system can take from a month to several years, depending on the approach and the scope of the collection.

The next step in the work plan includes production work that happens before the taping of each interview or presentation. This work includes choosing speakers, getting appropriate releases, and doing the research needed to write interview scripts and/or set up the presentation shoot. Once the pre-interview work is completed, the video shoot or audio taping itself actually takes the least amount of time, in comparison to other aspects of the project. With setup and break down, the shoot (production) time will take about 2 times the length of the actual taping. The post-production tasks (such as compressing, transcribing, editing, outputting to various formats, and translating and subtitling (if needed), can take much longer, depending on the extent of metadata and the need for subtitles. Furthermore, if the collection is intended for use beyond the educator himself, the final steps of the project plan should involve marketing, promotion and distribution, all of which can also be resource-intensive.

Presentations or Interviews?

The most convenient approach to generating rich media content can be to capture presentations that are already occurring at a conference or in a lecture room. Such events can provide a cost effective alternative to interviewing; however, speakers do not always divide comments into clear sections,

Table 1. Workplan for creating digital media collection

	Tasks	Approximate duration
Initial work – Pre-Production	• Study opportunity for using video in specific settings ○ Talk to educators ○ Talk to potential learners • Set mission and goals • Choose size and scope of project ○ Number of interviews or presentations ○ Audio vs. video ○ Set timeline for the project • Choose methods for: ○ capture ○ storage ○ delivery • Create budget and secure funding • Build team for content creation and processing • Create materials ○ Invitation to interview ○ Information about the collection ○ Release form	Several weeks up to ~3 months
Pilot	• Optional: run small pilot	1 month
Infrastructure	• Choose or create storage and delivery mechanisms	6months-2 years
Production work – Pre-Interview or presentation	• Set up Interviews or presentations • Choose portfolio of speakers ○ Obtain permission and releases ○ Obtain bios ○ Research speakers ○ Line up technology • Writing Interview scripts (2 hours/interview)	1-6 months
Production work - Shoot	• Conduct interviews and followup activities or tape presentation	1.5 hours per interview
Post Production	• Digitize, transcribe, translate (if needed) edit, tag/index (create metadata), upload	2-4 weeks per interview
Marketing	• Market to educators and learners	ongoing
Distributing	• Deliver content to end users ○ Finalize product scope ○ Seek out distribution channels (including strategic partnerships) both traditional and non-traditional	

so if there is a desire to clip material into shorter pieces (see next section for whether or not to clip), post-production editing of presentations can be problematic. It can also be challenging to capture rich media in a setting where you may not have control over lighting or the sound system. Panels provide an especially challenging situation for the videographer and/or sound engineer.

As shown in Figure 1, presentations, panel discussions and sit-down interviews present a different look and feel for the user. Although typically more resource-intensive than presentations, a sit-down interview can provide a good interviewer with the perfect opportunity to craft very focused material and, with the help of a talented videographer, the result can be a very intimate one-on-one feel for the user.

Audio or Video?

Choosing the type of rich media for the intended audience is a strategic choice. The decision between audio and video should be based on the following factors:

1. **Ability to Create Video at a High-Quality Level.** If there is no access to good videographers who can follow standards, it may be preferable to create audio content, which requires a simpler setup and avoids the need for an experienced eye behind the camera. Bad video quality is distracting and takes away from the credibility of a speaker. However, whenever the resources and talent are available for doing a video shoot, it is the first choice, since good quality video is effective and engaging. Producing the original in video format still leaves the option to use only the audio if needed.

2. **Playback Capability.** If only a few of the end users have video playback capabilities, then creating audio files makes the most sense. If end users have access to high bandwidths and mobile or computer devices, then video is a good choice.

3. **Cost.** While creating audio is cheaper than video in terms of recording costs, the actual creation of raw content makes up only about 25% of the overall costs of producing and using rich media, and the postproduction activities are about the same for each format.

4. **Culture.** In some environments, interviewees are less willing to be videotaped and prefer audio-only recording, which can provide them with a higher degree of anonymity.

Clip or Not to Clip?

Editing rich media into small pieces costs more money and time in postproduction as compared to long form video and audio. However, if done correctly, creating more digestible "nuggets" of a speaker's storyline can create highly useable material. With so many sources of competition for the learner's attention, it is important to be able to signal that an initial investment in time for the listener to engage with the video is not burdensome. Providing the listener/viewer with smaller, sequential pieces may be more successful than asking him to tackle a full-length piece of rich media. In other words, it may be easier to get a user to watch ten 3-minute clips than one 30-minute clip. Thus, editing longer pieces of video or audio into shorter, focused clips, and storing them in a searchable database, provides flexibility for the educator and learner. Still, the editing process is cost intensive and can make up more than half the cost of content creation.

A key aspect of effective clip editing is to use a transcript when editing. Cost-effective transcription is available both domestically and overseas. A content expert can edit an hour-long video into shorter clips more easily using the text of the transcript than trying to edit straight from the content. It may be tempting to skip the cost of transcription, but using transcripts will actually save resource expense later in the post-production process.

Figure 1. Presentations, panels and interview all provide a different look and feel

CREATING RICH MEDIA THROUGH INTERVIEWS

Interviews are especially important sources of video content because of the ability to choose a particular expert and extract specific aspects of his story for use in education. Included below are some best practices in interviewing developed by the Cornell eClips team.

Creating a Budget

Table 2 contains the cost categories that should be considered when drawing up a budget for rich media collection focused on sit-down interviews (as opposed to taping presentations). The assumption is made that the interview will involve a professional videographer and that the shoot is done in a studio or at the site of the interviewee.

Building a Good Team

Since content creation is always the work of more than one individual, the team is an important factor the project from the very beginning. To create a collection with a predictable level of quality, all the players need to have a good understanding of the project and how their work fits into the collection. Some of the roles to be played are:

- **Director**. This individual is responsible for setting the mission of the project, overseeing the selection of the rest of the team, choosing and communicating with the interviewees, helping with the creation of the interview scripts, and coordinating and overseeing the post production work.
- **Interviewer**. In many cases, the interviewer role can be played by the Director. When choosing the Interviewer, consider whether he/she has a demeanor that will be accessible and comfortable when conversing with the interviewees. The individual should have some combination of the qualities of a researcher and a journalist:

natural curiosity, ability to infer, systematic approach to recordkeeping, and knowledge of qualitative research ability to listen proactively and to adjust to and deal with the unexpected.

- **Videographer**. It may be tempting to use an amateur to run the camera in a shoot, but it is highly recommended to find a professional, since the quality of the audio and video will make a big difference to the end user. The Videographer must be committed to meeting the established quality standards (suggested quality standards follow in a later section). The Videographer must be professional in interacting with the interview and remain flexible and adaptable, able to use natural lighting or to set lights strategically and be pro-active in creating the best setting for the interview.
- **Post-Production Team**. There are many elements to the post-production process: digitizing, dubbing a backup copy, transcribing, translating (when needed), editing, compressing, subtitling (when needed), tagging, uploading and long term hosting. While members of the team may handle some of these functions, other functions may be outsourced. However, it is important to have a full team, including subcontractors if needed, to handle every step of the post-production so that the Director can concentrate on the management role. The tagging aspect of post-production is especially critical and easy to overlook. It entails titling, and assigning keywords, topics and/or themes to each clip. Together with the transcript, these tags are what determine how easy it is for users to find the clips in your collection. In assembling the post-production Team, the Director should think about standardizing the workflow so post-production work can be done in a timely manner with predictable quality.

Table 2. Consider all costs when putting together a budget

Cost Category	Special comments
Interviewer	Consider labor requirements and costs for communication required for interview: • preparation, • interview execution • interaction with subjects after the interview.
Videographer	If shooting video (rather than just audio), budget for at least one trained person to run the shoot from a technical side.
Location expense	Sometimes the only way to get high quality audio and video is to rent a conference room or studio.
Supplies and equipment for video shoot	Include cost of professional or "prosumer" equipment rentals or purchases required to do high quality audio and video production: • camera • lights • microphones • tripod • high quality video tapes • portable hard drives • amenities for the interviewee (such as water bottle, lunch or small thank you gift)
Travel	Include travel for both interviewer and videographer to the site (consider extra baggage charges imposed by airlines, bus or rail).
Post production - equipment	To edit and process minimum requirements include: • A powerful desktop computer with expanded memory, • Hard drive or asset server with plenty of storage space (500 gigabytes to 15 terabytes depending on anticipated collection size) • Editing software (such as Apple's FinalCut Pro or Adobe'sPremiere Pro) • Compression software (something with batch compression capabilities)
Post production - labor	Consider the labor costs involved in: • Digitizing • Editing • compressing • quality control. Note: Different levels of training are needed at each step.
Transcription	This is done first in the original language. You will need to evaluate various options, including outsourcing. The transcript is **critical** in creating the metadata that will enrich the user's searching experience, so this is not a place to skimp.
Translation and Subtitling	If the original language is not the one most comfortable for your users, include translation costs to convert. There are various options for subtitling. *Note: the translation and subtitling expenses will likely at least in-* ***crease*** *your cost per clip* ***by factor of 5*** *as compared to simple transcription.*
Tagging and uploading - labor	Creating the right set of metadata is critical. Include labor costs associated with someone doing quality control, careful titling and keyword assignment, as well as assigning clips to any topics or themes you are building. That person also finalizes the bio and company information that will be associated with the clip.
Web programmer	Even a collection of the smallest size will benefit from a web presence.
Database programmer	More than a few dozen clips on a web page will require organization and searchability. A database will help facilitate that. Consider planning for scalability as it will pay off when your collection grows.

Choosing a Good Subject and Preparing to Create a Digital Story

A good interview can come from a subject in any stage in life or from any industry or sector. But if a series of interviews are planned, it is important to think through the composition of the interviewee pool. For example, students and young entrepreneurs enjoy stories of individuals close to them in age, but they also find name-brand speakers highly credible. In addition, the team should determine whether to concentrate on a single industry for depth or target a variety of industries to get a broad sample. The team should also give thought to gender, racial, and ethnic composition along with other dimensions of diversity.

The interviewer should research the interviewee thoroughly, starting with his/her personal or professional webpages, blogs or podcasts. Listening to or reading interviews done with your prospective candidates can help provide a sense of what is important to them. Sites such as Linkedin and Zoominfo can be helpful, but the information found there is not necessarily accurate and/or endorsed by the interviewee.

The goal of the interview is to capture a story in digital format. Based on my experiences, keeping a digital story framework is important even when the goal is primarily to get factual information. The objective information you gather is more likely to stick with students if imbedded in a storyline. By identifying critical turning points in the life of the individual, the interviewer can more easily get the subject to open up during their conversation. The research phase can also be helpful in identifying where the interviewee can inform (talk about their subject matter expertise) and where they can inspire (report how they survived the bumps in the road to accomplish their goals). Each stage of a person's professional journey brings its own "teachable moment" and it is important to design questions that feel relevant to the interviewee and illustrate that the interviewer understands where the speaker is in his/her journey (early startup, about to exit, moving into entrepreneurship after a corporate career, etc.).

Always Write a Script

It might be tempting to have a free-flowing conversation with an expert, but creating and sharing a written interview script with the interviewee ahead of time organizes the interview and provides a sense of safety for the speaker. In the case of a series of interviews, a database of questions can be developed and serve as the source of 80% of most interview scripts, leaving about 20% to be written and tailored for the specific individual. An efficient process can include a template for use each time an interview script (to be shared with the interviewee) is constructed. The template can include:

- a short explanation of the project.
- a reminder of how the interview will be conducted and what not to wear on camera (bold striping, black and/or white).
- whatever bio information available have for the interviewee (to verify).
- initial set of standard questions.

When interviewing an expert with a specific course outline or set of topics in mind, it is important to create questions that will evoke the comments, insights and wisdom relevant to the need. One technique is to ask the interviewee to first comment on a particular topic and then give a specific example or relate it directly to his/her personal experience, which helps steer an interview away from a long series of empty platitudes. Although the general comments on particular topics can be useful, specificity brings the material alive for the listener and provides the real-world context that makes the speaker credible.

What truly interests users about an interview, in the end, is the personal and professional journey of the person him/herself. Humans relate to stories, so the eClips collection, more than anything else, is about the insights the entrepreneurs/experts have gained as they have lived out their personal stories. An interview with ten standard questions and little room for variation will result in material that will feel quite sterile. On the other hand, if the interviewer provides a chance for the individual to talk more broadly about his/her life, unexpected gems may appear along the way.

Planning the Shoot

One of the first decisions when planning the shoot is the pacing of the interviews. Although it is possible to do an intensive number of interviews over a 1-2 week period, the eClips experience has shown that it may be more efficient to schedule blocks of 4-5 interviews at a time. When planning the pace of the interviews, take into account basic logistics - the availability of the team, the physical distance between interviewees, etc.

The interviewer, depending on the level of experience, will spend 1-2 hours preparing for the interview. After creating an interview script, the interviewer should plan how to use the 15-20 minutes with the interviewee while the videographer is setting up and checking lights, and getting the speaker wired up. This time provides an opportunity to check in with the interviewee, clarify any questions about the process or where/how the interviews will be used, and to relax the individual ahead of the official beginning of the interview.

Selecting an appropriate interview location makes a difference in the look and feel of the clips, and most importantly, the quality of the sound. There are two primary options – onsite at the interviewee's offices or at a studio. There are many advantages to doing the shoot on the site of the interviewee's company. First, the environment itself will provide clues about the entrepreneur/expert and may suggest additional questions. Second, it is more convenient for the interviewee, which makes him more likely to agree to an interview. Finally, the collection will be filled with different backdrops for each speaker, which will be more interesting to users. The disadvantage is that the interviewer and videographer have to travel to the site and set up in uncertain circumstances.

When working with the interviewee to choose the site, some considerations include:

1. **Light**. The degree of control over lighting can make a considerable difference in the quality of a shoot. Flourescent lights are dif-ficult to work with, and windows with too much natural light (and no curtains) can be equally challenging.

2. **Sound**. It is very difficult to shoot with good audio if there is a lot of ambient noise. Typical culprits: loud air conditioning, roofs that are noisy if it rains, and office environments with a lot of activity. The interviewee should be alerted that a relatively quiet space will be needed, free of these types of noises.

3. **Privacy**. It is important that the interviewee remain relaxed and natural during the interview. That is unlikely to be the case if partners and/or employees surround him.

4. **Size**. Small rooms are difficult for the videographer, who will be looking for flexibility in terms of camera placement.

5. **Seating**. Two comfortable chairs are needed, preferably ones that do not allow movement, such as rocking or leaning backward.

6. **Backdrop**. The videographer may choose to hang a backdrop or to use existing surfaces as a background for the shoot. Creating an effective backdrop is an art rather than a science and the videographer should take the lead in doing this while the interviewer converses with the interviewee.

7. **Studio setting**. If a studio setting is available and it is easy for interviewees to travel to the location, it can provide consistent, predictable quality in terms of backdrop, lighting, and audio. The disadvantages are usually cost (which may be counterbalanced by the fact that the videographer and interviewer have no travel expenses) and the risk the shoot may look too sterile or "overproduced."

The Interview

At the beginning of the interview, interviewer should explain that it is very helpful for the interviewee to include some aspect of the question in the answer they give. Since the interviewer's voice is typically edited out, the clips need to start with some context. For example, if asked: "What is your definition of an entrepreneur?" speakers should not start with "Someone who is independent," but rather "I think an entrepreneur is someone who is independent."

The interviewer should pay attention to his own demeanor and interaction with the speaker. To create clean clips, the interviewer should not interrupt the speaker until the thought is finished. Interviewers who have a conversational style in which the tendency is to encourage someone in a dialogue by giving verbal cues (e.g., "I see", "Oh, that's interesting", "I know what you mean"), should learn the discipline of giving those cues with body language, eyes, and facial expression in order to avoid clips with extraneous interviewer noise. Relaxing the interviewee is an important task for the interviewer. This can be achieved by reminding the speaker that the interview will be conversational and post-editing will help if there are any slip-ups. If the interviewer maintains a relaxed but attentive demeanor, the interviewee may feel more at ease. The interviewer should be aware of any restlessness on the part of the speaker and provide breaks as needed. Also, most interviews will touch upon a subject not anticipated by the interview script, so the interviewer must stay alert to take advantage of these key moments.

Although it may seem self-evident, the interviewer should write a note of thanks as soon as possible after the interview and follow up later with a copy of the clips. Interviewing is an important networking activity and can help the educator connect to other interesting subjects.

Post Production

Postproduction activities vary depending on the goal of the collection. For example, the eClips process begins with making a backup copy of the original footage. Then the team creates an audio file, gets a transcript produced, edits the clips, and compresses the clips in various file formats (for use with PCs, Mac and the Web). The results

are then reviewed for quality control, tagged with keywords and other metadata, and then uploaded to the eClips site.

CONCLUSION

Understanding the cognitive, psychological and neurological aspects of why rich media is a powerful tool for educators was the starting point for this chapter. Advances in technology have allowed educators the opportunity to use storytelling, a powerful tool in education, in a very effective manner to engage students and create meaningful learning. The digitization of material and the ability to edit media into digestible bites has made it possible, for the first time, to insert real world wisdom into classroom presentations and lesson plans. Learning to use audio and video inside and outside the classroom is an ongoing adventure. As educators become more adept at blending the chaos of the real world with the discipline of the classroom, they will seek more and more customized content. In the process, motivated educators have the opportunity to generate high-quality content and organize and tag the material for quick and easy access. The journey of the eClips team has shown that the process for creating and using rich media is becoming more and more accessible. While the technology capabilities increase and prices decrease, a teacher's creative mind still plays the fundamental role in continuing to explore how digital stories can be used to effectively engage and inform students.

REFERENCES

Barrett, H. C. (2005, June). *Researching and evaluating digital storytelling as a deep learning tool*. The REFLECT Initiative. Retrieved December 12, 2009, from http://www.electronicportfolios. com/portfolios/SITEStorytelling2006.pdf

Bongey, S. B., Cizadlo, G., & Kalnbach, L. (2006). Explorations in course-casting: Podcasts in higher education. *Campus-Wide Information Systems, 23*(5), 350–367.

Bumpus, M. A. (2005). Using motion pictures to teach management: Refocusing the camera lens though the infusion approach to diversity. *Journal of Management Education, 29*(6).

Champoux, J. E. (1999). Film as a teaching resource. *Journal of Management Inquiry, 8*(2), 206–218.

Choi, H. J., & Johnson, S. D. (2005). The effect of context-based video instruction on learning and motivation in online courses. *American Journal of Distance Education, 19*(4), 215–227.

Clark, R. E. (1983). Reconsidering research on learning from media. *Review of Educational Research, 53*(4), 445.

Copyright Clearance Center. (2009, June). *Video use and higher education: Options for the future.*

Cuban, L. (2001). *Oversold and underused: Computers in the classroom.* Harvard University Press.

David, J. (1994). Realizing the promise of technology: A policy perspective. In *Technology and education reform* (pp. 169–189). San Francisco, CA: Josey-Bass.

Diamond Jr, A. M. (forthcoming, 2010). Using video clips to teach creative destruction. *Journal of Private Enterprise.*

Edirisingha, P., & Salmon, G. (2007). Pedagogical models for podcasts in higher education. In *Conference Proceedings from In Beyond - Distance Research Alliance Conference.* Retrieved on March 1, 2010 from https://lra.le.ac.uk/handle/2381/405

Fletcher, C., & Cambre, C. (2009). Digital storytelling and implicated scholarship in the classroom. *Journal of Canadian Studies. Revue d'Etudes Canadiennes, 43*(1), 109–130.

Gallos, J. B. (2007). Artful teaching: Using the visual, creative and performing arts in contemporary management education. In Armstrong, S., & Fukami, C. (Eds.), *Handbook of management learning, education and development.* Thousand Oaks, CA: Sage.

Griffin, D. K., Mitchell, D., & Thompson, S. J. (2009). Podcasting by synchronising powerpoint and voice: What are the pedagogical benefits? *Computers & Education, 53*, 532–539.

Hastings, N. B., & Tracey, M. W. (2004). Does media affect learning: Where are we now? *TechTrends, 49*(2), 28–30.

Hiemstra, R. (1991). *Creating environments for effective adult learning.* San Francisco, CA: Jossey-Bass Inc., Publishers.

Hooper, S., & Hannafin, M. J. (1991). Psychological perspectives on emerging instructional technologies: A critical analysis. *Educational Psychologist, 26*(1), 69–95.

Howard, W. G., Ellis, H. H., & Rasmussen, K. (2004). From the arcade to the classroom: Capitalizing on student' sensory-rich media preferences in disciplined-based learning. *College Student Journal, 38*(3), 431–440.

Karppinen, P. (2005). Meaningful learning with digital and online videos: Theoretical perspectives. *AACE Journal, 13*(3), 233–250.

Kolb, D. A. (1981). Learning styles and disciplinary differences. In *The modern American college: Responding to the new realities of diverse students and a changing society* (pp. 232–255). Jossey-Bass Inc., Publishers.

Leet, D., & Houser, S. (2003). Economics goes to Hollywood: Using classic films and documentaries to create an undergraduate economics course. *The Journal of Economic Education, 34*(4), 326–332.

Marshall, J. M. (2002). *Learning with technology: Evidence that technology can, and does, support learning. A white paper prepared for cable in the classroom.* Retrieved on April 1, 2010, from http://www.medialit.org/reading_room/article545.html

Meadows, D. (2003). Digital storytelling: Research-based practice in new media. *Visual Communication, 2*(2), 189–193.

Miller, M. V. (2009). Integrating online multimedia into college course and classroom: With application to the social sciences. *MERLOT Journal of Online Learning and Teaching, 5*(2), 395–423.

Ohler, J. (2007). *Digital storytelling in the classroom: New media pathways to literacy, learning, and creativity.* Corwin Press.

Pappas, J. P. (1990). Environmental psychology of the learning sanctuary. *New Directions for Adult and Continuing Education, 46*(Summer), 41–52.

Richardson, K., & Glosenger, F. (2006). *7 strategies to enhance video use in the college classroom. Teaching Professor.* August/September.

Sexton, R. L. (2006). Using short movie and television clips in the economics principles class. *The Journal of Economic Education, 37*(4), 406–417.

Skiba, D. J. (2008). Nursing education 2.0: Twitter & tweets. Can you post a nugget of knowledge in 140 characters or less? *Nursing Education Perspectives, 29*(2), 110–112.

Snelson, C. (2008). YouTube and beyond: Integrating web-based video into online education. In K. McFerrin, R. Weber, R. Carlsen & D. A. Willis (Eds.), *Proceedings of Society for Information Technology and Teacher Education International Conference* 2008 (pp. 732-737). Chesapeake, VA: AACE.

Standley, M. (2003). Digital storytelling. *Cable in the classroom.* Retrieved on March 1, 2010, from http://its.ksbe.edu/dst/#Resources.

Swap, W., Leonard, D., Shields, M., & Abrams, L. (2001). Using mentoring and storytelling to transfer knowledge in the workplace. *Journal of Management Information Systems, 18*(1), 95–114.

Tobolowsky, B. F. (2007). In practice - thinking visually: Using visual media in the college classroom. *About Campus, 12*(1), 21–24.

Ventura, S., & Onsman, A. (2009). The use of popular movies during lectures to aid the teaching and learning of undergraduate pharmacology. *Medical Teacher, 31*(7), 662–664.

Vosko, R. S. (1991). Where we learn shapes our learning. In *Creating environments for effective adult learning.* Jossey-Bass Inc., Publishers.

Chapter 11
Unleashing Dormant Diversity:
Insights on Video, Culture, and Teaching Diverse Student Groups

Amanda E.K. Budde-Sung
The University of Sydney, Australia

Anthony Fee
The University of Sydney, Australia

ABSTRACT

Given the increasing diversity of many workplaces, as well as the rise in the number of international student enrollments around the world, the subject of cross-cultural management has increased in importance in many business education programs. As it has grown, the academic literature available on the subject has also grown, and much has been learned about the importance of cultural differences in the general area of international business. However, while we have recognized the importance of the subject, questions still remain regarding how we teach the subject (Bell & Kravitz, 2008; Kulik & Roberson, 2008). Many concerns make teaching cross-cultural management issues more challenging than teaching other business courses. These include inconsistencies in textbook contents, a lack of standardized understanding of useful concepts (Tipton, 2008), and an increasingly diverse student body studying the topic (Gallos, Ramsey & Associates, 1997). To complicate matters, while we have only a limited understanding of what teaching techniques work with an American audience, we have even less understanding of the teaching techniques that are effective within a non-U.S. context (Bell & Kravitz, 2008). Many studies of cross-cultural learning agree that learning styles may differ from one culture to the next (e.g. Hayes & Allinson, 1988; Ruksasuk, 2000; Yamazaki, 2002), neither the convenient and traditional 'chalk and talk' didactic approach, nor the more interactive, experiential approaches preferred by North American students, is likely to suit all students' learning preferences. In brief, instructors need to be more flexible and considerate in teaching diverse groups.

This chapter aims to add insight to the teaching of cross-cultural management within a non-U.S. context. It draws on contemporary research to highlight the benefit of using video in teaching cross-cultural management to a diverse student audience. Educators have examined the use of video as a teaching tool (e.g. Kraemer, 1973; Hicks & Essinger, 1991; Greenlee-Moore & Smith, 1996; Metros, 2008) and specifically in teaching culture (Fontenot & Fontenot, 2008; Molinsky & Perunovic, 2008).

DOI: 10.4018/978-1-60960-800-2.ch011

In this chapter, we extend this analysis to explore the particular benefits of teaching cultural issues to culturally diverse student groups. We argue that effective and prudent use of video can help all students to benefit from the opportunities for cross-cultural interactions that a culturally diverse class can provide.

The chapter will begin with a discussion of the increasing diversity in today's classrooms and the current pedagogies in higher education, and then move to the challenges of a diverse student audience, followed by the benefits of using video to meet these challenges, finally offering some practice-based suggestions on using video in the cross-cultural classroom.

DIVERSE LEARNING AUDIENCES

Diversity in the Global Classroom

The 21st century campus is a truly diverse place. International student enrollments are at record levels, especially in countries with English as the primary language of instruction. In the United States, for example, almost 650,000 international students were enrolled in university education programs in 2008 (Monaghan, 2009), a rise of more than seven percent from the previous year (Institute for International Education, 2008). Other countries have similarly impressive figures. In Australia, where international education is the third largest export earner, more than half a million international students from 199 different countries were enrolled in educational institutions in 2008, a rise of 12% over the preceding year (AEI, 2008). Canada hosted 180,000 international student enrollments in its educational institutions, a figure almost double that of a decade earlier (Monaghan, 2009), while Singapore, with a population base of under five million, educated over 100,000 international students in 2007 (Stearns, 2008). Recent data suggests that the U.K. is nearing the U.S. in numbers of international students at its universities: a 2009 report by the Higher Education Statistics Agency in the U.K. noted that there were 513,570 international students in British universities in 2008, and that at the postgraduate level, 80% of business students were international students, and 70% of social science and biological science students in the U.K. were international students.

The perceived social and actual economic benefit of this diversity[1], as well as the cultural importance placed upon formal education in major source countries, notably China (Sterns, 2008), India and South Korea (Monaghan, 2009), suggests that the trend is likely to continue.

This diversity on campus, as well as in most workplaces and many communities, has contributed toward the growing recognition of the need for students to develop greater cultural awareness. As cross-cultural educators, we aim to help learners develop this cultural awareness that underpins effective cross-cultural management. This can be done in multiple ways, and as outlined in this volume (Fee & Budde-Sung). The current preference is for 'experiential learning' approaches which are believed to more accurately replicate real world situations. Yamazaki & Kayes (2004), in considering cross-cultural learning, assert that methods for developing cross-cultural learning skills include an individual assessment of one's values and beliefs (Kayes, 2002); behavioral skills and emotional development (Mainemelis, Boyatzis, & Kolb, 2002), as well as immersion in different, and possibly challenging, cross-cultural situations (Mintzberg & Gosling, 2002). They note "these experiential approaches are not simply tangential to conceptual approaches; they are a primary component of cross-cultural learning" (Yamazaki & Kayes, 2004: 376). In cross-cultural education, experiential pedagogies involve students participating in meaningful interactions with people from other cultures as a way to develop cultural knowledge and understanding, and to observe and practice culturally-appropriate behaviors. These interactions can be either authentic cross-cultural experiences, in which students solve problems, discuss ideas, or share experiences, or simulated cross-cultural experiences in the form of role-plays.

The diverse cohorts that make up many university classes are tailor-made for experiential learning activities. Surrounded by cultural differences, in-class discussions and group work can provide authentic cross-cultural interactions that can be used to develop capabilities related to cultural intelligence (CQ). The presence of students from a variety of countries and cultures has the potential to make the cross-cultural lecture room a particularly potent experiential learning laboratory. However, if not managed correctly, the benefits of this diversity may remain unachieved and the opportunity to turn this diversity into a learning tool goes unrealized. There are several reasons for this missed opportunity. Some of these are pragmatic; successful cross-cultural interaction does not occur by accident (Allport, 1979) and creating an environment that is conducive to experiential learning among students from many different cultures can take time, effort, resources, and energy that are often beyond those available to instructors. More pertinent, however, are a number of characteristics embedded in the learners themselves relating to differences in values, language, communication, and learning expectations that can impede the extent to which diverse groups might engage in productive cross-cultural interaction. In a team environment, many of these impediments are called 'process losses' that hinder the performance potential of the team (Steiner, 1972). In a cross-cultural classroom, such process losses can result from improper or inadequate harnessing of the diversity within the classroom, and can cause a weakening of the potential learning experiences of the class. In analyzing this situation, we must first consider the challenges that diverse student cohorts bring to the classroom.

CHARACTERISTICS OF DIVERSE STUDENT COHORTS

Diverse Cultural Values

Culture has been defined variously as "a shared system of meanings" (Trompenaars & Hampden-Turner, 1998) or collective mental programming (Hofstede, 1980). It incorporates all of the visible and invisible forces that shape the members of a given society. At the core of a culture are the attitudes, values, and beliefs that underpin the way that members of a culture think, how they act, and what they notice. Most cross-cultural studies differentiate cultural groups by examining the differing values that form the core of the culture. Values are beliefs that we hold about what is right and wrong, or good and bad, and thus directly influence our attitude towards particular situations, actions, and objects, and our behaviors in given situations. By examining the different cultural values of groups of people, researchers have begun to understand the different value sets that are common to members of a particular culture, and which differentiate them from members of other cultures.

In studying and recording these differing value sets, researchers have identified dimensions along which cultures, and their differences, can be classified. One widely used dimension is that of individualism and collectivism (e.g. Hofstede, 1980, 2001; House, Hanges, Javidan, Dorfman, & Gupta, 2004). Individualistic societies are those in which the connections between people are loose, in which people are expected to consider and protect themselves and their immediate families before considering others, and in which rewards and benefits, as well as blame and punishments, are given for individual efforts and achievements. Collectivism, as envisioned by Hofstede (2001), refers to a society in which "people from birth onwards are integrated into strong, cohesive in-groups, which throughout people's lifetime continue to protect them in exchange for unquestioning

201

loyalty" (Hofstede, 2001: 225). In a collectivistic society, individuals would be expected to subvert personal goals for the greater goals of the group, and rewards, as well as blame, would be expected to accrue to the group, rather than to any given individual within the group.

Group activities, in which teams of students work together for a communal grade or mark, may appeal to students from more collectivistic cultures, but may engender social loafing among students from individualistic cultures (Karau & Williams, 1993). A learner from a highly collectivistic culture may view silence in the classroom as indicative of strength, or possibly disagreement, whereas a learner from a highly individualistic culture may view that same silence as a sign of trouble or weakness (Liu, 2001). Students in the host English-speaking countries, such as the USA or Australia, may expect international students to adjust to their cultural norms and values, and behave as they do in the classroom, but international students may not adapt to those norms and values as quickly as the English-speaking students expect, and may instead respond with silence in the classroom (Marginson, 2002). This silence on the part of international students from collectivistic cultures may result in a classroom discussion involving only the domestic students from culturally similar backgrounds. Learners from collectivistic cultures may feel less comfortable engaging in direct interaction with out-group members, as the in-group versus out-group distinction is more distinct for people from collectivistic cultures than it is for individualistic cultures (Earley, 1993; House *et al*, 2004). This cultural difference extends to classroom communication styles, as well. Students from individualistic countries may perceive silence in the classroom to be weakness or shyness, whereas students from collectivistic cultures may perceive that same silence to be indicative of strength or disagreement (Liu, 2001).

Another way in which cultures differ is in the attitudes of people towards the distribution of power. Following Hofstede (2001), the GLOBE study (House *et al*, 2004) defines power distance as the "degree to which the less powerful members of an organization or society expect and agree that power should be shared unequally" (House *et al*, 2004: 517). Cultures with higher power distance place a heavier emphasis upon hierarchy, titles, and roles than do cultures with lower power distance. People from cultures with higher power distance tend to be less likely to directly challenge those in power, and tend to be more likely to give greater levels of respect to those in authority. Power distance may thus influence the interaction between student and instructor. Students from a culture of lower power distance may be more willing to challenge and/or question an instructor than will students from higher power distance cultures. Different attitudes towards power distance can cause particular problems for instructors seeking to use 'western style' participatory teaching methods. Students who come from cultures where power distance is high, or where gender roles are clearly defined, or from highly collectivistic cultures, may feel uncomfortable engaging in class discussions, particularly if these discussions are structured as debates or if they involve challenging a professor's comments. Many cultures value a high level of respect given to teachers, (reflecting greater power distance), which suggests that students will not challenge teachers, and will be less willing to share ideas with people they perceive to be more senior to them. Students from higher power distance cultures expect teachers to have the answers, and expect those with less power (in this case, students), to listen, learn, and respond, rather than suggest their own ideas as solutions. Thus, those students will not be satisfied with teachers answering questions via class discussion:

"If a lecturer does not answer a student's question in class, but asks the other students what they think, in my country we would think that the teacher is either poorly qualified or lazy. But in Australia this way of not giving the answer...it is common in our class" (Ballard & Clanchy, 1997, p.1).

Nisbett (2003) gives the example of Lao-tzu, the ancient Chinese philosopher, who said "he who knows does not speak, he who speaks does not know," (p.211) as highlighting the eastern equation of knowledge with silence rather than with discussion. In Western education, these same discussions are often structured as a link between didactic and experiential learning. Asking for a student's opinion, in a lower power distance culture, may encourage class discussion, but that same request for a personal opinion, to a student from a higher power distance culture, may be perceived as impolite, and the student may feel that his/her peers in the classroom are arrogant for offering their opinions (Wang, 2006). Engaging students in class participation, and encouraging academic debate, are teaching methods associated with lower power distance cultures. While these can be effective teaching tools within those lower power distance cultures, they become problematic when applied to a more diverse student audience that includes learners from higher power distance cultures.

The cultural dimension of assertiveness refers to a culture's belief or attitude as to "whether people are or should be encouraged to be assertive, aggressive, and tough, or nonassertive, nonaggressive, and tender in social relationships" (Den Hartog, 2004: 395). Learners from cultures with lower assertiveness scores tend to speak indirectly, relying on greater context and nuance in communications (Den Hartog, 2004). Like their peers from high power distance cultures, these students would be less comfortable expressing opinions or beliefs that directly challenge other students or a teacher in a classroom, rendering class discussions, a common teaching tool in Western education, less useful.

Culture emerges as an important influencer of classroom expectations and behaviors. Cultural differences may lead to different perceptions of the sharing of personal opinions in class (Wang, 2006), and cultural indicators such as in-group versus out-group distinctions may influence class cohesiveness and levels of participation.

Differences in Learning Styles and Expectations

Teaching any subject to a culturally diverse student audience can be challenging. Ironically, teaching the subject of cross-cultural management to a culturally diverse student audience can be even more complex. This is because the skills involved in learning cross-cultural management lessons are subtle and hard to articulate, even when working within one culture and one learning style. When the student audience, to which a teacher is attempting to convey these subtle lessons, is itself comprised of cultural diversity with different learning styles and preferences, the teaching methods become more critical to properly use the diversity that lies within the classroom. In order to engage in effective cross-cultural training, instructors need to consider the preferred learning style(s) of the learners (Rodrigues, Bu, & Min, 2000; Kelly, 2009). Problems can arise, though, with culturally diverse learning audiences, in which some students prefer a passive learning style, and others prefer a more active learning style. Rodrigues (2005) states that teachers will be ineffective if they do not consider students' culturally-influenced learning preferences in designing classes.

Students bring expectations regarding education (how to achieve it, what it means, and the roles of teacher and student) that were derived from experiences in their home countries (Pincas, 2001). Some scholars have suggested that learning style is influenced by national culture (e.g. Lindsay & Dempsey, 1983; Pun, 1989; Ladd & Ruby, 1999; Merriam & Caffarella, 2007; Kelly, 2009). Linday and Dempsey (1983) proposed that students from Asia have different pedagogical preferences than Western students do. Jarrah (1998) and Ladd & Ruby (1999) suggest that, while Western students prefer to engage in active or experiential learning through their own discovery and exploration, Chinese students prefer a more teacher-led form of learning, in which an instructor provides information in a structured didactic-style of teaching. Learning styles are reinforced through educational systems as well as through socially-accepted child raising processes. Different learning styles emerge between cultures because people sharing a common culture must "collectively adapt to a unique set of environmental demands" (Rodrigues, 2005:609).

Earlier research on international students suggests that student participation in Western classes with a large number of non-native English speaking international students is considerably less than in those classes made up largely of native English-speakers (Ryan, 2000). There are several possible reasons underlying this phenomenon, including a lack of experience in discussion-based learning activities, anxiety over the classroom expectation to speak publicly, inhibition over language capabilities (Anderson & Moore, 1998), as well as cultural expectations of the classroom environment. While classroom discussions and debates may be a useful educational tool in western learning for reinforcing analytic thought processes and encouraging self-reflection of ideas and concepts, non-western students may find these discussions and debates intimidating and actually deleterious to their learning (Nisbett, 2003).

As there may be students from different cultures in one single classroom, thereby suggesting more than one preferred learning style among the students in that classroom, teaching techniques that work for students of one culture may not work for students of other cultures. To further add to the challenge, even within one culture, Stewart (2004) and Kelly (2009) assert that there is no single, parsimonious explanation for how students learn, as personality characteristics influence preferred learning styles, as well. Certainly, it is difficult, if not impossible, to teach exclusively to each student's individual learning style in a diverse classroom, but it is not necessary to do that in order to successfully accommodate the different learning styles present. Felder (1993) and Kelly (2009) note that as long as a teacher spends some of the time addressing each learning style using a wide array of teaching methods, then

all students in a culturally diverse classroom will have their learning needs attended to during the course of a class.

Language Differences

More than half of all international students studying in Western education (such as Australia, the U.S.A., and New Zealand) come from cultures whose main language is not English (Dalglish & Evans, 2008). Increasingly, domestic students may also come from non English-speaking households. The consequence is that most classrooms today comprise several students using the language of instruction as a second language. While all students should be reasonably expected to speak English sufficiently well to be able to cope in the classroom environment due to English-testing admissions requirements, our experiences are that the levels of comfort using English can vary widely. This can create challenges in an English-instructed cross-cultural management classroom. For students from non-English speaking backgrounds, didactic lectures can be difficult to fully absorb. Language skill challenges may go beyond difficulty understanding an oral lecture, and may extend to such problems as difficulty effectively participating in group discussions or group work efforts; problems understanding humor used in the classroom (e.g. "why was that funny?"); language problems in giving oral presentations; a lack of familiarity with technical jargon; and possible struggles with the cultural ramifications of subtle variations in wording (e.g. "we need to talk" versus "there's something I would like to discuss with you").

Furthermore, in all languages, there exist words or phrases that do not have exact equivalents in other languages. One concept used in cross-cultural training is that of leadership. In English, the concept of leadership seems clear and has positive connotations, and yet the concept of "leader" is not as clear, and does not have such positive connotations, across linguistic divides.

For example, for some Europeans, "…everything seems to indicate that leadership is an unintended and undesirable consequence of democracy" (Grauman & Moscovici, 1986: 241).

The language issue intersects with the assertiveness and collectivistic cultural dimensions, as many international students come from highly collectivistic cultures that have low assertiveness scores, such as Japan. These students may already struggle with language difficulties, which, when combined with a culturally-influenced hesitation to engage in classroom debates or heated discussions, may result in the native English speaking host country nationals dominating class discussions. This possibility causes the diversity present in the classroom to remain unused, an untapped resource. Moreover, it causes the host country nationals to miss out on intercultural dialogues, as it causes these international students to assume the role of classroom observer, rather than classroom participant, jeopardizing the learning potential of all students.

Attitudes Towards Sensitive Subjects

Even if students from diverse cultures are willing to equally and actively engage in those participatory or experiential teaching approaches, there may be a taboo-avoiding tendency among group members; in other words, students may not be comfortable discussing sensitive or politically-incorrect issues about their home culture with other students. All cultures have taboo subjects, topics that are not discussed in polite company. These can include, for example, religious beliefs, politics and political opinions, sex, human rights, or particularly contentious or painful national histories. Many of these taboo subjects may, however, be central to classroom discussions of cross-cultural management as they are directly relevant to the culture being considered. For instance, the issue of special payments or bribery has direct relevance to all managers operating across cultural boundaries,

irrespective of one's home culture. Taboo subjects are difficult for learners to discuss in the best of circumstances; when combined with challenges of language and cultural differences, they can become almost impossible to approach. In a diverse student audience, the number of taboo topics increases, as many cultures will be represented, each with its own taboo topic(s). Thus, there may be difficulty finding common subjects to discuss in experiential or didactic lessons.

Token Representatives

Finally, all teaching approaches to cross-cultural training must endeavor to avoid a 'token representative' phenomenon, in which the experiences and attitudes of one person from Culture X is taken to be representative of all people from Culture X. In a diverse classroom, learners may encounter a few members of a given culture and assume that all members of that given culture behave in the manner that the token representatives behave. Moreover, some students may not fully appreciate the diversity of perspectives that exists within multicultural classrooms (e.g. projected similarity), and thus interaction may cause stereotypes and prejudice to be reinforced, rather than reduced.

These characteristics of diverse student groups suggest that this immense diversity present in today's university classrooms, which is, in itself, an invaluable resource that is beneficial to the study of cross-cultural management, may lay dormant. The potential benefits that this diversity can bring may fail to be realized, causing what we term "dormant diversity." Interaction in and out of the classroom can be stifled, lacking the openness and equality needed for it to be productive. In such conditions, students may convey, and perceive in others, only superficial characteristics. Consequently, experiential learning intended to promote cross-cultural understanding can actually lead to reinforcement of stereotypes, mistrust and limited learning. Part of the process of unleashing the dormant diversity in a cross-cultural management class involves fully exploring the ranges of acceptable behaviors and values of various cultures.

While there are challenges involved in teaching issues of cross-cultural management to student audiences that are themselves culturally diverse, including cultural differences, differences in learning styles and expectations, language difficulties, and taboo-avoiding tendencies, there are ways to unleash the dormant diversity present in the classroom. This diversity resource can greatly enhance the learning experience of all students, but the challenges of teaching to that diverse student audience need to be addressed in order to properly maximize the benefits of this dormant diversity. In our experiences, the use of video can help to address these challenges in teaching cross-cultural management to a diverse learning audience, not as a replacement for genuine cross-cultural interaction, but as a valuable and pedagogically sound companion. Table 1 outlines a number of benefits of video and lists how video can help overcome the above-mentioned challenges.

Cultural Differences

Visual images can be powerful methods to challenge preconceived ideas (Tipton & Tieman, 1993), as well as provide opportunities for case decision-making exercises and the development of assessment skills (Myers et al., 2009). This is particularly beneficial when teaching a diverse audience, as many adult learners may approach cross-cultural learning as a redundant topic when the student audience itself represents multiple cultures. It allows instructors to introduce examples that differ from the expected cultural norm, encouraging students to examine their preconceived ideas about other cultures as well as their own.

People from different cultures view situations differently (Masuda & Nisbett, 2001). Having a culturally diverse group view (and re-view if necessary), and then analyze a video of a cross-cultural interaction, enables the instructor to draw out differences or similarities in perception within and across cultures. This creates an authentic experiential learning activity, whereby learners play the role of 'cultural detectives', identifying

Table 1.

Challenges	Benefits of Video in Overcoming Challenges
1. Cultural Differences	• Provides shared concrete experience for all students • Allows instructors to draw out similarities and differences between cultures by highlighting situations in a multi-context manner • Forms bridge between purely participative classroom and purely didactic classroom can engage more students, deepening their thinking on the topics being presented.
2. Differences in Learning Styles & Expectations	• Provides context to topics being discussed/presented • Allows instructors to teach to many different learning styles due to multi-sensory format of video • Provides highly engaging medium • Offers multiple uses—flowing from instructor to students = more didactic; flowing from students to instructor = more participative
3. Language Differences	• Provides subtitle options • Helps facilitate understanding, as video is easier to understand due to multicontextual format, including non-verbal communication as well as verbal communication • Allows watch and re-watch options • Offers pause and play option
4. Taboo-avoiding tendencies; token representatives	• Effects empathy • Allows introduction of sensitive subjects in a safe environment through a shared experience • Provides ability to challenge pre-conceived notions by giving alternative perspectives • Imports additional people's perspectives and opinions via vicarious guest lecturers, speeches from experts, and virtual visits.

patterns in interpretation (both similarities and differences). The video serves as a shared concrete experience, and the learners are able to experience differences in how this experience is processed and interpreted. In this manner, instructors are better able to tap into and exploit the diversity inherent in these diverse classrooms, and use that diversity to enhance the learning of all participants.

Video can be particularly effective for highlighting some of the more abstract concepts of cross-cultural management, such as ethical (or unethical) behavior, corporate citizenship, nonverbal communication, and the individual's relationship to society (Fontenot & Fontenot, 2008). These concepts can be highlighted by showing video clips or full-length films to students, and having them consider the issues presented in them. Furthermore, research in cognitive science suggests that students both prefer, and learn better, from visual media than from verbal lectures (Hicks & Essinger, 1991; Metros, 2008). Requiring students to consider video media in their writing on classroom topics helps to reinforce the concepts in students' minds, as well as deepen their thinking on those topics (Murphy, 2004). The use of video in teaching cross-cultural management can help improve both the delivery of the teaching as well as the absorption of the material by the learners:

The use of video-based materials "quickens the cadence of learning, heightens the immediacy of the experience for those who are participating in the conversation, and makes tangible both the experience and the message that we wish to convey. Needless to say, videos also play directly in our "mental cinemas," and, in doing so, open up a world of unlimited possible connections on which to build effective managerial conversations (Fischer & Boynton, 2007: 413).

This benefit is especially important for diverse learning groups, as video provides a bridge between the didactic presentation of those abstract concepts and an experiential approach to learning.

This bridge may provide students of differing cultural backgrounds with multiple learning opportunities with which to help them fully absorb the lessons.

Differences in Learning Styles and Expectations

Video provides a rich, multi-sensory learning experience that is more cognitively and emotionally engaging than standard didactic approaches, while enabling a shared and concrete experience capable of circumventing problems of risk aversion or perceived shyness (addressing cultural issues in learning). While a student may be reluctant to share his/her opinion or experiences with classmates, or to directly challenge an instructor, he/she may be far more comfortable discussing the situation of a character in a video or finding online video sources to serve as examples of what he/she would like to say in a discussion.

Yet another benefit of using video in teaching cross-cultural management to a diverse class is that of contextualism. A common assumption in educational theory and practice is that decontextualizing human experiences allows for better understanding of the elemental components of the subject matter (South *et al., 2008)*. That may be true when teaching some subjects, but cross-cultural skills depend on an understanding not only of the parts of the whole, but of the whole itself. In other words, it is not enough to know how to exchange business cards in a culturally-appropriate form; individuals with highly developed understandings of culture's impact on business understand *when* that exchange should happen, *how* it should happen, *where* it should happen, and *why* it should happen. Video allows students of all cultures to engage in a multi-sensory learning experience in contextualizing that lesson, in a way that a written case study or a standard instructor-based lecture cannot. In essence, a picture paints a thousand words, and a film/video paints still more, which is especially helpful when working with learners who may not be completely comfortable in the language of instruction. Moreover, the multi-contextual medium of video may better address all students' learning expectations and styles. Students who are uncomfortable asking for clarification on a point made in a lecture may gain additional clarification by watching a reinforcement of the lesson in video format. Students who prefer a more participative approach to learning will be participating in knowledge absorption via a highly engaging medium.

Language Differences

The use of video in cross-cultural training can be especially helpful when the learners are not native English speakers (or are not native speakers of the language of the instruction). Many films have subtitle options, and learners whose language skills lie outside of the dominant language used in the films and the classroom may choose to re-watch the film segment in order to better process the film's information. Whereas didactic lectures can be difficult for a non-native speaker to fully absorb, a video can be watched and re-watched, until the main content is absorbed and understood, thus allowing for greater holistic learning by non-native speakers. Moreover, video may help all students, including non-native speakers, to feel more engaged in the learning (South et al., 2008). Students may find that they are able to identify with, or empathize with the characters they see in the videos, which helps improve student engagement and overall understanding.

Furthermore, the multi-sensory experience of video can help better communicate subtle nuances of language, addressing the impact of wording differences mentioned above. Watching people's reactions to subtle wording differences can convey the enormity of those differences in ways that a textbook or text-based case cannot.

Taboo-Avoiding Tendencies; Token Representative Problems

Video can help students experience cultural learning and differing cultural situations in a secure and comfortable environment, through empathy. Particularly when viewing fictional films, such as motion pictures, students may identify and empathize with the characters and universal themes, regardless of the ethnicity or culture of the characters. The empathy effect, in which a viewer identifies with a fictional, on-screen character, has been used to help students learn about behavior in child and adolescent psychology (e.g. Longo & Longo, 2003; Weber & Haen, 2005), and students of cross-cultural management may find that they learn subtle cultural skills by identifying with fictional on-screen characters. For example, a student might feel uncomfortable either role-playing or discussing a taboo or sensitive cultural topic, but will be able to learn about and understand the topic by empathizing with a character in a film who is in some way dealing with this sensitive cultural issue. This empathy can then form the basis of a discussion relevant to the topic as shown in the video, which can be less uncomfortable for students than a direct dialogue about the sensitive subject. Students may find that discussing a scene in a film or documentary is less confronting than is trying to express their own opinions in a public forum, lessening their inhibitions over public speaking or class participation. Moreover, cultural considerations that might prevent a student from offering his/her opinion, especially if that opinion differs from the teacher or other classmates, are somewhat mitigated when the student is referring only to scenes or characters presented in visual media.

Video can be used to present situations or contexts that can stimulate cognitive rehearsal. For instance, learners can be shown a segment of a cross-cultural interaction and then asked to imagine themselves within this situation (the empathy effect). After this empathy-inducing experience, students can then discuss the video contents in a safe manner. And because the discussion is not a debate, nor does it involve offering opinions that might challenge the instructor's opinions, which might cause cultural hesitation on the part of some of the students, the discussion format may be more fruitful. Moreover, video can be used to model both appropriate and inappropriate cultural behavior, allowing for a more complex learning scenario.

Instructors may be able to challenge preconceived ideas regarding culture within a diverse classroom by bringing in additional perspectives in the form of vicarious guest lecturers, speeches from experts, and virtual visits. As mentioned earlier, the possibility of a token representative effect is magnified in a diverse classroom. Students may (incorrectly) assume that, because the classroom is already culturally diverse, student members of a given culture are authentic and complete representatives of that culture. An example might be something that many instructors will have heard: *"I know about Chinese culture—there was a Chinese guy in my class."* In order to challenge that idea, and expose students to multiple perspectives, guest lecturers or virtual visits may be brought in to the classroom vicariously, through previously-recorded video clips. This activity exposes students to multiple perspectives involving more people than are present only within the classroom, helping all students to embrace a deeper understanding of culture and its impacts on business.

SUGGESTIONS FOR USING VIDEO

While many instructors recognize the benefits that video can bring to their classrooms, some are unsure of how to best use video to unlock its benefits within the learning experience. Below are some suggestions for using video in a diverse classroom.

One approach used by one of the authors is to use a video as a stimulus for a classroom deliverable. After learning concepts of cultural dimensions or cultural differences in motivation in a traditional (textbook and lecture) manner, students in a very diverse cross-cultural management class are shown a film highlighting some of these differences and dimensions. Students are then asked to reflect on those differences, critique the behavior shown in the film, and discuss how the film relates to the reading and lecture material in a written paper. This method attempts to make issues of diversity more salient to the students by taking the learning beyond the realm of the textbook and into the realm of modeling behavior. This video can be a short non-fiction video, showing specific cultural behaviors, or a full-length film dealing with issues of diversity in international business. Using videos in this manner helps students build awareness of cross-cultural issues, by giving students examples of contextually appropriate and inappropriate behavior, which students can observe and critique. Furthermore, it helps students improve cross-cultural awareness, by highlighting dimensions of culture, such as issues of personal space or the concept of the individual, which helps students increase their sense of self-efficacy in cross-cultural situations. For example, a student may learn, in a class reading and/or lecture, about the cultural dimension of power distance (e.g. Hofstede, 1980; House *et al*, 2004). To reinforce the reality of that dimension, an instructor may opt to show a video that highlights the issue of power distance, reinforcing the cognition, or "what" aspect of learning. That video may also show appropriate and inappropriate behavior regarding power distance in a given context, which will reinforce a student's awareness, or the "why" aspect of learning, as well as emphasize the skills aspect of learning, or the "how to" aspect in shaping culturally intelligent behavior.

This video use need not be uni-directional, flowing from the teacher to the student. With today's modern technologies, the use of video can flow in the other direction, from student to student cohort to teacher. One means of increasing the relevance of video content is to involve learners in the process by, for instance, asking them to search online video content sites in order to find and share pertinent examples demonstrating a particular concept. This method of video use can help cement cultural concepts in students' minds, as well as provide another opportunity to unleash the dormant diversity within a class. For instance, one author asked students in a postgraduate Cross-Cultural Management cohort comprising students from 32 different cultures to search freely accessible online AV media sources for examples where particular cultural values – e.g. high/low context communication (Hall, 1976), or high/low power distance (Hofstede, 1997) - were evident in either the content, narration or presentation of one part of a video clip (Cortés, 2003). This activity was structured as a (multicultural) team activity, so learners needed to explain and discuss their selection with team members. Once the teams had identified their clips, links to each of the chosen sources were shared with other groups, and these formed the basis of an 'in-class' discussion that provided a rich experiential learning activity in its own right. The contents of the video helped learners by providing models of appropriate and inappropriate culture-specific behavior, while the activity itself provided an authentic multicultural team experience.

The traditional model of showing a full-length film in a classroom format, while still valid, need not be the only method of using videos in a classroom environment. Certainly, showing full-length video case studies, or documentaries, or even motion pictures, can be an effective way of teaching these subtle skills, but that need not be the only way. Video material found online can often consist of short film segments, which can be used to highlight a particular behavior or underscore a given concept. For example, in showing the proper physical distance between people when shaking hands, an instructor could stream video content of several short clips showing people shaking hands.

Written cases often discuss cultural blunders in international business, but the very act of writing about a cultural error brings attention to the error. Many instructors of cross-cultural management have heard exclamations along the lines of "but I'd never do something as stupid as that!" Indeed, putting an error into written form necessitates a focus upon that error, but real life is rarely so one-dimensional. Opportunities for cross-cultural blunders exist not necessarily because people are ignorant, but because reality is multi-dimensional. A written case scenario in which a Western businessman writes on and folds a Japanese employee's *meishi*, or business card, putting it in his pants pocket, draws attention to that error. Cross-cultural textbooks would caution students against committing such a blunder. However, in reality, that Western businessman may be thinking about hundreds of things all at the same time, and may be so focused upon another area of etiquette that he completely overlooks the proper handling of a *meishi*. Showing a video case study, instead of a written case study, to help students develop those proper *meishi* skills can introduce students to the multidimensional nature of cross-cultural interactions, and students from many cultures can identify the error and place it in its proper context. In this way, context is given to the development of cross-cultural skills in a manner that helps develop skills, rather than relying on a general class discussion of the concept, or allowing the lesson to fall into token generalizations, (e.g. "why can't people from Country X learn to respect other cultural traditions" and the response argument "why is the business card thing such a big deal?").

Lessons involving video use can be structured in many ways. The lecture can open with a video, followed by a lecture or a question-and-answer format. Another option is for an instructor to present textbook concepts in a traditional lecture format, cutting to short video clips to emphasize those concepts as he/she lectures. Videos can be placed after a traditional lecture or experiential exercise, to help underscore the lessons being taught. These methods teach to the students who prefer a more passive approach to teaching, whose learning styles tend to be less participative and more reflective. Students can present their own videos that highlight various cultural dimensions or other textbook concepts, using their laptop computers or mobile phones, to other students in small groups as a way of fostering discussion in a culturally-safe manner. Students can also work alone or in groups to create their own podcasts regarding issues related to cross-cultural management. For example, students could create a video presentation on job motivation across countries by interviewing workers, professors, human resource personnel, etc., instead of a written text-based paper. This teaching method favors the learning styles of students who prefer more active, experiential teaching techniques. A longer video can be shown instead of a lecture, and students can write papers reflecting on issues raised in the video, encouraging an individual form of learning.

These suggestions are by no means exhaustive. Instructors can incorporate video into their classes with diverse student audiences through a variety of methods. The benefit of doing so addresses Felder's (1993) suggestion to ensure that everyone's learning needs are attended to in some manner within the duration of a course.

Some practical suggestions to bear in mind when incorporating video into the classroom experience include the following:

1. Clearly outline the purpose of viewing the video in advance, highlighting the learning aspects of the activity.
2. Provide written transcripts, if needed, so that students can read along with the video if they are experiencing language difficulties.
3. In general, limit intra-lecture use of video to brief segments of no longer than 6-7 minutes. We have used longer clips, but find that students can become restless when longer segments are embedded in a class lecture.
4. Ensure students recognize the relationship between the video and (1) the related topic/

theme and 2) their broader lives as students, workers, or community members.
5. For video use outside of the main lecture (either before, after, or replacing the main lecture), aim to balance entertainment films, which often exaggerate cultural characteristics, with documentaries, showcase authentic cultural behaviors.
6. Choose video content from a variety of cultures.
7. Involve students in creating, finding, or suggesting content. As well as enriching the video content available, this serves to highlight positive aspects of the diversity present in the classroom.
8. Pre-screen all video content to assure its appropriateness for class viewing. If necessary, edit out (or fast-forward past) any content that could be seen as inappropriate content for classroom viewing. As one instructor's judgment can differ from another's, it is helpful to get a second opinion on any possibly controversial content before class viewing. Some controversial content may be an integral part of the lesson; that which is not need not be shown.

DISCUSSION

Teaching cross-cultural management can be challenging in a monocultural environment, and even more so in a multi-cultural environment, as a diverse student learning audience presents unique characteristics that instructors must consider in helping students to develop the subtle skills of cultural intelligence. Little has been discussed in the teaching literature about how to teach these skills in a diverse, non-U.S. setting, and this chapter attempts to begin to fill that gap. Many of today's students are accustomed to instructors incorporating video content in their lectures, but that tool becomes even more useful when addressing a diverse student audience. Teaching cross-cultural management involves helping students develop subtle skills, and these skills can be difficult to communicate to a multi-cultural and multi-linguistic audience. Video content can be used to help unleash the dormant diversity present in the modern classroom, while avoiding some of the pitfalls that experiential learning sometimes encounters in that multi-cultural classroom. Video can help enhance the overall learning of all students in a diverse learning audience and can help that audience unleash and benefit from its dormant diversity.

REFERENCES

Al-Arishi, A. Y. (1994). Role-play, real-play, and surreal-play in the ESOL classroom. *ELT Journal, 48*(4), 337–346. doi:10.1093/elt/48.4.337

Allport, G. W. (1979). *The nature of prejudice.* Reading, MA: Addison-Wesley.

Australia Education International. (2008). *End of year summary of international student enrolment data: Australia – 2008.* Canberra, Australia: Department of Education, Employment and Workplace Relations.

Australian Department of Foreign Affairs and Trade. (2009). *Tourism and international students.* Retrieved August 1, 2009, from www.dfat.gov.au/aib/tourism_studnets.html

Ballard, B., & Clanchy, J. (1997). *Teaching international students.* Deakin, ACT: IDP Education Australia.

Bandura, A. (1977). *Social learning theory.* Englewood Cliffs, NJ: Prentice-Hall.

Bandura, A. (1982). Self-efficacy mechanism in human agency. *The American Psychologist, 37*(2), 122–147. doi:10.1037/0003-066X.37.2.122

Bell, M. P., & Kravitz, D. (2008). What do we know and need to learn about diversity education and training? *Academy of Management Learning & Education, 7*(3), 301–308. doi:10.5465/AMLE.2008.34251669

Bhawuk, D. P. S., & Brislin, R. W. (2000). Cross-cultural training: A review. *Applied Psychology: An International Review, 49*(1), 162–191. doi:10.1111/1464-0597.00009

Black, J. S., & Mendenhall, M. (1989). A practical but theory-based framework for selecting cross-cultural training methods. *Human Resource Management, 28*(4), 511–539. doi:10.1002/hrm.3930280406

Black, J. S., & Mendenhall, M. (1991). The U-curve adjustment hypothesis revisited: A review and theoretical framework. *Journal of International Business Studies, 22,* 225–247. doi:10.1057/palgrave.jibs.8490301

Black, J. S., & Mendenhall, M. E. (1990). Cross-cultural training effectiveness: A review and a theoretical framework for future research. *Academy of Management Review, 15,* 113–136.

Brissett, D., & Edgley, C. (1990). *Life as theatre.* Hawthorne, NY: Walter de Gruyter.

Bruschke, J. C., Gartner, C., & Seiter, J. S. (1993). Student ethnocentrism, dogmatism, and motivation: A study of BAFA BAFA. *Simulation & Gaming, 21*(1), 9–20. doi:10.1177/1046878193241003

Citizenship and Immigration Canada. (2009). *Facts and figures 2008: Summary tables—permanent and temporary residences.* Retrieved June 2, 2009, from www.cic.gc.ca

Cortés, C. E. (2003). Media and intercultural training. In Landis, D., Bennett, J. M., & Bennett, M. J. (Eds.), *Handbook of intercultural training* (3rd ed.). Thousand Oaks, CA: SAGE.

Dalglish, C., & Evans, P. (2008). *Teaching in the global classroom.* UK: MPG Books.

Den Hartog, D. N. (2004). Assertiveness. In House, R. J., Hanges, P. J., Javidan, M., Dorfman, P. W., & Gupta, V. (Eds.), *Culture, leadership, and organizations: The GLOBE study of 62 societies* (pp. 395–436). Thousand Oaks, CA: Sage Publications.

Earley, P. C. (1993). East meets West meets Middle East: Further explorations of collectivist and individualist work groups. *Academy of Management Journal, 36,* 319–348. doi:10.2307/256525

Earley, P. C. (2002). Redefining interactions across cultures and organizations: Moving forward with cultural intelligence. *Research in Organizational Behavior, 24,* 271–299. doi:10.1016/S0191-3085(02)24008-3

Earley, P. C., & Ang, S. (2003). *Cultural intelligence: Individual interactions across cultures.* Stanford, CA: Stanford University Press.

Earley, P. C., & Mosakowski, E. (2004, October). Cultural intelligence. *Harvard Business Review,* 139–146.

Earley, P. C., & Peterson, R. S. (2004). The elusive cultural chameleon: Cultural intelligence as a new approach to intercultural training for the global manager. *Academy of Management Learning & Education, 3*(1), 100–115. doi:10.5465/AMLE.2004.12436826

Egan, M. L., & Bendick, M. (2008). Combining multicultural management and diversity into one course on cultural competence. *Academy of Management Learning & Education, 7*(3), 387–393. doi:10.5465/AMLE.2008.34251675

Feinstein, A. H., Mann, S., & Corsun, D. L. (2002). Charting the experiential territory: Clarifying definitions and uses of computer simulation, games, and role play. *Journal of Management Development, 21*(10), 732–744. doi:10.1108/02621710210448011

Felder, R. (1993). Reaching the second tier: Learning and teaching styles in college science education. *Journal of College Science Teaching, 23*(5), 286–290.

Fischer, B., & Boynton, A. (2007). Out of this world high performing teams: A video tour. *Academy of Management Learning & Education, 6*(3), 412–428. doi:10.5465/AMLE.2007.26361630

Fontenot, M. J., & Fontenot, K. A. (2008, March). Incorporating film into the research paper. *Business Communication Quarterly, 55*–58. doi:10.1177/1080569907312872

Fowler, S. M., & Blohm, J. M. (2004). An analysis of methods for intercultural training. In Landis, D., Bennett, J. M., & Bennett, M. J. (Eds.), *Handbook of intercultural training* (3rd ed., pp. 37–84). Thousand Oaks, CA: Sage.

Gallos, J. V., & Ramsey, V. J. (1997). *Teaching diversity: Listening to the soul, speaking from the heart.* San Francisco, CA: Jossey-Bass.

Garcia, R. (2008). *Integrating video clips in classroom teaching.* In 'Knowledge Development and Exchange in International Business Networks': 50th Annual Meeting of the Academy of International Business, Milan, Italy, 30 June to 3 July 2008: Academy of International Business.

Grauman, C. F., & Moscovici, S. (1986). *Changing conceptions of leadership.* New York, NY: Springer-Verlag.

Greenlee-Moore, M. E., & Smith, L. L. (1996). Interactive computer software: The effect on young children's reading achievement. *Reading Psychology: An International Quarterly, 17,* 43–64. doi:10.1080/0270271960170102

Gudykunst, W. B., Guzley, R. M., & Hammer, M. R. (1996). Designing intercultural training. In Landis, D., & Bhagat, R. (Eds.), *Handbook of intercultural training* (2nd ed., pp. 61–80). Thousand Oaks, CA: SAGE.

Hall, E. T. (1976). *Beyond culture*. New York, NY: Doubleday.

Harrison, R., & Hopkins, R. L. (1967). The design of cross-cultural training: An alternative to the university model. *The Journal of Applied Behavioral Science, 3*, 431–460. doi:10.1177/002188636700300401

Hayes, J., & Allinson, C. W. (1988). Cultural differences in the learning styles of managers. *Management International Review, 28*, 75–80.

Hicks, R., & Essinger, J. (1991). *Making computers more human-designing for human computer interaction*. Oxford, UK: Elsevier Advanced Technology.

Hofstede, G. (1980). *Culture's consequences*. Newbury Park, CA: Sage Publications.

Hofstede, G. (1997). *Cultures and organisations: Software of the mind, intercultural cooperation and its importance for survival*. New York, NY: McGraw-Hill.

Hofstede, G. (2001). *Culture's consequences, comparing values, behaviors, institutions, and organizations across nations*. Thousand Oaks, CA: Sage Publications.

House, R. J., Hanges, P. J., Javidan, M. J., Dorfman, P. W., & Gupta, V. (Eds.). (2004). *Culture, leadership, and organizations: The GLOBE study of 62 societies*. Thousand Oaks, CA: Sage Publications.

Institute of International Education. (2008). *Open doors: Report on international education exchange*. New York.

Jarrah, F. (1998, April 23). New courses will target transition to university. *China Morning Post*, p. 28.

Karau, S. J., & Williams, K. D. (1993). Social loafing: A meta-analytic review and theoretical integration. *Journal of Personality and Social Psychology, 65*, 681–706. doi:10.1037/0022-3514.65.4.681

Kayes, D. C. (2002). Experiential learning and its critics: Preserving the role of experience in management learning and education. *Academy of Management Learning & Education, 1*(2), 137–149. doi:10.5465/AMLE.2002.8509336

Kelly, P. (2009). Group work and multicultural management education. *Journal of Teaching in International Business, 20*, 80–102. doi:10.1080/08975930802671273

Kolb, D. (1984). *Experiential learning: Experience as the source of learning and development*. Englewood Cliffs, NJ: Prentice-Hall.

Kraemer, A. J. (1973). Development of a cultural self-awareness approach to instruction in intercultural communication. Alexandria, VA, Human Resources Research Organization. (Technical Report #73-71: 60).

Kulik, C. T., & Roberson, L. (2008). Common goals and golden opportunities: Evaluations of diversity education in academic and organizational settings. *Academy of Management Learning & Education, 7*(3), 309–331. doi:10.5465/AMLE.2008.34251670

Ladd, P. D., & Ruby, R. Jr. (1999). Learning style and adjustment issues of international students. *Journal of Education for Business, 74*(6), 363–367. doi:10.1080/08832329909601712

Langer, E. J. (2000). Mindful learning. *Current Directions in Psychological Science, 9*(6), 220–223. doi:10.1111/1467-8721.00099

Leary, M. R. (1996). *Self-presentation: Impression management and interpersonal behavior*. Boulder, CO: Westview Press.

Lindsay, C. P., & Dempsey, B. L. (1983). Ten painfully learned lessons about working in China: The insights of two American behavioral scientists. *The Journal of Applied Behavioral Science, 19*(20), 265–276. doi:10.1177/002188638301900305

Lipsett, A. (2009, May 21). More overseas students than thought. *The Guardian*. Retrieved June 2, 2009, from http://www.guardian.co.uk/education/2009/may/21/more-overseas-students-than-thought

Liu, J. (2001). *Asian students' classroom communication patterns in U.S. universities: An emic perspective*. Norwood, NJ: Ablex.

Longo, R. E., & Longo, D. P. (2003). *New hope for youth: Experiential exercises for children and adolescents*. Holyoke, MA: NEARI Press.

Mainemelis, C., Boyatzis, R. E., & Kolb, D. A. (2002). Learning styles and adaptive flexibility: Testing experiential learning theory. *Management Learning, 33*(1), 5–33. doi:10.1177/1350507602331001

Marginson, S. (2002). The phenomenal rise of international degrees down under. *Change, 34*(3), 34–43. doi:10.1080/00091380209601854

Masuda, T., & Nisbett, R. E. (2001). Attending holistically vs. analytically: Comparing the context sensitivity of Japanese and Americans. *Journal of Personality and Social Psychology, 81*(5), 922–934. doi:10.1037/0022-3514.81.5.922

Merriam, S. B., & Caffarella, R. S. (2007). *Learning in adulthood*. San Francisco, CA: Jossey-Bass.

Metros, S. E. (2008). The educator's role in preparing visually literate learners. *Theory into Practice, 47*(2), 102–109. doi:10.1080/00405840801992264

Mintzberg, H., & Gosling, J. (2002). Educating managers beyond borders. *Academy of Management Learning & Education, 1*(1), 64–76. doi:10.5465/AMLE.2002.7373654

Molinsky, A. L., & Perunovic, W. Q. E. (2008). Training wheels for cultural learning: Poor language fluency and its shielding effect on the evaluation of culturally inappropriate behavior. *Journal of Language and Social Psychology, 27*, 284–289. doi:10.1177/0261927X08317959

Monaghan, P. (2009, April 8). Minds in the marketplace. *The Australian*. Retrieved on April 8, 2009, from http://www.theaustralian.news.com.au/story/0,25197,25304815-25192,00.html

Murphy, P. (2004). Observations on teaching marketing ethics. *Marketing Education Review, 14*(3), 14–21.

Myers, D. R., Sykes, C., & Myers, S. (2009). Effective learner-centered strategies for teaching adults: Using visual media to engage the adult learner. *Gerontology & Geriatrics Education, 29*(3), 234–238. doi:10.1080/02701960802359466

Nisbett, R. (2003). *The geography of thought: How Asians and Westerners think differently… and why*. New York, NY: Free Press.

Pedersen, A., & Pedersen, P. (1989). The cultural grid: A framework for multicultural counseling. *International Journal for the Advancement of Counseling, 14*(4), 299–307. doi:10.1007/BF00123258

Pincas, A. (2001). Culture, cognition and communication in global education. *Distance Education, 22*, 30–51. doi:10.1080/0158791010220103

Pun, A. S. L. (1989). *Developing managers internationally: culture-free or culture-bound?* Presented at the Conference on International Personnel and Human Resource Management, Hong Kong, December 13.

Rodrigues, C. (2005). Culture as a determinant of the importance level business students place on ten teaching/learning techniques. *Journal of Management Development, 24*(7), 608–611. doi:10.1108/02621710510608740

Rodrigues, C., Bu, N., & Min, B. (2000). Learners' training approach preference: National culture as a determinant. *Cross Cultural Management: An International Journal, 7*(1), 23–32. doi:10.1108/13527600010797048

Ruksasuk, N. (2000). *Effects of learning styles and participatory interaction modes on achievement of Thai students involved in Web-based instruction in library and information science distance education.* Unpublished doctoral dissertation, University of Pittsburgh, Pittsburgh, PA.

Ryan, J. (2000). *A guide to teaching international students.* Oxford, UK: Oxford Centre for Staff and Learning Development.

Shiffrin, R. M., & Schneider, W. (1977). Controlled and automatic human information processing: Perceptual learning automatic attending and a general theory. *Psychological Review, 84*(2), 127–190. doi:10.1037/0033-295X.84.2.127

Shirts, R. G. (1977). *BAFA-BAFA: A cross-cultural simulation: Director's guide. Del mar.* CA: Simile II.

South, J. B., Gabbitas, B., & Merrill, P. F. (2008). Designing video narratives to contextualize content for ESL learners: A design process case study. *Interactive Learning Environments, 16*(3), 231–243. doi:10.1080/10494820802114044

Steiner, I. D. (1972). *Group process and productivity.* New York, NY: Academic Press.

Stewart, E. C. (1966). The simulation of cultural differences. *The Journal of Communication, 16*(4), 291–304. doi:10.1111/j.1460-2466.1966.tb00043.x

Stewart, M. (2004). Learning through research: An introduction to theories of learning. *JMU Learning & Teaching Press, 4*(1), 6–14.

Tan, J.-S., & Chua, R. Y.-J. (2003). Training and developing cultural intelligence. In Earley, P. C., & Ang, S. (Eds.), *Cultural intelligence: Individual interactions across cultures* (pp. 258–303). Stanford, CA: Stanford University Press.

Thomas, D. C. (2006). Domain and development of cultural intelligence: The importance of mindfulness. *Group & Organization Management, 31*(1), 78–99. doi:10.1177/1059601105275266

Thomas, D. C., & Inkson, K. (2003). *Cultural intelligence: People skills for global business.* San Francisco, CA: Berrett-Koehler Publishers.

Thompson, N. (2006). *Anti-discrimination practice* (4th ed.). New York, NY: Palgrave Macmillan.

Thompson, N. (2006). *Promoting workplace learning.* Bristol, UK: Policy Press.

Tipton, D. B., & Tiemann, K. A. (1993). Using the feature film to facilitate sociological thinking. *Teaching Sociology, 21*, 187–191. doi:10.2307/1318642

Tipton, F. B. (2008). Thumbs-up is a rude gesture in Australia: The presentation of culture in international business textbooks. *Critical Perspectives on International Business, 4*(1), 7–24. doi:10.1108/17422040810849730

Trompenaars, F., & Hampden-Turner, C. (1998). *Riding the waves of culture.* New York, NY: McGraw-Hill.

Wang, H. (2006). Teaching Asian students online: What matters and why? *PAACE Journal of Lifelong Learning, 15*, 69–84.

Weber, A. M., & Haen, C. (2005). *Clinical applications of drama therapy in child and adolescent treatment.* New York, NY: Routledge.

Yamazaki, Y. (2002). *Learning styles and typologies of cultural differences: A theoretical and empirical comparison.* Working paper.

Yamazaki, Y., & Kayes, D. (2004). An experiential approach to cross-cultural learning: A review and integration of competencies for successful expatriate adaptation. *Academy of Management Learning & Education*, *3*(4), 362–379. doi:10.5465/AMLE.2004.15112543

ENDNOTE

[1] International students contribute somewhere in the vicinity of US$15 billion to the U.S. economy (Monaghan, 2009).

Chapter 12

Streaming Media for Writing Instruction:
Drexel's Streaming Media Server and Novel Approaches to Course Lessons and Assessment

Scott Warnock
Drexel University, USA

ABSTRACT

The Information Resources and Technology Department of Drexel University has developed an ambitious, flexible streaming media system to help Drexel faculty use various types of media in their teaching. This system, Drexel DragonDrop, allows faculty to upload a wide variety of file types and then encodes and converts them to media files that students (and others) can easily access and view. DragonDrop provides media options that can be used in any academic discipline, but this chapter focuses on how the system simplifies the use of video applications specifically for those who teach writing or writing-centered courses. As has been discussed throughout this book, video enables innovative teaching practices, but instructors have had to solve core issues including creating and distributing files and ensuring that students can access that material. Drexel's system eliminates many of these logistical obstacles, allowing faculty to focus on creative teaching uses of technology.

INTRODUCTION

Using streaming video, instructors of writing can engage in teaching-centered practices such as

- Assessing, evaluating, and responding to their students' writing in innovative ways, creating "virtual conferences."
- Modeling the writing process for students.

- Creating activity-oriented workshops in which students follow short instructions and then engage in self-paced, workshop-like activities.
- Conducting course lessons and introducing course materials.

I will focus on the uses of this technological application in perhaps the most novel and

DOI: 10.4018/978-1-60960-800-2.ch012

course-specific ways first—using AV methods for modeling and to provide responses to students about their writing—and I will then describe some other teaching strategies. Because writing is an interdisciplinary activity, I will also discuss how writing teachers and administrators can use streaming media to open new instructional methods for teachers across the disciplines who want to enhance the practice of using writing in their courses.

The uses of streaming media that I discuss here all involve creating media presentations with screen capture software, so in demonstrating the value of these streaming media applications I am also advocating for the value of screen capture software itself. This type of software—and while there are a number of products, I used Camtasia for everything I describe—facilitates creative teaching activities for the writing course. By capturing via video, with accompanying audio, the movements and activities on their computer screen, writing instructors can develop teaching approaches and specific tools that enhance their teaching. While some of these practices are ways of expanding what teachers do in a face-to-face classroom to the virtual environment, the use of video itself, as with most thoughtful uses of learning technologies, also provides an opportunity for teachers of writing to re-think what they are doing in their classes, how they teach, and why they teach in that way. As Klass (2003) said, streaming media inherently can help learners understand complex concepts and procedures by helping instructors move beyond the use of just text or even graphics: "The immediacy of the moving image and the impact of the human voice is powerful [sic]."

I also want to note that I am primarily talking about these types of applications in terms of conducting asynchronous course experiences—and by that I mean courses that do not require students to all be in the same place with you at the same time. A basic function of streaming media, as the editors of this book point out in the beginning, provides students with control over the progress of a video, and this can greatly enhance the asynchronous course experience.

DREXEL DRAGONDROP

First, I want to describe the Drexel DragonDrop system's operation. For those of you strictly interested in the pedagogical applications of streaming media, this section may be only of passing interest, as it describes in some detail the technological scaffolding of the system. You may want to skip ahead to "Special media needs for writing teachers." The system was featured in *Campus Technology* as a 2007 Campus Technology Innovator, which described the initial version of it (called then RMCP—the Rich Media Conversion Project) in this way: "Built entirely inhouse (originally written in PERL and now being converted to ASP.NET2), RMCP is a user-friendly web-based graphical user interface (GUI) that automates the rich media deployment process" ("Technology…", 2007). Drexel's Information Resources and Technology (IRT) further describes DragonDrop:

as a feature-rich, multi-institution enabled, web-based application for capturing, encoding and publishing rich media for web access. It significantly simplifies the process of getting audio, video, text and other rich media formats into highly compressed and streamable formats suitable for web delivery. (Drexel, 2009)

According to a series of PowerPoint materials created by Drexel's IRT Department, "DragonDrop is a home-grown, internally developed Drexel software." Faculty and staff began using an early version of the system in 2004, and the first Web-based version became available in 2006. Drexel's IRT says that the "raison d'etre" for DragonDrop is to simplify the handling and accessing of rich media: "This project was developed as a response to the need to minimize the staff handling time necessary to encode and publish rich media destined for web delivery, and to make access to Drexel's current archive of web-based on-demand rich media as simple as possible." The DragonDrop system, in a nutshell, enables the following basic functions:

- *Capture*: The system allows faculty to author rich media content.
- *Drop*: Faculty can upload that content via a Web application.
- *Encode*: The system automatically converts to and from a variety of Web-ready formats.
- *Publish*: The system "pushes" media to the Web as HTML and RSS (Really Simple Syndication, a format for distributing and updating information on the Web).
- *Play*: The system provides access to published media content from anywhere on the Web. (C. Dennis, personal communication, October 1, 2009)

As you can see, DragonDrop's primary function is to allow users—mainly instructors—to upload media files and have them converted into a streaming format for easy, efficient access by students. The *Campus Technology* article that recognized DragonDrop (again, originally called RMCP) as a top innovation said, "RMCP's complexity is transparent to the user; [Drexel developer John] Morris and his team worked closely with faculty and staff content authors to create a system that does not overwhelm users with too many choices, yet retains flexibility and power" ("Technology…", 2007). For users, the basic steps in this process are:

- Users can select rich media or text files from their hard drives to upload.
- Users enter metadata, which describes the file being uploaded (keywords, etc.).
- Users select output formats to be created from the input source.

- The output types provided are optimized formats for Web delivery. (C. Dennis, personal communication, October 1, 2009)

As an example, through Camtasia I create the videos for the teaching applications that I describe below (although, as mentioned above, DragonDrop actually includes a capture function that allows users to record directly in the DragonDrop Web application; those videos can be published automatically to a user's playlist). I often create these videos in a generalized.avi (audio video interleave) format, a universal audio video format[1], and then I upload the file to the DragonDrop system, the interface of which is shown in Figure 1.

The system allows the user to choose from a variety of formats for output:

- 3GPP (3gp): Video format optimized for cell phone and PDA delivery.
- Flash Video (flv): Adobe video format (which can also be played DragonDrop's built-in Flash player).
- MP3 (mp3): Popular audio format used for music and podcasts (these files are iTunes/iPod/iPhone compatible).
- MP4 (mp4): Video format used for video-podcasts (these files are also iTunes/iPod/iPhone compatible).
- Real Media (rm): Real Networks streaming video format.
- Windows Media Video (wmv): Microsoft streaming video format.

For the applications I describe below, I typically request Real Media output, since.rm files are a flexible file format that can be played on any type of computer.

The system not only solves conversion issues, but it also addresses almost equally cumbersome delivery issues. One feature of DragonDrop that makes it so user-friendly for faculty is that the system not only processes the file, converting it

Figure 1. DragonDrop Web interface

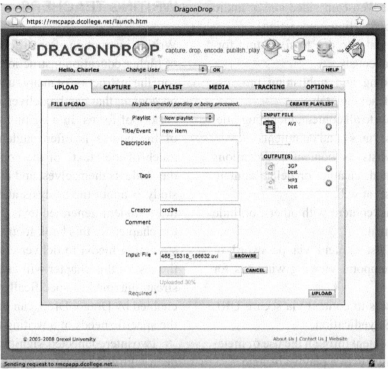

into the desired format, but it makes the delivery of the material simple by automatically creating a Website for students to access the media materials; in the system, this list of links is called a "playlist." Users can manage these playlists in several ways, including creating passwords to access material on the site "playlist."[2] In fact, the system creates both a URL for the particular media file as well as one for the entire site. Usually within an hour of your upload, the system generates an automatic email with the information about how to access the file, such as this one:

Hello Scott,
Your file, 'Introduction to classEngl101195,' has been successfully published as a 'medium' quality 'rm.'
The URI for your published file is:
http://rmcp.dcollege.net/playlists/***

The HTML URI for the playlist containing your published file is:
http://rmcp.dcollege.net/playlists/***
The RSS URI of the playlist containing your published file is:
http://rmcp.dcollege.net/playlists/***
Sincerely,
Your Friendly Neighborhood Transcoder

In most of the pedagogical applications I describe below, I upload all the materials to the same Website or playlist for a given class. However, if you wanted to password-protect certain files or separate files in a course, the system easily allows you to create different playlists.

While I am focusing on the file transcoder and playlist features of the system, DragonDrop also offers much more functionality, again as described from Drexel's IRT site. It allows instructors to

221

- Utilize the built-in Camtasia Relay recorder to capture Web-cam video and/or audio for ad-hoc podcasting /vodcasting.
- Encode content into one to six output formats simultaneously.
- Track encoding and publishing progress through a "Tracking" tab.
- Add metadata to all content, including title, descriptions, "tags" and comments.
- Create playlists as content aggregations and freely add, change, or delete content from playlists at will.
- Share playlist content with others, or, hide playlist content.
- Secure playlist content via password or by setting temporal viewing windows for access.
- Provide access to content via secure URL and via RSS syndication.
- Search for content through the use of metadata associated with a playlist or item.
- Create surrogate users who can act on your behalf. (Drexel, 2009)

Using Camtasia Relay, a user can greatly simplify the capture of videos. The newest version of the DragonDrop system, which follows from an earlier generation (I took part of the beta testing for this new version), allows users to organize data and add metacontent through tags so to provide for a searchable archive of media. Figure 1 shows the DragonDrop Web interface, and one of the system fields automatically asks users to create a playlist; the creation of these different sites can help to organize the files that are created by the system.

Ultimately, DragonDrop is a powerful, flexible way of helping teachers introduce media into their courses. Now turning from quasi-technological explanations, I will approach the use of the system specifically as a teacher of writing, and from that perspective I found what I think of as novel uses for streaming media that are especially enabled by the DragonDrop system.

SPECIAL MEDIA NEEDS FOR WRITING TEACHERS

Writing instruction often differs from other types of higher education instruction for a simple reason: the instruction of many subjects is dependent on *content* that can be delivered to students in a variety of forms. In a writing class, the content of the course is often student-generated; i.e., much of the "text" of the course is created by the students themselves, and much of the course study is about the analysis and development of these student-generated texts. So while many of the chapters in this book focus on ways of using streaming media to deliver content to students, the rest of this chapter will talk about ways that streaming media, specifically the applications enabled by DragonDrop, can be used to enhance the specific needs of a writing course.

Two interconnected, significant issues must be dealt with if a teacher is going to use streaming media (or any learning technology, for that matter): *access* and *distribution*. Students must be able to access easily the media materials, and, along the same lines, teachers must solve the problem of how to distribute often quite-large media files. The premise of this book is that streaming media helps solve these problems for many students, allowing them to overcome the access and distribution issues that make rich media sometimes difficult to use. DragonDrop further simplifies the process, as it provides Web-based access for students, thus making the distribution of media files simple and straightforward. While access and distribution issues must be solved by any teacher, the applications I describe below, especially the "virtual conference" application, demand solutions to access and distribution barriers because students will often have their own personal videos, and they may receive such videos multiple times in the course. By automatically encoding and creating an access site, DragonDrop helps writing teachers, who may create dozens of response videos for a round of student papers.

A FEW GENERAL SCREEN CAPTURE AND RECORDING THOUGHTS

The applications described below are designed to minimize screen activity, which by reducing the file size can provide an advantage when encoding and using the videos. When creating your own videos, you will want to experiment with the settings of your screen capture software so that the media you create are as simple and clean as possible. Although DragonDrop has a very high file size limit, minimizing file size is almost always a good thing, as it allows you to more easily upload and also store the files locally on your own computer if you wish. As Hartsell and Yuen (2006) said of using streaming media, "Use motion only where it clearly compliments [sic] the learning experience" (p. 38).

Also, in creating the videos, as I discuss in more detail below, I do not feel that you need to strive for studio-level perfection with your recordings. If you become uncertain about what to say, you can simply pause the recording. The worst that could happen when you are recording is that you make a glaring mistake and have to begin recording again, but if you use a program like Camtasia (which you can purchase on the TechSmith site for $299), you can quickly become adept at editing out bits of audio, so you can clip out mistakes instead of having to re-record the whole video. While some (e.g., Klass, 2003) recommend that you record in a studio, there are advantages—aside from the obvious logistical advantages for you—for recording in a normal setting. If I am interrupted when creating a response or workshop video, I can pause the recording; and because I am not recording these videos in a studio, interruptions are part of the experience, just as they would be if students met me in my always-busy office. Not only are interruptions inevitable in the environment in which I record—few of us have dedicated studio space—but limited interruptions might even create a relaxed atmosphere for the students viewing the media. A student of writing instructor J. Sommers said that when listening to audio comments he created about her writing, she could hear the instructor's pet birds in the background. Now he was a real person, not just the "guy with the ax" (Mellen and Sommers, 2003, pp. 22-3). An informal AV recording environment can create the same effect.

AND A FEW GENERAL ADVANTAGES

All of the applications below share similar advantages, which I wanted to describe briefly here. Some are inherent advantages of streaming media itself, and others are enhancements provided by using DragonDrop. For one, most of the applications provide some time savings once users become adept at simple-to-use screen capture technologies such as Camtasia. DragonDrop's automatic encoder reduces the time that faculty must spend "producing" videos for student viewing. More specifically, the "virtual conference" application saves instructors response time. Many of the other applications, if used in face-to-face courses, can save classroom time or allow instructors to dedicate class time to other matters. Another obvious advantage of all streaming media applications is reproducibility: When you have a video record of a lesson, students can view and listen to that lesson repeatedly. And, finally, DragonDrop offers tremendous advantages in terms of organization: The files are all on a Website that can be simply bookmarked and referred to by the student whenever needed.

VIRTUAL CONFERENCES

One key area of interaction between writing teachers and their students is *response*: The backbone of many writing courses is the conversation that takes place between instructors and students,

223

oftentimes in the context of drafts of work that students are developing into a final product. As anyone who has used writing extensively in a classroom situation would attest, response is complex and can be arduous and demanding, with teachers reading hundreds of pages of student work and writing thousands of words during only one assignment cycle.

When exploring technologies of response, the interrelated issues of access and distribution are crucial. The traditional form of response, writing comments back to a student, makes access easy: You simply hand the paper back (and if you reflect on this process for a moment, you might marvel at what great technologies the pen/pencil and paper are). For decades (for example, see Fitzpatrick [1968]) instructors have tried audio technologies to help make response less difficult, and that history is also a history of dealing with access issues. How did instructors 40 years ago get audio-recorded comments into the hands of students? This was not an easy task, and teachers solved it in a variety of ways. Sometimes the class would just be a workshop-like work space, and students would take turns listening to the audio. Some improved on the process by asking students to purchase an audio cassette in the beginning of the term and then asking the students to turn in that cassette with each written project, a solution with obvious pitfalls, including the juggling of dozens and perhaps as many as a hundred tapes.

One of the more interesting uses of streaming media may be in this realm of response: Using media technology to facilitate the conversation between teacher and student. As I described in a recent book chapter in *Writing and the iGeneration: Composition in the Computer-Mediated Classroom* (Warnock, 2008), audiovisual commenting is a fairly novel application for writing instruction, and I will extract from that chapter here. While they are discussing using streaming media for computer course applications, I agree with Hartsell and Yuen (2006), who say, "Using video streaming as a form of feedback is another

instructional application to help distant learners understand problem solving procedures and abstract concepts" (p. 40). As anyone who has ever tried to assess writing or has had his or her writing assessed can affirm, the process of communicating about writing between assessor and student is indeed a "problem-solving procedure" that can be incredibly "abstract" and complex. Simply put, it is difficult to communicate how to improve writing, and thus, thinking, to another person. Using streaming media, instructors can create comprehensive, clear, and time-saving commentary about their students' writing, replacing written commentary with spoken. By recording the simple visual of an on-screen paper and the accompanying audio, teachers can reproduce a talked-through writing conference, with the added advantage that the contents of that "conference" are recorded and accessible to the student for multiple viewings.

To create response videos, teachers need to have the proper technological scaffolding: some type of screen capture program (as I mentioned, I use Camtasia to create the videos I am describing); a microphone, and while computers increasingly have sophisticated built-in microphones, audio can be optimized by using an inexpensive, plug-in desktop microphone; and enough computing power and memory to allow for video—this latter constraint is rapidly evaporating in an environment in which computers are now designed to handle multimedia applications.

The process of creating the videos is straightforward once you have the technology in place. I take about five minutes for each draft, as I have found when transcribing samples of my written comments that five minutes creates about 2.5 times more feedback when compared with my normal written comments (and it is worth my pointing out here that I spend a lot of time on my written comments and have been told by many students that I give a lot of focused commentary). I will reiterate what I said above about production quality: I think for these response videos that you need not worry too much about making the production quality professional level. What I mean by that is that if you are using streaming response videos for your class, you will be creating dozens of these videos. You need to gain the minor confidence to turn on the screen capture recorder after having read and lightly annotated the text. From there, you will essentially think out loud about the text while talking to the student. Like Anson (1999), I feel this type of extemporaneously speaking can spark "many spontaneous discoveries" (p. 168) and actually further creates a conference-like experience for the student.

Here is a brief description of how you can provide AV feedback using Camtasia, although, again, the process will be similar with any type of screen capture software. First, you have to collect your students' drafts electronically, whether via your course management system's (CMS) electronic drop box, email, USB memory drive, or CD. You will open Camtasia and click through a brief instructional wizard, and then you will be ready to record. (The Camtasia interface includes more options than most instructors will need, especially for your initial forays into this type of response methodology.)

Before I record, I give the student document a brief read-through, lightly annotating key areas I will discuss during the recording. After this initial reading, I am ready to begin recording. I activate Camtasia and talk through the essay, using the cursor to highlight areas being discussed or typing in particular points of emphasis I wish to make: for instance, "What does this topic sentence mean?" The recording can always be paused if need be. If you have a tablet computer, and I have used a tablet for this process, you can use the tablet functions to handwrite commentary on the draft, perhaps lending an even more personalized feel to the process.

When I am finished reviewing the student document, I end the recording. Camtasia then requests a name for the newly created file. I use a simple naming process (student last name, assignment, etc.) that helps me archive and access the file on my computer, and I save the file to a specific folder, often as an.avi (as mentioned,.avi stands for "audio video interleaved," a common format for video files with sound). Camtasia plays the recorded video back for you right away, allowing you to review the video that you have created. Once you become skilled at creating these videos, you will probably not watch the entire recording again; at this point I feel experienced enough that I just watch the beginning and the end to make sure the production quality is satisfactory. If you are dissatisfied with the results, you can edit the file using Camtasia's production tools, clipping out bits of erroneous audio or video. I seldom edit my comments. If you made many glaring mistakes, you can simply re-record the video—remember, these videos should only take a few minutes to create, so you do not lose that much time re-recording.

When you have finished, you can then open a new document file and start the process anew with the next student document. Periodically, I upload the files to the DragonDrop server, a process that is fine from my fast cable connection at home and is nearly instantaneous from my very fast server at work. Because most of the writing of my class is "public" in terms of the class, I upload all of the files to the same Website/playlist, but, if you wanted privacy, especially if you discussed grades in the videos, you could use DragonDrop to password-protect files.

Streaming video offers, as I mention above, a reliable solution for providing students with access to these videos. I think after a brief learning period, many instructors will find creating the videos to be simple. But access and dissemination issues are ever-present. The AV video files can be quite large (10 to 50 mb for a three- to eight-minute video), certainly too large to move around the Internet via email, even with the geometric progression of the speed of the Web, so using AV feedback depends on having a means of providing students with access to the video files. Others have noted this, and, in fact, a good portion of Still's (2006) article about using Word audio-only files for feedback is dedicated to a discussion of methods of file compression. To distribute the Camtasia-produced AV videos, instructors could ask each student to provide a CD or USB memory drive (much as instructors who have used audio use tapes), or they could even load the videos to a video-sharing site such as YouTube or TeacherTube. Drexel DragonDrop, of course, solves these problems.

SOME ADVANTAGES TO AV RESPONSE

AV feedback provides several potential advantages for teachers and students. AV feedback can be quite conversational and might let students feel connected to a real reader, while at the same time allowing students to see specifically where a comment is directed, helping instructors depict the "movie-in-your-mind" (Elbow, 1973) approach to response, in which instructors describe what they are seeing/experiencing as they go through the piece of writing. In discussing audio-only methods, Sipple and Sommers' (2005) research suggests those methods offer

text-specific commentary on student writing in more substantive and affective detail than would ever be possible in the small space provided by a paper's margins or even the larger space of a letter or email. In addition, it conjures up for both parties the moment of a face-to-face conference without the problems inherent in such a meeting.

It would seem that AV would only expand on this conference-like feeling.

I think the conversation I need to have with students about their writing is facilitated at least as well by AV feedback as with written comments. As I mentioned above, AV response also allows me to give students a lot of feedback, often between

750 and 1,200 words for these short videos. That is a lot of writing. Also, providing AV feedback is much less onerous for me. I feel less fatigued, less of a "psychological drain." Anson (1999) notes that when giving taped comments, he "no longer dreaded the process of reading my students' work," and he feels that he gave more "help" (p. 166). Think what this means for students: As N. Sommers (1982) discovered decades ago in a still-influential article, many students have experienced the "mean-spiritedness" (p. 149) of response comments made by frustrated teachers burned out from reading piles of essays. Perhaps because creating response is less difficult in this way, AV comments may help teachers include more praise and break the habit of finding "error more attractive than excellence" (Daiker, 1999, p. 153). Research does show that "praising whatever a student does well improves writing more than any kind or amount of correction of what he does badly," especially for "less able writers who need all the encouragement they can get" (Diederich, 1974, p. 20). In listening to my AV responses, I realize how much I do in fact compliment students, repeatedly saying things like "really great," "nice," and "cool thought." This method of response allows me to be more supportive at least partially because I do not try to economize as we all must do when writing comments.

But while I am not economizing, I am working faster. Based on my own mini-study of my class experiences, when I provide written comments for a standard three- to four-page writing assignment, I review about four drafts an hour. With Camtasia AV comments, I can respond to six (or more) an hour. This might not seem dramatic until you consider what it means for one round of papers for one of the many—actually, it is more typical than not—instructors who have 90 students: regular written comments: 22.5 hours; AV comments: 15 hours. Then calculate this out over several papers. If we can decrease the response process time by a third while giving the same—and perhaps better—feedback, we have an opportunity to improve significantly the work of those teaching writing (Warnock, 2008).

While indeed many teachers do now type comments, AV also avoids the problem of unreadable teacher scrawl on a draft. That scrawl is often reflective of the strain described above. AV feedback also may help address the fact that some students' writing troubles stem from reading troubles (Petite, 1982)—yet the primary means of communication teachers have with students about their writing *is* writing. Multimedia commentary such as that provided by AV comments would seem to help avoid that problem. It is worth noting here that I agree with other writing teachers that spoken feedback (audio or AV) works best when used as part of the writing process (Anson, 1999; Sipple and Sommers, 2005). I use AV to provide revision comments, not summative/evaluative comments, which means I do not give the students grades in this way.

In a perfect world, instructors would meet all students to discuss their writing, providing, as Rose (1982) says, the "liberating effect on both teacher and student when the isolation of paper grading and the anxiety of facing the graded paper alone are exchanged for the openness of discussion and even confrontation" (p. 331). Yet, unsurprisingly, Stern and Solomon (2006) say that few teachers "have the time, energy, or inclination to meet one-on-one with all of their students […]". Similarly, in discussing his experimentation with Word-embedded audio comments, Still (2006) says conferences are best but unworkable: "I did not have time to hold 80 student conferences for every one of the seven or eight writing assignments" (p. 462). Therefore, maximizing the intentionality, power, and effect of the comments that faculty do make may be all the more important in providing helpful feedback to students" (p. 39). AV comments may provide a means for faculty to offer good feedback without the difficulties of conferences, in effect providing a technological means of breaking the isolation Rose discusses.

Finally, for administrators, in light of the onerous nature of response, there may even be an ethical responsibility to explore these technologies. Using the above numbers in a class with three or four papers, during a term teachers using response technologies get back *half a week* of their lives. This is a lot of time administrators may not be making available to their faculty (Warnock, 2008).

AV feedback could provide a useful feedback alternative, helping writing teachers provide response to student writing in ways that help them do this crucial part of their jobs more efficiently, effectively, and, perhaps, humanely. The advantages to this use of streaming media are manifold: Once teachers secure the technological applications, they can simplify the process, lessening or even eliminating many of the traditional problems of written response. Students can use the media files to access a teacher's comments, repeatedly viewing the video if need be, and teachers could even use a podcasting option to provide audio-only comments for students who have long commutes or other need to listen only to the audio portion of comments.

Using streaming media for response is unlike many other types of media applications because, again, this application allows instructors to simulate a conversational environment. Having students access the comments on a streaming server, plain and simple, facilitates their use in this way. If teachers and students were forced to use the videos as the large type of files they are, while certainly the creative instructor would find ways around access and dissemination issues, these issues would be ever-present and provide an obstacle to using video for response.

WORKSHOP-LIKE WRITING LESSONS

Instructors can also use streaming media to create writing workshops. This is another method of using streaming media in the writing classroom that differs from content delivery; instead, it is about creating a writing class *environment*. By "workshop" here I mean that students are not only viewing content but are participating in various activities described and sometimes modeled (I talk more about modeling below) by the video. The way I have applied these workshops requires that students be actively engaged in their own learning, as they themselves are responsible for "playing along" with the workshop rules to make it most effective. (Of course, there are many options for writing software that guides students through heuristics to help them with invention, revision, or editing: Just perform a Web search for "writing software"; also, see McDaniel, 1986).

The workshop method I am describing capitalizes on the flexibility of the streaming media applications created by DragonDrop, which provides the student with basic control of the video they are watching, as they can start and stop the video at will and return back to earlier parts as they wish. Instructors can use these simple navigational advantages to provide students with a kind of simulated writing workshop. I have tried different versions of how to re-create the workshop environment, settling on a straightforward PowerPoint

presentation during which I ask students to pause the video to engage in workshop–like activities (as depicted in Figure 2). While you could certainly have an archive of such workshops that you use each term, I always make a new video for my particular courses, so students are having more personalized instruction based on the particular writing assignment on which they are working.

My process for conducting the workshop is again straightforward. After I have reviewed a particular set of student writing, I create a PowerPoint in which I provide all of the students with general comments about their drafts, as you can see in the example in Figure 2.

After I have made an observation/comment on some aspect of their draft, I then ask them to *do* something related to that comment. So, in the example above, I discuss peer review comments they received from their colleagues in the class as well as the comments they received from me. But then using simple PowerPoint animation I call up the next bullet point, which asks them as an action item to go through and answer every question posed to them by the reviewers and by me (my response strategy involves posing plenty of questions in my response comments to students).

Figure 2. Example PowerPoint workshop slides

Project 1 Workshop

1. ## Peer reviews and my comments
   ➢ Go through and answer every question posed to you and respond to every comment.

2. ## What is the **purpose** of the project?
   ➢ Write out the main idea of your project.

3. ## Does your project have a visual?
   ➢ If not, where can you place a visual?

Again, I ask them to self-pace this activity, so I tell them to pause the video for about five minutes while they do the deep, workshop-style thinking that I am asking for.

As you can see from the example, my presentation is not fancy. I use basic slides with minimal movement of the mouse cursor in an effort to reduce the video file size. I use simple bullet points to structure my comments, and I typically differentiate the list or bullet points that indicate my comments from the action items points in some easy-to-follow way: Normally by creating a different type of bullet, often accompanied by a different font color; in the example, the "action" items appear with red arrow bullet points. This way the students know that they are supposed to be doing something when they see a certain bullet format. Also, and this of course is not reflected in the static image of the slide above, I use a simple PowerPoint animation scheme so they only see one point at a time, and hopefully this encourages them to focus on the task at hand. Initially they would see and listen to a few comments I made about peer review, and then the animation introduces the arrow bullet point indicating it is time for them to now work through their project to answer those questions.

These workshops should be relatively short and straightforward. I do not strive for overly elaborate instructions, and this entire approach is, again, based on the idea that students can use streaming media technology to take responsibility for their own learning. The whole workshop often only takes 30 minutes or so, with my lesson typically providing between six and ten different action items that they will respond to. What I am ultimately hoping as an instructor of writing is that they will internalize the process we use in this workshop and, as I say to them repeatedly, realize how much they can accomplish in a short period of intensive revision work.

In class such a workshop can make for a great session, with a group of students working through the workshop materials in a room that can feel pretty intense, as the instructor walks around providing structure and guidance as well as answering questions; another use of streaming media, of course, is to record the actual workshop that you facilitated in class and then to provide access to the video for those who were unable to attend the in-person workshop or who want to reinforce their learning or to revisit the lesson.

Why are streaming media applications valuable for conducting workshops like this? As I mention above, students need to have control over the flow of the video. Hartsell and Yuen (2006) point out, "Finally, being in charge of when to start, pause, skip, and review the visual material is another way that students can contend with the material. In short, the primary advantage of streaming video is the ability for students to self-pace their learning" (p. 37). Indeed, students must be able to stop and start the video easily if they are to maximize the experience of the workshop. Also, streaming media, as is so often represented in this book, provides easy access for the students. Again, Drexel's DragonDrop system creates an automatic Web link for the use of these videos, greatly simplifying student access as well as instructor dissemination and future archiving of the material.

MODELING THE WRITING PROCESS

Another writing class-specific application is the use of streaming media to model the actual writing process. Here, I differentiate "modeling" from "model," where the former is the active process of creation and the latter is a fixed demonstration of some thing, its product. Using video, instructors can *show* students how they actually write. There is long history in the writing and composition literature of discussions of using modeling in the writing process as a teaching technique (for example, see Harris, 1983 and Schunk, 2003), and, in fact, some early discussions of using modeling even included suggestions for videotaping modeling sessions (Harris, 1983). By modeling the writing process, I mean that instructors will record their own screen while they actually write, thus creating a demonstration of the process of writing and showing students a variety of traits and strategies, including how a "pro" goes about writing. This is along the lines of a cognitive modeling approach, which provides an important form of observational learning, as with this type of modeling the model incorporates explanations and demonstrations while verbalizing the thoughts and reasons for performing certain actions (Meichenbaum, 1977). Schunk (2003) said, "Teachers often employ cognitive modeling when teaching new skills and concepts" (p. 162). This helps students see a concept in action, and, in a general sense, cognitivists believe adding multimedia to instruction can improve learning through such demonstration approaches (Michelich, 2002). More specifically, as Harris (2003) has shown, this kind of modeling in the writing instructional milieu can be effective in helping students see how another writer—in this case one with the imprimatur of "instructor"—works through a writing task. Harris said, "Seeing how something is done can indeed be interesting and can demystify processes too long considered arcane. And what better way is there to convince students that writing is a process that requires effort, thought, time, and persistence than to go through all that writing, scratching out, rewriting, and revising with and for our students?" (p. 81). This approach can be useful in a number of pedagogical settings, showing students not just the product but the process, but it can be especially intriguing for writing, as what students learn while watching an experienced writer is not only how that writer goes about writing but also the inevitable error-filled path to a finalized product. If you record every step of the process, students may be stunned to see how complicated the process of arriving at a final product is.

Modeling can be a useful activity to perform in a face-to-face classroom—I've done it, almost

in a game show-like way, challenging students to give me a topic and working through that topic in 20 minutes or so—but once again streaming video technology allows teachers to expand on ways this pedagogical strategy is used. Teachers can show students *products* of their writing, and that too can be a useful teaching strategy, but the use of streaming media allows them to show the *process* as well. Certainly teachers have done this type of exercise in class, but using streaming media allows you to model writing as an out-of-class homework assignment, with the added advantage that students can watch it at their own pace.

Here is a specific example of how I used modeling in a lesson. In helping students to write a compare-contrast essay, I have used a grid structure that I show in Table 1,

(I owe credit for this chart to Shaughnessy [1977].) With this exercise, I modeled my efforts to fill out sections of the grid, demonstrating how I actually worked my own way through the assignment. On one hand, I am showing them how I would approach a complex assignment like this. But, as I mentioned above, more importantly for the lessons in my class, I am also showing them how I *draft* and *brainstorm*, which includes the stops and starts of the initial writing process. Students often run into problems with writing because of their inability to break up writing into

Table 1. Compare-contrast essay planning grid for modeling lesson

Generating A Topic Sentence Structure For Your Comparison/Contrast Essay			
Essay Topic:			
Points of comparison/ contrast: (+) for comparison; (-) for contrast (be careful that the contrasts give you something good to work with)	**INPUT: First text**	**INPUT: Second text**	**OUTPUT: Topic sentence**

a variety of tasks (Berkenkotter & Murray, 1983) and differentiate different parts of the process. Actually *showing* them this sort of process changes the way that they can learn to understand what we mean by process: They can watch me and listen to the accompanying narrative as I make some blunders—the kind of blunders all skilled writers make (N. Sommers, 1980) on their way to framing out a piece of writing.

This method of using streaming video can be productive in showing the natural, often error-filled process of writing, but it can also be useful if you want to show students, basically, how *well* you write. They may be surprised you have so many false starts when you start writing, but they may also see how skillfully you navigate a writing task and how quickly and expertly you write. Schunk (2003) differentiates this between *coping models* and *mastery models,* and it can depend on students' learning styles to see which model they may benefit from most:

At times, it may be important to use coping models who initially portray learning difficulties and express low self-efficacy for learning but gradually improve as a result of persistence, effort, effective strategy use, and verbalizing coping statements [...] Coping models contrast with mastery models who perform the task flawlessly from the outset. Students who typically learn easily in school may benefit from mastery models, but those who often have difficulty may perceive themselves more similar in competence to the coping models. (p. 169)

Either way, the use of streaming media to model the writing process can be a powerfully productive tool to show students how writing looks. When we think about it, students are asked to write all the time, but they may never see how someone who writes well actually does it. Harris (2003) said that "the success of modeling" as indicated by teachers' experiences "implies that we need to think long and hard about showing, not telling, students about composing processes.

What does planning look, feel, and sound like? What do we do when we revise?" (79). One of the great advantages of streaming media applications is that they make this *showing* easier to facilitate.

COURSE INTRODUCTION AND INTRODUCTION TO COURSE MATERIALS

The courses that we teach often meet initially or solely online. Streaming media can help us introduce students to our classes in ways that welcome them to the environment of our course. I make rudimentary screen videos of the course management system (CMS) of my courses and then talk students through a brief tour of the CMS Website for these courses. I think hearing my voice helps provide a more humanistic introduction to the class, and the 10 to 15 minutes I spend talking them through key aspects of the course are well worth it.

This type of exercise is particularly useful for my writing courses because the CMS interface is interactive. I am not just explaining to them where they are going to download relevant course documents; instead, I can walk them through how they will work on the course message board environment and show them some of the other interactive tools in the class.

DragonDrop again facilitates this type of streaming media use, especially if you prepare and distribute the videos before classes start. You can simply send the students to a URL; you do not need any other way of distributing a bulky media file to them. Also, that URL is sturdy, so they can re-visit the class orientation any time they are confused or need reinforcement.

GUEST WRITERS

Bringing guests directly to your students via video is discussed far more thoroughly in other parts of this book, so I will just touch on it here, but you could use streaming media to bring guest writers or other visitors to your virtual classroom. Streaming media, as mentioned in the introduction, provides a means of engaging your students with live events, and in a writing class you may want to bring a guest writer in to talk with your students. With a basic technological set-up—Webcam and screen capture—you can have someone talk with your students about their work, perhaps even having this person read some examples of the students' own writing and comment on that writing. As I once learned when a guest speaker failed to come to my class because he got a flat tire on the way—true story—technology can be a great partner in facilitating these kinds of connections in your teaching.

COURSE LESSONS

Because the use of course lessons is also dealt with thoroughly in other parts of this book, I will only briefly discuss this use of streaming media here. As with any other course, streaming media can still be used to deliver writing course content, with the advantage of allowing the participation involved in so much writing course learning. So while you may not want to engage in the type of activity described in the workshop lesson above, you can still engage students in participatory, asynchronous experiences by having them pause the video and do their own work or even contribute to an asynchronous posting environment such as a message board that is set up in conjunction with the video. Aside from that, there are still plenty of course lessons that we can deliver to students clearly and efficiently using streaming media, specifically the automatic encoding of DragonDrop.

HOW STREAMING MEDIA CAN ENCOURAGE WRITING OPPORTUNITIES AROUND AN INSTITUTION

The ways I described using streaming media above not only can enhance the classroom, but many of these teaching techniques also may expand the use of writing across the university, for a variety of reasons.

For one, technologies of response that help teachers respond to student writing can lessen one of the biggest obstacles to using writing in interdisciplinary settings: responding to student writing. I have conducted numerous writing across the curriculum-type workshops, and one of the first questions faculty ask is this: "How am I going to manage the grading burden?" Evaluating writing and responding constructively to a student are hard tasks, but technologies of response can lessen the burden significantly, especially for instructors who are tech savvy yet are not inherently teachers of writing. The video response method I describe above not only reduces the strain but, point blank, it reduces the amount of time one spends responding.

Also, the ability to save and re-play model-type writing lessons can be a powerful way to demonstrate writing in different disciplines. One could envision creating a variety of such lessons, perhaps showing how writing "pros" from around campus tackle various writing tasks. These videos, with some minimal production work, can be made into brief, entertaining lessons that demonstrate to students how experienced writers tackle the writing task. Using the easy recording, storing, and organizing functions of DragonDrop, a writing program could have short, simply produced writing demonstration tutorials in which expert writers from different fields and disciplines show how they go about tackling a writing task.

CONCLUSION

I introduced my discussion of the various teaching applications with some general advantages, but the use of video does have limitations. Recently our first-year program has had the opportunity to provide orientation sessions to incoming freshman to welcome them to our program and help them understand what Drexel first-year writing was about, especially because we offer so many hybrid and online courses. The person coordinating and presenting these workshops asked me to produce a short video about our hybrid courses to show during her 10-minute presentation to business faculty. At first, I thought of this as a good idea, since I make similar videos, as I mention above, to introduce my own courses. However, I then got cold feet, because of the context of this presentation. This was a dynamic faculty member who was going to talk to freshman about the importance of writing in their careers using some very cleverly created visuals. And then she was going to derail her presentation to offer a one-minute clip of my voice talking over some screen captures of my hybrid course. I cringed at the thought of it.

The problem of course is that when we explore streaming media, we are entering a very real cultural context in which students are accustomed to seeing and hearing professionally produced materials. My gravelly voice and rudimentary walk-through of a sample class, while perhaps appropriate and certainly at least adequate as a way of introducing *my own* course to *my own* students, might not hold up to a large audience of freshman. I balked on producing the video, telling my colleague that we needed to work higher-level production skills if we were to hold their interest. After all, the use of this type of media explodes in our faces if students pay more attention to what they perceive as amateurish production qualities than to the content.

Of course, as mentioned, some institutions may have to invest in the type of technology infrastructure that we have at Drexel so that faculty can overcome access issues involved with these large media files created by screen capture programs (some programs, like Impatica, help get around this problem). The Internet's ongoing evolution would seem to indicate that these issues will some day be behind us, but, as of the first decade of the new millennium, bluntly put, we are not there yet. Part of the purpose of this chapter is an elaborate argument for DragonDrop: The system facilitates the technology side of using streaming media for me and many other Drexel faculty; it allows us to get past the technical and logistic issues and be creative pedagogically with the technology.

Interestingly, those who want to use streaming media in higher education might want to explore interacting with the many companies involved in this endeavor. There is a market out there for streaming media in higher education, and it is apparent when you research the background of these applications how connected with industry so many of the offerings are. For instance, in researching streaming media applications on the Web via engines like Google Scholar, I was struck by how many of the links I found went to .com sites with a definite stake in the use and improvement of streaming media. Why "streaming" as opposed to any use of video? As the authors discuss in the introduction, streaming allows users to take small bits of media at a time, allowing more ubiquitous use of video. In fact, for applications like the use of response videos for all of your students, the many videos make usage other than streaming problematic.

By using a streaming media system like Drexel DragonDrop, you create a variety of pedagogical advantages in a writing course, but I cannot emphasize enough that you are saving time as well. We cannot downplay this, especially those of us in the position of trying to encourage faculty to explore new technologies, as I am as the director of a 60+ faculty writing program. The time spent disseminating video files and dealing with students' subsequent access issues can be a deal-killer for many faculty who are seeking turn-key technological solutions. DragonDrop avoids those types of problems. For instance, in the fall 2009 term I used a streaming RealMedia video to introduce my hybrid course to students. Several students emailed me that they were having trouble viewing the video, but these problems all seemed to be addressed by having the students download free RealPlayer software. The problems had nothing to do with creating the video, finding the video, or with clunky distribution issues.

I call the video response above a "virtual conference," but the thoughtful reader will question my use of the word "conference": After all, this is a conference only if my student is not allowed to talk during our meeting. There is no true interaction. The use of streaming media is being conflated with the use of telecommunication tools to provide truly interactive conferencing. This would be the kind of interactivity people have in mind when using the term Web 2.0. There are of course applications that allow for real-time video interaction: I'm thinking of now well-established technologies like Skype and other video conferencing and document-sharing tools. However, the use of streaming media in the way I describe here is designed for students to have, as I mentioned, an asynchronous experience in their writing-centered course.

It is easy to think of streaming media applications for the delivery of traditional course lessons and other "text-like" materials, but for those who teach writing, streaming media also opens up a variety of other teaching opportunities. With the ease of delivery facilitated by streaming applications, faculty can use media in other ways to augment their classes. Drexel's DragonDrop System provides even greater teaching flexibility, as it allows teachers to create, encode, and distribute media in ways that allow students easy access and use. As streaming media applications continue to catch on in higher education, institutions may want to explore developing hardware infrastructure similar to what Drexel has created. Of course, faculty input about the development of these systems can serve as a way to encourage a campus conversation with the goal of eventual technology implementation.

In other venues (especially my book, *Teaching Writing Online: How and Why* [Warnock, 2009]), I have argued that the online environment holds great potential for those who teach writing. After all, in this environment, students write all of the interactions in the class, not just with me but with the other students. Some of the video applications I describe here can be helpful in further developing the pedagogical goals of the course, and when those applications can be deployed via a system like Drexel's DragonDrop, writing teachers can do that amazing thing: Begin to use technologies in that constructive way, as a tool to help them expand their pedagogical reach, allowing them to help students learn in ways previously unimagined.

REFERENCES

Anson, C. (1999). Talking about text: The use of recorded commentary in response to student writing. In Straub, R. (Ed.), *A sourcebook for responding to student writing* (pp. 165–174). Cresskill, NJ: Hampton Press, Inc.

Berkenkotter, C., & Murray, D. M. (1983). Decisions and revisions: The planning strategies of a publishing writer, and response of a laboratory rat: Or, being protocoled. *College Composition and Communication, 34*(2), 156–172. doi:10.2307/357403

Campus Technology. (2007). *Innovator: Drexel University technology area- rich media*. Retrieved August 31, 2009, from http://campustechnology. com/articles/2007/08/2007-campus-technology-innovators-rich-media.aspx?sc_lang=en

Daiker, D. A. (1999). Learning to praise. In Straub, R. (Ed.), *A sourcebook for responding to student writing* (pp. 153–163). Cresskill, NJ: Hampton Press, Inc.

Diederich, P. B. (1974). *Measuring growth in English*. Urbana, IL: NCTE.

Drexel University. (2009). *DragonDrop*. Retrieved August 20, 2009, from http://www.drexel.edu/irt/coursetools/toolList/dragonDrop.aspx

Elbow, P. (1973, 1998). *Writing without teachers,* 2nd ed. New York, NY: Oxford UP.

Fitzpatrick, V. (1968). An AV aid to teaching writing. *English Journal, 57*(3), 372–374. doi:10.2307/812235

Harris, M. (1983). Modeling: A process method of teaching. *College English, 45*(1), 74–84. doi:10.2307/376921

Hartsell, T., & Yuen, S. (2006). Video streaming in online learning. *Association for the Advancement of Computing In Education Journal, 14*(1), 31–43.

Klass, B. (2003, May 30). Streaming media in higher education: Possibilities and pitfalls. *Campus Technology*. Retrieved September 20, 2009, from http://www.campustechnology.com/Articles/2003/05/Streaming-Media-in-Higher-Education-Possibilities-and-Pitfalls.aspx

McDaniel, E. (1986). A comparative study of the first-generation invention software. *Computers and Composition, 3*(3), 7–21.

Meichenbaum, D. (1977). *Cognitive behavior modification: An integrative approach*. New York, NY: Plenum.

Mellen, C., & Sommers, J. (2003). Audio-taped response and the two-year-campus writing classroom: The two-sided desk, the guy with the ax, and the chirping birds. *Teaching English in the Two-Year College, 31*(1), 25–39.

Michelich, V. (2002). Streaming media to enhance teaching and improve learning. *The Technology Source*. January/February. Retrieved June 20, 2009, from http://technologysource.org/article/streaming_media_to_enhance_teaching_and_improve_learning/

Petite, J. (1983). Tape recorders and tutoring. *Teaching English in the Two-Year College, 9*(2), 123–125.

Rose, A. (1982). Spoken versus written criticism of student writing: Some advantages of the conference method. *College Composition and Communication, 33*, 326–331. doi:10.2307/357501

Schunk, D. H. (2003). Self-efficacy for reading and writing: Influence of modeling, goal setting, and self-evaluation. *Reading & Writing Quarterly, 19*, 159–172. doi:10.1080/10573560308219

Shaughnessy, M. (1977). *Errors and expectations*. New York, NY: Oxford University Press.

Sipple, S., & Sommers, J. (2005). *A heterotopic space: Digitized audio commentary and student revisions*. Retrieved March 24, 2006, from http://www.users.muohio.edu/sommerjd/

Sommers, J. (2002). Spoken response: Space, time, and movies of the mind. In Belanoff, P., Dickson, M., Fontaine, S., & Moran, C. (Eds.), *Writing with elbow*. Logan, UT: Utah State Press.

Sommers, N. (1980). Revision strategies of student writers and experienced adult writers. *College Composition and Communication, 31*(4), 378–388. doi:10.2307/356588

Sommers, N. (1982). Responding to student writing. *College Composition and Communication, 33*(2), 148–156. doi:10.2307/357622

Stern, L., & Solomon, A. (2006). Effective faculty feedback: The road less traveled. *Assessing Writing, 11*, 22–41. doi:10.1016/j.asw.2005.12.001

Still, B. (2006). Talking to students: Embedded voice commenting as a tool for critiquing student writing. *Journal of Business and Technical Communication, 20*(4), 460–475. doi:10.1177/1050651906290270

Warnock, S. (2008). Responding to student writing with audio-visual feedback. In Carter, T., & Clayton, M. A. (Eds.), *Writing and the iGeneration: Composition in the computer-mediated classroom* (pp. 201–227). Southlake, TX: Fountainhead Press.

Warnock, S. (2009). *Teaching writing online: How and why*. Urbana, IL: NCTE.

ENDNOTES

[1] For more technical information about.avi files, see the Microsoft Developer Network site http://msdn.microsoft.com/en-us/library/ms779636(VS.85).aspx.

[2] While beyond the scope of this article, DragonDrop was developed as a composite of various applications and technologies including ASP.NET 3. 5 (C#), Perl, Flash, XML, JavaScript (AJAX), Windows Server 2008, IIS 7, SQL Server 2005, Real; Helix Server, Flash Media Server; Lucene, Sorenson Squeeze, TechSmith Relay, TextAloud, PDFCamp, VideoCharge, and Flash Syndrome.

Chapter 13

Effective Online Courses in Business Administration:
Expanding Course Design to Activate Diverse Learning Styles

David L. Sturges
University of Texas-Pan American, USA

ABSTRACT

Technologies used to enhance, augment, or replace traditional course content have been widely examined. With few exceptions, study of these technologies focuses on the effects of the technologies in isolation. Only a few discussions have attempted to evaluate multi-technologies and their contribution to effective learning for online students. This chapter looks at the traditional learning styles and creates a model for robust, multi-technology, student learning-centered approach to optimize student learning in online classes in a business school. It finds that a well-designed, multi-technology approach results in better student performance, more satisfied students, and greater cost-benefit for the business school. The results have been adapted into course design to create a new kind of resource for online course deployment.

INTRODUCTION

Higher education is in a crisis. Between 1995 and 2005, enrollments have increased by twenty-three percent (US Dept. of Education, 2008). President Obama is on record encouraging every American to add college education to his or her résumé (Obama, 2007). These facts suggest that college and university capacities are to be under serious assault. Current student enrollments serve a minority of the American population (US Dept of Education, 2008). Increased demand by Americans

DOI: 10.4018/978-1-60960-800-2.ch013

will tax higher education capacities well beyond the breaking point.

Access for students and retention of students are primary concepts to meet the enrollment challenge. Optional methods to traditional brick-and-mortar facilities must be created to deliver course content ensuring that access to the population is available and that contents and implementation are such that students are more likely to complete courses and, eventually, degree requirements.

To be successful in creating educational content to meet these challenges, learning styles of students must be studied to ensure that the optimum learning experience is made available to students to attract them and to ensure that activities in the course contribute to course completion and, eventually, degree completion.

LEARNING STYLES

Work done by Grasha and Riechmann on learning styles is different from much of the learning styles research in that it focuses on students' responses to activities in the classroom (Montgomery and Groat, 1998). Table 1 shows the six learning styles that were identified along with their characteristics and classroom preferences. (Grasha, 1996)

Further, Grasha suggested teaching methods that were appropriate to clusters of these learning styles. Table 2 shows the Primary Teaching Styles that were found most successful with specific combinations of learning styles (Grasha, 1996).

According to Montgomery and Groat, Grasha does not advocate trying to include all learning styles preferences at all times (Montgomery and Groat, 1998). Such an attempt could result in a mishmash and complicated course content structure that overburdens all students. Instead, they suggest that Grasha's components can be used in a cafeteria-style menu to select from to enhance course content to attract and engage students with different learning types. (Montgomery and Groat, 1998)

Making an assumption that students in our business school are not significantly different from the students in Grasha and Riechmann studies, then the implication for online course design is that the content of courses should be designed to incorporate the most advantageous learning components to ensure student attraction and retention to the courses.

DISTANCE EDUCATION

One realization that occurs to many trying to understand what is happening in the current state of adoption of technologies in the delivery of educational courses is a confusing application of terms exists. A general label, "Distance Education," is applied to the use of technology to supplement or enhance educational opportunities. But, the activities and concepts encountered in the world of "distance learning" are diverse and, in some instances, contradict the connotation of the label.

Table 1. Characteristics of Grasha-Reichmann learning styles

Style	Characteristics	Classroom Preferences
Competitive	Compete with other students	Teacher-centered, class activities
Collaborative	Share ideas with others	Student-led small groups
Avoidant	Uninterested, non-participant	Anonymous environment
Participant	Eager to participate	Lectures with discussion
Dependent	Seek authority figure	Clear instructions, little ambiguity
Independent	Think for themselves	Independent study and projects

Table 2. Teaching methods associated with each cluster of teaching and learning styles

Cluster 1	**Primary Learning Styles** Dependent/Participant/ Competitive	**Cluster 2**	**Primary Learning Styles** Participant/Dependent/Competitive

	Primary Teaching Styles Expert/Formal Authority
	• Exams/Grades emphasized
	• Lectures
	• Mini-lectures +triggers
	• Teacher-centered questioning
	• Term papers
	• Technology-based presentation
			Primary Teaching Styles Personal Model/Expert/Formal Authority
			• Role modeling by illustration
			  o Sharing thought processes
			  o Sharing personal experiences
			• Role model by direct example
			  o Demonstration of ways of doing
			• Teacher/Coaching/Guiding Students

Cluster 3	**Primary Learning Styles** Collaborative/Participant/ Independent	**Cluster 4**	**Primary Learning Styles** Independent /Collaborative/Participant

	Primary Teaching Styles Facilitator/Personal Model/Expert
	• Case Studies
	• Guided Readings
	• Key Statement Discussions
	• Laboratory projects
	• Problem-based learning
	  o Group inquiry
	  o Guided design
	  o Problem-based tutorials
	• Role Plays/simulations
	• Roundtable discussions
			Primary Teaching Styles Delegator/Facilitator/Expert
			• Helping trios
			• Independent Study/research
			• Jigsaw groups
			• Learning pairs
			• Practicum
			• Small group work teams
			• Student journals

The label "distance learning" traces its genealogy to the adoption in the 1970s and 1980s of television or audio linkages to offer classroom connections between a central production point and one or more off-site technology centers equipped with appropriate electronic production capabilities. Once distance centers were installed and dedicated connections established, additional students for any one course could be added for little marginal increase in cost.

College and university extension programs were quick to capture the technology as its development corresponded with the increase in public television outlets, which tended in many instances to be associated with colleges and universities. This marriage made delivery of courses to students in separated geographic locations at once easy and, secondly, attractive to potential students. Until this time, extension programs were limited to printed course lessons distributed by mail or other physical delivery methods. The concept of viewing a lecturer and seeing demonstrations and applications of concepts made television courses a major step forward in improving the quality of extension offerings.

However, schools using this technology found that attracting students who could not be on campus, the driving motivation behind "distance learning," was not the operative motivation in practice. Residential students used these offerings as a method to accelerate degree completion. Students who were not given permission by administrators to take heavy loads could take fifteen to eighteen hours in a semester in residence and could supplement the workload with one or two courses via extension. These courses could be transferred to the residential record to apply against degree credit at any time.

The phenomenon of students using "distance learning" course offerings to supplement regular class offerings led to the introduction of the terms "flexible learning" or "flexible scheduling." This concept recognizes that a prime target for delivery of these courses is the traditional student who seeks additional opportunities. Their desire may be to accelerate degree completion or to provide scheduling flexibility when course times do not meet student needs.

In general, comments by students enrolled in Flexible Schedule courses suggest that the population falls into two categories. First are students who have the skills and capacity to be successful in on-line courses that are dominated by written study materials. The course content focuses on textbooks, written notes presented on an Internet site, on-line quizzes, and other written support materials. Students who have the ability to read and comprehend effectively are successful in this approach (Sturges, 2003).

The second group is students who find the on-line experience to be troublesome. These students are those who developed their educational techniques from years of courses built on personal association with faculty members. These students tend to be "visual learners" who require visual components to course content as well as lecture and written components. Many faculty incorporate visual components into class content using video tapes to show illustrations or to include content from sources not readily available. (Sturges, 2003)

A review of the types of web-based course materials and techniques suggests a hierarchy of course types based on criteria such as the degree of technical expertise required to produce the web-based materials and the degree of computer literacy required to function in a web-based environment. In general these criteria produce five categories of web-based course material. The five categories are illustrated in Figure 1 (Sturges, 2003).

Successful implementation of On-line learning depends on systemic recognition of the levels of production and use and their differences. More importantly, on-line learning will not achieve the projected level of service envisioned by administrators until recognition is made in academic policy considerations. As the techniques of production evolve from OL-1 to OL-5, the time, effort, equipment, personnel resources, and faculty expertise needs go up as well. The result is that producing an OL-5 course offering is a major commitment in terms of fact-finding, content writing, and creative presentation.

In order to produce a resource to meet the needs of increasing student access exponentially to the availability of faculty, then OL 5 courses are the target. It is only at this level of production that the ability to enroll more and more students for limited faculty resources is possible. The concern has been that developing courses at this level is designed to remove faculty from the process for delivery and, therefore, reduces the learning-style components that make traditional college experiences more successful. The goal then, in order to create a robust educational experience, is to create OL 5 courses that include considerable faculty personality in the course's content and a selection of components to create attractive, robust course that are nearly the equal of face-to-face courses.

NEW TECHNOLOGY PROVIDES THE TOOLS

During the past few years, technology has introduced tools that may provide access to meeting the need to create robust, personalized, educational experiences that will make the on-line educational experience with OL5 courses more effective and efficient.

Development of virtual classroom software has opened a new world of online learning that comes as close to face-to-face teaching as is possible with today's computer technology. (WIMBA and Second Life)

Virtual Classrooms contain powerful discussion boards for students to use in individual discussion of course topics. (WIMBA, BlackBoard, Breeze, Second Life, and others)

Textbook suppliers have recognized the video tool as an important contribution as more and more publishers place support video on DVD for electronic distribution.

Figure 1.

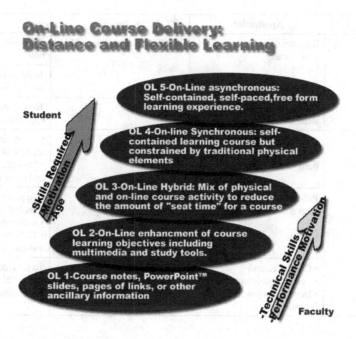

Electronic presentation software and support files have blossomed in their capability to easily produce visually attractive and communicative audio/visual support for classroom presentations. The capabilities of this class of software (Microsoft PowerPoint™, and Apple Keynote™) have created a graphics environment that students can easily use to produce advanced A/V support for online virtual classes.

New streaming video technology will permit incorporation of video into course content that previously was unavailable (Ingebritsen et al, 2009). This is potentially a major leap in the learning experience from what has been the delivery techniques developed during the past few years. (QuickTime™, Realvideo™, Flash™ and other proprietary systems for streaming video)

These tools provide the opportunity for instructional design to open online courses to multiple learning styles. A taxonomy for the application of these concepts is called "Technology Application for Critical-Thinking," or TACT (see Table 3) and

proposes course content to access assumed Clusters in the Learning Styles inventory (see Table 2)

ONLINE STEAMING VIDEO AND TACT COMPONENT

Of the TACT components, Steaming Video is the one that is least used by online faculty (Shephard 2003). Of course, the intervening five years since Shephard's assessment have provided opportunity for expansion of Streaming Video as course content as broadband access and video production have become more compatible and easier to access.

A review of steaming video literature suggests that it can be used for three basic learning-components.

1. Online lectures to introduce topics, provide demonstration, and illustrate concepts.
2. Archives of lectures for learning reinforcement

Table 3. Taxonomy of "technology application for critical-thinking" (Sturges and Ozuna, 2006)

Technology	Application	Software	Objective
Virtual Classrooms	Real-time contact for students/faculty	WIMBA, Breeze, Second Life	To provide student/faculty interaction
			To provide face-to-face student/faculty contact
	Creation of a time and place students must attend		To provide online students a required schedule to keep
Online Discussion Boards	Sharing with classmates to develop ideas and applications of course content	BlackBoard, Second Life	• To provide student/student learning reinforcement, • To foster a sense of collaboration and cooperation.
Electronic Presentations	Presentation support for lectures and student projects	Microsoft PowerPoint™ Apple Keynote™	• To provide Increased attractiveness and communication of audio/visual support material • To foster a sense of collaboration and cooperation.
Online Steaming Video	• Course lectures • Learning Reinforcement • Demonstrations and illustrations	Apple Quicktime™ RealVideo™ Adobe Flash™	To provide virtual access to visual presentation of demonstration, illustration, and lecture

3. Video presentation of case study, demonstrations, and illustration to form the base of student discussion.

(So and Pun, 2002; Cofield, 2002; Keefe, 2003; McCrohon, Lo, Dang, and Johnson, 2001; Hartsell and Yuen, 2006; Reisslein and Reisslein, 2005; Shephard, 2003: Gibbs et al, 2001, Leijen et al, 2009)

Each of these applications becomes an essential component of course design in order to expand a course's learning-style access. In fact, streaming video, as a primary component of course design, can provide influence to all four of the learning-style clusters proposed by Grasha (See Table 2).

Incorporating streaming video into online class design opens the course to a broader spectrum of students of diverse learning-styles. Such robust course development requires dedication from faculty or course designers to learning new techniques and to ensure the streaming video meets the course objectives and not just to be gratuitous "fluff."

CONSTRUCTING A ROBUST ONLINE COURSE (OL5)

Many faculty have developed skills in design of instructional courses that classify as OL4 and OL5. Once skills in authoring courses are acquired, the process of assembling new courses is easy. The only challenge with each new course is incorporation of textbook material and ensuring a complete understanding of the topic. In fact, a rising industry is third-party production of online courses ranging from textbook publishers providing modular components for course creation to independent producers, which contract to educational institutions to produce courses. The primary concerns for this resource is cost and time.

Thousands of OL5 courses have been created that solely use text-based learning materials for course content. In these courses, textbook readings are assigned, assignments requiring responses to specific questions are made, and assessments are created with textbook readings as the basis. These courses are usually designed on the faculty's face-to-face course content in the traditional lecture/

Table 4. Steaming video influence on learning-style clusters

Steaming Video Type	Objective	Cluster Influence
Online Lectures	Video and Audio concept introduction	1- Lectures and Technological presentation
Archives of lectures	Provide learning reinforcement	1 and 2-Lectures, Faculty guidance, demonstration
Video Presentation	Provide visual and audio demonstration, illustration and case student	2, 3, and 4- Demonstrations, illustrations, case study, small group work

interaction/test method. (Keefe, 2003) Unfortunately, they rarely are successful in introducing interaction other than written assignments that students must respond to. These are the digital-age equivalent of mail-based extension courses prevalent for decades.

An effective OL5 course that will contain content and rigor equal to a face-to face course must contain elements to ensure all learning-style clusters are addressed. This suggests that incorporating streaming video is vital to course design and implementation.

Each of the three types of steaming video creates its own set of challenges. Examining each one can provide a better understanding of its use.

Online Lectures

Online lectures are one of the basic building blocks for a robust course to access a number of learning-style clusters. They can be produced in one of two ways. First, recording of lectures that are then edited in postproduction software to add visual support such as electronic presentation slides, text support, illustrative video, or demonstrations. Second, lectures in person can be recorded during a class, post produced and placed as lectures for future sections of a class.

Production of video lectures can be a function of use of video production resources on the institutions' campuses. Third-party producers can be employed. Or, faculty members can produce lectures with help from a teaching assistant. This Option requires acquisition of equipment and software to accomplish similar results to the first two options.

Equipment required includes a digital camera of good quality (minimum of CCD technology), wireless microphone, lights, post-production software, graphics software, electronic preparation software, video capture software, translation software (if Adobe Flash format is to be used). In addition, if the institution does not have streaming service software, then a steaming video server is needed. For a complete list and estimated costs of a lecture streaming lecture production and delivery system, please contact the author.

Production of streaming video resources can be accomplished in one of two methods. First, arrangements can be made to videotape actual lectures in a course and the resulting video can serve as the basis for post-production into an appropriate presentation of the topics.

This method has served in developing resources including class lectures and guest presentations in classes that were, with the permission of the guest, converted to streaming video for access by class members or general public. For an example see http://www.baclass.panam.edu/mmib/video.html.

Second, lectures can be produced in a studio environment using more standard videotaping techniques. This includes lighting, multiple cameras, and sound recording technologies and techniques. The resulting videotapes tend to appear more professional in production values and easier to edit in post-production into very accomplished product. For example, see http://www.baclass.panam.edu/login3/chapter03.php. (QuickTime required)

Archives of Lectures

In addition to self-production, a number of third-party contractors offer the lecture as reinforcement model. In this type of production the goal is to record real time lectures to make them available in an archive for class students to access at whatever time is available for the student to listen and view the lectures.

One of the easiest and most effective of these third party archiving solutions relating to building online courses is WIMBA, a software package for creating virtual classrooms. When using a WIMBA virtual classroom, the archiving process is as simple as pressing a button and the virtual classroom is recorded including any visuals, multimedia, or other enhancements to course content placed in the online virtual classroom. Once recorded the archive can be opened so any enrolled student in the class can access the archive to listen to and to view the online lecture. For example, see http://www.baclass.panam.edu/regentsaward/ra2.html (QuickTime required).

In addition to WIMBA, Second Life, Adobe Breeze, and other class development software packages allow creation of archives for student access.

Course Support

And thirdly, the streaming video technique opens a tremendous resource for enhancing course content with robust support material such as case studies, group activity, concept illustrations or demonstrations of techniques that could otherwise only be included in a face-to-face class meeting for students to view the demonstration (Stilborne et al, 2001).

Most textbook publishers distribute ancillary support material including videos that support or illustrate concepts. These, of course, are designed to be presented in a face-to-face class since they typically are DVD-format. But textbooks adopted for online do not have face-to-face meetings for these resources to be incorporated in the course content.

However, a close assessment of the publishers copyright on these videos suggests they can be incorporated into content with care to meet the publisher's intent in copyright. For an example, see http://www.baclass.panam.edu/mana4361video/ch05videob.html. (QuickTime required)

CONCLUSION

The increase in online courses is the result of students' flextime scheduling of courses in their degree programs. This increasing role suggests that online courses must meet the rigor and learning effectiveness of face-to-face courses to ensure quality and, for many programs, accreditation compliance. In order to create online courses that are quality and educationally based, then the design effort is one to ensure that multiple learning styles are addressed in online courses in the same way they may be intuitively applied in physical courses.

One of the development components available for online course design to address multiple learning styles is streaming video. Incorporating streaming video as a course component permits building elements that attract and motivate varied learning styles in students enrolled in online courses.

Streaming video addresses a number of learning style clusters in its application. In all, streaming video carefully built in to content seamlessly provides content access to students who have traditionally found online courses based on text difficult to navigate.

Streaming video is not a free-to-produce component, but it can be cost effective in creating resources for courses. Once the techniques are incorporated, the courses, in our case, result in demand that increases with every semester.

Streaming video as a course component is a resource that must be evaluated to serve students of the 21st Century!

REFERENCES

Gibbs, W., Bernas, R., & McCann, S. (2001, November 1). *Using a video split-screen technique to evaluate streaming instructional videos.* (ERIC Document Reproduction Service No. ED470087). Retrieved March 6, 2009, from ERIC database.

Grasha, A. F. (1996). *Teaching with style: A practical guide to enhancing learning by understanding teaching and learning styles.* Pittsburgh, PA: Alliance Publishers.

Hartsell, T., & Yuen, S. (2006, January 1). Video streaming in online learning. *AACE Journal, 14*(1), 31–43.

Ingebritsen, T., & Flickinger, K. (1998, January 1). *Development and assessment of Web courses that use streaming audio and video technologies.* (ERIC Document Reproduction Service No. ED422859). Retrieved March 6, 2009, from ERIC database.

Keefe, T. (2003). Enhancing face-to-face courses with online lectures: Instructional and pedagogical issues. In *Teaching, Learning & Technology: The Challenge Continues. Proceedings for the Annual Mid-South Instructional Technology Conference.* (8th, Murfreesboro, TN, March 30 to April 2003).

Leijen, A., Lam, I., Wildschut, L., Simons, P., & Admiraal, W. (2009, January 1). Streaming video to enhance students' reflection in dance education. *Computers & Education, 52*(1), 169-176. (ERIC Document Reproduction Service No. EJ819465). Retrieved March 6, 2009, from ERIC database.

McCrohon, M., Lo, V., Dang, J., & Johnston, C. (2001, December 1). *Video streaming of lectures via the Internet: An experience.* (ERIC Document Reproduction Service No. ED467957). Retrieved March 6, 2009, from ERIC database.

Montgomery, S., & Groat, L. (1998). *Student learning styles and theory implications for teaching.* Center for Research on Learning and Teaching. CRLT Occasional Papers. University of Michigan. Retrieved, March 6, 2009 from CRLT database.

Obama, B. (2007). Remarks of Senator Barack Obama: Reclaiming the American dream. Bettendorf, IA. Retrieved from http://www.barackobama.com/2007/11/07/remarks_of_senator_barack_obam_31.php.

Reisslein, J., Seeling, P., & Reisslein, M. (2005, January 1). Video in distance education: ITFS vs. Web-streaming--evaluation of student attitudes. *Internet and Higher Education, 8*(1), 25-44. (ERIC Document Reproduction Service No. EJ803748). Retrieved March 6, 2009, from ERIC database.

Shephard, K. (2003, June 1). Questioning, promoting and evaluating the use of streaming video to support student learning. *British Journal of Educational Technology, 34*(3), 295-308. (ERIC Document Reproduction Service No. EJ670076). Retrieved March 6, 2009, from ERIC database.

So, S., & Pun, S. (2002, June 1). *Using streaming technology to build video-cases that enhance student teaching on IT.* (ERIC Document Reproduction Service No. ED477095). Retrieved March 6, 2009, from ERIC database.

Stilborne, L., MacGibbon, P., & Virginia Commonwealth of Learning. (2001, January 1). *Video/videoconferencing in support of distance education. Knowledge series: A topical, start-up guide to distance education practice and delivery.* (ERIC Document Reproduction Service No. ED479026). Retrieved March 6, 2009, from ERIC database.

Sturges, D. (2003). *Creating student access and retention model.* Unpublished manuscript. Grant Application FIPSE.

Sturges, D., & Ozuna, T. (2006). Using technology to increase critical-thinking in undergraduate study. *Journal of College Teaching & Learning, 3*(3). ISSN 1544-0389

U.S. Department of Education, National Center for Education Statistics. (2008). *Digest of education statistics, 2007.* (NCES 2008-022), Chapter 3.

Chapter 14
Utilitarian and Hedonic Motivations in the Acceptance of Web Casts in Higher Education

Peter van Baalen
Rotterdam School of Management/Erasmus University Rotterdam, The Netherlands

Jan van Dalen
RSM/Erasmus University Rotterdam, The Netherlands

Ruud Smit
RSM/Erasmus University Rotterdam, The Netherlands

Wouter Veenhof
Capgemini, The Netherlands

ABSTRACT

Today, many universities offer e-learning programs to reach new student markets and improve the efficiency and effectiveness of learning. A key component in e-learning programs are webcasts: condensed, live- and studio-recorded lectures made available, by streaming video technology, via the Web as multimedia presentations that combine videos, audio, lecture slides, and a table of contents (Day, 2008). Web lectures have the potential to become a vital technology in higher education as they enable students to take courses in a convenient and flexible way, at a time and place they prefer. The success of Web lectures in higher education depends to a large extent on the acceptance of the technology by students. To investigate these influencing factors we use the technology acceptance model (TAM), which has originally been developed by Davis, Bagozzi, and Warshaw (1992) and Davis and Venkatesh (1996) to explain the intention to make use of Information Technology. In this study, we are interested in the question what motivates students to use webcast? Most technology acceptance studies have focused on extrinsic (utilitarian) motives (increase in efficiency, ease of use and effectiveness, etc.) to explain the use of e-learning systems. However, recent research suggests that intrinsic (hedonic) motivations, like attractiveness and enjoyment play an important role as well.

DOI: 10.4018/978-1-60960-800-2.ch014

1 INTRODUCTION

This chapter reports on a study of the intended use of web lectures by students of the Rotterdam School of Management, Erasmus University. Web lectures have been introduced in 2004 and have been progressively used by students, mostly in addition to the regular lectures. The aim is to deepen our understanding of the factors that influence the use of web lectures by students.

2 NO SIGNIFICANT DIFFERENCE?

The role, the use, and the impact of educational technologies have been discussed in educational research for a long time. In his book Teachers and Machines, Cuban (1986) reviews the use of educational technologies since the 1920s. Typically, the rise of any new technology (motion pictures, radio, TV, computer) was accompanied with high expectations about the potential of improving the effectiveness of learning. However, in all cases the great promises of the new technologies were followed by disappointments and unmet expectations (Mayer, 2003).

The well-known quote of Cisco Systems' CEO John Chambers in 1999 is only a recent illustration of the high expectations about e-learning technologies: "The next big killer application for the Internet is going to be education. Education over the Internet is going to be so big, it is going to make e-mail look like a rounding error". On the wave of these high promises the interest in e-learning grew exponentially during the late 1990s, but it imploded with the internet bubble in the early 2000s. The widely cited report Thwarted Innovation (Zemsky & Massy, 2004) reports on the causes of the unrealized promises of e-learning technologies during the internet bubble.

There is a multitude of factors that potentially determines the success of e-learning initiatives. The most fundamental question in the debate on e-learning technologies is whether technology and media can influence learning outcomes. The debate about the influence of modern media on learning effectiveness was initiated by Clark (1983) who reviewed the results of comparative research on educational media and claimed that there are "no learning benefits to be gained from employing any specific medium to deliver instruction" (p. 445). In Clark's view media are "mere vehicles that deliver instruction but do not influence student achievement any more than the truck that delivers our groceries causes changes in nutrition" (p. 445). His main argument is that it is not possible to isolate the effects of a medium from the effects of the instructional design. In like spirit, other researchers argued that technology alone does not 'cause' learning to occur (Piccoli, Ahmad, & Ives, 2001, Mayer, 2003). It is the instructional method embedded in the media presentation that causes learning to take place (Jonassen, Davidson, Collins, Campbell, & Haag, 1995).

Kozma (1994) criticized Clark's claim for not considering the relationship between media and learning. Learning is not just a receptive response to instruction's delivery, but an active, constructive, cognitive and social process. He therefore rephrased Clark's original question whether media influence learning into "in what ways can we use the capabilities of media to influence learning for particular students, tasks, and situations?" (Kozma, 1994, p. 7). It should be possible to identify clusters of attributes of technologies, e.g. customization, hyperlinking, for different instructional design. Jonassen, Campbell, and Davidson (1994) critiqued Clark for focusing on media attributes and less on the attributes of the learner in constructing knowledge. According to Jonassen et al. (1994) learning is a holistic, constructive process which cannot be understood by studying responses to attributes of media. Media are part of the learning context which functions within a larger context in which the interaction between problems, relevance and meaning determine the direction and effect of learning.

In 1999, Russell published a comprehensive review on educational research concerning the impact of media on learning performance. In this study he found ample support for Clark's original claim and concluded there is no significant difference between distance and traditional, classroom education.

The 'no significant difference'-debate still continues in academic communities (see Piccoli et al., 2001, Zhang, Zhao, Zhou, & Nunamaker Jr, 2004, Sitzmann, Kraiger, Stewart, & Wisher, 2006, Tallent-Runnels et al., 2006). One problem with the debate is that technology and media are used in a rather generalized way. Over the last decade a variety of e-learning technologies have been developed, which vary in information richness, synchronicity, instructional design, complexity, et cetera. The question therefore is to what extent statements can be made about the influence of e-learning technologies in general. Moreover, the 'no significant difference' debate focuses on the distinction between technology-based learning and traditional classroom learning (face-to-face). Much research has been focused on the question to what extent classroom learning can be replaced by e-learning (Zhang et al., 2004, Brown & Liedholm, 2002). However, most higher education institutions use e-learning technologies only to a certain degree and combine it with traditional classroom learning (hybrid or blended learning). Only a few institutions offer courses that are completely delivered via the Internet. Furthermore, e-learning technologies comprise a variety of technologies and communication modalities (multimedia) and should not be presented as a single technology. Finally, most educational media research has taken the attributes of the technology or the instructional design as the starting point of the research which assumes a rather deterministic (stimulus-response) perspective on learning.

The 'no significant difference'-debate illustrates the complex relationship between learning and (e-)learning media. In his theory of multimedia learning, which we will discuss in the next sec-tion, Mayer attempts to formulate in an interesting way how different media interact with different cognitive information processes in the human brain. Mayer's multimedia learning theory is interesting because it theorizes about the match between different media within e-learning appli-cation (as in the case of webcasts) with different human information processes.

3 MULTIMEDIA LEARNING AND WEB CASTS

In his multimedia learning theory, Mayer (2003) integrates different perspectives from instructional design- and cognitive learning theories. According to Mayer the main cause of the failures of using technologies to learning environments is that learners were forced to adapt to the demands of cutting-edge technologies instead of helping people to learn through the aid of technology. Mayer's cognitive theory multimedia learning is based on the idea that instructional messages should be designed in the light of how the human mind works. Mayer's theory assumes that human information processing systems include dual channels for visual/pictorial and auditory/verbal processing, that each channel has limited capacity for processing, and that active learning implies running a coordinated set of cognitive processes during learning. When information is presented to the eyes, humans process that information in the visual channel. When information is presented to the ears, humans process that information in the auditory channel. Traditional classroom teaching has emphasized verbal information processing by presenting the learning material in words, while ignoring the potential of the visual information processing system. Mayer argues that both human information systems can complement each other and that human understanding takes place when learners are able to mentally integrate visual and verbal representations (Mayer, 2003, p. 4-5).

The problem however is that the human brain is limited in the amount of information that can be processed in each channel at one time. Sweller' cognitive load theory (Sweller, 1994, Mousavi, 1995, Sweller, 1998, Tuovinen & Sweller, 1999) further helps to explain the limited-capacity assumption. The cognitive load theory distinguishes between the long-term memory and the working memory. The long-term memory has an almost unlimited capacity to store information, whereas the working memory has a limited capacity to deal with no more than a few (seven) elements of information simultaneously (Miller, 1956). The working memory is the vehicle which enables humans to think (both logically and creatively), to solve problems and to be expressive (Cooper, 1998). The cognitive load refers to the total amount of mental activity imposed on the working memory at an instance in time (Cooper, 1998). A distinction is made between intrinsic load and extrinsic load. The intrinsic load depends on the inherent difficulty of the information, i.e. the number of elements and how they interact. The extraneous cognitive load depends on the way the instructional message is organized and presented. Based on the cognitive load theory, Mayer seeks to develop instructional designs of multimedia material that reduce the extraneous cognitive load.

The strength of Mayer's cognitive theory of multimedia learning is that it takes the human information processing capacity as the starting for instructional design instead of the attributes of the technology. However, an instructional design, based on the multimedia learning principles assumes that students will accept and use the multimedia for learning. Research in the management education literature suggests that the acceptance and adoption of new learning technologies in educational settings cannot be taken for granted (Arbaugh, 2000, Martins & Kellermanns, 2004). So, prior to the discussion about the role of multimedia on educational outcomes it is important to understand the motives of students to accept and use multimedia technologies for learning.

Student acceptance of new e-learning technologies is prerequisite for an instructional design of the e-learning environment to become successful.

Technology acceptance has been studied in the field of information systems for more than two decades. In our study we seek to contribute to the understanding of the students' motives to accept the use of video web lectures and video web assignments. We theoretically base our research on the technology acceptance model that has been successfully used for a wide variety of information technologies over the last decades. The background of this model will be explained in the next section.

4 TECHNOLOGY ACCEPTANCE MODEL

The technology acceptance model (TAM) is based on the theory of reasoned action (TRA) of Fishbein and Ajzen (1975) and Ajzen (1991), which explains a broad range of behaviors on situation-specific combinations of personal beliefs and attitudes. Later, additional factors have been integrated into this model in order increase its explanatory strength. The underlying idea of TAM is that user acceptance can be explained by two dominant beliefs: perceived usefulness (PU) and perceived ease of use (PEOU). Perceived usefulness is defined as the extent to which people believe that using a particular system would enhance his or her performance. Perceived ease of use can be defined as the degree to which a person believes that using a particular technology would be free of effort (Davis, 1989). A central factor in TAM is the individual's intention to perform a given behavior. As Ajzen argues, "intentions are assumed to capture the motivational factors that influence behavior; they are indications of how hard people are willing to try, of how much an effort they are planning to exert, in order to perform behavior." (Ajzen, 1991, p. 181). User's intention have been found to be better a predictor of system usage than other factors like realism of expectations, motivational force, value, user information satisfaction and user involvement (Venkatesh & Davis, 1996).

In its primordial form TAM posits that information system usage is determined by a behavioral intention to use the system, where the intention to use the system is jointly determined by a person's attitude toward using the system and its perceived usefulness (Amoako-Gyampah & Salam, 2004). The intermediate role of attitude has been subject to debate since the early application of TAM to technology acceptance research. While Fishbein and Ajzen (1975) argued that beliefs influence behavior only via indirect influence on attitudes, others found that beliefs and attitudes are co-determinants of behavioral intentions. Davis (1986, 1989) found that attitudes do not fully mediate the effect of perceived usefulness and perceived ease of use on behavior. Other researchers found strong evidence for the mediating role of attitude between perceived usefulness and intention to use (e.g., Heijden, 2003).

Davis (1989) emphasizes that perceived usefulness and perceived ease of use are people's subjective appraisal of performance and effort and do not necessarily reflect objective reality. Beliefs are viewed as "meaningful variables in their own right, which function as behavioral determinants, and are not regarded as surrogate measures of objective phenomena". The main implication is that TAM emphasizes that user acceptance is not a universal goal and is actually undesirable in cases where systems fail to provide clear performance gains (Davis, 1989).

TAM has been widely adopted in information system research and applied to a broad variety of information technologies. The popularity of TAM is explained by its simplicity and understandability (King & He, 2006). Over time, TAM has been adapted and changed. King and He (2006) sum up four main categories of modifications:

1. The inclusion of external precursors (prior factors) of perceived usefulness and perceived ease of use, like situational involvement, prior usage or experience, and personal computer self-efficacy.
2. The incorporation of factors that are intended to increase TAM's predictive power, like subjective norm expectation, task-technology-fit, risk and trust.
3. The inclusion of contextual factors like gender, culture, technology characteristics that may have moderating effects.
4. The inclusion of consequence measures like attitude, perceptual usage, and actual usage.

In this study we include computer self-efficacy and factors, which are expected to enhance the predictive power of TAM. The mentioned inclusion of contextual and consequence measures, also known as hedonic motivators, will be explained in the next section.

5 HEDONIC MOTIVATORS IN USER ACCEPTANCE

The original technology acceptance model (TAM) departs from a utilitarian perspective assuming that people make their decisions to adopt new technologies for pragmatic reasons, that is expected benefits against a minimal effort to attain these benefits. In the context of TAM, the perceived usefulness of a technology would be considered a benefit and the perceived ease of use an indication of minimum effort. The assumption basically implies that the decision to use information systems is largely based on a rational calculation of the benefits relative to the costs incurred (Igbaria, Parasuraman, & Baroudi, 1996).

However, as Igbaria, Iivari, and Maragahh (1995) argue, even though many people recognize the potential gains of the use of information systems, many people still resist using them. Apparently, extrinsic motivators, like usefulness (benefit) and ease of use (minimal effort), cannot completely explain computer adoption behavior. For this reason some researchers have integrated non-instrumental, that is intrinsic motivators, into technology acceptance models. Davis et al. (1992) assume that extrinsic and intrinsic motivation influence technology acceptance. Extrinsic motivation is defined as the performance of an activity because it is perceived to be instrumental in achieving outcomes that are distinct from the activity itself. Intrinsic motivation can be defined as the performance of an activity for which no reinforcement other than the process of performing the activity per se (Teo, Lim, & Lai, 1999). Different types of intrinsic motivators have been studied. Davis et al. (1992) introduced perceived enjoyment into TAM and found in their two case studies a positive impact of enjoyment on the intention to use information systems. Agarwal and Karahanna (2000) examined the role of cognitive absorption in the student's use of the World Wide Web. They defined the multidimensional concept of cognitive absorption as "a state of deep involvement with software" (p. 665) and found strongly significant correlations between perceived usefulness, perceived ease of use and behavioral intention to use the World Wide Web. Venkatesh (2000) studied, among other factors, the impact of computer playfulness on the perceived ease of use. Computer playfulness does not only refer to the desire for fun but also involves exploration and discovery. In this study he found support for his hypothesis that more playful individuals will rate any new information system as being easier to use than those who are less playful.

Due to the increasing use of the internet and the gaining popularity of computer games and virtual worlds, there has been a growing interest in hedonic, intrinsic motivators, of information systems. The study of hedonic factors, as these intrinsic motivators are called, is rooted in marketing research that investigates the reasons why individuals develop the intention to consume aesthetic products (Holsapple & Wu, 2007). The terminology of hedonic factors is related to hedonic consumption, which refers to "those facets of consumer behavior that relates to the multi-sensory, fantasy and emotive aspects of one's experience with products" (Hirschman & Holbrook, 1982, p. 92). Recently, IS researchers have incorporated hedonic factors into information technology acceptance research (Heijden, 2003, 2004, Holsapple & Wu, 2007, Saeed, Yang, & Sinnappan, 2009). These factors capture the entertainment nature of information systems that evoke imaginal and emotional responses to the user.

A few studies have applied the technology acceptance model to e-learning systems and courses (e.g., Arbaugh, 2000, Martins & Kellermanns, 2004, Gong & Du, 2004, Lee, Cheung, & Chen, 2005, Van Raaij & Schepers, 2008). In general, these studies found support for the predictive power of the two main variables perceived usefulness and perceived ease of use. Gong and Du (2004) enhanced the traditional TAM by including computer self-efficacy which appeared to have strong direct and indirect effects on the intention to use. Martins and Kellermanns (2004) adopted a set of change-motivators and a set of change-enablers as antecedents of perceived usefulness and perceived ease of use. They found that change motivating factors led to a greater perceived usefulness and that change enablers influenced the perceived ease of use. With their extended TAM, Van Raaij and Schepers (2008) found that personal innovativeness and computer anxiety have direct effects on perceived ease of use. Perceived ease of use only had an indirect effect on perceived usefulness.

So far, we haven't found studies that applied the technology acceptance model with hedonic factors to e-learning technologies. Moreover, most research on e-learning is applied to nonvoluntary learning settings in which the use of the proposed technology was mandatory. By contrast, we will apply the model to technology acceptance in a voluntary learning context. This means that the webcast lectures and assignments were not a required part of the courses, but were provided as an additional service to the students. So, the use of the webcast lectures and assignments were left to the will of the students Based on recent research on TAM we extended the model and aim to find out to what extent utilitarian factors, hedonic factors and computer self-efficacy explain the acceptance of webcast lectures and webcast assignment by students in higher education. An overview of the hypotheses implied will be subject of the next section.

6 HYPOTHESES AND RESEARCH MODEL

6.1 Traditional TAM Hypotheses

As there is strong empirical support for TAM in the technology acceptance literature, we take the original TAM as the basis for the webcast research model. So, perceived usefulness (benefit) and perceived ease of use (minimum effort) are expected to exert a significant impact on the intention to use webcasts. In our model the impact of perceived ease of use is mediated by the attitude toward using webcasts. Following the original TAM, we also assume that perceived ease of use influences perceived usefulness. In line with the discussion in the previous section, the following hypotheses are formulated:

H1: A positive attitude (ATT) towards the usage of webcasts has a positive impact on the intention to use (INT).

H2: The perceived ease of use (PEOU) has a positive impact on the attitude to use webcasts (ATT).

H3: The perceived usefulness (PU) has a positive impact on the intention to use (INT).

H4: The perceived usefulness (PU) has a positive influence on the attitude to use webcasts (ATT).

H5: The perceived ease of use (PEOU) has a positive influence on the perceived usefulness of webcasts (PU).

6.2 Computer Self-Efficacy

An important extension to TAM is the adoption of computer self-efficacy as an antecedent of perceived ease of use. The perception of the ease of using webcasts depends on the computer competence level of the student. Skilled computer users will experience less problems in running webcast programs compared to less skilled students. However, as Bandura (1977), 1982) points out, competence levels are necessary, but not sufficient for accomplished performances. People often do not behave optimally, even though they know well what to do. Bandura (1982) argues that motivation and behavior are affected by how people judge their own capabilities to execute tasks, or more in general, how they regulate events in their lives. This self-referent thought is called self-efficacy, which can defined as "the judgments of how well one can execute courses of action required to deal with prospective situations" (Bandura, 1982, p. 122). Compeau and Higgins (1995) applied and extended Bandura's concept of self-efficacy to computer usage (CSE), which refers to a judgment of one's capability to use a computer. Researchers that have integrated computer self-efficacy into TAM found relatively strong correlations between computer self-efficacy and perceived ease of use (Venkatesh & Davis, 1996, Gong & Du, 2004). The following hypothesis can be formulated:

H6: Computer self-efficacy (CSE) has a positive impact on perceived ease of use (PEOU).

6.3 Perceived Enjoyment

Davis et al. (1992) extended the technology acceptance model with an intrinsic motivator called perceived enjoyment (PE). Perceived enjoyment is defined as "the extent to which the activity of using the computer is perceived to be enjoyable in its own right, apart from performance consequences that may be anticipated" (Davis et al., 1992, p. 1113). Perceived enjoyment was expected to influence the intention directly. They found that people's intentions to use computers is mainly influenced by the perceived use of improving their performance and less by the degree of enjoyment in using computers. Similar results were found by Igbaria et al. (1995) and Teo et al. (1999). In contrast, Heijden (2003) found rather strong support for the impact of perceived enjoyment on attitude towards using (ATT).

We adopted perceived enjoyment in TAM as we are interested to learn whether enjoyment influences to use of webcasts by the students. Webcasts may be enjoyable to students, especially compared to traditional lectures, even apart from any anticipated performance consequences (Igbaria et al., 1996). There is a practical implication here. If we find a positive impact of enjoyment on attitude or intention to use, future producers of webcast should take this enjoyment factor into account. The following three hypotheses can be formulated:

H7: Perceived enjoyment (PE) will have a positive impact on the intention to use webcasts (INT).

H8: Perceived enjoyment (PE) will have positive impact on the attitude toward using webcasts (ATT).

H9: Perceived ease of use (PEOU) will have positive impact on perceived enjoyment (PE).

6.4 Perceived Attractiveness

Heijden (2003), 2004) has introduced the concept of perceived visual attractiveness (PA) into TAM. He assumes that aesthetics may play a role in the decision to use an information system, which is based on empirical results found in the psychology and marketing research. In psychological research on the role of aesthetics a strong cor-

relation was found between perceived physical attractiveness with several personality characteristics. In consumer marketing research there is compounding evidence that attractive products create more favorable attitudes towards purchasing than unattractive products. Heijden hypothesizes that perceived attractiveness influences information systems usage indirectly through perceived usefulness, perceived ease of use, and perceived enjoyment.

We assume that aesthetic attributes of webcasts may indeed induce students to use them more intensively. It is reasonable to think that the multimedia and 'information rich' format of webcasts will appear relatively attractive, especially compared to 'information lean' electronic learning media, and thus stimulate the usage of webcasts. Perceived attractiveness also relates to the current tendency toward 'edutainment' that seeks to educate as well as to amuse people. The following hypotheses can be formulated:

H10: Perceived attractiveness (PA) will have a positive impact on perceived usefulness (PU).

H11: Perceived attractiveness (PA) will have a positive impact on perceived ease of use (PEOU).

H12: Perceived attractiveness (PA) will have positive impact on perceived enjoyment (PE).

6.5 Control Variables

We consider three control variables in our model: gender, the distance between campus and home, and the use of webcasts as a substitute for attending classes.

There exists a long tradition in computer behavior research investigating the role of gender differences on computer attitude and usage (Shashaani, 1993, 1994, Colley, 1994, Whitley, 1997, Meelissen & Drent, 2008). The consistent finding in this research is that in many countries girls and women are often behind in ICT use, ICT knowledge and skills (Meelissen & Drent, 2008). Women tend to have less positive attitudes toward IT and show less confidence in using information systems compared to men. We therefore will control for this gender variable. Furthermore, e-learning technologies allow students to take courses independent from time and place. We expect that students that live at a long distance from the university will use the webcasts more frequently as a substitute for traditional classroom courses than students that live near to the university. Finally, we control for students that view webcasts as a substitute. The more students hold this view, the more they will make use of the webcasts. (Figure 1)

7 METHODS AND MEASUREMENT

7.1 Sample

Our empirical application of the TAM model is concerned with two types of webcasts: video and assignments. The video webcasts consist of live recordings of lectures synchronized with the

presentation slides. The assignments webcasts are recordings of solutions to exercises.

After pre-testing, the electronic survey was distributed among undergraduate business students at RSM/Erasmus University to collect measurements of the various TAM constructs. The survey for the video webcasts was sent to 1474 students, of which 132 gave a usable response, yielding a response rate of about 9%. The assignment webcast survey was sent to 1679 students, of which 165 gave usable responses, thus giving a response rate of 9.8%. These relatively low response rates are likely due to the facts that these surveys were presented as part of a thesis project and were not associated with the lecturing activities in any formal way, which may have limited the sense of urgency among the target population.

The descriptive characteristics of the two samples are very similar. In the video webcasts sample, 37.0% of the respondents is female and 47.3% lives within 20 kilometers from campus. As for usage, 14.4% of the respondents tried these applications only at the beginning of the courses, 37.7% checked them only at the end, 34.9% used

Figure 1. Research framework

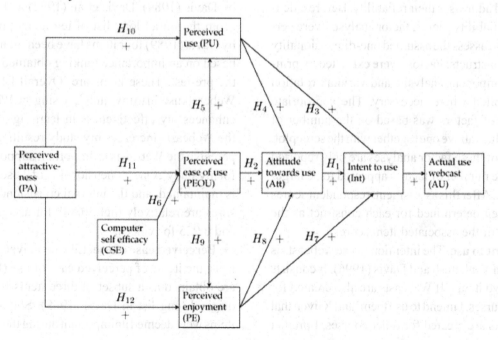

the webcasts throughout the course, and 13.0% made no use of the webcasts at all. In the case of the assignment webcasts, the percentage of female students is 35.0% and 46.7% lives within a 20 kilometer range. The use of these webcasts was confined to the beginning by only 3.8% and to the end by 68.5%; 17.4% of the respondents used these webcasts throughout the courses, while 9.8% ignored them altogether.

Larger differences are observed for the functional role of both types of webcasts. In the case of assignments, the vast majority of respondents, 91.7%, perceives the webcasts as complementary to class lectures, whereas in the case of video webcasts a substantial percentage of respondents 39.0% considers the webcasts as a replacement of the lectures.

7.2 Measurements

The constructs used in our TAM model are largely adapted from Davis (1989), Davis et al. (1992) and Venkatesh and Davis (1996). All constructs have been measured as multi-item Likert scales using 7-point agreement scales with outcomes ranging from -3 to +3. This section reviews the measures used and addresses their reliability. Before calculating reliability scores, factor analyses were performed to assess the assumed one-dimensionality for all constructs. Factors were extracted by principal component analysis, and varimax rotation was applied where necessary. The appropriate number of factors was based on the number of eigenvalues above one together with the screeplot. Results of these factor analyses are only reported when the number of factors appeared to be larger than one. After this assessment, respondent scores have been determined for each construct as the average of the associated item scores.

Intent to use. The intention to use webcasts is based on Venkatesh and Davis (1996). It consists of the two items 'If Webcasts are also created for other courses, I intend to use them' and 'Given that Webcasts are created for other courses, I predict

that I would use them'. The Cronbach alpha for this construct is relatively high: 0.823 for assignments and 0.859 for the video webcasts.

Attitude towards usage. The attitude toward usage (ATT) consists of four items which appear to reflect two attitude dimensions. The formulation of the items has been adapted from Heijden (2001). Factor analysis of the four attitude items results in a two factor solution, which is shown in Table 1. The items 'I have a positive attitude towards the Webcasts' and 'I perceive the Webcasts as a good addition to the regular lectures' reflect a general attitude toward webcasts as complementary material to the lectures (ATTC). Their Cronbach alpha is 0.775 for assignments and 0.785 for video. The other two items 'I prefer the Webcasts to regular lectures' and 'I perceive the Webcasts as a good replacement for regular lectures' reflect the attitude towards the potential of webcasts to substitute regular lectures (ATTS). Their reliability scores are equal to 0.875 (assignments) and 0.839 (video). Both sub-dimensions may be expected to have different effects on the intention to use webcasts, as will be explored below.

Perceived usefulness. The perceived usefulness construct (PU) has been extensively tested by Davis (1989), Davis et al. (1992) and others. From the initial long list of ten items proposed by Davis (1989) four items have been maintained based on an importance ranking obtained during the pre-test. These items are 'Overall I find the Webcasts useful to my study', 'Using the Webcasts enhances my effectiveness in learning', 'Using the Webcasts increases my study results', and 'I perceive the Webcasts as important support tools for my study'. One-dimensionality of these factors is maintained, and the internal consistency measures are relatively high: 0.888 for assignments and 0.925 for videos.

Perceived ease of use. Like perceived usefulness, the items of perceived ease of use (PEOU) are obtained as a subset of three items from the original long list in Davis (1989). Some of the items were deemed unimportant during the pretest,

Table 1. Factor analysis results for attitude (after Varimax rotation)

Items	Assignments		Videos	
	Factor 1	**Factor 2**	**Factor 1**	**Factor 2**
ATT1	0.024	0.904	0.312	0.851
ATT2	0.940	0.083	0.900	0.199
ATT3	0.944	0.013	0.929	0.084
ATT4	0.067	0.901	0.012	0.932
Eigenvalues	1.779	1.636	1.770	1.640
Percentage Explained Variance	35.574	32.711	35.408	32.809
Cumulative Explained Percentage	35.574	68.285	35.408	68.217

others were simply not applicable to webcasts. The remaining three items 'Overall I find the Webcasts easy to use', 'I find it cumbersome to use the Webcasts', and 'Interacting with the Webcasts is often frustrating' are only moderately reliable: the Cronbach alpha values are equal to 0.617 for assignments and 0.604 for videos.

Additionally, we explored the convergent and discriminant validity of the perceived usefulness (PU) and perceived ease of use constructs (PEOU) for the two samples. The outcomes in Table 2 show that the estimated factor loadings are all quite high for the items belonging to the same construct (convergent validity), and low for the other construct (discriminant validity). Cross loadings are mostly well below 0.25 with an exception for the first item of the perceived ease of use construct in the case of assignments, where it is equal to 0.426. Yet, we decided to maintain the item to remain consistent with existing applications, but also to facilitate comparability of the results for the two types of webcasts. Moreover, the concerning item 'Overall I find the Webcasts easy to use' directly appeals to the notion of perceived easy of use and its removal would be somewhat counterintuitive.

Perceived enjoyment. The perceived enjoyment (PE) was introduced to the TAM model by Davis et al. (1992) and has been later applied by Venkatesh (2000) and Heijden (2001). The construct measures the extent to which the use of

webcasts is enjoyable in addition to being useful. It consists of three items 'I find the webcasts entertaining', 'I find using the webcasts pleasurable' and 'I find learning with the help of the webcasts more enjoyable than learning without the webcasts'. The internal consistency of this construct is relatively high as can be observed by the Cronbach alpha values equal to 0.828 (assignments) and 0.778 (videos).

Perceived attractiveness. Perceived attractiveness (PA) measures the extent to which webcasts are considered to look attractive. It was introduced to the TAM model by Heijden (2001). It consists of three items 'Overall I find that the webcasts look attractive', 'The lay-out of the Webcasts is attractive' and 'The colors that are used for the webcasts are attractive'. The internal consistency of this scale is relatively high: 0.932 for assignments and 0.917 for videos.

Computer self-efficacy. The computer self-efficacy construct (CSE) has been developed by Compeau and Higgins (1995) and applied in a TAM context by Venkatesh and Davis (1996). It measures how webcast users feel about their ability to use the facility. Our survey contained ten items to measure this construct, which upon factor analysis appeared to reflect two distinct dimensions; see Table 3. The three items 'I could complete the job using the software package, if there was no one around to tell me what to do as I go', '…if I had

Table 2. Factor analysis results for perceived usefulness and ease of use (after Varimax rotation)

Items	Assignments		Videos	
	Factor 1	**Factor 2**	**Factor 1**	**Factor 2**
PU1	0.834	0.245	0.903	0.042
PU2	0.887	0.136	0.914	0.129
PU3	0.789	0.111	0.872	0.060
PU4	0.902	0.149	0.915	0.134
PEOU1	0.426	0.681	0.214	0.674
PEOU2	0.144	0.791	0.003	0.781
PEOU3	0.024	0.743	0.025	0.781
Eigenvalues	3.120	1.756	3.295	1.714
Percentage Explained Variance	39.000	21.946	41.190	21.421
Cumulative Explained Percentage	39.000	60.945	41.190	62.612

never used a package like it before' and '…if I had just the built-in help facility for assistance' reflect peoples belief in their ability to master the webcast functionality on their own, without further support (CSEO). With Cronbach alpha's equal to 0.744 for assignments and 0.751 or videos, it is fairly reliable. The five items 'I could complete the job using the software package, if I could call someone for help if got stuck', '…if someone else had helped me get started', '…if I had a lot of time to complete the job for which the software was provided', '…if someone showed me how to do it first', '…if I had used similar packages before this one to do the same job' measure a person's ability to work with webcasts given initial support of some kind (CSES). The Cronbach alpha values for this second scale are equal to 0.885 for assignments and 0.906 for video webcasts.

Table 3. Factor analysis results for self-efficacy (after Varimax rotation)

Items	Assignments		Videos	
	Factor 1	**Factor 2**	**Factor 1**	**Factor 2**
CSE1	0.157	0.802	0.065	0.848
CSE2	-0.158	0.888	-0.055	0.902
CSE8	0.198	0.733	0.319	0.670
CSE5	0.820	0.122	0.810	0.196
CSE6	0.864	0.018	0.920	0.014
CSE7	0.813	0.134	0.766	0.065
CSE9	0.848	-0.064	0.887	0.041
CSE10	0.781	0.155	0.840	0.169
Eigenvalues	3.498	2.031	3.691	2.054
Percentage Explained Variance	38.866	22.571	41.014	22.819
Cumulative Explained Percentage	38.866	61.437	41.014	63.834

The two remaining items 'I could complete the job using the software package, if I had only the software manual for reference' and '...if I had seen someone else using it before trying myself' showed ambiguous loadings and have accordingly been dropped from the scale constructions.

7.3 Descriptive Summary of the Measures

Table 4 provides a summary of the main sample characteristics of the measures obtained. A few outcomes are worth mentioning. First, respondents appear to be very positive about the perceived use and ease of use of the webcasts technology and their intention to use it; the observed mean scores are significantly positive (p<0.001). Similar positive outcomes are observed for perceived enjoyment, perceived attractiveness and computer self-efficacy, both supported and unsupported. Secondly, students express a significantly positive attitude to webcasts when the complementary use is concerned. By contrast, respondents have a somewhat negative attitude towards webcasts as a replacement for regular classes and tutorials. Thirdly, strongly significant positive zero-order correlations are obtained for the intention to use webcasts and almost all other constructs except computer self-efficacy. Computer self-efficacy seems hardly related with the other constructs. Computer self-efficacy with some support (CSES) only appears to have a negative association with perceived ease of use of assignment webcasts and a positive correlation with perceived usefulness of video webcasts. Fourthly, respondents' attitudes toward the complementary use of webcasts is significantly positively related with perceived use, ease of use, enjoyment and attractiveness, whereas their attitude towards the supplementary use of webcasts is much less strongly related with these variables, particularly in the case of assignments.

8 RESULTS

In line with previous TAM applications we evaluate the hypotheses of the TAM model using linear regression. The results in Table 5 show that the goodness-of-fit of the models reflected by the adjusted is comparable with those reported elsewhere, and even somewhat more favorable; see e.g. Venkatesh (2000), Horton, Buck, Waterson, and Clegg (2001), and Moon and Kim (2001). Below, we discuss the consequences of the estimation results for the various hypotheses.

8.1 Evaluation of the Hypotheses

Concerning the intention to use webcasts (INT) we find that the attitude towards the complementary use of webcasts (ATTC) and the perceived usefulness (PU) have significantly positive effects for both assignments and lectures, which is in line with hypotheses H1 and H3. The attitude towards the ability of webcasts to substitute for tutorials and lectures has no significant influence on intention to use webcasts for assignments. It has a moderate influence in the case of videos, which vanishes though when respondent characteristics are included in the model. Perceived enjoyment has no significant influence on intention to use contra hypothesis H7. Its significant zero-order effect in Table 4 suggests that the influence of enjoyment is mediated by attitude (ATTC). Respondent characteristics do not significantly contribute to the explanation of variation in intention to use webcasts.

The results for attitude towards webcast usage differ with respect to complementary and substitutable use. In the case of attitude towards the complementary use of webcasts (ATTC) significantly positive effects are observed for perceived usefulness (PU), perceived ease of use (PEOU) and perceived enjoyment (PE) in accordance with hypotheses H4, H2 and H8. An exception is the insignificant influence of perceived enjoyment for videos. An explanation might be that video

Table 4. Descriptive summary of the measurement scales, including zero order correlations

Construct	Mean	StdDev	Alpha	Int	Attc	Atts	Pu	Peou	Pe	Pa	Cseo	Cses	dGesl	Afstand
Assignments (n = 165)														
Int	2.148	1.074	0.823											
Attc	2.206	0.804	0.775	0.704***										
Atts	-0.315	1.569	0.875	0.226**	0.043									
Pu	1.832	0.954	0.888	0.713***	0.687***	0.354***								
Peou	1.554	0.958	0.617	0.344***	0.462***	0.053	0.397***							
Pe	0.954	1.111	0.828	0.504***	0.564***	0.170*	0.581***	0.436***						
Pa	1.224	1.196	0.932	0.297***	0.423***	-0.071	0.365***	0.458***	0.494***					
Cseo	0.822	1.277	0.744	0.075	0.070	0.060	0.120	0.091	0.076	0.118				
Cses	1.336	1.173	0.885	-0.094	-0.036	-0.056	-0.071	-0.209**	-0.088	-0.086	0.175*			
dGender	0.345	0.477	n.a.	0.000	0.068	-0.110	-0.019	-0.007	0.019	0.198*	0.011	0.016		
Distance	3.200	1.358	n.a.	0.126	0.065	-0.083	0.091	0.008	-0.036	0.052	0.087	0.044	-0.051	
dReplace	0.085	0.280	n.a.	-0.052	-0.065	0.207**	-0.038	-0.108	-0.007	0.089	0.003	0.054	0.190*	-0.157*
Videos (n = 136)														
Int	2.066	1.223	0.859											
Attc	2.298	0.861	0.785	0.711***										
Atts	-0.007	1.752	0.839	0.436***	0.254**									
Pu	1.794	1.172	0.925	0.776***	0.716***	0.418***								
Peou	1.250	1.109	0.604	0.356***	0.382***	0.222**	0.219*							
Pe	1.047	1.034	0.778	0.632***	0.536***	0.442***	0.679***	0.322***						
Pa	1.424	1.172	0.917	0.282***	0.339***	0.249**	0.343***	0.379***	0.439***					
Cseo	0.841	1.308	0.751	0.081	-0.021	0.170	0.060	0.034	-0.039	-0.078				
Cses	1.296	1.315	0.906	0.004	-0.028	0.086	0.102	-0.047	-0.076	-0.167	0.278**			
dGender	0.375	0.486	n.a.	-0.148	-0.083	0.012	-0.120	0.003	-0.060	0.044	-0.193*	0.166		
Distance	3.066	1.497	n.a.	-0.017	-0.007	-0.001	-0.115	0.115	-0.007	-0.005	-0.124	-0.035	-0.034	
dReplace	0.390	0.489	n.a.	0.204*	0.039	0.569***	0.154	0.174	0.198*	0.179*	0.117	0.038	0.066	-0.147

$*\ p < 0.05,\ **\ p < 0.01,\ ***\ p < 0.001$

Table 5. Regression results of the relations implied by the TAM model with and without respondent characteristics

Dependent variable: intention to use (INT)

	Assignments		Videos	
Intercept	0.107	0.137	0.110	0.192
Attc	0.562 ***	0.566 ***	0.450 ***	0.477 ***
Atts	0.046	0.057	0.089 *	0.080
Pu	0.428 ***	0.364 ***	0.425 ***	0.324 ***
Pe	0.033	0.059	0.152	0.162 *
dGender		0.025		-0.137
Distance		0.063		0.025
dUseAtStart		-0.565		-0.574 **
dUseAtEind		-0.170		0.051
dReplace		-0.068		0.183
R2adj	0.590 ***	0.593 ***	0.669 ***	0.692 ***
F		1.233		2.931 *

Dependent variable: attitude complementarity (ATTc)

	Assignments		Videos	
Intercept	1.063 ***	0.996 ***	1.196 ***	1.101 ***
Pu	0.425 ***	0.420 ***	0.480 ***	0.520 ***
Pe	0.140 **	0.142 **	0.015	0.013
Peou	0.149 **	0.147 **	0.181 ***	0.195 ***
dGesl		0.143		-0.001
Afstand		0.015		0.017

Dependent variable: perceived usefulness (PU)

	Assignments		Videos	
Intercept	1.157 ***	1.247 ***	1.223 ***	1.964 ***
Peou	0.289 ***	0.304 ***	0.110	0.068
Pa	0.184 **	0.165 *	0.304 ***	0.302 ***
dGender		-0.023		-0.263
Distance		0.062		-0.106
dUseAtStart		-1.185 **		-1.389 ***
dUseAtEind		-0.314		-0.342
dReplace		0.002		0.235
R2adj	0.190 ***	0.232 ***	0.114 ***	0.289 ***
F		2.792 *		7.520 ***

Dependent variable: perceived enjoyment (PE)

	Assignments		Videos	
Intercept	0.052	0.361	0.370 **	0.431
Peou	0.308 ***	0.297 **	0.169 *	0.125
Pa	0.346 ***	0.361 ***	0.326 ***	0.320 ***
dGesl		-0.129		-0.126
Afstand		-0.054		-0.002

continued on following page

Table 5. continued

	Assignments		Videos	
dGebruikBegin		-0.048		0.213
dGebruikEind		-0.011		0.004
dVervangen		-0.108		-0.209
R2adj	0.529 ***	0.522 ***	0.556 ***	0.558 ***
F		0.540		1.141
Dependent variable: attitude supplementarity (ATTs)				
Intercept	-1.259 ***	-1.010 *	-1.238 ***	-2.269 ***
Pu	0.669 ***	0.709 ***	0.326 *	0.401 **
Pe	-0.033	-0.064	0.449 *	0.289
Peou	-0.162	-0.122	0.141	0.028
dGenderl		-0.509 *		0.061
Distance		-0.111		0.125
dUseAtStart		0.192		0.417
dUseAtEnd		0.081		0.084
dReplace		1.295 **		1.792 ***
R2adj	0.119 ***	0.170 ***	0.210 ***	0.440 ***
F		3.004 *		11.847 ***

	Assignments		Videos	
dGebruikBegin		0.024		-0.461
dGebruikEind		-0.117		0.059
dVervangen		-0.095		0.269
R2adj	0.291 ***	0.278 ***	0.209 ***	0.226 ***
F		0.410		1.602
Dependent variable: perceived ease of use (PEOU)				
Intercept	1.284 ***	1.262 ***	0.688 ***	0.177 ***
Pa	0.348 ***	0.379 ***	0.363 ***	0.328 ***
Cseo	0.054	0.074	0.055	0.031
Cses	-0.150 **	-0.156 **	-0.001	-0.007
dGender		-0.192		0.057
Distance		-0.032		0.117
dUseAtStart		0.499		-0.295
dUseAtEnd		0.216		0.312
dReplace		-0.425		0.333
R2adj	0.230 ***	0.245 ***	0.128 ***	0.163 ***
F		1.635		2.098

$* \ p < 0.05$, $** \ p < 0.01$, $*** \ p < 0.001$

R2adj refers to the adjusted R2, the associated asterisks indicate the significance values of the corresponding F-test

F refers to the multipe F-test on the contribution of the respondent characteristics webcasts require much less involvement on behalf of the users than assignments. It also suggests that effort should be made to design assignment webcasts such that student's enjoyment of the application is stimulated. Students who actually use video webcasts as a replacement for attending lectures have a weakly significant negative effect on attitude towards complementarity (p=0.074), which is consistent with its positive influence on attitude towards substitutability.

Results for the attitude toward the potential of webcasts to substitute for tutorials or lectures (ATTS) are somewhat different. Perceived usefulness does have a significantly positive influence on attitude, but its influence is slightly less significant in the case of video webcasts. Contrary to the attitude towards complementarity, perceived enjoyment (PE) has no significant effect in the case of assignments, whereas it significantly influence the attitude towards substitutability in the case of videos. Furthermore, the attitude towards substitutability is the only situation in which respondent characteristics play a significant role. Female students are significantly less positive about the substitutability potential of assignment webcasts than male students. Moreover, students who actually use the webcasts as a substitute for tutorials and lectures have a significantly more positive attitude towards their substitutability potential than other students, which is intuitive.

The perceived usefulness (PU) of the webcasts is positively influenced by their perceived attractiveness (PA) in accordance with hypothesis H10. The perceived ease of use (PEOU) also has a significantly positive effect on usefulness in the case of assignment webcasts, but not in the case of videos. For video webcasts, female students perceive the usefulness of webcasts slightly less positively than male student (p = 0.078).

Furthermore, perceived enjoyment (PE) is positively affected by perceived ease of use (PEOU) and attractiveness (PA), thus supporting hypotheses H9 and H12. The more attractive these webcasts are perceived, the more their us-

age is enjoyed. Respondent characteristics have no significant influence on perceived enjoyment.

Lastly, the perceived ease of use (PEOU) of webcasts is positively affected by their attractiveness as hypothesized (H11). The results for computer self-efficacy are somewhat mixed. Respondents' belief about their unsupported ability to work with webcasts (CSEO) has no significant influence on perceived ease of use. But the effect of self-efficacy with some kind of support or previous experience is unexpectedly negative for assignment webcasts. Students who used the assignment webcasts instead of attending tutorials are seen to perceive these webcasts less easy to use than other students (p=0.062). Distance is seen to have a weakly positive effect in the case of video webcasts (p=0.081): the larger the distance dwelling and campus, the more positive the user friendliness of webcasts are perceived. No other effects are observed for the respondent characteristics.

9 DISCUSSION

Webcasts, both videos of lectures and assignments, are intensively used by students that participated in this study. We used TAM to find out what students motivate to use these webcast. We enhanced and modified the original TAM framework with computer self-efficacy and two hedonic factors: perceived enjoyment and perceived attractiveness. We tested the model in a voluntary usage context, which means that there were no requirements set by the lecturers to use these webcasts during the courses. This section summarizes the main findings of our study and discusses the results. We conclude with implications of our findings.

9.1 Main Findings

A summary of the findings regarding our hypotheses is presented in Table 6. Although we were not able to compare the impact of voluntariness separately, previous research found differences between mandatory and voluntary usage contexts (Venkatesh, 2000, Martins & Kellermanns, 2004). In spite of the absence of a mandatory context we found a strong, direct impact of perceived usefulness on the intention to use the webcasts.

The strong support for the hypotheses about the traditional TAM factors is consistent with other recent research that applied TAM to e-learning systems (Van Raaij & Schepers, 2008, Martins & Kellermanns, 2004, Gong & Du, 2004) and other information systems. In our study some interesting results were found concerning the intermediating role of attitude. After conducting a factor analysis we split up attitude into two variables, one which measures students' perception of webcasts as complementary material to the lectures and one that measures students' perceptions about replacement of lectures by webcasts. The results show that students do not view webcasts as a substitute for traditional lectures. Our research further confirms that attitude is a relevant variable in TAM (see also Heijden, 2003), but also that care should be taken when defining the object of the attitude.

Table 6. Main findings for the hypotheses about webcasts acceptance

	Independent Variable	Dependent Variable	Expected sign	Supported?
H1	Att	Int	+	Yes
H2	PEOE	Att	+	Yes
H3	PU	Int	+	Yes
H4	PU	Att	+	Yes
H5	PEOU	PU	+	Yes
H6	CSE	PEOU	+	No
H7	PE	Int	+	No
H8	PE	Att	+	Yes
H9	PEOU	PE	+	Yes
H10	PA	PU	+	Yes
H11	PA	PEOU	+	Yes
H12	PA	PE	+	Yes

The absence of significant effects of computer self-efficacy on perceived ease of use is surprising because strong direct effects were demonstrated in previous studies (Compeau & Higgins, 1995, Igbaria et al., 1995, 1996, Gong & Du, 2004). Martins and Kellermanns (2004) also didn't find a significant influence of computer self-efficacy and explain this by the differences in age between the respondents in the different studies. For example, in the studies of Igbaria et al. (1995) and Igbaria et al. (1996) the average age of the respondents was 39, while the average age in Martins and Kellermanns (2004) study was only 22. It is reasonable to assume that the latter group was more acquainted with computers and had more computer skills than the former group. The absence of a significant influence of computer self-efficacy in our study can be explained similarly. Furthermore, Compeau, Higgins, and Huff (1999) point at the continuous reciprocal interaction (reciprocal determinism) between computer self-efficacy and computer usage, by which they suggest that self-efficacy is not only an antecedent of computer usage but also a result of it. The main implication is that computer usage and computer self-efficacy interactively develop over time. It also means that, without longitudinal research in which hypothesized causes can be separated from effects, it becomes hard to draw conclusions about the causality in this interaction.

Our study found strong support for the impact of the hedonic factors perceived enjoyment and perceived attractiveness. Perceived attractiveness appears to influence the usefulness, enjoyment and ease of use directly and indirectly the intention to use, both in the case of assignments and videos. It implies that when the attractiveness of the webcasts can be enhanced the intention to use will increase as well, because of the causal relationship between usefulness and enjoyment and the intention to use.

We hardly found any impact of the control variables gender, distance home-campus, and webcast as a substitute. The absence of gender differences may be explained by the population under study (higher education). Also, special computer skills are not required to use webcasts and therefore do not differentiate between male and female students. With respect to distance home-campus we expected that students who live at a greater distance from the university might have a higher propensity to use webcast. In our study we did not found support for this assumption.

WRAP-UP AND IMPLICATIONS

The use, the role and the impact of e-learning in higher education have been discussed extensively over the last two decades. Research by educational technologists about the impact of the use of e-learning systems on learning success shows mixed results. Information system researchers did not attempt to measure the impact of the use of e-learning systems on learning but have tried to explain the usage of these systems in the student's learning environment. Our research contributes to the latter stream of research. We used the technology acceptance model to gain insight in the factors that help to explain the usage of webcasts by students. We extended TAM with so called hedonic factors (enjoyment and attractiveness). We found a strong influence of the traditional (utilitarian) TAM factors and of the newly introduced hedonic factors on the intention to use the webcasts. An important implication of our study is that intrinsic motivation to use webcast should be taken into account in the design of webcast.

However, the usage of webcast in learning environments does not necessarily imply an increase of the pedagogic effectiveness. Technology acceptance models do not include instructional design dimensions, nor do they measure pedagogic impact. For this reason it is important to bring together research on instructional design, multimedia learning and technology acceptance. Costabile, De Marsico, Lanzilotti, Plantamura, and Roselli (2005) provide an example of a framework (Systematic Usability Evaluation) which integrates usability dimensions and learn-

ing effectiveness. We think that further research is needed to explore the ways in which technology acceptance dimensions, instructional design, and multimedia learning aspects can be integrated. We studied the use of webcasts in a voluntary setting. Webcasts were provided supplementary to traditional class room lectures. It is clear that a mandatory use of webcast and an explicit role of the instructor will influence the usage (Martins & Kellermanns, 2004).

Finally, webcasts are just one example of e-learning applications. There is a myriad of e-learning technologies that can be applied in higher education systems. It is hard to predict how these different technologies will be applied and adopted by new generations of teaching staff and students. We expect that new interactive and collaborative technologies will invade higher education and will dissolve the sharp distinction between traditional and virtual learning environments. Future research on the acceptance of e-learning technologies should therefore not be limited to individual technologies but should be applied to the broader concept of new learning environments.

REFERENCES

Agarwal, R., & Karahanna, E. (2000). Time flies when you're having fun: Cognitive absorption and beliefs about information technology usage. *Management Information Systems Quarterly*, 665–694. doi:10.2307/3250951

Ajzen, I. (1991). The theory of planned behavior. *Organizational Behavior and Human Decision Processes*, *50*, 179–211. doi:10.1016/0749-5978(91)90020-T

Amoako-Gyampah, K., & Salam, A. (2004). An extension of the technology acceptance model in an ERP implementation environment. *Information & Management*, *41*(6), 731–745. doi:10.1016/j.im.2003.08.010

Arbaugh, J. (2000). Virtual classroom characteristics and student satisfaction with Internet-based MBA courses. *Journal of Management Education, 24*(1), 32. doi:10.1177/105256290002400104

Bandura, A. (1977). Self-efficacy: Toward a unifying theory of behavioral change. *Psychological Review, 84*(2), 191–215. doi:10.1037/0033-295X.84.2.191

Bandura, A. (1982). Self-efficacy mechanism in human agency. *The American Psychologist, 37*(2), 122–147. doi:10.1037/0003-066X.37.2.122

Brown, B., & Liedholm, C. (2002). Can Web courses replace the classroom in principles of microeconomics? *The American Economic Review*, 444–448. doi:10.1257/000282802320191778

Clark, R. (1983). Reconsidering research on learning from media. *Review of Educational Research, 53*(4), 445.

Colley, A. (1994). Effects of gender role identity and experience on computer attitude components. *Journal of Educational Computing Research, 10*(2), 129–137. doi:10.2190/8NA7-DAEY-GM8P-EUN5

Compeau, D., & Higgins, C. (1995). Computer self-efficacy: Development of a measure and initial test. *Management Information Systems Quarterly, 19*(2), 189–211. doi:10.2307/249688

Compeau, D., Higgins, C., & Huff, S. (1999). Social cognitive theory and individual reactions to computing technology: A longitudinal study. *Management Information Systems Quarterly*, 145–158. doi:10.2307/249749

Cooper, G. (1998). *Research into cognitive load theory and instructional design at UNSW.* Retrieved from http://www.arts.unsw.edu.au/education/clt.html

Costabile, M., De Marsico, M., Lanzilotti, R., Plantamura, V., & Roselli, T. (2005). On the usability evaluation of e-learning applications. In *Proceedings of the 38th Hawaii International Conference on System Sciences.*

Cuban, L. (1986). *Teachers and machines: The use of classroom technology since 1920.* Columbia, NY: Teachers College Press.

Davis, F. (1986). *A technology acceptance model for empirically testing new end-user information systems: Theory and results.* Unpublished doctoral dissertation, Sloan School of Management, Massachussets Institute of Technology.

Davis, F. (1989). Perceived usefulness, perceived ease of use, and user acceptance of information technology. *Management Information Systems Quarterly*, 319–340. doi:10.2307/249008

Davis, F., Bagozzi, R., & Warshaw, P. (1992). Extrinsic and intrinsic motivation to use computers in the workplace. *Journal of Applied Social Psychology, 22*, 1111–1132. doi:10.1111/j.1559-1816.1992.tb00945.x

Davis, F., & Venkatesh, V. (1996). A critical assessment of potential measurement biases in the technology acceptance model: three experiments. *International Journal of Human-Computer Studies, 45*(1), 19–46. doi:10.1006/ijhc.1996.0040

Day, J. (2008). *Investigating learning with Web lectures.* Unpublished doctoral dissertation, Georgia Institute of Technology.

Fishbein, M., & Ajzen, I. (1975). *Belief, attitude, intention and behavior: An introduction to theory and research.* Reading, MA: Addison-Wesley.

Gong, M., & Du, G. (2004). E-learning: Redefining tomorrow's education: Case study of e-learning in Hong Kong University of Science and Technology. In New Horizon in Web-Based Learning: Proceedings of the Third International Conference on Web-Based Learning, Beijing, 8-11 August 2004 (p. 151).

Hirschman, E., & Holbrook, M. (1982). Hedonic consumption: Emerging concepts, methods and propositions. *Journal of Marketing, 46*(3), 92–101. doi:10.2307/1251707

Holsapple, C., & Wu, J. (2007). User acceptance of virtual worlds: The hedonic framework. *ACM SIGMIS Database, 38*(4), 86–89. doi:10.1145/1314234.1314250

Horton, R., Buck, T., Waterson, P., & Clegg, C. (2001). Explaining intranet use with the technology acceptance model. *Journal of Information Technology, 16*(4), 237–249. doi:10.1080/02683960110102407

Igbaria, M., Iivari, J., & Maragahh, H. (1995). Why do individuals use computer technology? A Finnish case study. *Information & Management, 29*(5), 227–238. doi:10.1016/0378-7206(95)00031-0

Igbaria, M., Parasuraman, S., & Baroudi, J. (1996). A motivational model of microcomputer usage. *Journal of Management Information Systems, 13*(1), 127–143.

Jonassen, D., Campbell, J., & Davidson, M. (1994). Learning with media: Restructuring the debate. *Educational Technology Research and Development, 42*(2), 31–39. doi:10.1007/BF02299089

Jonassen, D., Davidson, M., Collins, M., Campbell, J., & Haag, B. (1995). Constructivism and computer-mediated communication in distance education. *American Journal of Distance Education, 9,* 7–26. doi:10.1080/08923649509526885

King, W., & He, J. (2006). A meta-analysis of the technology acceptance model. *Information & Management, 43*(6), 740–755. doi:10.1016/j.im.2006.05.003

Kozma, R. (1994). Will media influence learning? Reframing the debate. *Educational Technology Research and Development, 42*(2), 7–19. doi:10.1007/BF02299087

Lee, M., Cheung, C., & Chen, Z. (2005). Acceptance of Internet-based learning medium: The role of extrinsic and intrinsic motivation. *Information & Management, 42*(8), 1095–1104. doi:10.1016/j.im.2003.10.007

Martins, L., & Kellermanns, F. (2004). A model of business school students' acceptance of a web-based course management system. *Academy of Management Learning & Education, 3*(1), 7–26. doi:10.5465/AMLE.2004.12436815

Mayer, R. (2003). The promise of multimedia learning: using the same instructional design methods across different media. *Learning and Instruction, 13*(2), 125–139. doi:10.1016/S0959-4752(02)00016-6

Meelissen, M., & Drent, M. (2008). Gender differences in computer attitudes: Does the school matter? *Computers in Human Behavior, 24*(3), 969–985. doi:10.1016/j.chb.2007.03.001

Miller, G. (1956). Human memory and the storage of information. *I.R.E. Transactions on Information Theory, 2*(3), 129–137. doi:10.1109/TIT.1956.1056815

Moon, J., & Kim, Y. (2001). Extending the TAM for a World-Wide-Web context. *Information & Management, 38*(4), 217–230. doi:10.1016/S0378-7206(00)00061-6

Mousavi, S. (1995). Reducing cognitive load by mixing auditory and visual presentation modes. *Journal of Educational Psychology, 87*(2), 319–334. doi:10.1037/0022-0663.87.2.319

Piccoli, G., Ahmad, R., & Ives, B. (2001). Web-based virtual learning environments: A research framework and a preliminary assessment of effectiveness in basic IT skills training. *Management Information Systems Quarterly,* 401–426. doi:10.2307/3250989

Russell, T. (1999). *The no significant difference phenomenon: As reported in 355 research reports, summaries, and papers: A comparative research annotated bibliography on technology for distance education.* North Carolina State University.

Saeed, N., Yang, Y., & Sinnappan, S. (2009). *User acceptance of Second Life: An extended TAM including hedonic consumption behaviours* (Research-in-Progress Paper). 17th European Conference on Information Systems.

Shashaani, L. (1993). Gender-based differences in attitudes toward computers. *Computers & Education, 20*(2), 169–181. doi:10.1016/0360-1315(93)90085-W

Shashaani, L. (1994). Gender-differences in computer experience and its influence on computer attitudes. *Journal of Educational Computing Research, 11*(4), 347–367. doi:10.2190/64MD-HTKW-PDXV-RD62

Sitzmann, T., Kraiger, K., Stewart, D., & Wisher, R. (2006). The comparative effectiveness of web-based and classroom instruction: A meta-analysis. *Personnel Psychology, 59*(3), 623–664. doi:10.1111/j.1744-6570.2006.00049.x

Sweller, J. (1994). Cognitive load theory, learning difficulty, and instructional design. *Learning and Instruction, 4*(4), 295–312. doi:10.1016/0959-4752(94)90003-5

Sweller, J. (1998). Can we measure working memory without contamination from knowledge held in long-term memory? *The Behavioral and Brain Sciences, 21*(6), 845–846. doi:10.1017/S0140525X98371769

Tallent-Runnels, M., Thomas, J., Lan, W., Cooper, S., Ahern, T., & Shaw, S. (2006). Teaching courses online: A review of the research. *Review of Educational Research, 76*(1), 93. doi:10.3102/00346543076001093

Teo, T., Lim, V., & Lai, R. (1999). Intrinsic and extrinsic motivation in Internet usage. *Omega, 27*(1), 25–37. doi:10.1016/S0305-0483(98)00028-0

Tuovinen, J., & Sweller, J. (1999). A comparison of cognitive load associated with discovery learning and worked examples. *Journal of Educational Psychology, 91*(2), 334–341. doi:10.1037/0022-0663.91.2.334

Van der Heijden, H. (2001). Measuring core capabilities for electronic commerce. *Journal of Information Technology, 16*(1), 13–22. doi:10.1080/02683960010028447

Van der Heijden, H. (2003). Factors influencing the usage of websites: The case of a generic portal in The Netherlands. *Information & Management, 40*(6), 541–549. doi:10.1016/S0378-7206(02)00079-4

Van der Heijden, H. (2004). User acceptance of hedonic information systems. *Management Information Systems Quarterly, 28*(4), 695–704.

Van Raaij, E., & Schepers, J. (2008). The acceptance and use of a virtual learning environment in China. *Computers & Education, 50*(3), 838–852. doi:10.1016/j.compedu.2006.09.001

Venkatesh, V. (2000). Determinants of perceived ease of use: Integrating control, intrinsic motivation, and emotion into the technology acceptance model. *Information Systems Research, 11*(4), 342–365. doi:10.1287/isre.11.4.342.11872

Venkatesh, V., & Davis, F. (1996). A model of the antecedents of perceived ease of use: Development and test. *Decision Sciences, 27*(3), 451–481. doi:10.1111/j.1540-5915.1996.tb01822.x

Whitley, B. (1997). Gender differences in computer-related attitudes and behavior: A meta-analysis. *Computers in Human Behavior, 13*(1), 1–22. doi:10.1016/S0747-5632(96)00026-X

Zemsky, R., & Massy, W. (2004). *Thwarted innovation, what happened to e-learning and why. A Final Report for The Weatherstation Project of The Learning Alliance at the University of Pennsylvania.* Pittsburgh, PA: The Learning Alliance at the University of Pennsylvania.

Zhang, D., Zhao, J., Zhou, L., & Nunamaker, J. Jr. (2004). Can e-learning replace classroom learning? *Communications of the ACM, 47*(5), 75–79. doi:10.1145/986213.986216

Chapter 15
Streaming Live:
Teaching New Media with New Media

Ana Adi
University of the West of Scotland, UK

ABSTRACT

In an increasingly interconnected world, it is highly important that professors and researchers alike not only find cost-effective solutions to further their work, but also methods to inspire their students to go beyond the traditional methods. This chapter aims to show a couple of examples of successfully integrating new media features in the teaching and research of new media emphasizing their effectiveness, as well as their innovation, involvement, and surprise factors. Furthermore, the methods suggested are easy-to-use and mostly accessible on a non-fee basis. Additionally, the chapter reviews a series of platforms that allow live video broadcasting such as Yahoo! Messenger, Windows Live Messenger, Skype, Oovoo, Google Talk, PalBee, TokBox, PalTalk, TinyChat, TimZon, VoiceThread, Ustream.tv, and Livestream, giving some examples where they could be used in the daily teaching process. Finally, a call for more cross-cultural teaching and collaborative projects is launched.

INTRODUCTION

The Internet, up to some extent, can be considered an academic creation. After all, the first email implementation was done as part of research undertaken at California University from Los Angeles, USA (Gugoiu, 2002). Ever since then the Internet has remained both a source of inspiration and a research topic although it has grown into a

dynamic and dialogical medium whose influence spreads far beyond the academic realm. Moreover, nowadays there is almost no area of activity in the professional world that isn't using the Internet or that isn't influenced by its development, a reason strong and good enough to keep universities interested in the development of the internet and its related technologies.

In an attempt to adapt the teaching and learning process to the changes in the professional world as well as to the new challenges posed by

DOI: 10.4018/978-1-60960-800-2.ch015

the emergence of new media and web 2.0, this chapter aims to present several case studies where new media has been successfully integrated into the daily teaching process. The chapter focuses on three main topics: a) a review of the free online platforms currently available that enable live video streaming and that have a potential to be used in academia; b) the lessons learned from using freely and readily available platforms for live video guest lectures and c) a model for a new media course using new media.

EDUCATION IN THE INTERNET AGE

Changes in the professional world have a strong influence on the educational environment. After all, the universities' aim is to prepare students for a smooth immersion in the professional world by providing them with skills, by helping them refine aptitudes and by enabling them to expand their knowledge while discovering their strengths.

The emergence of new technologies and the expansion of the Internet use have been studied by many authors and researchers in an attempt to provide better education as well as improve current pedagogic practices. Some have focused on improving the teaching process (Angelo, 1993; Braxton et al., 1998; Chickering & Gamson, 1987; Terenzini, 1999), while others looked at ways to adapt the teaching to the different learner types and learning processes (Conner et al. 1996). Debates on the role of and balance between media and pedagogy in the design of a technology-mediated class also emerged, Clark (1983, 1994) arguing, for example, that it is the pedagogical methods and the application of instructional design principles that influence and affect student learning rather than the medium used. Charman and Elmes (1998) as well as Ritter and Leuke (2000) support Clark's argument. Others however, such as Kozma (1994) and Ullmer (1994) believe that it is the different attributes of each media that have the potential

to influence a positively or negatively a learning experience.

The rise of new technologies has influenced academia as well. Distance education for example is one of the fields that benefited most from the changes in technology. It is therefore no wonder that most of the studies dedicated to technology-mediated learning are done from a distance learning perspective. According to Lou, Bernard and Abrami (Lou et al., 2006) distance education knows several stages of development: from mail-in correspondence studies to broadcast-integrated programs, to teleconferencing and hypertext reliant courses. To these Taylor (2001) added two more stages: flexible learning and interactive courses both of them using Internet accessible courses, computer-mediated communication as well as a wider variety of resources available online.

Current studies explore modes of delivery, course structure (Dutton et al. 2001), the quality of the classes (Muirhead, 2000, 2001), applying a business model and strategy approach to the design, promotion and delivery of online education (Granitz & Greene, 2003) or questions about interactivity in an online context (McNabb, 1994; Moore, & Kearsley, 1996; Moore, 1991, 1992, 1993; Spitzer, 2001). However, only few articles present and assess the use of new technologies in a distance learning context and even fewer provide a comparison between traditional and online teaching environments (Mehlenbacher et al., 2000; Ponzurick et al., 2000; Smith, 2001). Fernandez, Simo and Sallan (2009) for example present the advantages and disadvantages of using podcasting in a university learning environment and conclude that podcasting is a powerful tool as a complement to the traditional resources on a course, but not a substitute for them. Similarly, Hauber et al. (2006) explore ways to combine video of a remote person to best emulate face-to-face collaboration showing that some benefits emerge from spatial videoconferencing interfaces. Nowadays the Internet is characterized by dynamic websites with increased interactive features, by the presence of dialogical platforms, and the emergence of collaborative working environments. Taking into account these features there is therefore a great need for further research into how universities could tap into such resources. Moreover, efforts into integrating technology in on campus courses and day-to-day student-professor meetings should be made. This chapter aims to explore such options.

VIDEO IN ACADEMIA

The current online landscape is much more diverse than a decade ago. Apart from the social aspect of the web – social networking, social bookmarking, social sharing, social collaborative creation – an exciting feature that has been perfected during the past years is video. It is a rich and dynamic medium that allows incorporation of a variety of cues and information formats. Furthermore, video can be live or recorded or both giving the viewer more flexibility as well as more information. However, when applied to an education environment video instruction presents both benefits as downfalls.

Armstrong-Stassen, Landstrom and Lumpkin (1998) emphasized the need of both students and instructors to be better prepared in order to have a videoconferencing session run smoothly. The authors show that students who were introduced to videoconferencing as an instructional method at the beginning of the semester and had no prior experience with the medium before reported significantly less positive attitudes towards taking a course through videoconferencing if they perceived faculty and administration to be ill-prepared or unresponsive.

In an early study on video-based instruction, Gibbons, Kincheloe & Down (1977) showed that learning can suffer when students watch lectures individually. However, by supporting discussion and collaboration around the video using the "Tutored Video Instruction" (TVI) model, learning improved over traditional lectures. Subsequent research, such as that reported in Cadiz et al. (2000), has begun to investigate distributed versions of the TVI model, where physically remote students are connected to each other by multiple audio/video feeds. (Bell et al., 2001)

A similar initiative taken by Murphy (2001) aimed to determine the students' preferred delivery method for different kinds of content. The Berkeley Digital Chemistry course, the experiment platform, was therefore made available both online as well as in a traditional classroom setting.

A few conclusions can be reached so far: a) video instruction requires thorough preparation and a good knowledge and understanding of the medium, b) interactive video instruction is better than individual video-lecture consumption and c) video can be a powerful tool to complement course traditional resources.

The nature of video though needs to be discussed and questions about which form of delivery and interaction give best results in an academic setting need to be addressed. Furthermore, more research into the resources to be used to render video within the classroom should be made available. Instead of trying to use the resources readily available online, most studies describe institutional efforts to create customized university platforms and solutions.

Bell et al. (2001) described the design and evaluation of a system that automatically captures and indexes audio and video streams of traditional university lectures without demanding any changes in the style or tools used by teachers. While they are more preoccupied with easy storage and retrieval of recorded lectures their approach could provide a solution for flexible learning and for reducing the technological pressure on the instructors.

The experiement of Hauber et al. (2006) focused on delivery of spatial videoconferencing. However it is 2D live video transmission that can be declared the winner in the study, as the overall task performance parameters are shown to be the closest to face-to-face communication.

Rowe, Harley, and Pletcher (2001) describe the webcasting system developed and operated by the Berkeley Multimedia Research Center: The Berkeley Internet Broadcasting System (BIBS). Liu and Zimmermann (2006) successfully implemented ACTIVE, a peer-to-peer audio streaming system that significantly reduces end-to-end delay experienced among active users while at the same time being capable of providing streaming services to very large multicast groups. And Pullen and Snow (2007) describe their successful and growing experience of more than a decade using Network Education Ware (NEW), an open source synchronous delivery tool blended with a variety of asynchronous capabilities and classroom instruction.

All these efforts have proven to be time-consuming and costly for each institution. Additionally most of them increase the academics' work rather than minimize it while maximizing pedagogical benefits. Finally, in most of the situations described in the literature, technology is just a pretext for a new form of presentation rather than a purpose for knowledge acquisition and skills development. With new media uses growing at a rapid speed it is highly important that universities not only integrate these technologies in their classroom delivery but prepare their students to work independently with them. Teaching the teachers how to use new technologies, encouraging exploration of existing tools before the creation of custom-made solutions as well as identifying how technology can support learning and help meet set learning objectives, are just some of the issues that higher education institutions should also address in the future.

ONLINE VIDEO: CURRENT PRACTICES

An article published by Mashable in 2009 (Lavrusik, 2009) some examples can be found on how universities, both in Europe and the USA, use social media. In emphasizing that most universities use social media as a platform for showcasing the work of their faculty and students the article also shows that social media is also used to gather and share general information relevant to students. Facebook and Twitter are the preferred platforms. YouTube is also among the favorites, the platform being used by universities such as Stanford University[1], University of California, Berkley[2], University of Missouri-Kansas City[3], or the National Programme on Technology Enhanced Learning funded by Ministry of the Human Resource Development of India[4], to upload among others course lectures and office hours responses. These initiatives represent already an advancement when it comes to integrating video, social media and online readily available solutions in the traditional teaching, however they still use asynchronous communication systems – the lectures are recorded, uploaded online, reactions are made to the recording and then more time passes until the uploader of the lecture can send his/her own response.

Research has shown that live video has similar impact on student achievement as in-class instruction (Lou et al., 2006). Under these circumstances, the author believes that a blend between in-class instruction and distance education methods could be easily achieved by using free online resources. In fact, synchronous live video is already being successfully used in areas such as language training, surgery and marketing-communication courses so it is only a question of time until it will be more openly adopted by academic institutions.

In medicine, Dr Adrian Lobontiu, surgeon at Henri Mondor Hospital and professor at Paris 12 University in France in the Cardio-Thoracic and Vascular Surgery Department, is among the first doctors to have used telesurgery, also known as remote surgery. A live synchronous audio and video stream is the key to this method that combines elements of robotics, medical know-how and high-speed data connections. It is a revolutionary method that requires specialized equipment but that has the potential of giving patients around the world access to the expertise of specialized surgeons without the need to travel beyond their local hospital (Lobontiu, 2007).

Also ChineseVoice[5], a language training company specialized in distance-learning, invites people to learn Chinese from Beijing based teachers. The virtual platform of ChineseVoice offers students voice and video streaming together with a shared blackboard enabling students and teachers alike to communicate live and view the same content, in the same window, in real-time.

Unlike the previous two examples, O'Dowd (2007) used available technologies for his qualitative study carried out in university level English as Foreign Language classes in Germany. He used a combination of email, chat and videoconferencing in order to engage students in exchanges with different partner classes in Ireland and the USA.

Finally, inviting prominent professionals to virtually join marketing classes is no longer impossible. C.C. Chapman[6], a Boston based media consultant and active public speaker that helps companies of all sizes figure out how to smartly and strategically leverage social media in their marketing initiatives, is one of such individuals. He joined remotely marketing classes from Canada and USA and shared with them his experience and ideas using platforms such as Skype or Second Life.

USING ONLINE LIVE VIDEO IN HIGHER EDUCATION: THE BACKGROUND OF AN IDEA

Integrating video in a classroom setting is an effective method (Liu & Zimmermann, 2006; Rowe, Harley & Pletcher, 2001). Embedding live video in the teaching process follows the same trend and the literature reviewed so far shows examples of successful implementation (Conner et al., 1996; Lou et al., 2006; Moallem, 2003; Murphy, 2001; Pullen & Snow, 2007).

Furthermore, creating, sharing and transmitting video online is now easier than ever. Yet, the ideas of integrating live online video in a traditional classroom and teaching media using new media were strongly influenced by the author's personal experiences. Being an international exchange student to several institutions around the world, in Belgium, Romania, USA and UK, in some cases following courses in parallel, the author was always confronted with the problem of maintaining close contact with each academic institution. The efforts of coupling the universities existing technologies with readily and freely available online communication tools have influenced the author's research as well as her professional work that heavily focuses on new media and emerging technologies.

One particular event however is the stepping-stone for the initiative that inspired this chapter. It took place in February 2006 and is related to the author's master's thesis defense to the Faculty of Communication and Public Relations in Romania whose online course in Management and Business Communication she was about to graduate. According to the university's regulation the students, irrespectively of the form of study - on-campus, online or distance – have to submit and defend in person a thesis, a paper that combines theory and practice. The author however, starting August 2005, was also enrolled as a Fulbright scholar and full-time master's student at the Missouri School of Journalism of the University of Missouri-Columbia and was therefore residing in the United States. Furthermore, the month of February was an examination month in the American institution as well, which meant that the author had to either postpone defending her thesis or postpone her American exams in order to travel to Romania. Either solution would have brought some harm or delay to the other program, therefore neither one was deemed acceptable. A good knowledge of both institutions, their technical equipment and technological possibilities, the fact that the Romanian master's was online and the fact that the author's thesis was investigating online public relations led the author to suggest defending the thesis online, using a platform that would enable live video calls. This meant that the author would comply with all university rules and regulations and the defense would take place at the scheduled time with the author virtually joining the evaluation committee. The proposal was accepted marking a first for the Faculty of Communication and Public Relations, a first probably for higher education in Romania as well as a first for the Fulbright Program. Needless to say none of the two programs was disrupted.

This is what inspired the author's quest for a way of delivering classes that combine traditional instruction with online resources, online live video being among them. Additionally, having benefited from instruction at various universities around the world, the author believes that new technologies used in the classroom could help broaden the students' learning horizons, expose them to current practices and bring them fresh ideas without burdening financially the home institutions and without requiring extensive preparations from either the host lecturer or the guest.

FREE LIVE VIDEO RESOURCES

As stated previously, one of the aims of this chapter is to present and review the online platforms that enable live video streaming that could be used in academia in general and to the in-class teaching in particular. The platforms will be classified according to their type: instant messaging with video capability, free computer-to-computer calling platforms, online chat rooms with video capability, and other such as live streaming platforms or collaboration platforms with video. Other characteristics related to the video transmission options of each platform that are discussed include: the type of live video they enable – synchronous or asynchronous-, and the number of users they allow to stream at the same time.

Providing a review of such platforms emphasizes the variety of resources freely available online. It also gives lecturers interested in adopting new media for the chance to choose the platform that meets best their course and program requirements. Finally, in order to test or use any of the platforms reviewed in this chapter lecturers should ensure that the following criteria are met: they have a broadband or higher internet connection, a working webcam, a working microphone and either a set of headsets or a working sound system.

Instant Messaging with Video Capabilities

There are many instant messaging (IM) platforms available online, however only few of them have the potential of being considered global providers: *Yahoo! Messenger, Windows Live Messenger (formerly known as MSN Messenger),* and *iChat.* These platforms are among the first and have the advantage of being affiliated with bigger companies committed to delivering online solutions that enhance communication.

These platforms were initially known for their real-time text-based communication and for being a customizable alternative to chat rooms. As the Internet and technology evolved the features of IM platforms spanned from simple text-based exchanges, to customizable fonts and window appearance, to emoticons, avatars and even calls that enable two-way live streaming of both audio and video signals.

All three platforms are free but need to be downloaded and installed on the host computer – iChat is pre-installed on every Apple computer – and require the person to set up an account and password in order to use them. People who do not have an account cannot get in touch via messenger with those who do. Furthermore, in order to join someone's contact list one needs to send an invitation and be accepted. This tightens security and increases privacy, making users responsible at the same time for their decisions to add to or block other users from their lists. The messengers' general features are mostly the same, users having the possibility to choose a display photo or avatar, to customize the appearance of their window and font, to organize their contacts in groups, to update and customize their status, and to share files.

In regards to video transmission it is only *iChat* that enables multiple user video calls of up to three people without any extra charges. It is also iChat alone that allows users to share and visualize documents in the same window while they speak, the formats supported though being those of Apple Software. Furthermore, iChat's screenshare option grants users remote access to their co-speaker's screen, making collaborative work possible and therefore making iChat a great solution for academic work, collaborative projects as well as for remote guest lectures.

Yahoo! Messenger (YM) webcam stream works in a 4-step process. First users need to connect their webcams and either send a single invitation to another contact or advertise that they are broadcasting their webcam via their status. Then, their contacts need to click on the "view my webcam" invitation. A notification is sent to the webcam streaming user asking them to accept or deny granting access to the contacts attempting to view their webcam. This gives users the chance to further control where and to whom they want their live video feed to be accessible. Once permission is granted the user is seen live. The streaming comprises both audio and video and is opened in a new window allowing therefore further communication via chat or further sharing of links, images and videos. The newest version of Yahoo! Messenger now embeds the preview of the shared links, images and videos in the chat widow, which is still separate from the video window. It also enables users to swap video windows, position them side-by-side, mute the call or place it on hold. As for visualization and collaboration in real-time on documents such as spreadsheets, presentations or text documents are not possible,

YM allowing only for files to be transmitted and downloaded on the other user machine.

With YM one user can live broadcast and grant access to their complete list of contacts. This feature makes Yahoo! Messenger a potential academic platform as remote guest lecturers could be seen both by an in-class audience as well as by a scattered audience at the same time. While it is clear that one user can stream live to a large group of people who do not necessarily need to have a camera themselves it is still unclear whether a user can simultaneously watch multiple broadcasts. If this were possible interaction with Yahoo! Messenger would be taken to a level that would blur the boundaries between distance and in-class learning.

Finally, *Windows Live Messenger (WLM)* presents similar features with YM. The 2011 version of the software, which is compatible with Windows 7 and Windows Vista, offers extended video features compared to the Messenger for Windows XP edition. The 2011 edition includes HD video, and photo and video sharing while in the video chat. For those who have purchased the Office Communication Server access multi-party audio and video conferencing options is included in the price. Alternative Microsoft conference services include Microsoft Lync platform which provides an interface that bring together audio, video and webconferencing.

Apart from downloadable instant messaging platforms, several browser-based solutions are also available. They are relatively newer in the instant messaging scene and base their concept on the chat-room model. The most promising platforms are *Google Talk*, *TokBox* and *PalBee* but there are many other providers offering similar services.

Google Talk is part of the big family of Google products but unlike iChat, YM and WLM it can both downloaded or accessed online via Gmail. Initially Google Talk was instant messaging service but now, like most of its competitors Google has included a live video call feature as well. As an instant messaging platform Google Talk works similarly with the platforms already presented and it is its online availability that gives it an advantage. In order to use Google Talk from any computer users need to log into their Google email account, Gmail. Google Talk is embedded in the email window so when logged in one can check its new emails but also see who is online at the same time. The video of Google Talk works only on a peer-to-peer basis and has limited features compared to the downloadable IM versions. Futhermore, a plug-in needs to be downloaded in order to make the video transmission possible. While this is a handy feature for having video conversations from virtually anywhere in the world and any computer, the need to install a plug-in becomes a shortcoming when thinking to use Google Talk for academic purposes. Most universities have strict regulations and policies related to the use of their computers and generally do not allow downloads on their machines without the approval of the head of the department and support of the IT team. Therefore, instead of making the process easier and access to live video straightforward, Google Talk, although available via any browser, meets the same challenges as other IM platforms.

Additionally, for project or teamwork Google offers a great platform via Google Docs, which enables real-time collaboration on presentations, spreadsheets and text documents. Google Docs also has an embedded chat in its platform that allows users that have access to the documents to exchange thoughts and information. However, the Google Docs chat is different from Google Talk and therefore if people were to use both platforms simultaneously they would either face the challenge of resizing the windows in order to view both platforms or choose between which platform to view - the video talk or the collaborative document. An alternative that enabled video conversations to be embedded in the same window and allow sharing of documents was Google Wave. No longer actively developed by Google, Google Wave remains a promising platform for collabora-

tion that includes synchronous and asynchronous video solutions.

A more integrative solution, which includes email, calendar, collaboration and communication tools is Google Apps for Education, a package offered for free to universities and colleges[7]. However, evaluating and recommending new IT systems is not the aim of this chapter, the readers therefore being left here with an opportunity to explore them further if they want to.

Free Computer to Computer Calling Platforms

Free PC-to-PC calling platforms are similar with the instant messaging ones but have a different emphasis. They generally use the same technologies and offer users the same functions while displaying similar requirements: download, creating an account, broadband or higher Internet connection. It is only during the past years that the line between instant messaging platforms and calling platforms has blurred, the last ones being the first to implement live video calling. Skype is the veteran in the field and Oovoo is its newest contender.

Both Skype and Oovoo allow free computer-to-computer calls between their registered users. The video and sound quality of Skype are considerably better to those of Oovoo: sharper image, and crisper, clearer sound with a reduced echo effect but variations on how the services are experienced can be expected to vary from user to user depending on Internet connection. Oovoo's free version offers as many features as Skype yet, unlike Skype, Oovoo displays advertising almost forcing them into buying their monthly plans. Since its launch in 2009, Oovoo has added a lot of features to its offer to include mobile solutions or web-based calls. The free version includes 3-way video-calls for Oovoo to Oovoo users, recording to video messages, embed of a video chatroom in a website as well as video and audio calls with non-Oovoo users.

Figure 1. Skype video guest lecture at the University of Missouri – Columbia, April 2009

By comparison Skype offers its users a screen sharing option, which works both with Macs and PCs. (Figure 1)

Skype will be further analyzed in this chapter, the case studies presented evaluating its impact and performance in a classroom setting.

Browser-Based Video Chat Platforms

TokBox started a service for video chatting and video mailing that didn't require any download and worked with every browser and operating system. It required registration but enabled registered users to import contacts from their existing free email accounts and instant messaging services such as YM, WLM or Google Talk as well as to add new ones from the TokBox users groups. This therefore gave more choice for the user when setting up a video-call. At the time of testing during 2009 and 2010, TokBox's remarkable features included: unlimited multi-user live video chat, the ability to invite unregistered users to join an ongoing video chat via a unique URL sent to them via email, Twitter or Facebook as well as the ability to watch YouTube videos, Picasa or Flickr uploaded photos or SlideShare presentations from within the same video chat window. The platform ran smoothly and the video quality was high the registration easing access to all the platform's interactive features.

However, after offering alternative group and web-conferencing options for purchase for a while, TokBox took its service offline on April 2011 and now uses the same technology to enable websites to embed video chats. While moving away from the traditional browser-based solution and losing a considerable amount of the features that made it so promising, ToxBox multi-user technology can be still used by academic institutions by either having video chats embedded in their websites or by embedding the video-chats in the virtual learning platforms they use. (Figure 2)

Still, there are several situations when using TokBox could add value to the teaching process. With its multi-party video broadcasting it is easy to have distance students or online students join and interact with an on-campus lecture and its audience. Similarly, multi-party video broadcasting would allow conference speakers to virtually join a conference and deliver a presentation without having to travel to it.

For lecturers that rely on external guests, TokBox offers the opportunity of organizing live debates between experts and for those that assign group work to their classes, TokBox could be work as an alternative meeting point.

PalTalk and *TinyChat* are two other platforms that offer similar services with TokBox and use the same Adobe Flash technology. PalTalk, like Oovoo, has expanded its offer beyond the web-based chat-room to integrate desktop and mobile application, small business solutions and embeddable chat-rooms. The platforms were not subject to thorough testing therefore there are no specific recommendations the author can make.

Another promising platform is South Korean developed *PalBee* launched in 2007 as a free online video meeting tool. As TokBox, PalTalk and TinyChat, PalBee is browser-based, uses Adobe Flash technology and requires registration. The platform is sometimes loading slow and is often the victim of server disconnections due to constant updates. But PalBee could be an ideal solution for small project work or remote

Figure 2. TokBox screenshot with embedded SlideShare Powerpoint of online live video guest lecture given to Florida Southern College in September 2009

classroom meetings as it allows up to 10 people to live broadcast simultaneously. Moreover, users joining a PalBee meeting don't have to be all registered users but rather they can join via the meeting's unique URL. (Figure 3)

There is a virtual whiteboard space as well where users can display, draw, write, highlight and erase elements from the uploaded spreadsheets, documents, presentations and photos. Moreover, there is a library list function where multiple documents in a.PPT or.PDF or photos in.JPG,.PNG and.GIF can be uploaded by the meeting initiator and used in the desired sequence. Furthermore, the chat area of the screen allows users to share links to external, online sources. However, the recording function of PalBee is the one that adds value to the platform and expands its potential for academic use. The meetings can also be recorded and then shared online or embedded where desired or necessary. While there is no indexing function yet that would give PalBee a

flexible learning application (Bell, Cockburn, McKenzie, & Vargo, 2001) meetings can be saved under specific names making at least their archival and later retrieval easier.

Other Video Platforms

Up to now the platforms reviewed allowed live synchronous video calls between at least two "talking-heads" no matter if download or registration is required. They were chosen and analyzed having as main aim the delivery of a lecture when either the class or the lecturer are not in the same place. Direct and unmediated interaction and dialogue were therefore the fundamental criteria.

The academic process though doesn't always take place in a classroom setting. Students having team assignments as well researchers working on joint projects could benefit, apart from direct interaction for their talks and brainstorming, using platforms where they can collaborate and amend

Figure 3. PalBee test screen with chat and whiteboard

documents at their own pace. While there are many collaborative platforms online (Adi, 2009), this chapter will only present those that use video as a working tool.

Furthermore, in some situations such as lecturing to big classes or inviting students to a viewing, multi-party video streaming can become noisy and difficult to manage. Therefore other solutions might be needed: having either a) multiple video streaming with one audio channel or b) having only one party streaming and allowing the others to interact via text chat might be work better.

One example of a video platform successfully used in academia is *FlashMeeting*, powered by the Open University in Great Britain. Registration is free yet the Open University representatives do not activate an account until are made aware of the reasons and purposes for which one intends to use the platform. This can be solved through via email or phone. Once granted access, setting up meetings is easy, yet unlike any platform this chapter has reviewed so far, meetings have to be scheduled. Non-registered users can also join meetings using a direct link and logging-in with

as guests. Also, unlike any platform, FlashMeeting records all meetings by default and stores them on the server of the Open University, which can later use them as research material.

The platform also has chat, URL and file sharing and voting areas and annotation possibilities. The author has used FlashMeeting for qualitative research and found its asynchronous video and audio transmission useful. The author also found the quality of both the sound and video transmitted to be poorer than that provided by any of the platforms tested and reviewed here.

Although all users are online and logged in the meeting, there is only one streaming audio and video channel. This means that users need to queue to speak. While at first dialogue seems to be truncated, in reality dialogue is thriving as all video-meeting participants need to find ways to react to what was previously discussed while also expressing their thoughts. There are, of course, risks of having participants attempt to monopolize the discussion and this is why the author recommends that meetings assign a moderator before they start. However, it was noted that due to the asynchronous nature of the dialogue and the low video refresh rate of the participant images, users pay closer attention to the dialogue. Moreover, they are more careful to how they structure their speech so that it is both concise and in line with what has been previously discussed.

FlashMeeting is no doubt a platform with multiple applications in the academic sphere. It is designed to be a great tool for remote qualitative research as well as a meeting place for distance students. Its recording with annotations feature allows FlashMeeting to render flexible learning student-friendly materials. Furthermore, the meeting reports are a valuable post-meeting analysis resource and great research support.

VoiceThread has an academia-friendly approach visible through the several solutions for education institutions it offers. The author has used VoiceThread in 2009 as a new media, out-of-classroom, remote interaction platform for her new media class at Katholieke Hogeschool Zuid-West-Vlaanderen (KAHTO-HANTAL) and has received positive feedback from students as well as a high level of interaction. Figure 4 presents a screen capture of the discussion about print and online resumes using the author's resumes and a series of questions as a starting point. The author left a welcome video message explaining the task. To answer students could choose from the platform's five options to reply: leave a video message recorded with their webcams, leave an audio recorded message, call in to leave a message, upload an audio file as comment or type a text. Most students preferred the type-in option. (Figure 5)

VoiceThread security and privacy settings, like those of TokBox at the time, gave the user plenty of control. In addition, VoiceThread's education licenses allow lecturers to share content with all or a selection of their students while keeping content private. This not only protects the students but also keeps the classroom content safe from any undesired connection with or interference coming from the wider web. In terms of publish-

ing a project, the platform doesn't only allow choosing between public or private, embedding or sending a link to it but also has a download option. This means that all comments in all forms together with all uploaded files can be downloaded in either.mp3 or DVD video archive. The online projects can therefore be stored or used offline as well as further instructional materials or as technology examples.

Finally, because of the wide range of formats that VoiceThread allows to be uploaded –.PDF,. PPT,.DOC,.XLS, photos and movies – as well as to its enabling the import of image and videos from social media platforms, the platform can be used by almost any department of a university in activities that range from collaborative assignments to historical research.

Online Live Broadcasting

The last category of this review is represented by live broadcasting platforms: Livestream and Ustream.tv. They generally permit one user to stream live and be watched by a large number of viewers. Interaction with viewers is possible via a real-time chat associated with the show. Such platforms can be a convenient, accessible, easy-to-use solution for broadcasting major university relevant events, competitions, ceremonies, symposia, seminars, and conferences.

Ustream.tv is better suited for streaming live events where it's the event or the speaker that matter most (Good, 2007). Like all resources presented up to now it has a free version and, like most, requires registration. Broadcasting however is very easy and can be done with a single click. Its has controls for recording, broadcast and reception, frame rate, audio and video quality as well as sound volume, all very user-friendly and all with a positive impact of delivering a good quality audio and video feed. Interaction possibilities are many, besides chat Ustream.tv allowing insertion of live polls, linked subtitles and even an embed of Twitter live postings. As for accessibility,

Figure 4. FlashMeeting screen capture of meeting review

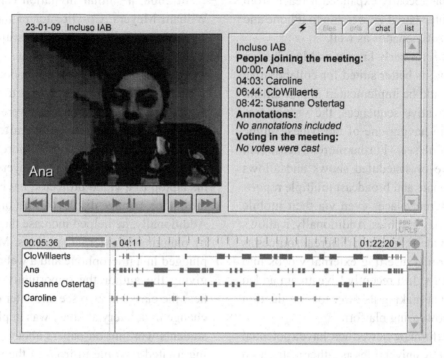

Figure 5. VoiceThread project[8] with video and text comments

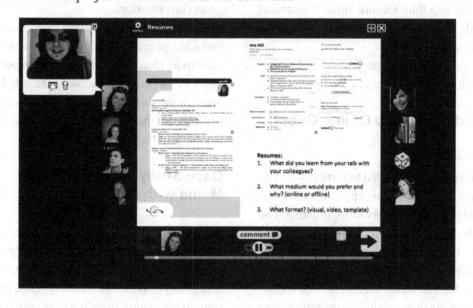

Ustream.tv has recently expanded it reach from online computer-based viewership to iPhone and mobile video aficionados as well.

Livestream, formerly known as Mogulus, on the other hand, is better suited for collaborative projects. It could be implemented in journalism, media and creative sequences, the virtual production studio having one of the widest online production tool sets. Furthermore, Livestream can have live or scheduled shows and allows one to coordinate and broadcast multiple reporters from different places even via their mobile phone or overlay graphics. Additionally, it allows aggregating video clips from different sources as well as it permits inserting external videos into a live broadcast. Just recently Livestream added interactive chat making its offer to a production and video showcasing platform.

All the platforms reviewed here have a potential of being used by universities as either instruction tools or as instruction media. They were all tested and used by the author before being included in this chapter. They are all free of charge or have free versions and thus require little investment – technical, financial and training – from the academic institutions.

Table 1 presents a summary of what the platforms mentioned in these pages can offer.

Case Study: The Live Online Guest Lecture

In 2007 the author was invited to virtually join an "EU Policies and Institutions" class offered to students of the University of Missouri-Columbia. The platform chosen for the class delivery was Skype since at the time, from the author's experience, Skype was the most stable platform offering good quality of video and audio streaming. The lecture however had some shortcomings: connectivity was weak and therefore sound and image quality were poor. Furthermore, due to low Internet bandwidth the connection was lost a couple of times and the video-call dropped.

In 2008, a similar invitation came from Dr William Meyers, Co-Director of the Food and Agricultural Policy Research Institute and Professor of Agricultural Economics at the same university. In order to join his Honors Colloquia "Challenges of EU Enlargement to Central and Eastern Europe" a few changes were made. Both Dr Meyers and the author ran several tests to ensure connectivity was good. Furthermore, to enhance the students' experience Dr Meyers connected his laptop to a video projector, having therefore the author's image displayed on a bigger screen. Additionally, he helped increase the sound level by plugging in external speakers. Moreover, he plugged in a microphone and a webcam as well, giving the author the opportunity not only to hear the class but also see and interact with it. A change in delivery strategy was in place as well, students working on papers about Romania being invited to come in front of the webcam and directly address their questions to the author. This ensured that both parties heard and understood each other's messages and it generated a really good conversation.

In a later letter Dr Meyers expressed his belief that a Skype mediated interaction, which is in fact a 2D live video simultaneous stream between two users, is "as close as possible to actually having the guest in person". He added that he will certainly use this method again when the desired guest cannot join the class in person.

Case Study: Teaching New Media with New Media

Joining Dr Meyers class and its success led the author to further consider using new media technologies in the teaching process. She turned to her area of expertise, communication and public relations, which saw struggling to adapt to new media and its requirements and which she considered that could have benefited most from international guest lectures, cross-cultural contacts and live interaction. Furthermore, delivering lectures on

Table 1.

Platform	Type	Download	Browser-based	Registration required	Accessible to non-registered guests	Video call	Interaction	Real-time collaboration	Online sharing	Other features	Potential Use in Academia
Yahoo Messenger	instant messenger	yes	no	yes	no	one-to-one; one-to-many	chat; preview links in chat window; send files	no	no			live remote lectures
Windows Live Messenger	instant messenger	yes	no	yes	no	one-to-one; one-to-many	chat; preview links in chat window; send files	no	no			live remote lectures
iChat	instant messenger	yes (pre-installed on Macs)	no	yes	no	one-to-one; 4-party video	share view of Apple compatible text, spreadsheet, presentation, video and photo programs; share screen	yes	no			team work; remote lectures; guest speakers; research
Google Talk	instant messenger	yes	yes within Gmail	yes	no	one-to-one	chat	via Google Docs	no			in conjunction with Google Apps
Skype	voice messenger	yes	no	yes	no	one-to-one	screenshare; send files; chat; moile version	yes	no			remote lectures; collaborative research
Oovoo	voice messenger	yes	yes but needs link	yes	yes	one-to-one and up to 3 simultaneous audio/video broadcasts with free version	chat; send files; mobile version; send URL to non-user	no	link to call	record; send video messages		remote lectures; collaborative research
TokBox	video chat	no	yes	yes	yes	up tp 20 multi-party	chat; link preview in chat window;	yes	embed			distance education; live debates; conferences; seminars; sympozia; ceremonies
PalBee	video meeting	no	yes	yes	yes	up to 10 simultaneous audio/video broadcasts	whiteboard; library list; chat	yes	link to meeting			distance education; project/assignment team work
PalTalk	video chat	no	yes	yes	yes	unlimited multi-party	chat	no	link to meeting			
TinyChat	video chat	no	yes	yes	yes	up to 12 simultaneous audio/video broadcasts	chat	no	link to meeting			
VoiceThread	group conversations	no	yes	yes	yes	no	text, video, audio, call-in	no	link to project; embed; download			team work; discussions; debates;

continued on following page

Table 1. continued

Platform	Type	Download	Browser-based	Registration required	Accessible to non-registered guests	Video call	Interaction	Real-time collaboration	Online sharing	Other features	Potential Use in Academia
Livestream	broad-cast plat-form	no	yes	yes	yes	no	chat, facebook	no	link to broadcast; facebook; on-demand; embed	multi-camera broad-cast; video aggre-gation	creative media practice
Ustream. tv	broad-cast plat-form	no	yes	yes	yes	no	chat, polls, twitter	no	link to broadcast; twitter; embed		distance education; live debates; conferences; seminars; sympozia; ceremonies

new media using new media could have covered the current technical instruction gap made by courses that approach new media just by talking about them. In constructing her model aiming at enhancing skills through practice, she followed the examples of the Convergence and Strategic Communication sequences offered at the Missouri School of Journalism whose practice she has observed both from a student as well as from a lecturer's perspective.

When the offer to teach her own class on new media at the Business and Languages School of Katholieke Hogeschool Zuid-West-Vlaanderen in Kortrijk (KATHO – HANTAL), Belgium, came in summer 2008, the author saw an opportunity to experiment and put to test her teaching through practice ideas. The course called "New Media - the challenge for traditional media, advertisers and communicators –" was set to be a 2 credit intensive course offered in English only to Erasmus exchange students.

Erasmus students in Europe are either in their last two years in university or follow a master's program at their home institutions. Through the Erasmus program students can go to partner uni-

versities around Europe from one semester up to one year, time during which they have to follow the courses and pass the exams of their host institutions. The instruction language is usually that of the host country however there are exceptions.

To ensure good conditions for interaction, communication and cultural exchange, only 15 places were made available for the class in each semester. There were 3 hours of teaching daily, the course lasted a week out of which only 3 days had traditional, in-class meetings based mostly on instructor-student interaction and providing very student-centered content delivery. The remaining two were a practice-based day where student-to-student interaction was encouraged and a visit to a successful company in the new media field where students received insights from those already in an industry about which they had gained theoretical insights during the week. The course and assignments were organized having in mind Biggs' (2003) constructive alignment theory and Angelo's (1993) principles for improving higher learning such as:

1. active learning is more effective than passive learning,
2. learning requires focused attention, and awareness of the importance of what is to be learned,
3. learning is more effective and efficient when learners have explicit, reasonable, positive goals, and when their goals fit well with the teacher's goals,
4. to be remembered, new information must be meaningfully connected to prior knowledge, and it must first be remembered in order to be learned,
5. unlearning what is already known is often more difficult than learning new information,
6. information organized in personally meaningful ways is more likely to be retained, learned, and used,
7. learners need feedback on their learning, early and often, to learn well,
8. the ways in which learners are assessed and evaluated powerfully affect the ways they study and learn,
9. mastering a skill or body of knowledge takes great amounts of time and effort,
10. learning to transfer, to apply previous knowledge and skills to new contexts, requires a great deal of practice,
11. high expectations encourage high achievement,
12. to be most effective, teachers need to balance levels of intellectual challenge and instructional support,
13. motivation to learn is alterable, and
14. interaction between teachers and learners is one of the most powerful factors in promoting learning.

The summer semester of 2010-2011 academic year is the sixth consecutive semester when the class is offered. Furthermore, due to positive student evaluations the class was extended from one intensive to two intensive weeks of teaching after its first semester delivery. The presentation below focuses on the differences implemented between the first three consecutive deliveries.

Although the theoretical content was only updated, there were structural differences between the courses delivered each semester. The first lecture was an introduction into the course and aimed to the main concepts with the course operated with: media, convergence and web 2.0. The lectures of days two and thee focused on presenting and discussing the challenges faced traditional journalism, advertising, marketing and public relations due to the emergence of new media, their reactions to it and potential solutions. Very current examples were given throughout the lectures, most of them coming from an international background. Throughout the lectures in-class exercises encouraged students to share their experiences with traditional and new media, analyze their home country's media landscape and compare it with that presented by other students. Critical thinking was encouraged through frequent analyses and discussions that also enhanced intercultural dialogue.

Second semester students were also asked to bring to class their laptops and any recording devices they owned: photo cameras, camcorders, mobile phones with audio or video recording options or with image capture features. Laptops were constantly used for documentation purposes and many in-class exercises required Internet searches. The recording devices were used to gather data for the team project about which more information will be given shortly.

Similarly, the students who took the course in the winter 2009-2010 semester used their own technology in the class. However, unlike previous sessions, they had two-practice days, one for individual assignments and one dedicated to teamwork.

For the individual task students were split into three randomly selected groups, each of them belonging to an online platform: wordpress, wiki and posterous. Students were asked to create content that reflected their interest and fit the platform they were assigned to. The materials had to be live and online by the end of the class.

For the team assignment, students were asked to study and come up with recommendations for improving the online presences of three given entities: The International Boxing Association (AIBA), NeoLingo, a productivity tool for translators and translation companies, and the Wave Machines, an aspiring band from Liverpool, UK. Similar with the previous practice session, the output of the teamwork had to be live and online at the end of the class.

Student results can be seen on the Wiki page[9], the Wordpress blog[10] and the Posterous blog[11] as well.

Based on student evaluations and suggestions, the number of assignments however was reduced from 4 to 2 in the second semester, after the students voted for the change. In the third semester the final assignments were maintained to two – one practical and one academic – but practice day assignments were graded as well. Therefore, a more balanced distribution between assignments focusing on academic skills and critical thinking and those aimed at providing students with employability aptitudes was obtained. The syllabus course is available for consultation on the author's Slideshare[12] page.

Students were also required to generate a new media project using new media platforms presented in class or discovered by themselves. The deadline of the project was tight and the finished product had to be presented to the class. The project required students to describe the new media class they were part of using as many convergent and web 2.0 features. The nature of the project was not set students having plenty of freedom in choosing the nature of their project, format and creative directions. However they were advised to keep their project rather short and dedicate some time to presenting their work, the process, the platforms used and highlight the lessons learned as well as emphasize good and bad experiences. In this way team work, first-hand exploration and

experimentation of technology, critical thinking and presentation skills were brought together in one assignment. Similarly learning outcomes and employability skills also met in one assignment.

Finally, the academic assignment consisted of three one page long commentary and summary of three of the assigned readings. Its aim was to provide students with further exposure to academic thinking, writing as well as different research approaches.

The course also featured a day dedicated to building online resumes, discussing about their relevance, and about preparing to work in a web 2.0 environment. For materials students submitted before the class started were used: their own online resumes and cover letters explaining their reasons for choosing the class. The cover letters also had to highlight their experience with new media and their expectations from the class and lecturer before the actual beginning of the class. Recruiting students for future classes in now under consideration.

Another novelty element introduced in the course was an online live video guest lecture. In the second semester, the summer of 2008-2009 academic year, Dr Mugur Geana, Assistant Professor of Strategic Communication at the William Allen White School of Journalism and Mass Communication of the University of Kansas in the USA joined the class talking about social media. Dr Geana joined the students via Skype, a platform that he and the author found to be most reliable and best suited for the occasion and after having tested and obtained poor results with Oo-voo. Drawing on previous experience, when the author was a guest lecturer to Dr Geana's class using the same technique, a test connection was made prior to the scheduled meeting. The aims were to ensure there is a good and steady internet connection that can support a 30-50 minutes of uninterrupted video-call; that the sound system available at KATHO-HANTAL was enriching communication rather than produce echo and static; that the projector was compatible with the author's computer and that displaying the guest lecturer's video simultaneously with a PowerPoint presentation was possible. Unlike the author's lecture to Dr Geana's class when he had two projectors in the room connected to two computers, one for the video and one the PowerPoint, the author had to proceed to resizing the Skype and Powerpoint windows to accommodate simultaneous display.

Dr Geana also joined the third semester class, of the winter 2009-2010. He gave an introduction to mass communication research and connected with the class via TokBox. Unfortunately, the connection was dropped and couldn't be re-established even if both parts choose to stream only audio. Skype was the only platform through which connection could be maintained, although with difficulty, for the duration of the complete lecture.

Finally, the last day of the course was a company visit to Netlog[13], one of Europe's biggest social networks very popular with youth, had given students a direct and unmediated insight into the new media industry. The visit comprised a company tour where students were introduced to each department and their role and had the opportunity to ask questions about the nature of the job, employment techniques, challenges, dos and don'ts and rewards. Additionally students received three presentations about Netlog's community management, recruiting techniques and marketing strategy and techniques, all presentations complementing the information they had already come across to during the previous days of the course.

Lessons Learned and Thoughts for the Future

The Netlog visit was considered a highlight in both semesters, students identifying it in their evaluations as the visit that changed their opinion about new media companies in general. The live video guest lecture done via Skype received very good evaluations. Most students saw it as a vivid example of the new media advancements and for some it was for the first time in their lives that

have been part of a live video call. Furthermore some indicated that they would like to have such guest lectures more often. Coupled with empirical observations that noted the students' enthusiasm and positive surprise when the test was ran a day prior the guest lecture and that all teams included the live video in their rendition of the new media class it can be argued that online live 2D guest lectures introduced in the daily teaching process keep engage students with new media in a way that goes beyond the classroom setting.

Similar reactions to Skype live video lecturers were received both from Dr Meyer's and Dr Geana's classes. In a letter sent to the author on January 24, 2009 Dr Geana was writing about the author's lecture on new media's impact on creative industries:

"(...) lecturing from 5,000 miles away using an audio-video connection over the Internet was a complete success and a main attraction that generated a lot of discussions among students after the class."

During the months of September and November 2009 the author has delivered four more online video guest lectures to institutions in USA and Belgium and since then she holds or facilitates several lecturers every year. In 2009 participants to the online guest lectures were given qualitative questionnaire. Students indicated that they found the online live video guest lecture to be innovative. They mentioned enjoying the versatility of the platforms used and how they make time and space feel insignificant. They also appreciated the interaction that Skype and TokBox enabled.

Integrating new media in the teaching process and turning it into an omnipresent educational support has had a positive impact on all students of the KATHO-HANTAL course. From personal talks with the students, the author found out that using new media so heavily in and out of the class, for the instruction and assignments, made several students consider focusing more on new media aspects for their honors degrees. Furthermore, some indicated that they were strongly considering pursuing a career in a new media field both the course and the company visit contributing to their decision.

However, there are several pitfalls that need to be overcome before adopting such an initiative. The Internet adoption rate in European school is quite high yet WIFI connections aren't yet as widely accessible as in the USA. Furthermore, security settings differ from institution to institution, and downloading and using free platforms readily available online such as the ones previously presented in this chapter, most often requires agreement and/or installation support from the IT departments.

When it comes to making the guest lecture possible, scheduling conflicts and technical capabilities need to be considered. For the author's guest lectures to the USA it was always the time zone difference that posed a challenge, however a challenge considerably smaller than that of scheduling a whole trip from Scotland to the USA. As for technical capabilities, as stressed numerous times in this chapter, it is highly necessary that both lecturers have good and steady internet connections, and functional cameras, microphones and sound systems. For excellent delivery additional devices are needed such as projectors and sound amplifiers. Ideally, zooming cameras or multiple streaming cameras present in the lecture room would enable the remote lecturer to better see the class and interact with the students.

There are also cultural barriers to overcome. A call to establishing a network of lecturers and researchers interested in testing and implementing online live guest lectures using available platforms being thus made. The Skype in the classroom program launched at the end of 2010 partly answers this call by enabling teachers and speakers to connect based on their location, language and area of specialty. For now the Skype project it is free and its is hoped that its network will grow to include academic and business speakers. Similarly, it is hoped that at some point, universities will also consider paying online guest lecturers, cost however considerably smaller when compared to that of covering transport and lodging of the speaker.

Language barriers also have to be taken into consideration. In an increasingly interconnected world when exchange programs are striving, attention needs to be paid to integrating international students. This among others means tackling with language difficulties. While an online live guest lecture can be as close as possible as a face-to-face meeting, a poorer Internet connection can create understanding difficulties. This is why, it is recommended to lecturers to have a presentation that would support their speech and help overcome such barriers. This support could be made available prior to the talk via email, a sharing platform such as SlideShare or Isuu, in a print format or during the talk by displaying it in parallel with the video: TokBox, Palbee, iChat have such a feature.

As for using new media platforms in the class, it is recommended that lecturers are familiar with them and can bring reality-driven examples where such technologies are used. Furthermore attention to security and privacy settings is a must, platforms with a higher degree of security and privacy control being recommended. While in some cases receiving feedback from people outside the classroom or the university environment might be needed, the author would advise using platforms that have a comments moderating option keeping thus inappropriate references to a minimum.

The two case studies presented here show that live video can be successfully used in on-campus, in-class teaching and not only in distance education or online studies. The chapter argues that online live video can be a meaningful addition with positive impact to the class content as well as an alternative delivery method. Furthermore, integrating live video and other new media platforms that enable students, among others, to use and interact through video should be considered as alternative and complementary delivery platforms similar to podcasting (Fernandez et al., 2009; Skira, 2006), Second Life classes or recorded and annotated lectures are now (Bell et al., 2001; Conner, 1996; Ellin, 2000). Moreover, integrating live video guest lectures in the teaching process as a means of exposing students to collaborative effort to prepare well trained professionals for the world of tomorrow also meets the principles of good practice (Angelo, 1993; Braxton et al., 1998; Chickering & Gamson, 1987; Ritter & Lemke, 2000).

Platforms such as TokBox that enable emailing video messages or platforms such as VoiceThread that allow collaboration on projects could be used as feedback mechanisms that encourage contact between students and faculty. Furthermore collaborative platforms such as VoiceThread, Google Docs or chat and video chat platforms such as Skype or iChat, help develop reciprocity and cooperation among students but also encourage active learning, and respect diverse talents and ways of learning. Furthermore, using new media platforms readily available online, including social networking, social bookmarking and social collaborative tools, delivers the information in personally meaningful ways making it therefore more likely to be retained, learned and used (Angelo, 1993).

CONCLUSION

This chapter addressed the alternative of including live video streaming in the daily teaching process using platforms freely and readily available online. It argued that live video is a suitable delivery method for on-campus teaching that could have similar positive results with those obtained when applied to distance or online learning. It also showed the advantage of using freely and readily available platforms online by emphasizing on their low cost, better-said lack of additional costs, on their ease of use and accessibility, and on their ability to promote dialogue between lecturers, students, professionals with great implications

for intercultural, international, professional, and research relations. Several platforms that offer live video calling, streaming or multi-user streaming were reviewed in an attempt to raise awareness of the wide variety of options available.

The chapter also presented two case studies: one of a guest invited to virtually and remotely join from Scotland a class in the USA and one of an intensive, one-week long course on new media using new media as part of the instruction methodology, student assignments, and student communication and feedback. Both of them support the idea of integrating live video in the daily process as a method of bringing further and where possible international expertise into the classroom making students aware of the worldwide research, professional and academic trends. Both case studies showed that the implementation of live video was successful and communication between students and the guest lecturer was effective. Potential positive effects on broadening cultural horizons as well as enhancing exploration of new media were also mentioned. The case studies also emphasize that platform testing and teacher training are essential for the success of an online live lecture.

The chapter launched a call for more integration of live video as well as of other new media technologies usually perceived as synonymous with flexible, distance or online learning, into day-to-day teaching taking place in a traditional setting. Another call to establish a network of scholars and researchers interested in testing the concept of a new media class using new media was also made.

REFERENCES

Adi, A. (2009). *Collaborative platforms*. Retrieved July 22, 2009, from http://anaadi.wordpress.com/2009/07/12/collaborative-platforms/

Angelo, T. A. (1993). A teacher's dozen: Fourteen general, research-based principles for improving higher learning in our classrooms. *AAHE Bulletin, 45,* 3–13.

Bell, T., Cockburn, A., McKenzie, B., & Vargo, J. (2001, June 25-30). *Flexible delivery damaging to learning? Lessons from the Canterbury digital lectures project.* Paper presented at the ED-MEDIA 2001: Proceedings of the World Conference on Educational Multimedia, Hypermedia and Telecommunications, Tampere, Finland.

Biggs, J. B. (2003). *Aligning teaching and assessment to curriculum objectives.* LTSN Generic Centre, Imaginative Curriculum. Retrieved March 2, 2009, from www.ltsn.ac.uk/genericcentre

Braxton, J. M., Olsen, D., & Simmons, A. (1998). Affinity disciplines and the use of principles of good practice for undergraduate education. *Research in Higher Education, 39*(3), 299–318. doi:10.1023/A:1018729101473

Charman, D., & Elmes, A. (1998). A computer-based formative assessment strategy for a basic statistics module in geography. *Journal of Geography in Higher Education, 22*(3), 381–385. doi:10.1080/03098269885787

Chickering, A. W., & Gamson, Z. E. (1987). Seven principles for good practice in undergraduate education. *AAHE Bulletin, 39,* 3–7.

Clark, R. E. (1983). Reconsidering research on learning from media. *Review of Educational Research, 53*(4), 445–459.

Clark, R. E. (1994). Media will never influence learning. *Educational Technology Research and Development, 42*(2), 21–29. doi:10.1007/BF02299088

Conner, M. L., Wright, E., De Vries, L., Curry, K., Zeider, C., Wilmsmeyer, D., et al. (1996). *Learning: The critical technology.*

Dutton, J., Dutton, M., & Perry, J. (2001). Do online students perform as well as lecture students? *Journal of Engineer Education, 90,* 131–136.

Ellin, A. (2000, August 6). The battle in cyberspace. *New York Times,* p. 4.

Fernandez, V., Simo, P., & Sallan, J. M. (2009). Podcasting: A new technological tool to facilitate good practice in higher education. *Computers & Education, 53,* 385–392. doi:10.1016/j.compedu.2009.02.014

Good, R. (2007). *Ustream vs. Mogulus: Which live video streaming and broadcasting service is better?* Retrieved July 22, 2009, from http://www.masternewmedia.org/video_internet_television/live-video-streaming/ustream-vs-mogulus-which-is-live-video-streaming-service-is-better-20071008.htm

Granitz, N., & Greene, S. C. (2003). Applying e-marketing strategies to online distance learning. *Journal of Marketing Education, 25*(1), 16–30. doi:10.1177/0273475302250569

Gugoiu, T. (2002). *Internet - mijloc de informare si comunicare (internet - medium of information and communication).* Bucharest, Romania: SNSPA Printing House.

Kozma, R. B. (1994). Will media influence learning? Reframing the debate. *Educational Technology Research and Development, 42*(2), 7–19. doi:10.1007/BF02299087

Lavrusik, V. (2009). *10 ways universities share information using social media.* Retrieved July 15, 2009, from http://mashable.com/2009/07/15/social-media-public-affairs/

Liu, L. S., & Zimmermann, Roger. (2006). Adaptive low-latency peer-to-peer streaming and its application. *Multimedia Systems, 11*(6), 457–512. doi:10.1007/s00530-006-0030-4

Lobontiu, A. (2007). Robotic surgery and tele-surgery: Basic principles and description of a novel concept. *Journal de Chirurgie, 3*(3), 208–214.

Lou, Y., Bernard, R. M., & Abrami, P. C. (2006). Media and pedagogy in undergraduate distance education: A theory-based meta-analysis of empirical literature. *Educational Technology Research and Development, 54*(2), 141–176. doi:10.1007/s11423-006-8252-x

McNabb, J. (1994). Telecourse effectiveness: Findings in the current literature. *TechTrends, 39*(4), 39–40. doi:10.1007/BF02763631

Mehlenbacher, B., Miller, C. R., Covington, D., & Larsen, J. S. (2000). Active learning and interactive learning online: A comparison of web-based and conventional writing classes. *IEEE Transactions on Professional Communication, 43*, 166–183. doi:10.1109/47.843644

Moallem, M. (2003). An interactive online course: A collaborative design model. *ETR&D, 51*(4), 85–103. doi:10.1007/BF02504545

Moore, M., & Kearsley, G. (1996). *Distance education: A systems view*. Toronto, Canada: Wadsworth Publishing Co.

Moore, M. G. (1991). Editorial: Distance education theory. *American Journal of Distance Education, 5*(3), 1–6. doi:10.1080/08923649109526758

Moore, M. G. (1992). Three types of interaction. *American Journal of Distance Education, 3*(2), 1–6. doi:10.1080/08923648909526659

Moore, M. G. (1993). Theory of transactional distance. In Keagan, D. (Ed.), *Theoretical principles of distance education* (pp. 22–38). London, UK & New York, NY: Routledge.

Muirhead, B. (2000). Interactivity in a graduate distance education school. *Journal of Educational Technology & Society, 3*(1).

Muirhead, B. (2001). Enhancing social interaction in computer-mediated distance education. *Ed at a Distance Journal, 15*(4).

Murphy, C. (2001). Taking chemistry online with digital video. *Syllabus Magazine, 36*(1), 28–29.

O'Dowd, R. (2007). Evaluating the outcomes of online intercultural exchange. *ELT, 61*(2), 144–153. doi:10.1093/elt/ccm007

Ponzurick, T. G., France, K. R., & Logar, C. M. (2000). Delivering marketing graduate education: An analysis of face-to-face versus distance education. *Journal of Marketing Education, 22*, 180–187. doi:10.1177/0273475300223002

Pullen, M. J., & Snow, C. (2007). Integrating synchronous and asynchronous internet distributed education for maximum effectiveness. *Education and Information Technologies, 12*, 137–148. doi:10.1007/s10639-007-9035-7

Ritter, M. E., & Lemke, K. A. (2000). Addressing the seven principles for good practice in undergraduate education with internet-enhanced education. *Journal of Geography in Higher Education, 24*(1), 100–108. doi:10.1080/03098260085171

Rowe, L. A., Harley, D., & Pletcher, P. (2001). *Bibs: A lecture webcasting system*. Berkley, CA: Berkeley Multimedia Research Center, Shannon Lawrence, Center for Studies in Higher Education, University of California.

Skira, D. J. (2006). The 2005 word of the year: Podcast. *Nursing Education Perspectives, 27*(1), 54–55.

Smith, L. J. (2001). Content and delivery: A comparison and contrast of electronic and traditional mba marketing planning courses. *Journal of Marketing Education, 23*(1), 35–44. doi:10.1177/0273475301231005

Spitzer, D. R. (2001). Don't forget the high-touch with the high-tech in distance learning. *Educational Technology, 41*(2), 51–55.

Taylor, J. C. (2001, April 1-5). *Fifth generation distance education. Keynote address delivered at the ICDE 20th World Conference.* Paper presented at the ICDE 20th World Conference, Dusseldorf, Germany.

Terenzini, P. T. (1999). Research and practice in undergraduate education: And never the twain shall meet? *Higher Education, 38*(1), 33–48. doi:10.1023/A:1003709230179

Ullmer, E. J. (1994). Media and learning: Are there two kinds of truth? *Educational Technology Research and Development, 42*(1), 21–32. doi:10.1007/BF02298168

ENDNOTES

1. http://www.youtube.com/user/stanforduniversity
2. http://www.youtube.com/user/ucberkeley
3. http://www.youtube.com/user/UMKC
4. http://www.youtube.com/iit
5. http://www.chinesevoice.com
6. http://www.cc-chapman.com
7. http://www.google.com/a/help/intl/en/edu/index.html
8. http://voicethread.com/share/514912/
9. http://kathonewmedia.pbworks.com
10. http://kathonewmedia.wordpress.com
11. http://kathonewmedia.posterous.com
12. http://www.slideshare.net/ana_adi/katho-new-media-syllabus-dec09-ana-adi
13. http://www.netlog.com

Chapter 16
The New Chalk and Slate?
Public Online Video in Higher Education

Christopher Barnatt
Nottingham University Business School, UK

ABSTRACT

This chapter explores the rise of public online video in higher education as both a compliment to and a potential replacement for more traditional means of teaching students. It also proposes that the publication of public online videos has the potential to turn some academics into powerful online brands in a manner that was only previously open to those who excelled in the research or consultancy parts of a higher education career, or to those who published best-selling textbooks.

INTRODUCTION

It used to be said that a picture was worth a thousand words. In terms of static information provision this may indeed still be true. However, when it comes to delivering higher education it is today perhaps more useful to muse that an online video can be worth a thousand chalked boards or PowerPoint slides.

As both a factual and an emotional delivery mechanism, the multimedia of film or video have long been a potentially powerful educational tool.

It is therefore somewhat unfortunate that, in the first hundred years following the invention of the movie camera, few working in higher education had any opportunity to communicate using recorded moving images and sound. Of course, since around 2005 all this has started to change. Today anybody in the world with a personal computer, an Internet connection and a $20 webcam can make a video and put it online. At least some pioneering higher education institutions and academics are also starting to take advantage of this. In turn their students are discovering that they can access their lecturer when wish, with content delivery for the first time under their control. By making some

DOI: 10.4018/978-1-60960-800-2.ch016

of their content available in the form of public online video, some higher education academics are thereby beginning to challenge the traditional broadcast lecturing model. In the process many are also transcending institution boundaries. A whole new set of higher education academic practices may therefore emerge as a result.

What follows is divided into six sections. Firstly there is a brief history of the recording and delivery of the moving image from the zoetrope to the launch of YouTube. Following this there is a review of the public video platforms currently available and being used by academics. The use of public online video in higher education is then examined from the perspective of the students who may watch such videos, the academics who may make them, and the institutions for whom these academics may work. Finally, some conclusions are presented as a potential guide to future strategy and action.

FROM THE ZOETROPE TO YOUTUBE

The first device capable of creating the illusion of a moving image was the zoetrope. Literally translated as a 'living wheel', this comprises a cylinder with slits in its sides and a succession of still images within. When spun at an appropriate rate the zoetrope presents its viewer with the illusion of a moving image. Zoetropes were first created in China around 180AD, although the first 'modern' zoetrope was invented in 1833 by the British mathematician William George Horner. By the 1860s Horner's 'Daedalum' had become popular in the United Kingdom, with William F. Lincoln successful promoting his own zoetrope in the United States. It took, however, until 1882 for the movie camera to be invented by Étienne-Jules Marey. This recorded images on strips of photographic paper. However, by 1894 sprocketed 35mm celluloid film had replaced paper in

the 'Kinetoscope' movie machines pioneered by Thomas Edison and William Dickson.

Kinetoscopes soon became popular in New York, London, Berlin and Paris. In 1895 the French capital also hosted the first paying film show when brothers Louis and Auguste Lumière projected ten short films in a Parisian cafe. As one man who attended this first ever cinema presentation remarked many years later, its 'marvelling' and 'extraordinary' sights had to imply that 'the world had changed' (Hodgson, 1995: p.172).

Over the next three decades silent movies spread around the world. For the first time people became free to experience ideas and happenings that they could never witness in person. Perhaps most notably in terms of education, Pathé's famous newsreel gazettes commenced their communication of world events internationally from 1909.

By the late 1920s sound was being added to movies and television was being born. John Logie Baird demonstrated a system for capturing and transmitting pictures electronically in 1926, whilst Al Johnson then spoke and sang to cinema audiences a year later. Television services where then set up across both Europe and the United States in the 1930s, although they did not become popular until the 1950s. However, from that decade forward the hold of electronic sounds and moving images as the dominant mass media has never really faltered. Indeed, by 1977 less than one in five words published or broadcast in the United States were being delivered by print media (de Sola Pool, 1982).

Whilst the screening of educational films in schools and universities had been growing in popularity since the 1950s, and the first video recorder become commercially available in 1956, it was not until the early 1980s that the widespread availability of consumer video decks and cameras started to make the recording and playback of moving images with synchronised sound a realistic possibility for at least some academics. This said it took the arrival of high performance personal computers and a high-speed Internet in the early

21st century to start to turn video into a potentially mainstream, many-to-many educational media. In other words, higher education had to wait for the invention and consumerization of video technology, as well as the emergence of public video distribution channels, before the majority of academics really had the option to follow the Lumière brothers into their own arena of extraordinary sights and sounds that may change the world.

Highly acceptable digital video can now be shot on a camera costing a few hundred dollars, and broadcast quality video on one with a price tag of no more than a few thousand. Desktop video editing of such footage is then possible on most personal computers using applications ranging from *Windows Movie Maker* or *iMovie* (as included with Windows or Apple computers respectively), right up to sophisticated packages including Adobe's *Premiere Pro* for Windows and Apple's *Final Cut Pro*. Since the launch of YouTube in February 2005, it has also been increasingly easy to upload at least a short video to the Internet and just as importantly for other people to actually find it. It is also now perfectly possible to bypass the entire traditional shoot-edit-distribute process and to record a video live from a webcam directly to YouTube or several other video sharing websites. The medium of the moving image for so long dominated by its production and delivery technology is finally in the hands of those who just want to communicate.

THE NEW PLATFORM FOR HIGHER EDUCATION

When anybody wants to put a video online they have two choices. One is to host their precious movie somewhere on their own webspace or private video server, whilst the other is to use a public video sharing website. The majority of people and increasingly many organizations now also tend to go for the later option. The particular reasons why this may be the best decision for academics and higher education institutions are discussed later in this chapter. However, first we will explore some of the main public video hosting options both generally, as well as specifically for the higher education sector.

There are now a whole host of websites that allow pretty much anybody to upload video files for free, to arrange their content into 'channels', and to place their movies on any other website via an embedded player. Such public video sharing websites free users from having to pay for and maintain dedicated video servers. They also crucially provide a means for other people to actually locate public online video content.

Back in the 1990s many commentators became obsessed with the idea that the Internet was turning everybody into a publisher. Unfortunately, what was sadly missed was that being a publisher is one thing, whilst being a distributor is quite another. Granted, from around 1990 it did indeed become possible for anybody to write a novel or to record rudimentary audio or video and put it online. However, in most cases such content was about as likely to be discovered as a self-published book sitting in a large pile of unsold volumes in an author's garage.

When it comes to public online video, sites including Vimeo, Blip.tv and YouTube have changed all this. Not only do such sites enable anybody to be a video publisher, but just as crucially they also enable most uploaders to find an audience. Like it or loathe it, YouTube is a now cultural phenomenon and the online video platform of first choice for the majority. Indeed, many people now begin with a YouTube rather than a Google search when they want to learn about something *precisely because* they know of the quantity and often quality of material available on the site. Some still judge and dismiss YouTube on the grounds of the technical quality of its videos. However this is no longer really justifiable as YouTube now offers pretty high quality public video streaming, including full high definition.

Others also still moan than YouTube movies are limited to 10 minutes, which is also untrue.

Via invitation or application YouTube has for some time being promoting its most successful channels to the status of 'Partner'. Partner channels are able to host videos of any length (subject only to an upload file size of 20Gb), and to brand their channels with custom graphics. In only a few years YouTube has not only managed to stay in business (something that many initially higher quality competitors have not achieved), but has matured into an online video platform that hosts everything from cameraphone spam to full-length TV shows. YouTube also allows its Partners to obtain income from a variety of advertising as well as the sale of downloadable video files paid for via Google Checkout. There are also now different versions of the YouTube interface optimized for different kinds of player devices, such as YouTube.com/xl for watching videos on a television via a mediaplayer PC or nettop box.

When it comes to the particular needs of higher education, YouTube has also not been idle. At the end of 2007 YouTube launched its initial university channels service, with institutions 'nearly tripping over themselves' to establish custom-branded channels devoid of advertising yet free of the 10 minute upload constraint (Riismandel, 2009, p.2). March 2009 then saw the launch of YouTube EDU (YouTube.com/edu) which initially brought together content from over 100 universities and colleges. Via YouTube EDU anybody with an Internet connection can access lectures by professors and other world-renowned thought leaders, as well as new research and campus tours. At launch, over 20,000 videos covering over 200 full courses were available from leading universities, including MIT, Stanford, UC Berkeley, UCLA and Yale (Colman, 2009). The University of Michigan School of Dentistry, for example, now offers 463 videos via YouTube EDU, including programmes on anatomy and prosthodontics, as well as a significant historical archive.

YouTube is also not alone in wooing higher education with its public video hosting facilities. Most notably, in May 2007 Apple announced the launch of iTunes U, a dedicated area within the iTunes Store featuring video as well as audio podcast content from colleges and universities including Stanford, UC Berkeley, Duke and MIT. As Eddy Cue, vice president of iTunes said at the time, 'education is a lifelong pursuit and we're pleased to give everyone the ability to download lectures, speeches and other academic content for free' (Apple, 2007: p.1). iTunes U content is now also being brought together on other websites that integrate the best lectures on a topic from a range of top institutions. For example, in March 2009 Learn-Gasm published a list of '50 Terrific iTunes U Lectures to Get You Through the Economic Crisis', including content from Cambridge, Berkley, Princeton, Yale, Warwick and the Open University (BachelorsDegreeOnline.com, 2009).

Alongside YouTube and iTunes, a number of smaller players offering public access to video content at the higher education level are also worthy of a mention. For example, the superb TEDTalks programme at TED.com 'single-handedly popularized the phenomenon of brainy [video] programming' with over 50 million viewings in its first year (MacIntyre, 2008, p1.). Via Edge.org, the Edge Foundation also offers great educational video content at a graduate level, with its mandate 'to promote inquiry into and discussion of intellectual, philosophical, artistic, and literary issues' (Edge.org, 2009: p.1). Interesting higher education level content can also be found at Fora.tv and Bigthink.com.

Whilst TED.com, Edge.org, Fora.tv and Bigthink.com are not public video hosting websites, they nevertheless serve as good examples of how publicly-accessible higher-level educational video can be very usefully amalgamated and presented. Indeed, any academic or institution with the time and the will can now create such a resource within, for example, a YouTube partner channel.

A PROFESSOR YOU CAN PAUSE AND REWIND

The traditional model of higher education requires students to turn up to a lecture theatre at a time of their institution's choosing. They then have to listen for a length of time their institution also determines to an academic who is in almost total control of what is delivered in that teaching session.

The above is, of course, hardly good customer practice. To a millennial generation who are used to regularly engaging in the social networking interplay of the Web 2.0 revolution, it is also just not an expected or acceptable state of affairs. What is therefore needed is for higher education institutions to start tailoring their product to their students rather than requiring their students to conform to the institution's broadcast model. The use of online video as an additional or even replacement delivery mechanism to traditional talk-and-chalk or bullet-point-and-project face-to-face lectures also provides one of the most powerful mechanisms for making this happen.

It is worth reflecting in some depth on the reasons why students — and in particular today's students — may be highly receptive to and may even expect public online video to be used in their higher education. Such reasons can also be grouped under the following headings:

- Multimedia expectations of the MTV Generation
- Consumption at a time, place and pace of a student's own choosing
- Engagement with and retention of video content
- Bringing academic literature to life
- A tutorial with the world
- Known relative ease of production

Multimedia Expectations of the MTV Generation

Today virtually all young people — and hence almost all higher education students — have grown up with television and the Internet as the wallpaper of their lives. Some educational commentators like this and some would clearly like to sledge-hammer every TV set and PC in existence. However, pragmatically, those delivering higher education have to accept that before they can change the world they have to work within its current reality. And one of those realities is that television and the Internet are now two of the most fundamental conduits for human interaction. Or, as Douglas Rushkoff put it so nicely in his book *Children of Chaos*:

Today's 'screenager'—the child born into a culture mediated by the television and the computer — is interacting with the world in at least as dramatically altered a fashion from his grandfather as the first sighted creature did from his blind ancestor, or a winged one from his earthbound forebears. Human beings have evolved significantly within a single creature's lifespan, and this intensity of evolutionary change shows no signs of slowing down (1997, p.3).

If higher education is going to compete successfully with all of those information outlets that deliver their messages via sophisticated audio-visual media, then it simply has no choice but to tech-up and to saturate itself with all of those technologies that its screenage customers already live and breathe. And one of those is without doubt public online video.

A Choice of Consumption Time, Place and Pace

One of the potentially greatest advantages for students of being able to access higher education content via online video is that such material can pretty much be consumed at a time and place of their own choosing. This is in stark contrast to teaching performances delivered via live lectures which students have no choice but to consume at a precise time in a single location and at a pace usually entirely beyond their control. Students can also consume online video content more than once, and can stop the video and replay sections as their individual educational needs dictate. For example, many of the author's students have reported the advantage of having video content available for revision.

Given that a whole host of recording and on-demand delivery options now enable the majority of film and television content to be consumed at a time and at a pace of the viewer's own choosing, it is perhaps not surprising that higher education may now be expected to be consumed in a similar fashion. Media engagements as ritualistic, mass-attendance events are simply no longer the norm the way they were in the days before the video recorder, DVD player or YouTube. And higher education simply has to take account of this fact.

The growing proliferation of next generation computing devices — including tablets, smart-phones, netbooks, and in time e-book readers capable of handling video — will increasingly also mean that there will be fewer and few occasions in which access to video content will not be possible. In turn, this is likely to drive a demand for video content — including higher education video content—to actually be available. The web is rapidly in the process of 'going video', with the divide between television and the Internet also increasing to blur. In five years it is likely that all forms of media content will be accessible via Internet protocol (IP) enabled devices anytime, anyplace and anywhere. To stay in touch with their customer base, higher education institutions therefore need to be planning how all such devices may serve as a form of student interface.

Engagement With and Retention of Video Content

There is also already some evidence that material delivered either solely online or via some form of 'blended' format that integrates both online materials and traditional lectures can lead to improved student learning. For example, a recent report for the United States Department of Education that conducted a meta-analysis of a number of studies, found that students taught in whole or part online on average performed better than those reliant solely on traditional face-to-face interaction (InsideHigherEd, 2009). As the report make clear, using technology to give students 'control of their interactions' had a positive effect on student learning, with studies indicating that 'manipulations that trigger learner activity or learner reflection and self-monitoring of understanding are effective when students pursue online learning as individuals' (Means *et al*, 2009 p.xvi).

Where online video is used in a blended learning content, the level of student engagement with materials outside of the classroom can also be significantly improved. For example, in the author's recent teaching experience a set of undergraduate tutorials were based around a playlist of YouTube videos that participants were asked to view in advance (see youtube.com/techandorg). Other tutorial classes for the same student cohort had typically involved the pre-reading of academic journal articles. It is perhaps not surprising that the students involved rapidly embraced video-centric as opposed to hardcopy-centric tutorial preparation. Student feedback on this initiative was also very positive.

A particularly welcome outcome of the above experiment was a significant increase in the level of student attendance. In addition, all students who turned up to the tutorials were aware of the material being discussed and had good recall of what they had viewed. This was in comparison to previous tutorial sessions in which typically only half of the students in attendance had done any pre-reading at all. The apparent evidence that students are far more prepared to *view ahead* than to *read ahead* is therefore perhaps something that more academics need to reflect on and to make use of in attempting to engage their classes.

Bringing Academic Literature to Life

One of the reasons that students may be more prepared to view online video than to read traditional textbooks or academic articles is that video delivery humanizes academic content. Psychology has long informed us that around eighty per cent of human communication is non-verbal. On paper, the names of those famous academics that students cite in their essays may be just words. However, once individual academics have been seen and heard on video they almost inevitably become 'real human beings' whose contribution is far more likely to be remembered.

The video-centric tutorial described above also very much highlighted the value of formally prompting students to watch even short public online videos made by at least some of the academics whose work they were studying. Indeed, once names on the page became 'the man with the beard' or 'the blonde woman in the blue suit', discussion of their academic work became significantly easier, the academic's passion for their subject was more effectively communicated, and they became somebody to whom the students could more easily relate. When later in their studies most of these students did read traditional journal materials by these individuals they were therefore learning from and citing somebody 'they knew', as opposed to a faceless and voiceless block of text.

In the above context it is very important to see public online video as highly complimentary to traditional academic literature. Already the academic practice of posting a video on YouTube or iTunes U to summarize the ideas presented in a new book or journal paper is starting to take hold. As this becomes more mainstream, such easy-access video material will also prove extremely helpful when it comes to engaging students not just with the subject they are studying, but also with individual distant professors and in turn their traditional forms of academic output.

A Tutorial With the World

As students start to use public online videos as teaching resources, opportunities will also start to exist for barriers to fall between academic institutions and for 'tutorials to take place with the world'. YouTube and most public online video websites allow comments to be posted, and such forums can get very busy on successful academic videos. It is also both logical and understandable for students used to seeking answers from the best online source to go straight to the author when they have a question, rather than routing it via their own professor.

It may of course not be possible for the producers of very successful public online videos to communicate individually with all of their viewers. However, not everybody will ask a question, and fairly rapidly all of the questions a video may raise are likely to have been asked. Some champions of online higher education videos are also already eliciting questions and addressing them in additional videos. Just one example is Professor Martyn Poliakoff whose 'Periodic Table of Videos' on YouTube (a set of movies covering every chemical element) has already attracted over fourteen million hits (see youtube. com/periodicvideos).

As in a traditional academic tutorial, the forum associated with an online public video can also become an arena in which viewers/students answer each other's questions. This practice is also already alive and kicking on some YouTube academic videos, with the students involved in the discussions interacting based on what they have watched rather than who is in their class or what higher education institution they attend. For the Facebook generation, this is also perfectly natural. It also has to be an excellent higher education development.

Known Relative Ease of Incorporation and Production

A final reason that students may increasingly demand the use of public online video is their everyday knowledge of how easy it now is to locate and produce. When it comes to straight-forward provision, there is no excuse for any professor not to do a YouTube search of the subject area covered in their classes and to embed or otherwise provide links to those videos that they deem useful. Indeed, it could now be argued that academics need to do this if only to avoid students conducting such searches themselves and perhaps consuming inaccurate or less appropriate content. There may still be a very great deal of very poor video content online. However, that does not mean that all online educational and related content is poor, with the pool of good public educational video improving all the time. Academics therefore almost have a duty to help their students watch what is most appropriate for their learning.

Today's screenage students are also fully aware of now easy it is to produce at least basic video content. Like anybody else, all any academic needs is a computing device with a webcam to start putting video content online. The growing minority of academics who do take the trouble to put video content on the Internet are therefore likely to generate student pressure on all of their academic colleagues to do the same. This point noted, resistance to putting video content online does remain very significant. Reasons for not engaging with students in this manner range from time pressure, to not wishing to be seen on camera, to a view that video dumbs-down educational delivery and panders to student whim. The next section therefore addresses why academics as well as students may benefit from making and publishing public online videos.

THE ACADEMIC PERSPECTIVE

As already noted, there is now little or no excuse for any academic not to at least check what public video content is available in their subject area and to refer their students to it. This section will therefore focus on why any individual academic may decide to become a video presenter and producer in addition to amalgamating existing video content. So what, then, may be the personal paybacks of sticking one's head above the parapet? The answer is perhaps best found under one or more of the following headings:

- Professional role and philosophy
- Improvement of internal profile
- Content quickly judged on its own merits
- Establishment of an individual academic brand

Professional Role and Philosophy

Perhaps the most obvious reason why academics may make public online videos is that communicating knowledge is supposed to be the central tenet of their role and professional philosophy. Almost by definition, academics are employed to create, synthesise and present knowledge. As new media become available, there is therefore an implicit professional expectation that academics will embrace such media as part of their individual communications toolset. No medical doctor would reasonably resist a new technological development that would allow them to improve the healthcare they could offer. In terms of professional practice, the same therefore ought to apply to the use of public online video by individuals engaged in delivering higher education.

Whilst many dispute the fact, most academics also ought — at least in theory — to be good video producers and presenters. Unlike most people, academics are used week-in and week-out to preparing structured material and presenting it to an audience. That's simply their job. Once editing is embraced, explaining something in a video can also be easier and more powerful than explaining it in a live lecture. Graphics sequences, illustrations, archive materials, interviews and location work can also be included. Anybody capable of preparing a competent traditional lecture, let alone writing a journal article or book, just really ought to be able to be a decent public online video producer. The skills of synthesising and structuring material and communicating it to an audience are pretty much the same. Academics with a strong passion for their subject are also likely to find that this will come over as strongly in video as it usually does in a traditional lecture setting.

Improvement of Internal Profile

A second reason that may drive academics to create online public videos is that doing so is likely to rapidly improve their profile in their own institution. As already noted, students tend to respond very positively to online videos and hence to the staff who make them. Above and beyond the actual content communicated, placing videos online also provides a clear signal to students and colleagues that serious efforts and being made to expand educational horizons. Any academic today wondering what (else) they could do to improve their chances of promotion would therefore be foolish to not at least dabble in public online video.

As one student posted on one of the author's early online educational videos, 'Finalement (sic), a lecturer who can be bothered to make a clip and put it online'. Granted, many colleagues worry that they may look stupid and be ridiculed for their initial public online video efforts. However, that does not tend to be the culture of sites like YouTube where a respect for the effort involved in actually making a video is reflected in the vast majority of posted comments.

Content Quickly Judged On Its Own Merits

Another key payback from placing academic videos in the public domain is that it is an excellent way of getting rapid feedback on new ideas. Communicating a new theory or research finding to the world is indeed far easier on YouTube than via publishing a paper in an academic journal. The latter is likely to involve a substantial period of writing and review, with a several year gap between idea, research and publication not being uncommon. In contrast, a public online video can be written in the morning, shot and edited in the afternoon, and viewed and commented upon globally that evening.

The rise of the Internet, and in particular the Web 2.0 developments of the past few years, are moving more and more human activities into real time. As more and more objects and sensors also join people online in an emerging 'Internet of Things', so both businesses and individuals also increasingly expect to receive information pretty much instantly. In a world in which only real-time information is starting to be judged as good enough, the idea that academics will be able to continue to trade in months- or years-old information is simply ludicrous. No research can be considered cutting-edge if it takes 12, 18 or 24 months to be communicated. One of the strongest reasons for some academics to make public online videos may therefore be because they offer the best opportunity to remain relevant in a world that demands immediacy as well as richness and interactivity in its communications.

Establishment of an Individual Academic Brand

For some academics their single greatest reason to create public online video may be to build a personal brand and a level individual intellectual identity not necessarily open to them via other means. It is difficult to establish whether anybody has decided to make public online videos with higher educational content purely for this reason. However, it is already undeniable that some individuals have established a considerable, global academic reputation through public online video that they may well not have otherwise achieved.

Perhaps most notably, Michael Wesch, Assistant Professor of Cultural Anthropology in Kansas State University, has become famous for producing YouTube videos that explore the impact of new media on human interaction. In January 2007 Wesch posted a video entitled 'Web 2.0... The Machine is Us/ing Us' that, in its initial and final versions, has now achieved over eleven million hits. Another video by Wesch called 'A Vision of Students Today' explores the hopes, dreams and lives of higher education students and has received over three million viewings. Wesch has subsequently won several awards for his work with video, including a Rave Award from *Wired Magazine* and the Media Ecology Association's John Culkin Award for Outstanding Media Praxis. However, it is the online fame that Wesch has achieved through 'Web 2.0... The Machine is Us/ing Us' that has both made his name and demonstrated to others how a single academic can use the YouTube public online video platform to communicate with the world (see youtube.com/mwesch).

Another example of a single individual who has established their own online brand via public online video is the previously mentioned Professor Martyn Poliakoff. Via the 'Periodic Table of Videos' (featuring a YouTube video for each chemical element), Professor Poliakoff has obtained an international reputation. For example, in addition to attracting an global online audience and international press, in 2008 the Periodic Table of Videos won IcemE's Petronas Award for Excellence in Education (see youtube.com/periodicvideos).

Whilst not everybody may achieve the success of Michael Wesch or Martyn Poliakoff, no academic should underestimate what they can achieve

with public online video so long as they are capable of clearly communicating relevant expertise. For example, in a just a few years the author's own ExplainingComputers YouTube videos have obtained over 450,000 hits globally and generated over 1,700 subscriptions or other information requests (see youtube.com/explainingcomputers). These have included personal messages, offers of speaking engagements, consultancy work, research collaboration opportunities, case study information from companies, radio and hardcopy press interviews, and a book deal. Some academics may not like the idea that a YouTube video or few can in terms of volume of exposure eclipse decades of traditional academic communication. However, this is now very much what the use of public online video can achieve for higher education academics even at this embryonic stage in the medium's evolution.

THE INSTITUTIONAL PERSPECTIVE

Having looked at public online video from the perspectives of students and individual academics, we may now sensibly consider the resultant implications for higher education institutions and those who run them. However, to do this it is important to first step back a little to examine the broader impact of Web 2.0 developments. We will then be able focus our attention back on public online video and its implications for higher education strategy and operations in a more informed context.

The term Web 2.0 was coined by O'Reilly (2005), and refers to the use of the Internet for interpersonal content sharing and online service delivery. Interpersonal content sharing is associated with wikis (collaborative document authorship websites, such as Wikipedia), blogs (online journals, as facilitated by websites like Blogger), social networking sites (including MySpace and Facebook), as well as public online video. However, whilst interpersonal content sharing still gains the most popular attention, the service delivery aspect of Web 2.0 is at least as significant.

Developments in online service delivery include the rise of SaaS and web services. Specifically, SaaS (software as a service) involves the delivery of software application functionality online, with examples including the Google Docs online word processor, spreadsheet and presentation package, as well as the Pixlr online photo editing application and the Jaycut online video editor. Other SaaS offerings include project management, CRM and HR applications available from suppliers such as Zoho, Clarizen, Salesforce and Employease.

The web services aspect of online service delivery refers to the development and application of discrete building blocks of online functionality that can be seamlessly embedded or 'mashed' from one website into another. Examples include PSP (payment service provider) web services from the likes of Worldpay, Netbanx and Paypal, and which allow other websites to easily take credit card payments. Other common web services enable the integration of maps from Google or Microsoft Virtual Earth, or the embedding of a news or Twitter feed. Websites such as Google Gadgets, Yahoo Pipes and Zoho Marketplace now offer literally hundreds of web services for others to mash into their own sites and to customise as they see fit.

The rise of SaaS and web services is already starting to have a great many organizational implications. Most significantly, SaaS and web services are already enabling organizations of all scales to gain access to software, services and online functionality that they could not previously have afforded to purchase or to develop and maintain in-house. The idea that IT services and expertise have to be internal to an organization is therefore starting to be questioned across a wider and wider range of industries. This wave of new thinking and practice will sooner or later also have a major impact on the often quite insular activities of higher education institutions.

Already there is some discussion of 'Higher Education 2.0' (HE 2.0) to signal the potential implications of Web 2.0 developments across the higher education sector (Barnatt, 2009). Three key agendas already being discussed under the HE 2.0 banner are specifically:

- The 'looser-coupling' of educational resources to a single institution,
- The 'piggybacking' of higher education content on public Web 2.0 sites, and
- The achievement of infrastructure independence.

The above developments are already evident on a number of fronts. For example, an increasing number of universities are now abandoning internal student data centers in favour of providing their students with Google Apps Education Edition (an educational version of Goole Docs). However, as earlier sections have hopefully already begun to signal, the rise of public online video is already also starting to play a major role in all three of the above spheres of HE 2.0 activity.

The 'Looser-Coupling' of Educational Resources

A loosely-coupled system is one in which any particular component part can easily be replaced without significant implications for the rest of the system. For example, an e-commerce website that uses the web service provided by WorldPay to take credit card payments can fairly easily switch to using NetBanx with minimal operational disruption. Loose coupling is made possible due to the open Internet technologies used to mash web services together. It is also in stark contrast to many pre-Internet business systems and processes that were tightly-coupled, or which in other words did not permit the rapid replacement or exchange of one or more operating components.

Traditionally higher education has been fairly tightly coupled, with both people and other resources constrained within the boundaries of single institutions. Whilst research information may – if slowly – have flowed freely between different ivory towers, when it comes to teaching activities most academics and students have generally been tightly-coupled to the dictates of their own single college or university. Student exchanges have and continue to take place. However, in the main most students have continued to register at single institutions for significant periods of time and have received their instruction solely from that institution and its academics for that period. One implication of this is that students have generally only been taught by the academics at a particular higher education institution after they have formally enrolled, and have not been taught by them again after they have left.

Public online video is, however, one of the Web 2.0 developments starting to challenge tightly-coupled tradition. Initiatives such as YouTube EDU and iTunes U — let alone the growing number of academics running their own YouTube channels — are allowing not just students *but anybody* to obtain quality higher educational contact from an institution and its academics not just whilst they are in residence, but also before they arrive and after they have graduated. Whilst they are being formally educated, students are also increasingly able to view relevant lectures and other video content made by academics from institutions at which they are not registered. Granted, academics who have written textbooks and journal articles have always had some input into the education of students beyond their own institution. However, as Michael Wesch and Martyn Poliakoff have shown, the opportunities for teaching inputs from academics employed by one institution to be loosely coupled into the teaching activities of another have no previous parallel.

Those managing higher education need to wake up to this new reality and fast. In particular, policy needs to be put in place concerning the extent to which any institution will support their academics in posting public online video, as well as how it is

to be branded and what institutional affiliation it ought to carry. At present we are in the age of the public online video pioneer, with all academics venturing into the Brave New World of showcasing their wares online likely to win praise. However, whilst establishing an individual online education brand is always likely to be positive for the academic(s) concerned, as the trend accelerates not all institutions may want to mass-cross-subsidise the education of others beyond their boundaries. As courses and modules become loosely-coupled webs of resources mashed from academics and institutions elsewhere, some colleges and universities will also have to take care to signal to their students just where they are offering institutional value added.

Soon no academic will sensibly be able to claim that there are no public online videos that do not improve the teaching of their particular courses and modules. Presenting their students will a loosely-coupled web of public online video from a range of contributors will therefore simply become good higher education practice. However, the role of many an academic will have to be redefined if it is discovered that everything they teach is better explained in video by somebody else. Such a development suggests that being able to mash a web of loosely-coupled educational resources may become a more important educational skill than lecturing for perhaps the majority. Whether this is alarming or liberating of course depends on your point of view. Either way it has to have major implications for the kinds of individuals higher education institutions will in future employ.

At the other end of the spectrum, colleges and universities will have to decide how they will support, promote and retain their public online video stars. Future universities could become more like movie studios vying for affiliation with the performances of A-List online video academics. This said, the most established public online video educators will not necessarily even need such institutional affiliations. Not least this is because the financial paybacks from running, for example, a successful YouTube partner channel can be considerable. Such paybacks may derived directly via advertising income. However, and even more significantly, financial paybacks for individuals also accrue from the offers of work that positive online academic exposure tends to generate.

Those well known for making good public educational videos are also likely to be in high demand to make real-life lecture performances. Traditional lecturing is absolutely not going to be entirely killed off by public online video or any other form of electronic media. However, it is likely that more and more warm breath lectures will have to become signature events in order to justify why all students are expected to be in the same room at the same time to receive information in a linear stream at a pace beyond their control. It is also worth remembering that at present those employing academics also often have too little information on each candidate's lecturing ability before they consider an offer of employment. Public online video will change this too, with those academics without a solid portfolio of popular content potentially finding themselves to be less and less employable. It also cannot be long before academic promotion panels start to consider and even expect public online video portfolios.

Piggybacking on Public Websites

The looser-coupling of both academics and students to single institutions is a major issue for those running higher education to manage. However, it will also drive the requirement for broader strategies that embrace the 'piggyback-ing' of institutional content on public websites.

Back in the Dot Com days of the unnamed Web 1.0, almost all online attention was focused on building great websites and attempting to generate traffic. In other words, everybody was focused on getting those people surfing the Internet to come to them. In contrast, little attention was

directed into seeking out where potential content consumers actually congregated online.

Whatever many web designers may still mistakenly believe, Web 2.0 is all about challenging the highly-user-unfriendly way of thinking that characterised Web 1.0. Indeed, a competent Web 2.0 strategy — and hence any competent HE 2.0 strategy — ought to be a strategy for how an institution uses the web, rather than an internalistic plan for the design and use of its own website. Those managers still obsessing about the graphics on their homepage have today really well and truly lost the plot.

Far too many colleges and universities still apparently believe that the development of an institutional website and internal web resources is where e-learning is at. Unfortunately this is Web 1.0 thinking in spades. Those institutions who believe that they can offer their students and staff the best deal by doing everything in-house are simply trying to lock the stable door long after the horse has bolted. And nowhere more is this the case than when it comes to the hosting and dissemination of educational video.

In a world in which it is finally being realized that no college or university can compete with Google *et al* when it comes to offering e-mail, file space and basic office applications, any belief that higher education institutions ought to be hosting video internally has to be equally naïve. Piggybacking on public video hosting infrastructures such as those offered by YouTube is simply a far, far better option. This is also the case for two reasons.

Firstly, hosting video on public websites like YouTube will almost certainly prove less time consuming, less technically demanding, and more successful, than trying to host the content on an institution's own internal web servers. This is simply because providing tools for video hosting is the core business of public online video websites and not the core business of higher education establishments. It is therefore strategically sensible for colleges and universities to adopt a 'mashup mentality' and to host video on public online video websites. Granted, many a university IT department may argue to the contrary, but then they've got a vested interest in maintaining the status quo of running everything in-house.

Those running internal IT departments sometimes argue that hosting video on public sites is risky and unreliable. This is bizarre given that, due to their usually modest funding, educational IT departments boast such poor levels of service continuity that many dare not even compare themselves to commercial providers. For example, an uptime for web provision of 99.9% is considered acceptable by many universities. However, accepting such a potentially high level of outage would rapidly put many a commercial Internet hosting provider out of business, with such companies typically advertising an uptime of between 99.99% and 99.999%. The bottom line is therefore that hosting video content on major public websites such as YouTube is at least as reliable as hosting content on most higher education web servers, and often by an order of magnitude.

The second reason for educational institutions to open up their boundaries and host their video publicly is perhaps even more important than the first, and involves the maximisation of traffic. As has already been noted, the logic of Web 1.0 was to strategically focus too heavily on building a great website and to ignore where potential visitors actually congregated online. Today any organization that internally hosts any video that it wants to communicate as widely as possible is also making this mistake.

YouTube is one of the most popular websites in the world. Hosting a video on YouTube and then embedding it back onto an organization's own website as a web service is therefore almost by definition going to lead to more viewings. This is because anybody conducting a search on YouTube will have a chance of finding the video if it is hosted on YouTube, and yet no chance at all of finding it via that search if it is hosted on an institution's own web server. Just as importantly,

YouTube videos tend to rank highly in Google searches (perhaps because Google owns YouTube!), whilst most other online video content does not. Once a video is hosted on YouTube it will also gather associations with related content. This means that when anybody watches a related video — be it on YouTube or embedded from YouTube on another site — there will once again be a chance of obtaining a viewing.

The importance of hosting public video on those 'magnet' video hosting websites which large numbers of people are known to regularly visit and search cannot be over stated. To illustrate this, consider the viewings obtained for the author's educational video 'Explaining Cloud Computing'. This is hosted on YouTube and also embedded back into the ExplainingComputers.com website. After its first three years online this had attracted 229,487 views. Of these only 12,620 were of the video embedded on the ExplainingComputers or other websites, with the remaining 94.5 per cent of viewings being on YouTube. This is perhaps not surprising when you discover that 84,989 viewings resulted directly from a search on YouTube or Google, with a further 47,917 viewings being direct referrals from related YouTube videos. As this simple but stark example shows, it is gaining access to a powerful distributor that everybody visits (here YouTube), rather than simply getting a video on the Internet, that really matters.

Achieving Infrastructure Independence

A final implication of hosting higher education videos publicly rather than on internal servers is that it enables the achievement of infrastructure independence. In his seminal paper on Web 2.0, Timothy O'Reilly (2005) talks of the Web 2.0 revolution moving software beyond the level of a single device. What this means is that an online SaaS application such as Google Docs can run on any Internet-enabled piece of hardware capable running a browser, rather than being limited to running on a PC with a particular operating system. In the same way, hosting video on public sites separates an institution's educational delivery from a reliance on its own hosting infrastructure.

Infrastructure independence is likely to make most undertakings more accessible, less risky, and more global. Once again convincing an internal IT department that it is a good idea to let an institution's educational content take on a life of its own out on the web – rather than being safely 'caged' on an institution's own servers – may at present prove a hard sell. However, an acceptance that delivery infrastructure ownership no longer needs to be integral to educational delivery is one of those mindset shifts that will inevitably flow from the growing use of public online video in higher education.

In a conversation following one of the author's YouTube-based tutorials discussed earlier in this chapter, a student with a good knowledge of the material being taught stated how much he was enjoying the module. He then noted that he had not attended any of the lectures. The initial reaction of most academics to such a statement is one of shock. However, whether such a reaction is justified when the student in question was clearly engaging with the module online (in this case via online handouts, journal papers, audio podcasts and public online videos) is something we all perhaps need to question. In terms of higher education, infrastructure independence is not just about the acceptance and use of online technology. Far more fundamentally it also involves an acknowledgement that traditional, physical methods of educational delivery are becoming something that students may legitimately abandon as their requirements dictate. Such an argument starts to open up far broader debates. However, it is important to recognise that in becoming the new chalk-and-slate, public online video is triggering other evolutions in a much broader educational context.

CONCLUSION

By 2020 we are likely to look back and be amazed that there was ever a text-based Internet that largely required us to read and type. In 2007 the Internet slowly started to 'go video'. A few years later, and the transformation to an online world in which users have the choice of whether to view, read or listen is rapidly accelerating. By 2015 all manner of e-book readers, netbooks, mobile devices and surface computers are also likely to have seriously reduced the volume of information currently smeared onto slabs of dead tree. Today, embedding a video in most books or magazines can only be achieved by the horrifically environmentally unfriendly solution of including a slimline video player within hardcopy pages (Mirchandani, 2009). However, as handling more and more information electronically becomes the norm, so the embedding of video into all manner of publication formats will become an easy option. In turn video is destined to become a more and more dominant mode of human communication. All of this has to have major implications for higher education. Imagine, for example, how useful it would have been if the pages in this book could have been embedded with some of the videos discussed herein...

In this chapter we've focused on the reasons why students, academics and institutions may benefit from the use of public online video. As has been discussed, such a revolution is now well beyond theory and may become mainstream within a few years. This said, a great many academics are still extremely hostile to the idea of appearing in video online.

Perhaps the greatest concern voiced by colleagues is that once they place a video on a site like YouTube 'everybody will see it'. This is quite a bizarre worry for two reasons. For a start, anybody claiming this has clearly never attempted to generate web traffic. As the pre-Web 2.0 Internet so clearly taught us, whilst the Dot Com revolution allowed everybody to be a publisher, the simple act of putting anything online in no way guarantees that anybody will ever see it. Even today, the fear that when Professor Jones posts a video online it will immediately be seen by the whole world is simply not true. There are, in fact, likely to be more people wandering into university buildings for a visit than will ever randomly happen across the average academic's public online video. What an academic posts on YouTube is therefore no more likely to be viewed 'by everybody' that the contents of the noticeboard outside their office. It is also worth reminding colleagues of this fact when trying to convince them to take their first steps in public online video.

Of course, what will really drive the growth of public online video will be the demands of our customers—or in other words students—coupled with the potential of public online video to make a better quality of education more widely available. Granted, even the best online video is never likely to compete with a perfect lecture theatre performance by a top professor. However, we need to remember that most lecture performances are usually far from perfect and that few academics really are at the top of their game.

There is, perhaps, some value in returning to our consideration of media developments in the last century when trying to figure out how public online video may transform higher education. In this context, a case can still be made that the theatre offers a better live entertainment experience than watching a film at a cinema, and in turn that watching a film in a cinema is a far richer experience than watching a programme or indeed the same film on television. This is generally argued to be because of the relative intensity of these different modes of media delivery, coupled with the heightened experience of attending any presentation as part of a live audience. However, as we all know, in comparison to the volume of content watched on a television or computer screen, most people consume very little media content in the cinema and even less in a theatre.

The fact that people favour the potentially less effective media of television over cinema and theatre is usually explained by the fact that watching television is more convenient and far cheaper than attending a cinema or theatre. However, even if all three media had the same level of cost and ease of access it is extremely unlikely that all live theatre experiences would actually rival cinema and television presentations. Good live theatre would almost certainly always be the most electric. However, good live theatre performances could also never realistically become a mass-produced product. In other words, theatre only maintains its quality of delivery by being a minority media.

The above ought to remind us of two things of significant relevance to the delivery of higher education. The first is that on the face of it the cost and accessibility of any form of media is likely to determine its mass appeal. The second is that whilst recorded moving image presentations can be mass delivered at high quality, the mass delivery of high quality presentations in person is in comparison exceptionally difficult to achieve. It is indeed for these reasons that most people most of the time forgo the experience of a live or at least co-experienced media presentation in favour of sitting at home before a television or computer screen. Or to put in another way, we know we could not see a good play in a theatre every night even if we wanted to and could afford it.

Today the mechanism used for the delivery of the majority of higher education remains the lecture. This makes higher education one of the few industries that does attempt to mass produce its product on a craft production basis. Each lecture delivered is unique for its own student audience. This can also be a great thing. However, trying to take a more objective stance it can sensibly be argued that the craft production delivery of tens of thousands of lectures on exactly the same topic in exactly the same language each week is crazy and a very poor use of resources. Even worse, given that it is likely that most such lectures are at best mediocre—and that forcing students to consume them at a fixed time in a fixed place at a fixed pace is hardly consumer-centric — the current higher education model of mass-craft-production is not serving most students well.

On so many levels public online video provides a major part of the 'answer' to the above. In comparison to live lectures, public online educational videos are the equivalent of television versus a theatre performance. Public online videos may never quite match the quality of the very best live lectures. But then we are foolish if we really believe that most students today are receiving very high quality live lecture performances most of the time. If, however, higher education institutions encourage more of their star academics to record and update world-class public videos, so everybody may get a better education. Universities and colleges also need to remember that whilst schools have a requirement to gather their pupils together all day to in order to provide childcare, socialisation and crowd control *in addition* to education, that such a 'constraint' does not have to be a feature of higher education.

The above does not mean that live lecturing will cease. However, it does imply that the role of most academics will evolve to include a great deal of online content mashing and one-to-one learning support, with live one-to-many class performances taking up a smaller proportion of their time. In turn this means that the ties between students and single higher education institutions are likely to be more loosely-coupled and that institutions have to be far clearer what they are providing to students for their fees.

Potentially the rise of public online video may mean that at least some higher education institutions become more like television companies that broadcast 24/7, but which do not attempt to produce in-house all of their programming. Rather, they will produce and deliver in the lecture theatre or on video their own bread-and-butter — the equivalent of local news programming — as well as those types of educational content in which they specialise. However, their students will then obtain as a mashup from an open educational marketplace the rest of their lectures/programmes, with such mashups almost certainly including the equivalent of most prime-time content. Such a model means that all and more viewers will tend to get a better service. And that is what the increased used of public online video in higher education ought to be about.

REFERENCES

Apple. (2007). *Apple announces iTunes U on the iTunes store: Free content from universities now available.* Press release 30th May. Retrieved on October 6, 2009, from http://www.apple.com/pr/library/2007/05/30itunesu.html

BachelorsDegreeOnline.com. (2009). *50 Terrific iTunes U lectures to get you through the economic crisis*. Retrieved on October 6, 2009, from http://www.bachelorsdegreeonline.com/blog/2009/50-terrific-itunes-u-lectures-to-get-you-through-the-economic-crisis/

Barnatt, C. (2009). Higher education 2.0. *The International Journal of Management Education*, 7(3). Retrieved on October 6, 2009, from http://www.heacademy.ac.uk/IJME/ijme/business/resources/detail/ijme/IJME_vol7_no3_barnatt

Colman, D. (2009). Introducing YouTube EDU! *Open Culture*. Retrieved on October 6, 2009, from http://www.openculture.com/2009/03/introducing_youtube_edu.html

de Sola Pool, I. (1982). *Technologies of freedom: On free speech in an electronic age*. Cambridge, MA: Harvard University Press.

Edge.org. (2009). *About edge*. Retrieved on October 6, 2009, from http://www.edge.org/about_edge.html

Hodgson, G. (1995). *People's century*. London, UK: BBC Books.

InsideHigherEd. (2009). *The evidence on online education*. Retrieved on October 6, 2009, from http://www.insidehighered.com/layout/set/print/news/2009/06/29/online

MacIntyre, J. (2008). *Want a free education: A brief guide to the burgeoning world of online video lectures*. Retrieved on October 6, 2009, from www.boston.com/bostonglobe/ideas/articles/2008/11/02/u_tube/

Means, B., Toyoma, Y., Murphy, R., Bakia, M., & Jones, K. (2009). *Evaluation of evidence-based practices in online learning: A meta-analysis and review of online learning studies*. Center for Technology in Learning for the U.S. Department of Education. Retrieved on October 6, 2009, from http://www.ed.gov/rschstat/eval/tech/evidence-based-practices/finalreport.pdf

Mirchandani, R. (2009, 17 September). Video screens hit paper magazines. *BBC News*. 17th September http://news.bbc.co.uk/1/hi/technology/8255729.stm

O'Reilly. (2005). *What is Web 2.0: Design patterns and business models for the next generation software*. Retrieved on October 6, 2009, from http://www.oreillynet.com/lpt/a/6228

Riismandel, P. (2009). Advanced learning: Education year in review. *Streamingmedia.com*. Retrieved on October 6, 2009, from http://www.streamingmedia.com/article.asp?id=10966

Chapter 17
IFRS Cyber–Guest Lecturers:
A Pedagogical Resource for Professors and an Inspiration for Student Online Video Projects

Mark Holtzblatt
Roosevelt University, USA

Norbert Tschakert
Salem State University, USA

ABSTRACT

In early 2011, 117 nations mandate or allow the use of International Financial Reporting Standards (IFRS). On November 14, 2008, the SEC issued its proposed roadmap for U.S. companies to adopt the new international accounting standards. As a result firms nationwide are beginning to prepare for adoption of IFRS. However, many U.S. business schools are still lagging in the teaching of the new standards and attribute their slow movement to the lack of educational materials. While several IFRS textbooks are beginning to appear on the worldwide market and several innovative curriculum developments are occurring, the teaching materials are still considered sparse. This chapter examines an emerging and impressive source of IFRS teaching materials that includes professional and institutional webcasts and online videos. The available IFRS webcasts are first surveyed and then pedagogical strategies are suggested for a variety of accounting courses. This technology based media offers both professors and students alike numerous educational benefits and opportunities. Our experience with these "cyber-guest" lecturers has inspired an innovative Inter-University IFRS Online Video Competition amongst our two universities.

DOI: 10.4018/978-1-60960-800-2.ch017

INTRODUCTION

The globalization of business and finance has led to the successful mass adoption of International Financial Reporting Standards (IFRS) by more than 117 countries. Other countries are expected to follow suit over the next few years, including India (2011), Canada (2011) and Mexico (2012). IFRS are set by the International Accounting Standards Board (IASB) in London, the international equivalent of the U.S.'s Financial Accounting Standards Board (FASB).

The G20, in their April 2009 Leaders' Statement, called on accounting standard setters to work urgently to achieve a single set of high-quality global accounting standards. At the September 2009 Pittsburgh summit, the leaders of the G-20 called on "international accounting bodies to redouble their efforts to achieve a single set of high quality, global accounting standards within the context of their independent standard setting process and complete their convergence project by June 2011" (Lamoreaux, 2009). Sir David Tweedie, Chairman of the IASB, expects that as many as 150 out of the 195 independent countries in the world will mandate or allow IFRS in the near future (Pickard, 2007).

Despite this global progress, U.S. IFRS education efforts are in a state of flux and transition (Nilsen, 2008) as business schools now have to start teaching IFRS (Iwata, 2009). Donna Street, president of the International Association for Accounting Education and Research (IAAER) said in a 2009 University of Dayton press release, "Many business schools are not moving quickly enough to teach international standards and equip accounting graduates with the knowledge they'll need to be competitive." Street also said "Recent graduates report that knowledge of IFRS is useful in their careers. Graduates of schools providing substantial IFRS training are definitely going to be ahead of the game and sought out by employers" (University of Dayton, 2009).

According to survey results from September 2008 by KPMG and the American Accounting Association, a dearth of IFRS educational materials was delaying IFRS incorporation into many syllabi (KPMG, 2008); 79 percent of respondents said the key challenge for them was developing curriculum materials. In terms of what materials would be needed to support teaching IFRS: 89 percent noted textbooks as the highest priority, followed by case studies at 76 percent. Faculty members surveyed predicted that the first class of graduating seniors likely to have a substantial amount of IFRS education will be the class of 2011. Jim Young, the accountancy chair at Northern Illinois University recently stated in a 2009 interview (ICPAS, 2009), "…we're also realizing we're going to have to self-develop materials to adequately teach IFRS right now. There just isn't enough material out there. What we really need is more specific guidance and classroom materials."

The second annual KPMG-AAA Faculty Survey, conducted during July and August 2009, showed that nearly half of the 500 professors who responded believe the United States should transition to IFRS to remain competitive, and three-quarters think IFRS needs to be immediately incorporated into their school's curricula. 70 percent said they have taken significant steps to incorporate IFRS into the curriculum. Further, 83 percent believe IFRS needs to be incorporated into their curricula by 2011 (KPMG, 2009).

"The findings of the KPMG-AAA survey suggest that we have made progress, but there is still much work to be done in optimizing how IFRS is taught in our university classrooms," said Philip M. J. Reckers, Ph.D., recent Chair of the American Accounting Association's Education Committee and Professor of Accountancy at Arizona State University's W. P. Carey School of Business. "Professors, university administrators, regulators and thought leaders in the accounting profession need to work together to make sure the curricula is timely and relevant."

If we examine the development of IFRS teaching materials on a global basis, we can see there are signs of pedagogical development. In Australia, where IFRS has been applied since 2005, a Wiley book entitled "Applying International Financial Reporting Standards" (Alfredson, 2007) has been widely used in university classes. In Canada, another Wiley book authored by Wiecek and Young, entitled "IFRS Primer: International GAAP Basics" has just been published in 2009 (Wiecek, 2009). Thus, IFRS textbooks are slowly starting to appear on the market. IFRS textbooks in the European Union are plentiful and of high quality, but they are mostly written for an individual country within the European Union and published in that country's language, focusing on differences between the still existing local GAAP and IFRS. Significant research projects led by Virginia Tech University and Ohio State University (Ghose, 2008) within the past year have led to innovative IFRS curricula for both the Intermediate Accounting course and a separate one term IFRS course. Global Accounting firms such as Deloitte and Ernst & Young have recently released high quality IFRS curricula for use by university professors.

In addition to these emerging books and professional curricula, there exists another valuable and perhaps underappreciated source of IFRS teaching materials. This includes the rapidly growing body of professional and institutional IFRS webcasts and online videos. The number of webcasts and videos dealing with the international standards has accelerated sharply within the past year. When viewed as a group, the entire collection is impressive.

The objective of this chapter is to shine a light upon this engaging body of pedagogical material. To begin, the IFRS videos and webcasts will be organized and classified by source and category type. Detailed strategies will then be suggested for integration into a variety of accounting courses ranging from the introductory level to the most advanced classes. Finally, a new innovative paradigm in university-level accounting education, inspired by IFRS "cyber-guest lecturers" will be introduced and discussed.

IFRS WEBCASTS AND ONLINE VIDEOS

The creators and hosts of the majority of IFRS webcast presentations include the major global accounting firms, the American Institute of Certified Public Accountants (AICPA), the Canadian Institute of Chartered Accountants (CICA), the SEC and educational institutions. The accounting firms' efforts have been led by the "Big 4" firms including Deloitte & Touche, Ernst & Young, KPMG, and PricewaterhouseCoopers. Other accounting firms that have created and archived IFRS webcasts include BDO Seidman, Grant Thornton and McGladrey and Pullen. Let's now take a look at the various sources and available topics.

Deloitte provides a link on their main IFRS homepage entitled "Dbriefs: IFRS Webcasts". There are currently twenty different IFRS webcasts available, ranging from general discussions of IFRS differences to specific webcasts focusing upon selected industries (i.e., Oil & Gas, Real Estate, and Insurance). The Deloitte presentations are primarily audio casts accompanied by synchronized power point presentations. A current and archived list of the Deloitte webcast titles is shown in Table 1.

Ernst & Young has a link on their global IFRS homepage for all current and archived IFRS webcasts. The webcasts range from audio/power point to full video/power point presentations. Like Deloitte, the Ernst & Young (EY) webcasts deal with industry specific issues related to IFRS, but EY also has sessions that focus upon specific accounts (i.e., IFRS revenue recognition, IFRS tax, IFRS hedging). The level of EY production quality is so high that they were awarded three 2007 Telly awards. Current, forthcoming and archived Ernst & Young webcast IFRS titles are presented in Table 2.

Table 1. Deloitte Dbriefs: upcoming and archived IFRS webcasts (www.deloitte.com/us/IFRS)

Title	Date
IASB and FASB Financial Instruments Project: A Closer Look	12/09/09
The People Challenges of IFRS Conversion	09/10/09
IFRS: A Deeper Dive into Revenue Recognition	07/29/09
IFRS: Working Toward a More Cost Effective Transition	07/07/09
IFRS: A Deeper Dive on Tax Accounting Methods	05/18/09
IFRS: The Impact be in the Real Estate Arena	04/30/09
IFRS: Is It More Complex Than Many Suspect?	02/25/09
IFRS: New Year, New Updates	02/17/09
IFRS: Why Private Companies Should Take Note	01/28/09
IFRS: Should TMT Companies Sign On?	12/17/08
Converting from U.S. GAAP to IFRS	11/24/08
IFRS: Implications for Life Sciences Companies	10/22/08
IFRS Conversion: Process, People, Controls	10/15/08
IFRS: What Does the Latest SEC Activity Mean?	09/19/08
GAAP and IFRS Convergence: Bridging the Divide	09/03/08
Consumer Business – IFRS: Opportunities and Challenges	07/24/08
Real Estate – IFRS: What Will the Impact Be	06/03/08
Oil & Gas – IFRS: What's the Road Ahead?	04/16/08
IFRS: Time for U.S. Insurers to Get On Board	03/25/08
IFRS: Strategies for Adopting a Single Set of Standards	02/01/08

Table 2. Ernst & Young thought center IFRS webcast series (http://webcast.ey.com/thoughtcenter/ default.aspx)

Title	Date
Replacement of IAS 39- Financial Instruments: Recognition and Measurement	11/24/09
Preparing for year-end reporting under IFRS	10/27/09
IFRS Developments in the US	10/15/09
The Changing Landscape of IFRS	09/22/09
Accounting for Rate-Regulated Activities Under IFRS	09/03/09
Lessons for Year-End Reporting: A Webcast for Companies Currently Using IFRS	06/23/09
IFRS Convergence for the Pharmaceutical Industry	06/01/09
IFRS 1: Focus on New Converting Countries	05/28/09
Proposed Changes to Accounting for Income Taxes Under IFRS	05/14/09
Accounting for Income Taxes: Differences Between US GAAP and IFRS	05/07/09
Remuneration Packages: IFRS 2 and Pension Fund - Issues Related to Restructuring	04/28/09
Consolidations and the Effect of the New Business Combinations Standard	03/31/09
IFRS Convergence for the Pharmaceutical Industry	03/09/09

continued on following page

Table 2. continued

Title	Date
IFRS: Proposed Changes to Revenue Recognition Requirements	02/17/09
Mergers and Acquisitions Under IFRS: the New Business Combinations Standard	01/20/09
IFRS: Fair Values and Financial Instruments	12/15/08
Accounting for Consolidations in an IFRS World: Similarities, Differences	12/05/08
Conversion Considerations for IFRS: Implications for Energy Companies	12/03/08
Journey to IFRS: the SEC's Roadmap	11/20/08
Accounting for Financial Instruments in an IFRS World – Focus on Hedging	11/06/08
Accounting for Pensions and Restructuring Charges in an IFRS World	10/30/08
Share-Based Payments in an IFRS World: Similarities and Differences	10/23/08
Conversion Considerations for IFRS: Implications for Automotive Companies	09/29/08
Goodwill and Long-Lived Assets in an IFRS World: Recognition and Impairment	09/19/08
Conversion Considerations for IFRS: Implications for US Power and Utility Co.'s	09/18/08
Conversion Considerations for IFRS: Implications for Real Estate Companies	09/16/08
Is Your Company Ready for IFRS? What Audit Committee Members Need to Know	09/15/08
The Forward-Thinking Guide to IFRS Revenue Recognition	08/26/08
Financial Statement in an IFRS World – Are They Really Comparable?	07/17/08
Conversion Considerations for IFRS (for the Media and Entertainment Industry)	07/09/08
Why Tax Departments Need to Pay Attention to IFRS Now	06/11/08
Are You Ready for IFRS? What US Companies Need to Think About	06/06/08

KPMG launched their KPMG IFRS Institute on April 24, 2008 to raise awareness and to address the information needs of companies, investors and academics that may be affected by a transition to IFRS. A link on the institute's homepage connects to the upcoming webcasts and on-demand events. The majority of the KPMG webcasts are audio accompanied by synchronized power point presentations, which are also available for separate downloading. KPMG has webcasts dealing with both IFRS industry issues and specific IFRS accounts. In addition they currently have five archived webcasts geared to presenting IFRS information to professors. These sessions have information on incorporating IFRS into classrooms and various faculty IFRS surveys, as seen in Table 3.

PricewaterhouseCoopers (PwC) hosts three separate and distinct websites of IFRS webcasts and online videos. Their newest source is perhaps the most exciting development in the whole sphere of IFRS cybercasts. This is their newly created PwC IFRS Video Learning Center. As announced on November 20, 2008, the center is designed to assist companies in assessing the impact of transitioning to IFRS. The center is free to the public and offers a series of videos to help companies understand IFRS. As the press release of Nov. 20, 2008 stated:

A conversion to IFRS is a challenging exercise, and companies will need to ensure they have allowed themselves sufficient time to prepare for that change. The Video Learning Center is one way PwC is helping to guide business and accounting professionals through the implementation and adoption processes.

The Video Learning Center features a series of videos, available on-demand and viewable

Table 3. KPMG IFRS institute webcasts (www.kpmgifrsinstitute.com)

Title	Date
Update on the IFRS Convergence Process and IASB Rulemaking	12/17/09
IFRS for Financial Instruments and Exposure Draft Update Webcast	10/15/09
IFRS – Synergies with Finance Transformation	09/24/09
IASB Rate Regulated Activities	07/31/09
IFRS for Small & Medium Sized Entities: A New Choice for Many U.S. Private Co's	07/24/09
Consolidations, Derecognition, and Off Balance Sheet Activities	07/01/09
U.S. Tax Implications of Adopting IFRS: Accounting for Income Taxes	06/24/09
U.S. Tax Implications of Adopting IFRS	06/04/09
Live Interview with IASB Chairman, Sir David Tweedie	05/27/09
IT Implications of Conversion to IFRS	05/07/09
IFRS Institute Comment Period Webcast	04/21/09
Implications of IFRS for Consumer Products Companies and Retailers	04/08/09
IFRS Financial Reporting for Pharma & Biotech Industries	03/31/09
Insights into IFRS in the Oil and Gas Sector	03/17/09
Proposed Roadmap Survey Results and International Adoption Update	03/10/09
Technology Companies: The R&D and Intangible Assets Transition from US GAAP to IFRS	02/04/09
IFRS Webcast for Natural Gas and Electric Utilities	01/15/09
International Update on Accounting for Financial Instruments, Fair Value Measurements	12/18/08
KPMG Faculty Forum IFRS Roadmap Webcast	11/24/08
SEC Proposed Roadmap for the Potential Use of Financial Statements Prepared in Accordance with IFRS by U.S. Issuers	11/19/08
IFRS for Technology Companies: Closing the GAAP	10/08/08
The SEC August 27 Meeting to Consider Adoption of IFRS by U.S. Public Companies and Highlights of AAA/KPMG IFRS Faculty Survey On Incorporating IFRS Into the Curriculum	09/04/08
Insights on the SEC Meeting and Possible Implications to U.S. Public Companies	08/28/08
IFRS: Tax Considerations When Converting from U.S. GAAP	06/16/08
Key IFRS Standards and Topics and How to Incorporate Them Into Classroom Discussions	05/27/08
IFRS Institute Webcast: IFRS: Insights on Adoption and Potential Impact in the U.S.	05/01/08
Similarities and Differences Between U.S. GAAP and IFRS	04/14/08
IFRS: U.S. Adoption and the Impact on Academia	03/26/08

individually at www.pwc.com/usifrs/vlc. In the videos, PwC IFRS specialists discuss key differences between US GAAP and IFRS, and provide practical examples of what companies should consider as they embark on their transition to IFRS. (PricewaterhouseCoopers LLP, 2008)

There are 6 sessions, containing a total of 16 separate 20 to 30-minute video courses. The courses contain a combination of full video, along with synchronized power point slides. There is also a special session of three separate panel discussions from the PwC IFRS Senior Executive Conference, held in September 2008.

PwC also offers three excellent short IFRS videos of approximately 7 minutes each at their PwC.tv website which has various programs and issues geared specifically and directly to students. On channel 3 of PwC.tv the videos discuss the "What? Why? and How?" of IFRS. In addition

Table 4.

PWC IFRS video learning center (www.pwc.com/usifrs/vlc)	
Session 1 – First-Time Adoption, Revenue Recognition, Provisions & Contingencies	First-Time Adoption Revenue Recognition Provisions & Contingencies
Session 2 – Impairments and Noncurrent Assets	Impairments of Nonfinancial Assets Internally Generated Intangibles Property, Plant, and Equipment
Session 3 – Business Transactions	Consolidations Leases Business Combinations
Session 4 – Employee Benefits	Pensions Share-based Payment
Session 5 – Financial Instruments	Derecognition Hedge Accounting Debt vs. Equity Classification, Measurement, Impairment
Session 6 – Income Taxes	Income Taxes
Special Sessions: IFRS Senior Executive Conference Highlights	Standard-Setter &Regulator Perspectives Views of the Capital Markets A Registrant's Perspective
PWC IFRS Webcasts (http://www.pwc.com/us/en/issues/ifrsreporting/webcasts/index.jhtml)	
Title	**Date**
Similarities and Differences Between IFRS and US GAAP	11/17/09
IFRS in the US: The impact of continued global adoption and IFRS for SMEs	09/23/09
IFRS Webcast: Exploring the Revenue Recognition and Leasing Discussion Papers	07/15/09
IFRS in the US: The Next Steps to Adoption of IFRS	04/28/09
IASB's Exposure Draft on Income Taxes: Understanding Conversion Considerations	04/17/09
IFRS Conversion: Understanding the Systems Impact	04/09/09
IFRS Conversion: Pension, OPEB and Stock-Based Compensation Issues	02/10/09
IFRS Conversion: Understanding the Key Tax Issues for Pharmaceuticals	01/27/09
Converting to IFRS: Process and System Implications for Pharmaceutical Companies	12/15/08
IFRS Conversion: Understanding the Impact on Your Global Tax Footprint	12/11/08
What Manufacturers Need to Know About IFRS	12/08/08
IFRS Conversion Process: Phase 1 Preliminary Study	11/20/08
IFRS in the US: One Step Closer to Adoption of IFRS	09/04/08
Accounting for Income Taxes Under IFRS: Convergence & the Path Forward	08/21/08
PWC IFRS Ready Videos (http://www.pwc.com/us/en/careers/pwctv/ch3-ifrs-ready.jhtml)	
PWC.tv IFRS Ready Video Series	What? Why? How? (3 short videos, each about 7 minutes)

PwC has developed a separate IFRS Webcast series which discusses industry and specific rule issues. This consists of a monthly series of webcasts, each featuring a panel of PwC professionals and IFRS specialists. Table 4 presents the three sources of webcasts and videos offered by PricewaterhouseCoopers.

In addition to the global public accounting firms' webcasts, the American Institute of Certified Public Accountants (AICPA) and the Canadian Institute of Chartered Accountants (CICA) have produced numerous high quality IFRS videos. The AICPA announced on May 20, 2008 the creation of their new website IFRS.com. It serves as their hub for updates, publications and videos related to IFRS. There are currently 16 short video clips ranging from 1 to 13 minutes in duration. A variety of perspectives can be observed from senators, practitioners, and institute officers. Also, in Canada which is adopting IFRS in 2011, the CICA has three excellent, very detailed videos ranging from 30 to 90 minutes that combine video with synchronized power points. The videos, entitled "Get Ready", "Go Deep", and "Even Deeper" were from the June 2008 conference of the Canadian Academic Accounting Association (CAAA), which was scheduled to help academics

prepare for International Financial Reporting Standards. The CICA also hosts two videos of approximately 10 minutes each, featuring Tricia O'Malley, a member of the IASB discussing the structure and standard setting process of the London based organization. The Institute of Management Accountants (IMA) has recently initiated an IFRS Webinar series which has five sessions from March to November of 2009. These IMA webinars consist of audio with synchronized power point presentations. Table 5 summarizes the available presentations by the AICPA, CICA and IMA.

Two excellent sources of IFRS webcasts of a more theoretical nature include the productions of the Securities and Exchange Commission, and the University Forums offered each year by the

Table 5. IFRS webcasts and videos by professional accounting institutes

American Institute of Certified Public Accountants (AICPA) (http://www.ifrs.com)	
Title	**Duration**
IFRS Highlights – Second Quarter	5 minutes
IFRS for SME's	3 minutes
SEC Roadmap for Adoption of IFRS	6 minutes
IFRS: Experts Answer	7 minutes
IFRS: Experts Answer Questions About Adoption	4 minutes
IFRS: Christopher Cox at a Recent AICPA Conference	8 minutes
SEC Releases Proposed IFRS Roadmap, Arlene Thomas Sr. VP, AICPA	3 minutes
IFRS: Roadmap for a Possible Transition	11 minutes
IFAC President Ferdinand Del Vale	1 minute
IFRS: Adopting Global Standards	8 minutes
IFRS: Who is IASB? Arleen Thomas, Sr. VP, AICPA	4 minutes
IFRS: Three Questions for a Company, Bob Laux, CPA, Microsoft Corp.	11 minutes
Bob Bunting on IFRS, President of the IFAC	13 minutes
IFRS: An Overview	3 minutes
SEC Chair Christopher Cox on IFRS, January 2008, to AICPA Conference	3 minutes
SEC Roundtable Prospect for U.S. Adoption of IFRS	2 minutes
Canadian Institute of Chartered Accountants (www.cica.ca/index.cfm/ci_id/39172/la_id/1.htm)	
2008 CAAA Conference Presentations Chartered Accountants of Canada 6/08	IFRS: Get Ready, Ian Hague of the ASB, (90 minutes)
	IFRS: Go Deep, Ian Hague, Karen Jones, (70 minutes)
	IFRS: Even Deeper, Ian Hague, Karen Jones (31 min.)

continued on following page

Table 5. continued

Tricia O'Malley, FCA member of IASB presents two videos with slides	The IASB – Introduction (9 minutes)
	The IASB – Standard Setting Process (10 minutes)
Institute of Management Accountants (http://www.imanet.org/development_webinar_inside_ifrs.asp)	
Title	**Date**
IFRS Financial Reporting: Liabilities Section	Nov. 19, 2009
IFRS Financial Reporting: Assets and Revenue	Sept. 23, 2009
IFRS Financial Reporting Entities	August 13, 2009
IFRS Financial Reporting Presentation Considerations	May 20, 2009
An Overview of IFRS	March 25, 2009

Lubin School of Pace University. The SEC has archived roundtables that have occurred within the past several years that deal with the SEC U.S. IFRS "Roadmap" and the use of IFRS by foreign registrants. The Lubin School has also archived their various forums dealing with IFRS issues. The 2007, 2008 and the recent April 30, 2009 webcasts are currently available for viewing. The specific webcast titles of these two organizations can be seen in Table 6.

In addition, IFRS videos may be accessed on numerous websites. YouTube.com hosts video clips on many subject areas including those that relate to International Financial Reporting Standards. These video clips range from very brief one minute videos to more lengthy interviews. One aspect of the YouTube.com collection is the presence of a great number of IFRS videos created in India. Thus, students from around the world can easily gain awareness of the problems that India faces in meeting their proposed IFRS conversion date of 2011. However, a common problem with the IFRS videos on YouTube is the different levels of quality in terms of video production and audio variations.

Another interesting website that can be a good source for IFRS videos is Blinkx.com. This company bills themselves as the world's largest video search engine. They claim to have access to more than thirty five million hours of videos.

Table 6. SEC roundtables on IFRS and the university forums of the Lubin School, Pace University/IASB

The SEC Roundtables on IFRS (www.sec.gov/spotlight/ifrsroadmap.htm)	
Title	**Date**
Proposing a Roadmap Toward IFRS, remarks by former SEC Chairman Christopher Cox	08/27/08
Roundtable on the Performance of IFRS and U.S. GAAP During the Subprime Crisis	08/04/08
SEC Roundtable on Practical Issues Surrounding the Use of IFRS in the U.S.	12/17/07
SEC Roundtable on IFRS in the U.S. Markets	12/13/07
SEC Staff Roundtable on International Financial Reporting Standards "Roadmap"	03/06/07
University Forums on IFRS Issues (www.pace.edu/page.cfm?doc_id=24187)	
Lubin School, Pace University/ IASB	International Accounting Standards: Going From the Talk to Doing the Walk (April 30, 2009)
	Global Integration of Accounting Standards: How Do We Get it Done (April 29, 2008)
	Convergence in Global Financial Reporting and Corporate Governance: Charting a Course for the Future (April 27, 2007)

Blinkx.com has built a reputation as the "Remote Control for the Video Web" with more than 530 media partnerships, including national broadcasters, commercial media giants, and private video libraries. At www.blinkx.com, users can search for video content, create personal video playlists, or build a customized Video Wall for their blog or MySpace page. An upcoming competitor to Blinkx.com is Microsoft's Bing.com search engine which also has an extensive collection of IFRS related video links.

Another more focused innovative website for finding IFRS videos and webcasts is the new TeachingIFRS.com website. This website was conceived in 2009 and currently provides easy access to more than 100 IFRS video clips, videos and webcasts. Accounting teachers from around the world can simply walk into a smart classroom, access the TeachingIFRS.com video clip collection and choose from a multitude of video presentation of varying topics and lengths.

Since new videos are constantly being added, TeachingIFRS.com is a dynamic pedagogical source of engaging IFRS multimedia material that can enliven and inspire accounting students and professors worldwide.

CLASSIFICATION OF CURRENTLY AVAILABLE IFRS WEBCASTS AND ONLINE VIDEOS

As noted, this proliferating body of IFRS webcasts and videos is vast in quantity and varied in perspectives. An analysis of the numerous online media reveals seven separate and distinct categories. These categories, along with related descriptions and examples are presented in Table 7.

STRATEGIES FOR INCORPORATING IFRS WEBCASTS AND VIDEOS INTO THE CLASSROOM

The webcasts and videos offer a significant source of pedagogical supplementary material that can

Table 7. Classification of IFRS webcasts and online videos

Categories/Types	Description and Examples
(1) IFRS Principles	These webcasts are created primarily by the global public accounting firms and focus upon specific IFRS principles (i.e., Tax Accounting, Revenue Recognition, Goodwill, Intangibles, Property, Plant and Equipment, etc.)
(2) IFRS Industry Issues	These webcasts discuss IFRS issues that are unique to various industries (i.e., IFRS in the Insurance Industry, IFRS for the Automotive Industry, IFRS for the Telecommunications Industry, etc.)
(3) IFRS Conversions	These webcasts discuss procedures and timelines that should be considered by corporations when contemplating the transition from U.S. GAAP to IFRS. Also, the significant non-accounting impacts of conversions are addressed.
(4) IFRS Teaching Issues	These webcasts include the KPMG Faculty Forum Webcast Series which is directed towards professors seeking ideas for curriculum changes, and also the IFRS Ready videos of PwC.tv that are addressed directly to students.
(5) SEC "Roadmap" U.S. GAAP-IFRS	The archived SEC roundtable webcasts give background on the "Roadmap" whereas the "Big Four" public accounting firms each have responses and analysis of the SEC proposal for switching from U.S. GAAP to IFRS.
(6) Short IFRS Clips	This includes the brief clips (1 to 13 minutes) found on the AICPA's new website IFRS.com, the PricewaterhouseCoopers IFRS Ready videos on their PWC.tv website, and the CICA video clips with Tricia O'Malley of the IASB.
(7) IFRS Conferences	Includes the 2008 Canadian Academic Accounting Association conference, the Lubin School of Business at Pace University/ IASB joint conferences of 2009, 2008, 2007 and the PWC IFRS Senior Executive Conference of September 2008.

enrich IFRS classroom presentations and discussions. The following analysis offers a variety of strategies for incorporating these webcasts into different levels of courses. Professors can consider showing several videos or portions of webcasts during class sessions. Alternatively, students may be assigned homework that can include viewing the webcasts in conjunction with a written assignment, team project or subsequent class discussion.

Introductory Accounting, Finance and Survey of International Business Courses

For the introductory courses, the short IFRS video clips are ideal. The PwC.tv IFRS Ready videos and several of the short AICPA videos located at the IFRS.com website are excellent supplements to introductory business courses to efficiently raise student awareness of IFRS. Student response is very positive when viewing the IFRS Ready: "What? Why? and How?" videos. Their eyes are opened to the changing world of standard setting via "Big 4" partners, multinational executives, managers and other levels of staff. When the AICPA video, "IFRS: Adopting Global Standards" (8 minutes) is shown to Introduction to Accounting classes, it really makes the point that IFRS is forthcoming via the words of a Senator, AICPA and IFAC officers and other experts. Finance majors, Introduction to International Business students and other business classes should also be made aware of the coming IFRS revolution. These short videos provide an excellent source of "cyber-guest lecturers" that really grab students' attention.

Intermediate Accounting and Advanced Accounting Courses

These higher level classes will benefit from all the short video clips mentioned above, especially during early class sessions as a preliminary introduction to IFRS. In addition, the specific

rule webcasts (i.e., Tax IFRS, Goodwill IFRS, PP&E IFRS, etc.) are available supplements to the various topics and chapters covered within Intermediate Accounting courses. Since various financial accounting topics are covered in depth with relevant FASB rules cited, the insertion of professional webcasts with partners discussing the related IFRS principle is a natural fit. For example the PWC IFRS Video Learning Center: Sessions I to VI are excellent supplements to the corresponding Intermediate Accounting topics. The other international accounting firms also offer in-depth and timely IFRS webcasts dealing with various rules. Student's attention is enhanced when viewing experienced "hands on" experts analyzing the IASB pronouncements and implementation rules.

A suggested schedule of IFRS webcast supplements for an Intermediate Accounting course using the 13th edition of Wiley's Kieso Intermediate Accounting textbook (Kieso, 2010) could be structured as follows in Table 8 (additions or deletions could be made depending upon time available and professor discretion). As a caveat, in some cases the webcast excerpt or video will be too long for showing in-class. If there is a portion of a webcast that a professor would like to show, advance preparation would have to be done to find and isolate that segment. In other cases, a professor may only want videos and omit audio webcasts. Thus, some productions will be of more value than others depending upon available class time, and the goals of the professor. The PWC Video Learning Center with its 20 to 30 minute videos that are synchronized with power point slides provides state of the art IFRS teaching supplements. While the number of subjects is currently limited, as time goes on the number of topics included in the PWC VLC collection will undoubtedly expand.

Table 8. Suggested IFRS webcast supplements for intermediate and advanced accounting topics

Intermediate Accounting Topic	IFRS Webcasts and Online Videos
Ch. 1 Financial Accounting and Standards	IFRS: Adopting Global Standards, AICPA (8 minutes) Who is IASB?, Arleen Thomas, Sr. VP AICPA(4 minutes)
Ch. 2 Conceptual Framework	PwC.tv IFRS Ready Videos: What? Why? How? (21 min.) IASB: Introduction, Patricia O'Malley, IASB (9 minutes) Standard Setting Process, Patricia O'Malley (10 minutes)
Ch. 10&11 Property, Plant & Equipment Depreciation and Impairments	PwC Video Learning Center: Session 2- P, P & E. (30 min.) 2008 CAAA: IFRSs-Go Deep, Ian Hague- P, P & E. E&Y: Goodwill, Long Lived Assets: Recognition Impairment
Ch. 12 Intangible Assets	KPMG: R&D and Intangible Assets Transition (2/4/09) PwC Video Learning Center: Session 2- Intangibles 2008 CAAA:IFRSs-Go Deep, Ian Hague- Intangibles
Ch. 13 Current Liabilities, Contingencies	PwC VLC: Session 1- Provisions & Contingencies
Ch. 17 Investments	2008 CAAA:IFRSs-Go Deep, Financial Instruments PwC VLC: Session 5: Financial Instruments E&Y: Fair Value and Financial Instruments (12/15/08)
Ch. 18 Revenue Recognition	PwC VLC: Session 1: Revenue Recognition E&Y: Proposed Changes-Revenue Recognition Requirements E&Y: Forward-Thinking Guide- IFRS Revenue Recognition
Ch. 19 Accounting for Income Taxes	E&Y: Tax Departments Need to Pay Attention to IFRS Now KPMG: Tax Consideration When Converting from US GAAP PwC: Income Taxes-IFRS: Convergence & the Path Forward
Ch. 20 Accounting for Pensions	E&Y: Accounting for Pensions in an IFRS World PwC VLC Session 4: Employee Benefits
Ch. 21 Accounting for Leases	PwC VLC Session 3: Leases
Advanced Accounting Topics	
Accounting for Consolidations	PwC VLC Session 3: Consolidations E&Y: Accounting for Consolidations (Dec. 12, 2008)

International Accounting Courses and Accounting Theory Courses

The AICPA short videos and webcasts, along with the PWC.tv IFRS videos serve as good introductory supplements in these higher level courses. The SEC "Roadmap" to IFRS and "Big 4" responses and analysis provide excellent theoretical background foundation material for in-depth class discussions. Within our Fall 2008 International Accounting class, we viewed the former SEC Chairman Christopher Cox laying out the rationale for the IFRS roadmap during an August 2008 roundtable (AICPA, 11 minutes). This was followed by the PWC partners webcast (Sept. 4, 2008, 60 minutes) analyzing and responding to the SEC proposal, and a very interesting class discussion about all the related issues was generated. During the Spring 2009 semester, the Ernst & Young webcast of November 20, 2008 entitled "Journey to IFRS: the SEC's Roadmap" was shown following the 11 minute AICPA video. This substitution was made because the more recent webcast incorporated developments that had occurred since the PWC September webcast. This illustrates the fact that this body of educational material is not static, but rather dynamic and constantly changing as new events occur.

Also, the IFRS Conferences such as the annual Lubin School of Business at Pace University/

IASB joint conference, the 2008 CAAA Conference or the PWC IFRS Senior Executive Conference provide a rich source of classroom teaching material of a more advanced theoretical nature with various perspectives offered. In addition, a professor can draw upon the webcasts in Table 8 depending upon the topics and direction that are included in the class syllabus.

Separate Newly Created IFRS Courses

These separate IFRS courses which are just beginning to emerge focus solely and specifically on IFRS theoretical and practical implementation issues. The entire spectrum of the seven available groups of IFRS webcasts and online videos may be considered ripe for incorporating into this course depending upon the topics and direction the professor intends to utilize. For the two graduate and undergraduate IFRS courses that Roosevelt University offered in the Summer 2009, supplementary segments of webcast presentations from each of the seven aforementioned categories were shown. There was more than 36 total contact hours with the students. The courses focused solely upon the history, structure, and processes of the IASB, and the specifics of IFRS rules.

The IFRS videos and webcasts enlivened the class by introducing the students to IFRS experts from public accounting, industry, standard setting bodies, government regulators and a variety of professional accounting societies from around the world. For example, the 2009 summer IFRS graduate students at Roosevelt University heard and saw Sir David Tweedie, Chairman of the IASB, 10 to 15 partners and managers from PricewaterhouseCoopers, KPMG and Ernst and Young, former Securities and Exchange Commissioner Christopher Cox, the Director of IFRS Policy and Implementation for IBM Aaron Anderson and the Technical Director of the ICAI of India Dr. Kamal Gupta. As "virtual" guest speakers these "visits" involved absolutely no cost to Roosevelt

University and the students were able to review the videos and webcasts multiple times via archived links. See Appendix A for the videos and webcast excerpts incorporated into the summer/2009 course at Roosevelt University entitled "Global Accounting: The IASB and IFRS".

A suggested schedule of IFRS webcast supplements for a separate one term IFRS class could also be structured as follows in Table 9. For this table the various topics covered by the aforementioned Ohio State-Deloitte separate one term IFRS course were utilized as the outline of the subject matter.

EXPANSION OF IFRS CYBER-GUESTS INTO AN INNOVATIVE STUDENT VIDEO PROJECT

The videos and webcasts described thus far still leave students in their traditional role and do not add a new interactive component that truly engages the student. Students are still able to 'consume' the class and the 'performance' of the professor without being forced to actively participate in it. Let's now examine emerging areas that have been used in accounting that will be promising to further observe and evaluate in the future.

Tom Hood, CEO of the Maryland Association of CPA's, initiated 'CPA Island' (www.cpaisland. com), a place in the virtual community Second Life (www.secondlife.com) where CPA's can attend conferences in the virtual world and even gather CPE credits.

Steven Hornik teaches accounting at the University of Central Florida and he sometimes teaches in his office in Second Life (www.mydebitcredit.com). Hornik also built a virtual learning environment for his students where the students can learn accounting in a more playful setting. Students have to walk with their avatar from one side of the T-Account to the other for different business transactions - until the concept of book entries of debit and credit is well understood. It is possible to use these tools as homework as-

Table 9. Suggested IFRS webcast supplements for the newly created one term IFRS courses

Class Topic	Suggested IFRS Webcast
1: Introduction, First time Adoption and Financial Presentation	AICPA: IFRS: Adopting Global Standards PwC.tv IFRS Ready Videos: What? Why? How? PWC VLC Session 1: First-Time Adoption
2: Revenue, Inventory and Income Tax	PWC VLC Session 1: Revenue Recognition EY: Revenue Recognition Requirements (2/17/09) KPMG: Tax Considerations When Converting PWC: Understanding the Impact on Global Tax
3: Business Combinations, Discontinued Operations and Foreign Currency	PWC VLC Session 3: Business Combinations EY: Mergers and Acquisitions Under IFRS
4: Intangibles and Leases	KPMG: R&D and Intangible Transition (02/04/09) PWC VLC Session 2: Internally Generated Intangibles PWC VLC Session 3: Leases
5: Property and Asset Impairment	EY: Long-Lived Assets: Recognition and Impairment PWC VLC Session 2: Property, Plant and Equipment PWC VLC Session 2: Impairments of Nonfinancial Assets
6: Provisions, Pensions and Share Based Payments	EY: Accounting for Pensions in an IFRS World EY: Share-Based Payments in and IFRS World PWC VLC Session 1: Provisions & Contingencies PWC VLC Session 4: Employee Benefits
7. Financial Instruments	EY:IFRS: Fair Values and Financial Instruments(12/15/08) KPMG: Financial Instruments, Fair Value (12/18/08) PWC VLC Session 5: Financial Instruments
8. Consolidation and Joint Ventures	EY: Accounting for Consolidations in an IFRS World PWC VLC Session 3: Consolidations
9. Convergence and Standard Setting Activities	Deloitte: GAAP & IFRS Convergence: Bridging the Divide SEC: Proposing a Roadmap Toward IFRS-Christopher Cox Lubin School: Global Integration of Accounting Standards

signments and to receive verification whether students successfully performed the book entries for a certain percentage of transactions.

Resorting back to the idea of Cyber Guest Lecturers, it is possible to establish certain Cyber Guest Lecturers as role models for the students and to motivate students to actively participate in their learning experience by using the medium of videos. Students could post video responses to Cyber Guest Lecturers and could interact with them and with each other. The advancements in the availability of powerful and affordable software products and cameras for video production are significant and make it possible to assign such products without overstraining students.

During the Fall Semester of 2009, Norbert Tschakert and Mark Holtzblatt are co-innovators of a new program/competition involving student produced IFRS videos that will ultimately be posted on a special Student IFRS Video Competition online channel.

This innovative program was the brainchild of Norbert Tschakert who is a collaborator with Mark Holtzblatt on a variety of IFRS educational initiatives. We have chosen an easy to use and entry-level camcorder, the Kodak Zi8, to demonstrate that this video program can be run at any University around the world regardless of their financial situation. The goal was to reduce costs and complexity as much as possible without sacrificing output quality. We did not want to waste the student's time by dealing with mediocre, non-standardized, and old equipment. Students should be able to focus their attention and energy on content and quality comments. Despite the low costs, the outcome will be the first IFRS video series that is available online exclusively recorded with external microphones for superior sound quality and viewable in High Definition (HD).

The students of both universities are being encouraged to seek out expert interviewees in their chosen IFRS topic. Appendix B includes a complete list of the Student IFRS Video topics. The expert interviewees may be from any city in the United States and for that matter from any country of the world. Both Professor Norbert Tschakert and Mark Holtzblatt had an Adobe Connect license available. Adobe Connect allows conference video calling with Adobe's proprietary Flash Technology. The interviewee only needs to have a standard flash-enabled browser and a high-speed internet connection. Faculty university internet connections are much faster compared to standard DSL connections. For this reason the student interviews will be conducted together with the professors being present. With the Adobe Connect solution the students will be able to schedule interviews with IFRS experts from around the globe and use these interviews in their videos in an acceptable quality.

Another feature of the student video assignments is the creation of a special Discussion Board and Assignment area. Students from the same group and also from other groups will be able to communicate questions, solutions and other areas of common concern as the video project progresses. Also, various community experts in video production will be able to conduct brief Q & A sessions to provide students support regarding technical production questions. We have also prepared a comprehensive and continuously updated list of helpful resources to aid students. Appendix C includes a list of the online resources being provided to the student groups.

CONCLUSION: BENEFITS FOR PROFESSORS AND STUDENTS

As we have seen, the proliferating body of IFRS webcasts and online videos allows professors to sidestep traditional obstacles of finding and bringing quality IFRS guest lecturers into classrooms. Numerous guest speakers that are IFRS experts are much more accessible. Whether a university is located in a rural location far from a big city or in the smallest village in the furthest corner of the world, experts in IFRS may be brought in to address a class, as long as the requisite equipment and internet connection exists. This presentation has consolidated into one study the majority of IFRS webcasts and online videos currently available. Professors have readily available access to a growing and organized body of stimulating and timely information that relates to and facilitates IFRS discussions.

On the other hand, students respond enthusiastically to innovative technology applications in the classroom, which these IFRS multimedia presentations can certainly be classified as. These webcasts and online videos help students grasp the IFRS subject matter. Students tend to have a heightened interest in presentations knowing that they are learning from a recognized expert (i.e., "Big 4" Partner, Regulatory Commissioner, Professional Institute Officer). In addition, students can watch the online webcasts repeatedly as all the presentations are archived. Students can also be assigned innovative IFRS video group projects to help them gain experience with leading edge communication technologies and first-hand interaction with IFRS experts worldwide.

In a sense online videos and IFRS have a lot in common. Just as online videos are new and exciting and symbolize change and growth, IFRS has been a success and growth story of its own that promises far reaching changes. Bringing online videos and IFRS together leads to an astonishing effect with students. They immediately understand that IFRS is new, will quickly replace the old status quo and simply symbolizes change and adoption in a changing world.

Thus, professors and students alike should benefit from exploring the numerous IFRS webcasts and videos that have been created and which will undoubtedly multiply as the world progresses towards the adoption of IFRS.

REFERENCES

Alfredson, K., Leo, K., Picker, R., Pacter, P., Radford, J., & Wise, V. (2007). *Applying international financial reporting standards* (1st ed.). Milton, Australia: John Wiley & Sons Australia.

Ghose, C. (2008). *Business schools ramping up for switch to global accounting rules*. Retrieved August 29, 2008, from http://www.bizjournals.com/columbus/stories/ 2008/09/01/story8.html

Illinois, C. P. A. Society – ICPAS. (2009). Academics ask for more classroom materials. *INSIGHT Magazine* Jan. & Feb. 2009, p. 32.

Iwata, E. (2009). *U.S. considers costly switch to international accounting rules*. Retrieved September 28, 2009, from http://www.usatoday.com/money/companies/regulation/2009-01-05-international-accounting-rule-switch_N.htm?loc=interstitialskip

Kieso, D. E., Weygandt, J. J., & Warfield, T. D. (2010). *Intermediate accounting* (13th ed.). Hoboken, NJ: John Wiley & Sons.

KPMG. LLP. (2008). *University professors weigh in on building IFRS into curricula: Small number of universities will be ready for 2008-2009 academic year*. Retrieved October 27, 2009, from http://www.financialexecutives.org/eweb/upload/FEI/ KPMG%20AAA%20IFRS%20Professor%20Survey%20Press%20Release_9.4.08.pdf

KPMG. LLP. (2009). *Faculty in KPMG-AAA survey see U.S. economy, students impacted without adoption of global accounting standards*. Retrieved September 22, 2009, from http://news.prnewswire.com/DisplayReleaseContent.aspx?ACCT=104&STORY=/www/story/09-22-2009/0005098454&EDATE=

Lamoreaux, M. G. (2009). *G-20: Achieve single set of global accounting standards by June 2011*. Retrieved September 27, 2009, from http://www.journalofaccountancy.com/ Web/20092188.htm

Nilsen, K. (2008). *On the verge of an academic revolution: How IFRS is affecting accounting education*. Retrieved December 20, 2009, from http://www.journalofaccountancy.com/Issues/2008/Dec/OnTheVergeOfAnAcademicRevolution

Pickard, G. (2007). *Simplifying global accounting: IASB chair discusses the future of IFRS, U.S. GAAP and the global accounting profession*. Retrieved November 12, 2009, from http://www.journalofaccountancy.com/Issues/2007/Jul/SimplifyingGlobalAccountingSirDavidTweedieInterview.htm

PricewaterhouseCoopers LLP. (2008). PricewaterhouseCoopers launches online video resource for transitioning to IFRS. Retrieved November 20, 2008, from http://www.pwc.com/us/en/press-releases/pwc-launches-online-video-resource-for-transitioning-to-ifrs.jhtml

University of Dayton. (2009). *Credit crisis adds uncertainty to international accounting transition, most business schools not preparing students*. Retrieved January 16, 2009, from http://www.udayton.edu/News/Detail/?contentID=22352

Wiecek, I. M., & Young, N. M. (2009). *IFRS primer: International GAAP basics* (1st ed.). Hoboken, NJ: John Wiley & Sons.

APPENDIX A: Partial Syllabus with Assigned Videos and Webcast Excerpts from the Roosevelt University Course "Global Accounting: The IASB and IFRS"

IFRS e-Learning Modules, Homework Assignments and
IFRS Online Videos and Webcasts to be Viewed

May 30

Introduction to the Course Materials, the IASB and IFRS. How to access the e-IFRS and the IFRS e-learning modules. In-class viewing of introductory IFRS videos by the AICPA & PricewaterhouseCoopers. Review the six articles assigned for reading regarding the demand for IFRS expertise.

AICPA Video: IFRS: Adopting Global Standards

http://www.ifrs.com/video.html

PricewaterhouseCoopers PWC.tv IFRS Videos

Go to attached link and click on (1) "See What's On", (2) "Channel 3", and (3) IFRS Ready videos "What" "Why" "How" http://www.pwc.tv/

June 6

1. IFRS Module "Framework for Preparation of Financial Statements"
2. IFRS Module for IAS 1 "Presentation of Financial Statements" Do these two modules for homework. Hand in assessment results for both modules.
3. Read Wiecek Ch. 1 and 2, and hand in answers for Ch. 1: Question 3 Ch. 2: Questions 1, 3, 6

Video Interview with Sir David Tweedie, Chairman of the IASB (May 27, 2009)

Go to this link and register to view the webcast, which lasts for 60 minutes. For Week 2 we will view the first 18 minutes during the class session. http://www.visualwebcaster.com/event.asp?id=57978

June 13

1. IFRS Module for IAS 7 "Cash Flow Statements" (Only do the "Overview" and "Preparation of Cash Flow Statements", not the other parts)
2. IFRS Module for IAS 2 "Inventories" Hand in the module assessments for the Inventories module only.
3. Read Wiecek Ch. 3 and Ch. 7 and hand in Ch. 3 Question 2 and 4 Ch. 7 Question 4

June 20

1. IFRS Module for IAS 16 "Property, Plant and Equipment"
2. IFRS Module for IAS 40 "Investment Property"
3. Read Wiecek Ch. 10, 11, and 13 and hand in Ch. 10 Question 2, 4 Ch. 11 Question 2, 3 Ch. 13 Question 1, 2

PWC Video from the IFRS Video Learning Center - Property, Plant, and Equipment

Go to the following link for the PWC IFRS Video Learning Center and view the Session 2 video dealing with Property, Plant and Equipment http://www.pwc.com/usifrs/vlc

June 27
1. IFRS Module for IAS 38 "Intangible Assets"
2. IFRS Module for IAS 36 "Impairment of Assets"
3. Read Wiecek Ch. 15 and 16 and hand in Ch. 15 Question 2, 3 Ch. 16 Question 2, 3

PWC Video from the IFRS Video Learning Center - Impairment of Assets

http://www.pwc.com/usifrs/vlc Session 2 – Impairments of Non-Financial Assets

PWC Video from the IFRS Video Learning Center – Internally Generated Intangibles

http://www.pwc.com/usifrs/vlc Session 2 – Internally Generated Intangibles

July 11
Mid-Term Exam

July 18
1. IFRS Module for IAS 18 "Revenue"
2. IFRS Module for IAS 11 "Construction Contracts"
3. Read Wiecek Ch. 6 and 8 and hand in Ch. 6 Questions 1, 2, 3 Ch. 8 Questions 1

Webcast from EY Thought Center - Proposed Changes to Revenue Recognition Requirements

This webcast (2/17/09) discusses the joint Discussion Paper issued on December 19, 2008, by the FASB and the IASB. The paper proposed a new model for the recognition of revenue, thereby changing the landscape for both US GAAP and IFRS. http://webcast.ey.com/thoughtcenter/default.aspx

Video from PWC IFRS Video Learning Center – Revenue Recognition

http://www.pwc.com/usifrs/vlc Session 1 – Revenue Recognition. This video discusses both IAS 18 and IAS 11.

July 25
1. IFRS Module for IAS 8 "Accounting Policies Changes in Estimates and Errors"
2. IFRS Module for IAS 37 "Provisions, Contingent Liabilities and Contingent Assets"
3. Read Wiecek Ch. 5 and 21 and hand in Ch. 5 Questions 1, 3, 5 Ch. 21 Question 2

Video from PWC IFRS Video Learning Center – Provisions, Contingencies

http://www.pwc.com/usifrs/vlc Session 1 – Provisions Contingencies. This video discusses IAS 37.

Aug. 1
Research Paper due on Accounting for Financial Instruments

KPMG IFRS Institute Webcast

International Update on Accounting for Financial Instruments, Fair Value Measurements. From December 18, 2008. www.kpmgifrsinstitute.com

Video from PWC IFRS Video Learning Center – Financial Instruments

http://www.pwc.com/usifrs/vlc Session 5 – Classification, Measurement and Impairment. This video discusses IAS 39 and related recent developments.

Aug. 8

1. IFRS Module for IAS 21 "Foreign Exchange Rates"
2. IFRS Module for IAS 28 "Investments in Associates"
3. Read Wiecek Ch. 35 and 30 and hand in Ch. 35 Question 1, 2, 3, 4 Ch. 30 Question 1 and 2

Aug. 15

Exam II

APPENDIX B: Topics for the Student IFRS Video Projects

IFRS video topics San Diego State University

Group #	Topic
1	**The U.S. Roadmap to IFRS** Present and explain the content of the SEC 'Roadmap for the Potential Use of Financial Statements Prepared in Accordance with International Financial Reporting Standards by U.S. Issuers'. Discuss the seven milestones. Discuss Mary Shapiro's position on adopting IFRS in the U.S. Discuss to what degree market forces might dwarf the SEC's decision authority. Focus your work on a discussion of selected pro and con comment letters that were due on April 30, 2009. http://www.sec.gov/spotlight/ifrsroadmap.htm
2	**FASB & IASB Conceptual Framework Project** *"The objective of the Conceptual Framework Project, a joint project of the FASB and IASB, is to develop an improved common conceptual framework that provides a sound foundation for developing future accounting standards. Such a framework is essential to fulfilling the Boards' goal of developing standards that are principles-based, internally consistent, and internationally converged and that lead to financial reporting that provides the information capital providers need to make decisions in their capacity as capital providers."*http://www.fasb.org/project/conceptual_framework.shtml The current IASB Framework is 20 years old and it is challenging to resolve accounting issues with the current framework as prescribed by IAS 8 (Accounting Policies, Changing in Accounting Estimates and Errors). During the Conceptual Framework Project, the FASB and IASB discovered that revising the Frameworks is not a trivial task. The 'final' publication date has been delayed multiple times and is now stated as 'End of 2011'. Describe the scope and importance of this project and focus your work on the many problems involved.
3	**IFRS in Canada and Mexico** Explain the rationale behind Canada's (2011) and Mexico's (2012) decision to adopt IFRS. Why did these countries make this decision despite the uncertainty of the events in the U.S.? How do they benefit from it? What is the current status on the transition? Do companies in Canada or Mexico need more time?
4	**IFRS for Small and Medium Sized Entities (SMEs)** Provide an overview of the new Standard 'IFRS for Small and Medium-sized Entities (SMEs)' and compare selected accounting rules to IFRS for public companies. Is it attractive to use this standard? What are potential problems? What nations have approved the use of 'IFRS for SMEs' to date? What is the AICPA's perspective on this new standard for U.S. companies? What are opinions of managers in medium sized businesses in the U.S.? What is the IASB doing to promote this Standard? Should additional steps be taken?
5	**Standard Setting and Political Lobbying** Explain 'highlights' of the political threats and lobbying that the FASB and the IASB had to go through since their inception. How did the IASB react in each of those incidents? How was this different for the FASB? Has the IASB learned from these events and is the IASB independent for the future as requested in the Roadmap? A focus of your work should be Sir David Tweedie's responses in the U.K. Parliament regarding changes to fair value accounting.

Group #	Topic
6	**IFRS and Accounting Scandals** Briefly present some of the biggest Accounting Scandals that have occurred throughout the world under US-GAAP and under IFRS. Are these really Accounting Scandals or rather breakdowns of Corporate Governance? Describe what has happened in each case and if the applicable set of accounting standards might have contributed to these scandals. Focus your work on the questions whether IFRS would have made matters worse or better in the particular case under review.
7	**IFRS and International Auditing Standards** *"The International Auditing and Assurance Standards Board (IAASB) serves the public interest by: setting, independently and under its own authority, high quality standards dealing with auditing, review, other assurance, quality control and related services, and facilitating the convergence of national and international standards."* http://www.ifac.org/IAASB What is the importance of International Auditing Standards and explain in how far these standards relate to U.S. Auditing Standards. Find citations for IFAC President Robert L. Bunting that indicates his opinion on IFRS. To what extent are International Auditing Standards important for IFRS? Provide an overview of current IAASB projects.
8	**Non-Accounting Implications of Adopting IFRS** Adopting IFRS is not purely an accounting exercise. For example, consultants frequently advise to also upgrade and harmonize all IT Systems as part of the Transition to IFRS. Is this really necessary? How about implications for HR and Top Management? Show in detail what areas of a company are affected by the transition to IFRS.
9	**IFRS and XBRL** Extensible Business Reporting Language (XBRL) is understood to have the potential to 'revolutionize' business information. Explain how this 'Revolution' would impact Financial Reporting under IFRS. Refer to the IASB Exposure Draft 'IFRS Taxonomy 2009'. Show examples of how companies are using XBRL in Financial Reporting. Simplify the complex issues behind the two different taxonomies (IASB and U.S.), so that a person with little technical background is able to understand the challenges involved. What are problems surrounding XBRL?
10	**IFRS Implications and Experiences for a major So Cal-based Multinational Corporation** Identify a multinational Southern California-based Corporation and investigate their background and history of global growth. Examine the mention and application of IFRS in their annual report. Potential interviewees include executives in Accounting, Finance, IT and HR. To what extent are they impacted by IFRS and what is their overall view on IFRS?

IFRS video topics Roosevelt University

Group #	Topic
1	**"IFRS as written by the IASB" vs. "IFRS as adopted"** Different nuances in IFRS Application around the world are currently a major concern that jeopardizes the comparability of Financial Statements, frequently cited to be the main benefit of Global Accounting Standards. Why have such modifications arisen? Give examples of such nations. What are current approaches to mitigate these concerns and how realistic is it that these will be sufficient to establish a standardized application around the world? What are additional options?
2	**IFRS Expertise and the Employment Market Impact** Research job search websites such as Indeed.com. Survey job descriptions and describe the positions and IFRS related duties that companies are looking for. Contact local executive recruiters for their perspectives and interview them. Gather, list and evaluate all available IFRS Certificates and Diplomas. What should students do now to ready themselves for IFRS related careers?
3	**Educational Implications of the IFRS Revolution** What is the current status of IFRS education in the U.S.? Compare the infusion approach (full curriculum integration approach) to the stand-alone approach. Give examples of schools using each approach. Compare the development of U.S. IFRS education with that in Canadian universities. What insights into IFRS education progress in the U.S. is offered by area professors.
4	**Valuation Under IFRS: Fair Value vs. Historical Cost** IFRS allows the use of fair value or historical cost valuation for a variety of accounts. Research the various valuation alternatives allowed under IFRS. Survey the use of the alternative valuation methods in the European Union, U.S. and other nations. What are considerations in choosing and implementing a valuation method? Survey actual financial statement excerpts of corporations that have incorporated fair values into their financial statements. Discuss the costs vs. benefits in the application of fair value.
5	**IFRS Enforcement Issues** The creation of IFRS is only one part of the equation. There is also the question of how to enforce the standards. Research how enforcement of IFRS takes place within the countries of the European Union and other nations. What is IOSCO? Trace the history of IOSCO's involvement with the IASB. Research the prospects for effective uniform enforcement of IFRS in the future under a global regulatory system rather than the fragmented nationalistic structure currently in place.

Group #	Topic
6	**IFRS Implications and Experiences for a Major Chicago based Multinational Corporation** Identify a multinational Chicago-based Corporation and investigate their background and history of global growth. Examine the mention and application of IFRS in their annual report. Potential interviews include executives involved with the Accounting, Finance, HR and Information Technology functions as to the impact and planning related to IFRS and their overall view on IFRS.
7	**IFRS Critics** Several very prominent regulators, practitioners and professors have been harsh critics of IFRS. Examine the arguments of these IFRS critics and also the negative comments to the Roadmap by respondents that were due April 20, 2009. Research and discuss the U.S. judicial and legal considerations related to arguments against IFRS in the U.S. Are these valid considerations...why or why not?
8	**IFRS and the Implications of Lifo Elimination in the U.S.** Examine the issues involved in the U.S. of the potential elimination of Lifo. Interview tax experts in addition to performing background research into this issue. What are the opinions of various U.S. executives of corporations, public accounting firms and government tax authorities and regulators? What are possible solutions to this problem?

APPENDIX C: Online IFRS Student Video Competition: Helpful Resources

YouTube.com Producer Handbook:

http://www.youtube.com/t/yt_handbook_produce

Please review this handbook closely for technical requirements (accepted file formats etc.), and define technical standards for your group. This will greatly improve the workflow in your group.

Videomaker.com Tips and Tutorials:

http://www.videomaker.com/learn

Student Film Makers:

http://www.studentfilmakers.com

Access to Non-Copyrighted Material:

http://digitalmedia.jhu.edu/learning/documentation/opensource

Windows Movie Maker (included in Windows Vista):

http://www.microsoft.com/windows/windows-vista/features/movie-maker.aspx

Apple iMovie '09:

http://www.apple.com/ilife/imovie

Apple Final Cut Express:

http://www.apple.com/finalcutexpress

Apple Final Cut Pro:

http://www.apple.com/finalcutstudio/finalcutpro

Adobe Premiere Elements 7

http://www.adobe.com/products/premiereel

Online Media Technologies Ltd.: AVS Video Editor

www.AVS4You.com

Chapter 18
Developing Interactive Dramatised Videos as a Teaching Resource

Alastair Tombs
University of Queensland, Australia

Doan Nguyen
University of Queensland, Australia

ABSTRACT

This chapter presents a reflection of the development of dramatized video cases as a resource for use in teaching marketing. It explains the benefits of developing and the pitfalls with making this sort of interactive media. The benefits of using dramatized video scenarios as a teaching resource are: a) they facilitate problem based learning; b) they provide the student with a realistic view of the ethical decisions that are faced by marketing managers, and c) they keep the class learning at the same pace. The development of a multi-platform format means that the videos can be streamed into lectures and tutorial groups, published as streaming content on Web based platforms such as Blackboard and/or downloaded onto students' cell phones and iPods. However, the problems associated with developing this sort of resource are the cost and time required to make a high quality and credible dramatized case study.

INTRODUCTION

A common challenge faced by educators of applied courses such as marketing is to combine theory and practice into the learning activities of students. Students are commonly taught the

concepts and theories that underpin 'real world' marketing activities and so build up a toolbox of skills from which they can draw upon in a given circumstance. However they are rarely challenged in marketing courses to choose specific skills from that toolbox and apply these skills to an actual business situation (Diamond, Koernig, & Iqbal, 2008). Students' lack of ability to select

DOI: 10.4018/978-1-60960-800-2.ch018

the method appropriate for a given situation and apply these concepts in their post graduation employment has been widely criticized, both here in Australia and overseas (Business Council of Australia, 2006; Bennett, 2002; McClymont, Volkov, Gardiner, Behjat, & Geoghegan, 2005). Yet it is considered a major goal of most tertiary institutions to produce graduates that are able to deal with a complex and dynamic world, solve problems in a rational and reasoned manner, and do this within ethical and moral guidelines (Choi & Lee, 2008). Dacko (2006) identified decision making, problem formulation, persuasion and negotiation as important skill weaknesses that need developed among future marketers. These are skills that go beyond content knowledge yet are critical in the students' ability to use the specific course content. This lack of real-world problem solving ability is surprising considering the pro-liferation of literature from all disciplines on the benefits of problem-based and active learning and its underlying philosophy of constructivism (Dalsgaard & Godsk, 2007). In other words as educators we should provide a learning environ-ment that encourages students to question, analyse and problem solve for themselves and so actively construct knowledge.

"The competencies that employers and educators value most include critical thinking, problem solv-ing, working in teams and with diversity, leader-ship, creativity, written and oral communications, etc. Grounding competencies in the real world helps ensure they are relevant to students now and after they graduate" (Mendenhall, 2009 p. 22).

We contend that many of these issues relating to students having the content or course specific knowledge but not knowing how or when to use it comes down to the resources (both in time and tools) available to marketing educators. While the resources for the delivery of theory in marketing courses are readily available, both in hard copy (text books) and online, the resources to help

students relate this theory into practice are more difficult to find. With the increasing demands on academic's time the ability to develop such resources is reduced greatly. Hence academics are increasingly looking for more 'off the shelf' tools to help increase the students' learning and make them ready to meet the demands of future employment. This chapter discusses the rationale for and development of dramatized video scenarios as a teaching resource that will not only increase the students' knowledge of the subject but will also challenge them by showing them realistic situations that need an in-depth knowledge of the topic to enable them to problem solve. It provides a case study of the authors' experience in developing videos to help highlight the issues of developing an 'off the shelf' teaching resource.

THE RATIONALE FOR DEVELOPING PROBLEM BASED LEARNING MATERIALS

The ubiquitous access to the internet has opened up a wealth of video material that can be used as a 'streaming' resource in classroom teaching. On YouTube alone, ten hours of video is uploaded every minute (YouTube.com, 2009a). Access to the internet and hence the delivery of streaming video is relatively simple these days with most classrooms and lecture theatres in tertiary institu-tions having the IT capability to facilitate immedi-ate downloading of video material. Likewise the instructor can easily embed streaming video into their PowerPoint presentations, so now has the ability to play video at any time relevant to the content delivered in that particular class. Unfortu-nately, not all video material available is of high quality, unbiased or even of a length suitable for use in the classroom (Carlson, 2009). While the length of streaming videos is increasing with the increasing capacity of the internet bandwidth most streaming videos is less than 5 minutes duration so doesn't cause length issues yet. More importantly for educators however, is that most streaming video websites such as YouTube, Hulu, Google Video, Blip.tv, Metacafe and Dailymotion provide no vetting as to the content of the video (other than limiting illegal or pornographic content). Therefore, while material is available to cover almost any topic, the validity of the information provided cannot be assumed.

Access to the plethora of video clips that may have the potential to be teaching resources also means that considerable time is involved in searching for and screening of suitable material. For example, a key marketing concept such as 'market segmentation' brings up over 2,100 videos on a YouTube search (YouTube.com, 2009b) and about 3,880 hits on Google Videos (GoogleVideos, 2009a). More specific concepts such as 'customer satisfaction' score over 13,000 hits on Google Videos (GoogleVideos, 2009b). Moreover, concepts like 'service failure' bring up videos that, just on the first page of 10, ranged from three different clips of the George Bush shoe assault (a *secret* service failure) to a six minute rant about spam on YouTube and even a fake video on how to rip-off gas station pumps (GoogleVideos, 2009c). The time required to vet suitable material for their classes is time that must be made by academics already under time pressure to both teach and research. Again finding suitable material that is relevant and can be used as stimulation for students to question and to learn from is becoming more and more difficult. As an example, at the time of writing the top 10 streaming videos related to the "value chain" on YouTube.com include seven video clips of other academics' lectures (either video of them lecturing or just the PowerPoint slides with audio of the lecture), one company promotional video, and one conference panel discussion (YouTube.com, 2009c). While these are informative they are hardly inspiring or likely to capture the students' attention more than the instructor's own performance. So, of the top ten videos that could be streamed into the classroom only one, a documentary style video, is likely to capture students' attention sufficiently to be of benefit in their acquisition of knowledge.

Another issue that must be considered when using steaming or web sourced videos is the issue of copyright. The contents of all videos uploaded onto sites, such as YouTube, are the property of the original producers and are subjected to copyright. Therefore while it appears to be legal to show streaming videos in class provided that a) the class is not conducted for profit and b) the video is streamed directly from a website (Australian Copyright Council, 2009), it becomes illegal if the streaming video is downloaded and saved without prior consent from the respective copyright holder[s]. Likewise if lectures that include streaming video are recorded for students to download at a later date then this may also be a breach of copyright.

The video resources that accompany many of the marketing textbooks don't have these issues associated with running streaming videos from commercial sites such as YouTube.com. Academic publishers' videos are normally course specific. In the case of marketing subjects they generally provide students with an insight into the real-life activities that marketing managers undertake on a day to day basis. However, they are usually filmed in a documentary style which means the content is very descriptive rather than actively engaging. Most of the content is restricted to interviews with marketing managers interspersed with film of the activities of the firm as a backdrop. In other words, these videos present closed ended case studies of a specific firm without challenging the viewer to come up with some explanation or solution. Therefore, while these resources may be instructive and professionally made, the content material doesn't actively engage the student in anything more than passive learning. Videos such as these just become an extension of a one-way teaching method where information is delivered with the assumption that the student will understand without any further explanation or interaction with the instructor (Lee & Sharma, 2008). Moreover, the length of many of these videos exceeds 10 minutes and covers several concepts (in each episode) relative to the chapter they are linked to. Hence students run the risk of cognitive overload (Sweller, van Merrienboer, & Pass, 1998): being exposed to too many new concepts at one time to take in and remember them all. In situations like this it is not possible to turn the video on, let the students take notes while watching (which most of them will not) and expect them to not only retain the material but to reconstruct the ideas in a way that enables understanding and actively constructs knowledge. An active learning approach involves showing the video in short segments each covering one key concept and allowing time to engage the students in discussions or group activities about what they have just seen (Lee & Sharma, 2008).

The other criticisms of the video resources that accompany textbooks are that they are generally American centric and use American terms rather than terms commonly used in Australia and other countries outside the USA. They are also often out of date. An example of this is the same video series has been supplied as a supplement for the 5th, 6th and 7th edition of the main 'principles of marketing' text book used in many introductory marketing courses. While the message may not have changed, students are aware of dated material especially those that are linked to events that anchor them in a particular point in time. The first author's own teaching evaluations have borne evidence of this even though the videos used were only five years old: "use more updated materials" and "some of the videos provided were not that relevant".

Having criticized the currently accessible video resources there are still major benefits that can be obtained by the use of visually stimulating material that engages students and supports learning. In fact video is seen as an integral part of the resources that can be provided to students to support learning (Hill & Hannafin, 2001). However the use of documentary style video presentations where the students are still 'lectured at', is

surprising considering that marketing educators have acknowledged that they are trying to move away from techniques that foster passive learning toward approaches that are seen to improve active or problem based learning (Daly, 2001; Young, Klemz, & Murphy, 2003). Carlson (2009) suggests that the use of video material should be purposeful rather than just taking up time and reducing the effort put in by instructors. Instructors should "integrate the video or multimedia with lectures, frame with discussion questions, show short clips only or otherwise use it to work for you not as a *substitute* for you," (Carlson, 2009, p. 205). One way of doing this is to create or use videos portraying open-ended dramatized case studies.

ARE LECTURES THE APPROPRIATE FORMAT FOR THE DELIVERY OF STREAMING VIDEO?

Despite a growing body of literature that suggests that the didactic lectures so prevalent in our tertiary institutions fail to deliver deep and effective learning experiences it is still the most common way of delivering knowledge (see Jones, 2007 for a review). Choi and Lee (2008) make the observation that many students exposed to a lecture based education "are neither engaged in reflective thinking nor deepening their understanding of the topics taught. Consequently, we suspect some of the knowledge acquired in the lecture-based college class cannot be spontaneously utilized in real-world problem-solving situations" (Choi & Lee, 2008, p. 27). This may be due to the non-interactive nature of most lectures. They are non-interactive because students are given the answers already embedded in the knowledge presented, therefore not allowing the student time or resources to problem solve and/or find the answers themselves (Dalsgaard & Godsk, 2007). We are not saying that all lectures, per se, are detrimental to student learning; we are just suggesting that different ways of delivery must be considered beyond the traditional one-way delivery of information. In fact there are several advantages of the lecture. The experience of the live performance especially from an inspirational lecturer will often linger in the student's memory and stimulate further enquiry and learning (Jones, 2007). Hodgson (2005) refers to this as 'experiences of relevance' in the minds of the student where the student thinks more about the meaning and implications of what has been said. This is taken one step further with 'vicarious experience of relevance' where the student empathizes with the lecturer's enthusiasm for the topic which then stimulates the students' further interest in the subject (Hodgson, 2005). The lecturer is also able to monitor the student's interest and adjust the delivery of content accordingly. Likewise the student can sense cues from the lecturer which can enhance the meaning and relevance of the particular topic (Jones, 2007). These benefits of live performance are not able to be reproduced by books or other recorded media. Despite the advantages of the lecturer's live performance students are still faced with the issue of cognitive overload, especially where vast amounts of information dense material is covered in a short period of time (Cronin Jones, 2003). This issue of cognitive overload also applies to many information rich or long videos that present material in a one-way format. To avoid the problems associated with one-way lectures, and the cognitive overload that is usually associated with them, the lecturer can intersperse the lecture with breaks that allow the students to discuss what was just covered and even have the students' peers explain the material (Cronin Jones, 2003; Larson, 2000). Allowing time for discussion and group activities also allows time for the students to construct their own personal understanding of what has been said or presented. Another possible way of creating breaks in lectures and to encourage interaction, discussion and even group work into the classroom and hence facilitate active learning and problem solving is to use open ended case studies.

BENEFITS OF CASE STUDIES

Case studies that offer open ended scenarios encourage the students' involvement and yet allow the instructor to then direct the discussion of possible endings. This assertion is in line with Dacko's (2006) recommendations that a marketing education framework should be based on classroom debate and discussion, and oral presentations. However, to gain maximum benefit from class discussions Sautter (2007) has suggested that students' expectations must be set regarding the content and the requirement for students to actively listen to other students' comments as part of the learning experience. By guiding students in this way, while still allowing them the freedom to expose their own and their fellow students' creativity in problem solving helps build critical thinking skills and deep learning (Sautter, 2007). Learning then develops through students engaging in problem solving and social negotiation. Problems that arise in most real-life work situations are ill-structured. That is, they are not always simple, governed by stable rules that converge on single solutions but contain all of the interconnections, complexities, randomness and uncertainty that is the world we live in (Zane, 2009). Therefore to prepare students to become practitioners in the real-world we need to expose them to problems and situations that can't be answered through direct reference to a text book. Zane (2009) describes the role we should be training our students for:

In the real world, competent practitioners resolve problems by gathering information, considering pros and cons of situations, using social interaction and or collective problem solving, confronting ineffective strategies as needed, exploring misconceptions, making decisions, self-evaluation and self-correcting mistakes. Exactly how the competent practitioner responds to the problem may include taking certain actions, writing a report, or responding in some other way (Zane, 2009, p. 88).

Unlike closed or structured case studies open-ended case studies are a technique that can be used to present ill-structured problems and so build the competencies of our students. Structured case studies will either provide all of the answers to lead students to one finite solution or just highlight changes that have occurred within a firm due to some intervention (much the same as documentary style video). Therefore they are little more than passive learning approaches. Both sorts of case based videos allow a number of responses to be used, whether they are addressed written or verbally by individuals or groups of students. However open-ended case studies don't provide immediately recognizable solutions. To find a solution requires higher order thinking skills such as interpretation, analysis and manipulation of information. This makes open-ended case studies ideally suited to encouraging class room discussion. Through classroom discussion students become active participants, engaging with the topic and being exposed to multiple perspectives (Larson, 2000). As the problem is addressed the solution comes from the student by using the cognitive processes of constructing outcomes, and hence knowledge, from the range of techniques, concepts and theories that are contained in each student's toolbox of skills. The knowledge of how these techniques, concepts and theories are used enables the student to understand how solutions can be informed by theory and hence see the link between theoretical concepts taught in the classroom and applications in the real world.

As discussed earlier, problem based learning is student-centred and tends to promote deep learning as opposed to traditional lecturing that is teacher-focused and tends toward passive learning (Ma, O'Toole, & Keppell, 2007; Ramsden, 2003). Choi and Johnson (2007) describe this in more detail by proposing that "problem based learning, which uses contextualised problems as the starting point of learning, encourages student-centred learning, utilizes collaborative learning via group discussions, and allows learners to handle more complex and difficult cases by actively and socially constructing knowledge, " (Choi & Johnson, 2007, p. 885) Therefore learning is developed by embedding instruction in authentic, everyday problems (Jonassen, 2004).

ISSUES WITH IN-CLASS DELIVERY OF CASES

From the authors' personal experience, providing students with the opportunity to work through and discuss case studies is easier said than done in a lecture environment where time is limited and large amounts of theory need to be covered. The first author has been trying to encourage case based learning in his sales management classes by each week giving the students ill-structured ethical dilemmas to solve. The material is text based and either projected as a densely written slide as part of a PowerPoint presentation or delivered by a written handout. Due to the variation in reading ability within the student cohort some students are finished reading the case very quickly while others take a long time to read and comprehend the information given. This is the case even when relatively short scenarios are given. The problem of differential comprehension rates is compounded in classes with a high proportion of international students where English is a second language. Therefore, it becomes difficult for the instructor to know when to start discussing the ethical problem. The differential rates of reading also poses the dilemma of either catering to the lowest common denominator and having the students wait until everyone has finished reading, or starting at an earlier point and have only have half the class in a position to interact and participate. This has resulted in the instructor reading aloud the cases to the class. Although the content and purpose of the case is transmitted to the students, reading doesn't often create the dynamic portrayal of the ethical dilemma the way a video would. Hence engagement of the students is sometimes questionable. The use of video stimuli that portray real-life problems are more effective for learner satisfaction, comprehension and retention than the use of text based instruction (Choi & Johnson, 2007; Shyu, 2000). Therefore, this format of delivering case studies in class has advantages over text based material as it overcomes the variation in reading ability within the student cohort. The development of a multi-platform format means that the videos can be streamed into lectures and tutorial groups, and so all students are exposed to the material at the same rate. The other advantage of this form of delivery is that it can be published as streaming content on web based platforms such as Blackboard and/or downloaded onto the students' cell phone and iPod. Moreover making the video available as streaming media, students can access the content again at a later time. Students can use the material individually to guide a written component such as a set assignment or as the focus for informal study groups and so further extend the effectiveness beyond the classroom. Streaming videos may also be used in formal study situations such as tutorials where the problem solving and solutions may be constructed under the guidance of a tutor/facilitator. It also provides valid material that has been written and produced specifically to engage students with one particular concept and therefore helps eliminate the need for students to view or download material from the internet that may not be conceptually correct.

The benefits of using dramatized video scenarios as a teaching resource are: a) they facilitate problem based learning, b) they provide the student with a realistic view of the ethical decisions that are faced by sales and marketing managers in a format that is easy to comprehend, and c) keeps the class learning at the same pace. More importantly dramatized video cases appear to be far more engaging of the students' attention and imagination than the documentary style video. As the characters in dramatized videos are fictitious then it becomes easier to remove any temporal location. In other words it avoids an issue common to case studies: that is references to specific events in a company that may fix a specific date to the time when the scenarios were made. This non-time specific aspect that can be designed into dramatized videos has the advantage that it can expand the effective life of these videos.

The next section of this chapter outlines the authors' experience with the production of streaming video compatible resources for teaching marketing to second and third year tertiary students. As such it discusses in detail the development issues and pitfalls associated with a series of dramatized case-based scenarios. The goal of this project was to encourage problem based learning. Any resource should provide the students with an opportunity to: a) gain an insight into the decision making activities business managers face on a day to day basis, b) make the students aware of the ethical issues that business managers must deal with, and c) help provide an interactive and engaging format to enhance the students' learning. These goals were able to be achieved by producing a pedagogically sound set of examples that help students construct the knowledge and ability to apply theoretical concepts to situations the students are likely to encounter once they graduate. By using characters in the video series of similar age to the student cohort we hoped that the students would relate to the situations in each episode better than they would relate to watching older sales and marketing managers talking about their respective firms as is the case with many videos that accompany the marketing text books. Dramatization should also overcome the issues with documentary style resources so often used for teaching into an applied subject such as marketing.

PRODUCING DRAMATIZED CASE-BASED VIDEOS: A HOW TO GUIDE

This part of the chapter will review what we believe are the five important steps that should be taken in order to produce streaming video for higher education students.

1. Overcoming the inertia.
2. Pulling the money together.
3. Designing the story.
4. Producing the videos.
5. Distributing the videos.

For each of these steps an example of producing a dramatized case-based video (The Internship Series) will be provided as a case study.

Step 1: Overcoming the Inertia

Although marketing educators understand the importance of using streaming videos as an integral resource in their teaching, there are several inertia related factors that prevent this process from happening. These factors include the instructor's motivation (or lack of), the energy to push the envelope and hence drive the project through many bureaucratic hurdles that are the system of large tertiary institutions, to overcoming the 'impossible-to-break' hesitation from the management to provide the financial resources necessary to adopt innovative approaches to teaching. Teaching using an active learning or problem based approach does require a lot more effort and organization on behalf of the instructor than just delivering a pre-prepared lecture (especially where the lecture has been delivered many times before). Therefore to develop and drive a change to this format of delivery requires energy, motivation, and time from the instructor. These are often hard things to find in an already heavy workload.

The production of case-based videos raises two main issues that must be addressed before such teaching resources can be developed. First and most importantly is the credibility of the scenarios. Because of the high levels of exposure to film and television that students experience in their everyday lives anything less that a professional standard of production would be treated with cynicism and mistrust by the students. This in itself takes a large amount of thought to ensure the story lines are believable and relevant, and that they portray issues that are likely to be seen by the students as the issues that they may encounter in their postgraduate employment. Second, even once the content of the videos has been decided the next most significant hurdle that needs to be overcome is the costs involved with production. To produce a series of case-based videos to a professional standard requires considerable expense both financially and in the time and effort of those involved.

The Internship Series Case: Overcoming the Inertia

Hesitation from management to adopt innovative approaches to teaching was experienced by the authors. An attempt to apply for a teaching grant to construct a series of 12 video scenarios to teach into a Selling course and International Marketing course was turned down by the department. The reason given was that the department saw no value added to the students' learning by producing these videos. The grant was later picked up by Pearson Publishing who commissioned the production of the entire series. In so doing, the ownership and rights to the resource were lost to the school.

These inertia factors often destroy video projects before they can be even developed. However it is not recommended that instructor's intent on producing these resources ignore these inertia factors and move straight ahead to the next stage. The ideal solution is to outline all factors that are likely to occur with the development team and address each of them. Any project development will be underdone and will result in damage to the project in the long run unless all the stakeholders understand and believe in the rationale of the project. After the entire team agrees on the rationale of the project, the project leader must ensure that all members have the appropriate level of commitment and resources required to pursue and complete it.

Tips:

Write down a series of WHYs. Why do we need this project? Why can't we use current resources? Why can't we do something simpler, written material for example? If the marketing educators think that all the WHY questions can be satisfactorily answered, they will be better prepared to take this video proposal to the senior management to seek funding.

Step 2: Pulling the Money Together

For several reasons funding an educational video project is much more difficult than corporate or training videos in the private sector. First, educational institutions are generally in a more fiscally restrained situation than companies in the private sector. Second, an educational video is typically used to accompany other teaching material such as textbooks or other paper-based reading resources. A good quality video is expensive to produce, and yet only adds an incremental value to the final teaching resource. Third, video production reaches into another area which is totally beyond academia. Thus, academic "in house" expertise is seldom available. When the production relies on out-sourced labor, the expense will start mounting up. Finally, there will always be a debate about how professional the video should look. The more professional the video is and the more complicated the content is, the more expensive the production is going to be. However, with the development of technology and the reduction in relative costs of amateur equipment, technology savvy students can easily produce their own videos with respectable quality. Therefore, this must set the benchmark for marketing educators. If video resources are to be produced, they need to appear more professional than those produced by students to gain sufficient credibility.

There are three stages in a typical video production: pre-production, in-production and post-production. Pre-production includes conceptualizing the story, storyboarding, casting, meetings between the production company and the client, and defining the brief. Production companies typically will not charge the clients for pre-production meetings. However, if the pre-production involves field trips, auditions, casting, and negotiating access to locations for filming then these factors should be considered when budgeting. The in-production stages are the most costly process for a typical educational video. It includes all filming activities. Upfront expenses are required to pay director and producer's fees, some venue/location hire, props and costumes. During filming expenses (on set expenses) include catering, makeup/costume and incidentals. Expenses incurred after the filming process will be the actual hours of work from actors, technical crew and time spent for transferring film stock. Post-production includes editing and publishing the videos. The post-production for educational videos is relatively inexpensive compared to in-production costs. Pitfalls for this stage will be discussed later.

Although budget is a "must" in producing good quality educational videos, it should not be a prohibitive factor. Funding can be obtained from multiple sources; the amount of, access to, and competition for this funding will vary with different institutions. It is beyond the scope of this chapter to recommend how to apply for funding suffice to say that there are funding opportunities (grant schemes) at an institutional, state or federal level as well as corporate sponsorship.

Tips:

To minimise the cost in the pre-production stage, marketing educators could: a) try to use as much free resources as possible (for example: free loca-

tions, drama students as cast, student extras); b) try to choose as many internal locations as possible (opposed to choosing external locations) as it is easier to eliminate factors such as background noise (e.g. the noise of a car passing the building) or effects of the sun (time of day) that mean that the scenes must be filmed again or even on another day; c) choose shooting locations that are logistically close to one another (saves on time being lost and additional costs incurred in travel between locations); d) reduce the number of different locations to as few as possible (saves on set-up costs); e) choose the production house that can handle the whole filming process (this is often cheaper than using several different firms); and f) know exactly the story the instructor wants to tell via the video (this avoids costly changes to production schedule, or even re-filming sections after completion if changes are made once the production starts).

To minimize the cost during the filming process, choose a production company that has worked with educational institutions before as this specific experience is invaluable to the instructor looking to develop video-based teaching resources. It helps the instructor achieve an appropriate outcome within a reasonable price. Experienced production companies can help choose the most appropriate location and recommend appropriate tools/equipment suitable for an educational purpose. For example, an experienced production company will know that filming in a natural classroom setting will save the cost of paying extra actors. However, they will not recommend it as being the overall most cost effective way of capturing the scene. Filming in a natural classroom environment will take more time and coordination effort therefore, off setting any cost savings on extras. Shots in a natural classroom environment cannot be re-taken therefore there is only one chance to capture the scene. If there are any factors that may interrupt the filming such as external noise or a student interrupting then the

opportunity to retake this scene is lost. This will have an affect on the final product as these things often can't be edited out in post production. Further, the crew has to work out of their comfort zone to make the filming activities as least intrusive as possible. In sum, using natural and free resources from schools would typically be recommended by less experienced production companies in order to save costs, however it will not be the most cost effective solution for the instructors.

Choosing an un-professional or inexperienced production company may appear affordable at the beginning. However, the cost will come later with in-efficiency, poor results or the possibility of having to re-film parts. The total cost might be higher than the choice of a professional and experienced production company.

The Internship Series Case: Pulling the Money Together (Funding)

Funding seeking activities for the Internship Series appeared to be difficult for the very reasons outlined in the first step. The inertia of senior management was impossible to break and so internal funding was not available. This meant that we had to look for corporate funding to produce this series of teaching videos. One organization that was known to fund the development of teaching resources (albeit in the form of written texts) was Pearson Higher Education: the publishers of many of the textbooks used in Australian universities. The concept of the series was pitched to a resource development manager (not the book representative) from Pearson Higher Education. Fortunately the resource development manager was open to the concept and went through the 'front-line-battle' with the senior management on our behalf and got the concept approved.

This was a unique case to start with as there was no precedent in Australia. For markets where these sorts of precedents already have occurred funding sources for this type of project should not be that difficult.

Step 3: Designing the Story

The production of case-based videos raises two main issues that must be addressed before such teaching resources could be developed. The first and most important issue is the credibility of the scenarios. Because of the high levels of exposure to film and television that students experience in their everyday lives anything less that a professional standard of production would be treated with cynicism and mistrust by the students. Moreover, the story lines have to be believable and relevant. They have to portray issues that are likely to be seen by the students as the issues that they may encounter in their postgraduate employment. Second, writing an educational story that carries pedagogical value requires not only creative writing skills but theoretical knowledge about the subject of interest. However, unlike other forms of creative writing, screen writing requires specific training and experience. Inexperience potentially leads to an in-executable script. As previously discussed, for the video to be an effective learning tool students must be able to gain enough information so as to understand the problem or issues raised but not be so structured that the solution is obviously identifiable. Ideally, the concept comes from an academic, and the writing comes from a trained script writer. This collaboration between the two parties leads to sensible scripted educational videos. Apart from getting the script to accurately portray the ethical dilemma or other teaching problem, writing a well developed script is also critical for the costing of the production. An academic or a lay person is more likely to develop a script that is not technically executable or a script that is expensive to complete. Marketing educators should accept that video production including scripting is a professional field, and therefore should leave the work for the professionals regardless of how knowledgeable the marketers are about the subject of interest. For example, an academic would write a story about a marketing case study. To make a nice

and convincing story the academic would have multiple characters with complicated dialog and include detailed description of the product, the brand, and store setting. The amateur script writer could simply write "the customer walks into a popular restaurant, glances at a glass cabinet full of inviting food. She looks up, smiles at a friendly young employee at the counter and slowly orders the food". An experienced script writer on the other hand would write: "A customer approaches the counter at a restaurant. The customer (smiles at the employee): "May I have …" The difference between the two pieces of writing is that the first one will require more resources for: a) getting extra cast to set up a popular restaurant, b) setting up the food cabinet, and c) getting cast based on specific requirements such as a young and/or friendly looking employee. These things have been eliminated by the experienced script writer without detracting from the message to be portrayed. Therefore by using the professional scriptwriter, the video production will cost less in terms of cast, props and time. Moreover complicated scripting can only be convincingly delivered by professional actors, who in most cases will not do pro bono work: this again adds to the cost. Unless these extra costs provide some pedagogical advantage or value they should not be included. A simple script costs less and also gives the producers flexibility to execute the shooting on schedule.

The Internship Series Case: Designing the Story (Pre-Production Work)

A series of video scenarios based on ethical situations faced by managers and relating to the current week's teaching was produced. The scenarios were conceived by a marketing academic based on previous work experience and the relevant theory to be covered in the teaching week. An experienced script writer was then employed to turn these ideas into a workable script. The outcome of this collaboration was a 60 page long script written in the form of a TV drama series. This series was broken in to 10 different marketing dilemmas. Each of the 10 different scenarios followed on from each other using the same two main characters in each case. This meant that the instructor could use one per week for the majority of the semester. The characters are involved in changing situations that mirrored the learning objectives of that week. To ensure a professional looking product was produced a professional film production company was employed for the filming and post production editing. The series of videos clips are called the Internship Series. The story line was developed around the following synopsis:

Two graduates apply for job at a marketing firm. The firm specialises in several aspects of marketing including event marketing, integrated marketing communication, and marketing research. Both graduates are top class, well trained and very competitive. They are both offered internship positions in the firm. Their first assignment is to work as a team and win an account with a global giant in the hi-tech telecommunication industry. To win that account, the two graduates not only have to use the skills they have learnt at university, but also have to handle ethical issues and dilemmas that were not mentioned in their textbook. Their lives are not getting any easier when they have to work together everyday to win the account with the aim to secure a long term position in the firm – a position that might accommodate only one of them.

The scripts were written in such a way that the activity on the screen was dramatized rather than the normal documentary style video. The intention of this format was to avoid students guessing the results of the marketing dilemma without considerable thought and discussion. For example the characters might be faced with the dilemma of whether or not their marketing firm should use sex appeal in advertising. The drama is designed to last approximately three minutes

then stops to allow the instructor time to encourage the students to continue the debate. If required the instructor could then restart the video to show the final sequence that reveals a recommended solution to the dilemma. All of these issues were decided on before any attempt at script writing was made so that once in production the video creation would run smoothly with no additional ideas or changes.

The following script provides an example of how the interaction between the two interns (Dylan and Yvonne) is written in a dramatized format yet still outlines the dilemma the students must then solve.

Ext. Tennis Court - Offensive Ads – Episode 5

Dylan is practicing tennis. Yvonne enters the court.
Dylan: It's my day off Yvonne.
Yvonne: I'm sorry. I know. But I need your help.
Dylan: What's up Yvonne? Can't stand a day at work without seeing me?
Yvonne: Have a look at this ad. It's an M2MN's ad.
Dylan looks. He's astonished.
Yvonne: I know. Bad isn't it?
Dylan: That's disgusting. I mean nothing's wrong with the product, but an ad like that is unacceptable....
Yvonne: What should we do? Tell them?
Dylan: But, if we tell them now that their ads are bad and doesn't fit our style, we might never win that account.
Yvonne: How do you know?
Dylan: No one wants to hear people telling them that their ads suck.
Yvonne: I don't think we should tell them.
Dylan: I'll tell them.
Yvonne: Why?
Dylan: If we win the account, we'll be associated with their products and their marketing. If we are not telling them now, we can't turn around a change their marketing philosophy.
Yvonne: There is no philosophy behind these poor taste sexist ads.

Dylan: Yes there is Yvonne. You don't know advertising, but I do. If we win the account, it'll be our task to help them improve the ads.

Yvonne: Can we just deal with this later?

Dylan: Yvonne, ads for adult products have to be very tasteful. It will affect consumer's purchase decision, big time!

Yvonne: Yeah, but we won't win the job if we tell them now.

Dylan: I'll tell them. I have to. It's my professional conduct.

Yvonne: Yeah right. You mean I don't have any professional conduct?

Dylan: I didn't say that.

Yvonne: It's not just this account that we are losing. It's our internship position; it's our jobs at ZAP.

Dylan: No, it's either my job or your job at ZAP, not ours. Keep that in mind

Yvonne: I'm telling the client anyway.

Yvonne stands up walks away frustrated.

INSERT: TO BE CONTINUED

Step 4: Producing the Videos

This step is where a professional production company who has experience with educational video production and those who do not have the experience makes a difference in terms of value for money. There are however, several types of professional production companies. These companies range in expertise from those who produce simple productions such as wedding videos to those more experienced in the most advanced level of producing feature films. The key point we highlight here is that it is the experience with work in the educational sector that will work for the marketing educator, not the experience in the film and media industry per se. Only production companies who have interacted with the educational sector would understand the specific needs of an instructor. That experience will save a significant amount of cost and give the instructor the most appropriate final product. This is a

critical point for educational video production as educational videos are always produced on a tighter budget compared to the production of corporate videos. Still, the quality of the production must be maintained at a professional level. Media is a volatile industry. Most workers in this industry work freelance with unstable incomes thus, their tolerance and understanding for small budget educational production is limited. Taking that into consideration, instructors are better off trying to build long term relationships with experienced production companies with whom they have earned trust and a good rapport, rather than selecting freelancers for each new project.

Tips:

Take care when looking for script writers and production people. Demand to see examples of previous work and charges. A wedding video production company or an amateur script writer may appear a cheaper option. However the lack of experience in writing or producing educational videos may lead them to either mis-quote the clients or carry out the production in in-efficient manner. Hence, there may be a greater demand for additional costs to complete the work to your satisfaction. Therefore it is likely to cost more money in the end, or worse still get a product that is of minimal use for the instructor.

The Internship Series Case: Producing the Videos (In-Production Process)

To ensure the final outcome was produced to a professional standard Pearson Higher Education contracted Passage Entertainment – a professional production company – to execute the series. Professional actors were employed to fill the roles of the two interns. Professional actors were deemed necessary for two reasons. First, they had the ability to portray believable and credible characters in front of the camera and second, they could ensure consistency in their portrayal of the characters for the entire week of filming that was required to produce the 10 videos. The time involved in retakes is something that is often under estimated by the amateur film maker. Even when the actors perform perfectly there are often external factors (e.g. the noise of a car passing the building) which mean that the scene must be filmed again. The actors who played the protagonists in the background story (as detailed in the synopsis above) were cast to reflect the diversity of the student demographic in Australia. They were played by an Asian male and a Caucasian female. The male character is called Dylan. He is into sports and gadgets and is an extrovert. The female character is called Yvonne. She is a nerdy and conservative person. A still shot from one of the videos is shown in Figure 1.

As well as employing professional actors a professional film crew was also employed. This consisted of a team of eight including a director, a director of photography, a sound operator, a lighting technician, a set designer, a camera assistant, an assistant director, and a continuity

person. Again this was deemed necessary to enable a professional outcome rather than having amateurs filming with a standard camcorder. The professional cameraman and director were able to capture the action so that the finished film clips looked more like a TV drama rather than the front-on standard documentary film format that is used by most amateur film makers. Hence, the end result should be more engaging for the students and therefore evoke a more involved response from them. To produce the final 10 x three minute video clips approximately 50 hours of filming took place over five consecutive days. Again this is something that is easily under estimated by the amateur film producer.

To reduce this amount of raw material into something that could be made available to the publishers a large amount of editing and post production work was required. The post production editing took two weeks. While editing can be done using off the shelf software the processing power of most computers (and the readily downloadable software) would not have the capacity

Figure 1. The Interns: Yvonne and Dylan

to run such a large amount of data at once. The raw data to produce a high definition film of this size occupied 300 GB hard drive. The DVD took 24 hours to print on an ordinary office computer (2 GB Ram). This was after several unsuccessful attempts where the computer crashed under the high processing load. In hindsight it would have been cheaper and a lot easier to use a professional post-production company for this task.

When the production was completed, Pearson Higher Education received 10 three minute video clips in a DVD with multiple formats. The different formats will allow the series to be played in lectures on a DVD player or inserted into Power-Point using QuickTime Player and downloadable files from the internet onto a student's computer, IPod, or cell phone. More detailed information about the production process, a trailer of the video series and summary of episodes filmed are available on the Passage Entertainment website: http://passageentertainment.com.au/projects/educational-videos/13-internship-series.

Finding a production company that has experience with educational video production is not complicated. One can simply Google or look at a local directory. However, by just looking up a directory the instructor could easily end-up contacting a wedding or music video production company. One effective way of finding an appropriate production company is to contact academic publishers as they often have local contacts that they have previously used. With the development of technology and internet medium, production now can be cheaply achieved through international collaboration. For example, prior to the advent of high speed internet and digital cameras, filming would be conducted in a one location and the reels of film would need to be physically shipped some where else to edit. Now, the footage can be uploaded into a main server and downloaded on the other side of the world. Certainly this process should be done by a professional production house but global technology does open up the choice considerably.

Occasionally, to save costs, a client will employ the production company's technical crew only. This means paying only for the camera, sound and light operator. However, this means being in charge of managing the process on set. This is relatively straight forward with a good crew who know what they are doing but project managing the film production needs to be planned carefully. For example a simple matter such as catering can become problematic. By law (in Australia) film crew need a break approximately every five hours. A typical production day goes for 10 hours. Extra rates will be charged after the 10 hour block. Ill-planned catering will interrupt the production schedule and make the shooting days last longer.

Tip:

Where possible try not to intervene in the process. When an instructor uses a professional to produce the educational video, the instructor is a client. Effectively, the production company will do whatever is required by the client to make the project happen. Although it is often tempting to have some hands on involvement in the process of filming and editing this can add to the cost of production. These can be the personal costs of physically getting to the production place or extra costs of having to redo work due to changes that may be suggested by the client after the initial quote has been received. The best way to avoid this is to be very clear about what is wanted at the beginning (pre-production) and leave the process to the professionals.

Consumer cameras that are available now can produce HD quality footage. The drawback with these cameras is that the audio quality recording is not up to the same professional quality as the image recording. However, the most significant drawback is that the video files are not always compatible with professional editing programs therefore the ability to edit to a professional standard is lost. Saving the cost by filming using a consumer camcorder is more likely to produce a home-made quality production. Two examples of the use of cameras are provided on the Passage Entertainment website: http://passageentertainment.com.au/projects/educational-videos. The website provides the trailer of the Internship Series and the whole clip of a video called the Chase. The Internship Series was produced using a professional camera. The Chase was shot as a student project and used a high end hand held consumer camcorder. The Internship Series cost 5 days filming and 2 weeks editing to produce a 1.5 hour final production. The Chase cost $1000 and involved 1 day planning, 1 day filming and 2 days editing to produce a 3 minute final production. Both productions used the same professional editing program. While the Internship Series was a straight import and edit, the Chase had to have each individual clip manually copied and all sounds had to be re-recorded post production. This additional work was due to the incompatibility between the camera that shot the Chase and the professional editing program.

Pitfall

While images can be manipulated to a level that is suitable for an educational video and still achieve a respectable look, audio or sound is the fatal failure of cheap production. No consumer camera to date can hide the "home-made" effect of the production. Unless the "home-made" feel is desirable by the instructor, no cost saved by cheap production can compensate for the compromise in sound quality.

Step 5: Distributing the Videos

Distributing educational videos includes streaming the videos online and printing to DVDs. In addition to the actual video, educational videos are typically accompanied by teaching notes provided by the writer and the academic. As the client, the instructors will have the complete ownership of the final production. The production company is entitled to use part of the footage for their show reels. Writers, directors and other crew members will have no right to the production except using part of it for their own credit (proof of experience).

The distribution of on-line or streaming videos requires some technical aspects that instructors should know.

1. Video clips should be less than 3 minutes. Longer clips will be too heavy to download and watch online. (YouTube guides)
2. Exported format should be web friendly. There is an option in movie editing programs to export to the web. Depending on the program, if the option is selected, the files should be ready for web upload. Web format for streaming and downloadable video to iPhones and other cell phones are different. An iPhone will not take a cell-phone formatted file, and vice versa. QuickTime Player will give users different formats for iPhone and for cell phone. Web format for streaming and downloadable video to iPhones and other cell phones are different. If a multi platform is intentional then the instructor must upload videos in multiple formats.
3. YouTube and MySpace have conditions regarding copyright and ownership of the clips upload on their site. Instructors have to ensure they have read and agreed to all conditions to avoid any possible future litigation.
4. It is much better to have multiple small clips rather than one large clip. YouTube's new measurement tool indicates that viewer's attention span drops significantly after 1.5 minutes.
5. In addition to YouTube many users will not have a flash program installed on the computer and/or the program is not up-to date. That makes flash video un-watchable to those viewers.

For DVD distribution there are potential issues that instructors should note. First, DVD videos are often not easily inserted into PowerPoint. This formatting problem with DVD's is used to protect videos and movies from being pirated. To allow the user to insert video into their PowerPoint the files should be exported as normal Windows Media Player files or QuickTime Player files. An issue with burning videos to DVDs is that not all features of a professional video production are able to be copied for example, 'Flash' introductions or pirate protected chapters. Second, not all computers have a DVD player installed or have up-to-date drivers. Therefore, instructor produced videos should be formatted to give users more options than just DVD.

Online streaming video has good potential for social networking and file sharing and hence be able to increase the effectiveness of using streaming video as a tool to help students socially construct knowledge. Social networking and file sharing is one of the most engaging ways of online communication to date. The majority of students are internet and social network savvy. This can be an additional way of engaging students in the material: they can comment and discuss with their fellow friends the issues raised in the video. They can also tag important concepts and can even rate the importance of concept for examination preparation.

The Internship Series Case: Distribution the Videos

The completed series was printed on to a DVD in multiple format files. Each episode was saved into a separate folder. In each folder there are 2 video files: the main episode and a suggested episode ending. This suggested ending gives the instructor the option of whether or not they want to show the ending to the students or let the students come up with different possible answers themselves. Each file has 3 formats: a QuickTime player file, a cell phone file and an iPhone file. The instructor can up-load all three formats of the files on to any educational web-based platform for example, Blackboard. Accompanying each of these episodes are teaching notes and a list of possible questions that may be used by the instructor. Below is a sample extract from the teaching notes for one episode in the Internship Series.

Episode: 2
Suggested topic: Secondary data
Suggested associated textbook chapter(s): 3 and 4
Scenario: Dylan and Yvonne argue about the use of primary data and secondary data.
Suggested points for discussion:

1. Pros and cons of using a generic database from a client's perspective and the marketing firm's perspective.
2. Compare and contrast the use of secondary data and primary data in this case?
3. Pros and cons of using a primary database from a client's perspective and the marketing firm's perspective.
4. What are the potential ethical concerns when the marketing research firm use generic database to form their structured survey in a later stage.

As the Internship Series is now owned by Pearson Higher Education it will be used as an instruction resource to accompany the textbooks of their choice. Whether the series is complimentary to the book user is entirely Pearson's decision as they commissioned the entire series. Getting funding in this way may limit our use of the resources as we no longer own the series. However it opens this resource up to a much larger audience and so benefits the marketing education sector in general.

Passage Entertainment uses a small component of the series for their show reel portfolio. They also published the trailer of the series as per Pearson's request. The contract conditions state that Passage Entertainment has no ownership or rights to the Series.

CONCLUSION

In this chapter we have examined the need for interactive teaching aids that will encourage the students to not only know the concepts of what we teach but how and when to use these concepts. Producing such interactive case-based videos has been shown to be yet another tool in the marketing lecturer's arsenal of tools that will encourage deep learning. The main benefits of this form of teaching resources are: a) they provide the student with a realistic view of the ethical decisions that are faced by sales and marketing managers in a format that is easy to comprehend and keeps the class learning at the same pace, b) they facilitate problem based learning, and c) they provide an up to date image of business that is also Australian focused. While the benefits of producing a teaching resource such as this are obvious the problems of producing a top quality video series must also be considered. A large amount of time and resources are required.

REFERENCES

Australian Copyright Council. (2009). *Q&As on using YouTube for education.* Retrieved September 17, 2009, from http://www.copyright.org.au/information/cit005/cit073/wp0032

Bennett, R. (2002). Employers' demands for personal transferable skills in graduates: A content analysis of 1000 job advertisements and an associated empirical study. *Journal of Vocational Education and Training, 54*(4), 457–475. doi:10.1080/13636820200200209

Business Council of Australia. (2006). *New concepts in innovation: The keys to growing Australia.* Melbourne, Australia: BCA.

Carlson, J. D. (2009). Who are you wearing? Using the red carpet question pedagogically. *International Studies Perspectives, 10*(2), 198–215. doi:10.1111/j.1528-3585.2009.00370.x

Choi, H. J., & Johnson, S. D. (2007). The effect of problem-based video instruction on learner satisfaction, comprehension and retention in college courses. *British Journal of Educational Technology, 38*(5), 885–895. doi:10.1111/j.1467-8535.2006.00676.x

Choi, I., & Lee, K. (2008). A case-based learning environment design for real-world classroom management problem solving. *TechTrends, 52*(3), 26–31. doi:10.1007/s11528-008-0151-z

Cronin Jones, L. L. (2003). Are lectures a thing of the past? *Journal of College Science Teaching, 32*(7), 453–457.

Dacko, S. G. (2006). Narrowing the skills gap for marketers of the future. *Marketing Intelligence & Planning, 24*(3), 283–295. doi:10.1108/02634500610665736

Dalsgaard, C., & Godsk, M. (2007). Transforming traditional lectures into problem-based blended learning: challenges and experiences. *Open Learning, 22*(1), 29–42. doi:10.1080/02680510601100143

Daly, S. P. (2001). Student-operated internet businesses: True experiential learning in entrepreneurship and retail management. *Journal of Marketing Education, 23*(3), 204–215. doi:10.1177/0273475301233006

Diamond, N., Koernig, S. K., & Iqbal, Z. (2008). Uniting active and deep learning to teach problem-solving skills: strategic tools and the learning. *Journal of Marketing Education, 30*(2), 116–129. doi:10.1177/0273475308317707

GoogleVideos. (2009a). *Market segmentation search*. Retrieved September 17, 2009, from http://video.google.com/videosearch?q=service+failure&emb=0&aq=f#q=market+segmentation&emb=0

GoogleVideos. (2009b). *Customer satisfaction search*. Retrieved September 17, 2009, from http://video.google.com/videosearch?q=customer+satisfaction&www_google_domain=www.google.com&emb=0&aq=0&oq=customer+sat#

GoogleVideos. (2009c). *Service failure search*. Retrieved September 17, 2009, from http://video.google.com/videosearch?q=service+failure&emb=0&aq=f#

Hill, J. R., & Hannafin, M. J. (2001). Teaching and learning in digital environments: The resurgence of resource based learning. *Educational Technology Research and Development, 49*(3), 37–52. doi:10.1007/BF02504914

Hodgson, V. E. (2005). Lectures and the experience of relevance. In F. Marton, D. Hounsell & N. Entwistle (Eds.), *The experience of learning: Implications for teaching and studying in higher education* (3rd ed., pp. 159–171). Edinburgh, UK: University of Edinburgh, Centre for Teaching, Learning and Assessment. Retrieved September 7, 2009, from http://www.ed.ac.uk/etl/docs/ExperienceOfLearning/EoL10.pdf

Jonassen, D. H. (2004). *Learning to solve problems: An instructional design guide*. San Francisco, CA: Pfeiffer/Jossey-Bass.

Jones, S. E. (2007). Reflections on the lecture: Outmoded medium or instrument of inspiration? *Journal of Further and Higher Education, 31*(4), 397–406. doi:10.1080/03098770701656816

Larson, B. E. (2000). Classroom discussion: A method of instruction and a curriculum outcome. *Teaching and Teacher Education, 16*(5-6), 661–667. doi:10.1016/S0742-051X(00)00013-5

Lee, K. J., & Sharma, M. D. (2008). Incorporating active learning with videos: A case from physics. *Teaching Science, 54*(4), 45–47.

Ma, A. K. F., O'Toole, J. M., & Keppell, M. (2007). The attitudes of teacher educators to the use of problem based learning: The video triggers approach. *In ICT: Providing choices for learners and learning.* Proceedings Ascilite Singapore 2007.

McClymont, H., Volkov, M., Gardiner, M., Behjat, N., & Geoghegan, N. (2005). Employer (dis) satisfaction with Australian marketing graduates: The development of a research framework. In *Australian and New Zealand Marketing Academy Conference Proceedings,* Perth, Australia.

Ramsden, P. (2003). *Learning to teach in higher education* (2nd ed.). Abington, UK: RoutledgeFalmer.

Sautter, P. (2007). Designing discussion activities to achieve desired learning outcomes: Choices using mode of delivery and structure. *Journal of Marketing Education, 29*(2), 122–131. doi:10.1177/0273475307302014

Shyu, H. C. (2000). Using video-based anchored instruction to enhance learning: Taiwan's experience. *British Journal of Educational Technology, 31*(1), 57–69. doi:10.1111/1467-8535.00135

Sweller, J., van Merrienboer, J. J. G., & Paas, F. G. W. C. (1998). Cognitive architecture and instructional design. *Educational Psychology Review, 10*(3), 251–296. doi:10.1023/A:1022193728205

Young, M. R., Klemz, B. R., & Murphy, J. W. (2003). Enhancing learning outcomes: The effects of instructional technology, learning styles, instructional methods, and student behavior. *Journal of Marketing Education, 25*(2), 130–142. doi:10.1177/0273475303254004

YouTube.com. (2009a). *YouTube fact sheet: Traffic and stats*. Retrieved September 18, 2009, from http://www.youtube.com/t/fact_sheet

YouTube.com. (2009b). *Market segmentation search*. Retrieved September 17, 2009, from http://www.youtube.com/results?search_query=market+segmentation&search_type=&aq=f

YouTube.com. (2009c). *Value chain search*. Retrieved September 17, 2009, from http://www.youtube.com/results?search_query=value+chain&search_type=&aq=f

Chapter 19
Higher Education in a Virtual World

Patricia Genoe McLaren
Wilfrid Laurier University, Canada

Lori Francis
Saint Mary's University, Canada

E. Kevin Kelloway
Saint Mary's University, Canada

ABSTRACT

Following years of discussion surrounding the characteristics, both positive and negative, of generations X and Y, we are seeing the emergence of what is referred to as the virtual generation, the net generation, or Generation V. To some, the virtual generation includes 15 to 24 year olds who spend significant amounts of time playing video games, browsing the Web, and communicating over the Internet (Proserpio & Gioia, 2007). Tapscott (2009) defines the net generation as the first generation to have grown up in the digital age. To others, Generation V is a generation that transcends age, gender, social demographic, and geography, and encompasses everyone who participates in a virtual environment (Sarner, 2008). Regardless of the exact parameters of the generation in use, as the virtual generation enters our academic institutions en masse, we need to ensure that we are providing educational environments that encompass the technological world in which they live, that defines who they are. Rather than requiring them to be confined solely to traditional lecture-based pedagogy, let the virtual generation learn in a virtual world.

INTRODUCTION

While the term virtual generation refers to individuals who are comfortable in an online environment, within that online environment it is possible to go beyond gathering and distributing information and goods over the internet and venture into a myriad of virtual worlds. Virtual world, alternate gaming reality (ARG), and massive multiplayer online game (MMOG) are all terms used to describe online environments in which real people, represented by avatars, interact in real-time. These environments are more broadly known as metaverses. Some metaverses are completely open to users, such as the virtual worlds Second Life and Entropia Universe, and interaction occurs for social, cultural, and information-seeking reasons.

DOI: 10.4018/978-1-60960-800-2.ch019

Users have the ability to shape the landscape of the world themselves, creating lands, homes, and businesses. Other metaverses exert control over the users, such as the MMOGs Everquest and World of Warcraft, with specified tasks to complete, problems to be solved, goals to be met, and winners and losers. In all metaverses activity continues even when an individual member is offline, which increases the draw of the community to the members.

Virtual worlds have been gaining in popularity since the launch of Second Life in 2003, and are beginning to be seen as innovative new learning environments. Users of Second Life value the ability to interact with people and information resources at the same time within a virtual world (Ostrander, 2008). Although the internet generally holds vast amounts of information that users can access, virtual worlds go one step further and allow for real-time discussion about that information, visual inspection of three-dimensional cultural artifacts, buildings, and events, and the opportunity to learn through watching others learn. Virtual worlds also facilitate learning by allowing users to engage in activities and behaviours that have observable outcomes in an environment in which the effects of mistakes or wrong decisions can be experienced, but without the tangible repercussions that would take place in the real world.

The extent to which virtual technologies are embedded in the lives of the average university student, combined with the breadth in age of the virtual generation and the potential educational benefits of learning in a virtual world, calls out for higher education institutions and instructors to make use of these burgeoning technologies. To ensure a full understanding of the potential uses, benefits, concerns, and outcomes of learning in a virtual world we have undertaken an analysis of the opportunities provided by virtual worlds and their associated technologies in conjunction with the current literature on learning theory and teaching strategies. As any pedagogical technique can only be as effective as the quality of its imple-

mentation, we also discuss some of the factors that need to be taken into consideration when designing and implementing a virtual learning environment. Throughout the chapter we use examples from actual virtual world implementations to illustrate clearly our thoughts, observations, and discussions.

TEACHING THE VIRTUAL GENERATION

The days of post-secondary students accepting that sitting in seats and frantically taking notes, while being lectured to by professors, constitutes a valuable education have ended (Tapscott, 2009). Students of the virtual generation want to learn through teaching strategies that emphasize interaction, technology, experience, and activity (Zeliff, 2004), and they want entertainment and play to be part of their education and work (Tapscott, 2009). As a generation they believe more strongly in a meritocratic environment than preceding generations, and they place great value on collaboration and sharing, as can be seen by the success of open-source technologies such as Linux (Sarner, 2008). Student-centered learning, in which students take an active role in their education and instructors become both learning facilitators as well as content deliverers (Shrivastava, 1999), has emerged in the forefront of education. High levels of exchange, including the free exchange of ideas and opinions among and between students and instructors, have been linked to increased levels of motivation, positive attitudes toward learning, and lasting learning outcomes (Brower, 2003; Sitzmann, Kraiger, Stewart, & Wisher, 2006).

Teaching strategies that emphasize interaction and experience over instructor-based content delivery have been developed and refined over the previous two to three decades. Among the most prevalent of these is experiential learning. When individuals undertake experiential learning they examine and strengthen "the critical linkages among education, work, and personal development" (Kolb, 1984, p. 4), creating new knowledge through the transformation of experience. Thus, the content of a class-based course is linked to the outside world, be that the workplace or personal life, giving more relevance to the material, showing the importance of formal education, and also showing how learning can occur outside, as well as inside, the classroom. Experiential learning emphasizes the process of learning, rather than content or outcomes, and considers knowledge as being continuously created and recreated, not an independent entity to be acquired (Kolb, 1984). As students engage in experiential learning they build understanding and expertise, and they are engaged in active critical learning. Knowledge received from an instructor is practically applied, and in doing so students have a far greater chance of understanding and remembering what they are learning (Taber, 2008). Examples of ways in which experiential learning can be offered to students include internships, field placements, structured exercises and role plays, games, and simulations (Kolb, 1984).

Online Learning

Online learning, sometimes referred to as e-learning, involves the use of online technologies such as web sites, discussion boards, chat rooms, and email for the delivery of information and instruction in an educational setting (Welsh, Wanberg, Brown, & Simmering, 2003). Online learning can be either asynchronous or synchronous. Asynchronous online learning refers to content posted on a website that students can access when convenient to their schedule. Synchronous online learning occurs when both students and the instructor are online at the same time, and communicate through live streaming media, instant message, chat rooms, or technologies such as web cameras and Skype that allow users to see and hear each other. One of the most fundamental benefits of online learning is that it provides students with the ability to access the learning environment at the time and location of their choice (Shrivastava, 1999).

Online learning has become more prevalent in post-secondary classrooms and distance education programs, and teaching strategies have evolved, or emerged, in order to make use of the new technological resources available to instructors. Where technology is well integrated into the classroom, and students are extremely comfortable in the use of the technology, student-centered learning strategies become easier to implement and students can become facilitators as well as instructors (Zeliff, 2004).

Yohon (2004) discusses the strategies of collaborative learning, problem-based learning, inquiry-based learning, and situated learning as methods that lend themselves well to online learning and allow students to take active control of their education. In collaborative learning students work together in small groups to solve problems, complete projects, or achieve common goals. Online learning can increase opportunities for collaborative learning as it can create spaces, in the form of chat rooms and discussion boards, for students to collaborate outside of the classroom setting (Yohon, 2004). These spaces allow students to communicate in a medium in which most of them are extremely comfortable and at times when their schedules allow. They also give students time to process lecture-based material and think about others' comments before responding, which can be difficult to do in a classroom based setting.

Both problem- and inquiry-based learning involve finding answers to questions, for which the internet is a vast informational resource. In situated learning students both learn and live subject matter that is embedded in their ongoing lives. The internet allows access to a greater set of real-world resources, such as practitioners, experts, or consultants.

Effectiveness of Online Learning

Most of the research on the effectiveness of online instruction has focused on declarative, rather than procedural, knowledge and learning (Sitzmann, et al., 2006). Declarative knowledge consists of declarable data and facts, and the associations between them, that can be acquired through learning (Squire, 1987). Retrieval of declarative knowledge is generally unconscious and extremely selective, and requires directed attention (ten Berge & van Hezewijk, 1999). Procedural knowledge, on the other hand, consists of knowledge about how to perform skills and cognitive operations (Squire, 1987). Like riding a bike or playing chase, acquiring procedural knowledge usually takes many trials, and once acquired it is difficult to express verbally (ten Berge & van Hezewijk, 1999). Meta-analytic evidence suggests that online instruction is more effective than classroom-based instruction for teaching declarative, but not procedural, knowledge (Sitzmann, et al., 2006).

Although some argue that online learning increases the control that students retain over their own education, thereby providing a benefit over classroom-based instruction (Yohon, 2004; Zeliff, 2004), recent evidence suggests that student control of their learning has a negligible effect on the actual learning that occurs (Sitzmann, et al., 2006). Online learning that removes students from the classroom also removes the potential for face-to-face interaction between both students and students and instructors. Where online learning simply involves reading course content that has been provided over the internet there is little difference from sitting in a lecture-based class. In order for online learning to be effective it needs to be carefully designed and implemented so that the potential benefits can be realized (Welsh, et al., 2003).

To help students achieve practical learning that is transferable to their own lives, online learning needs to provide context, be embedded in everyday experiences, and require students to use their existing knowledge (Slotte & Herbert, 2008). Communication among students and between students and instructors is critical, and instructors need to understand that teaching online requires different skills and techniques than teaching in the classroom. To achieve the interaction and engagement that is critical to learning, instructors need to develop learning communities, rather than simply presenting course content online and expecting students to operate independently of each other and the instructor (Peltier, Schibrowsky, & Drago, 2007). Where online learning communities are formed, students engage in collective inquiry, sharing knowledge, and finding ways to use that knowledge, in order to meet their interests and needs. Learning occurs from both interaction and the information resources available on the internet (Shrivastava, 1999). A defined structure is also important for online courses, as the built-in time and location structures of classroom-based courses is missing (Arbaugh & Benbunan-Fich, 2006).

Immediacy

Concerns with online learning as it is implemented today include the difficulty in providing immediacy to students. Immediacy refers to "the extent to which learners feel connected to the learning experience" (Hutchins & Hutchison, 2008, p. 372), and is manifest in both verbal and nonverbal behaviours such as feedback, praise, discussion, use of student names, eye contact, smiling, and open gestures. Many of the currently used online teaching strategies, such as asynchronous downloadable and streaming media, online case studies, and discussion boards decrease the amount of immediacy that students experience. Online courses do not always have instructors teaching them. These courses can be set up so that all content, assignments, tests, and grading is automated. If there is a live instructor teaching or administering the course students must wait for that instructor to be online to receive feedback on their work, clarification on topics, and answers to questions.

Instructors of online courses need to be active guides in the online learning environment, encouraging student involvement in discussion, asking questions, clearly communicating expectations, and directly communicating with students individually. Rather than simply supplementing textbook material with added content in the form of PowerPoint slides and embedded links, instructors need to provide actual enhancements to the material through the use of case studies, creative assignments, and real-world applications of knowledge (Marks, Sibley, & Arbaugh, 2005).

Blended Learning

Blended learning environments are those in which students are given both classroom-based and online instruction. These types of environments can incorporate the benefits of both types of instruction, with student and instructor interaction in the classroom environment, opportunities for immediate feedback, information and communication resources of the internet, and students' ability to participate in a course as suits their own schedule. Blended learning is particularly valuable in training settings because it is more effective than classroom use alone, has a high learner value/impact, is more effective than non-blended approaches, and learners like it (Kerres & De Witt, 2003). In contrast to online instruction, blended learning environments are effective for teaching both declarative and procedural knowledge (Sitzmann, et al., 2006).

LEARNING IN A VIRTUAL WORLD

There is much research and guidance on online teaching strategies and techniques. These techniques, however, make only cursory use of the potential power provided by the online environment. Classroom web sites, discussion boards, chat rooms, live or recorded streaming or downloadable media, internet video conferencing and power

point presentations can all enhance a traditional classroom-based course when used effectively, but these options tend to be underutilized by students (Proserpio & Gioia, 2007). Although the basic online teaching strategies make it easier for students to learn at their own time and location, they offer only slight differences from learning in the classroom, and they provide little in the way of enhanced excitement and engagement.

Learning in a virtual world, on the other hand, opens a whole new realm of possibilities for students and instructors. Through games, simulations, and directed tasks such as developing, opening, and running a functional business in Second Life, students can have the opportunity to learn through doing, to experience all the ramifications of decisions – both good and bad – without causing real-world repercussions, and to do so in an immersive medium in which more and more individuals are actively participating in their leisure time (Wagner, 2008). Virtual worlds allow instructors to deliver content, teach how to apply principles, and evaluate performance in the preferred learning styles of their students, and in far more realistic situations than the classroom (Proserpio & Gioia, 2007). Learning while in a virtual world also allows students to go beyond the information resources of the internet and interact with people other than the course's students and instructor (Ostrander, 2008). Searching in an information-based environment requires students to formulate the correct questions, or keywords, to find the answers to their questions. Interacting with people while searching for information allows students to refine and focus their questions in discussion with subject experts.

There are several examples of the successful use of virtual worlds for learning environments. For instance, the United States military relies heavily on online simulations to train its members (Aldrich, 2004). Virtual worlds are being used in training for emergency response professionals (Taber, 2008); sales staff (Slotte & Herbert, 2008); and university students (Jarmon, Traphagan,

Mayrath, & Trivedi, 2009; Wagner, 2008), particularly for nursing and medical students (Lafsky, 2009; Skiba, 2009). Various universities, including Edinburgh, Harvard and Princeton, have virtual classroom space in Second Life (Jacoby, 2009). The University of Salerno (DMI) has created a virtual campus for their Department of Mathematics and Informatics (De Lucia, Francese, Passero, & Tortora, 2009).

What, Exactly, Will Students Do?

Expounding on the excitement and innovation of learning in a virtual world is of little value without providing a clear picture of what students are asked to do. Within virtual worlds, learning can be enhanced through the use of virtual classrooms, games, simulations, and tasks that students are assigned to complete within boundaries defined by the instructor or within the virtual world as a whole. A virtual world being used for a course could be a specific space within an open virtual world, it could be a world designed and built specifically for the course itself or for the department or university, or it could be the highly controlled environment of a simulation or game incorporating specific characters, rules, actions, constraints, and outcomes that have been built into the world. Simulations and games can also be built so that they are entered via a course's virtual meeting place, or a virtual classroom. In addition to designing and using virtual worlds for specific tasks defined by the instructor, students can also be sent out into open virtual worlds such as Second Life to find information, meet new people, and apply the declarative content of their course while interacting within the world.

Games and Simulations

Today's generation of computer games and simulations are set in highly-complex, graphically-detailed, fully realized virtual worlds. For students who have grown up playing the latest and greatest computer games, it is a mistake to expect overly simple and dated educational games and simulations to be engaging. Computer games are full of complexity, alternative strategies, multiple paths to the end goal, and realistic consequences to decisions. Students will expect the same in courses that purport to harness the power of online technologies (Aldrich, 2004). Simulations and games offer cost-effective approaches to experience-based learning, with emphasis on both declarative and procedural knowledge (Roman & Brown, 2008). The inclusion of games and/or simulations in training and education environments results in greater positive behaviour change and greater learning than the use of case studies. Students who use games and/or simulations experience greater course enjoyment, and perceive the usefulness of the course to be higher, than those who use case studies (Kenworthy & Wong, 2005). The multiple strategies and complexity of online games and simulations set the stage for critical learning to take place (Proserpio & Gioia, 2007).

Games and simulations are similar in that they immerse participants in the virtual world and provide spaces in which students can apply course content and develop procedural knowledge within a directed setting. Games always have a pre-defined goal that must be met to win the game, such as finding the treasure or amassing the strongest army. On the other hand, winning or losing is not a facet of simulations (Aldrich, 2004). Simulations may have a pre-defined goal set by the instructor, such as to receive satisfactory feedback from at least five customers, but students may also be sent into a simulation with instructions simply to explore and interact.

Games and simulations differ mainly in the extent to which they mimic reality. Games are not expected to do so and are often set in worlds that are contrived or fantastical, such as outer space or a mythical land. Games used in educational settings are generally applied in team building types of exercises, and their value lies in drawing on skills required to work together such as decision-making, collaboration, and communication (Aldrich, 2004). The contrived nature of the game permits semi-structured experiences in which students progress through a series of levels, each requiring an understanding of more complex concepts and solving more challenging problems, while expecting students to master skills more previous levels. Games structured in this way give students a sense of progressive learning (Proserpio & Gioia, 2007).

In contrast, simulations always mimic some aspect of reality and they provide students with an understanding of a system or process, such as a city that has experienced a natural disaster. When participating in a simulation, students can directly observe and analyze the effects of their and others' actions on various factors of the system. Students can purposely act in ways that might cause negative outcomes, such as creating a run on a bank, in order to experience and react to the results (Aldrich, 2004). Authenticity within a simulation is critical to its effectiveness as a learning tool (Slotte & Herbert, 2008).

Truly effective and engaging games and simulations must provide multiple routings to participants, particularly in situations where students may encounter complex situations that do not have predetermined outcomes, such as emergency response, health care, and urban planning. Students will have been taught procedures and rules that need to be followed in particular situations. They may, however, forget to apply them while in the midst of the simulation experience. It is also highly possible that, due to personal preferences, interpretations, and strengths, any two people may apply what are ostensibly the same procedures and rules and still make different decisions. Multiple routings within a simulation means that the simulation progresses naturally from each possible decision that a student might make. Within the virtual world there is no one right answer, and students must be allowed to make mistakes (Taber, 2008).

It is also critical that games and simulations provide feedback so that students can see the results of their actions and understand what they did well and where they made mistakes. Online simulations provide excellent opportunities for students to experience the consequences of their actions without having to experience an actual, potentially dangerous real world failure. Students are free to take the risks that may cause death or financial ruin, or may save lives or make millions. All of these decisions can be made and actions taken without instructors ever needing to take control of the situation to divert potential catastrophe (Taber, 2008).

For the full value of an online game or simulation to be achieved, students must have access to an instructor or a live coach. The instructor needs to provide students with the required concepts and skills for them to function within the online environment, and needs to ensure that students identify enough with the content and the game or simulation that they are motivated to become fully engaged (Slotte & Herbert, 2008). Following participation in a game or simulation it is important that students undertake a debriefing process with each other and their instructor. Through debriefing, students can discuss their experiences, connecting them to similar experiences that have happened, or will happen, in the real world. Decisions that were made, and their consequences, can be analyzed, with both students and the instructor discussing what they had done, suggesting other actions that could have been taken, and dissecting the reasons behind decisions and consequences (Taber, 2008). Discussing the game or simulation with fellow students and the instructor increases the enthusiasm that students feel towards the skills being learned (Slotte & Herbert, 2008).

Directed Tasks in a Virtual World

Open virtual worlds such as Second Life mimic the real world in many ways. Users can own and rent property, purchase products and services such as clothing, shoes, and entertainment, run businesses that produce and sell goods, attend rock concerts, visit museums, and travel to Stonehenge. Students can be sent into these worlds with tasks to complete, such as starting and running a business (Wagner, 2008) or practicing and developing communication strategies (Jarmon, et al., 2009). Directed tasks like these have similarities to online simulations in that many aspects of the real world are present, yet the consequences of mistakes are not severe. Students have the opportunity to apply concepts and skills learned in the course and to develop procedural knowledge and experience. The environment, however, is far less controlled. Where the simulation designer foretold all possible eventualities and essentially created the reactions and responses of the simulation characters, students working within Second Life will interact with individuals completely independent of the course itself. Instructors will only be able to attempt to predict the difficulties that may arise. Access to instructor support and guidance, feedback, and debriefings is even more critical in this type of environment to ensure that students are not being frustrated by issues such as technical glitches (network downtime, loss of data, etc.), and that the instructor knows the types of interactions students are encountering.

Benefits

Using the powerful technology and potentially addictive and immersive nature of virtual worlds in an educational setting has a variety of benefits for both students and instructors. We have already alluded to many of these benefits, such as students being able to experience the consequences of their decisions and actions, and to purposely take and recover from actions that may have negative repercussions. Learning within a virtual world through tasks that go beyond virtual classes and discussion can bring experiential learning, double-loop learning, and the acquisition of tacit knowledge

into the higher education environment to an extent which has never before been possible.

Tacit Knowledge

Tacit knowledge is a difficult construct to grasp. It was introduced by Michael Polanyi with his statement "we can know more than we can tell" (1966, p. 4). Even Polanyi himself acknowledged that while on the surface the statement makes sense, "it is not easy to say exactly what it means" (1966, p. 4). Polanyi described the act of tacit knowing as attending from one thing in order to attend to something else. Since Polanyi's introduction of tacit knowledge, researchers have continued to clarify certain aspects of it. Tacit knowledge is said to have a personal quality based on experience, context, and judgment (Lam, 2000), and to reside in the unconscious (Leonard & Sensiper, 1998). It is evident when an individual successfully executes a skill, yet cannot fully codify or articulate the reason for his or her success (Mooradian, 2005; Smith, 2001). This inability to effectively articulate the knowledge required can result from the individual not being fully conscious of all of the aspects of the skill, or from insufficiently developed codes of language (Gertler, 2003; Leonard & Sensiper, 1998). The aspect of tacit knowledge that makes it difficult to articulate, however, also makes it difficult to ascertain whether an individual possesses a level of tacit knowledge, or is simply unaware (Li & Geo, 2003).

Tacit knowledge and skills that are required in the workplace can be difficult both to teach and to assess in a classroom-based setting. Students can, however, acquire and display tacit knowledge in a virtual world (Wagner, 2008). A physician can teach medical students the lists of symptoms of various illnesses and can provide checklists of questions to ask and symptoms to look for, but she cannot teach her students, while lecturing in a classroom, how to develop rapport with a patient. She can, however, within a virtual hospital show students how she interacts with patients, give them the time and the space to practice, and provide feedback on bedside manner.

Double-Loop Learning

In double-loop learning students correct errors by first changing the governing values that caused those errors and then changing the associated actions. This is in contrast to single-loop learning, in which students correct errors only by changing the actions, not the underlying values (Argyris, 2002). Double-loop learning is primarily concerned with determining the differences between an individual's theories of action: espoused theory versus theory-in-use. An espoused theory is that action we believe we will take in a given situation and tell others we would do. A theory-in-use is what we actually do when we are in the situation. For any given situation our theories in action may differ, but neither we, nor those around us, know what these differences are until we can observe our theory-in-use (Argyris & Schon, 1974). When double-loop learning occurs, espoused theory and theory-in-use become the same.

Virtual worlds, by giving students an opportunity to actually witness their own theories-in-use, offer an environment in which double-loop learning can be achieved. Many people believe their espoused theories and theories-in-use to be the same. Actions taken within a virtual world and later analyzed and assessed with fellow students and the instructor, can show students where the differences in their espoused theories and theories-in-use exist. Students can then alter one or both of their theories to bring them into congruence, thereby leading to the correct actions in future situations. Consider a law student who espouses the theory that every individual deserves the best defense, regardless of their guilt or innocence. He may find, when called upon within a simulated courtroom to defend a serial killer who he knows to be guilty, that he is unable to provide a worthy defense due to his disgust at the crimes and their perpetrator. The law student's theory-in-use is that

everyone does not deserve the best defense. As he realizes the discrepancies between his espoused theory and his theory-in-use he can take the time to determine how he wants to align those theories. He may go with his theory-in-use and become a prosecuting or non-litigating attorney, or he may go with his espoused theory and work at quelling his emotions when preparing cases for court.

Experiential Learning

Learning within virtual worlds provides students with the opportunity to learn through experience without ever having to leave the comfort of their desks. Virtual games, simulations, and directed tasks all require students to apply course concepts and declarative knowledge in practical situations. As they apply these concepts, and experience them in ways that are similar to how they will be experienced in the real world, students create new knowledge and strengthen the linkages between that taught in the classroom and that lived in the world.

Even when virtual worlds are used for simple information-seeking, as opposed to more in-depth tasks, the information-seeking process is itself experiential. Students asked to research life in a mental hospital can experience walking through the hallways, being a patient, being an employee, or being a psychiatrist, rather than simply reading about another's perspective as would be done in more traditional online environments (Ostrander, 2008).

Research has shown the effectiveness of virtual worlds such as Second Life when used for a project-based experiential learning approach. Characteristics of virtual worlds that facilitate experiential learning include virtual social interactions and collaborations, hypothesis testing through actual projects and actions minus the risks and costs of the real world, potential for relevance of actions in the virtual world to the real world, practice and demonstration of procedural knowledge, exploration, and tangible experience.

Students found that working within Second Life helped them understand the connections between education and experience. The three-dimensional nature of the environment makes students' experiences more real and enhances their experiential learning (Jarmon, et al., 2009).

Immediacy

Courses or course assignments offered in a virtual world provide greater immediacy to students than more traditional online courses. Where the classroom itself exists in the virtual world, and students and the instructor meet on a regularly scheduled basis, the opportunity for feedback, praise, discussion, and use of names is the same as that in a traditional classroom. Where the students use virtual worlds for course components such as games, simulations, and directed tasks, students experience immediacy through interactions with other individuals within the virtual worlds, be they characters created for the game or simulation, or actual members of the virtual world. Students may also come across fellow students and their instructor as they navigate through the virtual world, and can receive feedback, ask questions, or engage in discussion outside of official class hours. All of these opportunities for interaction increase the connection that students feel to their learning experience.

Collaborative Learning

The highly collaborative nature of the virtual generation lends itself well to collaborative learning styles (Tapscott, 2009). The use of collaborative teaching and learning approaches within an online environment give students increased social presence in the course, and an increased sense of belonging to an online community (Arbaugh & Benbunan-Fich, 2006). Open virtual worlds provide a wide array of communication tools that make it easy for interaction and collaboration to occur within its borders. Collaboration is also

aided by the fact that normally occurring social boundaries, such as gender, ethnicity, race, age, and personality, do not intrude into virtual worlds. When two avatars communicate they have no idea if the person on the other computer is someone whom they would normally scorn in a real world social setting - only their immediate interest of and knowledge about the topic at hand come into play. Likewise, social anxiety, shyness, and introversion can be mitigated through an online environment. Students who would normally be too shy or anxious to speak in class can speak through their avatar and feel protection from potential social embarrassment (Jarmon, et al., 2009).

Areas of Concern

No teaching strategy or tool is ever going to be the complete answer to effective higher education, and virtual worlds are no exception. While the use of virtual worlds for education purposes is growing, empirical research on its effectiveness is still minimal. Much of the literature touts collaborative learning as the most appropriate for online education, but this is done without a thorough consideration of other learning strategies or comparing collaborative learning to other possibilities (Arbaugh & Benbunan-Fich, 2006). In the same vein, Kenworthy and Wong (2005) found that for all of the claims as to the effectiveness of teaching through games and simulations, there is very little supporting empirical research. Claims of effectiveness are mainly anecdotal or based on poorly designed research studies. Constructs are not well-defined, and evaluation tends to rely mainly on the reactions of students, as opposed to a measurement of performance or learning outcomes.

Traditional online technologies, such as email, websites, and discussion boards, lack the richness of face-to-face conversation as non-verbal cues such as eye contact, physical gestures, and emotions are not visible. This lack of connection to fellow students and the instructor can lead to feelings of emotional detachment from the course (Brower, 2003). Virtual worlds do allow for some expression of emotion and physical gestures, but they must be consciously instigated by the user and as such lack the naturalness and potential usefulness of seeing the unconscious and spontaneous physical reactions of people with whom we are communicating.

Not all students in a course will have equal levels of comfort and familiarity with virtual world technologies, and for some the expectation to function within a virtual world may invoke a steep learning curve. Students who spend most of a course familiarizing themselves with the technology and learning how to navigate and interact within a virtual world will be at a great disadvantage to other students in terms of participation, completing assigned tasks, and achieving course goals (Brower, 2003). The associated frustration and feelings of isolation that come from not being able to use the technology effectively may lead to disengagement and poor performance.

As with more traditional online learning environments, learning within a virtual world will be most effective when offered in a blended learning environment. Students can reap the experiential and double-loop learning benefits of acting on the declarative knowledge learned in the classroom, and still have fellow students and an instructor for discussion, interaction, feedback, clarification, and immediacy (Roman & Brown, 2008).

CREATING A VIRTUAL LEARNING ENVIRONMENT

A poorly designed and implemented virtual learning environment will not only lack any benefits for students and instructors, but may have a negative impact on the learning outcomes of the course. The frustration and lack of perceived usefulness that result from attempting to function in a virtual world that is slow, unreliable, poorly detailed, and unrelated to the course content may lead to poor

participation and disengagement from the course. Careful planning and consideration must be given to integrating virtual worlds into the classroom, and integrating course content into virtual worlds, be that through games and simulations, virtual classrooms, or directed tasks within open virtual worlds (Jarmon, et al., 2009).

The act of creating a game or simulation within reasonable time and cost parameters, and at a level of complexity that users can navigate, requires that the number of variables represented in the game be lower than the number of variables existing in the environment (Proserpio & Gioia, 2007). A bridge-building simulation for civil engineering students can account for variables of span length, wind patterns, temperature and precipitation ranges, and materials. Including the personalities of all of the individual construction workers, however, is far too complex even though one of those individuals doing shoddy work could influence the stability of the bridge. Reducing the complexity of the actual environment into a usable simulation can affect its face validity. To help determine the validity of a game or simulation Proserpio and Gioia (2007) present a set of heuristics for choosing, or designing, a good simulation.

(a) is it based on good educational principles?; (b) is it framed around an engaging story?; (c) does it put some mystery and continuity into the simulation story?; and (d) does it lend itself to conducting a good "pre-briefing" of the simulation (oral or written) so that the student can run the simulation *and* be prepared to learn from it? (p72)

Learning Curve

Both students and instructors are going to experience learning curves when they first begin navigating through virtual worlds. Instructors, while probably not designing and implementing games and simulations themselves, will need to be extremely comfortable navigating through the virtual world and be aware of all the possible permutations and combinations of action within the game or simulation. Instructors who teach in a virtual classroom, or assign directed tasks within open virtual worlds, will need to have created an avatar and be familiar enough with the virtual world that they know how to communicate and lecture effectively, allowing them to assign tasks that it is possible for students to successfully complete within the constraints of the world itself. An instructor who intends to assign students the task of opening a business within Second Life needs to understand the economy, land ownership or rental, customer patterns, and infrastructure of Second Life to ensure that students can be successful in completing the task. Instructors need to be trained in the use of the virtual world, and they must be given opportunities to experience the world themselves. They need to play games (Aldrich, 2004). Experiential learning is required for the instructors to be able to use virtual worlds effectively. Instructors must also accept the fact that some of their students may be more comfortable with and knowledgeable about the technology meaning that the instructor may no longer be the expert in all facets of the course (Zeliff, 2004).

Courses need to be developed with the range of students' virtual world experience in mind. For games and simulations designed specifically for the course, all students will need to invest some time in learning how to use the interface. Students who frequent virtual worlds or play computer games regularly will be able to comfortably navigate through the world much more quickly than those students whose online experiences are restricted to email and the internet. To avoid creating high frustration for students, and needing to spend the bulk amount of course time on learning how to navigate through a virtual world, the interface needs to be simple and streamlined and learning how to use the interface needs to be part of the learning for the course. In the case of simulations, where the open-ended nature can make it difficult for those who are used to a more linear style of learning, one option is to provide new players with the option to follow an automated, annotated walk-through of some of the key sections of the virtual world (Aldrich, 2004).

Content

One of the greatest challenges of developing successful virtual world learning environments lies in ensuring that the desired content is effectively integrated into the virtual world. It is important that the technology used is not obsolete, but beyond that requirement content plays the greatest role in effective online learning (Aldrich, 2004; Slotte & Herbert, 2008).

When using a virtual classroom within a virtual world content considerations will be the same as in a traditional classroom, with only the method of delivery changing slightly. Assigning directed tasks within open virtual worlds will require instructors to tailor the assignment to the content of the course and to determine beforehand that the virtual world has the infrastructure required to support the assignment. Asking students to open and run a business requires the virtual world to have an economy and customers. Asking students to treat a certain number of patients requires the virtual world to have a hospital and sick or injured people.

Developing games and simulations that make effective and realistic use of content in a way that complements the course is difficult. Technical experts who can create and program the virtual world are generally unfamiliar with both the course content and pedagogical techniques. Their interests lie in the latest technologies and creating engaging, immersive environments, not creating effective teaching and learning environments or considering the learning styles of potential users (Aldrich, 2004).

Course instructors or subject matter experts will know the required content but generally will not understand how that content needs to be structured to integrate into the virtual world. They may also be insufficiently grounded in effective game and simulation pedagogical techniques. Where content is delivered in a linear fashion in the classroom, it needs to become a set of rules that can be integrated into the artificial intelligence of the game or simulation, preferably in the form of cyclical or open-ended content (Aldrich, 2004; Lynch & Tunstall, 2008). This is difficult to do without a fundamental understanding of artificial intelligence and game theory.

Pedagogical experts will not know the course content, and will have varying levels of understanding of the technical aspects based on their experience working with virtual worlds. Assembling a team of subject matter, technical, and pedagogical experts is a start, but there is often so little overlap between the expertise of the three areas that effective communication and integration can be challenging (Lynch & Tunstall, 2008).

Customization and Localization

Where games and simulations are developed for course purposes, or existing games and simulations are used, it is important that the background, dialogue, and character reactions and responses are specifically customized to the locale of the students and the simulated environment (Aldrich, 2004). Cultural norms in organizations differ in various countries. Where in Canada it may be acceptable for a front-line supervisor to question a vice-president, in Japan it may not. Norms also differ between types of workplaces. It may be common for a software developer fresh out of university to raise technical concerns with a manager, but a newly graduated physician may not feel comfortable questioning the work of a more experienced doctor. When creating a simulation for training bookstore employees in customer service, the Finnish Bookstore started with dialogue based on generic sales theories, but then customized that dialogue specifically to what would be heard in the Finnish Bookstore itself (Slotte & Herbert, 2008).

The virtual characters within games and simulations may also need to be customized for their intended users. A group of undergraduate students may relate to, and be engaged by, a different type of character than a group of executive MBA students. People have different communicative styles and games and simulations should provide characters with whom everyone can communicate. Instead of customizing a game or simulation for each use, designers can include multiple virtual characters of various types and communicative styles and have users select the characters with whom they would like to interact (Gulz, 2005).

Interaction and Evaluation

Virtual individuals with whom students interact within the game or simulation need to react and respond to the actions around them in a realistic way. This realism is a factor of both the content and the technology. The reactions of avatars need to look like the reactions of humans in a physical sense, in order to avoid throwing students out of their immersion in the virtual world. At the same time the reactions and responses need to be realistic and useful in the context of the course being taught. Medical students who are treating virtual patients need to hear the same complaints, symptoms, and responses to questions that they would hear in an actual hospital. Management students who are leading virtual teams need to hear complaints, questions, problems, and excuses that they would hear in an actual workplace.

There is no obvious way to evaluate the performance of students who are completing tasks within virtual worlds, and it is more difficult to test the material learned than that learned in the classroom (Aldrich, 2004). When designing a game or a simulation one must ask if students will be graded solely on the final outcome or also on individual tasks along the way. Will progress through a simulation be tracked, so that students can debrief, and instructors can provide feedback on, the entire experience? Perhaps only participation will be graded, so that students can take risks that may lead to negative outcomes but that will better prepare them for their workplace. In one nursing school, faculty role-play the administrator and the staff nurse in the simulation (Skiba, 2009), thereby being present for the entire experience and able to provide extensive feedback and evaluate the experience as a whole.

Having students complete defined tasks within open virtual worlds can also pose evaluation challenges. Marks can be assigned for the outcomes – a successful business opening, healthy and satisfied patients, or well-designed and functional architecture. If some of the greatest benefits of learning within a virtual world are experiential and double-loop learning, interaction, and risk-taking, however, basing evaluations solely on outcomes will not motivate students to take full advantage of the technology and all that it offers. Students who know that only the final outcome of their work is being graded may not be as willing to implement innovative new ideas or make high-risk decisions at the risk of failing the assignment.

CONCLUSION

In the twenty-first century, with vast amounts of information always at our fingertips, "the ability to think and learn and find out things is more important than mastering a static body of knowledge" (Tapscott, 2009, p. 127). We suggest that the use of virtual environments allows the possibility of enacting principles of learning that are both engaging and powerful. These environments allow us to structure and experience educational environments in ways that have not been previously possible. In particular, they provide a powerful medium through which learners can think, acquire new knowledge and, ultimately, learn. Double-loop, collaborative, and experiential learning are all valuable learning styles that are inherent in students learning through doing in a virtual world. While exploring virtual worlds,

students also have the opportunity to benefit from the acquisition of tacit knowledge and immediacy in responses to their actions. Using virtual worlds as an educator will require a considerable upfront commitment of time to both fully understand the opportunities available and to create environments that provide value to specific courses. Over time the initial commitment, however, will reap the benefits of engaged, excited students and a more interesting and interactive teaching environment for educators as well.

REFERENCES

Aldrich, C. (2004). *Simulations and the future of learning: An innovative (and perhaps revolutionary) approach to e-learning.* San Francisco, CA: Pfeiffer.

Arbaugh, J. B., & Benbunan-Fich, R. (2006). An investigation of epistemological and social dimensions of teaching in online learning environments. *Academy of Management Learning & Education, 5*(4), 435–447. doi:10.5465/AMLE.2006.23473204

Argyris, C. (2002). Double-loop learning, teaching, and research. *Academy of Management Learning & Education, 1*(2), 206–218. doi:10.5465/AMLE.2002.8509400

Argyris, C., & Schon, D. A. (1974). *Theory in practice: Increasing professional effectiveness.* San Francisco, CA: Jossey-Bass, Inc., Publishers.

Brower, H. H. (2003). On emulating classroom discussion in a distance-delivered OBHR course: Creating an on-line learning community. *Academy of Management Learning & Education, 2*(1), 22–36. doi:10.5465/AMLE.2003.9324013

De Lucia, A., Francese, R., Passero, I., & Tortora, G. (2009). Development and evaluation of a virtual campus on Second Life: The case of SecondMI. *Computers & Education, 52*, 220–233. doi:10.1016/j.compedu.2008.08.001

Gertler, M. S. (2003). Tacit knowledge and the economic geography of context, or the undefinable tacitness of being (there). *Journal of Economic Geography, 3*, 75–99. doi:10.1093/jeg/3.1.75

Gulz, A. (2005). Social enrichment by virtual characters - differential benefits. *Journal of Computer Assisted Learning, 21*(6), 405–418. doi:10.1111/j.1365-2729.2005.00147.x

Hutchins, H. M., & Hutchison, D. (2008). Cross-disciplinary contributions to e-learning: A tripartite design model. *Journal of Workplace Learning, 20*(5), 364–380. doi:10.1108/13665620810882950

Jacoby, D. (2009). SecondLife, second strife? *Intellectual Property & Technology Law Journal, 20*(9), 7–10.

Jarmon, L., Traphagan, T., Mayrath, M., & Trivedi, A. (2009). Virtual world teaching, experiential learning, and assessment: An interdisciplinary communication course in Second Life. *Computers & Education, 53*, 169–182. doi:10.1016/j.compedu.2009.01.010

Kenworthy, J., & Wong, A. (2005). Developing managerial effectiveness: Assessing and comparing the impact of development programmes using a management simulation or a management game. *Developments in Business Simulations and Experiential Learning, 32*, 164–175.

Kerres, M., & De Witt, C. (2003). A didactical framework for the design of blended learning arrangements. *Journal of Educational Media, 28*(2-3), 101–113.

Kolb, D. A. (1984). *Experiential learning: Experience as the source of learning and development*. Englewood Cliffs, NJ: Prentice-Hall, Inc.

Lafsky, M. (2009). Can training in Second Life teach doctors to save real leaves? *Discover: Science, Technology, and The Future*. Retrieved from http://discovermagazine.com/ 2009/jul-aug/15-can-medical-students-learn-to-save-real-lives-in-second-life.

Lam, A. (2000). Tacit knowledge, organizational learning and societal institutions: An integrated framework. *Organization Studies, 21*(3), 487–513. doi:10.1177/0170840600213001

Leonard, D., & Sensiper, S. (1998). The role of tacit knowledge in group innovation. *California Management Review, 40*(3), 112–132.

Li, M., & Geo, F. (2003). Why Nonaka highlights tacit knowledge: A critical review. *Journal of Knowledge Management, 7*(4), 6–14. doi:10.1108/13673270310492903

Lynch, M. A., & Tunstall, R. J. (2008). When worlds collide: Developing game-design partnerships in universities. *Simulation & Gaming, 39*(3), 379–398. doi:10.1177/1046878108319275

Marks, R. B., Sibley, S. D., & Arbaugh, J. B. (2005). A structural equation model of predictors for effective online learning. *Journal of Management Education, 29*(4), 531–563. doi:10.1177/1052562904271199

Mooradian, N. (2005). Tacit knowledge: Philosophic roots and role in KM. *Journal of Knowledge Management, 9*(6), 104–113. doi:10.1108/13673270510629990

Ostrander, M. (2008). Talking, looking, flying, searching: Information seeking behaviour in Second Life. *Library Hi Tech, 26*(4), 512–524. doi:10.1108/07378830810920860

Peltier, J. W., Schibrowsky, J. A., & Drago, W. (2007). The interdependence of the factors influencing the perceived quality of the online learning experience: A causal model. *Journal of Marketing Education*, *29*(2), 140–153. doi:10.1177/0273475307302016

Polanyi, M. (1966). *The tacit dimension*. Garden City, NY: Doubleday.

Proserpio, L., & Gioia, D. A. (2007). Teaching the virtual generation. *Academy of Management Learning & Education*, *6*(1), 69–80. doi:10.5465/AMLE.2007.24401703

Roman, P. A., & Brown, D. (2008). *Games - just how serious are they?* Paper presented at the Interservice/Industry Training, Simulation, and Education Conference.

Sarner, A. (2008). Generation virtual. *Forbes*. Retrieved from http://www.forbes.com/2008/04/30/genv-gartner-marketing-oped-cx_asa_0430genv.html

Shrivastava, P. (1999). Management classes as online learning communities. *Journal of Management Education*, *23*(6), 691–702. doi:10.1177/105256299902300607

Sitzmann, T., Kraiger, K., Stewart, D., & Wisher, R. (2006). The comparative effectiveness of Web-based and classroom instruction: A meta-analysis. *Personnel Psychology*, *59*(3), 623–644. doi:10.1111/j.1744-6570.2006.00049.x

Skiba, D. J. (2009). Nursing education 2.0: A second look at Second Life. *Nursing Education Perspectives*, *30*(2), 129–131.

Slotte, V., & Herbert, A. (2008). Engaging workers in simulation-based e-learning. *Journal of Workplace Learning*, *20*(3), 165–180. doi:10.1108/13665620810860477

Smith, E. A. (2001). The role of tacit and explicit knowledge in the workplace. *Journal of Knowledge Management*, *5*(4), 311–321. doi:10.1108/13673270110411733

Squire, L. R. (1987). *Memory and brain*. New York, NY: Oxford University Press.

Taber, N. (2008). Emergency response: E-learning for paramedics and firefighters. *Simulation & Gaming*, *39*(4), 515–527. doi:10.1177/1046878107306669

Tapscott, D. (2009). *Grown up digital: How the net generation is changing your world*. New York, NY: McGraw Hill.

ten Berge, T., & van Hezewijk, R. (1999). Procedural and declarative knowledge: An evolutionary perspective. *Theory & Psychology*, *9*(5), 605–624. doi:10.1177/0959354399095002

Wagner, C. (2008). Learning experience with virtual worlds. *Journal of Information Systems Education*, *19*(3), 263–266.

Welsh, E. T., Wanberg, C. R., Brown, K. G., & Simmering, M. J. (2003). E-learning: Emerging uses, empirical results and future directions. *International Journal of Training and Development*, *7*(4), 245–258. doi:10.1046/j.1360-3736.2003.00184.x

Yohon, T. (2004). Internet use in classroom instruction. In Christopher, D. (Ed.), *E-world: Virtual learning, collaborative environments, and future technologies* (pp. 42–66). Reston, VA: National Business Education Association.

Zeliff, N. D. (2004). Pedagogical and technological challenges of the Internet. In Christopher, D. (Ed.), *E-world: Virtual learning, collaborative environment, and future technologies*. Relston, VA: National Business Education Association.

Chapter 20

Use of Blended E–Learning Resources in Higher Education:
An Innovation from Healthcare Training

Catharine Jenkins
Birmingham City University, UK

Andrew Walsh
Birmingham City University, UK

ABSTRACT

This chapter discusses the challenges for higher education raised by socio-cultural, technological, and pedagogical developments. The authors' response as experienced healthcare educators was to develop videos and e-learning objects as part of a blended approach to training mental health nursing students. The authors describe the initiative, discuss progress, analyse outcomes, and highlight implications for practice. The chapter ends by drawing wider conclusions about use of streaming media within professional education.

INTRODUCTION

The purpose of this chapter is to discuss and share our reflections, experiences and opinions on developing and using digital streaming media. We suggest that theoretical understandings have yet to catch up with practice; to some extent those of us working with this media are pioneers. This

DOI: 10.4018/978-1-60960-800-2.ch020

is our contribution to the ongoing debate on how best to use these resources.

Now is an exciting and challenging time to be working in higher education. Not only is a vast range of new knowledge and understanding being created, but new resources enable us to share these and learn from each other. Higher education is expanding all over the world, and the groups that we teach are so diverse that any interaction benefits from a multitude of perspectives. The push for active learning means that any lesson can be full of surprises and generate new ideas for teachers as often as students. Living as we do in an age of rapid technological development, there are innovations waiting to be explored and applied in every lesson. The opportunities for students themselves to design and develop their own learning means that many come to class enthused by new research and wishing to share it with their colleagues. Classroom time is freed up for discussions, arguments and challenges, making each interaction more exciting and leading to further generation of theories and ideas. Not long ago we felt we were being creative when playing a record to students as they entered class, nowadays we and they have 24 hour access to a huge range of multimedia resources to stimulate and entertain. Learning as a result has become so much more fun – and so an experience that we are keen to repeat.

In this chapter we will be focusing on video-streaming in its use within mental health nurse training. In the UK, mental health nurses are specialists from day one, and draw all their experiences from this area. The University where we work, Birmingham City University, is a leading educator of all branches of nurses. Our background is as nurses ourselves, and our understandings are very much rooted in this tradition. The professionalization of nursing has meant that this practical understanding now must be underpinned with vast amounts of knowledge and theory, and nurses must be able to explain the relevance of the theory, and account for any interaction using values and evidence. So for us, nursing has become both an intellectual and emotional subject – care is difficult to define, when it is done well or badly this is clear to the recipient, but unpacking the whys and wherefores is quite a task. The recent emphasis on the perspectives of service users (previously known as patients!) and their family members, sometimes known as carers, has led to a more balanced power dynamic, although we still have a long way to go.

In our teaching, we need to develop multi-faceted abilities in the nurses of the future. Of course, they come to us having selected themselves on the basis of feeling that their personal characteristics matched what they imagined would be needed for the role, and they tend to be empathetic, skilled communicators with a commitment to social justice.

Their values and skills are applied in the context of government policy and theoretical approaches. Over the three years of nurse education, they learn about different specialities – older people's mental health, which is Catharine's area, community mental health care, which is Andrew's, and others such as rehabilitation, crisis management, addiction and so on. The modular system of teaching means that students can study hard and do well in a module, but then forget about it afterwards! We realised that by their third year they may have strong discrete areas of understanding, but these tended to be disconnected and some previous learning was being wasted. As we teach them Community Mental Health Care in their final year, it seemed a good idea to tackle this issue and make a virtue out of the opportunity to revise and apply previous learning to a variety of realistic scenarios representing the sort of common problems people in their care could face.

The use of e-learning tools such as digital film has provoked a great deal of interest in recent years. We recognised an opportunity to use this new technology to enliven our teaching and promote greater engagement. We felt that this had great potential, and were keen to explore this further. As we looked into it, one thing led to another, and the ideas snowballed into one whole which has proven to be very exciting for us, as well as being very positively received by the students.

The learning we have gained from the innovation has been immense, and in this chapter we plan to share the process and tactics we used, together with the technological and theoretical background, so that colleagues will be able to take and apply what is useful for their own areas. This chapter also reflects our response to the impact on our work overall and to evaluations of subsequent student learning. We hope that in sharing this we will be contributing to broadening debate and contributing to this exciting innovative – and also practical and applicable, new educational approach.

Our experiences as mental health nurses have taught us that the most important aspect of our work with service users is the quality of the relationship with them. For us there is huge congruence between the role of the nurse as facilitator, and educator as facilitator. In this chapter we will be explaining how technology can be used to enhance rather than distance inter-personal relationships with clients, whether they be service users or students.

THE CONTEXT OF CHANGES IN HIGHER EDUCATION

In recent years, there has been a worldwide increase in the numbers of people entering higher education. For educators there is an expectation that they will not only manage these greater numbers but also enhance the quality of student learning, their experiences and outcomes. A recent report (Association of Graduate Recruiters, 2007) highlighted the fact that employers believe that graduates generally lack essential abilities, especially the so-called "soft skills" such as team working and the ability to negotiate with others. In mental health nursing there is an expectation (DH, 2004) that as well as having a basic knowledge framework, people should be able to practice collaboratively with service users and their families and work in partnership with a variety of other professionals.

As UK based health care educators the authors are aware of these pressures. As mental health nurses we are also conscious of the need to manage expectations imposed upon us by our professional body, the Nursing and Midwifery Council (2008). As will be discussed, in recent years there

have been changes in the organisation and ethos of mental health care in the UK, and it was also necessary to reflect these changes in our teaching.

Professional education for nurses is a relatively recent phenomenon. The heritage of our profession involves staff being chosen on the basis of their size and their ability to play in the hospital band! We hasten to reassure you that we are talking about the distant past, but our own learning experiences were mainly practice based, and involved learning while working, generally through modelling our own behaviour on senior colleagues' that we respected. Theoretical aspects were recognised only in so far as they provided a justification for the interventions favoured at the time, and nursing, as an occupational group, was not seen as enjoying the status of autonomous professionalism. Fortunately, there have been vast changes over the past twenty years. Nowadays, the role of the mental health nurse is seen as one of enabler, supporting people through a process of regaining their mental health in ways that they themselves find most useful. In coming relatively late to nurse education, we find that this reflects the current focus on teaching as facilitation, in which we enable students to reach goals in ways which are most suitable for them.

The worlds of both healthcare and education are changing in response to demographic, social and economic factors. The diversity of patients, nurses, students and educators reflects twenty first century urban society. Increased student numbers following widening access policies have led to greater student diversity in terms of ethnicity, age and maturity, social background and previous educational experience (Carr, 2008). Recent government policy (Department of Health, 2004 and 2006) consistently highlights the centrality of valuing diversity and social inclusion for good mental health.

This is the context within which we provide mental health nurse education. In this chapter we will outline how we use digital film as a tool in enhancing learning opportunities for student nurses, how it fits in with educational theory and government policy, how we went about this, the advantages and potential pitfalls, and where we see the future developments to be leading us.

APPROACHES TO TEACHING MENTAL HEALTH NURSING

The course on which we teach is run on modular lines. Themes run throughout the modules, and students spend 50% of their time in each of practice areas and the University setting. At times they appear to struggle in linking theory with practice, and with integrating learning from earlier modules with that subsequent ones. In response to this one of the authors (Andrew) designed an e-learning resource, the 'Mental Health Learning Community website'. This site is situated on the university virtual learning environment, 'Moodle' and offers students a one-stop link to all on-line learning related to the course, and aims to unify the e-learning provision and promote continuity between the various aspects of the course. The intention is to provide a scaffold around which the student can construct their understanding of mental health-nursing (Cowan, 2006). A series of scenarios were developed by the teaching team, which would enable students to apply their learning at different stages to the various aspects of service-users difficulties. These scenarios lend themselves perfectly to digital film, and we proceeded to design, and make, videos of fictional characters playing the part of Mental Health service users.

The process of developing the scenarios will be described in detail below, but our priorities are to promote positive values around mental health, and to respect the diversity of both students and service-users, making the films engaging, authentic and relevant to practice decision-making, and able to respond to policy developments.

We recognise that issues such as inclusion and exclusion, communication styles, learning styles and the management of a therapeutic (learning)

environment are equally applicable to education as to mental health care provision. Indeed, evidence supporting the need for attention to diversity issues in nursing (Fernando, 2003) is matched by that suggesting education faces similar problems (Allen, Bonous-Hammarth, & Teranishi, 2006). Brunson, D., Jarman, B. and Lampl, L. (2007) outline how minority students feel marginalized both inside and outside the classroom. Unresolved, these problems mean that services, whether education or health and social care, provide a lesser and possibly damaging service to those who come from diverse backgrounds, particularly in relation to recognised strands such as age, ethnicity, gender, sexuality disability and religion (Stickley and Bassett, 2007).

In developing the module ethos, and the digital films that are central to its success, we prioritise sensitivity to diversity issues. The films are streamed online, and this is a potential obstacle to students who do not have easy access to the internet. Older students, those who cannot afford broadband, and those with heavy home commitments find it more difficult to get online and view the films 'any time, anywhere' than others. In order to promote confidence and access we need to develop tactics not only to enable access, but also to motivate students to engage and improve their IT skills. The University has a large computer department and a library also well-stocked with PCs. At the beginning of each module we demonstrate the logon process, and are able to check via the Moodle site so as to monitor who is struggling and may need extra support.

There is a suggestion that e-learning approaches can help to improve learning by making resources more readily available. For example, for mature students who have other family commitments or students who have to work and may have to study after long or unsocial hours (Niederhauser, VP. Bigley, MB. Hale, J. Harper, D. (1999). Phillips (2005) discusses the benefits of access, convenience, enhanced quality, and swift feedback, while emphasising the importance of an active experiential approach which can combine to work well with a variety of learning styles.

IT skills are a part of modern home and professional life, but even nowadays, it is surprising how many students report poor access to computers on placement and at home (Gilchrist and Ward, 2006). Similarly, service users have a range of understandings related to their access to online information sources. Many are well-informed, and expect to be partners in rather than recipients of care. Some of course are not, and depend on staff for understandable information, assistance with solving problems and using technology. The context of delivery of the module is therefore one of a changing and diverse world, in which students are expected to be able to use sensitivity and good judgement in applying multi-faceted learning to complex and often difficult situations.

We realise that we need to be thoughtful and reflective about the outcomes we require and sensitive to the identified needs of our students, guided by educational theory in preparing a consistent programme. Following Biggs (2003), we are determined to provide alignment from our assessment of the complex learning needs, to designing the related learning outcomes, and from there to the teaching programme and assessment approach. Our motivation is to provide students who are 'fit for purpose' – ready and capable of becoming not only mental health nurses, but also self-directed, motivated professionals.

Our own experiences of mental health nursing in community settings certainly contribute to the learning outcomes, as well as the hidden agenda on our wish list. Although knowledge of medical, social and psychological approaches to well-being features strongly, we also want to include 'soft' transferable skills (that are perhaps more difficult to teach). Skills such as the ability to think on your feet and to respond appropriately to a crisis, taking in masses of complex information and prioritising actions whilst also acknowledging the concerns of families. We also feel that it is important that students recognise their own part in any situation.

How they fit into a team, how they learn and teach others, how they keep themselves and others safe, and how they manage their own emotional responses to challenging situations.

Narrative Approaches

One of the ways that nurses deal with these issues informally is by telling each other stories. We both have a wealth of stories of our own that have gathered over the years, and even now sometimes reminisce and try to make sense of what happened in relation to incidents from the past. We use these stories to illustrate points in classroom teaching, and have found that students respond very positively to them, enjoying the vicarious thrill of the dilemmas involved, empathically identifying with the issues raised, and working effectively and collaboratively in coming up with ideas for solutions to problems. The 'narrative' approach to teaching is very engaging, and congruent with and traditional to the culture of the caring professions, with its case conferences and oral handovers (McDrury and Alterio, 2002), and one we feel could be used successfully in promoting formation of conceptual links.

Problem-Based Learning

Problem based learning (PBL) is used increasingly to develop the higher order cognitive activities required for professional practice and is associated with higher engagement and enthusiasm, as students can see the learning is meaningful and worthwhile (Biggs, 2003). PBL is enhanced by the opportunities raised by technological improvements used complementarily with traditional approaches, and emphasises a social, collaborative approach (Jochems, W, Van Merrienboer, J, and Koper, R (2004). In developing the narratives, we keep the learning outcomes, the desired learning processes and interests of stakeholders (for example, service users and professional colleagues) in mind, designing suitable problems as triggers into the scenarios.

We also consider what students want. Traditionally they are viewed as 'assessment driven' (Biggs, 2003). As outlined earlier, they are a diverse group with wide-ranging abilities and responsibilities. Their study has to be fitted in with paid work, family time and other responsibilities. Despite commitment to the professional qualification, they really need to understand the point of an activity before designating time and energy to developing their knowledge and understanding beyond the basic that will enable a passed assessment (Biggs, 2003). Like many of our students, we aspire to high grades, but recognise the variety of factors that could limit this. We need to increase the factors that would promote intrinsic motivation and excellence within this context. Our conclusions are that a narrative approach, using PBL, combined with an assessment that was strongly linked to realistic, thought-provoking practice issues would increase motivation, leading to enhanced immediate outcomes in grades, together with long-term outcomes for professional practice (JISC, 2009).

Emotional Intelligence

We recognise that learning, perhaps especially in a care orientated profession is an emotional process, and that students benefit from positive relationships with us and with each other. Learning can be a sociable, fun and enjoyable activity, and we want the module to reflect an enthusiasm for our work as both teachers and nurses. Some motivation is provided by a negative emotion – fear! Anxieties about knowing what to do and how in tricky situations, and about how as a result one is viewed by colleagues, do focus the mind. In common with most novice professionals, establishment of a professional reputation is often central to student nurses' concerns.

The need for feedback, both positive and negative is recognised by Race (2001) who includes it in a list of factors underpinning successful learning.

Others are the opportunity to practice and learn from mistakes, to learn with others, collaborating in developing understanding from different perspectives, and making sense of learning, or developing a sense of ownership. The module is planned so as to offer opportunities for the application of theory to a variety of challenging scenarios, so that students can build self-esteem as a competent practitioner.

Responding to Stakeholders

Our learning outcomes are also designed to respond to other stakeholders, in particular service users and professional colleagues. Warne and McAndrew (2005) suggest that 'how nurses are prepared for practice should be shaped by practice' and our own links with service providers and users certainly support the process. All parties agree that nurses should be well-informed, basing care on a strong evidence base and values, and should take a person-centred approach. In addition service users require respect, empathy, to be listened to, that their perspective be acknowledged, and to be cared for in their own home environment by knowledgeable, skilled practitioners (Clarke and Walsh, 2009). Practitioners emphasise safety, interpersonal skills, confidence and professional consideration, as well as punctuality! They also expect their colleagues to know the basics thoroughly, and operate safely, legally and ethically in a challenging environment. (Clarke and Walsh, 2009)

Constructivist Approaches

Traditional approaches to teaching, such as power-point lectures, are limited in their impact on learning (Bligh, 2000) and do not meet the students', service users' or employers' needs described above. The complexities of modern professional practice require a multi-faceted approach that allows students to take charge of their learning needs and approaches to meeting them, in a way that enables them to test application of theory to realistic challenging situations. Sometimes theory learnt earlier can be called to mind, on other occasions students recognise a gap in learning and that they need to address this 'just-in-time' (Thorne, 2003). Through this process they build a bridge from their previous knowledge and understanding to the next level. This 'constructivist' approach to learning is based on the work of Piaget (1954, cited in Gagnon and Collay 2006) and emphasises the role of the teacher as facilitator, enabling and guiding students while they build their learning collaboratively and socially using relevant and realistic activities (Phillips, 2005, Gagnon and Collay, 2006)

The learning process mirrors the practice environment in that the students will be working in teams, supporting each other and contributing to each other's development. The focus is very much on active engagement with the narratives and issues raised, with an expectation that theory be tested and challenged, and solutions created that are both realistic and evidence and value-based. The narratives that have been developed, outline challenging, complex situations that are not easily managed, either emotionally or practically. Mental health nursing, in common with other high-pressure professions, requires an individual to be able to manage their own emotional responses and assist others in coping with theirs, while simultaneously working towards agreed goals. Emotional intelligence is therefore central to professional success, and a positive learning environment in which educators show empathy, genuineness and unconditional positive regard (Mortiboys, 2005) models these characteristics for students and offers a safe place for risk-taking while building understanding. The philosophy underpinning this approach values students' ownership of their development and recognises that learning is a social, collaborative process in common with a profession with values such as promotion of autonomy, growth, and safety.

The scenarios and narratives based around them are constructed too. A mixture of script, films and simulations (interactions with actors) offer opportunities for a blended learning experience and use of a variety of approaches to learning. The different perspectives shown by the characters in the scenarios mean that no scenario is one dimensional. Depending on their own agenda, a character from a scenario may hide or reveal information, thus forcing the student to assess the motivations of each and a range of possible solutions. This problem-based learning approach is particularly creative and engaging, and promotes intrinsic motivation and a deeper approach to learning (Ramsden, 2003), particularly in alignment with a realistic assessment (Biggs, 2003, Laurillard, 2002).

How the students engage with the online and written material is entirely up to them. They may access the resources at any time, and watch the films as often as they wish. Some students report a more reflective, intuitive approach, as they like to imagine the characters as real people on a real caseload, whereas others will take a more focused approach, structuring their work around prioritising, planning and delegating. The combination of online and classroom interactions facilitates each learning style, whether reflector, activist, theorist or pragmatist (Honey and Mumford, 1992). Indeed, in working to their strengths, students gain confidence, and are able to experiment with different approaches in response to both the on-line material and collaborative classroom work. This 'blended' approach to learning (Thorne, 2003) makes full use of the video-streaming possibilities. Complemented by further e-learning resources available on the virtual learning environment (VLE) (Moodle) such as quizzes, discussion forums, journal articles and face-to-face in tutorials and lessons they make a highly useful educational resource. As module leaders we watch the films in classroom time, using them as a trigger to prompt the students into further analysis of the issues at stake. The pre-work that the students do before class means that they are able to work with us at a deeper level than had been possible previously. Time is freed-up for the more creative levels of learning – conceptualisation, analysis critique and evaluation. This academic stretch challenges students, both those who struggle to apply theory to practice and those who are theoretically strong but less confident in practice. Support is provided mutually by students, through the VLE and through staff availability.

Students' Approaches to Learning

The students' own characteristics also affect their learning. Factors such as their previous experience of education, their starting points, their approaches to learning and learning styles all make a difference (Race, 2001, Ramsden, 2003). The approach to learning may be deep or superficial (Ramsden, 2003) and refers to how a student deals with a learning task. It depends at least partly on the problem set and how the student perceives the teacher's wishes (Laurillard, 2002) As deep learning is associated with understanding of arguments and connections, as opposed to collection of unrelated facts, deep learning is desirable for situations where the learning is meaningful, such as is the case with health professionals. Experiential learning is considered more likely to promote a deep approach because the student uses their knowledge to solve realistic problems. The role of the teacher here is to facilitate opportunities for the student to engage with and challenge knowledge and theory, to adapt to student progress and to support reflection which leads to understanding (Ramsden, 2003). These theoretical considerations influence our determination to promote an active, experiential approach throughout the module, which we achieve by exploiting the online learning potential afforded by the combination of video-streaming and narratives, which enabling contact time to be used to reinforce analysis and application of learning.

There is considerable debate surrounding the extent to which learning approach influences outcomes. Many authors have written positively about the 'deep' approach. For example, Moon (2002), states that it is desirable because it results in more successful learning involving clearer understanding of meaning, interpreting, and reasoning. Bain (2004) and Ramsden (2003) would add problem solving, intrinsic motivation, setting the new knowledge in the context of what has already been learnt, and commitment and transferability. It is also more rewarding, fun, and gains higher marks, according to Ramsden (2003). However, the concepts of learning styles and approaches are challenged by other authors (see Haggis, 2003) below, while Maclellan (2005) notes that the diversity of the UK population means that one size does not fit all and people have differing approaches in how they could achieve deep learning. Upon reflection it seems clear that students who are interested and enthusiastic will benefit more from a learning situation.

STUDENTS' APPROACHES TO LEARNING: A CRITIQUE

As discussed, we have to acknowledge the influence of student learning style theories – (especially Biggs, 2003) upon our work. In this we are not alone, ideas about students 'deep' or 'surface' approaches to study permeate many discussions within higher education. These theories continue to be widely influential in informing higher education teaching practice and the preparation of newly appointed lecturers. However, questions have been raised; for example, Haggis (2003) argues that these ideas have been accepted uncritically by many within higher education. She argues that acceptance of this theory has minimised attention to alternative ideas about how people learn. Haggis also makes a point that a great deal of research simply sets out to confirm existing theory.

In the UK, an influential report which examines learning style theories Coffield, F, Moseley, D, Hall, E and Ecclestone, K (2004) is critical about the research basis for much of this work. They highlight the fact that many studies were small in scale and confined themselves to the examination of responses of groups of students in particular contexts. The study authors find little in the way of robust research studies that would justify wider generalisations or that could be used to suggest recommendations for improvements in teaching practice.

An argument favouring qualified use of learning styles is provided by Rayner (2007). Examining Coffield et al's (2004) critique, Rayner agrees that over – rigid application of this theory, where learners are given labels such as 'deep' or 'surface' – is a mistake. He rebuts criticism that there is little consensus amongst proponents of learning style theory by arguing that in common with any good teacher – understanding of pedagogy and individual learning is a work in progress. Good teachers it is argued are constantly making and breaking their own models of what is effective teaching practice. The fact that learning style theorists disagree indicates that this area has developed by an empirical process of testing and falsification. It is therefore, natural that disagreements become apparent. Rayner concludes that assessments of student learning style are 'a tool and not an end in itself' – useful for helping educators to consider pedagogical improvements.

An interesting perspective is offered by Malcolm & Zukas' (2001) review of literature surrounding the general application of pedagogical ideas in higher education. The authors conclude that the most dominant ideas are drawn from psychology. This suggests that education is something that focuses upon the learner as an individual. The authors argue that there is an assumption that students learn (or fail to learn) because of their individual characteristics or because of the qualities (or failings) of individual teachers. They argue that this approach ignores possible social, politi-

cal, gender or class issues. An attempt by higher education managers to focus upon 'knowable' facts that can lead to policy changes is suggested as a reason for this focus Malcolm & Zukas' (2001).

Feedback from Students

In light of this critique of learning approaches we decided to take a cautious approach to the application of these theories and to carefully consider how best we could engage our students. Whilst it seemed reasonable to consider development of resources that would engage the student's interest we did not want to get too preoccupied with an over – reliance on learning style theory. As part of this consideration we decided to examine evaluations already provided to us by students used in a study investigating student interactions with digital learning resources (Walsh, 2009)

An important theme is the way in which students approached studies. There were several suggestions that students changed study approaches depending upon whether or not the content of the learning task was considered interesting; a typical response was one student who said:

'If something grabs my attention then I am interested in it and more likely to want to do it, if it doesn't then it is boring and more of a chore'

Students generally agreed that a subject was defined as 'interesting' if they could see its relevance to mental health nursing practice. If this link wasn't clear then students would very often take a different approach;

'I do the very minimum that I think will get me a pass if I think it is not relevant to my being a nurse. If I think it is interesting and relevant then I go above and beyond what is needed'

Another theme was the effect that the group had upon individual learning. Group members appeared to act as a shared memory when students were unsure about what was required;

'The group helps you, if you are struggling and unsure what to do, other people help you'

It was also reassuring to check if individuals shared understanding of course work. The students mentioned the importance of social support and friendship as having influenced their University experience. Another suggestion was that group interactions encouraged students to broaden ideas;

'..it is good that you have got a wide range of people that you can bounce things off and get other angles and things you wouldn't consider otherwise, and obviously you have got other cultures within the group giving you feedback so I think that is fantastic'

We therefore decided that whatever was developed would need to consider both our own responsibilities to make learning interesting and enjoyable and how the student's social group could influence learning. This attention to social factors is clearly something vital to the preparation of mental health nursing students. We conclude that our learning resources benefit from being a blend of online and class based material, and that both should have a warm, welcoming feel. Whilst it would be important to encourage individual learning it is also necessary to use the opportunity to encourage students to collaboratively work upon learning tasks.

Our discussions with students suggested that the nature of the task presented to them is crucial. As we have seen above, if the students feel that they are being presented with learning that is irrelevant to their future practice then they are much less likely to engage with this. It was therefore decided to ensure that learning tasks presented to students were of clinical significance – they should be studying and being assessed upon relevant material.

Aligned Assessment

Students take our module towards the end of their course. This means that they have a wide range of previous experience from placements, together with a similarly wide range of background theory. Unfortunately they are not always able to tie the two together effectively. The assessment for our module attempts to drive this process through requiring synthesis of previous knowledge and understanding, applied to realistic scenarios. Each scenario covers the problems faced by a fictional service-user. Laurillard (2002) recommends that assessment should reflect complex performances that are relevant to the field of study. Our assessment is authentic in reflecting practice and ties in well to the video scenarios and other triggers. Use of a viva echoes the practice situation of requirement to give a verbal summing up of the factors involved in problem development, theory and values behind intervention decisions, and evaluations of alternative approaches. This may well be similar to many professional situations, in that the novice worker needs to be able to offer a confident, reasoned account of their approach to a problem, expected goals, and perhaps a plan B! Of course they also need to be able to outline recent relevant policy and guidelines as well. The viva assessment provides a realistic (nerve-wracking, some say) approximation of accounting for oneself in a multi-disciplinary team meeting. Similarly feedback is rapid and so more effective (Gibbs, 2006). However, in the viva, students are expected to use evidence in the form of reading, research results and policy to back up their points, which generally speaking there is not the time for in the real-life version. Echoing the findings of Bickerstaffe, P. Hannigan, B. Wood, S. Young, N. (2007), students respect the assessment format, and have been known to say in retrospect how useful it has been in their professional preparation, despite their initial anxieties. Thus the assessment contributes to learning for the future, but we feel that it also has an impact, prior to the assessment, over the course of the module. This effect, known as 'backwash' (Biggs, 2003) occurs because students are motivated by the assessment, and because the assessment, curriculum and outcomes match, our intentions for learning, and students' actual learning, tend to correlate.

Our intentions are to produce competent, confident practitioners who are able to apply their knowledge and understanding to a variety of problems in order to produce effective, sensitive outcomes that will support people in returning to mental health. This involves syntheses of practical, intellectual and soft skills, underpinned by a sound knowledge of theory and policy, the ability to think critically and express their views articulately. We believe this is what the students wish for too.

The ambitious outcomes outlined above require a clearly thought out, well planned and structured approach. The digital films are central to the modules approach, and are entirely integrated into the approach to teaching and learning and the assessment process. In the next part of this chapter we will outline the creative imaginative and technological processes behind development of the stories and their presentation in the films.

USING DIGITAL FILM: RESEARCH AND PEDAGOGY

As part of developing the digital film to support our modules we considered what has already been written about their application within a health care setting. We were aware of a great deal of activity to produce these resources both within our own institution as well as more widely. However, we were less sure about how best to go about this in practice. Great claims have been made about the benefits of digital media and e-learning generally. For example, according to Slater (2005) these developments have the potential to 'transform' Higher Education Institutions although they may need support to do so. Acknowledging this need,

JISC (2009) state that whilst the link between technology and the enhancement of learning is well established, the link between pedagogy and technology is less clear. It is argued that despite little consideration of practicalities a vast amount of money has already been spent in the production of computerised resources – many of which have failed to find any use (Liber 2005). We were keen to avoid repeating such mistakes and set out to try and develop resources that were sound from a pedagogical perspective.

It is necessary to consider pedagogy because our reading suggested that the pedagogical basis of learning objects is infrequently considered, Mason, R, Pegler, C and Weller, M (2005). According to Maddux CD, Johnson, D & Willis, J (1992) the possibility of computer mediated learning and teaching has been around since at least the 1970's. Initially this technology assumed a fact transmission and instructional pedagogy (Parrish, 2004). Similarly, within nurse education Lewis M, Davies, R, Jenkins, and Tate, M, (2005) suggest that technological development to date has occurred in two distinct phases, a text only system, replaced by text and graphics. These authors argue that only recently have attempts been made to develop computer based learning resources to their full potential.

We initially considered whether there was any difference in outcomes between e-learning resources as opposed to traditional face to face teaching. A great many studies seek to investigate the comparative effects of e-learning resources as compared to traditional teaching methods and we found several that were of general relevance to our practice. Of several studies looking for evidence of effectiveness, four report no significant difference between groups using learning objects compared to more traditional approaches (DeAmicis, 1997, Gadanidis and Schindler, 2006, Jeffries, 2001, and Nugent, Soh & Ashok, 2006). This appears to be a common finding when evaluating e-learning courses, and Russell (1999) found nearly 400 studies confirming this.

However, it is possible to question the methodological rigour of many studies accessed and this appears to be a general criticism of much of this work. A recent literature review (Lewis et al 2005) sets out to critically evaluate 25 studies which report upon the effects of computerised resources in nurse education. Their review highlights a range of basic methodological problems which include design flaws, small sample groups and lack of control groups. The review (whilst acknowledging the difficulty of such measurement) finds that studies generally avoid investigating the effectiveness of knowledge transfer or knowledge retention. It concludes that there was a need for further studies into the use of computer based learning within nurse education. Similarly, another study (Bloomfield, While & Roberts 2008) which investigates the use of computerised resources on the acquisition of specific nursing clinical skills finds fault with many studies accessed and concludes that there is a need for more rigorous research into this area.

It is important to recognise that whilst all of the above studies sought to investigate the possible effects of e-learning, such studies are problematised by Clark's (2001) critique of assumptions made in such studies. As stated, it can be argued that there is little evidence to suggest that e-learning outcomes are any different to other forms of learning. Clark (2001) suggests that this is because there *is* no difference between the two. He argues that instructional media make no difference to student learning. What is important is teaching methods, it doesn't matter how this teaching is delivered any more "than the truck which delivers the groceries has an influence on our nutrition". Clark (2001) also argues that educational studies showing an advantage to e-learning are methodologically flawed.

We also considered evidence about the possible effect of e–learning resources upon student learning approaches. In a study involving 95 Open University psychology undergraduates Jelfs and Colbourn (2002) found some correlation between 'deep' learners and positive perceptions of e-learning. Students identified as 'surface' learners tended to complain about time constraints and engaged less with online resources. This study found a stronger correlation between confidence of using IT and student perceptions of e-learning. Students who are less confident at using IT are correspondingly less likely to positively evaluate e-learning. The authors acknowledge that this was a small study and that therefore findings could not be considered very widely relevant.

A study into student satisfaction with e-learning was conducted by Nian-Shing, Lin and Kinshukc (2008). This Taiwanese research study did not look specifically at student learning approaches. Instead, a consumer satisfaction questionnaire was used to study attitudes amongst 230 (88% response rate) students. This identified four important areas, which influenced student's views on e-learning. Course administration, ease of e-learning use/ access, quality of educational materials and perceived quality of group and instructor interaction were the most critical factors. Overall, the study recommends that IT support is especially important to quality of e-learning experienced.

Another Taiwanese study reached similar conclusions (Sun, P. Tsai, R. Finger, G. Chen, Y. Yeh, D. (2008). This study of 295 students (45% response) attempted to identify the most critical factors which may influence learner satisfaction with e-learning. Less emphasis was placed on factors such as IT support and technical ability, the most important variable was perceived quality of educational materials. The study concludes that perhaps students are now more comfortable with technology use. The authors acknowledge however that this study is limited in that it only examines satisfaction, there is no indication of the effect that use of this technology might have on learning outcome such as course grades.

We are interested in the suggestion (Sit, J. Chung, J. Chow, M. Wong, T, 2005) that whilst nursing students subjectively consider online learning resources to be useful they also value personal contact. In a study of 198 nursing students the authors find that whilst students value the convenience of this resource they highlight the need for human contact. The study concludes that technology (whilst valuable to learning) does not influence the learning process and it is important to maintain a focus on the quality of teaching input.

Muirhead (2007) is critical of e-learning that is developed 'top down' by institutions, arguing that this type of resource restricts critical thinking amongst students, while Wright (2009) suggests that an over-reliance on technology in multi-media presentations might actually obscure messages and hinder the transfer of ideas.

We reflected on the progress we had made in understanding our possible applications of this technology. Whilst it seems clear that there had been a growth in the uptake of these resources the evidence for their effectiveness is equivocal. Reflection upon our own teaching experience confirms that whilst our students find these to be helpful they also highly value class and group interaction. We therefore decided that:

- Any resources produced should be used to enhance existing teaching.
- Student responses to films should be developed and discussed as part of taught sessions. Although they would also be used as part of private study this would not be at the expense of class and group based interaction.
- Filmed resources should approximate as closely as possible the students actual clinical experience.
- Long term, we would commit to attempting an evaluation of this work.

We also had to consider the practicalities of actually making digital film. Until relatively recently we were both working within community mental health nursing services, neither of us have any specific technical training. This is a point raised by several commentators (Fallows and Bha-

not, 2005, Moisey, S, Mohamed, A, Spencer, B, 2006) who have commented that lack of technical skills are a significant barrier to the production of any kind of e-learning resource. Discussing the problems of efficient deployment of technology, the Association for Learning Technology (ALT, 2005) have highlighted the need for there to be co-operation between researchers, practitioners, developers as well as budget holders.

In response to these concerns the authors' institution has developed a system of support for educators who wish to develop learning resources. The aim of The Centre for Enhancement of Teaching and Learning (CELT) is to work across the University in developing multi media resources. A significant part of this work is undertaken by media students from Birmingham Institute of Art and Design who undertake practical placements within the department. Working in conjunction with the CELT it was possible to discuss the learning support that we wanted to develop (see Mackenzie and Walsh, 2009 for more detail). The first part of the process of working with CELT involved a discussion and agreement about what was to be produced, An important proviso is a consideration of the underlying pedagogy, staff are not encouraged and assisted to simply video record lectures. It is also agreed that any learning resources produced are made available as shared resources (see http://shareville.bcu.ac.uk/ for details of the most recent developments).

Our working partnership benefits from the diversity of our different perspectives, approaches and personalities. We can share skills and ideas, and offer friendly supportive but direct critiques of each other's work. Nursing is a highly gendered profession -10% of nurses are male (The Information Centre, 2007). There is similarly a perception that use of IT is has gender-based differences, but in the opposite proportions, in that men are more likely to be positive and confident about using computers (Gilchrist and Ward, 2006). In considering our own approaches, it is certainly the case that Andrew is an 'early adopter', taking an enthusiastic and pro-active approach to the potentials of new technology, and indeed having characteristics associated with this role, being an experienced user of IT, male and an opinion leader! (Bates, Manuel, and Oppenheim, 2007). Catharine, on the other hand, is more of a pragmatist (Moore, 1999) and has little interest in computers for their own sake, but is keen on how they can help her achieve exciting innovations for learning. In working through our own differences, it is helpful to be mindful of how these may have parallels with our students ease with use of technology, and the encouragement and support they may require.

USING DIGITAL FILM: CONTENT DESIGN

The scenarios constructed for the module are designed specifically with a variety of learning outcomes in mind (Race, 2001), to fit the specifics of development of the competent, aware professional described above. We intentionally decided to include the 'lowest common denominator' of replicating a soap opera feel. The stories of the different characters, representing service users on a mental health nurses caseload, deliberately overlap, in some cases the problems of one character having an impact on another. This also enables us to develop further characters that the students can meet earlier in their training, and who can then shed light on the situations their friends and relatives were encountering later, in our module. So for example, in the care of older people module, students meet Albert, an elderly man with dementia. They practice specific communication techniques and develop an appreciation of the skills and patience required. When they meet his stressed wife, Vera, in our module, they already have an insight into some of the causes of her distress, and realise that she probably does not understand his condition or the reasons for his unpredictable behaviour. The film in which Vera outlines her fears for the future is engaging and genuinely moving. At a later stage, we added a son for Vera and Albert, making him a dubious and devious character inclined towards the abuse of his parents. Nothing is said explicitly, but students pick up on his threatening manner, and are able to deduce that some of his parents' financial problems and anxieties are due to his behaviour.

It is interesting that despite the relatively late arrival of Mark on the scene, from our perspective, this potential lack of continuity is interpreted differently by the students. They will often comment that Vera does not mention the abuse because of shame, stigma and fear of her son, and that as a result they will have to approach this touchy subject particularly sensitively!

Preparation and experience of the actors seems to be a crucial factor. The actors were recruited using a 'snowballing' approach, beginning with a friend who acted in an amateur company, who then introduced us to other suitable people. We met with them beforehand to discuss the relevant issues, the types of problems we wanted to be conveyed, and how the character might express him or her self. We also gave them some reading material from the British organisation, MIND, which is a campaigning organisation for mental health, run by and for people with mental health problems and the public. Their material is highly thought of, clearly written, and respects and represents the points of view of service users. We also used other organisations such as the Alzheimer's Society. We discussed how side effects of medications might appear, and how signs of emotional distress could be demonstrated non-verbally and verbally. The actors were asked to talk about their experiences, as if speaking with a mental health professional; describing recent events and their feelings about them. We were able to prompt the actors occasionally, and also used a number of sticky-notes arranged out of sight of the cameras, with pointers for crucial aspects to be included. We were fortunate in being able to work collaboratively with students and staff studying media and film, who made the films as part of their own development.

It is important to include enough detail to work with, but also allow a certain vagueness so as to promote a feeling of curiosity and engagement by the students, together with the feeling that there are gaps in service provision which require their attention. As far as possible, complementary trigger resources, such as General (medical) Practitioner referral letters, reflect their real counterparts, in this case by being brief, rather unclear and written somewhat untidily! As did Bickerstaffe et al (2007), we feel it is important to promote a range of possible perspectives on each scenario. Some aspects are deliberately ambivalent. For example, in the film, one character hints at childhood sexual abuse, and now as a young adult has alcohol and drug problems, and behaves in ways which can be felt by staff to be extremely challenging and difficult. People with such behavioural problems (and associated history) are sometimes described as having a 'personality disorder' (Clarke, V and Walsh, A, 2009). The stigma and negativity this arouses can now be analysed from a more person-centred and critical perspective. In addition, it appears that the kindly, confused and avuncular character of 'Albert' may have been involved. Again, the students need to re-evaluate their pre-conceived ideas and clarify their value systems. Concepts such as 'social exclusion' seem to have more meaning when discussed in relation to someone the students feel they have come to know.

In preparing students for roles such as Community Mental Health Nurse, their development is not restricted to clinical aspects. Transferable professional skills such as teamwork, supporting colleagues, collaborating across professional boundaries and managing junior staff all have an impact, as in any other professional field. In many respects these professional aspects worry students as much as the welfare of the people in their care. Students also have to consider a code of conduct, (NMC, 2008) and ensuring that they act within

the law. A huge amount of learning has to be synthesised before they can feel safe and competent to take on these roles. Use of video-streaming encourages a mental rehearsal by the learner in being a person with these responsibilities. The virtual caseload begins to feel more real, and on each watching of the film, there is the opportunity to take more out of it. Sometimes in viva assessments, students will say, 'as Vera told me…'

The learning outcomes include the ability to apply policy to practice and to practice ethically. While some values may be eternal (the duty to do no harm, for example), policy seems to escalate in the rapidity of its development (Warne and McAndrew, 2005). So far the scenarios have proven able to withstand the fluctuating priorities of policy. Generally, as outlined above, the trend in the UK is increasingly service-user led and person-centred (Stickley and Bassett, 2007). The emphasis is on facilitating change rather than 'looking after' – but this is expected while simultaneously prioritising safety. This does cause a clash between ethical principles of valuing autonomy and beneficence, but importantly, it also heightens awareness of the cultural values of the profession, the dangers of enculturation, and the struggle students may face in challenging practice norms. It is at these times that they realise how great the need is for mutual support, networking and finding key figures in organisations who can become role models for good practice. As the students are so well prepared in advance, through prior engagement with videos, they are able to take classroom time, using staff as facilitators, to construct their understanding of these challenging aspects of practice, which previously had been difficult or impossible to address. In coming to recognise a professional identity of their own, students realise that they will be called upon to state their position on contentious issues. As part of a team, they also have individual accountability. This is reflected in the viva assessments. Students are aware that they will be asked questions that prove an ability to 'think on their feet' (authentic to practice!) but they do not know in advance what line specifically this will take. An example is whether or not a service-user, in a crisis situation, should be admitted to hospital. In their answer they should be able to demonstrate awareness of legal responsibilities, an ethical, sensitive and person-centred approach, courtesy and negotiating skills, adaptable communication skills and awareness of procedures. They should also be able to back their answers up with evidence, in the form of reference to their reading.

REFLECTION AND CONCLUSION

Having discussed evaluation of students, we will now turn to reflect on our own progress, and our conclusions drawn from the experience of using digital film.

In this chapter we look at the use of video-streaming in a UK healthcare education setting. We have discussed the process we followed in considering this initiative, in particular with reference to the needs of diverse students, the changing wider social context, theoretical considerations and technological aspects. We have reflected on how the evidence base is to some extent contradictory, and examined how, in these circumstances, much of our work has been based on the fortuitous overlap between our professional values and the philosophy of constructive learning approach. Part of this is the commitment to positive relationships with students in order to promote an emotional environment that is conducive to learning. Above all we emphasise that good teaching is central, regardless of whether this happens in the real world or the virtual one. We recognise that our work is still in progress; that our online learning endeavours are a part of our 'teaching toolbox' not the whole thing, but that it's complementary potential is vast, and as yet we are still beginning our explorations of its possibilities.

Future ideas include possibilities for more interactive resources, perhaps using 'Adobe Captivate', Macromedia Flash or possibly even virtual worlds in which students can interact with the environment as well as the service user. We have already begun to increase the use of simulation, in which, after further training, actors come to class 'in role' to challenge students about the impact of the interventions they suggest. Similarly service users themselves, together with their family members, have contributed to student learning in classroom time. Previous use of the digital films and related study has meant that students are more confident and feel more prepared for these sessions.

We feel that this blended, active and experiential approach, in which we value both diversity and social relationships, will stand our students in good stead. The commitment to lifelong learning, adapting to different learning approaches and interacting with a variety of media will be useful in their ongoing careers. Further research is indicated in order to confirm or refute this, for example in investigating the extent to which these resources may or may not have influenced eventual practice. Finally, we would like to add that we are relatively new as educators, that we have learnt a lot, but are still learning, and that we welcome feedback and sharing from others involved in similar endeavours.

REFERENCES

Allen, W. R., Bonous-Hammarth, M., & Teranishi, R. T. (2006). *Higher education in a global society: Achieving diversity, equity and excellence*. Amsterdam, The Netherlands & London, UK: Elsevier JAI.

Association for Learning Technology. (2005). *ALT learning technology research strategy*. Retrieved on September 20, 2009, from http://www.alt.ac.uk/ALT_2005_Research_Strategy_20050420.html

Association of Graduate Recruiters. (2007). *Winter survey 2007 – press release*. Retrieved on September 20, 2009, from http://www.agr.org.uk/Content/AGR-Winter-Survey-2007-Press-Release

Bain, K. (2004). *What the best college teachers do*. Cambridge, MA: Harvard University Press.

Bates, M., Manuel, S., & Oppenheim, C. (2007). *Models of early adoption of ICT innovations in higher education*. Retrieved on September 20, 2009, from http://www.ariadne.ac.uk/issue50/oppenheim-et-al/

Bickerstaffe, P. Hannigan, B. Wood, S., & Young, N. (2007). Chapter. In T. Stickley & T. Basset (Eds.), *Teaching mental health*. Chichester, UK: John Wiley and Sons.

Biggs, J. (2003). *Teaching for quality learning at university*. Maidenhead, UK: Open University Press.

Bligh, D. (2000). *What's the use of lectures?* San Francisco, CA: Jossey-Bass.

Bloomfield, J., While, A., & Roberts, J. (2008). Using computer assisted learning for clinical skills education in nursing: Integrative review. *Journal of Advanced Nursing, 63*(3), 222–235. doi:10.1111/j.1365-2648.2008.04653.x

Brunson, D., Jarman, B., & Lampl, L. (Eds.). (2007). *Letters from the future*. Sterling, VA: Stylus.

Carr, G. (2008). Changes in nurse education: Delivering the curriculum. *Nurse Education Today, 28*(1), 120–127. doi:10.1016/j.nedt.2007.03.011

Clark, R. (2001). *Learning from media: Arguments, analysis and evidence*. Boulder, CO: Information Age Publishing.

Clarke, V., & Walsh, A. (2007). Use of narrative in mental health nursing practice and its teaching. In *Proceedings of Conference-The Narrative practitioner,* (p. 22). June 11th – 13th North East Wales Institute of Higher Education, Wrexham UK.

Clarke, V., & Walsh, A. (2009). *Fundamentals of mental health nursing*. Oxford, UK: Oxford University Press.

Coffield, F., Moseley, D., Hall, E., & Ecclestone, K. (2004). *Learning styles and pedagogy in post 16 learning: Findings of a systematic and critical review of learning styles models*. London, UK: Learning and Skills Research Centre.

Cowan, J. (2006). *On becoming an innovative university teacher*. Buckingham, UK: Oxford University Press.

DeAmicis, P. (1997). Interactive video disc instruction is an alternative method for learning and performing a critical learning skill. *Computers in Nursing, 15*(3), 155–158.

Department of Health. (2004). *The 10 essential shared capabilities*. London, UK: DOH.

Department of Health. (2006). *From values to action. The Chief Nursing Officer's Review of Mental Health Nursing*. London, UK: DOH.

Fallows, S., & Bhanot, R. (2005). *Quality issues in ICT based higher education*. Oxon, UK: Routledge Farmer. doi:10.4324/9780203416198

Fernando, S. (2003). *Cultural diversity, mental health and psychiatry*. Hove, UK: Brunner Routledge. doi:10.4324/9780203420348

Gadanidis, G., & Schindler, K. (2006). Learning objects, type II applications and embedded pedagogical models. *Computers in the Schools, 23*(1-2), 14–17.

Gagnon, G. W., & Collay, M. (2006). *Constructivist learning design*. Thousand Oaks, CA: Corwin Press.

Gibbs, G. (2006). Why assessment is changing. In Bryan, C., & Clegg, K. (Eds.), *Innovative assessment in higher education*. London, UK: Routledge.

Gilchrist, M., & Ward, R. (2006). Facilitating access to online learning. In Glen, S., & Moule, P. (Eds.), *E-learning in nursing*. Basingstoke, UK: Palgrave MacMillan.

Haggis, T. (2003). Constructing images of ourselves? A critical investigation into approaches to learning research in higher education. *British Educational Research Journal, 29*(1), 89–105. doi:10.1080/0141192032000057401

Honey, P., & Mumford, A. (1992). *The manual of learning styles* (3rd ed.). Maidenhead, UK: Peter Honey.

Jeffries, P. (2001). Computer versus lecture: A comparison of two methods of teaching oral medication administration in a nursing skills laboratory. *The Journal of Nursing Education, 40*(7), 323–339.

Jelfs, A., & Colbourn, C. (2002). Do students approaches to learning affect their perceptions of using computing and Information Technology? *Journal of Educational Media, 27*(1-2), 41–53. doi:10.1080/0305498032000045449

JISC. (2009). Effective practice in a digital age: A guide to technology- enhanced learning and teaching. HEFCE. Retrieved September 2009, from http://www.jisc.ac.uk/media/documents/publications/effectivepracticedigitalage.pdf

Jochems, W., Van Merrienboer, J., & Koper, R. (Eds.). (2004). *Integrated e-learning*. London, UK: RoutledgeFalmer.

Laurillard, D. (2002). *Rethinking university teaching*. London, UK: Routledge Falmer. Lewis, M., Davies, R, Jenkins, D., & Tate, M. (2005). A review of evaluative studies of computer based learning in nursing education. *Nurse Education Today, 25*(8), 586–597.

Liber, O. (2005). Learning objects: Conditions for viability. *Journal of Computer Assisted Learning, 21*(5), 366–373. doi:10.1111/j.1365-2729.2005.00143.x

MacKenzie, N., & Walsh, A. (2009). Enhancing the curriculum: Shareable multimedia learning objects. *Journal of Systems and Information Technology, 11*(1), 1328–7265. doi:10.1108/13287260910932421

MacLellan, E. (2005). Conceptual learning: The priority for higher education. *British Journal of Educational Studies, 53*(2), 129–147. doi:10.1111/j.1467-8527.2005.00287.x

Maddux, C. D., Johnson, D., & Willis, J. (1992). *Educational computing: Learning with tomorrow's technologies*. Boston, MA: Allyn & Bacon.

Mason, R., Pegler, C., & Weller, M. (2005). A learning object success story. *Journal of Asynchronous Learning Networks, 9*(1).

McDrury, J., & Alterio, M. (2002). *Learning through storytelling in higher education*. London, UK: Kogan Page.

Moisey, S., Mohamed, A., & Spencer, B. (2006). Factors affecting the development and use of learning objects. *American Journal of Distance Education, 20*(3), 143–161. doi:10.1207/s15389286ajde2003_3

Moon, J. (2002). *The module and programme development handbook*. London, UK: Kogan Page.

Moore, G. (1999). *Crossing the chasm*. Retrieved on September 9, 2009, from http://blogs.knowledgegenes.com/home/2009/09/crossing-the-chasm-geoffrey-moore-coded-by-martin-wilcox.html

Mortiboys, A. (2005). *Teaching with emotional intelligence*. Abingdon, UK: Routledge.

Muirhead, R. (2007). E-learning: Is this teaching at students or teaching with students? *Nursing Forum, 42*(4), 178–184. doi:10.1111/j.1744-6198.2007.00085.x

Nian-Shing, C., & Kan-Min, L., & Kinshuk. (2008). Analysing users' satisfaction with e-learning using a negative critical incidents approach. *Innovations in Education and Teaching International, 45*(2), 115–126. doi:10.1080/14703290801950286

Niederhauser, V. P., Bigley, M. B., Hale, J., & Harper, D. (1999). Cybercases: An innovation in Internet education. *The Journal of Nursing Education, 38*(9), 415–418.

Nugent, G., Soh, L., & Ashok, S. (2006). Design, development and validation of learning objects. *Journal of Educational Technology Systems, 34*(3), 271–281. doi:10.2190/9BF6-1KBL-Y3CX-6QXG

Nursing and Midwifery Council. (2008). *The Code: Standards of conduct, performance and ethics for nurses and midwives.* London, UK: NMC Publications.

Parrish, P. (2004). The trouble with learning objects. *Educational Technology Research and Development, 52*(1), 49–70. doi:10.1007/BF02504772

Phillips, J. (2005). Strategies for active learning in online continuing education. *Journal of Continuing Education in Nursing, 36*(2), 77–83.

Piaget, J. (1954/1968). *The construction of reality in the child.* London, UK: Routledge & Kegan Paul. doi:10.1037/11168-000

Race, P. (2001). *The lecturer's toolkit: A resource for developing learning teaching and assessment* (2nd ed.). London, UK: Kogan Page.

Ramsden, P. (2003). *Learning to teach in higher education.* London, UK: Routledge Falmer.

Russell, T. (1999). *The no significant difference phenomenon.* Chapel Hill, NC: Office of Instructional Telecommunications, North Carolina State University.

Sit, J., Chung, J., Chow, M., & Wong, T. (2005). Experiences of online learning: Students' perspective. *Nurse Education Today, 25*(2), 140. doi:10.1016/j.nedt.2004.11.004

Slater, J. (2005). *Spent force or revolution in progress? E-learning after the e-university.* Report for the Higher Education Policy Institute Oxford. Retrieved September 2009, from http://www.hepi.ac.uk/466-1163/Spent-force-or-revolution-in-progress-eLearning-after-the-eUniversity.html

Sun, P., Tsai, R., Finger, G., Chen, Y., & Yeh, D. (2008). What drives successful e-learning? An empirical investigation of the critical factors influencing learner satisfaction. *Computers & Education, 50*, 118–1202. doi:10.1016/j.compedu.2006.11.007

The Information Centre. (2007). *NHS hospital and community health services non-medical staff: England 1996-2006.* Retrieved on September 9, 2009, from http://www.ic.nhs.uk/webfiles/publications/nhsstaff2006/non-med/Non-medical%20bulletin%201996-2006.pdf

Thorne, K. (2003). *Blended learning.* London, UK: Kogan Page.

Walsh, A. (2009). *How do e-learning resources influence student learning and assessment on a pre-registration mental health nursing course?* Unpublished Master's thesis, Birmingham City University.

Warne, T., & McAndrew, S. (2005). *Using patient experience in education.* Basingstoke, UK: Palgrave MacMillan.

Wright, J. (2009). The role of computer software in presenting information. *Nursing Management, 16*(4), 30–34.

Chapter 21
Medium Matters:
Experiences of Teaching Online In India[1]

Rajiv Kumar
Indian Institute of Management Calcutta, India

Abhishek Goel
Indian Institute of Management Calcutta, India

Vidyanand Jha
Indian Institute of Management Calcutta, India

ABSTRACT

Using three auto-ethnographies, in this chapter we have explored the experiences of teaching organizational behavior in an online environment. Before presenting the three auto-ethnographies, we have attempted to situate auto-ethnography as a tool in the domain of qualitative research. The analysis of these auto-ethnographies highlights the strengths and limitations of online medium in teaching organizational behavior. Our analysis shows that medium of teaching impacts the teaching style instructors adopt, poses challenges of mastering new technology, forces them to choose some content types over others, has an impact on their satisfaction with delivery and on their overall experience.

INTRODUCTION

In the last few years, there has been a growth in the spread of online education across the world. The revolution in Information Technology, the associated hardware and software, coupled with easier access to data transfer mechanisms around the world are understood to be the main drivers of such growth. The US and Europe, in particular, have seen growth in Web based interfaces. India

DOI: 10.4018/978-1-60960-800-2.ch021

too has not been far behind in terms of delivering higher education online. In late 1980s, the first experiments at online mass education were supported by a national open university (IGNOU) with the help of Educational Media Research Centers (EMRC) housed in various universities or other institutes of higher education across the country. These EMRCs recorded short video lectures on a select list of topics. These lectures were primarily meant to spread education to those with no or little access to physical classroom facilities. The programs were telecast over the national television channels in early morning or late night hours by the national television broadcasting service. The courses and delivery mechanisms have evolved a long way since then.

Today, India is witnessing a spurt in online education across various areas of expertise. Engineering institutes and science colleges are increasingly taking their faculty members online to spread higher education about various subjects, and universities in the online education domain are being set up. The online education has enabled reach to students located in farthest corners of the country, which is otherwise quite cumbersome for a large country like India. While the cost benefit analysis of online education, its utility for the students, and acceptance are getting more attention, there is little understanding of what an instructor goes through while teaching online (Webster & Hackley, 1997). The formulations or experiments in pure sciences have a tangible object on the screen that may change form, shape or color; soft subjects like behavioral training do not have such tangibles to bank upon. This paper presents instructors experiences about teaching "soft" organizational behavior courses to students of management and the challenges faced in delivering such behavioral courses online under the umbrella of a management institute in the country.

Offering Online Management Education

Initial forays into online education in business were suggested as innovative solutions to the problems of earning revenues to becoming self-reliant. Besides there were capacity constraints with existing facilities, and the time and resource required to pull up the existing infrastructure to meet market demand along with the benefit of a niche positioning in the virtual classroom/online education market provided an attractive option to follow. Some management institutes converted their on-campus long term management development programs in to online long term management

development programs to increase their reach and increase revenue streams for the institute (Das, Chittoor, & Ray, 2007). Initially, most such efforts took place with increased spread of delivery infrastructure. Collaborations were set up with technology and marketing partners who were usually firms in the technology solutions or in the field of software development. Within a period of five years, the revenues from online education in one institute, for example, have grown to Rs. 110 million and now contribute nearly one-fourth of the total revenue generated by the institute from its various programs. It has become an important contributor, and if one were to think rationally about running an expanding management institute, it is likely to stay.

Various categories of audience have put forth a demand for interactive education methodology especially in management (e.g., Abeysekara, 2008). The demand for interactive classes seems to be a common factor in the classroom as well as online teaching. This interaction has to be a two-way process if the dominant teaching philosophy is participant-centered learning and it uses case teaching or discussions as the vehicle for instruction. The best management institutes in India are known to use case method of instruction extensively across various sub-disciplines of management. Behavioral sciences in these institutes comprise mainly of organizational behaviour, organizational design, cross-cultural management and other soft-skills related subjects. Physical classroom instruction in these subject areas generally takes place through a mix of case based discussions, simulations and other exercises to facilitate interaction and experiential learning. All three authors of this paper are colleagues in the same area or sub-group of management studies and have been regularly dealing with online as well as physical classrooms.

AUTO-ETHNOGRAPHY AS A TOOL IN RESEARCH

As a systematic process of knowing about some phenomenon both quantitative and qualitative research methods have their own advantages as well as disadvantages (Strauss & Corbin, 1998). Though to some extent the choice of qualitative or quantitative research method is determined by personal liking, the state of knowledge of a particular phenomenon also governs this choice. When there is no well-established theory of a phenomenon, qualitative methods are more suitable as the requirement is first to build a theory, which can be subsequently examined by testing hypotheses employing quantitative methods (Eisenhardt, 1989). This paper uses qualitative research to understand and theorize more about instructor dilemma around online education. Among a host of methods available within the realm of qualitative mode of inquiry, auto-ethnography was chosen due to reasons specified subsequently.

As a term and a method of inquiry, auto-ethnography is almost 30 years old starting with Hayano (1979), a claim upheld by Ellis and Bochner (2000). Assuming that many readers may have positivistic research orientations, we describe the early history of the method and the term "auto-ethnography" and discuss its advantages and disadvantages as a method. As it emerges towards the end of this section, auto-ethnography in its current form validates and employs "self" as a source of data as well as an analyst of that data. While describing its history, strengths, and weaknesses, we also attempt to situate auto-ethnography as a method within the paradigm of qualitative research so that readers can have a fuller grasp of the method as well as the product that follows afterwards.

Paradigms in Research

In the domain of academic research, a paradigm is a set of beliefs that guide researchers' inquiry (Guba, 1990). Kuhn (1996) has described several features of a paradigmatic belief system. A paradigm has one (or a few) universally accepted scientific accomplishment(s) as its starting point. These scientific accomplishments also generate a variety of questions for further research. Recognizing these initial scientific achievements as valid and exemplary, several researchers subsequently get drawn to the inquiry of emerging questions. Besides providing legitimacy to questions and problems, a paradigm also establishes certain methods of research as legitimate. Therefore the researchers who view some scientific feats as exemplary also share a more or less uniform set of problems and methods as legitimate for the purposes of their further inquiry (Kuhn, 1996).

Guba (1990) considers the answers to three basic questions as central in understanding a paradigm. The *first question* is about the nature of reality to be understood through inquiry. Researchers who belong to positivistic paradigm, for example, believe that there is a single, immutable reality out there which is to be grasped through inquiry. Researchers from some other paradigm, for example constructivism, believe that there are multiple realities possible.

The nature of relationship between the inquirer and the reality constitutes the *second question*. Positivists, for example, believe that an inquirer should be detached and removed from the reality they are inquiring. Constructivists, on the other hand, believe that reality as viewed by different people can only be understood by being close to those people and not by practicing detached separation from them. The *third question* is about the legitimacy and superiority of the methods and tools of inquiry. Positivists believe in experimental manipulation and testing of hypotheses as the legitimate means of inquiry, while constructivists believe in eliciting multiple accounts in their original true form through observation or interviews, and enmeshing these accounts to see if one (or a few) more commonly agreed conceptions of realities emerge.

Qualitative Research as a Paradigm in Management Research

We are students of management, and qualitative research seems to meet the criteria of a paradigm enunciated by Kuhn (1996) for the purposes of our own inquiry. The *Administrative Science Quarterly* and *Academy of Management Journal* are noted to be the two top-ranked journals publishing empirical research in management (Adler & Harzing, 2009). A quick analysis of the articles winning the best article award in these two journals in the last 15 years of revealed that 35% of the best articles in *Academy of Management Journal* and 40% of the best articles in *Administrative Science Quarterly* are based on qualitative research. Such impactful articles and their proliferation over the last few instances lead to an inference that qualitative research is emerging as a valid paradigm for research in management. Within the paradigm of qualitative research, ethnography occupies a prominent position. In the next subsection, we briefly describe it and introduce the term auto-ethnography before offering a more detailed discussion of auto-ethnography.

Ethnography and Auto-Ethnography

Ethnography traditionally meant studying a culture different from one's own (Spradley, 1979). Noted ethnographers such as Mead, Malinowski studied cultures remote from their own setting. While doing so, they attempted to meet the demands of positivism such as objectivity and detachment from the people they studied (Tedlock, 1991).

Ellis and Bochner (2000) and Wolcott (1990) have credited Hayano (1979) to be the first published work in "auto-ethnography." The positivistic paradigm had influence over this work as well, as Hayano viewed the "auto" part of auto-ethnography as problematic because he believed that an intimate involvement of "auto" (or self) with the subjects studied could compromise the objectivity of scientific procedures employed (Hayano, 1979: 99).

He had also differentiated between traditional ethnographies which were the accounts of a culture by an outsider, and those ethnographies which described a particular culture from the lens of a *member* of that culture himself or herself. To illustrate, Hayano (1979) called the studies of Srinivas (1966) as auto-ethnography because he was more of an insider in the culture he studied as compared to any Western anthropologist. Similarly, Hayano (1979) viewed the study of Roy (1975) on Bengali women as an example of auto-ethnography; she was both a woman and a Bengali, and hence could be considered as an insider in the culture she studied.

Hayano (1979) succinctly describes how auto-ethnographies of the above nature became increasingly accepted within the traditional scholarship of Anthropology. He argued that as the remote field areas became increasingly unavailable to Western researchers due to breakdown of colonialism, auto-ethnography increasingly became a necessity. The other reason, in his opinion, was that isolated tribal regions too became increasingly rare as the forces of economics spread their wings. At the same time, a new set of people from developing societies started studying their own people, and their studies found place in the traditional Anthropological scholarship (Hayano, 1979). While these changes were taking place, scholars in the field of anthropology were also getting more sensitized to the fact that the interpretations of the same data from a native and non-native researcher may be different. This awareness partly contributed to the acceptance of studies of one's own people.

In his description, Hayano (1979) distinguishes between auto-ethnography and what he calls self-ethnography. Self-ethnography (e.g., Wallace, 1965) uses reflection on one's own experience as data and analyzes such data to create an account of one's culture. Wallace (1965) defends this approach in two ways. Firstly, he points out that the use of introspection as a source of data is present in virtually all so-called more objective sources of data. To illustrate, surveys or interviews invariably invoke introspection in respondents in order to generate data. Wallace (1965: 278), in fact, highlights the advantage of using self-introspection to generate data because such an approach permits "…high degree of thoroughness of inquiry and… directness…" Secondly, Wallace (1965) points out the inherent problem in being aware of the necessity to record one's experiences while also living those experiences. He argues that such simultaneity in being an observer—and chronicler—besides being an actor "…would change the experience itself" (Wallace, 1965: 278). Hence reflection as source of data, and analysis of the resulting data, is accorded legitimacy as a method of inquiry.

This approach to inquiry resembles what Levy and Hollan (1998) term as person-centered ethnography. In this approach, the researcher is encouraged to view people not as informants, but as respondents. Hence instead of seeking their opinions about the issues of interest to the researcher, their thoughts and feelings about the issue are given more importance. Such an approach, therefore, requires the researcher to spend more time with respondents in order to generate trust. The advantage of auto-ethnography becomes apparent in such an approach, as one's own self is always available for deeper scrutiny.

Auto-ethnography, therefore, is a highly personalized and reflective account drawing upon on the personal experiences of an author. In such narratives, the author poses his or her self in a social or cultural context and describes his/her experiences in a systematic manner. Such descriptions aim at highlighting some unique aspects of a phenomenon which otherwise either do not find voice in more traditional methods of even qualitative research, or get subdued because of attempts to meet the requirements of validity and reliability posed by reviewers and paradigms. To illustrate, Sutton (1997) recounts several such highly personal experiences which he had to downplay in order to look more "scientific" and

"acceptable." Auto-ethnography as a method allows such insights to come out in open and offers a humane account of both the process of inquiry as well as the inquirer.

Besides these features of auto-ethnography that provide more space to the inquirer and her/his process of inquiry, it also has the potential to offer new concepts and theories. For example, Hayano (1979: 101), while acknowledging the potential criticisms of auto-ethnography from a positivistic viewpoint, states that auto-ethnography may be useful in identifying new concepts and theories. Probably this is one of the reasons behind its increasing usage in social science research in last two decades (Anderson, 2006). This method has recently been used to understand a variety of contemporary issues such as workaholism (Boje & Tyler, 2009), workplace bullying (Vickers, 2007), value of customers (Holbrook, 2005), expatriate adjustment (Friedman, Dyke, & Murphy, 2009). A few noted examples of such reflective accounts can be found in distant past too. The classic work of Barnard (1938) that offered several insightful concepts and theories was based on his own experiences as an executive. He reflected upon, analyzed and offered a theory of the functions of executive which still excites managers and students alike (Mahoney, 2002).

Considering the above evidence, and recent calls of some scholars (e.g., Boyle & Parry, 2007) who have actively advocated the use of auto-ethnographic accounts in organization and management research, we have chosen auto-ethnography as a method to inquire the phenomenon of online teaching. In the remaining part of this chapter, we present thee auto-ethnographies that analyze our own experiences as online teachers.

THREE AUTO-ETHNOGRAPHIES

Several commentators (e.g., Coppola, Hiltz, & Rotter, 2002; Dykman & Davis, 2008; Palloff & Pratt, 2007) note that teaching in an online setting is quite different from teaching in a physical classroom. We intuitively agree with that teaching in a virtual mode is different from teaching students face-to-face in a physical classroom. However, we also believe that our experiences of teaching in virtual classrooms both match with, and differ from, what scholars have reported so far. The three auto-ethnographies that follow highlight these points of agreement as well as differences. We believe that these descriptions will help generate new theory. These are also appropriate considering that the subject of online teaching is at a nascent stage (Eisenhardt, 1989).

First Auto-Ethnography

Initial Comfort

I was often relieved to see just a computer in front of me as I enter into an online "classroom." At some level, I was aware of the presence of the camera and microphone, and hence the potential of getting electronically and "virtually" connected to more than a hundred students within minutes, but somehow it was less threatening than a physical classroom. The physical classrooms that I had taught in too occasionally had more than 100 students. But it was often daunting for me to see such a large number of sharp people who were mostly focusing on me and almost every movement of mine. It was an overwhelming task to assimilate all the cues available in that immediate environment and then react to them as well, suitably in time. Even in the smaller physical classrooms, I usually become aware of the scrutinizing and evaluating gaze of a number of people for the first few minutes. It usually takes me a while to forget the presence of people around me and come close to the topic I am supposed to deal with. Hence the initial distance available in the "virtual" classroom was comforting to some extent.

The personalized touch in the service of the employees who run the online studio was also reassuring. At least two employees were always present during my online classes. One was a technical person, while the other was a security guard who also used to help with small tasks such as bringing tea or coffee. It was relaxing to have someone who would care enough to ask about my choice of beverage, and bring it for me. Besides such seemingly insignificant but personally appealing niceties, the continuous presence of the technical person was also a considerable comfort. This person would not only upload the necessary materials for class (e.g., the presentation to be used), but would also help whenever something got stuck. For example, if some students complained about the current slide being invisible, he would come and correct it. His continuous presence used to assure me that in case the students or I face any technological difficulty, there was someone who could possibly solve it. Given these experiences of the initial few minutes, I disagree with Dykman and Davis (2008) who described the online experience to be "unforgiving."

Experience with Technology and Software

Dykman and Davis (2008) emphasize that the instructor should get acquainted with the software in order to improve the quality of online education. However, I could not get much orientation to the technology and software used. Before my first online class, the technical person had come and demonstrated different parts of the software for about half an hour. He showed how to change the slides being displayed, which in fact was similar to the mechanism used on any computer. He also sensitized me regarding my appearance to the students by pointing out a small portion of the screen before me which would play the video part of my lecture getting aired on real time basis. This made me conscious of the fact that I should look into the camera in order to appear looking at the individual students from their individual computer terminals.

The main aspects of familiarization, however, pertained to the facilities of video chat, text chat, and students' poll. Though the technical person did try to demonstrate these features, but I believe I learnt more by attempting to use them than from the short tutorial he had provided. For example, how to respond to a private text message of a student is something I learnt much later in my teaching. Similarly, the video chat mode required me to put on a headphone in order to converse. I often used to forget this initially, but after a few attempts of engaging in video chat, I was less forgetful of this aspect of technology.

The software also provided a facility of polling students, but I seldom used it initially. After a few months of my online teaching, however, the technical help in the studio told me about yet another usage of the poll facility which increased my frequency of using it. He demonstrated how it could be used to mark the attendance of students by asking the students to click on the "yes" button. This ensured that students who were only "virtually" present, but in fact were absent from the class[2], could be identified and removed from the class.

My experience with the entirety of technology and software remained similar to what Perreault, Waldman, and Zhao (2002: 315) report. In their survey of instructors teaching in similar environments, they found that more than half of them found the reliability of technology as the most problematic issue. In my own case, the reliability of technology such as establishing a video chat successfully, did improve with time. However, such improvements could not completely erase a sense of suspicion that the technology may fail anytime. Hence being able to have a class free from any technological glitches was a pleasant surprise, and not a norm.

Awareness of Students

I was aware of the students initially only as a long inventory of names before me, with their respec-tive centers written in front of their names. To me, their activities before the start of the session were only available in the chat box. I always felt curious to read the chat box to gauge the mood of the students towards the session topic and towards the course. The inevitable—and cursory—analysis of students' text messages among themselves also suggested to me the students who appeared more energetic and social, or more willing to engage and participate later on in the class.

After the classes began, my awareness of students was more or less limited to only those who asked questions using the chat window, or raised hands to seek a video chat with me. Video chat requests from students were quite infrequent compared to their participation in the text chat mode. Irrespective of the mode of their engagement with me, my attention was more or less confined to only those who had participated. For example, I would recount to the entire class—whenever an opportunity arose—the issues raised by a particular student who had previously participated. I would also attempt to weave the participation of a student into what I was about to say or had just said. Compared to a typical physical classroom, therefore, the online classes had more potential to push the non-participating students into oblivion. In a physical classroom, I could still see the faces of at least some non-participating students and occasionally even attempt to engage them. However, in an online classroom, I could not do that even to that "occasional" extent. I could go to non-participating students only when I had posed a question for the entire class, and I wanted to engage in a video chat with some students due to the expected difficulty in eliciting answers through text chat. But such occasions were rare during my online teaching.

Quality Issues

Unlike what Dykman and Davis (2008) state, as a teacher I did not struggle to ensure quality in my online teaching more than what I did while teaching in the traditional format. Dykman and Davis (2008) believe that due to the nature of online medium, faculty may not be able to receive information about trouble in time, and hence may not be able to correct the problem soon enough to the satisfaction of complaining students. Their contention is consistent with the theory of media richness (Daft & Lengel, 1986) which would suggest that face-to-face communication should be more helpful in ensuring quality as this is the richest medium of communication. Online communication is not as rich a communication medium as face-to-face communication is, and therefore is less munificent in terms of allowing instructors to ensure quality.

While my experience as an online teacher confirms these beliefs partly, it also goes against them in a significant way. I do recall instances when there were problems while I was teaching. Such problems included instances when the slide would not appear before some or all students, or the audio would not reach them. But unlike what Dykman and Davis (2008) suspect, students could always send their complaints to me regarding these problems almost instantaneously through the chat box. As soon as I would notice these complaints, I would ask the technical help available in the studio to rectify them. Occasionally such problems could not be rectified because of reasons beyond the control of studio people. To illustrate, if the machine at the remote center where the student was accessing my lecture was faulty, or the headphone was not working, the technical person in my studio could not do anything. Otherwise, I believe I could both, get to know, and solve, a significant number of the problems students faced.

There is another reason why my experiences do not completely reflect the contention of Dykman and Davis (2008). In traditional classroom, students coming to me after the class and commenting upon the quality of lecture was not a regular feature. Occasionally some students would come after the class was over to ask some question or discuss some of the points. But in

the online classes, I always got some idea of the quality of my session looking at the comments of students at the end of the chat box. The presence of such communication in an online class can be attributed either to the differences in my own delivery, or to the fact that many students would find it easier to leave their comments in the chat box than to personally approach the faculty and express their comments.

Post-Session Issues

During my online teaching, occasionally I encouraged students to withhold their immediate replies to my questions, and send them through e-mail subsequently. I usually did so for questions that required some reflection and assimilation of reading material. For example, I once asked students to think if money could reduce the motivation level of people. Many, but not all, students sent me their replies through e-mail. Their replies mostly suggested that they had taken time to think about the question. The advantage with such a scheme was that it also gave me time to reflect and respond to their e-mails, as Coppola et al. (2002: 177) point out.

Second Auto-Ethnography

I started teaching in 1995 in a physical classroom setting. My first classes were teaching part of an Organizational Development Course in an evening program for working executives. Later, I started teaching post graduate students; and working executives - in both short duration management development programs and longer duration quasi academic programs in class room settings topics related to organizational behavior and organization theory.

I was groomed into my teaching through participant centered experiential teaching- cases and experiential exercises being the most prominent methods. This required a higher degree of pre- class preparation by me and the students as well as a higher degree of in class participation by the students. Indeed my motto was what one teacher of mine said once: "a case teacher's task is to hear students learn." As I used cases mostly from secondary sources where teaching notes were not always easy to come by, the class followed a less structured more free flowing discussions. I, indeed, used to believe that the main learning came from listening to other's contributions and making ones' own contribution. The instructor's role was to hold the class together to facilitate the discussions ask right questions and not necessarily be the expert on the content. I hardly taught any theory or any standardized material consciously. My assumption was that I cannot be a good substitute for the books. That is why I always used to prescribe pre-class readings of theoretical content and also checked whether students are reading it by conducting in-class unannounced quizzes. So, my focus was on creating magic in the classroom together with the students.

This was the backdrop in which, an offer came from a large and globally respected publishing house's Indian arm to offer on-line courses to working executives. I floated a course on "Personal Effectiveness in the New Economy." I had read up about on-line teaching and had become a great fan of the flexibility which an asynchronous environment offered. The teacher and taught need not be present in the same geography and at the same time to learn together. However, the vision of the collaborating organization was different. It wanted to create content for the program to be put on the net and also held once a week classes where the students would login into a chat area. I found it different from my earlier teaching. Earlier, I did not have to generate or write up content for the classroom. The content came from many sources- books, papers, movies and I just assembled them together. Here, the expectation was to write a book and put it on the internet. I did not want to do that as it involved a great amount of work and mostly unoriginal work at

that. However, I did end up writing a kind of text book and we put it on the internet.

In addition, I devoted most of my time to holding the on-line chat classes which to me were the sites where most value could be generated as they were the proxy for a face to face classroom where students can participate. However, I realized that in a physical classroom students take cues from others' participation and await their turn, which was difficult in this set up. Similarly, their responses scrolled quite fast and it was very difficult to understand it if many people started responding at once: it was akin to too many people speaking at once in a physical classroom. Another thing which happened was that many a times, students used the public chat area to carry on dyadic discussions. It actually can happen in a physical classroom too. But there its ability to create distractions for the class is localized and one can always bring these discussions into the class by involving those dyadic participants. In chat mode, I found it difficult to do so as the speed of chat scrolling in itself was too much and to add to that these other issues of reducing distractions, it became virtually impossible to "control" the class.

Another discomfort arose in me as these classes were not fully asynchronous. Though the participants and I were in different locales, we had to be present at the same time. However, I was happy with the quality of class discussions. On the other hand, the students had an expectation of an expert telling them things about questions which were important to them. So, many of them were not happy if they were discussing things among themselves. This also had its root in another problem. In our cultural context, learning from an authority figure was expected, but learning from a peer was not very usual. So, these participants felt that discussions were not adding much value and they would rather listen to me.

We ran a few batches of this program and gradually it petered out as the collaborating organization wanted to get into a highly standardized class room experience which can be repeated time and again with very little incremental efforts. So, their model, as I inferred later, was to put standardized material which students can learn on their own and then they can clarify their doubts with somebody like me. I refused to continue to do this, as I myself did not have very precise answers to many of the questions faced by the participants and indeed, also believe that there may not be a right answer to many of the problems we grappled with during the course of the program.

Around same time, I was approached by an on-line university which wanted me to become an adjunct faculty. I did not know whether I would have time to devote to such an endeavor and the money which they were paying was also not very significant. However, I did want to see how does an on-line course floated by an international university run. So I got into it primarily to learn a new method of teaching.

I was first trained a great deal in the methods of on-line teaching. In this university's model there was true asynchronicity. The students were globally distributed. I never had any live inter-action with them. The university used threaded discussions quite a lot. It also taught the faculty as to how to establish an on-line presence in a medium where the students could not see or hear the instructor. Thus, the instructor was supposed to quite actively participate in and moderate the threaded discussions.

After an initial training, I taught two courses over a period of two years for the university. This experience was good. The university had put up some course content written by a group of experts on the internet which had to be read by the students. I could keep a tab on whether they had done their reading. In addition, a text book was provided to them. They also were given access to cases. As a teacher my task was to set up cases for them, set up examinations, participate in threaded discussions on cases and other top-ics which I set up for them and to evaluate their individual and group examinations. I also had to set up their individual and group examinations

and write a case exclusively for their end term examination. It was good fun the first time. Later it became boring. And it did take a long amount of time to teach and grade. Indeed my mobility during the course was quite limited. So, it was meant for working executives, but I could not be the working teacher. If I did not have a day job, then it wasn't bad. But otherwise, it did demand great time commitment. However, I did get to learn how to teach an on-line course and also had great benefit of interacting with a geographically diverse and dispersed student body.

After this, when I started teaching in satellite based courses, I was more confident. In retrospect it was a generalized confidence bereft of any roots in my previous experiences as the nature of teach-ing in my past two episodes of new technology teaching was quite different than the satellite based teaching. In satellite based teaching, I had to go to a studio and talk to the camera. The students could see me, but I could not see them. I could make students visible and audible one at a time. There was also a chat board where students could keep on posting their comments and which I could see. I could also conduct in-class opinion polls in a binary choice mode.

My initial experience of teaching in this me-dium was good, save the eerie feeling of talking to the camera and being conscious that others can see me, but I cannot see them. However, initially I did conduct exercises in the class and also had cases discussed. I talked very little and gave stu-dents chance to talk. Though, in the chat facility students also continued the dyadic conversations, I did not feel like disabling this faculty as I was told that some of my colleagues were doing to minimize distraction and bring undivided atten-tion to the proceeding of the class. I also got good response from the students. This was also due to the reason that not too many courses allowed this kind of interaction and the students found it novel (and I also like to think, empowering). Some of the students did find it disconcerting as they thought that the classes were meant for them to listen to the experts and not to listen to their peers. Many students later sent me mail telling me as to how much they enjoyed this method of teaching. However, there were two problems with this method. Firstly, the technology for two way communication, i.e. putting a student on-line was not up to the mark. The students could not be seen or heard with ease and it took long time to establish whether everybody in the class was able to hear and/or see the student who was making a point. This wasted a lot of class time. Second problem was regarding evaluations. Given the nature of the classes, the student expectation and indeed even my desire was to give write up kind of examinations. But the technology and logistics dictated that we conduct only multiple choice kinds of examinations. This made the students who were quite examination oriented wary of the class proceedings. I sold the teaching method to them saying that it would add to their learning and some of them agreed with me.

Later, when I started teaching in another program, which was also co-designed and co-directed by me, these problems took a new turn. Now when we took time to put a student on-line, I started feeling more responsible for it. More-over, some class time was devoted, and in some classes, lot of time was devoted in dealing with program related issues which had nothing to do with what I was teaching. This made me tired after some time. I also realized that may be this medium was more suited to a structured way of teaching and perhaps my methods were not very suited to this kind of a medium. I also realized that an average student was more interested in certification rather than class learning and there having an standardized material which could be useful for them to answer multiple choice questions easily was more required. In a sense I was not new to any of the arguments starting in my mind, but I was fatigued. I also realized that perhaps I can create more value in a face to face setting among working executives who did not attend the programs primarily for certification. I

did not feel valued enough in this mode of teaching. This made me declare one day to the students that I would stop teaching through case method to them and indeed stop teaching them. I did get some mails asking me to continue teaching and teaching with my interactive methods, but I did stop teaching in this course.

After that I have not taught in any other satellite based program.

Third Auto-Ethnography

I started my classroom and online teaching career almost simultaneously in 2008. Thus the differences due to adaptation of a honed teaching style for a particular medium were not so clear to me. I developed my own sense of teaching and was probably quite fresh and playful to try new media and technology out in my teaching. I had learnt and practiced case teaching as a post-graduate and doctoral student. In some of the top institutions the demand to teach through cases is quite high, though mostly the participants are not aware that the case teaching demands them to prepare as much as the instructor.

GETTING TO OB IN ONLINE MODE

To me the online experience was as big a novelty as the classroom. In the online mode, my initial few classes on OB were mostly interactive lectures because I could not figure out a way to discuss the cases. The system has in built capabilities of sending the messages through voice, video and written text messages through the chat window. The chat window also allows personal messages to be sent between two participants or between participant and instructor.

Phase 1: Getting Comfortable

I always wanted to have a screen where I can see people logged in to the classroom. In this case the

Figure 1. Outline of the screen available to the instructor

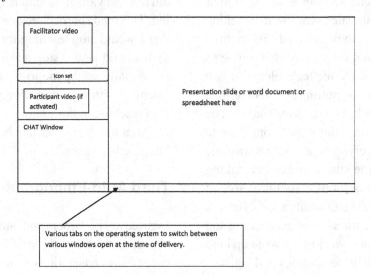

medium itself came in a big way to support the idea that video is for watching, and others would watch your actions and hear you, but you cannot see them. The whole sense of two-way communication was missing. Given my background of doing some theatre and on-stage performances, I would imagine that I am an actor on the stage, and the audience is sitting in a large dark hall. Of course, the lines need not be remembered; I just have to be well versed with the subject.

Figure 1 gives an idea of the facilitator screen.

That was the beginning. This is where I realized some of my strengths for the first time.

I always had an interest in trying out new software and platforms for computers, typing speed was alright, little did I realize that I would use it extensively for teaching and facilitating. The online "performance" required me to be alert about one half of me (the portion above the torso only was visible) and juggle between an array of gadgets laid out on my table. I had two monitors to look at, one keyboard, one mouse, one collar microphone, one headphone, one writing pad, a pen, a digital tablet pad, and a text digitizer. Then there were two cameras staring at me, and displaying me on a large screen right in the front.

The whole set up was quite overwhelming and to some extent intimidating.

Given my extensive training, comfort with, and intrinsic desire to discuss cases in the class, I was initially disappointed because the medium made me "feel" that there can be no discussion! I had no choice but to resort to "interactive" lectures. The institutional arrangements required instructors for the online classes. I was getting opportunities to teach via my interactive lectures. Within a few weeks I picked up the art of juggling various components on the table, on the screen, and maintain a fast pace on the chat window to answer queries. I had really mastered the art of reading the comment on the chat window and respond to it either by voice or chat, as was necessary.

Phase 2: Making Amends in Delivery

Typically there would be around 100 participants spread across several locations in India and abroad, some of them started getting enthused about my sessions and the interactions. Some days I used to come out with a feeling that there is a tussle between a young faculty and similar aged participants as to who would be faster. There was no other way but to persist and take the interactions to the next level. Once I eased in to the pace of discussions and developed a comfort I was more comfortable about trying new things.

I realized that though there was a provision of calling a person online and put him or her on video, most instructors felt that it took away a lot of time. I too shed my initial reluctance and decided to give it a try.

Little did I realize that I was instrumental in breaking the one-way communication barrier. Given the high power distance between ranks in our context, the students were hesitant in asking for an opportunity to talk. Once this step worked I decided to take the plunge to check if the participants would like to discuss cases.

Phase 3: Facing Dilemmas

Before I went to the participants, I talked to a senior faculty in my workgroup (also one of the authors of this paper). He was quite sure that the medium was ill suited to have a classroom like discussion. Given his extensive experience, pedigree and success at teaching in the institute, I became unsure of my understanding of my situation.

As the luck would have it, one of my colleagues decided to leave the online teaching mode, and the responsibility to run the online classes for a course on organizational design came to me. I knew the participants, knew the subject and the medium. We discussed and I decided to go ahead with the case studies in the online mode. Little did I know where I was stepping into.

Phase 4: Initial Euphoria in OB Case Teaching

The case discussion classes began with a bang. Everyone including me was enthused about taking the real world classroom to the online mode. So we started discussing cases. I would generally raise a question and look forward to participants to respond. Some responses would come on the chat window. However, some participants lacked

comfort with English and their variations in typing speed held the class back. They would want to communicate one thing, but end up conveying something else. This pulled the class back and the discussions went awry. At this juncture I decided to use the video facility. I would now call one person online based on interest, show of hands, or comments on the chat window and use our dialogue for some time to drive the case discussion ahead.

Phase 5: The Limitations

Soon I realized the technological and infrastructural limitations. Once the system was put under stress of communicating via two streaming live videos, the cracks started to show up. The complaints from participants about not being able to hear the discussion, missing audio or video or both, frequent system crashes, and receiving unclear video or voice became serious impediments.

Second set of restrictions came from the participant side. The participants were used to one-way communication and some interaction with the faculty over chat window. Here they were being pushed to pre-read, come with issues, and share their concerns and thoughts in open. Some participants definitely liked the idea, but most found it embarrassing to be picked up and unable to answer for having not read the case.

Phase 6: The Consequences

Despite the technological and participant restrictions there was some enthusiasm to pursue case discussions online. Most participants found it a bold step and were quite appreciative. As the course ended, I too had a mixed feeling about discussing cases online. May be the technique was not perfect, or the medium had severe limitations; or the combination was not working perfect.

Feedback given to course directors and program directors was that case discussion based classes had most points coming from the participants, and they were made to do the work. Thus, why should a faculty member be there? Though there was rebuttal from some participants, but it forced me to step away from my world and look within.

Phase 7: The Introspection

I was crestfallen. I had tried to do something new against all sorts of challenges. Case discussions were being well received in the physical classroom, and the record till the last course in online domain was good too. However, somewhere something had not worked. Over a period of time, several points of learning emerged:

1. Being executives in responsible positions, the participants might have faced difficulty in pre-reading for the class. I had conveniently forgotten that in my place of training and other similar places, the executive participants are given time to read and discuss cases. Here the structure of the program did not allow.

2. When discussions are held online, the instructor has to be comfortable with the slide, the video of the class on the large screen, own self, with the participant video, and the chat window. This requires tremendous energy and great deal of coordination. Once the discussion is on, the participants too have to be at the same pace. The complexity of interface and demands on the individual make it a huge investment for everyone in the room. Some participants may not be able to make the transition within the class, and thus lose out on the pace of discussion. Lecture method requires much lesser strain on the processing capacities of individuals.

3. The technological and infrastructure requirements to create a virtual classroom are probably too huge. There is a need for high speed connection capable of transmitting streaming video, servers, uplinks, hardware for each candidate, and so on. While the technological partners ensure availability of functional hardware, their business model of franchising may not be able to yield best results, especially for the faculty. This is more true when the faculty members are desirous of taking their own style to the online classroom. If the classroom is unable to provide the right platform, the delivery would be less than perfect and any discerning faculty would not like that.

4. Given the success of some top business schools in India in case based teaching, there is an aura and an enigma to learn through cases. The romance of case study and learning through cases seems to have reached gargantuan heights. The participants and in this case, the instructor as well, tend to get sucked in to the demand and glamour of teaching through cases. It might be useful for case discussion leaders and facilitators to check their urge in relation to the medium.

Phase 8: The Resurrection

After this instance, I had another opportunity to interact with the same set of participants for a course on cross-cultural management. The memories of organization design course feedback were fresh then. I had made considerable changes in the course delivery structure.

While the course content for physical classroom had mostly cases, the approach in this course was quite different. There was more visual experience that participants could relate to and understand. The online program participants were given a framework to acknowledge the differences and appreciate the similarities among various cultures. On the other hand, the physical classroom participants had a more experiential and grounding experience through discussions, live workshops, simulations and feedback sessions. The online participants had to make do with just sharing their experiences lectures on interpretation of my framework. We extensively used video and/or voice chat this time to create a dialogue.

The positive energy in the class due to sharing was infectious. While initial examples were about sharing success stories, later on participants came forward with vivid experiences and did not hesitate to put across their mistakes for the rest of the class. The focus was on building a positive attitude in cross-cultural interactions, and it seemed to work. In one session, for example, one participant discussed her problems due to cross-cultural interactions at work and home; and a set of 40 participants actively consoled her! The best part – they empathized with her and encouraged her to find her solutions.

If education is about liberation of mind and learning about new ways, means to achieve desired ends, skills – it was surely happening in the online medium.

DIFFERENCES AND SIMILARITIES

The biggest difference to me is at the perception level. Generally, in our context, as a facilitator walks into the classroom, the movements, the hum and din, minor conversations before the class begins reveal a lot about the mood of the group. Here it was all missing. The only reliable source available to gauge the mood or pick up the hot topic for the day was the chat window. The assumption here was that people were sharing their relevant thoughts on the public chat window. If this sharing did not happen, there was no other way to gauge or sense the mood of the class. As the typed in chat messages require some cognitive processing, untold expressions were completely missing from the transaction and interaction right from the beginning. This however had a positive externality.

There were some participants who were quite active, would generally arrive before time, and create an excitement due to their superior ability or interest or both. They would be the ones who would bring in social energy, spread enthusiasm, take lead in greeting everyone including the facilitator as soon as the facilitator arrival was an-

nounced, and share their experiences relevant to the course. Such conversations brought a bias in spreading positive energy to the classroom which facilitated learning. On the other hand, the gloomy or uninterested faces in the classroom sometimes drain the energy, and thus facilitator had to rely on sensory inferences to understand the mood of the class. Therefore, an extra effort is required to create a more positive learning atmosphere for the session. This limitation and extra effort in translating emotions into words made the picture clearer and the facilitator was more sure of the emergent mood in the session and the reactions.

Peer Based Learning

In my experience peer based learning did happen through discussions in the online classes, though a similar yet different route. Unlike physical classrooms where the room design, discussion tools, excitement and encouragement were infectious, the online classroom had just the written chat window to begin with. Slowly we pushed the system and each other to utilize the video conference facility. Once participants decided to open up, there was no looking back.

However, the biggest hurdle for a case discussion or simulation remained to be the absence of a common platform where one could see and learn from each other at the same point of time. The medium restricts everyone to be in one place and be there. The communication and interaction is by and large one way; even the video conference could not substitute the richness of face to face interaction. The future may have the answers for us to hold highly interactive and simultaneous exercises. Till then, the medium shall dictate the content and delivery methods adopted by faculty members.

CONCLUSION

There are quite a few insights emerging from the three auto-ethnographies. First and foremost the instructors seem have their own set of preferences, and it's the individual style and make-up that sets the tone for the experience. Individuals differ in their ability and interest to handle technological complexity at the first level.

Second, the infrastructure of the online classroom seems to be an issue at least in our experiences. There are obvious demand-supply gaps in an emerging market. This is largely a supplier's market. Even within the supplier market, it is the individual faculty whose skill is the scarcest. Thus, a faculty should logically be an important customer.

This is also important to take care of style differences. Well-functioning and highly regarded institutions generally give the faculty members the freedom to pursue their method and style to ensure an effective delivery of concepts and skills. The system in question should, ideally, be such that it can allow the faculty member to use his or her preferred set of tools. From the three auto-ethnographies, it emerged that while the participant is considered to be an important customer, the faculty who delivers hardly finds any concerted effort to have a system that adapts to his or her style.

It also emerged that while the medium does support transference of ideas and some exchange, it lacks the munificence of various perceptive experiences on offer in a physical classroom. From the auto-ethnographies, it clearly emerged that the physical classroom is more than "seeing" and 'hearing" students. There are several other experiences on offer from a faculty perspective.

Dykman & Davis (2008) have suggested about adopting a more-structure approach. It emerged from this study that such structured approach would depend on the pedagogy adopted by the faculty. It was quite evident that if the pedagogy is extensive discussion based or involves case discussions that survive on frequent exchange between different stakeholders, the medium just falls short of expectations. Besides, there is no possibility at least in our knowledge to hold simulations, role plays, and group exercises. Thus, subject matter at hand also poses an inherent set of challenges.

With the advent of time and advancement in technologies, there may be better solutions on offer, but if a faculty member is looking at a two-way communication of ideas, believes in learning with the participants and wants to learn by sharing – something all long-lasting teachers and researchers do – medium does matter.

REFERENCES

Abeysekeara, I. (2008). Preferred learning methods: A comparison between international and domestic accounting students. *Accounting Education, 17*(2), 187–198.

Anderson, L. (2006). Analytic autoethnography. *Journal of Contemporary Ethnography, 35*(4), 373–395.

Barnard, C. I. (1938). *The functions of the executive*. Cambridge, MA: Harvard University Press.

Boje, D., & Tyler, J. A. (2009). Story and narrative noticing: Workaholism autoethnographies. *Journal of Business Ethics, 84*(2), 173–194.

Boyle, M., & Perry, K. (2007). Telling the whole story: The case for organizational autoethnography. *Culture and Organization, 13*(3), 185–190.

Coppola, N. W., Hiltz, S. R., & Rotter, N. G. (2002). Becoming a virtual professor: Pedagogical roles and asynchronous learning networks. *Journal of Management Information Systems, 18*(4), 169–189.

Daft, R. L., & Lengl, R. H. (1986). Organizational information requirements, media richness and structural design. *Management Science, 32*(4), 554–571.

Dykman, C. A., & Davis, C. K. (2008). Part two - teaching online versus teaching conventionally. *Journal of Information Systems Education, 19*(2), 157–164.

Eisenhardt, K. M. (1989). Building theory from case study research. *Academy of Management Review, 14*(4), 532–550.

Ellis, C., & Bochner, A. (2000). Autoethnography, personal narrative, reflexivity: Researcher as subject. In Denzin, N., & Lincoln, Y. (Eds.), *The handbook of qualitative research* (2nd ed., pp. 733–768). Newbury Park, CA: Sage.

Friedman, P. A., Dyke, L. S., & Murphy, S. A. (2009). Expatriate adjustment from the inside out: An autoethnographic account. *International Journal of Human Resource Management, 20*(2), 252–268.

Hayano, D. M. (1979). Auto-ethnography: Paradigms, problems, and prospects. *Human Organization, 38*(1), 99–104.

Holbrook, M. B. (2005). Customer value and autoethnography: Subjective personal introspection and the meanings of a photograph collection. *Journal of Business Research, 58*(1), 45–61.

Levy, R. I., & Hollan, D. (1998). Person-centered interviewing and observation in anthropology. In Bernard, H. R. (Ed.), *Handbook of methods in cultural anthropology* (pp. 333–364). Walnut Creek, CA: Altamira Press.

Mahoney, J. T. (2002). The relevance of Chester I. Barnard's teaching to contemporary management education: Communicating the aesthetics of management. *International Journal of Organization Theory and Behavior, 5*(1&2), 159–172.

Palloff, R. M., & Pratt, K. (2007). *Building online learning communities: Effective strategies for the virtual classroom.* San Francisco, CA: Jossey Bass.

Perreault, H., Waldman, L., & Zhao, M. A. J. (2002). Overcoming barriers to successful delivery of distance learning courses. *Journal of Education for Business, 77*(6), 313–318.

Roy, M. (1975). *Bengali women.* Chicago, IL: University of Chicago Press.

Spradley, J. (1979). *The ethnographic interview.* New York, NY: Rinehart and Winston.

Srinivas, M. N. (1966). *Social change in modern India.* Berkeley, CA: University of California Press.

Sutton, R. I. (1997). The virtues of closet qualitative research. *Organization Science, 8*(1), 97–106.

Tedlock, B. (1991). The new anthropology of dreaming. *Dreaming, 1,* 161–178.

Vickers, M. H. (2007). Autoethnography as sensemaking: A story of bullying. *Culture and Organization, 13*(3), 223–237.

Wallace, A. F. C. (1965). Driving to work. In Spiro, M. (Ed.), *Context and meaning in cultural anthropology* (pp. 277–292). New York, NY: Free Press.

Webster, J., & Hackley, P. (1997). Teaching effectiveness in technology-mediated distance learning. *Academy of Management Journal, 40,* 1282–1309.

Wolcott, H. F. (1990). *Writing up qualitative research.* Newbury Park, CA: Sage.

ENDNOTES

[1] We thank Patti Law for her support. Her patience helped us in completing this work.

[2] There are a few ways in which students could do so. They could ask a friend to log in using their ID and password. Or, the staff at center could do so in collusion with students. Since the programs in which I taught had a minimum attendance requirement, students had a motive to engage in such practices.

Chapter 22

Online Business Education in India:
A Case Study[1]

Rajiv Kumar
Indian Institute of Management Calcutta, India

Abhishek Goel
Indian Institute of Management Calcutta, India

Vidyanand Jha
Indian Institute of Management Calcutta, India

ABSTRACT[2]

Several scholars have described the advantages of online education. The Indian market for business management education is also increasingly accepting this mode of delivery. This case presents the history and policy environment leading to the origin, design, and delivery of a one-year online management education program by a leading business school in India. The technological and marketing support received from a partner organization is presented. The structure of this program, along with the unique challenges faced in operationalizing such a program with limited resources is highlighted. The interplay between program administrators, business school, faculty members, program participants, and service provider is discussed. The authors illustrate various enablers and impediments faced, and provide some key points of learning.

INTRODUCTION

As suggested by Webster and Hackley back in 1997, the online medium for instruction and training appears to be here to stay 14 years later. Technological advances have enabled full-time students as well as working executives the world over to use online media to receive basic education and advanced training in subjects of their choice (Mueller, 2003; Wicklund & Gee, 2004). Virtual classrooms today include a repertoire of facilities such as video-conferencing, recorded lecture repositories, and text messaging exchanges among participants and faculty. Together they facilitate

DOI: 10.4018/978-1-60960-800-2.ch022

peer-based learning through synchronous as well as asynchronous discussions among participants (Lam, 2004). India too is currently witnessing a strong move to online education, especially in the domain of business education and training. In the next section, we briefly describe this Indian context for online learning.

BUSINESS EDUCATION IN INDIA

The demand for higher education has recently witnessed a boom in India (Pal, 2009). India and China are predicted to generate more than half of the demand for international higher education till 2025 (Bohm, Davis, Meares, & Pearce, 2002). A similar increase in demand is also predicted for formal business education as illustrated by nearly 10 times growth in the number of business schools offering Master of Business Administration (MBA) degree, or its equivalent, between 1988 and 2002 (Khurana, 2002). Besides the growing demand for an MBA from students, organizations are also providing impetus to demand for executive training. In order to build and further develop their human capital, organizations in India have considerably enhanced their training budgets in the recent past (Yadapadithaya, 2001). Apart from short-term training, many organizations also provide full or partial financial support to their employees to pursue higher education. There is also an increasing trend of individuals funding their own business management education to make better use of available opportunities in their work spheres, enabled by a widespread use of existing technologies.

Technology-enabled higher education in some form has been in existence in India for more than two decades. In the 1980's, educational media research centres (EMRCs) located in various universities across the country prepared several short video lectures on a variety of topics. These video lectures were routinely telecast over the national television network in non-primetime hours to supplement the higher education system of universities. With the rapid improvement in information and communication technology (ICT) infrastructure, people got used to interacting online and it facilitated the supply of online education. Top business schools in India took note of this opportunity, and some of them started offering online educational programs for working executives in 2000. However, these business schools did not have the required technological infrastructure, and they used the services offered by other organizations to offer such programs. Besides offering technological infrastructure such as virtual classrooms, these partners also provided marketing support to the business schools.

This mode of higher education is now poised to grow even further. The Government of India, through the Ministry of Human Resource Development (MHRD), has recently launched an ambitious program called "National Mission on Education through Information and Communication Technology" (2009) with the aim of enhancing the knowledge and skills of working adults. The government has plans to spend close to one billion US dollars in five years (from 2007 to 2012) to achieve its mission.

Considering this impetus and interest, it is an appropriate time to present a case study of an online program so that policy makers and others interested in using online media for offering higher education can understand some of the nuances involved in such an effort. This particular online program was recently offered by a top ranking business school in India. To ensure confidentiality, we label this business school as Renowned School of Business (RSB)[3]. In the next section, we provide a brief introduction to RSB and its executive education system.

Online Executive Education at RSB

Admission in the MBA program of RSB is through one of the toughest entrance examinations in the world. Less than 1% of the applicants are successful in securing admission into its MBA program. It has produced some of the best known business executives and teachers who have contributed significantly to industry and academia all over the world. The MBAs of RSB generally get multiple placement offers from reputed organizations even before they finish their studies. Industry and government regularly seek advice from RSB on important matters and also send their personnel for training at RSB. It should be noted here that unlike their counterparts in Europe, the UK and the USA, top Indian business schools such as RSB are independent institutes and are not housed under or governed by university system. They are autonomous organizations that run under the broad regulatory framework set—and modified from time to time—by the MHRD.

Historically, the central government supported RSB financially to ensure that the best business management education was available to everyone who could pass the admission test. Policy makers believed that such subsidies promoted equity in providing quality higher education. However, the scenario changed in the early 1990's when the government faced an alarming economic crisis, and hence had to reduce its burden of subsidies. Therefore, the government asked RSB and its counterparts to become financially self-sufficient.

RSB responded to this challenge initially by cutting costs through measures such as restricting faculty members' participation in international conferences, reducing library related expenses, and curtailing infrastructure expansion. It also tried to increase revenue by increasing the fees of its flagship MBA program, and more importantly for this case, by paying more attention to executive education and consulting. Over time, all of these activities contributed to the emergence of financial autonomy as an important organizational goal for RSB, tacitly as well explicitly. In due course, some faculty members at RSB tried to best leverage the two most important resources of RSB—its reputation and its faculty. Braving several initial difficulties, they started to offer a

few executive education programs of RSB in the online format. It should be noted here that RSB, like its counterparts around the world, was quite reluctant in the beginning to offer support to such an initiative due to non-familiarity with the medium and arrangements for online education (Dykman & Davis, 2008a, b). However, supporting individuals and their initiatives has always been a core value at RSB, so these efforts were allowed space to grow. The initial market response to such programs was quite encouraging. Soon several other faculty members also became involved in such programs, both as coordinators and teachers. Since then, online executive education programs have become a prominent feature within RSB. In recent years, such programs have contributed to about 20% of the annual revenue of RSB.

Policies and Infrastructure at RSB

As executive education courses, including the online ones, entailed teaching beyond the minimum expected teaching in the MBA and doctoral programs of RSB, faculty members received monetary compensation for it. Faculty members coordinating such programs too got monetarily compensated for their efforts. Having met certain academic and administrative requirements, faculty members were also free to design and launch an online program. It should be noted, however, that involvement in executive education as a faculty member or as a coordinator was completely voluntary. It is also important to note that even though participation in executive education often led to monetary gain, the decisions regarding tenure or promotion were guided mainly by publications in international journals of repute. Thus while participation in online education was monetarily lucrative, it was not helping the faculty to gain promotions. Thus, the time spent in teaching online had a considerable trade-off with time available for other institutional activities and research.

RSB entered into agreements with two different partners, National Technologies (NT) and

Interactive Technologies Limited (ITL) to provide technological infrastructure and marketing support for the online programs. Both these partners were for-profit organizations with global reaches in their areas of operation. These two organizations had a revenue sharing agreement with the institute to share the fees paid by program participants. Faculty members usually worked with one of these two to launch their programs. The program that we are going to describe, Online Program in Managing Global Businesses (OPMGB), was delivered with the support of ITL.

The administrative support available for online executive education at RSB could at best be called modest. Seeing the growth in this segment, the decision makers at RSB created a separate office to service online executive education. This office employed a manager and a few others who assisted the faculty coordinating various online programs. We describe the activities of this office in detail while describing the case of OPMGB in the next section.

ONLINE PROGRAM IN MANAGING GLOBAL BUSINESSES

As we mentioned earlier, there is a significant demand in India for business education as well as training. Many people reach the management cadre without having any formal education or training in business management. Some working executives find their skill-set inadequate due to the rapidly changing economy, but they do not have time for a full-time MBA. Even the option of an evening MBA is not available to many executives. As a participant[4] wrote in his statement of purpose while applying for OPMGB:

"...some executives have the option of joining the evening MBA programs, but such options are available to only those who reside in the cities where prestigious colleges offer evening MBA programs..."

Besides skill enhancement, completing programs such as OPMGB also improve a person's chances for promotion. As an executive who recently completed another online program from RSB put: "it enhances my chances to be a department head sooner." RSB being a prestigious business school, organizations value the certificate that students receive. In fact, some students of OPMGB did report getting better jobs after successfully completing the program.

Considering the nature of demand from various corners, OPMGB was launched as a general management program with a focus on managing global businesses. As mentioned earlier, OPMGB was launched with the support of ITL. In the next section, we briefly describe the nature of support provided by ITL.

SUPPORT OF ITL

ITL provided marketing support before the launch of OPMGB. After the program was launched, ITL also provided virtual classrooms to deliver the program.

Marketing Support

As per the policies of RSB, an online program could be launched only if a minimum number of participants enrolled in it. Despite the good image of RSB, it was necessary to put in some marketing and selling effort to launch a program. ITL provided this support. It had its own sales channel, and its sales staff reached the potential participants through various means such as newspaper advertisements, posters at the offices of different organizations and direct contacts. They explained the program content and benefits to potential participants, and once a prospective participant was willing to apply, her/his application along with testimonials was sent to the ITL office for initial scrutiny.

Virtual Classrooms

ITL provided a dedicated studio for the RSB faculty to broadcast their lectures which participants across India and overseas watched in dedicated classrooms. The technology provided by ITL allowed faculty and participants to communicate using audio, video and text chat. ITL had also developed an in-house learning management system to facilitate the content delivery from faculty.

Two Types of Classrooms

ITL had two types of classrooms that OPMGB participants used. Some classrooms were in the major cities of India and they are owned and operated by ITL itself. These remaining classrooms were located in smaller cities, and were typically owned and operated by franchisees selected by ITL. The technological infrastructure in ITL owned and operated these classrooms was generally better than that in the remaining classrooms.

Eligibility Criteria and Admission Process

Admission to OPMGB was based on certain selection criteria. As per the policy of RSB, the program coordinators were free to formulate the admission criteria. In the case of OPMGB, the following criteria were used to select participants. Firstly, applicant was required to have at least two years of full-time and paid work experience. Secondly, an applicant had to secure at least 50% marks or its equivalent grade in his or her graduation. Applicants also had to write a brief statement of purpose.

ITL did the initial review of applications to screen out the applicants who did not meet the eligibility criteria. After this initial screening, ITL sent the successful applications to program coordinators for their final approval. In the first year of its launch in 2008, OPMGB received a very good response from the field, and about 300 participants ultimately enrolled.

It is worth noting certain contradictions at this juncture of the OPMGB launch. Having a single large cohort was beneficial for both RSB and ITL in some ways. The administrators at RSB argued that a single cohort would save faculty time, and hence would be less of a strain on faculty. Similarly, running a single cohort reduced the demand on scarce studio hours that ITL was contractually obligated to provide to broadcast the lectures. However, a single cohort of such a large size was considered problematic for program coordinators for two reasons. Firstly, they sensed that despite running the program through virtual classrooms, the large number could adversely influence the educational experience for both program faculty and students. Secondly, the prevailing incentive system at RSB did not reward the program faculty or its coordinators for handling cohorts beyond the minimum specified number. Considering these reasons, the program coordinators were not in favor of running just one cohort with about 300 students. Ultimately the cohort of about 300 participants was divided equally into two – OPMGB-1 and OPMGB-2. They were now called OPMGB batch 1 and 2 respectively in line with RSB nomenclature. The two batches were launched in a staggered fashion with a gap of about a month separating the two.

Based on the feedback of participants of OPMGB 1 and 2 participants in these first two iterations, the program coordinators decided that it was important to ensure uniformity in them. Hence for the next round of OPMGB admissions cohort, they denied admission to a few candidates who did not match the general profile. To illustrate, someone with a PhD or having more than fifteen years of experience was deemed to not fit with the general profile of the students in the cohort.

Program Structure and Delivery

OPMGB had eleven modules which were delivered over a year. Most of these modules covered the foundational subjects such as marketing, finance and accounting, organizational behavior and economics, all of which are taught in any general business education program. However, considering the emphasis of the program on managing global business, there were some other modules on topics such as international business and cross-cultural management.

Every module had a pre-determined number of three-hour sessions. This number varied between 5 and 14. Scheduling from ITL allowed delivery of two sessions per week for a batch. Considering the faculty time and participant interest, it was decided to run two modules in parallel. Thus, every week there was only one 3-hour session per module. Each session had a 15 minutes break after the first ninety minutes. The sessions were held in the evenings and over weekends so that working executives could attend them without having to miss their regular work hours.

The program coordinators found it difficult to get faculty members to teach in modules. With the proliferation of online programs such as OP-MGB, faculty resources were getting stretched and hence faculty members were less willing to teach in such programs. Moreover, as noted earlier, teaching in programs such as OPMGB was not linked to promotion or equated with teaching in the core programs of RSB. Hence teaching in such programs remained more voluntary and less institutionally enforceable. Therefore, it was difficult for the program coordinators to get faculty involvement. At times, it required considerable persuasion and perseverance from the program coordinators to get faculty to teach in the OPMGB. The willing faculty members had their preferences for teaching in certain months in a year and on certain days of the week. Given the logistic concerns, the schedules were drawn to accommodate various requests. Such considerations and agreements had the potential to disrupt the learning of participants. In order to safeguard learning interests of the participants, the program coordinators had to continuously face the challenge to schedule different modules keeping in mind the availability of faculty as well as the natural sequence in which they should be taught. The negotiations with the faculty members were often tedious, but in the end someone would eventually support the initiative.

As it was easier for faculty members in a particular discipline to talk to his or her counterparts, faculty members were asked to take the role of course-coordinator to ensure delivery of respective functional modules. The program coordinators had no involvement in either designing the syllabi or actual delivery of these modules. They only conveyed the profile of the participants and sent a message to the program faculty that at least 30% to 40% of the time should be devoted to covering the global business related aspects in each module. To illustrate this, the faculty member teaching accounting was requested to spend about one-third of the time on topics such as international accounting practices and financial reporting standards. However, this faculty member was also free to design the content in any manner he or she deemed fit. The program coordinators and the faculty members both worked in a collegial system and the program coordinators had full faith in the judgment of individual faculty. There was no interference from coordinators once a particular faculty member agreed to teach in the program.

Once the program was underway, ITL and the program coordinators worked in tandem to ensure the smooth delivery of the program. Virtual classrooms and issues related to them were understood to primarily be the responsibility of ITL, while the program coordinators were responsible for academic content and concerns. The main responsibilities of program coordinators included: (a) designing the overall content and thrust of the program, (b) arranging for faculty to teach different modules in the course, and (c) completing the administrative formalities within RSB. The last responsibility of meeting the administrative requirements within RSB involved a significant interface with the newly established section within the office of executive education.

Role of the Program Assistants

As mentioned previously, a newly established office within RSB to support the online executive education employed a few young people as program assistants. Unlike many other staff of RSB, these program assistants were hired on a contractual basis. Each program assistant was usually associated with a few programs such as OPMGB. These program assistants worked closely with the program coordinators and helped deliver the program in many ways.

Firstly, the program assistant acted as an interface between participants and program coordinators. As program coordinators themselves were faculty members and had several other responsibilities, it was not possible for them to respond to every communication from participants. Program assistants usually responded to routine queries related to session or examination schedule. More important issues went to program coordinators. For example, if a participant wanted to take leave or was unable to appear for an exam, such matters were brought to the attention of program coordinators.

Secondly, the program assistant also worked as an interface between program coordinators and program faculty. Once a faculty member agreed to teach in the program, the program assistant took over and took care of routine matters such as getting the course syllabus and circulating it to participants, uploading course material, getting exams prepared in time, and circulating the final grades to participants. The program assistant also arranged for the transport to and from the studio for faculty. As in the case of participants, if some issues required the attention of program coordinators, such as rescheduling a session, the program assistant communicated them to the program coordinators.

The program assistant also helped in processing various payments such as honoraria to faculty and payments to book suppliers. RSB followed an elaborate system of approvals before any payment could be made. The program assistant generated the necessary requests for payments, got the required approvals, and sent papers to offices responsible for making final payments.

Considering the online nature of the program, faculty members distributed course materials in the electronic form too. The material distributed included presentations used in the session, some readings, and occasional case studies. Each group of OPMGB students was linked to an e-mail group, and the materials were sent to that group. The general practice was that the program faculty sent their material through the program assistant who worked for RSB. Though it would have been easier to upload some material—such as the PowerPoint presentations used for lectures—through ITL staff immediately after the lecture was over, faculty members routed their material only through the program assistant. At times doing so that way became inevitable as the faculty member had to add some slides based on class discussion.

Within RSB, only the program assistant knew the password necessary to upload the course material. This was to ensure one point of contact for all program related communication. At times such dependence on the program assistant was frustrating. As one program assistant normally handled more than one program, occasionally there were (a) delays in either sending course material or uploading some important information to the electronic group, and (b) mixing up of material between the two different cohorts of OPMGB.

Electronic vs. Physical Teaching Material

Initially, the program coordinators had not planned to offer any textbook in physical form. And as mentioned earlier, the instructors also distributed their material in electronic form. Occasional delays notwithstanding, distributing the electronic material was more or less easy to manage. However, this situation changed after a few months. A program similar to OPMGB offered by RSB had a provision to distribute textbooks. After knowing this, OPMGB participants also wanted textbooks for different modules, and program coordinators deemed the participants' demand as fair. Hence, they decided to distribute the textbook with the help of ITL. The program office at RSB asked faculty members to specify a textbook for their respective modules, and then purchased these textbooks in bulk and handed them over to a contact person within ITL. ITL took up the responsibility of sending these books to its centers across the country and overseas. While the distribution of electronic material posed no difficulty, the distribution of textbooks was considerably more difficult. At one point, the coordinators decided to use Internet-based book distributors for the next version of OPMGB with the expectation that procuring and distributing textbooks to a dispersed batch of participants should be easier through such means. However, the current institutional arrangements at RSB did not allow a new contract for a particular program. Hence, it was further decided to streamline the book distribution system by asking the faculty member's choice of text book at the time of scheduling itself. While this solution was administratively better, it took away the flexibility to check and suggest a newer or better book in a dynamic market.

Evaluation and Certification

As per the guidelines framed by RSB, a "Certificate of Successful Completion" was awarded to a participant who fulfilled the following criteria: (a) the participant had at least 66% attendance in each module of the program, (b) the participant had taken all exams, and (c) the participant did not have "Poor" grade (reflecting unsatisfactory academic performance) in more than two courses. The guidelines further specified that a "Certificate of Participation" would be awarded to the participant who failed to satisfy the above conditions. However, if a participant did not take all the examinations, his/her result will be "Incomplete."

Being an online program, the attendance records were automatically generated as students logged in to the virtual classrooms. The academic performance of students was assessed through examinations after the completion of modules. Typically, these examinations were multiple-choice type. The faculty concerned used to send a set of questions and answer key to the program assistant at RSB who would send the same to the contact person in ITL. This person in ITL used to set up the examination, and being an online examination, scores became available to participants immediately after finishing the test. Grading of the participants, however, was done by the faculty considering the overall scoring pattern, and then the program assistant communicated these grades to the participants. In accordance with RSB policies for such programs, a participant of OPMGB could get an "Excellent," "Good," "Average," or "Poor," depending on the deviation from the average score of the whole cohort. If a participant scored much lesser than the starting range of the average score, he or she was awarded a "Poor" grade.

This evaluation scheme had certain advantages and disadvantages. It was easy for the faculty to create a test, given the ubiquity of test banks available as instructor resources, and it also made the task of correction redundant. The computer instantly calculated the score once the test was over, and such efficiency helped participants too.

However, this efficiency had some hidden costs. Knowledge of a participant enrolled for online courses cannot be tested comprehensively in this type of exam. Moreover, a participant only gets to know that her/his answer is incorrect, but not the correct answer or why her/his original answer was incorrect (Borden, 2003). Besides such educational difficulties, there is another concern noted by Cooper (2000) that one can never be sure if the person who took the test is the genuine participant. In the case of OPMGB, there were institutional and technological mechanisms to minimize the possibility of occurrence of such events.

Borden (2003), therefore, advocates the use of more descriptive questions even in the online format. But the only experience of program coordinators with paper and pen exam was quite troubling. Considering the size of the exercise and the sophistication of support services required such as courier and secretarial assistance, it was a logistical challenge for program coordinators to get close to 150 answer scripts collected all across the country, and get them all sent to RSB. Due to several reasons, as the program coordinators later found out, the office at RSB was not well equipped to handle this task.

OPMGB also had a provision to administer a re-examination in all subjects towards the end of the program. This was primarily meant for those participants who wanted to improve on their grades received in the last examination. To ensure fairness, however, the grades obtained in the re-exam were reduced by one grade. Some illustrative portions of the rules of re-examination are given below:

- Those students who have received more than two poor grades so far could plan to appear for the re-exam.
- Students who want to attempt the re-exam to improve their original grade are allowed to do so. However, their grades in the make-up exam will be lowered by one level.

Campus Component

In a widely accepted model of understanding service quality, Parasuraman, Zeithaml, and Berry (1988) emphasized that tangibility –physical evidence of service and its delivery—is a dimension of service quality. In a recent study assessing the quality of service in higher education, Arambewela and Hall (2006) found that international participants of Indian origin placed the highest importance on quality, and the tangibility aspects of service was important to participants of all nationalities.

As per the general practice at RSB, this tangibility aspect was built into its online programs by having a mandatory on-campus component of typically a week. During this period, physical classes were held and participants got exposed to the conventional business education at RSB. In the case of OPMGB, the program coordinators tried to expose the participants to some inter-disciplinary topics, taught by an entirely new set of faculty besides facilitating the usual meeting with some of their virtual instructors. They also used this opportunity to get participant feedback regarding a variety of issues in a face-to-face discussion.

It also provided the participants an opportunity to interact with their classmates and network. The possibility of a much richer discussion during their time on campus formed a prominent tangible aspect of the service delivery. However, it was troublesome for some working executives to attend because of their work commitments.

The campus component was also more demanding for the program coordinators as they had to take care of several new activities. To illustrate this, program coordinators had to spend time to arrange for the lodging and meals of the participants. Additionally, the program directors needed to ensure that classrooms and course material were prepared and distributed to the visiting participants. Though secretarial help was available for almost all these activities, these activities were not *academic* in nature, they were rather managerial. Some RSB faculty members thus resisted from shouldering the responsibility of program administration because of their discomfort with such activities.

Project Component

OPMGB also required participants to work on a capstone project in a group of five or six. They received broad guidelines for the project once a few foundational modules were over. Some illustrative portions of the project guidelines are given below:

- Students will have to indicate the members of their group by … A group will have 5-6 participants.
- Project reports will have to be submitted within two weeks of the completion of the program.
- Students are strongly advised to choose project topics around the central theme of the programme – managing global businesses. Within this theme, they may choose to focus on one or more of the functional areas covered in the programme such as organisational behaviour, marketing, finance, etc. To illustrate, a team can opt to work on the talent management issues for an Indian organisation which plans to go global. Or, a group can formulate a concise business plan for a company planning to go global. In the previous case (talent management), we will expect in-depth treatment as the scope is well-defined. In the latter case (business plan), comprehensiveness as to different aspects of a business plan will be expected.
- Students are advised to communicate project topics along with a synopsis (of 200 words maximum) by …

Students then formed groups on their own, and in many cases, these groups were virtual groups. It also helped them experience working as a group in virtual mode. The project reports by participants were also graded.

CHALLENGES FACED

As the program went on, the coordinators faced several challenges. In this section, we describe these challenges to highlight how unanticipated and uncontrollable events affected the delivery of OPMGB.

Technological Glitches

In the initial few months of OPMGB, several instances of technological problems came to the fore. At times, the video link would stop working altogether, or the audio would not be available in some centers. The facility of video chat became notorious for its difficulty in using it, and several faculty members complained about it. On a few occasions, the entire session had to be called off because the studio could not get linked to the main server of ITL. In general, participants using the franchisee-operated classrooms faced more technological glitches during the course than those who used the classrooms owned and operated by ITL.

ITL tried to correct these problems. They invested in better technology. Over time, the technological problems became considerably infrequent, though they did not completely vanish. Some of the reasons behind technological problems were less under the control of ITL. As mentioned earlier, the classrooms owned and managed by franchisees had poorer infrastructure as compared to the classrooms ITL owned. Hence, if a participant could not get clear audio because of a faulty headset, it was easier for ITL to replace the headset in its own classroom. Forcing the franchisee owner to invest in new equipment was possible, but ensuring prompt action was more difficult.

Change of Program Assistants

The program coordinators faced a difficult situation because of frequent changes of program assistants. During the course of the program, the coordinators had to work with three different program assistants. Considering that (a) a general management program for one year was being offered for the first time, (b) the size of the OPMGB was quite large, and (c) all program coordinators were not used to "managerial" coordination jobs, maintaining continuity in program administration proved to be difficult. Each new program assistant naturally took some time before s/he could settle in and effectively handle the multiple responsibilities. As this person was the focal point of interface with all the stakeholders of OPMGB - participants, faculty, program coordinators, and ITL - any replacement of this person entailed difficulties for all of them.

Unique Demands of Participants

Some problems arose because of the nature of OPMGB participants. As they were all working executives, they were more mobile than typical students of a full-time residential program. This mobility created logistical challenges. For example, some of them got transferred from one city to another, or took up jobs in a new city. This necessitated changing their classrooms. To provide another example, a few participants had to go on overseas assignments for considerable amount of time, and hence they wanted leave from the program. This created a dilemma for program coordinators because launching the program the following year depended on lots of variables beyond their control. For example, even if they were willing to coordinate the program next year, it could not be guaranteed that the executive education committee would approve their proposal. Even after internal approval, the launch of the program depended on the market response, as the program could not be launched if the minimum number of participants did not enroll. Considering all this, it was not possible to assure them of enrolment in the next program. Hence the program coordinators explained their

predicament to such participants, and the choice was left to the participants. When the third batch of OPMGB did get launched in 2010, program coordinators got to know of one such participant's willingness to join OPMGB midway and complete the remaining course modules. These situations are examples wherein the program coordinators had to create new norms or even program-specific rules which took up considerable time.

Managing Faculty Resources

As mentioned previously, ensuring that faculty members would teach different modules was a difficult job[5]. To make matters worse, a few faculty members had to withdraw at the last moment because of logistical difficulties or personal constraints. Finding replacements and maintaining continuity was a challenge in a system where every individual was considered unique. A few faculty members who were reluctant to teach in the beginning itself became even more reluctant to spend time in evaluation, and it led to delays.

PARTICIPANTS' FEEDBACK

Program directors encouraged participants to send their feedback directly to them. In addition they kept track of feedback from the participants on the program and its facilities from various faculty members. Besides, an open house session was held during the campus visit to understand their problems and gauge expectations. Based on the information collected from these sources, one could say that the participants of the OPMGB 1 and OPMGB 2 generally had a positive experience with RSB. Some of them wrote e-mails expressing their positive sentiments, while others called on the program coordinators to report their achievements that they attributed to OPMGB and RSB. One such participant got an opportunity to work on a prestigious overseas assignment, while some other participants reported getting promotions or better job offers.

Many participants, however, did not have a positive experience in the beginning. Due to some of the problems described previously, some participants in fact were quite annoyed with the glitches and misses. The following e-mail received by the program coordinators reflects the annoyance and frustration of one such participant who could not receive textbooks in time:

Dear Program Assistant,

Prof. ..., in his capacity of program coordinator, in the ... class on ...made an announcement that the books for the rest of the subjects shall be made available to the students and students would not go about sourcing them. He also said that these expenses have been covered in the course fee and the students would not be required to pay anything for it. Can you please let us know when shall you be able to provide us the books? Please note that the course on economics starts on Tuesday, that's tomorrow. If you need to confirm this, please refer to the recording of the class held on ..., or have a word with Prof. ...

I would also request you to reply to this email at the earliest, even if you need time to have a discussion with the program coordinators, please reply back to us, at the earliest, setting an expectation (maximum time limit), as to when can you get back to us on this with a conclusive reply.

The same participant, however, wrote towards the end of the program:

Prof. ...,

Thank you very much for the quick action. I am sure my pain would have been fiercer had I not

called you, though I hate to trouble you for every little thing. I wish to also place my appreciation on record for the responsiveness with which you have always acted on our needs. I have known you writing emails at 10 at night from a far off place because something has not worked right in this set up. Words won't be enough to thank you. In the very early days I used to think that RSB and those at RSB are not responsive and most problems stem from there, but over time, I have realized that, THAT was a preconceived notion I had. RSB has been good to us, most of the time, and the responsiveness and sensitivity with which RSB, and you in particular Professor ..., have acted is no doubts commendable. It's something else that's not working right in this setup, it seems to me.

Hence it seems that at least some participants had a positive experience and at least some earlier mistakes could be corrected. It also seems that some previously aggrieved participants felt better by the time program came to a close.

VALIDITY AND RELIABILITY

There are often arguments about the "generalizability" of a case. It is worth noting here that this case is not meant to illustrate a statistical conclusion, but to inform policy makers and future coordinators of various exciting and challenging moments in running an online program. Our endeavor was to make it easier for them to understand what lies ahead, and start from a higher point rather than re-invent the wheel completely. This purpose of work guided our methods. It is quite well established that in the absence of a well-established theory of a phenomenon, qualitative methods are more suitable as the requirement is first to describe the phenomenon before attempting to theorize about the "why" and "how" questions (Eisenhardt, 1989). We have presented the case of OPMGB in that spirit.

The case presented here fulfills three purposes – exploration, description, and explanation (Yin, 1994). There are certain concerns about validity and reliability that we are sensitive to. The positivist view generally argues for one and only one representation of reality. The chief amongst various assumptions is the "naturalness" of the instrument applied (Kirk & Miller, 1986). Some of us were or are involved in running similar programs at RSB. We acknowledge the possible loss of objectivity while we collected and analyzed data to write this case. However, following the suggestions in the literature, this case study was reviewed by peers who were adjudged capable of understanding the differences between a case study for classroom discussion and a case study for research (Yin, 1994).

We have no reasons to believe that the experiences of other programs will be so different as to make this case completely extraordinary. Additionally, we believe that the descriptions of various features of an online business education program should be of interest to other people as well. Hence we believe that what we convey through this case could be further developed into an emerging theory (Yin, 1994) about the pedagogical and logistical decisions behind designing an online program.

SUMMARY AND CONCLUSION

Higher education in general, and business management education and training in particular, are increasingly going to use online media. Based on the experiences of OPMGB as presented in this case study, the following considerations emerge as worthy of attention of policy makers and other individuals who are going to be involved in such endeavors.

Importance of Robust Technology at Students' End

The technology used to deliver online education is one of the most important constituents of the delivery system. However, decision makers sometimes remain uninformed of various difficulties that students or other users face. It is easy for the program faculty and coordinators to point out deficiencies and demand improvements. As the decision makers are closer to this end of the technology, such improvements are more likely to happen. However, it is not enough because even simple problems (e.g., a non-functional headphone, an old computer that hangs frequently) significantly deteriorate the learning experience of participants. A robust system should ensure that the benchmark is a trouble-free education experience for the students, faculty members and other incumbents.

Importance of Customer or Student Orientation

It is also important to realize that this online education is akin to service delivery to students who demand value for their money. Program coordinators and the technology providers have to continuously strive to meet or exceed student expectations. Some non-action from the technology provider or program assistants could nullify the efforts of the program directors and the faculty members. It is a unique concept because faculty members generally set standards for the participants and ask the system to create a delivery infrastructure. We do acknowledge that it is indeed difficult for faculty members who are primarily teachers and researchers to change their outlook and become service providers, where they set demands for the participants and are also responsible for ensuring smooth delivery of the experience.

In our experience it would help to have periodic reviews of the program with open house sessions that can be held online. This would create a direct point of contact between the participants and the program directors, and thus allow for increased responsiveness to the participant need. Besides such open house sessions, it would be a good idea to develop a structured feedback form for such programs keeping in mind the unique propositions of the programs. However, as noted earlier, such activities would require additional time and effort on part of the program directors, who in turn might not find putting in additional efforts worth their while due to existing policies and internal consideration at the institute.

Size of the Cohort and Program

Cohort size is an important consideration, as Dykman and Davis (2008c) pointed out. Any aspect of technology, for example text chat, that permits dyadic interaction among all people present in a virtual classroom—participants as well as the instructor—is likely to get chaotic in a large cohort. Similarly, running multiple versions or cohorts has its own pros and cons. While it can be easier for a faculty member to teach multiple batches using the same material and preparation, it can be logistically difficult occasionally to arrange for such things as studio or secretarial support. It would be prudent for future administrators to strike an acceptable balance between the conflicting interests of saving faculty time, augmenting revenue for all service providers, and ensuring at least a satisfactory educational experience.

Limitation of Medium

As we describe in a separate chapter, the medium of online education has its own limitations. Business education is desired to be interactive, but the medium itself poses several challenges. Virtual classes cannot be made as interactive as what can occur in a physical classroom. While this limitation may not matter much while teaching some formula in mathematics or some equations in chemistry, it becomes more troublesome in

discussing case studies and in teaching "soft" subjects such as organizational behavior, human resource management, strategy, and marketing. Program designs would benefit if such limitations are kept in mind at the program design stage itself.

Uniformity of the Cohort

It seems important to have uniformity in a cohort. It is easier for both instructors and students to deal with heterogeneity in face-to-face classrooms as the medium of communication is richer (Daft & Lengel, 1986). Hence, the variety of communication cues and speedy feedback make it comparatively easier for students and instructors to deal with diversity of opinions and perspectives. In the case of using an online medium, it is more difficult, if not impossible. Thus, having more uniformity in batch could result in a better educational experience.

Evaluation

Evaluation is an important part of any educational program. So, it is critical to ensure that a fair and comprehensive evaluation can be administered. However, it becomes difficult to ensure that the candidate taking the online exam is genuine (Cooper, 2000). Moreover, the online format is more suited for multiple-choice type examinations and it is acknowledged that many aspects of students' knowledge cannot be fully tested in such an examination (Borden, 2003). But organizing a traditional paper-and-pen examination is logistically very difficult, especially in places where systems are largely informal and evolutionary in nature. Having a project component can overcome the limitations of multiple-choice type examination to some extent. But the problem of ensuring genuineness, at least of the effort, would still remain.

Faculty Members as Coordinators or Researchers?

While the experience was gratifying for program coordinators, it was a tough job that used up a lot of their time available for research. This is problematic considering both the intrinsic and extrinsic motivations. Intrinsically, research is a more satisfying activity for many faculty members as compared to handling the logistical challenges associated with managing programs such as OP-MGB. And extrinsically, research also has the most important influence on tenure and promotion decisions at RSB. Programs like OPMGB are not looked upon favorably by faculty members in general and important decision-makers in particular, even though they serve the important purposes of augmenting revenue and maintaining the social obligation to reach a wider audience. Yet it appears that at RSB, designing and delivering online courses may not count much in the decisions of promotion or tenure. Schell (2004: p.56) highlighted, a poignant consequence of such ambivalence: "… universities offer incentives other than promotion and tenure. Reduced class loads, monetary stipends, and other benefits may be provided to faculty. Yet faculty members are dismissed from the university if they cannot attain tenure." It might be necessary for the organizations to understand such contradictions and create systems that resolve them.

To conclude, we believe that the potential outreach of online educational technologies coupled with the unmet demand for business education may translate into unique opportunities for business schools in many countries. From the experiences narrated in this chapter, it seems that the potential students too have responded well to online business education (at least in India). But these programs may also create a few challenges, as discussed earlier. Decision makers at business schools seem to have an ambivalent attitude towards online programs. While they welcome the revenue these programs generate, they seem less willing to consider faculty members' involvement in online programs at par with traditional teaching or research. Such ambivalence creates dilemmas before faculty members who may want to—or have to—coordinate and teach in online programs. Technology employed to offer online programs may not always ensure a smooth experience for teachers and students, at least in India. Support services (e.g., office and secretarial help) required for effective coordination of these programs may take time to mature, compelling faculty members, students, and program administrators to deal with avoidable problems in the interim. Despite several advanced features of the online technologies, there are some limitations of this medium as we described earlier. These limitations may affect the quality of teaching, learning, and evaluation. This case study also highlights the fact that despite the outreach promised by technology, cohort size and cohort uniformity may play an important role in the overall educational experience. And lastly, we are aware that our conclusions stem from a single case study. Hence we believe that more research is required to understand the issues of online business education in depth.

REFERENCES

Arambewela, R., & Hall, J. (2006). A comparative analysis of international education satisfaction using SERVQUAL. *Journal of Service Research*, *6*, 141–163.

Böhm, A., Davis, D., Meares, D., & Pearce, D. (2002). *Global student mobility 2025: Forecasts of the global demand for international higher education*. Australia: IDP.

Borden, E. B. (2003). Getting schooled online at ESRI's virtual campus. *Geospatial Solutions*, *13*(2), 48–51.

Cooper, L. (2000). Online courses - tips for making them work. *T.H.E. Journal*, *27*(8), 86–91.

Daft, R. L., & Lengel, R. H. (1986). Organizational information requirements, media richness and structural design. *Management Science, 32*(5), 554–571. doi:10.1287/mnsc.32.5.554

Development, M. o. H. R. (2009). *National mission on education through information and communication technology: Mission document.* New Delhi, India: Ministry of Human Resource Development.

Dykman, C. A., & Davis, C. K. (2008). Online education forum: Part one – the shift toward online education. *Journal of Information Systems Education, 19*(1), 11–16.

Dykman, C. A., & Davis, C. K. (2008). Online education forum: Part two - teaching online versus teaching conventionally. *Journal of Information Systems Education, 19*(2), 157–164.

Dykman, C. A., & Davis, C. K. (2008). Online education forum: Part three - a quality online educational experience. *Journal of Information Systems Education, 19*(3), 281–289.

Eisenhardt, K. M. (1989). Building theories from case study research. *Academy of Management Review, 14*(4), 532–550.

Khurana, S. (2002). The mushrooming growth of management educational institutions and its impact of quality: A study of Haryana. *The Icfaian Journal of Management Research, 8*(3), 62–82.

Kirk, J., & Miller, M. L. (1986). *Reliability and validity in qualitative research.* Beverly Hills, CA: Sage.

Lam, W. (2004). Encouraging online participation. *Journal of Information Systems Education, 15*(4), 345–348.

Mueller, B. (2003). Online education in the corporate context. *Chief Learning Officer, 2*(6), 40–49.

Pal, Y. (2009). *Report of the committee to advise on renovation and rejuvenation of higher education.* New Delhi, India: Ministry of Human Resource Development.

Parasuraman, A., Zeithaml, V. A., & Berry, L. L. (1988). SERVQUAL: A multiple item scale for measuring consumer perceptions of service quality. *Journal of Retailing, 64*(1), 12–40.

Schell, G. P. (2004). Universities marginalize online courses. *Communications of the ACM, 47*(7), 53–56. doi:10.1145/1005817.1005821

Webster, J., & Hackley, P. (1997). Teaching effectiveness in technology-mediated distance learning. *Academy of Management Journal, 40*(6), 1282–1309. doi:10.2307/257034

Wicklund, G., & Gee, R. (2004). Learn on your time. *Office PRO, 64*, 24–25.

Yadapadithaya, P. S. (2001). Evaluating corporate training and development: An Indian experience. *International Journal of Training and Development, 5*(4), 261–274. doi:10.1111/1468-2419.00138

Yin, R. K. (1994). *Case study research: Design and methods.* Thousand Oaks, CA: Sage.

ENDNOTES

[1] This case is based on experiences and opinions of some people. We have attempted to conceal the names of organizations and individuals involved, and our description is not intended to showcase effective or ineffective handling of situations by any organization or individual.

[2] We thank Ms. Patti Law for her support while we prepared this manuscript. We also thank Dr. Venkatesh Pamu, Dr. Billy O'Steen and another anonymous reviewer for critiquing this work and offering useful suggestions.

Their suggestions have helped us improve the work. The weaknesses and limitations of this chapter are, however, entirely due to our own shortcomings.

3 We have changed all names to protect their identity. However, the data used are accurate and based on real events.

4 We use the words "participant" and "student" interchangeably in this case. OPMGB being a program in the domain of executive educa-tion programs, the word "participant" seems more apt. At the same time, the features of OPMGB also include evaluation of the executives' academic performance, grading, and certification. Considering these features, the word "student" also appears appropriate at times.

5 RSB had a policy of paying a fixed hourly rate for teaching such online classes, irre-spective of the nature of the work involved.

Compilation of References

Abeysekeara, I. (2008). Preferred learning methods: A comparison between international and domestic accounting students. *Accounting Education, 17*(2), 187–198.

Adams, J. (2006). The part played by instructional media in distance education. *SIMILE: Studies In Media & Information Literacy Education, 6*(2), 1–12. doi:10.3138/sim.6.2.001

Adler, N. J. (2002). *International dimensions of organizational behavior* (4th ed.). Cincinnati, OH: SWCP.

Admiraal, W., & Janssen, J. Pijls, M., & Gielis, A.M. (2008, May). *Transfer between learning and practice: The use of Web-based video in higher education.* Paper presented at the Annual conference on human resource development international. Lille, France. Retrieved October 30, 2009 from http://info.dividu.nl/docs/paper_HRDI.pdf

Agarwal, R., & Karahanna, E. (2000). Time flies when you're having fun: Cognitive absorption and beliefs about information technology usage. *Management Information Systems Quarterly*, 665–694. doi:10.2307/3250951

Ajzen, I. (1991). The theory of planned behavior. *Organizational Behavior and Human Decision Processes, 50*, 179–211. doi:10.1016/0749-5978(91)90020-T

Al-Arishi, A. Y. (1994). Role-play, real-play, and surreal-play in the ESOL classroom. *ELT Journal, 48*(4), 337–346. doi:10.1093/elt/48.4.337

Aldrich, C. (2004). *Simulations and the future of learning: An innovative (and perhaps revolutionary) approach to e-learning.* San Francisco, CA: Pfeiffer.

Alexander, C. (1979). *The timeless way of building.* New York, NY: Oxford University Press.

Alfredson, K., Leo, K., Picker, R., Pacter, P., Radford, J., & Wise, V. (2007). *Applying international financial reporting standards* (1st ed.). Milton, Australia: John Wiley & Sons Australia.

Allan, M., & Thorns, D. (2009). Being face to face - a state of mind or technological design. In Whitworth, B., & de Moor, A. (Eds.), *Handbook of research on socio-technical designing and social networking systems* (pp. 440–454). Hershey, PA: IGI Global Publications. doi:10.4018/978-1-60566-264-0.ch030

Allen, W. R., Bonous-Hammarth, M., & Teranishi, R. T. (2006). *Higher education in a global society: Achieving diversity, equity and excellence.* Amsterdam, The Netherlands & London, UK: Elsevier JAI.

Allport, G. W. (1979). *The nature of prejudice.* Reading, MA: Addison-Wesley.

Amoako-Gyampah, K., & Salam, A. (2004). An extension of the technology acceptance model in an ERP implementation environment. *Information & Management, 41*(6), 731–745. doi:10.1016/j.im.2003.08.010

Anderson, L. (2006). Analytic autoethnography. *Journal of Contemporary Ethnography, 35*(4), 373–395.

Anson, C. (1999). Talking about text: The use of recorded commentary in response to student writing. In Straub, R. (Ed.), *A sourcebook for responding to student writing* (pp. 165–174). Cresskill, NJ: Hampton Press, Inc.

Apple Inc. (no date). *Learning with iPod touch and iPhone. Apple in education.* Retrieved December 9, 2010, http://www.apple.com/education/ipodtouch-iphone/

Apple. (2007). *Apple announces iTunes U on the iTunes store: Free content from universities now available.* Press release 30th May. Retrieved on October 6, 2009, from http://www.apple.com/pr/library/2007/05/30itunesu.html

Arambewela, R., & Hall, J. (2006). A comparative analysis of international education satisfaction using SERVQUAL. *Journal of Service Research, 6,* 141–163.

Arbaugh, J. (2000). Virtual classroom characteristics and student satisfaction with Internet-based MBA courses. *Journal of Management Education, 24*(1), 32. doi:10.1177/105256290002400104

Arbaugh, J. B., & Benbunan-Fich, R. (2006). An investigation of epistemological and social dimensions of teaching in online learning environments. *Academy of Management Learning & Education, 5*(4), 435–447. doi:10.5465/AMLE.2006.23473204

Argyris, C. (2002). Double-loop learning, teaching, and research. *Academy of Management Learning & Education, 1*(2), 206–218. doi:10.5465/AMLE.2002.8509400

Argyris, C., & Schon, D. A. (1974). *Theory in practice: Increasing professional effectiveness.* San Francisco, CA: Jossey-Bass, Inc., Publishers.

Association for Learning Technology. (2005). *ALT learning technology research strategy.* Retrieved on September 20, 2009, from http://www.alt.ac.uk/ALT_2005_Research_Strategy_20050420.html

Association of Graduate Recruiters. (2007). *Winter survey 2007 – press release.* Retrieved on September 20, 2009, from http://www.agr.org.uk/Content/AGR-Winter-Survey-2007-Press-Release

Australia Education International. (2008). *End of year summary of international student enrolment data: Australia – 2008.* Canberra, Australia: Department of Education, Employment and Workplace Relations.

Australian Copyright Council. (2009). *Q&As on using YouTube for education.* Retrieved September 17, 2009, from http://www.copyright.org.au/information/cit005/cit073/wp0032

Australian Department of Foreign Affairs and Trade. (2009). *Tourism and international students.* Retrieved August 1, 2009, from www.dfat.gov.au/aib/tourism_studnets.html

Avid Learning Excellerator. (n.d.). *Alex.* Retrieved from http://learn.avid.com/alex/lms/

Baars, G., Wieland, A., Deinum, J. F., van de Ven, M., D'haese, I., & van de Linde, E. (2008). *Digitale didactiek: practische stappenplannen voor het gebruik van ICT in het hoger onderwijs* [Digital Didactics: practical procedures for using ICT in Higher Education]. Utrecht, The Netherlands: Lemma.

Bach, S., Haynes, P., & Smith, L. J. (2007). *Online learning and teaching in higher education.* New York, NY: Open University Press.

BachelorsDegreeOnline.com. (2009). *50 Terrific iTunes U lectures to get you through the economic crisis.* Retrieved on October 6, 2009, from http://www.bachelorsdegreeonline.com/blog/2009/50-terrific-itunes-u-lectures-to-get-you-through-the-economic-crisis/

Bain, K. (2004). *What the best college teachers do.* Cambridge, MA: Harvard University Press.

Ballard, B., & Clanchy, J. (1997). *Teaching international students.* Deakin, ACT: IDP Education Australia.

Baltes, B. B., Dickson, M. W., Sherman, M. P., Bauer, C. C., & LaGanke, J. S. (2002). Computer-mediated communication and group decision making: A meta-analysis. *Organizational Behavior and Human Decision Processes, 87*(1), 156–179. doi:10.1006/obhd.2001.2961

Bandura, A. (1977). *Social learning theory.* Prentice-Hall.

Bandura, A. (1982). Self-efficacy mechanism in human agency. *The American Psychologist, 37*(2), 122–147. doi:10.1037/0003-066X.37.2.122

Bandura, A. (1995). *Self-efficacy in changing societies.* Cambridge, UK: Cambridge University Press. doi:10.1017/CBO9780511527692

Bandura, A. (1977). *Social learning theory.* Englewood Cliffs, NJ: Prentice-Hall.

Bandura, A. (1977). Self-efficacy: Toward a unifying theory of behavioral change. *Psychological Review, 84*(2), 191–215. doi:10.1037/0033-295X.84.2.191

Bandura, A. (1982). Self-efficacy mechanism in human agency. *The American Psychologist, 37*(2), 122–147. doi:10.1037/0003-066X.37.2.122

Barnard, C. I. (1938). *The functions of the executive*. Cambridge, MA: Harvard University Press.

Barnatt, C. (2009). Higher education 2.0. *The International Journal of Management Education*, 7(3). Retrieved on October 6, 2009, from http://www.heacademy.ac.uk/IJME/ijme/business/resources/detail/ijme/IJME_vol7_no3_barnatt

Barrett, H. C. (2005, June). *Researching and evaluating digital storytelling as a deep learning tool*. The REFLECT Initiative. Retrieved December 12, 2009, from http://www.electronicportfolios.com/portfolios/SITEStorytelling2006.pdf

Bates, M., Manuel, S., & Oppenheim, C. (2007). *Models of early adoption of ICT innovations in higher education*. Retrieved on September 20, 2009, from http://www.ariadne.ac.uk/issue50/oppenheim-et-al/

Bateson, G. (1979). *Mind and nature: A necessary unity*. New York, NY: Ballantine Books.

Bateson, G. (1987). Men are grass. In Thompson, W. I. (Ed.), *Gaia, a way of knowing* (pp. 37–47). Hudson, NY: Lindisfarne.

Beldarrain, Y. (2006). Distance education trends: Integrating new technologies to foster student interaction and collaboration. *Distance Education*, 27(2), 139–153. doi:10.1080/01587910600789498

Bell, M. P., & Kravitz, D. (2008). What do we know and need to learn about diversity education and training? *Academy of Management Learning & Education*, 7(3), 301–308. doi:10.5465/AMLE.2008.34251669

Bennett, E., & Maniar, N. (2008). *Are videoed lectures an effective teaching tool? Biggs, J., & Tang, C. (2007). Teaching for quality learning at university: What the student does (Society for Research Into Higher Education)*. Mcgraw-Hill Publ.Comp.

Bennett, R. (2002). Employers' demands for personal transferable skills in graduates: A content analysis of 1000 job advertisements and an associated empirical study. *Journal of Vocational Education and Training*, 54(4), 457–475. doi:10.1080/13636820200200209

Bergin, J., Eckstein, J., Manns, M. L., & Sharp, H. (2009). *Patterns for active learning*. Retrieved October 23, 2009 from http://www.pedagogicalpatterns.org/

Berkenkotter, C., & Murray, D. M. (1983). Decisions and revisions: The planning strategies of a publishing writer, and response of a laboratory rat: Or, being protocoled. *College Composition and Communication*, 34(2), 156–172. doi:10.2307/357403

Bhawuk, D. P. S. (2001). Evolution of cultural assimilators: Toward theory-based assimilators. *International Journal of Intercultural Relations*, 25, 141–163. doi:10.1016/S0147-1767(00)00048-1

Bhawuk, D. P. S., & Brislin, R. W. (2000). Cross-cultural training: A review. *Applied Psychology: An International Review*, 49(1), 162–191. doi:10.1111/1464-0597.00009

Bickerstaffe, P. Hannigan, B. Wood, S., & Young, N. (2007). Chapter. In T. Stickley & T. Basset (Eds.), *Teaching mental health*. Chichester, UK: John Wiley and Sons.

Biggs, J. (1999). *Teaching for quality learning at university*. Buckingham, UK: Society for Research in Higher Education & Open University Press.

Biggs, J. (2003). *Teaching for quality learning at university*. Maidenhead, UK: Open University Press.

Billinghurst, M., & Kato, H. (1999). *Collaborative mixed reality- merging real and virtual worlds*. Paper presented at the First International Symposium on Mixed Reality (ISMR 99), Berlin.

Biocca, F., Harms, C., & Burgoon, J. K. (2003). Towards a more robust theory and measure of social presence: Review and suggested criteria. *Presence (Cambridge, Mass.)*, 12(5), 456–480. doi:10.1162/105474603322761270

Black, J. S., Mendenhall, M. E., & Oddou, G. (1991). Toward a comprehensive model of international adjustment: An integration of multiple theoretical perspectives. *Academy of Management Review*, 16(2), 291–317.

Black, J. S., & Mendenhall, M. (1989). A practical but theory-based framework for selecting cross-cultural training methods. *Human Resource Management*, 28(4), 511–539. doi:10.1002/hrm.3930280406

Black, J. S., & Mendenhall, M. (1991). The U-curve adjustment hypothesis revisited: A review and theoretical framework. *Journal of International Business Studies*, 22, 225–247. doi:10.1057/palgrave.jibs.8490301

Black, J. S., & Mendenhall, M. E. (1990). Cross-cultural training effectiveness: A review and a theoretical framework for future research. *Academy of Management Review, 15*, 113–136.

Blackboard. (n.d.). *Blackboard Inc* [Mobile technology software]. Retrieved from http://www.blackboard.com

Bligh, D. (2000). *What's the use of lectures?* San Francisco, CA: Jossey-Bass.

Bloomfield, J., While, A., & Roberts, J. (2008). Using computer assisted learning for clinical skills education in nursing: Integrative review. *Journal of Advanced Nursing, 63*(3), 222–235. doi:10.1111/j.1365-2648.2008.04653.x

Böhm, A., Davis, D., Meares, D., & Pearce, D. (2002). *Global student mobility 2025: Forecasts of the global demand for international higher education.* Australia: IDP.

Boje, D., & Tyler, J. A. (2009). Story and narrative noticing: Workaholism autoethnographies. *Journal of Business Ethics, 84*(2), 173–194.

Boler, M. (1999). *Feeling power: Emotions and education.* New York, NY: Routledge.

Boler, M. (2004). Teaching for hope: The ethics of shattering world views. In Liston, D., & Garrison, J. (Eds.), *Teaching, learning and loving: Reclaiming passion in educational practice* (pp. 117–131). New York, NY: RoutledgeFalmer. doi:10.4324/9780203465622_chapter_7

Bongey, S. B., Cizadlo, G., & Kalnbach, L. (2006). Explorations in course-casting: Podcasts in higher education. *Campus-Wide Information Systems, 23*(5), 350–367.

Bonk, C., & Zhang, K. (2008). *Empowering online learning: 100+ activities for reading, reflecting, displaying and doing.* San Francisco, CA: Jossey-Bass.

Bonk, C. J., Kirkley, J., Hara, N., & Dennen, V. (2007). Finding the instructor in post-secondary online learning: Pedagogical, social, managerial and technological locations. In J> Stephenson (Ed.), *Teaching & learning online: Pedagogies for new technologies.* London, UK: Kogan Page.

Borden, E. B. (2003). Getting schooled online at ESRI's virtual campus. *Geospatial Solutions, 13*(2), 48–51.

Bosch, L. T., Oostdijk, N., & Ruiter, J. P. (2004). *Durational aspects of turn-taking in spontaneous face-to-face and telephone dialogues.* Paper presented at the Text, Speech and Dialogue Conference. Retrieved from http://www.hcrc.ed.ac.uk/comic/documents/

Boyle, M., & Perry, K. (2007). Telling the whole story: The case for organizational autoethnography. *Culture and Organization, 13*(3), 185–190.

Brahler, C., Peterson, N., & Johnson, E. (1999). Developing online learning materials for higher education: An overview of current issues. *Educational Technology and Society, 2*(2). Retrieved on 5 October, 2009, from http://www.ifets.info/journals/2_2/jayne_brahler.html

Bransford, J. D., Brown, A. L., & Cocking, R. R. (Eds.). (2000). *How people learn: Brain, mind, experience and school.* Washington, DC: National Academy Press.

Brislin, R., & Yoshida, T. (1994). *Intercultural communication training: An introduction.* Thousand Oaks, CA: Sage.

Brissett, D., & Edgley, C. (1990). *Life as theatre.* Hawthorne, NY: Walter de Gruyter.

Brower, H. H. (2003). On emulating classroom discussion in a distance-delivered OBHR course: Creating an on-line learning community. *Academy of Management Learning & Education, 2*(1), 22–36. doi:10.5465/AMLE.2003.9324013

Brown, B., & Liedholm, C. (2002). Can Web courses replace the classroom in principles of microeconomics? *The American Economic Review*, 444–448. doi:10.1257/000282802320191778

Brunson, D., Jarman, B., & Lampl, L. (Eds.). (2007). *Letters from the future.* Sterling, VA: Stylus.

Bruschke, J. C., Gartner, C., & Seiter, J. S. (1993). Student ethnocentrism, dogmatism, and motivation: A study of BAFA BAFA. *Simulation & Gaming, 21*(1), 9–20. doi:10.1177/1046878193241003

Bumpus, M. A. (2005). Using motion pictures to teach management: Refocusing the camera lens though the infusion approach to diversity. *Journal of Management Education, 29*(6).

Burdet, B., Bontron, C., & Burgi, R. (2009). Lecture capture, what can be automated? *Educause Quarterly Magazine, 30*(2). Retrieved November 7, 2009, from http://www.educause.edu/EDUCAUSE+Quarterly/EDUCAUSEQuarterlyMagazineVolum/LectureCapture-WhatCanBeAutomat/157454

Burke, D. (2009). E-learning in dialogue: Using e-learning to explore the local religious environment. *Discourse: Learning and Teaching in Philosophical and Religious Studies, Special edition e-learning in dialogue, 8*(3).

Burke, D. (2009). *Using mobile devices to enhance fieldwork*. Presentation at Higher Education Academy Conference July 2009. Retrieved from http://www.techdis.ac.uk/index.php?p=2_1_7_26_29

Business Council of Australia. (2006). *New concepts in innovation: The keys to growing Australia*. Melbourne, Australia: BCA.

Caligiuri, P., Phillips, J., Lazarova, M., Tarique, I., & Bürgi, P. (2004). The theory of met expectations applied to expatriate adjustment: The role of cross-cultural training. *International Journal of Human Resource Management, 12*(3), 357–372.

Calimero. (2009). *Verkiezingsprogramma Calimero* [Election programme student fraction Calimero]. Retrieved October 21, 2009, from http://lijstcalimero.nl/verkiezingsprogramma-2009/

Campbell, G. (2005). Podcasting in education. *EDUCAUSE, Nov/Dec*, 5.

Campus Technology. (2007). *Innovator: Drexel University technology area- rich media*. Retrieved August 31, 2009, from http://campustechnology.com/articles/2007/08/2007-campus-technology-innovators-rich-media.aspx?sc_lang=en

Cape Town Open Education Declaration. (2010). *Unlocking the promise of open educational resources*. Retrieved from http://www.capetowndeclaration.org/read-the-declaration

Carlson, J. D. (2009). Who are you wearing? Using the red carpet question pedagogically. *International Studies Perspectives, 10*(2), 198–215. doi:10.1111/j.1528-3585.2009.00370.x

Carr, G. (2008). Changes in nurse education: Delivering the curriculum. *Nurse Education Today, 28*(1), 120–127. doi:10.1016/j.nedt.2007.03.011

Cassidy, S. (2004). Learning styles: An overview of theories, models, and measures. *Educational Psychology, 24*(4), 419–444. doi:10.1080/0144341042000228834

Cassidy, S., & Eachus, P. (2002). Developing the computer user self-efficacy (CUSE) scale: Investigating the relationship between computer self-efficacy, gender and experience with computers. *Journal of Educational Computing Research, 26*(2), 169–189. doi:10.2190/JGJR-0KVL-HRF7-GCNV

Champoux, J. E. (1999). Film as a teaching resource. *Journal of Management Inquiry, 8*(2), 206–218.

Chan, A., Lee, M., & McLoughlin, C. (2006). Everyone's learning with podcasting: A Charles Sturt University experience. *Who's learning? Whose technology? Proceedings ascilite Sydney 2006*.

Chang, C. (2004). Constructing a streaming video-based learning forum for collaborative learning. *Journal of Educational Multimedia and Hypermedia, 13*(3), 245–264.

Chang, S. (2007). *Academic perceptions of the use of Lectopia: A University of Melbourne example*.

Chiel, H. J., & Beer, R. D. (1997). The brain has a body: Adaptive behavior emerges from interactions of nervous system, body and environment. *Trends in Neurosciences, 20*, 553–557. doi:10.1016/S0166-2236(97)01149-1

Chizmar, J. F., & Williams, D. B. (2001). What do faculty want? *EDUCAUSE Quarterly, 24*(1), 18–24.

Chödrön, P. (1997). *When things fall apart: Heart advice for difficult times*. Boston, MA: Shambhala.

Chödrön, P. (2001). *The places that scare you: A guide to fearlessness in difficult times*. Boston, MA: Shambhala.

Choi, H. J., & Johnson, S. D. (2005). The effect of context-based video instruction on learning and motivation in online courses. *American Journal of Distance Education, 19*(4), 215–227.

Choi, H. J., & Johnson, S. D. (2007). The effect of problem-based video instruction on learner satisfaction, comprehension and retention in college courses. *British Journal of Educational Technology*, *38*(5), 885–895. doi:10.1111/j.1467-8535.2006.00676.x

Choi, I., & Lee, K. (2008). A case-based learning environment design for real-world classroom management problem solving. *TechTrends*, *52*(3), 26–31. doi:10.1007/s11528-008-0151-z

Chryssides, G. D., & Geaves, R. (2007). *The study of religion: An introduction to key ideas and methods*. London, UK: Continuum.

Chubb, J. E., & Moe, T. M. (2009). *Liberating learning: Technology, politics, and the future of American education*. San Francisco, CA: Jossey-Bass.

Citizenship and Immigration Canada. (2009). *Facts and figures 2008: Summary tables—permanent and temporary residences*. Retrieved June 2, 2009, from www.cic.gc.ca

Clark, R. E. (1983). Reconsidering research on learning from media. *Review of Educational Research*, *53*(4), 445.

Clark, R. (2001). *Learning from media: Arguments, analysis and evidence*. Boulder, CO: Information Age Publishing.

Clarke, V., & Walsh, A. (2009). *Fundamentals of mental health nursing*. Oxford, UK: Oxford University Press.

Clarke, V., & Walsh, A. (2007). Use of narrative in mental health nursing practice and its teaching. In *Proceedings of Conference-The Narrative practitioner*, (p. 22). June 11th – 13th North East Wales Institute of Higher Education, Wrexham UK.

Clotho Advanced Media Inc. (n.d.). *MediaLandscape* [Computer software]. Retrieved from http://www.media-landscape.com

Coffield, F., Moseley, D., Hall, E., & Ecclestone, K. (2004). *Learning styles and pedagogy in post 16 learning: Findings of a systematic and critical review of learning styles models*. London, UK: Learning and Skills Research Centre.

Colley, A. (1994). Effects of gender role identity and experience on computer attitude components. *Journal of Educational Computing Research*, *10*(2), 129–137. doi:10.2190/8NA7-DAEY-GM8P-EUN5

Collins, A. (1991). Cognitive apprenticeship and instructional technology. In Idol, L., & Fly Jones, B. (Eds.), *Educational values and cognitive instruction: Implications for reform* (pp. 121–138). Hillsdale, NJ: Erlbaum.

Collins, A., Brown, J. S., & Newman, S. E. (1989). Cognitive apprenticeship: Teaching the crafts of reading, writing and mathematics. In Resnick, L. B. (Ed.), *Knowing, learning, and instruction: Essays in honor of Robert Glaser* (pp. 453–494). Hillsdale, NJ: Erlbaum.

Collis, B. A., & Moonen, J. (2001). *Flexible learning in a digital world: Experiences and expectations*. London, UK: Kogan Page.

Collis, B. (1998). New didactics for university instruction: Why and how? *Computers & Education*, *31*, 373–393. doi:10.1016/S0360-1315(98)00040-2

Collis, B., & Moonen, J. (2005). *An on-going journey: Technology as a learning workbench*. Monograph (in Dutch, asfscheid rede) on occasion of their retirement from the University of Twente, Enschede, NL. (96pp). Retrieved 10th May 2008, from http://www.BettyCollisJefMoonen.nl/rb.htm

Colman, D. (2009). Introducing YouTube EDU! *Open Culture*. Retrieved on October 6, 2009, from http://www.openculture.com/2009/03/introducing_youtube_edu.html

Compeau, D., & Higgins, C. (1995). Computer self-efficacy: Development of a measure and initial test. *Management Information Systems Quarterly*, *19*(2), 189–211. doi:10.2307/249688

Compeau, D., Higgins, C., & Huff, S. (1999). Social cognitive theory and individual reactions to computing technology: A longitudinal study. *Management Information Systems Quarterly*, 145–158. doi:10.2307/249749

Cooper, L. (2000). Online courses - tips for making them work. *T.H.E. Journal*, *27*(8), 86–91.

Cooper, G. (1998). *Research into cognitive load theory and instructional design at UNSW*. Retrieved from http://www.arts.unsw.edu.au/education/clt.html

Coppola, N. W., Hiltz, S. R., & Rotter, N. G. (2002). Becoming a virtual professor: Pedagogical roles and asynchronous learning networks. *Journal of Management Information Systems*, *18*(4), 169–189.

Copyright Clearance Center. (2009, June). *Video use and higher education: Options for the future.*

Cornish, E. (2005). *Futuring: The exploration of the future* (p. 134). Bethesda, MD: World Future Society.

Cortés, C. E. (2003). Media and intercultural training. In Landis, D., Bennett, J. M., & Bennett, M. J. (Eds.), *Handbook of intercultural training* (3rd ed.). Thousand Oaks, CA: SAGE.

Costabile, M., De Marsico, M., Lanzilotti, R., Plantamura, V., & Roselli, T. (2005). On the usability evaluation of e-learning applications. In *Proceedings of the 38th Hawaii International Conference on System Sciences.*

Cover, R. (2006). Audience inter/active: Interactive media, narrative control and reconceiving audience history. *New Media & Society, 8*(1), 139–158. doi:10.1177/1461444806059922

Cowan, J. (2006). *On becoming an innovative university teacher.* Buckingham, UK: Oxford University Press.

Cranton, P. (2005). Learning styles. In English, L. M. (Ed.), *International encyclopedia of adult education* (pp. 111–117). New York, NY: Palgrave Macmillan.

Cronin Jones, L. L. (2003). Are lectures a thing of the past? *Journal of College Science Teaching, 32*(7), 453–457.

Cuban, L. (2001). *Oversold and underused: Computers in the classroom.* Harvard University Press.

Cuban, L. (1986). *Teachers and machines: The use of classroom technology since 1920.* Columbia, NY: Teachers College Press.

Dacko, S. G. (2006). Narrowing the skills gap for marketers of the future. *Marketing Intelligence & Planning, 24*(3), 283–295. doi:10.1108/02634500610665736

Daft, R. L., & Wiginton, J. (1979). Language and organisation. *Academy of Management Review, 4*(2), 171–191.

Daft, R. L., & Lengel, R. H. (1986). Organizational information requirements, media richness and structural design. *Management Science, 32*(5), 554–571. doi:10.1287/mnsc.32.5.554

Daiker, D. A. (1999). Learning to praise. In Straub, R. (Ed.), *A sourcebook for responding to student writing* (pp. 153–163). Cresskill, NJ: Hampton Press, Inc.

Dalglish, C., & Evans, P. (2008). *Teaching in the global classroom.* UK: MPG Books.

Dalsgaard, C., & Godsk, M. (2007). Transforming traditional lectures into problem-based blended learning: challenges and experiences. *Open Learning, 22*(1), 29–42. doi:10.1080/02680510601100143

Daly, S. P. (2001). Student-operated internet businesses: True experiential learning in entrepreneurship and retail management. *Journal of Marketing Education, 23*(3), 204–215. doi:10.1177/0273475301233006

Damrosch, D. (1995). *We scholars: Changing the culture of the university.* Cambridge, MA: Harvard University Press.

David, J. (1994). Realizing the promise of technology: A policy perspective. In *Technology and education reform* (pp. 169–189). San Francisco, CA: Josey-Bass.

Davis, B. (1995). Why teach mathematics? Mathematics education and enactivist theory. *For the Learning of Mathematics, 15*(2), 2–9.

Davis, B. (1996). *Teaching mathematics: Towards a sound alternative.* New York, NY: Garland.

Davis, B. (2004). *Inventions of teaching: A genealogy.* Mahwah, NJ: Lawrence Erlbaum.

Davis, B. (2005). Teacher as consciousness of the collective. *Complicity, 2*(1), 85–88.

Davis, B. (2008). Complexity and education: Vital simultaneities. *Educational Philosophy and Theory, 40*(1), 50–65. doi:10.1111/j.1469-5812.2007.00402.x

Davis, B., & Sumara, D. (1997). Cognition, complexity, and teacher education. *Harvard Educational Review, 67*(1), 105–125.

Davis, B., & Sumara, D. (2002). Constructivist discourses and the field of education: Problems and possibilities. *Educational Theory, 52*(4), 409–428. doi:10.1111/j.1741-5446.2002.00409.x

Davis, B., & Sumara, D. (2007). Complexity science and education: Reconceptualizing the teacher's role in learning. *Interchange, 38*(1), 53–67. doi:10.1007/s10780-007-9012-5

Davis, F. (1989). Perceived usefulness, perceived ease of use, and user acceptance of information technology. *Management Information Systems Quarterly*, 319–340. doi:10.2307/249008

Davis, F., Bagozzi, R., & Warshaw, P. (1992). Extrinsic and intrinsic motivation to use computers in the workplace. *Journal of Applied Social Psychology*, *22*, 1111–1132. doi:10.1111/j.1559-1816.1992.tb00945.x

Davis, F., & Venkatesh, V. (1996). A critical assessment of potential measurement biases in the technology acceptance model: three experiments. *International Journal of Human-Computer Studies*, *45*(1), 19–46. doi:10.1006/ijhc.1996.0040

Davis, B. (1993). *Towards an ecological view of mathematics education*. Paper presented at a meeting of the Canadian Society for the Study of Education, Ottawa, Canada.

Davis, F. (1986). *A technology acceptance model for empirically testing new end-user information systems: Theory and results*. Unpublished doctoral dissertation, Sloan School of Management, Massachussets Institute of Technology.

Day, J. (2008). *Investigating learning with Weblectures*. Unpublished doctoral dissertation, Georgia Institute of Technology.

Day, K. (2004, 24 January). Totally lost in translation. *The Guardian Newspaper*. Retrieved on December 11, 2008, from http://www.guardian.co.uk/world/2004/jan/24/japan.film

De Lucia, A., Francese, R., Passero, I., & Tortora, G. (2009). Development and evaluation of a virtual campus on Second Life: The case of SecondDMI. *Computers & Education*, *52*, 220–233. doi:10.1016/j.compedu.2008.08.001

de Sola Pool, I. (1982). *Technologies of freedom: On free speech in an electronic age*. Cambridge, MA: Harvard University Press.

DeAmicis, P. (1997). Interactive video disc instruction is an alternative method for learning and performing a critical learning skill. *Computers in Nursing*, *15*(3), 155–158.

Dekker, P. J., Wagemans, L., Winnips, J. C., Clement, M., Loonen, J., & Rasenberg, J. (2004). *Zelfstandig leren in een digitale leeromgeving: Handboek voor het ontwerpen van taakgericht onderwijs [Self-reliant learning in an electronic learning environment: Handbook for the design of task-based learning]*. Utrecht, The Netherlands: Digitale Universiteit. Retrieved November 6, 2009, from http://www.surffoundation.nl/nl/publicaties/Pages/DU-publicatie-Handboeken-Zelfstandig-Leren.aspx

DElight. (2008, July 8). *Adobe youth voices year end event – Delhi*. Retrieved from http://aifde.blogspot.com/2008/07/ayv-year-end-event-delhi.html

Demetriadis, S., & Pombortsis, A. (2007). E-lectures for flexible learning: A study on their learning efficiency. *Journal of Educational Technology & Society*, *10*(2), 147–157.

Den Hartog, D. N. (2004). Assertiveness. In House, R. J., Hanges, P. J., Javidan, M., Dorfman, P. W., & Gupta, V. (Eds.), *Culture, leadership, and organizations: The GLOBE study of 62 societies* (pp. 395–436). Thousand Oaks, CA: Sage Publications.

Dennis, A. R., & Valacich, J. S. (1999). *Rethinking media richness: Towards a theory of media synchronicity*. Paper presented at the 32nd Hawaii International Conference on System Sciences, Hawaii.

Denscombe, M. (2007). *The good research guide for small scale social research projects* (3rd ed.). Berkshire, UK: Open University Press.

Department of Health. (2004). *The 10 essential shared capabilities*. London, UK: DOH.

Department of Health. (2006). *From values to action. The Chief Nursing Officer's Review of Mental Health Nursing*. London, UK: DOH.

Desmedt, E., & Valcke, M. (2004). Mapping the learning styles "jungle": An overview of the literature based on citation analysis. *Educational Psychology*, *24*(4), 446–464. doi:10.1080/0144341042000228843

Development, M. o. H. R. (2009). *National mission on education through information and communication technology: Mission document*. New Delhi, India: Ministry of Human Resource Development.

Dewey, J. (1938). *Experience and education*. New York, NY: Collier Books.

Dewey, J., & Bentley, A. (1973). Knowing and the known. In Handy, R., & Harwood, E. C. (Eds.), *Useful procedures of inquiry* (pp. 89–190). Barrington, MA: Behavioral Research Council.

Diamond, N., Koernig, S. K., & Iqbal, Z. (2008). Uniting active and deep learning to teach problem-solving skills: strategic tools and the learning. *Journal of Marketing Education, 30*(2), 116–129. doi:10.1177/0273475308317707

Diamond Jr, A. M. (forthcoming, 2010). Using video clips to teach creative destruction. *Journal of Private Enterprise.*

Diederich, P. B. (1974). *Measuring growth in English*. Urbana, IL: NCTE.

Dimitriadis, Y., Goodyear, P., & Retalis, S. (2009). *Using e-learning design patterns to augment learners' experiences, 25*(5), 997-998.

Drexel University. (2009). *DragonDrop*. Retrieved August 20, 2009, from http://www.drexel.edu/irt/coursetools/toolList/dragonDrop.aspx

Duncan, C. (2004). *Leaning object economies: Barriers and drivers*. Retrieved August 10, 2009, from http://www.intrallect.com/index.php/intrallect/knowledge_base/white_papers/learning_object_economies_barriers_and_drivers

Dykman, C. A., & Davis, C. K. (2008). Online education forum: Part one – the shift toward online education. *Journal of Information Systems Education, 19*(1), 11–16.

Dykman, C. A., & Davis, C. K. (2008). Online education forum: Part two - teaching online versus teaching conventionally. *Journal of Information Systems Education, 19*(2), 157–164.

Dykman, C. A., & Davis, C. K. (2008). Online education forum: Part three - a quality online educational experience. *Journal of Information Systems Education, 19*(3), 281–289.

E4. (2009). *Skins mash-up*. Retrieved from http://www.e4.com/skins/doitandwin/2641f70985106483801215a7f901a42d/entry-terms.e4

Earley, P. C. (1993). East meets West meets Middle East: Further explorations of collectivist and individualist work groups. *Academy of Management Journal, 36*, 319–348. doi:10.2307/256525

Earley, P. C. (2002). Redefining interactions across cultures and organizations: Moving forward with cultural intelligence. *Research in Organizational Behavior, 24*, 271–299. doi:10.1016/S0191-3085(02)24008-3

Earley, P. C., & Ang, S. (2003). *Cultural intelligence: Individual interactions across cultures*. Stanford, CA: Stanford University Press.

Earley, P. C., & Mosakowski, E. (2004, October). Cultural intelligence. *Harvard Business Review*, 139–146.

Earley, P. C., & Peterson, R. S. (2004). The elusive cultural chameleon: Cultural intelligence as a new approach to intercultural training for the global manager. *Academy of Management Learning & Education, 3*(1), 100–115. doi:10.5465/AMLE.2004.12436826

Edge.org. (2009). *About edge*. Retrieved on October 6, 2009, from http://www.edge.org/about_edge.html

Edirisingha, P., & Salmon, G. (2007). Pedagogical models for podcasts in higher education. In *Conference Proceedings from In Beyond - Distance Research Alliance Conference*. Retrieved on March 1, 2010 from https://lra.le.ac.uk/handle/2381/405

Egan, M. L., & Bendick, M. (2008). Combining multicultural management and diversity into one course on cultural competence. *Academy of Management Learning & Education, 7*(3), 387–393. doi:10.5465/AMLE.2008.34251675

Eisenhardt, K. M. (1989). Building theory from case study research. *Academy of Management Review, 14*(4), 532–550.

Eisenhardt, K. M. (1989). Building theories from case study research. *Academy of Management Review, 14*(4), 532–550.

Elbow, P. (1973, 1998). *Writing without teachers,* 2nd ed. New York, NY: Oxford UP.

Ellis, C., & Bochner, A. (2000). Autoethnography, personal narrative, reflexivity: Researcher as subject. In Denzin, N., & Lincoln, Y. (Eds.), *The handbook of qualitative research* (2nd ed., pp. 733–768). Newbury Park, CA: Sage.

Entwistle, N. (2001). Promoting deep learning through teaching and assessment. In Suskie, L. (Ed.), *Assessment to promote deep learning* (pp. 9–20). Washington, DC: American Association for Higher Education.

Epstein, M. (1995). *Thoughts without a thinker: Psychotherapy from a Buddhist perspective*. New York, NY: Basic Books.

Epstein, M. (1998). *Going to pieces without falling apart: A Buddhist perspective on wholeness—lessons from meditation and psychotherapy*. New York, NY: Broadway Books.

Facebook. (n.d.). *Social networking website technology*. Retrieved from www.facebook.com

Fallows, S., & Bhanot, R. (2005). *Quality issues in ICT based higher education*. Oxon, UK: Routledge Farmer. doi:10.4324/9780203416198

Falsgraf, C. D. (1994). *Language and culture at a Japanese immersion school*. University of Oregon, Unpublished doctoral dissertation.

Feeney, L., Reynolds, P., Eaton, K., & Harper, J. (2008). *A description of the new technologies used in transforming dental education*.

Feinstein, A. H., Mann, S., & Corsun, D. L. (2002). Charting the experiential territory: Clarifying definitions and uses of computer simulation, games, and role play. *Journal of Management Development, 21*(10), 732–744. doi:10.1108/02621710210448011

Felder, R. (1993). Reaching the second tier: Learning and teaching styles in college science education. *Journal of College Science Teaching, 23*(5), 286–290.

Fernando, S. (2003). *Cultural diversity, mental health and psychiatry*. Hove, UK: Brunner Routledge. doi:10.4324/9780203420348

Ferraro, G. P. (2006). *The cultural dimensions of international business* (5th ed.). Upper Saddle River, NJ: Pearson Prentice Hall.

Fiedler, F. E., Mitchell, T., & Triandis, H. C. (1971). The culture assimilator: An approach to cross-cultural training. *The Journal of Applied Psychology, 55*(2), 95–102. doi:10.1037/h0030704

Filius, R. (2009). *Handleiding Weblectures in de Universiteit Utrecht*. [Weblectures manual at the university of Utrecht]. Utrecht, The Netherlands: Universiteit Utrecht, IVLOS. Retrieved October 19, 2009 from: http://cms.let.uu.nl/lecturenet/uploads/documents/Handleiding%20weblectures%20mei%202009.pdf

Fischer, B., & Boynton, A. (2007). Out of this world high performing teams: A video tour. *Academy of Management Learning & Education, 6*(3), 412–428. doi:10.5465/AMLE.2007.26361630

Fischer, K., & Immordino-Yang, M. H. (2008). Introduction. In Fischer, K., & Immordino-Yang, M. H. (Eds.), *The Jossey-Bass reader on the brain and learning* (pp. xvii–xxii). San Francisco, CA: Jossey-Bass.

Fishbein, M., & Ajzen, I. (1975). *Belief, attitude, intention and behavior: An introduction to theory and research*. Reading, MA: Addison-Wesley.

Fitzpatrick, V. (1968). An AV aid to teaching writing. *English Journal, 57*(3), 372–374. doi:10.2307/812235

Fleming, N. D., & Mills, C. (1992). *VARK: A guide to learning styles*. Retrieved from http://www.vark-learn.com/english/index.asp

Fletcher, C., & Cambre, C. (2009). Digital storytelling and implicated scholarship in the classroom. *Journal of Canadian Studies. Revue d'Etudes Canadiennes, 43*(1), 109–130.

Fontenot, M. J., & Fontenot, K. A. (2008, March). Incorporating film into the research paper. *Business Communication Quarterly, 55*–58. doi:10.1177/1080569907312872

Fotenos, S., Wiedemann, L., & Kautz, J. (2007). *Vamos blogar (let's blog): Integrating two worlds through technology*. Paper presented at DigitalStream 2007. California State University, Monterey Bay, Seaside, CA, USA, March, 2007. Retrieved June 30, 2009, from http://php.csumb.edu/wlc/ocs/viewabstract.php?id=34&cf=1

Fowler, C. J. H., & Mayes, J. T. (1999). Learning relationships from theory to design. *Association for Learning Technology Journal, 7*(3), 6–16. doi:10.1080/0968776990070302

Fowler, S. M., & Blohm, J. M. (2004). An analysis of methods for intercultural training. In Landis, D., Bennett, J. M., & Bennett, M. J. (Eds.), *Handbook of intercultural training* (3rd ed., pp. 37–84). Thousand Oaks, CA: Sage.

Frechette, J. D. (2002). *Developing media literacy in cyberspace: Pedagogy and critical learning for the twenty-first-century classroom* (p. 4). Westport, CT: Praeger.

Frederick, P. J. (1987). Student involvement: Active learning in large classes. In Gleason Weimer, M. (Ed.), *Teaching large classes well*. San Francisco, CA: Jossey-Bass Inc.

Freire, P. (2003). *Pedagogy of the oppressed*. New York, NY: Continuum.

Fricke, M., & Völter, M. (2000, July 10th). *Seminars: A pedagogical pattern language about teaching seminars effectively*. Workshop presented at the EuroPLoP2000 Conference, Irsee, Germany. Retrieved October 23, 2009 from: http://www.voelter.de/data/pub/tp/tp.pdf

Friedman, P. A., Dyke, L. S., & Murphy, S. A. (2009). Expatriate adjustment from the inside out: An autoethnographic account. *International Journal of Human Resource Management, 20*(2), 252–268.

Gadamer, H.-G. (1979). The problem of historical consciousness. In Rabinow, P., & Sullivan, W. M. (Eds.), *Interpretive social science: A second look* (pp. 82–140). Berkeley, CA: University of California Press.

Gadanidis, G., & Schindler, K. (2006). Learning objects, type II applications and embedded pedagogical models. *Computers in the Schools, 23*(1-2), 14–17.

Gagnon, G. W., & Collay, M. (2006). *Constructivist learning design*. Thousand Oaks, CA: Corwin Press.

Gallos, J. V., & Ramsey, V. J. (1997). *Teaching diversity: Listening to the soul, speaking from the heart*. San Francisco, CA: Jossey-Bass.

Gallos, J. B. (2007). Artful teaching: Using the visual, creative and performing arts in contemporary management education. In Armstrong, S., & Fukami, C. (Eds.), *Handbook of management learning, education and development*. Thousand Oaks, CA: Sage.

Garcia, R. (2008). *Integrating video clips in classroom teaching*. In Knowledge Development and Exchange in International Business Networks: 50th Annual Meeting of the Academy of International Business, Milan, Italy, 30 June to 3 July 2008: Academy of International Business.

Garcia, R. (2008). *Integrating video clips in classroom teaching*. In 'Knowledge Development and Exchange in International Business Networks': 50th Annual Meeting of the Academy of International Business, Milan, Italy, 30 June to 3 July 2008: Academy of International Business.

Gertler, M. S. (2003). Tacit knowledge and the economic geography of context, or the undefinable tacitness of being (there). *Journal of Economic Geography, 3*, 75–99. doi:10.1093/jeg/3.1.75

Ghose, C. (2008). *Business schools ramping up for switch to global accounting rules*. Retrieved August 29, 2008, from http://www.bizjournals.com/columbus/stories/2008/09/01/story8.html

Gibbs, G. (1992). *Improving the quality of student learning*. Bristol, UK: Technical and Educational Services Ltd.

Gibbs, G. (2006). Why assessment is changing. In Bryan, C., & Clegg, K. (Eds.), *Innovative assessment in higher education*. London, UK: Routledge.

Gibbs, W., Bernas, R., & McCann, S. (2001, November 1). *Using a video split-screen technique to evaluate streaming instructional videos*. (ERIC Document Reproduction Service No. ED470087). Retrieved March 6, 2009, from ERIC database.

Gilchrist, M., & Ward, R. (2006). Facilitating access to online learning. In Glen, S., & Moule, P. (Eds.), *E-learning in nursing*. Basingstoke, UK: Palgrave MacMillan.

Glader, P. (2009, June 22). The Jack Welch MBA coming to the Web. *The Wall Street Journal*. Retrieved from http://online.wsj.com/article/SB124562232014535347.html

Goffman, E. (1963). *Behaviour in public places: Notes on the social organisation of gatherings*. London, UK: The Free Press of Glenco.

Goldman, R. (1965). *Readiness for religion*. London, UK: Routledge.

Gommer, E. M. (2008, December). *Use and effectiveness of online video lectures.* Presentation at Online Educa 2008, Berlin.

Gommer, E. M., & Bosker, M. (2008). Videopilots UT: naar een standaarddienst voor registratie en aanbod van colleges via het Internet. [Videopilots UT: towards a standard service for registration and presentation of weblectures]. Unpublished project report. Enschede, The Netherlamds: University of Twente.

Gong, M., & Du, G. (2004). E-learning: Redefining tomorrow's education: Case study of e-learning in Hong Kong University of Science and Technology. In New Horizon in Web-Based Learning: Proceedings of the Third International Conference on Web-Based Learning, Beijing, 8-11 August 2004 (p. 151).

Goodyear, P. (2005). Educational design and networked learning: Patterns, pattern languages and design practice. *Australasian Journal of Educational Technology, 21*(1), 82–101.

GoogleVideos. (2009a). *Market segmentation search.* Retrieved September 17, 2009, from http://video.google.com/videosearch?q=service+failure&emb=0&aq=f#q=market+segmentation&emb=0

GoogleVideos. (2009b). *Customer satisfaction search.* Retrieved September 17, 2009, from http://video.google.com/videosearch?q=customer+satisfaction&www_google_domain=www.google.com&emb=0&aq=0&oq=customer+sat#

GoogleVideos. (2009c). *Service failure search.* Retrieved September 17, 2009, from http://video.google.com/videosearch?q=service+failure&emb=0&aq=f#

Grasha, A. F. (1996). *Teaching with style: A practical guide to enhancing learning by understanding teaching and learning styles.* Pittsburgh, PA: Alliance Publishers.

Grauman, C. F., & Moscovici, S. (1986). *Changing conceptions of leadership.* New York, NY: Springer-Verlag.

Greenlee-Moore, M. E., & Smith, L. L. (1996). Interactive computer software: The effect on young children's reading achievement. *Reading Psychology: An International Quarterly, 17*, 43–64. doi:10.1080/0270271960170102

Griffin, D. K., Mitchell, D., & Thompson, S. J. (2009). Podcasting by synchronising powerpoint and voice: What are the pedagogical benefits? *Computers & Education, 53*, 532–539.

Grimmitt, M. (Ed.). (2000). *Pedagogies of religious education.* Great Wakering, UK: McCrimmons.

Gudykunst, W. B., Guzley, R. M., & Hammer, M. R. (1996). Designing intercultural training. In Landis, D., & Bhagat, R. (Eds.), *Handbook of intercultural training* (2nd ed., pp. 61–80). Thousand Oaks, CA: Sage.

Gudykunst, W. B., Guzley, R. M., & Hammer, M. R. (1996). Designing intercultural training. In Landis, D., & Bhagat, R. (Eds.), *Handbook of intercultural training* (2nd ed., pp. 61–80). Thousand Oaks, CA: SAGE.

Gulz, A. (2005). Social enrichment by virtual characters - differential benefits. *Journal of Computer Assisted Learning, 21*(6), 405–418. doi:10.1111/j.1365-2729.2005.00147.x

Haggis, T. (2003). Constructing images of ourselves? A critical investigation into approaches to learning research in higher education. *British Educational Research Journal, 29*(1), 89–105. doi:10.1080/0141192032000057401

Hall, E., & Moseley, D. (2005). Is there a role for learning styles in personalized education and training? *International Journal of Lifelong Education, 24*(3), 243–255. doi:10.1080/02601370500134933

Hall, E. T. (1976). *Beyond culture.* New York, NY: Doubleday.

Hall-Matthews, J. C. (1993). *The collegiate Church of St. Peter's Wolverhampton.* Much Wenlock, UK: Smith Publishers.

Hanh, T. (2005). *Being peace.* Berkeley, CA: Parallax Press.

Haraway, D. (1991). *Simians, cyborgs, and women: The reinvention of nature.* New York, NY: Routledge.

Harris, H., & Kumra, S. (2000). International manager development: Cross-cultural training in highly diverse environments. *Journal of Management Development, 19*(7), 602–614. doi:10.1108/02621710010373278

Harris, M. (1983). Modeling: A process method of teaching. *College English, 45*(1), 74–84. doi:10.2307/376921

Harrison, R., & Hopkins, R. L. (1967). The design of cross-cultural training: An alternative to the university model. *The Journal of Applied Behavioral Science, 3*, 431–460. doi:10.1177/002188636700300401

Hartsell, T., & Yuen, S. (2006). Video streaming in online learning. *Association for the Advancement of Computing In Education Journal, 14*(1), 31–43.

Hartsell, T., & Yuen, S. (2006, January 1). Video streaming in online learning. *AACE Journal, 14*(1), 31–43.

Harvey, L., & Knight, P. (1996). *Transforming higher education*. Bristol, UK: Open University Press.

Hastings, N. B., & Tracey, M. W. (2004). Does media affect learning: Where are we now? *TechTrends, 49*(2), 28–30.

Hayano, D. M. (1979). Auto-ethnography: Paradigms, problems, and prospects. *Human Organization, 38*(1), 99–104.

Hayes, J., & Allinson, C. W. (1988). Cultural differences in the learning styles of managers. *Management International Review, 28*, 75–80.

Heeter, C. (1992). Being there: The subjective experience of presence. *Presence (Cambridge, Mass.), 1*(2), 262–271.

Hicks, R., & Essinger, J. (1991). *Making computers more human-designing for human computer interaction*. Oxford, UK: Elsevier Advanced Technology.

Hiemstra, R. (1991). *Creating environments for effective adult learning*. San Francisco, CA: Jossey-Bass Inc., Publishers.

Hill, J. R., & Hannafin, M. J. (2001). Teaching and learning in digital environments: The resurgence of resource based learning. *Educational Technology Research and Development, 49*(3), 37–52. doi:10.1007/BF02504914

Hirschman, E., & Holbrook, M. (1982). Hedonic consumption: Emerging concepts, methods and propositions. *Journal of Marketing, 46*(3), 92–101. doi:10.2307/1251707

Hodgson, G. (1995). *People's century*. London, UK: BBC Books.

Hodgson, V. E. (2005). Lectures and the experience of relevance. In F. Marton, D. Hounsell & N. Entwistle (Eds.), *The experience of learning: Implications for teaching and studying in higher education* (3rd ed., pp. 159–171). Edinburgh, UK: University of Edinburgh, Centre for Teaching, Learning and Assessment. Retrieved September 7, 2009, from http://www.ed.ac.uk/etl/docs/ExperienceOfLearning/EoL10.pdf

Hofstede, G. (1980). *Culture's consequences*. Newbury Park, CA: Sage Publications.

Hofstede, G. (2001). *Culture's consequences, comparing values, behaviors, institutions, and organizations across nations*. Thousand Oaks, CA: Sage Publications.

Holbrook, M. B. (2005). Customer value and autoethnography: Subjective personal introspection and the meanings of a photograph collection. *Journal of Business Research, 58*(1), 45–61.

Holsapple, C., & Wu, J. (2007). User acceptance of virtual worlds: The hedonic framework. *ACM SIGMIS Database, 38*(4), 86–89. doi:10.1145/1314234.1314250

Honey, P., & Mumford, A. (1992). *The manual of learning styles* (3rd ed.). Maidenhead, UK: Peter Honey.

Hooper, S., & Hannafin, M. J. (1991). Psychological perspectives on emerging instructional technologies: A critical analysis. *Educational Psychologist, 26*(1), 69–95.

Hopkins, R. S. (1999). Using Videos as Training Tools. In Fowler, S. M., & Mumford, M. G. (Eds.), *Intercultural Sourcebook: Cross-Cultural Training Methods* (Vol. 2, pp. 73–112). Yarmouth, ME: Intercultural Press.

Horton, R., Buck, T., Waterson, P., & Clegg, C. (2001). Explaining intranet use with the technology acceptance model. *Journal of Information Technology, 16*(4), 237–249. doi:10.1080/02683960110102407

House, R. J., Hanges, P. J., Javidan, M. J., Dorfman, P. W., & Gupta, V. (Eds.). (2004). *Culture, leadership, and organizations: The GLOBE study of 62 societies*. Thousand Oaks, CA: Sage Publications.

Howard, W. G., Ellis, H. H., & Rasmussen, K. (2004). From the arcade to the classroom: Capitalizing on student' sensory-rich media preferences in disciplined-based learning. *College Student Journal, 38*(3), 431–440.

Hull, D. (2009, June 17). Gov. Schwarzenegger wants California's schools to adopt digital textbooks. *San Jose Mercury News*. Retrieved from http://www.mercurynews.com/breakingnews/ci_12602248?source=rss

Hunt, C. S. (2001). Must see TV: The timelessness of television as a teaching tool. *Journal of Management Education, 25*(6), 631–647. doi:10.1177/105256290102500603

Hutchins, H. M., & Hutchison, D. (2008). Cross-disciplinary contributions to e-learning: A tripartite design model. *Journal of Workplace Learning, 20*(5), 364–380. doi:10.1108/13665620810882950

Igbaria, M., Iivari, J., & Maragahh, H. (1995). Why do individuals use computer technology? A Finnish case study. *Information & Management, 29*(5), 227–238. doi:10.1016/0378-7206(95)00031-0

Igbaria, M., Parasuraman, S., & Baroudi, J. (1996). A motivational model of microcomputer usage. *Journal of Management Information Systems, 13*(1), 127–143.

Ihde, D. (1974). The experience of technology: Human-machine relations. *Cultural Hermeneutics, 2*, 267–279.

Ihde, D. (1979). *Technics and praxis: A philosophy of technology*. Dordrecht, The Netherlands: Reidel.

Ihde, D. (1983). *Existential technics*. Albany, NY: State University of New York Press.

Ihde, D. (1990). *Technology and the lifeworld: From garden to earth*. Bloomington, IN: Indiana University Press.

Ihde, D. (1993). *Philosophy of technology: An introduction*. New York, NY: Paragon House.

Illinois, C. P. A. Society – ICPAS. (2009). Academics ask for more classroom materials. *INSIGHT Magazine* Jan. & Feb. 2009, p. 32.

Ingebritsen, T., & Flickinger, K. (1998, January 1). *Development and assessment of Web courses that use streaming audio and video technologie*s. (ERIC Document Reproduction Service No. ED422859). Retrieved March 6, 2009, from ERIC database.

InsideHigherEd. (2009). *The evidence on online education*. Retrieved on October 6, 2009, from http://www.inside-highered.com/layout/set/print/news/2009/06/29/online

Institute of International Education. (2008). *Open doors: Report on international education exchange*. New York.

Introduction to open education 2009. (n.d.). In *Wikipedia*. Retrieved March 16, 2009, from http://opencontent.org/wiki/index.php?title=Introduction_to_Open_Education_2009

Iwata, E. (2009). *U.S. considers costly switch to international accounting rules*. Retrieved September 28, 2009, from http://www.usatoday.com/money/companies/regulation/2009-01-05-international-accounting-rule-switch_N.htm?loc=interstitialskip

Jackson, R. (1997). *Religious education: An interpretive approach*. London, UK: Hodder & Stoughton.

Jacoby, D. (2009). SecondLife, second strife? *Intellectual Property & Technology Law Journal, 20*(9), 7–10.

Jadin, T., Gruber, A., & Batanic, B. (2009). Learning with e-lectures: The meaning of learning strategies. *Journal of Educational Technology & Society, 12*(3), 282–288.

Jarmon, L., Traphagan, T., Mayrath, M., & Trivedi, A. (2009). Virtual world teaching, experiential learning, and assessment: An interdisciplinary communication course in Second Life. *Computers & Education, 53*, 169–182. doi:10.1016/j.compedu.2009.01.010

Jarrah, F. (1998, April 23). New courses will target transition to university. *China Morning Post*, p. 28.

Jarvis, P., Holford, J., & Griffin, C. (2003). *The theory and practice of learning* (2nd ed.). Oxon, UK: Routledge.

Jeffries, P. (2001). Computer versus lecture: A comparison of two methods of teaching oral medication administration in a nursing skills laboratory. *The Journal of Nursing Education, 40*(7), 323–339.

Jelfs, A., & Colbourn, C. (2002). Do students approaches to learning affect their perceptions of using computing and Information Technology? *Journal of Educational Media, 27*(1-2), 41–53. doi:10.1080/0305498032000045449

Jenkins, H., Clinton, K., Purushotma, R., Robison, A., & Weigel, M. (n.d.). *Confronting the challenges of participatory culture: Media education for the 21st century*. Retrieved from http://digitallearning.macfound.org/atf/cf/%7B7E45C7E0-A3E0-4B89-AC9C-E807E1B0AE4E%7D/JENKINS_WHITE_PAPER.PDF

JISC. (2009). Effective practice in a digital age: A guide to technology- enhanced learning and teaching. HEFCE. Retrieved September 2009, from http://www.jisc.ac.uk/media/documents/publications/effectivepracticedigital-age.pdf

Jochems, W., Van Merrienboer, J., & Koper, R. (Eds.). (2004). *Integrated e-learning*. London, UK: Routledge-Falmer.

Johnson, M. (1987). *The body in the mind: The bodily basis of imagination, reason, and meaning*. Chicago, IL: University of Chicago Press.

Johnson, L., Levine, A., & Smith, R. (2009). *The 2009 horizon report*. Austin, TX: The New Media Consortium. Retrieved from http://www.nmc.org/pdf/2009-Horizon-Report.pdf

Jonassen, D., Campbell, J., & Davidson, M. (1994). Learning with media: Restructuring the debate. *Educational Technology Research and Development, 42*(2), 31–39. doi:10.1007/BF02299089

Jonassen, D., Davidson, M., Collins, M., Campbell, J., & Haag, B. (1995). Constructivism and computer-mediated communication in distance education. *American Journal of Distance Education, 9*, 7–26. doi:10.1080/08923649509526885

Jonassen, D. H. (2004). *Learning to solve problems: An instructional design guide*. San Francisco, CA: Pfeiffer/Jossey-Bass.

Jones, S. E. (2007). Reflections on the lecture: Outmoded medium or instrument of inspiration? *Journal of Further and Higher Education, 31*(4), 397–406. doi:10.1080/03098770701656816

Jorum. (n.d.). Retrieved from http://www.jorum.ac.uk/

Juwah, C. (Ed.). (2006). *Interactions in online education: Implications for theory and practice*. London, UK: Routledge.

Kamenetz, A. (2009, September 1). How Web-savvy edupunks are transforming American higher education. *Fast Company*. Retrieved from http://www.fastcompany.com/magazine/138/who-needs-harvard.html

Karau, S. J., & Williams, K. D. (1993). Social loafing: A meta-analytic review and theoretical integration. *Journal of Personality and Social Psychology, 65*, 681–706. doi:10.1037/0022-3514.65.4.681

Karppinen, P. (2005). Meaningful learning with digital and online videos: Theoretical perspectives. *AACE Journal, 13*(3), 233–250.

Kayes, D. C. (2002). Experiential learning and its critics: Preserving the role of experience in management learning and education. *Academy of Management Learning & Education, 1*(2), 137–149. doi:10.5465/AMLE.2002.8509336

Keefe, T. (2003). Enhancing face-to-face courses with online lectures: Instructional and pedagogical issues. In *Teaching, Learning & Technology: The Challenge Continues. Proceedings for the Annual Mid-South Instructional Technology Conference*. (8th, Murfreesboro, TN, March 30 to April 2003).

Kelly, P. (2009). Group work and multicultural management education. *Journal of Teaching in International Business, 20*, 80–102. doi:10.1080/08975930802671273

Kenworthy, J., & Wong, A. (2005). Developing managerial effectiveness: Assessing and comparing the impact of development programmes using a management simulation or a management game. *Developments in Business Simulations and Experiential Learning, 32*, 164–175.

Kerres, M., & De Witt, C. (2003). A didactical framework for the design of blended learning arrangements. *Journal of Educational Media, 28*(2-3), 101–113.

Ketterl, M., Mertens, R., & Vornberger, O. (2009). Bringing Web 2.0 to Web lectures. *Interactive Technology and Smart Education, 6*(2), 82–96. doi:10.1108/17415650910968099

Khurana, S. (2002). The mushrooming growth of management educational institutions and its impact of quality: A study of Haryana. *The Icfaian Journal of Management Research, 8*(3), 62–82.

Kieso, D. E., Weygandt, J. J., & Warfield, T. D. (2010). *Intermediate accounting* (13th ed.). Hoboken, NJ: John Wiley & Sons.

King, W., & He, J. (2006). A meta-analysis of the technology acceptance model. *Information & Management, 43*(6), 740–755. doi:10.1016/j.im.2006.05.003

Kirk, J., & Miller, M. L. (1986). *Reliability and validity in qualitative research*. Beverly Hills, CA: Sage.

Klass, B. (2003, May 30). Streaming media in higher education: Possibilities and pitfalls. *Campus Technology.* Retrieved September 20, 2009, from http://www.campustechnology.com/Articles/2003/05/Streaming-Media-in-Higher-Education-Possibilities-and-Pitfalls.aspx

Knowles, M. S., Holton, E. F., & Swanson, R. A. (1998). *The adult learner: The definitive classic in adult education and human resource development* (5th ed.). Houston, TX: Gulf Professional.

Kolb, D. A. (1981). Learning styles and disciplinary differences. In *The modern American college: Responding to the new realities of diverse students and a changing society* (pp. 232–255). Jossey-Bass Inc., Publishers.

Kolb, D. A. (1984). *Experiential learning: Experience as the source of learning and development*. Englewood Cliffs, NJ: Prentice-Hall, Inc.

Kozma, R. (1994). Will media influence learning? Reframing the debate. *Educational Technology Research and Development, 42*(2), 7–19. doi:10.1007/BF02299087

KPMG. LLP. (2008). *University professors weigh in on building IFRS into curricula: Small number of universities will be ready for 2008-2009 academic year*. Retrieved October 27, 2009, from http://www.financialexecutives.org/eweb/upload/FEI/ KPMG%20AAA%20IFRS%20Professor%20Survey%20Press%20Release_9.4.08.pdf

KPMG. LLP. (2009). *Faculty in KPMG-AAA survey see U.S. economy, students impacted without adoption of global accounting standards*. Retrieved September 22, 2009, from http://news.prnewswire.com/DisplayReleaseContent.aspx?ACCT=104&STORY=/www/story/09-22-2009/0005098454&EDATE=

Kraemer, A. J. (1973). Development of a cultural self-awareness approach to instruction in intercultural communication. Alexandria, VA, Human Resources Research Organization. (Technical Report #73-71: 60).

Krishnan, M. S., & Prahalad, C. K. (2008). *The new age of innovation: Driving cocreated value through global networks*. New York, NY: McGraw-Hill Professional.

Kuleshov, L. (1974). *Kuleshov on film: Writings by Lev Kuleshov*. Berkeley, CA: University of California Press.

Kulik, C. T., & Roberson, L. (2008). Common goals and golden opportunities: Evaluations of diversity education in academic and organizational settings. *Academy of Management Learning & Education, 7*(3), 309–331. doi:10.5465/AMLE.2008.34251670

L'Allier, J. J. (1997). *Frame of reference: NETg's map to the products, their structure and core beliefs.* NetG. Retrieved July 13, 2009, from http://netg.com/research/whitepapers/frameref.asp

Ladd, P. D., & Ruby, R. Jr. (1999). Learning style and adjustment issues of international students. *Journal of Education for Business, 74*(6), 363–367. doi:10.1080/08832329909601712

Lafsky, M. (2009). Can training in Second Life teach doctors to save real leaves? *Discover: Science, Technology, and The Future*. Retrieved from http://discovermagazine.com/ 2009/jul-aug/15-can-medical-students-learn-to-save-real-lives-in-second-life.

Lakoff, G. (1987). *Women, fire and dangerous things: What categories reveal about the mind*. Chicago, IL: University of Chicago Press.

Lakoff, G., & Johnson, M. (1980). *Metaphors we live by*. Chicago, IL: Chicago University Press.

Lakoff, G., & Johnson, M. (1999). *Philosophy in the flesh: The embodied mind and its challenge to Western thought*. New York, NY: Basic Books.

Lam, A. (2000). Tacit knowledge, organizational learning and societal institutions: An integrated framework. *Organization Studies, 21*(3), 487–513. doi:10.1177/0170840600213001

Lam, W. (2004). Encouraging online participation. *Journal of Information Systems Education, 15*(4), 345–348.

Lamoreaux, M. G. (2009). *G-20: Achieve single set of global accounting standards by June 2011*. Retrieved September 27, 2009, from http://www.journalofaccountancy.com/ Web/20092188.htm

Langer, E. J. (2000). Mindful learning. *Current Directions in Psychological Science, 9*(6), 220–223. doi:10.1111/1467-8721.00099

Larson, B. E. (2000). Classroom discussion: A method of instruction and a curriculum outcome. *Teaching and Teacher Education, 16*(5-6), 661–667. doi:10.1016/S0742-051X(00)00013-5

Laurillard, D. (1993). *Rethinking university teaching.* London, UK: Routledge.

Laurillard, D. (2002). *Rethinking university teaching.* London, UK: Routledge Falmer. Lewis, M., Davies, R, Jenkins, D., & Tate, M. (2005). A review of evaluative studies of computer based learning in nursing education. *Nurse Education Today, 25*(8), 586–597.

Leary, M. R. (1996). *Self-presentation: Impression management and interpersonal behavior.* Boulder, CO: Westview Press.

Lee, M., Cheung, C., & Chen, Z. (2005). Acceptance of Internet-based learning medium: The role of extrinsic and intrinsic motivation. *Information & Management, 42*(8), 1095–1104. doi:10.1016/j.im.2003.10.007

Lee, K. J., & Sharma, M. D. (2008). Incorporating active learning with videos: A case from physics. *Teaching Science, 54*(4), 45–47.

Leet, D., & Houser, S. (2003). Economics goes to Hollywood: Using classic films and documentaries to create an undergraduate economics course. *The Journal of Economic Education, 34*(4), 326–332.

Leijen, A., Lam, I., Wildschut, L., Simons, P., & Admiraal, W. (2009, January 1). Streaming video to enhance students' reflection in dance education. *Computers & Education, 52*(1), 169-176. (ERIC Document Reproduction Service No. EJ819465). Retrieved March 6, 2009, from ERIC database.

Leonard, D., & Sensiper, S. (1998). The role of tacit knowledge in group innovation. *California Management Review, 40*(3), 112–132.

Leoni, K., & Lichti, S. (2009). *Lecture capture in higher education.* Evanston, IL: Northwestern University. Retrieved November 6th, 2009 from http://www.it.northwestern.edu/bin/docs/classrooms/LC_survey.pdf

Levy, R. I., & Hollan, D. (1998). Person-centered interviewing and observation in anthropology. In Bernard, H. R. (Ed.), *Handbook of methods in cultural anthropology* (pp. 333–364). Walnut Creek, CA: Altamira Press.

Li, M., & Geo, F. (2003). Why Nonaka highlights tacit knowledge: A critical review. *Journal of Knowledge Management, 7*(4), 6–14. doi:10.1108/13673270310492903

Liber, O. (2005). Learning objects: Conditions for viability. *Journal of Computer Assisted Learning, 21*(5), 366–373. doi:10.1111/j.1365-2729.2005.00143.x

Linden Research Inc. (n.d.). *Second Life* [Virtual world technology]. Retrieved from http://secondlife.com/

Lindsay, C. P., & Dempsey, B. L. (1983). Ten painfully learned lessons about working in China: The insights of two American behavioral scientists. *The Journal of Applied Behavioral Science, 19*(20), 265–276. doi:10.1177/002188638301900305

Lipsett, A. (2009, May 21). More overseas students than thought. *The Guardian.* Retrieved June 2, 2009, from http://www.guardian.co.uk/education/2009/may/21/more-overseas-students-than-thought

Liu, J. (2001). *Asian students' classroom communication patterns in U.S. universities: An emic perspective.* Norwood, NJ: Ablex.

Longo, R. E., & Longo, D. P. (2003). *New hope for youth: Experiential exercises for children and adolescents.* Holyoke, MA: NEARI Press.

Lyman, P., & Varian, H. R. (2000). *How much information?* Retrieved July 10, 2006, from http://www.sims.berkeley.edu/how-much-info

Lynch, M. A., & Tunstall, R. J. (2008). When worlds collide: Developing game-design partnerships in universities. *Simulation & Gaming, 39*(3), 379–398. doi:10.1177/1046878108319275

Ma, A. K. F., O'Toole, J. M., & Keppell, M. (2007). The attitudes of teacher educators to the use of problem based learning: The video triggers approach. *In ICT: Providing choices for learners and learning.* Proceedings Ascilite Singapore 2007.

Maag, M. (2006). iPod, uPod? An emerging mobile learning tool in nursing education and students' satisfaction.

MacArthur Foundation. (2009, September 21). *Digital media are changing how young people learn*. Chicago, IL: The MacArthur Foundation. Retrieved from http://www.macfound.org/site/c.lkLXJ8MQKrH/b.4462309/apps/s/content.asp?ct=7510783

Macdonald, J. (2006). *Blended learning and online tutoring: A good practice guide*. Aldershot, UK: Gower.

Machemer, P., & Crawford, P. (2007). Student perceptions of active learning in a large cross-disciplinary classroom. *Active Learning in Higher Education, 8*(1), 11. doi:10.1177/1469787407074008

MacIntyre, J. (2008). *Want a free education: A brief guide to the burgeoning world of online video lectures*. Retrieved on October 6, 2009, from www.boston.com/bostonglobe/ideas/articles/2008/11/02/u_tube/

MacKenzie, N., & Walsh, A. (2009). Enhancing the curriculum: Shareable multimedia learning objects. *Journal of Systems and Information Technology, 11*(1), 1328–7265. doi:10.1108/13287260910932421

MacLellan, E. (2005). Conceptual learning: The priority for higher education. *British Journal of Educational Studies, 53*(2), 129–147. doi:10.1111/j.1467-8527.2005.00287.x

Maddux, C. D., Johnson, D., & Willis, J. (1992). *Educational computing: Learning with tomorrow's technologies*. Boston, MA: Allyn & Bacon.

Mahoney, J. T. (2002). The relevance of Chester I. Barnard's teaching to contemporary management education: Communicating the aesthetics of management. *International Journal of Organization Theory and Behavior, 5*(1&2), 159–172.

Mainemelis, C., Boyatzis, R. E., & Kolb, D. A. (2002). Learning styles and adaptive flexibility: Testing experiential learning theory. *Management Learning, 33*(1), 5–33. doi:10.1177/1350507602331001

Marginson, S. (2002). The phenomenal rise of international degrees down under. *Change, 34*(3), 34–43. doi:10.1080/00091380209601854

Marks, R. B., Sibley, S. D., & Arbaugh, J. B. (2005). A structural equation model of predictors for effective online learning. *Journal of Management Education, 29*(4), 531–563. doi:10.1177/1052562904271199

Marshall, J. M. (2002). *Learning with technology: Evidence that technology can, and does, support learning. A white paper prepared for cable in the classroom*. Retrieved on April 1, 2010, from http://www.medialit.org/reading_room/article545.html

Martins, L., & Kellermanns, F. (2004). A model of business school students' acceptance of a web-based course management system. *Academy of Management Learning & Education, 3*(1), 7–26. doi:10.5465/AMLE.2004.12436815

Mason, R., & Rennie, F. (2008). *E-learning and social networking handbook: Resources for higher education*. London, UK: Routledge.

Mason, R., Pegler, C., & Weller, M. (2005). A learning object success story. *Journal of Asynchronous Learning Networks, 9*(1).

Masuda, T., & Nisbett, R. E. (2001). Attending holistically vs. analytically: Comparing the context sensitivity of Japanese and Americans. *Journal of Personality and Social Psychology, 81*(5), 922–934. doi:10.1037/0022-3514.81.5.922

Maturana, H. (1975). The organization of the living: A theory of the living organization. *International Journal of Man-Machine Studies, 7*, 313–332. doi:10.1016/S0020-7373(75)80015-0

Maturana, H., & Varela, F. J. (1980). *Autopoiesis and cognition: The realization of the living*. Dordrecht, The Netherlands: Reidel.

Maturana, H., & Varela, F. J. (1987). *The tree of knowledge: The biological roots of human understanding*. Boston, MA: Shambhala Press/New Science Library.

Mayer, R. E. (2003). *Multimedia learning*. Santa Barbara, CA: Cambridge University Press.

Mayer, R. E. (Ed.). (2005). *The Cambridge handbook of multimedia learning*. New York, NY: Cambridge University.

Mayer, R. (2003). The promise of multimedia learning: using the same instructional design methods across different media. *Learning and Instruction, 13*(2), 125–139. doi:10.1016/S0959-4752(02)00016-6

McCarthy, B. (1987). *The 4MAT system: Teaching to learning styles with right/left mode techniques* (rev. ed.). Barrington, IL: Excel.

McClymont, H., Volkov, M., Gardiner, M., Behjat, N., & Geoghegan, N. (2005). Employer (dis)satisfaction with Australian marketing graduates: The development of a research framework. In *Australian and New Zealand Marketing Academy Conference Proceedings*, Perth, Australia.

McCrohon, M., Lo, V., Dang, J., & Johnston, C. (2001, December 1). *Video streaming of lectures via the Internet: An experience.* (ERIC Document Reproduction Service No. ED467957). Retrieved March 6, 2009, from ERIC database.

McDaniel, E. (1986). A comparative study of the first-generation invention software. *Computers and Composition, 3*(3), 7–21.

McDrury, J., & Alterio, M. (2002). *Learning through storytelling in higher education.* London, UK: Kogan Page.

McLuhan, M. (2003). *Understanding media: The extension of man - critical edition.* Berkeley, CA: Gingko Press.

McMillan, R. (2004, December 17). IBM researchers eye 100T-byte tape drive. *IDG News Service.* Retrieved from http://www.itworld.com/041217ibmtape

McPherson, M., & Baptista Nunes, M. (2004). *Developing innovation in online learning.* London, UK: Routledge. doi:10.4324/9780203426715

Meadows, D. (2003). Digital storytelling: Research-based practice in new media. *Visual Communication, 2*(2), 189–193.

Means, B., Toyoma, Y., Murphy, R., Bakia, M., & Jones, K. (2009). *Evaluation of evidence-based practices in online learning: A meta-analysis and review of online learning studies.* Center for Technology in Learning for the U.S. Department of Education. Retrieved on October 6, 2009, from http://www.ed.gov/rschstat/eval/tech/evidence-based-practices/finalreport.pdf

Meelissen, M., & Drent, M. (2008). Gender differences in computer attitudes: Does the school matter? *Computers in Human Behavior, 24*(3), 969–985. doi:10.1016/j.chb.2007.03.001

Mehrabian, A. (1971). *Silent messages.* Belmont, CA: Wadsworth.

Meichenbaum, D. (1977). *Cognitive behavior modification: An integrative approach.* New York, NY: Plenum.

Mellen, C., & Sommers, J. (2003). Audio-taped response and the two-year-campus writing classroom: The two-sided desk, the guy with the ax, and the chirping birds. *Teaching English in the Two-Year College, 31*(1), 25–39.

Merleau-Ponty, M. (1963). *The structure of behavior* (Fisher, A., Trans.). Pittsburgh, PA: Beacon Press. (Original work published 1942)

Merleau-Ponty, M. (1973). *The visible and the invisible* (Lingis, A., Trans.). Evanston, IL: Northwestern University Press. (Original work published 1948)

Merleau-Ponty, M. (1962). *Phenomenology of perception* (Smith, C., Trans.). London, UK: Routledge & Kegan Paul. (Original work published 1945)

Merriam, S. B., Caffarella, R. S., & Baumgartner, L. M. (2007). *Learning in adulthood: A comprehensive guide* (3rd ed.). San Francisco, CA: Jossey-Bass.

Metros, S. E. (2008). The educator's role in preparing visually literate learners. *Theory into Practice, 47*(2), 102–109. doi:10.1080/00405840801992264

Michelich, V. (2002). Streaming media to enhance teaching and improve learning. *The Technology Source.* January/February. Retrieved June 20, 2009, from http://technologysource.org/article/streaming_media_to_enhance_teaching_and_improve_learning/

Miller, M. V. (2009). Integrating online multimedia into college course and classroom: With application to the social sciences. *MERLOT Journal of Online Learning and Teaching, 5*(2), 395–423.

Miller, G. (1956). Human memory and the storage of information. *I.R.E. Transactions on Information Theory, 2*(3), 129–137. doi:10.1109/TIT.1956.1056815

Mintzberg, H., & Gosling, J. (2002). Educating managers beyond borders. *Academy of Management Learning & Education, 1*(1), 64–76. doi:10.5465/AMLE.2002.7373654

Mirchandani, R. (2009, 17 September). Video screens hit paper magazines. *BBC News*. 17th September http://news.bbc.co.uk/1/hi/technology/8255729.stm

Mishra, G. (2009, May 17). *The 4Cs social media framework*. Retrieved June 27, 2009, from http://www.gauravonomics.com/blog/the-4cs-social-media-framework/

MIT. (n.d.). *Open courseware system*. Retrieved from http://ocw.mit.edu/index.html

Moisey, S., Mohamed, A., & Spencer, B. (2006). Factors affecting the development and use of learning objects. *American Journal of Distance Education, 20*(3), 143–161. doi:10.1207/s15389286ajde2003_3

Molinsky, A. L., & Perunovic, W. Q. E. (2008). Training wheels for cultural learning: Poor language fluency and its shielding effect on the evaluation of culturally inappropriate behavior. *Journal of Language and Social Psychology, 27*, 284–289. doi:10.1177/0261927X08317959

Monaghan, P. (2009, April 8). Minds in the marketplace. *The Australian*. Retrieved on April 8, 2009, from http://www.theaustralian.news.com.au/story/0,25197,25304815-25192,00.html

Montgomery, S., & Groat, L. (1998). *Student learning styles and theory implications for teaching*. Center for Research on Learning and Teaching. CRLT Occasional Papers. University of Michigan. Retrieved, March 6, 2009 from CRLT database.

Moon, J., & Kim, Y. (2001). Extending the TAM for a World-Wide-Web context. *Information & Management, 38*(4), 217–230. doi:10.1016/S0378-7206(00)00061-6

Moon, J. (2002). *The module and programme development handbook*. London, UK: Kogan Page.

Mooradian, N. (2005). Tacit knowledge: Philosophic roots and role in KM. *Journal of Knowledge Management, 9*(6), 104–113. doi:10.1108/13673270510629990

Moore, G. (1999). *Crossing the chasm*. Retrieved on September 9, 2009, from http://blogs.knowledgegenes.com/home/2009/09/crossing-the-chasm-geoffrey-moore-coded-by-martin-wilcox.html

Morisse, K., & Ramm, M. (2007). *Teaching via podcasting: One year of experience with workflows, tools and usage in higher education.*

Mortiboys, A. (2005). *Teaching with emotional intelligence*. Abingdon, UK: Routledge.

Mousavi, S. (1995). Reducing cognitive load by mixing auditory and visual presentation modes. *Journal of Educational Psychology, 87*(2), 319–334. doi:10.1037/0022-0663.87.2.319

Mueller, B. (2003). Online education in the corporate context. *Chief Learning Officer, 2*(6), 40–49.

Muirhead, R. (2007). E-learning: Is this teaching at students or teaching with students? *Nursing Forum, 42*(4), 178–184. doi:10.1111/j.1744-6198.2007.00085.x

Multisilta, J. (2009). Activity theory approach to designing learning activities in social media. Accepted to *International Journal of Web Engineering and Technology* (IJWET).

Murphy, P. (2004). Observations on teaching marketing ethics. *Marketing Education Review, 14*(3), 14–21.

Myers, D. R., Sykes, C., & Myers, S. (2009). Effective learner-centered strategies for teaching adults: Using visual media to engage the adult learner. *Gerontology & Geriatrics Education, 29*(3), 234–238. doi:10.1080/02701960802359466

Nardi, B. A., & Whittaker, S. (2002). The place of face-to-face communication in distributed work. In Hins, P. J., & Kiesler, S. (Eds.), *Distributed work* (pp. 83–113). Cambridge, MA: The MIT Press.

Newberry, M. (2003). *A study of the UK designer fashion sector*. London, UK: DTI Publications.

Nian-Shing, C., & Kan-Min, L., & Kinshuk. (2008). Analysing users' satisfaction with e-learning using a negative critical incidents approach. *Innovations in Education and Teaching International, 45*(2), 115–126. doi:10.1080/14703290801950286

Niederhauser, V. P., Bigley, M. B., Hale, J., & Harper, D. (1999). Cybercases: An innovation in Internet education. *The Journal of Nursing Education, 38*(9), 415–418.

Nilsen, K. (2008). *On the verge of an academic revolution: How IFRS is affecting accounting education*. Retrieved December 20, 2009, from http://www.journalofaccountancy.com/Issues/2008/Dec/OnTheVergeOfAnAcademicRevolution

Nisbett, R. (2003). *The geography of thought: How Asians and Westerners think differently...and why*. New York, NY: Free Press.

Noel, W., & Breau, G. (2005). *Copyright matters!* 2nd edition. Ottawa, Canada: Council of Ministers of Education Canada, Canadian School Boards Association, and Canadian Teachers' Federation.

Nugent, G., Soh, L., & Ashok, S. (2006). Design, development and validation of learning objects. *Journal of Educational Technology Systems, 34*(3), 271–281. doi:10.2190/9BF6-1KBL-Y3CX-6QXG

Nursing and Midwifery Council. (2008). *The Code: Standards of conduct, performance and ethics for nurses and midwives*. London, UK: NMC Publications.

O'Reilly. (2005). *What is Web 2.0: Design patterns and business models for the next generation software*. Retrieved on October 6, 2009, from http://www.oreillynet.com/lpt/a/6228

Obama, B. (2007). Remarks of Senator Barack Obama: Reclaiming the American dream. Bettendorf, IA. Retrieved from http://www.barackobama.com/2007/11/07/remarks_of_senator_barack_obam_31.php.

Ohler, J. (2007). *Digital storytelling in the classroom: New media pathways to literacy, learning, and creativity*. Corwin Press.

Osland, J. S., & Bird, A. (2000). Beyond sophisticated stereotyping: Cultural sense-making in context. *The Academy of Management Executive, 14*(1), 65–77. doi:10.5465/AME.2000.2909840

Ostrander, M. (2008). Talking, looking, flying, searching: Information seeking behaviour in Second Life. *Library Hi Tech, 26*(4), 512–524. doi:10.1108/07378830810920860

Pal, Y. (2009). *Report of the committee to advise on renovation and rejuvenation of higher education*. New Delhi, India: Ministry of Human Resource Development.

Palloff, R. M., & Pratt, K. (1999). *Building learning communities in cyberspace: Effective strategies for the online classroom*. San Francisco, CA: Jossey-Bass Publishers.

Palloff, R. M., & Pratt, K. (2007). *Building online learning communities: Effective strategies for the virtual classroom*. San Francisco, CA: Jossey Bass.

Pappas, J. P. (1990). Environmental psychology of the learning sanctuary. *New Directions for Adult and Continuing Education, 46*(Summer), 41–52.

Parasuraman, A., Zeithaml, V. A., & Berry, L. L. (1988). SERVQUAL: A multiple item scale for measuring consumer perceptions of service quality. *Journal of Retailing, 64*(1), 12–40.

Parrish, P. (2004). The trouble with learning objects. *Educational Technology Research and Development, 52*(1), 49–70. doi:10.1007/BF02504772

Pedersen, A., & Pedersen, P. (1989). The cultural grid: A framework for multicultural counseling. *International Journal for the Advancement of Counseling, 14*(4), 299–307. doi:10.1007/BF00123258

Pedersen, P. B. (2004). *110 experiences for multicultural learning*. Washington, DC: American Psychological Association.

Pedersen, P. B., & Ivey, A. E. (1993). *Culture-centred counseling and interviewing skills*. Westport, CT: Greenwood/Praeger.

Pedersen, A., & Pedersen, P. (1989). The cultural grid: A framework for multicultural counseling. *International Journal for the Advancement of Counseling, 14*(4), 299–307. doi:10.1007/BF00123258

Peltier, J. W., Schibrowsky, J. A., & Drago, W. (2007). The interdependence of the factors influencing the perceived quality of the online learning experience: A causal model. *Journal of Marketing Education, 29*(2), 140–153. doi:10.1177/0273475307302016

Perreault, H., Waldman, L., & Zhao, M. A. J. (2002). Overcoming barriers to successful delivery of distance learning courses. *Journal of Education for Business, 77*(6), 313–318.

Petite, J. (1983). Tape recorders and tutoring. *Teaching English in the Two-Year College, 9*(2), 123–125.

Phillips, R., Gosper, M., McNeill, M., Woo, K., Preston, G., & Green, D. (2007). Staff and student perspectives on web based lecture technologies: Insights into the great divide. *Proceedings ascilite Singapore 2007*, (pp. 854-864).

Phillips, J. (2005). Strategies for active learning in online continuing education. *Journal of Continuing Education in Nursing, 36*(2), 77–83.

Piaget, J. (1954/1968). *The construction of reality in the child*. London, UK: Routledge & Kegan Paul. doi:10.1037/11168-000

Piccoli, G., Ahmad, R., & Ives, B. (2001). Web-based virtual learning environments: A research framework and a preliminary assessment of effectiveness in basic IT skills training. *Management Information Systems Quarterly*, 401–426. doi:10.2307/3250989

Pickard, G. (2007). *Simplifying global accounting: IASB chair discusses the future of IFRS, U.S. GAAP and the global accounting profession*. Retrieved November 12, 2009, from http://www.journalofaccountancy.com/Issues/2007/Jul/SimplifyingGlobalAccountingSirDavidTweedieInterview.htm

Pickford, R., & Brown, S. (2006). *Assessing Skills and Practice*. Oxon: Routledge.

Pincas, A. (2001). Culture, cognition and communication in global education. *Distance Education, 22*, 30–51. doi:10.1080/0158791010220103

Polanyi, M. (1966). *The tacit dimension*. Garden City, NY: Doubleday.

Prensky, M. (2001). Digital natives digital immigrants. *Horizon, 9*(5), 1–4. doi:10.1108/10748120110424816

PricewaterhouseCoopers LLP. (2008). PricewaterhouseCoopers launches online video resource for transitioning to IFRS. Retrieved November 20, 2008, from http://www.pwc.com/us/en/press-releases/pwc-launches-online-video-resource-for-transitioning-to-ifrs.jhtml

Projects, H. E. A. T. (2009). *Mobile technologies*. Techdis. Retrieved December 9, 2009, from http://www.techdis.ac.uk/index.php?p=2_1_7_27_2

Proserpio, L., & Gioia, D. A. (2007). Teaching the virtual generation. *Academy of Management Learning & Education, 6*(1), 69–80. doi:10.5465/AMLE.2007.24401703

Pun, A. S. L. (1989). *Developing managers internationally: culture-free or culture-bound?* Presented at the Conference on International Personnel and Human Resource Management, Hong Kong, December 13.

Qualifications and Curriculum Authority. (2004). *Religious education: The non statutory national framework*. London, UK: QCA.

Race, P. (2001). *The lecturer's toolkit: A resource for developing learning teaching and assessment* (2nd ed.). London, UK: Kogan Page.

Raman, N. (2003). *The practice and philosophy of decision making: A seven step spiritual guide*. North Charleston, SC: BookSurge Publishing.

Ramsden, P. (2003). *Learning to teach in higher education* (2nd ed.). Abington, UK: RoutledgeFalmer.

Reisslein, J., Seeling, P., & Reisslein, M. (2005, January 1). Video in distance education: ITFS vs. Web-streaming-evaluation of student attitudes. *Internet and Higher Education, 8*(1), 25-44. (ERIC Document Reproduction Service No. EJ803748). Retrieved March 6, 2009, from ERIC database.

Report, E. S. (2009, September 26). *Mobile marvels: A special report on telecoms in emerging markets*. Retrieved September 26, 2009, from http://www.economist.com/surveys/downloadSurveyPDF.cfm?id=14488868&surveyCode=%254e%2541&submit=View+PDF

Reynolds, J., Caley, L., & Mason, R. (Eds.). (2002). *How do people learn?* London, UK: CIPD.

Richardson, K., & Glosenger, F. (2006). *7 strategies to enhance video use in the college classroom. Teaching Professor*. August/September.

Ricker, T. (2006, June 22). *Toshiba's RD-A1 HD DVD recorder with 1TB disk*. Retrieved from http://www.engadget.com/2006/06/22/toshibas-rd-a1-hd-dvd-recorder-with-1tb-disk/

Riismandel, P. (2009a). *Advanced learning: Education year in review: The use of video in higher education has moved beyond mere lecture capture*. Streaming Media, Feb/Mar 2009. Retrieved August 26, 2010, from http://www.streamingmedia.com/Articles/ReadArticle.aspx?ArticleID=65390&PageNum=3

Riismandel, P. (2009b). *Class act: Making educational video more accessible*. Streaming Media, June/July 2009. Retrieved August 26, 2010, from http://www.streamingmedia.com/Articles/ReadArticle.aspx?ArticleID=65494

Rimer, S. (2007, December 19). At 71, Physics professor is a Web star. *The New York Times*. Retrieved November 8th, 2009, from http://www.nytimes.com/2007/12/19/education/19physics.html

RLO-CETL. (2009). *Reusable learning objects Centre for Excellence in Teaching and Learning*. Retrieved August 7, 2009, from http://www.rlo-cetl.ac.uk

Rodrigues, C. (2005). Culture as a determinant of the importance level business students place on ten teaching/learning techniques. *Journal of Management Development, 24*(7), 608–611. doi:10.1108/02621710510608740

Rodrigues, C., Bu, N., & Min, B. (2000). Learners' training approach preference: National culture as a determinant. *Cross Cultural Management: An International Journal, 7*(1), 23–32. doi:10.1108/13527600010797048

Roman, P. A., & Brown, D. (2008). *Games - just how serious are they?* Paper presented at the Interservice/Industry Training, Simulation, and Education Conference.

Rose, A. (1982). Spoken versus written criticism of student writing: Some advantages of the conference method. *College Composition and Communication, 33*, 326–331. doi:10.2307/357501

Rose, F. (2006, December). Commercial Break. *Wired, 14*(12). Retrieved from http://www.wired.com/wired/archive/14.12/tahoe.html

Roy, M. (1975). *Bengali women*. Chicago, IL: University of Chicago Press.

Rudestam, K. E., & Schoenholtz-Read, J. (2002). *Handbook of online learning: Innovations in higher education and corporate training*. London, UK: Sage.

Ruiz, J. G., Mintzer, M. J., & Issenberg, S. B. (2006). Learning objects in medical education. *Medical Teacher, 28*(7), 603–604. doi:10.1080/01421590601039893

Ruksasuk, N. (2000). *Effects of learning styles and participatory interaction modes on achievement of Thai students involved in Web-based instruction in library and information science distance education*. Unpublished doctoral dissertation, University of Pittsburgh, Pittsburgh, PA.

Rushowy, K. (2009, April 6). Profs blast lazy first-year students: Wikipedia generation is lazy and unprepared for university's rigours, survey of faculty says. *thestar.com*. Retrieved from http://www.thestar.com/News/Ontario/article/614219

Russell, T. (1999). *The no significant difference phenomenon: As reported in 355 research reports, summaries, and papers: A comparative research annotated bibliography on technology for distance education*. North Carolina State University.

Ryan, J. (2000). *A guide to teaching international students*. Oxford, UK: Oxford Centre for Staff and Learning Development.

Saeed, N., Yang, Y., & Sinnappan, S. (2009). *User acceptance of Second Life: An extended TAM including hedonic consumption behaviours* (Research-in-Progress Paper). 17th European Conference on Information Systems.

Salmon, G., Edirisingha, P., Mobbs, M., Mobbs, R., & Dennet, C. (2008). *How to create podcasts for education*. Maidenhead, UK: Open University.

Sarner, A. (2008). Generation virtual. *Forbes*. Retrieved from http://www.forbes.com/2008/ 04/30/genv-gartner-marketing-oped-cx _asa_0430genv.html

Sautter, P. (2007). Designing discussion activities to achieve desired learning outcomes: Choices using mode of delivery and structure. *Journal of Marketing Education, 29*(2), 122–131. doi:10.1177/0273475307302014

Schell, G. P. (2004). Universities marginalize online courses. *Communications of the ACM, 47*(7), 53–56. doi:10.1145/1005817.1005821

Schön, D. A. (1983). *The reflective practitioner. How professionals think in action*. London, UK: Temple Smith.

Schroeder, R. (2006). Being there together and the future of connected presence. *Presence (Cambridge, Mass.), 15*(4), 438–454. doi:10.1162/pres.15.4.438

Schroeter, R., Hunter, J., Guerin, J., Khan, I., & Henderson, M. (2009). *A synchronous multimedia annotation system for secure collaboratories*. 2nd IEEE International Conference on E-Science and Grid Computing (eScience 2006). Amsterdam, Netherlands. Retrieved November 6, 2009, from http://www.dart.edu.au/publications/escience2006.pdf

Schunk, D. H. (2003). Self-efficacy for reading and writing: Influence of modeling, goal setting, and self-evaluation. *Reading & Writing Quarterly, 19,* 159–172. doi:10.1080/10573560308219

Sexton, R. L. (2006). Using short movie and television clips in the economics principles class. *The Journal of Economic Education, 37*(4), 406–417.

Shashaani, L. (1993). Gender-based differences in attitudes toward computers. *Computers & Education, 20*(2), 169–181. doi:10.1016/0360-1315(93)90085-W

Shashaani, L. (1994). Gender-differences in computer experience and its influence on computer attitudes. *Journal of Educational Computing Research, 11*(4), 347–367. doi:10.2190/64MD-HTKW-PDXV-RD62

Shaughnessy, M. (1977). *Errors and expectations.* New York, NY: Oxford University Press.

Shephard, K. (2003, June 1). Questioning, promoting and evaluating the use of streaming video to support student learning. *British Journal of Educational Technology, 34*(3), 295-308. (ERIC Document Reproduction Service No. EJ670076). Retrieved March 6, 2009, from ERIC database.

Shieh, D. (2009, March 6). These lectures are gone in 60 seconds. *The Chronicle of Higher Education.* Retrieved from http://chronicle.com/article/These-Lectures-Are-Gone-in-60/19924

Shiffrin, R. M., & Schneider, W. (1977). Controlled and automatic human information processing: Perceptual learning automatic attending and a general theory. *Psychological Review, 84*(2), 127–190. doi:10.1037/0033-295X.84.2.127

Shirts, R. G. (1977). *BAFA-BAFA: A cross-cultural simulation: Director's guide. Del mar.* CA: Simile II.

Short, J., Williams, E., & B., C. (1976). *The social psychology of telecommunications.* New York, NY: John Wiley.

Shrivastava, P. (1999). Management classes as online learning communities. *Journal of Management Education, 23*(6), 691–702. doi:10.1177/105256299902300607

Shyu, H. C. (2000). Using video-based anchored instruction to enhance learning: Taiwan's experience. *British Journal of Educational Technology, 31*(1), 57–69. doi:10.1111/1467-8535.00135

Sipple, S., & Sommers, J. (2005). *A heterotopic space: Digitized audio commentary and student revisions.* Retrieved March 24, 2006, from http://www.users.muohio.edu/sommerjd/

Sit, J., Chung, J., Chow, M., & Wong, T. (2005). Experiences of online learning: Students' perspective. *Nurse Education Today, 25*(2), 140. doi:10.1016/j.nedt.2004.11.004

Sitzmann, T., Kraiger, K., Stewart, D., & Wisher, R. (2006). The comparative effectiveness of web-based and classroom instruction: A meta-analysis. *Personnel Psychology, 59*(3), 623–664. doi:10.1111/j.1744-6570.2006.00049.x

Sitzmann, T., Kraiger, K., Stewart, D., & Wisher, R. (2006). The comparative effectiveness of Web-based and classroom instruction: A meta-analysis. *Personnel Psychology, 59*(3), 623–644. doi:10.1111/j.1744-6570.2006.00049.x

Skiba, D. J. (2008). Nursing education 2.0: Twitter & tweets. Can you post a nugget of knowledge in 140 characters or less? *Nursing Education Perspectives, 29*(2), 110–112.

Skiba, D. J. (2009). Nursing education 2.0: A second look at Second Life. *Nursing Education Perspectives, 30*(2), 129–131.

Slater, J. (2005). *Spent force or revolution in progress? E-learning after the e-university.* Report for the Higher Education Policy Institute Oxford. Retrieved September 2009, from http://www.hepi.ac.uk/466-1163/Spent-force-or-revolution-in-progress-eLearning-after-the-eUniversity.html

Slotte, V., & Herbert, A. (2008). Engaging workers in simulation-based e-learning. *Journal of Workplace Learning, 20*(3), 165–180. doi:10.1108/13665620810860477

Smith, E. A. (2001). The role of tacit and explicit knowledge in the workplace. *Journal of Knowledge Management, 5*(4), 311–321. doi:10.1108/13673270110411733

Snelson, C. (2008). YouTube and beyond: Integrating web-based video into online education. In K. McFerrin, R. Weber, R. Carlsen & D. A. Willis (Eds.), *Proceedings of Society for Information Technology and Teacher Education International Conference* 2008 (pp. 732-737). Chesapeake, VA: AACE.

So, S., & Pun, S. (2002, June 1). *Using streaming technology to build video-cases that enhance student teaching on IT*. (ERIC Document Reproduction Service No. ED477095). Retrieved March 6, 2009, from ERIC database.

SOG. (2009). SOG Verkort verkiezingsprogramma [short election programme student fraction SOG]. Retrieved November 6, 2009, from http://www.studentenorganisatie.nl/new/index.php?library/download/16

Sommers, N. (1980). Revision strategies of student writers and experienced adult writers. *College Composition and Communication, 31*(4), 378–388. doi:10.2307/356588

Sommers, N. (1982). Responding to student writing. *College Composition and Communication, 33*(2), 148–156. doi:10.2307/357622

Sommers, J. (2002). Spoken response: Space, time, and movies of the mind. In Belanoff, P., Dickson, M., Fontaine, S., & Moran, C. (Eds.), *Writing with elbow*. Logan, UT: Utah State Press.

SonicFoundry. (n.d.) *Mediasite* [Webcasting and knowledge management software]. Retrieved from http://www.sonicfoundry.com/mediasite/

South, J. B., Gabbitas, B., & Merrill, P. F. (2008). Designing video narratives to contextualize content for ESL learners: A design process case study. *Interactive Learning Environments, 16*(3), 231–243. doi:10.1080/10494820802114044

Spradley, J. (1979). *The ethnographic interview*. New York, NY: Rinehart and Winston.

Squire, L. R. (1987). *Memory and brain*. New York, NY: Oxford University Press.

Srinivas, M. N. (1966). *Social change in modern India*. Berkeley, CA: University of California Press.

Standley, M. (2003). Digital storytelling. *Cable in the classroom*. Retrieved on March 1, 2010, from http://its.ksbe.edu/dst/#Resources.

Stein, J. (2008, April 9). *Defining "creepy treehouse."* Retrieved from http://flexknowlogy.learningfield.org/2008/04/09/defining-creepy-tree-house/

Steiner, I. D. (1972). *Group process and productivity*. New York, NY: Academic Press.

Stern, L., & Solomon, A. (2006). Effective faculty feedback: The road less traveled. *Assessing Writing, 11*, 22–41. doi:10.1016/j.asw.2005.12.001

Stewart, E. C. (1966). The simulation of cultural differences. *The Journal of Communication, 16*(4), 291–304. doi:10.1111/j.1460-2466.1966.tb00043.x

Stewart, M. (2004). Learning through research: An introduction to theories of learning. *JMU Learning & Teaching Press, 4*(1), 6–14.

Stiegler, B. (1994). Technics and time: *Vol. 1. The fault of Epimetheus* (Beardsworth, R., & Collins, G., Trans.). Stanford, CA: Stanford University Press.

Stilborne, L., MacGibbon, P., & Virginia Commonwealth of Learning. (2001, January 1). *Video/videoconferencing in support of distance education. Knowledge series: A topical, start-up guide to distance education practice and delivery*. (ERIC Document Reproduction Service No. ED479026). Retrieved March 6, 2009, from ERIC database.

Still, B. (2006). Talking to students: Embedded voice commenting as a tool for critiquing student writing. *Journal of Business and Technical Communication, 20*(4), 460–475. doi:10.1177/1050651906290270

Sturges, D. (2003). *Creating student access and retention model*. Unpublished manuscript. Grant Application FIPSE.

Sturges, D., & Ozuna, T. (2006). Using technology to increase critical-thinking in undergraduate study. *Journal of College Teaching & Learning, 3*(3). ISSN 1544-0389

Sumara, D., & Davis, B. (1997). Enactivist theory and community learning: Toward a complexified understanding of action research. *Educational Action Research, 5*(3), 403–442. doi:10.1080/09650799700200037

Summerfield, E. (1993). *Cross cultures through film*. Yarmouth, ME: Intercultural Press.

Sun, P., Tsai, R., Finger, G., Chen, Y., & Yeh, D. (2008). What drives successful e-learning? An empirical investigation of the critical factors influencing learner satisfaction. *Computers & Education, 50*, 118–1202. doi:10.1016/j.compedu.2006.11.007

Sutton, R. I. (1997). The virtues of closet qualitative research. *Organization Science, 8*(1), 97–106.

Swap, W., Leonard, D., Shields, M., & Abrams, L. (2001). Using mentoring and storytelling to transfer knowledge in the workplace. *Journal of Management Information Systems*, *18*(1), 95–114.

Sweller, J. (1994). Cognitive load theory, learning difficulty, and instructional design. *Learning and Instruction*, *4*(4), 295–312. doi:10.1016/0959-4752(94)90003-5

Sweller, J. (1998). Can we measure working memory without contamination from knowledge held in long-term memory? *The Behavioral and Brain Sciences*, *21*(6), 845–846. doi:10.1017/S0140525X98371769

Sweller, J., van Merrienboer, J. J. G., & Paas, F. G. W. C. (1998). Cognitive architecture and instructional design. *Educational Psychology Review*, *10*(3), 251–296. doi:10.1023/A:1022193728205

Taber, N. (2008). Emergency response: E-learning for paramedics and firefighters. *Simulation & Gaming*, *39*(4), 515–527. doi:10.1177/1046878107306669

Tallent-Runnels, M., Thomas, J., Lan, W., Cooper, S., Ahern, T., & Shaw, S. (2006). Teaching courses online: A review of the research. *Review of Educational Research*, *76*(1), 93. doi:10.3102/00346543076001093

Tan, J.-S., & Chua, R. Y.-J. (2003). Training and developing cultural intelligence. In Earley, P. C., & Ang, S. (Eds.), *Cultural intelligence: Individual interactions across cultures* (pp. 258–303). Stanford, CA: Stanford University Press.

Tapscott, D. (1996). *Growing up digital: The rise of the net generation*. New York, NY: McGraw Hill.

Tapscott, D. (2009). *Grown up digital: How the net generation is changing your world*. New York, NY: McGraw Hill.

Taylor, B. P. (1982). In search of real reality. *TESOL Quarterly*, *16*, 29–42. doi:10.2307/3586561

Tedlock, B. (1991). The new anthropology of dreaming. *Dreaming*, *1*, 161–178.

Tejeda, M. J. (2008). A resource review for diversity film media. *Academy of Management Learning & Education*, *7*(3), 434–439. doi:10.5465/AMLE.2008.37029279

Telegraph. (2009, Nov 25). Online education grows apace. *Telegraph*. Retrieved November 28, 2009, from http://www.telegraph.co.uk/education/expateducation/6588855/Online-education-grows-apace.html

ten Berge, T., & van Hezewijk, R. (1999). Procedural and declarative knowledge: An evolutionary perspective. *Theory & Psychology*, *9*(5), 605–624. doi:10.1177/0959354399095002

Teo, T., Lim, V., & Lai, R. (1999). Intrinsic and extrinsic motivation in Internet usage. *Omega*, *27*(1), 25–37. doi:10.1016/S0305-0483(98)00028-0

The Information Centre. (2007). *NHS hospital and community health services non-medical staff: England 1996-2006*. Retrieved on September 9, 2009, from http://www.ic.nhs.uk/webfiles/publications/nhsstaff2006/non-med/Non-medical%20bulletin%201996-2006.pdf

Thiagarajan, S. (2003). *Design your own games and activities: Thiagi's templates for performance improvement*. San Francisco, CA: Pfeiffer.

Thomas, D. C. (2006). Domain and development of cultural intelligence: The importance of mindfulness. *Group & Organization Management*, *31*(1), 78–99. doi:10.1177/1059601105275266

Thomas, D. C., & Inkson, K. (2003). *Cultural intelligence: People skills for global business*. San Francisco, CA: Berrett-Koehler.

Thomas, D. C. (2006). Domain and development of cultural intelligence: The importance of mindfulness. *Group & Organization Management*, *31*(1), 78–99. doi:10.1177/1059601105275266

Thomas, D. C., & Inkson, K. (2003). *Cultural intelligence: People skills for global business*. San Francisco, CA: Berrett-Koehler Publishers.

Thompson, E. (2001). Empathy and consciousness. *Journal of Consciousness Studies*, *8*(5/7), 1–32.

Thompson, E. (2007). *Mind in life: Biology, phenomenology, and the sciences of mind*. Cambridge, MA: Harvard University Press.

Thompson, N. (2006). *Anti-discrimination practice* (4th ed.). New York, NY: Palgrave Macmillan.

Thompson, N. (2006). *Promoting workplace learning.* Bristol, UK: Policy Press.

Thompson, E. (1996). The mindful body: Embodiment and cognitive science. In O'Donovan-Anderson, M. (Ed.), *The incorporated self: Interdisciplinary perspectives on embodiment* (pp. 127–144). Lanham, MD: Rowman & Littlefield.

Thompson, E. (1999). *Human consciousness: From intersubjectivity to interbeing.* Retrieved from http://www.philosophy.ucf.edu/pcs/pcsfetz1.html

Thorne, K. (2003). *Blended learning.* London, UK: Kogan Page.

Tiernan, S. L., & Grudin, J. (2001). *Fostering engagement in asynchronous learning through collaborative multimedia annotation* (MSR-TR-2000-91). Redmond, VA: Microsoft Research. Retrieved November 7, 2009, from http://research.microsoft.com/apps/pubs/default.aspx?id=69315

Tipton, D. B., & Tiemann, K. A. (1993). Using the feature film to facilitate sociological thinking. *Teaching Sociology, 21,* 187–191. doi:10.2307/1318642

Tipton, F. B. (2008). Thumbs-up is a rude gesture in Australia: The presentation of culture in international business textbooks. *Critical Perspectives on International Business, 4*(1), 7–24. doi:10.1108/17422040810849730

Tobolowsky, B. F. (2007). In practice - thinking visually: Using visual media in the college classroom. *About Campus, 12*(1), 21–24.

Toffler, A. (1980). *The third wave.* London, UK: Collins.

Tolbert, A. S., & McLean, G. N. (1995). Venezuelan culture assimilator for training United States professionals conducting business in Venezuela. *International Journal of Intercultural Relations, 19*(1), 111–125. doi:10.1016/0147-1767(94)00027-U

Torrance, S. (2006). In search of the enactive: Introduction to special issue on enactive experience. *Phenomenology and the Cognitive Sciences, 4,* 357–368. doi:10.1007/s11097-005-9004-9

Toye, M. (1989). Learning styles. In Titmus, C. J. (Ed.), *Lifelong education for adults: An international handbook* (pp. 236–232). Oxford, UK: Pergamon Press.

Triandis, H. C. (1995). Culture specific assimilators. In Fowler, S., & Mumford, M. (Eds.), *Intercultural sourcebook* (Vol. 1, pp. 179–186). Yarmouth, ME: Intercultural Press.

Triple, L. (2008). *Triple L Project Wiki tool.* Retrieved October 21st, 2009, from http://www.iis-communities.nl/portal/site/triple-l

Trompenaars, F., & Hampden-Turner, C. (1998). *Riding the waves of culture.* New York, NY: McGraw-Hill.

Tu, C.-H. (2000). On-line learning migration: From social learning theory to social presence theory in a CMC environment. *Journal of Network and Computer Applications, 23*(1), 27–37. doi:10.1006/jnca.1999.0099

Tuovinen, J., & Sweller, J. (1999). A comparison of cognitive load associated with discovery learning and worked examples. *Journal of Educational Psychology, 91*(2), 334–341. doi:10.1037/0022-0663.91.2.334

Twigg, C. (2001). *Innovations in online learning: Moving beyond no significant difference* [NCAT monograph]. Retrieved from http://www.thencat.org/Monographs/Innovations.html

U.S. Department of Education, National Center for Education Statistics. (2008). *Digest of education statistics, 2007.* (NCES 2008-022), Chapter 3.

University of Adelaide. (2008). *Research skill development and assessment in the curriculum* [Handbook for Research Skill Development Seminar]. Retrieved from http://www.adelaide.edu.au/clpd/rsd/otherfiles/RSD_hbk.pdf

University of Dayton. (2009). *Credit crisis adds uncertainty to international accounting transition, most business schools not preparing students.* Retrieved January 16, 2009, from http://www.udayton.edu/News/Detail/?contentID=22352

University of Southampton. (n.d.). *Edshare.* Retrieved from http://www.edshare.soton.ac.uk/

Van der Heijden, H. (2001). Measuring core capabilities for electronic commerce. *Journal of Information Technology, 16*(1), 13–22. doi:10.1080/02683960010028447

Van der Heijden, H. (2003). Factors influencing the usage of websites: The case of a generic portal in The Netherlands. *Information & Management, 40*(6), 541–549. doi:10.1016/S0378-7206(02)00079-4

Van der Heijden, H. (2004). User acceptance of hedonic information systems. *Management Information Systems Quarterly, 28*(4), 695–704.

Van Raaij, E., & Schepers, J. (2008). The acceptance and use of a virtual learning environment in China. *Computers & Education, 50*(3), 838–852. doi:10.1016/j.compedu.2006.09.001

Van Vianen, A. E. M., De Pater, I. E., Kristof-Brown, A. L., & Johnson, E. C. (2004). Fitting in: Surface- and deep-level cultural differences and expatriates' adjustment. *Academy of Management Journal, 47*(5), 697–709. doi:10.2307/20159612

Varela, F. J. (1996). Neurophenomenology: A methodological remedy for the hard problem. *Journal of Consciousness Studies, 3*(4), 330–349.

Varela, F. J., Thompson, E., & Rosch, E. (1991). *The embodied mind: Cognitive science and human experience*. Cambridge, MA: MIT Press.

Varela, F. J. (1987). Laying down a path in walking. In Thompson, W. I. (Ed.), *Gaia: A way of knowing—political implications of the new biology* (pp. 48–64). Hudson, NY: Lindisfarne Press.

Veeramani, R., & Bradley, S. (2008). *Insights regarding undergraduate preference for lecture capture*. Retrieved October 19th, 2009, from http://www.uwebi.org/news/uw-online-learning.pdf

Venkatesh, V. (2000). Determinants of perceived ease of use: Integrating control, intrinsic motivation, and emotion into the technology acceptance model. *Information Systems Research, 11*(4), 342–365. doi:10.1287/isre.11.4.342.11872

Venkatesh, V., & Davis, F. (1996). A model of the antecedents of perceived ease of use: Development and test. *Decision Sciences, 27*(3), 451–481. doi:10.1111/j.1540-5915.1996.tb01822.x

Ventura, S., & Onsman, A. (2009). The use of popular movies during lectures to aid the teaching and learning of undergraduate pharmacology. *Medical Teacher, 31*(7), 662–664.

Vickers, M. H. (2007). Autoethnography as sensemaking: A story of bullying. *Culture and Organization, 13*(3), 223–237.

Vosko, R. S. (1991). Where we learn shapes our learning. In *Creating environments for effective adult learning*. Jossey-Bass Inc., Publishers.

Wagner, C. (2008). Learning experience with virtual worlds. *Journal of Information Systems Education, 19*(3), 263–266.

Wagner, A., Chen, J., Shohamy, D., Ross, V., Reeves, B., & Wagner, A. D. (2009). *The impact of social belief on the neurophysiology of learning and memory*. Research work was supported by grants from the National Institute of Mental Health (5R01–MH080309), National Science Foundation, (NSF#0354453), and Stanford University's Media X program. Retrieved from http://hstar.stanford.edu/cgi-bin/?research_centers

Wainfan, L., & Davis, P. K. (2004). *Challenges in virtual collaboration: Videoconferencing, audio conferencing, and computer-mediated communications*. Santa Monica, CA: RAND National Defense Research Institute.

Wallace, A. F. C. (1965). Driving to work. In Spiro, M. (Ed.), *Context and meaning in cultural anthropology* (pp. 277–292). New York, NY: Free Press.

Walsh, A. (2009). *How do e-learning resources influence student learning and assessment on a pre-registration mental health nursing course?* Unpublished Master's thesis, Birmingham City University.

Wang, H. (2006). Teaching Asian students online: What matters and why? *PAACE Journal of Lifelong Learning, 15*, 69–84.

Warne, T., & McAndrew, S. (2005). *Using patient experience in education*. Basingstoke, UK: Palgrave MacMillan.

Warnock, S. (2009). *Teaching writing online: How and why*. Urbana, IL: NCTE.

Warnock, S. (2008). Responding to student writing with audio-visual feedback. In Carter, T., & Clayton, M. A. (Eds.), *Writing and the iGeneration: Composition in the computer-mediated classroom* (pp. 201–227). Southlake, TX: Fountainhead Press.

Watts, A. (2000). *What is zen?* Novato, CA: New World Library.

Weber, A. M., & Haen, C. (2005). *Clinical applications of drama therapy in child and adolescent treatment*. New York, NY: Routledge.

Webster, J., & Hackley, P. (1997). Teaching effectiveness in technology-mediated distance learning. *Academy of Management Journal, 40*(6), 1282–1309. doi:10.2307/257034

Weigel, V. B. (2002). *Deep learning for a digital age: Technology's untapped potential to enrich higher education*. San Francisco, CA: Jossey-Bass.

Weller, M. (2007). *Virtual learning environments: Using, choosing and developing your VLE*. London, UK: Routledge.

Welsh, E. T., Wanberg, C. R., Brown, K. G., & Simmering, M. J. (2003). E-learning: Emerging uses, empirical results and future directions. *International Journal of Training and Development, 7*(4), 245–258. doi:10.1046/j.1360-3736.2003.00184.x

Whitley, B. (1997). Gender differences in computer-related attitudes and behavior: A meta-analysis. *Computers in Human Behavior, 13*(1), 1–22. doi:10.1016/S0747-5632(96)00026-X

Wicklund, G., & Gee, R. (2004). Learn on your time. *Office PRO, 64*, 24–25.

Wiecek, I. M., & Young, N. M. (2009). *IFRS primer: International GAAP basics* (1st ed.). Hoboken, NJ: John Wiley & Sons.

Wieling, M. B., & Hofman, W. H. A. (in press). *The impact of online video lecture recordings and automated feedback on student performance*. Article accepted for publication, Computers & Education (2009).

Wilkinson, L. C. (2007). A developmental approach to uses of moving pictures in intercultural education. *International Journal of Intercultural Relations, 31*(1), 1–27. doi:10.1016/j.ijintrel.2006.08.001

Wilkinson, L. C. (2001). *Uses of moving pictures in intercultural education*. Seattle, WA: Seattle University, Unpublished dissertation (Ed. D).

Winnips, J. C., & McLoughlin, C. (2001, June). Six WWW based learner supports you can build. In C. Montgomerie & J. Viteli (Eds.), *Proceedings of EDMEDIA 2001*, (pp. 2062-2067). Chesapeake, VA: AACE.

Winnips, J. C., & Portier, S. (2008). *Creating content and not sharing it: Why is it so quiet in so many repositories?* Paper presented at Online Educa 2008, Berlin.

Winnips, J. C., & Verheij, G. J. (2009, June). *Didactic models for the use of videolectures*. Paper presented at Diverse 2009, Aberystwyth, UK. Retrieved on November 6th, 2009, from http://echo360.aber.ac.uk:8080/ess/echo/presentation/3e9be7dc-097d-4a83-a7c7-778d905cc314

Winnips, J. C., Verheij, G. J., & Beldhuis, H. (2009, December). *Interactive large scale lectures: From clothespins to Twitter mashups*. Paper accepted for the Conference: Student Mobility and ICT: Dimensions of Transition. Amsterdam, December 2009.

Wolcott, H. F. (1990). *Writing up qualitative research*. Newbury Park, CA: Sage.

Wright, J. (2009). The role of computer software in presenting information. *Nursing Management, 16*(4), 30–34.

Yadapadithaya, P. S. (2001). Evaluating corporate training and development: An Indian experience. *International Journal of Training and Development, 5*(4), 261–274. doi:10.1111/1468-2419.00138

Yamazaki, Y., & Kayes, D. (2004). An experiential approach to cross-cultural learning: A review and integration of competencies for successful expatriate adaptation. *Academy of Management Learning & Education, 3*(4), 362–379. doi:10.5465/AMLE.2004.15112543

Yamazaki, Y. (2002). *Learning styles and typologies of cultural differences: A theoretical and empirical comparison*. Working paper.

YFile. (2008, May 6). York recognized as a leader in distance education. *YFile*. Retrieved from http://www.yorku.ca/yfile/archive/index.asp?Article=10445

Yin, R. K. (1994). *Case study research: Design and methods*. Thousand Oaks, CA: Sage.

Yohon, T. (2004). Internet use in classroom instruction. In Christopher, D. (Ed.), *E-world: Virtual learning, collaborative environments, and future technologies* (pp. 42–66). Reston, VA: National Business Education Association.

Young, M. R., Klemz, B. R., & Murphy, J. W. (2003). Enhancing learning outcomes: The effects of instructional technology, learning styles, instructional methods, and student behavior. *Journal of Marketing Education*, *25*(2), 130–142. doi:10.1177/0273475303254004

Young, J. R. (2008, June 20). Short and sweet: Technology shrinks the lecture hall. *The Chronicle of Higher Education*. Retrieved from http://chronicle.com/article/ShortSweet-Technology/13866/

Young, J. R. (2009, October 29). Professor turns his online course into a role-playing game. *The Chronicle of Higher Education*. Retrieved from http://chronicle.com/blogPost/Professor-Turns-His-Online/4407

YouTube.com. (2009a). *YouTube fact sheet: Traffic and stats*. Retrieved September 18, 2009, from http://www.youtube.com/t/fact_sheet

YouTube.com. (2009b). *Market segmentation search*. Retrieved September 17, 2009, from http://www.youtube.com/results?search_query=market+segmentation&search_type=&aq=f

YouTube.com. (2009c). *Value chain search*. Retrieved September 17, 2009, from http://www.youtube.com/results?search_query=value+chain&search_type=&aq=f

Zeliff, N. D. (2004). Pedagogical and technological challenges of the Internet. In Christopher, D. (Ed.), *E-world: Virtual learning, collaborative environment, and future technologies*. Relston, VA: National Business Education Association.

Zemsky, R., & Massy, W. (2004). *Thwarted innovation, what happened to e-learning and why. A Final Report for The Weatherstation Project of The Learning Alliance at the University of Pennsylvania*. Pittsburgh, PA: The Learning Alliance at the University of Pennsylvania.

Zhang, D., Zhao, J., Zhou, L., & Nunamaker, J. Jr. (2004). Can e-learning replace classroom learning? *Communications of the ACM*, *47*(5), 75–79. doi:10.1145/986213.986216

Zorn, D. (1994). *A hermeneutics of technology: Don Ihde's postmodern philosophy of technology* (Unpublished master's thesis). McMaster University, Hamilton, Canada.

Zorn, D. (2010). *Enactive approach to education* (Unpublished doctoral dissertation). Ontario Institute for Studies in Education/University of Toronto, Toronto, Canada.

About the Contributors

Charles Wankel, Associate Professor of Management at St. John's University, New York, holds a doctorate from New York University where he was admitted to Beta Gamma Sigma, the national honor society for business disciplines in AACSB accredited universities. He serves at Erasmus University, Rotterdam School of Management on the Dissertation Committee and as Honorary Vice Rector at the Poznań University of Business and Foreign Languages. He was awarded the Outstanding Service in Management Education and Development Award at the Academy of Management's 2004 meeting. At the August 2007 meeting, he was awarded the McGraw-Hill/Irwin Outstanding Symposium in Management Education Development Award. Columbia University's American Assembly identified him as one of the nation's top experts on Total Quality Management. He co-authored a top selling textbook Management (Prentice Hall, 1986), published a St. Martin's Press scholarly book on interorganizational strategy development in Poland, and numerous scholarly articles, monographs, and chapters. The 18,000+ member Academy of Management, the world's premier academic society in this discipline, presented its Best Paper in Management Education Award to him in 1991, and he has been selected to serve as an officer of AOM divisions every year for more than a decade. He is the leading founder and director of scholarly virtual communities for management professors, currently directing seven with thousands of participants in more than seventy nations. (A Google search for "Charles Wankel" will provide you with an awareness of the scope of his online presence). He has led online international Internet collaborations in teaching and research for more than a decade.

J. Sibley Law is the creator of RocketsTail.com, a blog about the new media industry. In addition to co-editing this publication, he is the creator of numerous online video series, including: News for Blondes, Bonnie for President (Official Honoree of the 2007 Webby Awards), Dishes, The Oligarch Duplicity, Uncle Vic's Kitchen, and the online channel TangoDango. In addition, he has directed and produced numerous music videos. Law got his start producing when he was part of a small team of people who produced the numerous events celebrating the United Nations 50th Commemoration in San Francisco, its birthplace. Law has Chaired of the Stratford Arts Commission in Stratford, CT. There he founded and produced the Stratford Shakespeare Festival from 2005 to 2010. He co-founded SquareWrights Playwright Center, which has showcased more than 100 new works by emerging playwrights. Additionally, he has served on the boards of the New England Academy of Theatre and the Playwrights' Center of San Francisco. Law's stage-work as a director and playwright has been produced on stages from New York City to San Francisco to Valdez, AK, where he was a featured playwright at The Last Frontier Theatre Conference in 2006. Law has worked with Fortune 500 companies since 2000, helping to solve problems of margin loss and yield erosion through effective negotiation and strategy.

* * *

Ana Adi is an independent strategic communication consultant, specializing in new media and public relations. She is also a doctoral researcher in the Faculty of Business and Creative Industries at the University of the West of Scotland. Since December 2008, Ana also has been teaching an intensive class on new media to Erasmus students taking classes at Katholieke Hogeschool Zuid-West Vlaanderen in Kortrijk, Belgium. She is an active promoter of using new media to teach new media, and of integrating online live video guest lectures into the daily teaching process. She holds a BA Hons. MA (Bucharest), MA (Missouri). She blogs at http://anaadi.wordpress.com.

Mary Allan is an Adjunct Fellow in the School of Social and Political Sciences at the University of Canterbury in Christchurch, New Zealand. Her research interests are led by her key passion for studying relationships. One strand of her work focuses on the study of electronically mediated interactions and their potential for supporting collaboration across work, research, and study environments. In studying this field, she focuses on the socio technical relationships emerging against the backdrop of today's knowledge economy. The other strand of her work is the study of complex systems and the relationships at play in systems and subsystems. Working in this area, she developed an innovative model for the implementation and support of change in complex situations. She completed her PhD in 2005 at the University of Canterbury. Her thesis investigated Internet-mediated collaborative learning at tertiary level, and proposed a new methodology for micro and macro investigation of computer mediated collaborative activities. In her thesis, she developed a new concept for software that enables visualizing interactions in electronic communications and measuring their potential for supporting collaboration. The concept was patented in 2009.

Sarah Atkinson is Principal Lecturer in Broadcast Media at the University of Brighton. Sarah has a PhD from Brunel University; *Telling Interactive Stories* is her practice-based thesis, which theoretically and practically investigates the field of digital fictional interactive storytelling. She has also published articles around the area of interactive film, video, and cinema. Her own interactive film Crossed Lines has been exhibited internationally. It is an original fictional interactive AV piece, amalgamating multiform plots, a multi-screen viewing environment, an interactive interface, and an interactive story navigation form. It has been exhibited at the Electronic Literature Organisation conference at the Washington State University, US, the Digital Interactive Media in Arts and Entertainment conference arts show in Athens, The Interrupt arts show in Providence, US, the EuroITV arts show in Belgium, and the International Digital Interactive Storytelling conference in Portugal.

Brian Barber is a is a second year Religious Studies student at the University of Wolverhampto, who brought a range of subject combinations, different experiences, and backgrounds to the project worked on with Dierdre Burke. Brian drew upon skills developed in History and Deaf Studies in developing his iPod tour.

Christopher Barnatt has been teaching and researching in the area of computing, organizations, and future studies in Nottingham University Business School since 1990, where he is now Director of Teaching and Associate Professor of Computing & Future Studies. He is also a YouTube partner, the author of ExplainingComputers.com and ExplainingTheFuture.com, as well as five traditional books including "Cyber Business" (John Wiley & Sons, 1995). For six years he produced animation for the

BBC, and in 2009, produced the documentary series 'Challenging Reality' for Controversial TV (UK Sky channel 200). As a consultant, he has worked for a wide range of organizations including BT, Cisco, Discovery Channel, and the Clore Leadership Programme. Microsoft has integrated some of Christopher's ExplainingComputers.com video and other content into OfficeOnline.

Arin Basu is a Senior Lecturer in the Health Sciences Centre at the University of Canterbury in Christchurch, New Zealand. He is a medical doctor and an epidemiologist-health services researcher. In addition to teaching courses on research methods, he works as a senior researcher at the Health Services Assessment Collaboration (HSAC) at the University of Canterbury. Before joining Canterbury, he was working as the Associate Director of the Fogarty International Training Program in Environmental and Occupational Health at Kolkata, India. His primary research interests are in systematic reviews and meta-analyses in the context of health services and outcomes research. His area of interest in inter-disciplinary linkage between health services research and environmental epidemiology. He has published on health impacts and determinants of Arsenic toxicity in the India, and currently edits a systematic review on middle ear pain in airplane travelers for "Clinical Evidence" – a secondary evidence based journal.

Amanda Budde-Sung is a lecturer in International Business at the University of Sydney in Australia. Her research interests include issues related to cross-cultural management and intellectual property.

Deirdre Burke is course leader for Religious Studies at the University of Wolverhampton. She has a long-standing interest in pedagogical issues and was awarded a National Teacher Fellowship in 2005. The equipment for her iPod project was funded by the JISC TechDis HEAT scheme, to explore ways that mobile devices could support student learning during field visits. The project team was composed of second year Religious Studies students who brought a range of subject combinations, different experiences, and backgrounds to the project.

Anthony Fee (Ph D, University of Sydney) is a Lecturer in the Centre for International Security Studies at the Faculty Arts and Social Sciences, The University of Sydney, Australia. His research focuses on expatriate development and training, and has been published in international conference proceedings, edited books, and international journals. He has used video in his cross-cultural training programs for more than 15 years.

Lori Francis has a PhD in Industrial/Organizational Psychology from the University of Guelph. Lori is an Associate Professor in the department of psychology at Saint Mary's University in Halifax, Nova Scotia. Dr. Francis has broad research interests in occupational health psychology including work stress, aggression, and workplace fairness. Dr. Francis is a member of the CN Centre for Occupational Health and Safety and serves on the Board of Directors for the Nova Scotia Health Research Foundation. She is also an active member of the Nova Scotia Psychologically Healthy Workplace Awards program.

Abhishek Goel is a faculty of Organizational Behavior at the Indian Institute of Management Calcutta. He has been actively involved in teaching on different online platforms for the last few years. He has successfully evolved a style to use case-method, lecture, and discussion successfully over the online medium for teaching variety of subjects. He has now joined a successful team of colleagues to understand the intricacies of offering and managing online programs. Abhishek is a PhD in Management with specialization in Organizational Behavior. His current research work is focused on two broad themes - positive characteristics and positive behaviors at individual level; and attitudes in cross-cultural context. He finds consulting on organizational system design and culture to be refreshing and important for influencing practice of management in order to develop thought leadership. He has published in peer-reviewed international journals and also written cases. He was a visiting scholar to the University of Konstanz, Germany under the Young Scientists Program of the 29th International Congress of Psychology in 2008.

Lisa Gommer is consultant at the University of Twente, currently in charge of the Blackboard learning environment at this University. In the past she led projects on the implementation of wireless learning, videocommunication, and the use of weblectures. Lisa has published on activating learners via group communication, videocommunication and the use of electronic learning environments.

Sheila Griffiths, MA, is a Senior Lecturer and Pathway Leader at Birmingham City University's Institute of Art and Design, where she teaches Pattern Cutting to undergraduate students on all three levels of the BA (Hons) Fashion Design programme and is Garment Technology pathway leader to the final year undergraduates within the School of Fashion, Textiles & 3DD. Sheila is also seconded to the Faculty Learning and Teaching Development Centre, where she promotes the use of e-learning to staff within her school. Her research interests include e-learning and the development of online learning assets.

Mark Holtzblatt is an Associate Professor of Accounting at Roosevelt University in Chicago. He teaches the International Accounting courses at both the undergraduate and graduate levels. Recent research interests include the incorporation of online videos and webcasts into the teaching of International Accounting. He was awarded a 2009 PricewaterhouseCoopers IFRS Ready Grant to develop a new class dealing with International Financial Reporting Standards (IFRS), which is entitled "Global Accounting: The IASB and IFRS." He has also been the recipient of a 2009 best paper award from the American Accounting Association (AAA) and an honorable mention for the 2009 Mark Chain/Federation of Schools of Accountancy award for Innovation in Graduate Teaching Award. During the Fall 2009 semester he was a co-innovator of the Inter-University IFRS Online Video Competition. Mark has published articles and made numerous AAA and Academy of International Business conference presentations regarding IFRS. He is also a CPA in Illinois.

Catharine Jenkins holds BA (Hons), RMHN, Dip N, MSc, and PG Dip Education. Catharine Jenkins is a senior nurse lecturer at Birmingham City University and a qualified mental health nurse with many years experience in trans-cultural nursing care. She teaches pre- and post registration nurses, specialising in diversity issues, dementia care, and older people's mental health, and enjoys using a mix of active learning techniques including simulation, games, and online learning approaches.

Vidyanand Jha is an Associate Professor in Behavioural Sciences Group at Indian Institute of Management Calcutta. He teaches courses in Organizational Behaviour and related subjects to post graduate students and working executives. He has a Ph.D. in management from the Indian Institute of Management Ahmedabad. He launched the first online short duration executive programme of IIM Calcutta in 2001.

He has also been an adjunct faculty with Universitas 21 Global, an online university. He has actively contributed towards the design and delivery of various online executive education programmes offered by the Indian Institute of Management Calcutta.

Yvonne Johnson is a is a second year Religious Studies student at the University of Wolverhampton who brought a range of subject combinations, different experiences, and backgrounds to the project worked on with Dierdre Burke. Yvonne drew upon skills developed in Philosophy to identify and explore key concepts.

E. Kevin Kelloway received his PhD from Queen's University in 1991 and is the Canada Research Chair in Occupational Health Psychology as well as the Director of the CN Centre for Occupational Health and Safety at Saint Mary's University. An active researcher, he authored over 100 articles and book chapters in addition to authoring/editing 10 books. He is a Fellow of the Society for Industrial/Organizational Psychology and of the Association for Psychological Science. His current research interests include the role of leaders in occupational health and safety as well as issues related to workplace violence.

Rajiv Kumar is an MBA from Indian Institute of Forest Management, Bhopal and has earned his Ph.D. in Management (with specialization in Organizational Behavior) from Indian Institute of Management Ahmedabad. He has worked for about 6 years at an NGO (Society for Promotion of Wastelands Development), an international HR consulting firm (Hewitt Associates) and in academia (IMT Ghaziabad) before joining Indian Institute of Management Calcutta in March, 2008. He has been involved in online teaching both as an administrator and as a teacher. In his role as an administrator, he has co-directed two batches of a program meant for working executives in India and abroad. His online teaching is in the domain of Organizational Behavior. His research interests are varied, and his publications have appeared in peer reviewed journals, national and international conference proceedings, and edited books.

Nipan J. Maniar was born in Gujarat, India, 1977. He graduated from Gujarat University (BSc Mathematics) in 1998 and received his MSc (Multimedia Information Systems) from University of Portsmouth, United Kingdom in 2002, followed by PgC in Learning and Teaching in 2005. He is currently a part-time Principle Lecturer in eLearning and part-time Senior Lecturer in streaming media technologies at University of Portsmouth. As the inventor of C-Shock (www.c-shock.com), a gaming concept and the co-founder of www.sourcelearn.com, a pay per view educational video website, his research interests include the development of educational games and developing technical and pedagogical approaches to implement Digital Media Management and Delivery System. He has published over 30 peer reviewed articles, and his projects have contributed towards UK Research Assessment Exercise. Nipan was awarded the Learning and Teaching Fellowship by University of Portsmouth in 2007 based on his excellence in teaching and learning. Nipan was also awarded Enterprise Fellow award in 2007. He was nominated for UK Higher Education National Teaching Fellow award and UK Higher Education National e-tutor Fellow award. Nipan is a Teaching Fellow of the UK Higher Education Academy.

Patricia Genoe McLaren has a PhD in Management from Saint Mary's University. She is currently an Assistant Professor of Leadership at the Brantford Campus of Wilfrid Laurier University. Her research interests include the management and careers of professionals, the history of management theory and education, and gender and diversity within organizations.

Doan Nguyen teaches strategic brand management at the UQ Business School, University of Queensland, Australia. Doan's current research focuses on consumer emotion, sponsorship, cause related marketing, and creative communication in not-for-profit service sectors. Doan has published in Journal of Service Research, International Journal of Sports and Sponsorship Marketing, and Australasian Marketing Journal. Her research has been presented at several prestigious international conferences. Doan has consulted the educational sectors in Australia in developing creative communication contents for teaching and training using video streaming technology. Doan has produced a professional feature film to help Australian not-for-profit sectors raise funds. This project has been presented at the University of Melbourne as an example of connecting service research, sponsorship, and NGOs sector. Lastly, the film has been included in a prestigious State Arts and Cultural Heritage collection.

Aamir Nore is a second year Religious Studies student at the University of Wolverhampton who brought a range of subject combinations, different experiences, and backgrounds to the project worked on with Dierdre Burke. Aamir drew upon sociological awareness to explore the history of his selected community.

Billy O'Steen is a Senior Lecturer in Higher Education at the University of Canterbury in Christchurch, New Zealand. His teaching and research focus on innovative curriculum design and professional development, with a particular emphasis on experiential education and service-learning. He received his BA in English and History from Vanderbilt University and both MEd and PhD from the University of Virginia (Dissertation - *Experiential English: A Naturalistic Inquiry of Outward Bound in the Classroom*). Prior to his appointment at the University of Canterbury, he was a faculty member at North Carolina State University, served as a Peace Corps administrator, worked as a legislative aide to a US Senator, created and directed an intermediate school, taught English at a secondary school in Tennessee and two community colleges in California, guided whitewater raft trips in California, and facilitated multi-cultural education programs in Brazil and Tennessee.

Kelly Parke is adjunct faculty at the Schulich School of Business in Toronto, Canada. He has 30 years of experience with technology companies and in the broadcast television industry. As a media designer he has presented at conferences internationally on media streaming strategies. Please feel free to address questions to his email address: kparke@yorku.ca

Neerja Raman is a seasoned executive in technology based new business creation. At Stanford University, Ms. Raman is researching business models and metrics for sustainable development, and is coach and mentor for social entrepreneurs. Prior to joining Stanford, Ms. Raman was Director of Strategic Planning and founder of the Imaging Systems Lab at Hewlett Packard Labs, which delivered product ideas and advanced research for HP's flagship printing, imaging, and multi-media businesses. Ms. Raman has served on the advisory committee for Cyber-Infrastructure, National Science Foundation, an initiative to improve science education in the US. Among other awards, Ms. Raman was honored with *2009 Outstanding 50 Asian Americans in Business* and she has been inducted into the *Women in*

Technology International Hall of Fame. Ms. Raman is active in the blogosphere with *Digital Provide: from Good to Gold* and published the leadership book *The Practice and Philosophy of Decision Making.* Ms. Raman is a graduate of the Kellogg Executive Program, Northwestern University, and has Masters Degrees from S.U.N.Y Stony Brook, New York and Delhi University, India.

Andrew Saxon is Director of e-learning at Birmingham City University's Institute of Art and Design, and a University Senior Learning and Teaching Fellow. His research interests lie in the application of arts-based models of designing to software user interface development, the evaluation of the software user interface, and user experience design for software. The main focus of this work has been toward Web and multimedia software. He is also involved in the development of e-learning initiatives within the Institute's Learning and Teaching Centre, which he leads. These include the design and evaluation of reusable learning objects, and research into e-pedagogies for art and design. He supervises Doctoral and Masters' students in the School of Visual Communication.

Ruud Smit is assistant professor at Rotterdam School of Management, Erasmus University. He studied experimental psychology at the University of Amsterdam. His current research interests include agent-based modelling of the evolution of online social networks. His email address is rsmit@rsm.nl.

Deborah Streeter is the Bruce F. Failing Sr. Professor of Personal Enterprise and Small Business Management in the Department of Applied Economics and Management at Cornell. Entrepreneurship and small business management are the focus of Dr. Streeter's teaching, research, and outreach activities. She specializes in teaching business planning, small business management, and entrepreneurial leadership. Dr. Streeter received the Olympus Innovative Educator Award in 2007, Professor of Merit Award in 2002 and 2003, and was awarded the 2001 USDA National Food and Agricultural Sciences Excellence in College and University Teaching. In 2001, Dr. Streeter was named a Stephen H. Weiss Presidential Fellow in 2000, the highest teaching honor at Cornell University. She also received the SUNY Chancellor's Award for Excellence in Teaching in 2000 and the Innovative Teaching Award in 1996. A major project of Dr. Streeter's has been the development of Cornell's eClips, the world's largest collection of digital video clips on Entrepreneurship, Business, and Leadership, in use in over 1000 universities and more than 75 countries. She has created a variety of educational materials built on a database of digital video interviews with entrepreneurs from across the country. The video material is cut into clips by topic and used in a multi-media format to teach entrepreneurship and small business management. Dr. Streeter holds an M.S. (1980) and Ph.D. (1984) in Agricultural Economics from the University of Wisconsin Madison. She is a member of a university-wide program in entrepreneurship, the Entrepreneurship@Cornell program.

David Sturges, an Associate Professor at the University of Texas-Pan American, teaches and consults in strategic planning and organizational development based on Continuous Quality Improvement (CQI) concepts and practices. He holds a Ph.D. from the University of North Texas, an MBA from East Texas State University, and BBA from Abilene Christian University of Dallas. Prior to entering academics, Dr. Sturges spent 13 years in professional practice of advertising and public relations. His combination of professional experience, teaching CQI at the doctoral level, and advising educational institutions on application of concepts created the knowledge base that led to his being named to head the CQI task force for UTPA. His recent publications focus on educational reform and innovative education applications in higher education. His publication on educational reform proposed modification of higher education mindsets from traditional limitations to job responsibility to views of contribution to organizational (university) success as necessary in the changing world of public oversight and desires for accountability. The publications on innovation focus on incorporation of diverse course delivery techniques to make education more accessible, effective, and efficient for traditional and non-traditional students.

Alastair Tombs teaches sales and account management at the UQ Business School, University of Queensland, Australia. Alastair's teaching and research interests are in the area of the services marketing. Prior to gaining a PhD in Marketing Management in 2005, he has had extensive experience in both the commercial and public sectors. This included over 20 years of running his own businesses in areas such as retail, property management, and architectural/engineering design. His main area of research interest lies in the service environment and its impact on consumer behaviour, as well as the effects of emotional expression/recognition on customers' behaviour. To date, Alastair's work has been published in: academic journals (Marketing Theory, Journal of Management and Organisation); books (Research on emotions in organizations, Research companion to emotions in organizations) and at numerous international conferences. He has received "best paper" awards at Australasian, American, and European marketing conferences.

Norbert Tschakert is an Assistant Professor at the Salem State University. Norbert earned his Ph.D. from the Helmut Schmidt University, University of the Federal Armed Forces in Hamburg, Germany. He also holds the Certified Public Accountant (CPA) designation and received the "Certificate in IFRS" from both the Institute of Chartered Accountants in England and Wales (ICAEW) and the Association of Chartered Certified Accountants (ACCA). Norbert has published several articles in the area of US-GAAP, IFRS and XBRL and during the Fall 2009 semester he has been a co-innovator of the Inter-University IFRS Online Video Competition. His teaching interests are Auditing and International Accounting. Norbert is a member of the American Accounting Association, the Institute of Management Accountants, the Association of Certified Fraud Examiners and the Academy of International Business. Prior positions include San Diego State University, Sempra Energy and PricewaterhouseCoopers.

Peter J. van Baalen is Associate Professor of Knowledge, IT and Organization, academic director of the Centre of e-Learning and Knowledge Management (CELK). Peter van Baalen lectures in the fields of knowledge management, new worlds of work, new media and communication in business, and open innovation in the knowledge economy. His recent research focuses on knowledge exchange, IT-adoption, inter-organizational Information Systems, open source software development, e-communities, new media, and the evolution of global knowledge networks. Peter van Baalen published eight books and about 100 articles in national and international journals, chapters in books, and research papers and reports.

Jan van Dalen, PhD, is an Associate Professor of Statistics at RSM Erasmus University Rotterdam. He graduated Econometrics in 1986, and obtained his PhD in Quantitative models in wholesaling at the School of Economics at Erasmus University in 1992. His main research interests are in the quantitative analysis of information and logistics-related processes. He has written books on applied statistics and published in journals like JAE, JPIM and EJOR.

Wouter Veenhof studied Businesss Administration at the Rotterdam School of Management. He specialized in Business Information Management and wrote his Master's thesis on the adoption and use of Webcasts in higher education. Currently, he works as a project manager IT-Governance and Infrastructures at Capgemini – Consulting, Technology & Outsourcing.

Gert-Jan Verheij is consultant at the University of Groningen's Centre for Learning and Teaching since 2001. He has been leading and participating in projects around digital didactics, video, videoconferencing, and educational re-design of courses. From 1997 to 2001, he was employed at the Faculty of Educational Science and Technology at the Univerity of Twente. His job was to design and implement the electronic learning environment TeleTOP and do the re-design of an Interactive Classroom. Gert-Jan has studied Educational Science and Technology at University of Twente.

Clare Walker is a is a second year Religious Studies student at the University of Wolverhampton who brought a range of subject combinations, different experiences, and backgrounds to the project worked on with Dierdre Burke. Clare drew upon skills developed in Philosophy to identify and explore key concepts.

Andrew Walsh earned RNMH, LPE, BSc (Hons), PG Dip (Health Development), and MA Education certifications. Andrew Walsh is a Senior Nurse Lecturer at Birmingham City University where, after many years and a variety of roles in mental health settings, he now teaches pre-registration mental health nurses. Andrew has expertise in the development of online learning resources and is co-editor of the recent textbook Fundamentals of MH Nursing.

Scott Warnock, PhD, is an Assistant Professor of English and Director of the Freshman Writing Program at Drexel University, where he also helps coordinate Drexel's online and hybrid composition courses. He is interested in uses of technology in writing instruction, particularly how learning technologies can help student writers and can facilitate better methods of responding to student work. He is the author of *Teaching Writing Online: How and Why* (NCTE, 2009), and he has contributed chapters to a number of anthologies, publishing his work in venues such as *The Journal of Technical Writing and Communication, Kairos, Plagiary, Learning Technology, The Teaching Professor,* and *Science Communication.* He has spoken about teaching and technology issues and opportunities at many national conferences. Warnock maintains a blog about online writing instruction at onlinewritingteacher.blogspot.com. He was also co-founder of Subjective Metrics, Inc., a company created to develop Waypoint writing assessment and peer review software.

Koos Winnips did his promotion at the University of Twente in the Netherlands in 2001. The topic of his Ph.D. thesis is scaffolding of online learning. After his promotion, he was employed as an Assistant Professor at the University of Twente to apply models of online learning in industry. Some number of years in consultancy at Twente gave a more practical view of university education. During this time he was a project manager on projects to help close gaps on Maths via e-learning (http://www.mathmatch.nl) and on implementing weblectures at University. After a short period in Scotland at the Caledonian Academy, he moved on to become consultant and researcher at University of Groningen, where he is currently employed.

Diane Zorn teaches critical thinking in the Humanities Department and business ethics at the Schulich School of Business at York University, Canada. She designs, implements, and teaches fully online, rich media courses using Mediasite technology and audio and video podcasting. She was awarded York's University-Wide Teaching Award in 2007, the United States Distance Learning Association Excellence in Distance Learning Teaching Silver Award 2008, and York's Atkinson Dean's Award for Excellence in Teaching 2009. Please feel free to address questions to her email address: zorn@yorku.ca.

Index